EUROPEAN HISTORY

1848–1945

T A Morris

Collins Educational

An Imprint of HarperCollins*Publishers*

Published by CollinsEducational,
An imprint of HarperCollins*Publishers*
77–85 Fulham Palace Road, London W6 8JB

© HarperCollins*Publishers* 1995

This edition published 1995

Reprinted 1996 (twice), 1997

First published in 1985 by University Tutorial Press Ltd

ISBN 0 00 327275 3

Edited by Lorimer Poultney
Design by Derek Lee
Maps by Raymond Turvey
Production by Susan Cashin
Printed and bound by Scotprint Ltd, Musselburgh

Contents

Acknowledgements

The publishers would like to thank the following examination boards for permission reprint questions from past A-level History examination papers: the Associated Examining Board (AEB); Welsh Joint Education Committee (WJEC), Northern Examination and Assessment Board (NEAB)/Joint Matriculation Board (JMB); University of London Examination and Assessment Board (ULEAC); University of Cambridge Local Examinations Syndicate (UCLES).

The publishers would like to thank the following for permission for the use of statistical tables: two tables from *European Political Facts* by C. Cook and J. Paxton and two tables from *Industrialisation of Russia* by M. E. Falkus, by permission of Macmillan; a table from G. A Craig, *Germany 1866–1945*, © Gordon A. Craig, 1978, 1981, by permission of Oxford University Press; a table in abridged form from Alex Nove, *An Economic History of the USSR*, Penguin 1982; a table from M. Ferro, *The Great War 1914–18* by permission of Routledge, two tables from T. G. Charman, *Modern European History Notes*, by permission of Telles Langdon Publications.

Every effort has been made to contact holders of copyright material, but if any have been inadvertently overlooked the publishers will be pleased to make the necessary arrangements.

Illustrations

AKG London, 1, 96; AKG London/Michael Teller 228; AKG London, © DACS 1995 245; Robert Hunt Library 186; David King Collection 208,323; Popperfoto 270; Bildarchiv Preussischer Kulturbesitz, Berlin 78, 114; Cliché photothèque des musées de la Ville de Paris, © by SPADEM 1995 18, 38, 128 left; Süddeutscher Verlag Bilderdienst, Munich 286; Ullstein 148.

Cover photograph: The Battle of St Privat, 18 August 1870, by Alphonse de Neuville (Musée de l'Armée, Paris).

1

1815–48:
themes and problems

**A German cartoon showing a meeting of an intellectual society, the
'Thinkers' Club'. The notice on the wall reads: 'The important question to
be considered today: How long shall we go on being allowed to think?'.**

What sort of questions might such Germans have been debating had they not been
gagged?

How might a conservative such as Metternich have replied to the criticism implicit
in this cartoon?

1848–1945

The century between 1848 and 1945 formed in many respects an organic whole. Certainly the dramatic era of the French Revolution and of the Napoleonic conquests had drawn to a close in 1815, but the major political and ideological issues at stake in Europe in the following three decades were still very much those of the revolutionary period. The aspirations of liberal conspirators and of conservative politicians alike were the same that motivated them and their predecessors in the years since 1789.

Only in the years after 1848 did a new generation come to power that had not experienced at first hand the traumas of the 'Great Revolution'. Only then did the economic development of the major European states truly depart from the conditions of the 18th century.

1848, therefore, marked a significant stage in the development of problems that were not fully played out until the end of the Second World War, if then. It is impossible, nevertheless, to aspire to any real understanding of the Europe of 1848 without an outline of the events and forces which shaped that Europe. Many of these continued to influence the political, economic and philosophical development of the continent for many years thereafter.

A   The Vienna settlement

The restoration of the French monarchy

The political shape of Europe at the beginning of 1848 was predominantly the result of the great international settlement reached by the major powers, Britain, Russia, Prussia and Austria, upon the collapse of the Napoleonic Empire in 1814–15. The statesmen present had as their primary task the huge labour of providing for the political future of France and of those territories conquered by France. In addition they had to re-establish the balance of power shattered by the Napoleonic campaigns, and to ensure against any similar disruption in the future.

The cornerstone of the settlement was the fate of France herself. Although forcing the French to accept a restoration of the Bourbon monarchy deposed in 1792, the attitude of the allies in 1814 was one of wisdom and forbearance. They appreciated that harshness now would only store up trouble for the future. Only after substantial French support for Napoleon's last campaign in the 'Hundred Days' of 1815 did France lose those territories that she had occupied in 1790–92. Only then did the allies also impose a large war indemnity and an army of occupation. After the payment of the indemnity (1818) France was admitted to the alliance of the major powers, now the Quintuple Alliance, and became once more a full member of the diplomatic community. Even so, suspicion of French ambitions remained a constant feature of European diplomacy until France's definitive defeat in 1870.

The governmental settlement of France was also inspired by the need to ensure future stability. With both republican and Napoleonic forms of government generally unacceptable to the victorious allies, France was to undergo a restoration of the Bourbon dynasty deposed in 1792. However, that dynasty, in the person of Louis XVIII, was not to be restored unconditionally to all of its former powers. At the behest of the allies the Bourbon monarchy was to be transformed into a constitutional regime, adhering to a 'Charter' which guaranteed the maintenance of many of the primary achievements of the revolutionary and Napoleonic years.

Strengthening the borders of France

The wider territorial settlement achieved by the allies may be divided into three sub-sections. Firstly, the allies sought to prevent future French expansion by the creation of a cordon of relatively strong states around her borders. To this end, a new United Kingdom of the Netherlands was created, consisting of the old Dutch Republic and the Austrian Netherlands (now Belgium). The Italian border state of Piedmont was strengthened by the addition of Nice and Savoy, taken from France, and the formerly independent port of Genoa.

To the east, Prussia gained the greater part of the Rhineland, and thereby took on the role of front-line protector of Germany. This was partly compensation for the disappointment of her hopes of gains in central Europe, and partly because of the reluctance of the other allies to undertake the expensive and dangerous task of guarding the Rhine frontier against France. In this respect the

Rhineland settlement was, in the words of A. J. P. Taylor, 'a practical joke played by the Great Powers on the weakest of their number'. Although Prussia was reluctant to take on the responsibility for the industrial areas of the Rhineland, impregnated with both liberalism and Catholicism, their gain had the greatest significance for the future, both of Germany and of Europe as a whole.

The security of Germany and Italy

Secondly, this cordon was backed and supported by another. In Germany a loose confederation of 38 states known as the German Confederation (*Deutscher Bund*) was established to compensate for the collapse of the old Holy Roman Empire. Its task was to ensure that the mass of small German states would be less easy prey for a future expansionist power. Likewise, in Italy, a strong Austrian influence was maintained behind the enlarged state of Piedmont. This was based upon Austria's direct possession of Lombardy and Venetia, and also upon the reign in Tuscany, Parma and Modena of princes related to the Austrian Habsburg dynasty. Further south, the restoration of the Pope to his temporal power, and of the Bourbon family to rule in Naples, all aimed to counteract the strong French influence established in Italy over the previous two decades.

The wider balance of power

Thirdly, and largely independent of the fate of France, other territorial adjustments were necessary to satisfy the ambitions of certain of the allies, and thus to bind them more securely to the settlement as a whole. The most important of these concerned Saxony and Poland, where disagreements between the allies threatened at one time to precipitate further warfare. The peace conference ultimately agreed to the transfer of 40 per cent of Saxon territory to Prussia, further strengthening her German power, and leaving an independent 'rump' state.

A generally unsatisfactory agreement was also reached by which Poland became a kingdom under the rule of Tsar Alexander of Russia, nominally independent, but in all essentials subject to Russian control.

Lastly, largely upon the initiative of Great Britain, the victorious powers pledged themselves to further regular meetings with a view to diplomatic consultations upon whatever new causes of tension might arise in European politics. With the admission of France in 1818, this 'Concert of Europe' was perhaps the most lasting achievement of the statesmen of 1814–15. In the eyes of some commentators it earns comparison with the more sophisticated systems of collective security practised by the League of Nations after 1919, or by the United Nations after 1945.

Success or failure

The success, or the morality of the peace settlement has excited deep emotions among historians ever since its establishment. In a century in which liberalism and nationalism attracted wide support, the Vienna settlement was much criticised for ignoring those principles. The criticism made in an English radical pamphlet of 1821 was much repeated in the next century, and is still heard today. 'Public opinion was disregarded. National feeling was despised and the expression of it harshly repulsed. Whole countries were transferred from one prince to another, without any consideration of their wishes or habits.'

That these comments are less frequently heard today is due to two factors. Firstly, study of the settlement indicates that liberal principles were not invariably sacrificed to conservative ones. Constitutions were established or maintained in France, Spain, the Netherlands and Poland. Germany was a good deal less divided in 1815 than she had been in 1789. The shortcomings of the settlement lay less in the terms that it laid down than in the type of governors who, for the next three decades had perforce to be entrusted with the application of those terms.

Secondly, the experience of two world wars, and of a failed peace settlement in 1919 has led historians to a much rosier view of the treaties that kept Europe at peace for 40 years in the 19th century. Conscious now of the political weaknesses of liberalism, and of the potential disruptiveness of nationalism, many would now stress that the Congress was justified in its search for stability. They would echo the words of Sir Charles Webster: 'The primary need of Europe, once the Napoleonic tyranny was overthrown, was a period of peace; and this the statesmen of Vienna undoubtedly secured in a far greater degree than the publicists of the time dared to hope.'

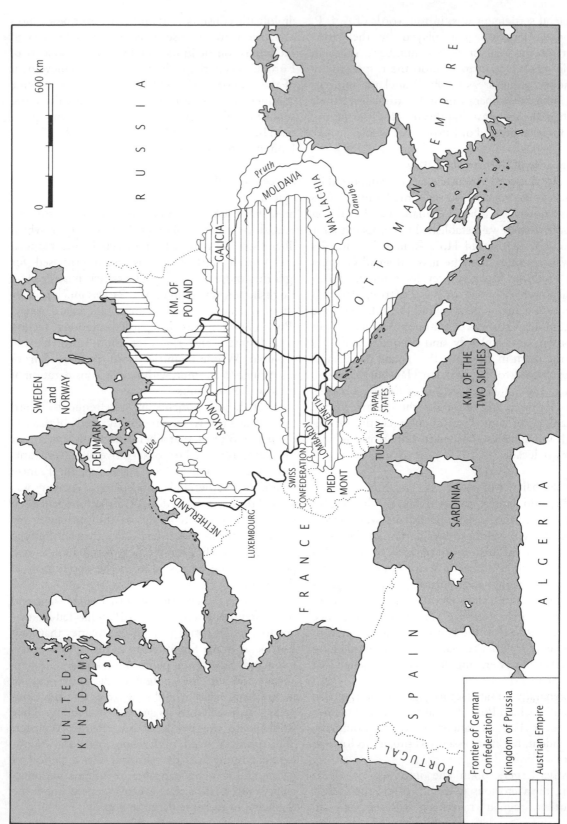

Europe after the Congress of Vienna, 1815

RUSSIA

OTTOMAN EMPIRE

MOLDAVIA

WALLACHIA

Pruth

Danube

GALICIA

KM. OF POLAND

SAXONY

SWEDEN
and
NORWAY

DENMARK

Elbe

NETHERLANDS

LUXEMBOURG

SWISS
CONFEDERATION

FRANCE

PIED-
MONT

LOMBARDY

VENETIA

TUSCANY

PAPAL
STATES

KM. OF THE
TWO SICILIES

SARDINIA

SPAIN

PORTUGAL

ALGERIA

UNITED
KINGDOM

600 km

0

Frontier of German
Confederation

Kingdom of Prussia

Austrian Empire

B Conservatism

Vested interests: legitimate monarchy

For all their startling successes before 1815, and despite their more modest achievements after that date, the liberal, constitutional and national ideas of the French revolutionaries were defeated and in opposition for most of the first half of the 19th century. In some states they remained so for the rest of the century. In Europe as a whole the dominant political ideas of the period were those of the conservatives whose triumph was at the very basis of the Vienna settlement.

European conservatism was based upon three main principles or interest groups. The first of these was the principle of hereditary monarchy, a principle so powerful that even the French revolutionaries had hesitated for three years before abolishing it, only for Napoleon to re-establish it throughout western Europe as the best guarantee of social and political stability. For some, the principle of monarchy was synonymous with the concept of 'legitimacy', the belief that in one state, one family alone was directly entrusted with power by God. Subsequent Russian tsars would not have differed much from Paul I (1796–1801) when he defined his absolute power as follows: 'Know that none in Russia is important except the person who is speaking to me; and that, only while he is speaking.'

Such notions of legitimism, however, were not widely held by the statesmen who served such monarchs. In the view of Metternich, who was often regarded as the personification of post-1815 conservatism, monarchy was desirable, not because it was the will of God, but because it seemed to offer the best hope of continuity and stability in human affairs. His view attracted widespread support. 'Monarchy,' concludes David Thomson, was at the time 'to most people the most natural form of government in the world.'

Vested interests: the nobility and the Church

Behind the monarchy in most European states stood the two groups who had suffered most, or had been most threatened by the upheavals of the last 25 years, the landowning nobility and the Church. In both cases the groups had been transformed by the French Revolution from being the rivals of the monarchy, mistrusting its centralising influence, into its close allies, aware now of far greater threats to their common interests. The role of the landowner is best illustrated in Prussia, where the feudal Junker class formed the staunchest support of the monarchy, or in Russia where, before the emancipation of the serfs (1861), the local control of the landlord formed the perfect complement to the central authority of the Tsar. In France, the pre-revolutionary authority of the landowner had not survived intact. His place had often been taken by richer tenant-farmers or by Napoleonic functionaries profiting from the break-up of the great estates. The events of 1848 well illustrate, however, that the new landowners had fully inherited the conservative interests of the old.

The Catholic Church had not only suffered assaults upon its property, but upon its doctrines too. In France, in Italy, in Spain, along with its Orthodox 'cousin' in Russia, it now ranged itself on the side of conservatism throughout the century. The maintenance of the temporal power of the Pope was to remain an emotive issue, and the philosophical clash between the rationalist ideas of *The Rights of Man* and the view of the human race as sinful creatures wholly subject to the will of God, formed one of the fundamental intellectual conflicts of the period.

Conservative theory: idealism and pragmatism

Two theoreticians of conservatism may be chosen to represent its main branches. For the Frenchman Joseph de Maistre (1753–1821), the supreme facts of human life were Original Sin, and man's consequent inability to create a good society by means of his reason. 'Mankind,' he proclaimed, 'is not progressing, it is groping back towards lost realms of light.' Monarchy was thus divinely ordained, in partnership with the Church, for the guidance of man, and the horrors of the French Revolution clearly showed how man lost his way when he rejected that guidance. Ultimately, because the authority of the monarch was derived from God, it was subordinated to that of God's main delegate on earth, the Pope. In the final analysis, de Maistre's Catholic conservatism owed a great debt to the medieval concept of universal Christendom.

Far more modern, and thus far more influential, was the conservatism of the Englishman Edmund Burke (1729–97). In his *Reflections on the Revolution in France* (1790) he laid his stress, not upon abstractions or mysticism, but upon the importance of experience as the chief guide in government. 'It is with infinite caution,' he wrote, 'that any man ought to venture upon pulling down an edifice which has answered in any tolerable degree for ages the common purposes of society.'

For Burke the tragedy of the revolution lay in the failure of questionable rationalist principles to take the place of institutions developed steadily through the experience of centuries. His was not necessarily an argument against change, merely against changing too fast and without due caution. In the hands of British Tories in the 19th century, Burke's was a philosophy of cautious advance, although elsewhere it was too often felt that any change at all was dangerous as tending to release anew the forces of revolution.

C Liberalism

The diversity of liberalism
In the first half of the 19th century the main rival to these conservative principles, and the other major governmental philosophy throughout the century, was liberalism. Although the concept of liberalism received coherent definition in Britain during these years, notably in the writings of Jeremy Bentham and John Stuart Mill, it remained a much broader one on the continent of Europe. The army officer in revolt against absolute government in Spain in 1820, the intellectual supporting the Decembrist rising in Russia in 1825, the German student participating in the demonstrations of the *Burschenschaften*, would all have found many points over which they disagreed. They were united, however, by a variety of factors: by their common negative aim to revise or undermine the conservative system of 'Vienna Europe', by common features of liberal political programmes, and by certain philosophical bases to their thought.

The legacy of the French Revolution
European liberalism drew much of its philosophical inspiration from the rationalist thought of the 18th century and from the early years of the French Revolution. From the former it inherited its primary point of contention with conservatism. Liberalism is based upon the conviction that people are essentially good and that to allow individual freedom will lead, not to anarchy and lawlessness, but to the ordered and rational progress of society.

From the latter came the classic statement of liberal thought on society and on politics, the *Declaration of the Rights of Man and of the Citizen* (26 August 1789). Essentially an expression of middle-class individualism, the declaration begins by establishing the 'natural and imprescriptible rights' of 'liberty, property, security and resistance to oppression'. It goes on to expand them into a full doctrine of equality of rights and equality before the law. Herein are to be found the elements that recur in every set of liberal demands presented during the next century.

The first demand was for a constitution. Indeed, as C. Breunig has pointed out, 'the word "constitution" took on an almost mystical significance for liberals in some German and Italian states, who assumed that by its mere existence such a document would solve all their problems'. Within such a constitution would be found requests for a consistent set of individual freedoms: freedom of speech, of worship, of assembly and of the press; freedom from arbitrary arrest, imprisonment and taxation; equality of opportunity. Parallel to these demands, especially in states with more advanced economies, ran the request for the freedom that critics such as Marx felt to be the end-product of all liberal thought, the freedom of trade and economic enterprise.

Liberalism and the poor
It will be clear that what 19th-century liberals drew from the French Revolution was the principle of *liberté* rather than that of *egalité*. In general, they were willing to accept material inequalities with the excuse that by equality of opportunity and the principle of 'self-help' any worthy man could aspire to material prosperity. The familiar slogan of British liberalism was that 'poverty is the divinely ordained consequence of a misspent life'. Thus European liberalism quickly ceased to be a radical political doctrine in the 19th century. 'We must preserve the political work that is the fruit of the Revolution,' wrote Chateaubriand, 'but we must eradicate the Revolution from this work.' Similarly Alexis de Tocqueville, in his influential work *Democracy in America* (1835–40), praised the American achievement precisely because it had created democratic

institutions without degenerating into mob rule.

Although aspiring to constitutional monarchy or to parliamentary rule as an ideal, liberals were increasingly resigned to accepting less democratic regimes, as in Russia or Prussia. They were also resigned to limiting themselves to detailed practical work on specific problems, such as legal procedures, or the improvement of living and working conditions. The essentials of the Vienna settlement were thus only threatened in a limited degree by liberalism. A more real threat was posed by the other great middle-class philosophy of the era, nationalism.

D Nationalism

Nationalism and the French Revolution

In many cases in 19th-century Europe, liberal political principles frequently went hand-in-hand with the desire for a free nation state. This was often because the conservative power that offended liberals was a foreign power. It is easy to appreciate how, to an Austrian governor in Italy, or to a Russian governor in Poland, the terms 'liberal' and 'nationalist' could appear to be almost interchangeable. However authoritarian and illiberal nationalism may have become in the 20th century, it was still reasonable in the 1830s and 1840s to equate the two ideals.

At this point in European history we may define nationalism as the belief that the natural division of humankind is the nation, as opposed to the social or economic class. A nationalist believed, in the words of Elie Kedourie, that 'the only legitimate type of government [for each division] is self-government'. In this form nationalism had its roots, like liberalism, in the rationalist thought of the 18th century. It also had roots in the French Revolution, which had stated in the *Declaration of the Rights of Man and of the Citizen* that 'the source of all sovereignty resides in the nation'.

The nation, in this sense, had no necessary racial connotation. It was not necessarily based upon a common language or upon common ethnic characteristics, but upon the factors identified by another French thinker, Ernest Renan, a century later (1882). 'A nation is a great solidarity, created by the sentiment of the sacrifices that have been made and those which one is disposed to make in the future.

It presupposes a past; but it resumes itself in the present by a tangible fact; the consent, the clearly expressed desire to continue life in common.' In this French tradition nationalism is not an excuse for aggression, for the division of humanity, but a bond uniting them in a spirit of fraternity. The greatest exponent of this form of nationalism was an Italian, Giuseppe Mazzini (1805–72), whose beliefs and political career are outlined in Chapter 2.

The German model: Herder

'I abhor,' wrote Mazzini in 1847, 'the usurping and monopolising nation, conceiving its own grandeur and force only in the inferiority and poverty of others.' Unfortunately, even as he wrote this, other currents in nationalist thought had led the movement very much in that direction. German nationalism was to show in 1848 some very different characteristics from those of its French counterpart. Partly this was due to the social and political circumstances of Germany, to the weakness of her middle classes and to her greater political diversity. There was also a substantial contrast between her cultural fruitfulness and her political impotence in the age of Beethoven, Goethe and Schiller. These characteristics found their expression in the writings of three dominant intellectual figures.

The first of these was a Lutheran pastor from Germany's most easterly provinces, Johann Gottfried von Herder (1744–1803). Reacting against what he felt to be the excessive dependence of German intellectuals upon French thought and fashion, Herder developed his theory of the uniqueness of each national group and of each set of national characteristics. Each was created by God with its own 'spirit' or 'genius' (*Volksgeist*) which it should preserve, cherish and develop, rather than slavishly imitate and pay homage to a foreign genius.

For Herder a major role of nationalism was the development of a nation's awareness of its own unique culture, for example in the famous collection of German folktales compiled by the brothers Grimm between 1811 and 1829. It must be stressed that Herder showed no interest in claiming the superiority of any one of these national cultures over the others. 'No nationality,' he specifically stated, 'has been solely designated by God as the chosen people of the earth; above all we must seek the truth and cultivate the garden of the common good.' His work had, however, instituted a radical development in the concept of 'the nation' by replacing the consenting community of French thought with the broadly racial concept of the *Volk*.

The German model: Fichte

Such generosity as Herder showed towards other nations could not survive the trauma of Napoleon's invasion of Germany and the humiliating defeat of the Prussian army at Jena (1806). The development of the thought of the Saxon university professor Johann Gottlieb Fichte (1762–1814) was characteristic.

Admiration for the ideals of the French Revolution turned to revulsion when those ideals were imposed upon a defeated German nation. In his *Addresses to the German Nation* (*Reden an die Deutsche Nation*, 1807–08), Fichte moved German nationalism away from its liberal origins by two important stages. Firstly, he stressed, not merely the diversity between peoples, but the superiority of the German 'spirit'. Adulteration of the national spirit, by imitation of or contact with foreign cultures, caused degeneration. Thus, by avoiding foreign domination since Roman times, the Germans had preserved their culture and their whole national identity in a much purer form than had the French, the Italians or the Slavs.

It was a case taken up with enthusiasm by a younger generation of agitators such as Friedrich Jahn and Ernst Arndt, who proclaimed unequivocally in 1818, 'let us hate the French strongly, and let us hate our own French who dishonour and ravage our energy and our innocence'. Here was a nationalism specifically directed against neighbouring states.

The German model: Hegel

Fichte's second innovation was to stress, in reaction to the political weakness that surrounded him, the importance of the state for the protection and development of the individual and of the national identity. This element was developed much further by his successor at the University of Berlin, Georg Wilhelm Friedrich Hegel (1770–1831). Although Hegel was primarily concerned with developing a general philosophical system, and not with the politics of either nationalism or of socialism, his influence upon both movements was profound. His

greatest contribution was his development of the theory of Dialectic.

According to this theory, all change and progress in history results from the clash of opposite ideas and forces. From such clashes between a 'thesis' and a diametrically opposed 'antithesis' results an end product, a 'synthesis', containing elements of both original ideas or forces. This synthesis will eventually come into conflict with its own opposite, and so change progresses. As an example, the French Revolution might be seen as a clash between a thesis (absolute monarchy) and an antithesis (radical democracy), producing the synthesis of Napoleonic paternalism.

The influence of this theory upon a Europe soon to receive Charles Darwin's message of scientific evolution was enormous, and the influence of Hegel upon Karl Marx's views of economic progress was especially important. For Hegel, however, the ultimate outcome of this dialectical development was not the victory of the working classes, but the emergence of the nation state. Sharing Herder's view that man's creative ability was limited when he acted as an individual, Hegel preached that man could truly fulfil himself only as part of the organic state. All this might have placed him closer to Mazzini than to Fichte, had it not been for two factors.

Firstly, Hegel was convinced of the special destiny reserved for Germany, and of the role of the Prussian monarchy. Secondly, he strongly implied that the conventional notion of legality and right in relations between states had little meaning if the positions of the nations represented inevitable stages in the dialectical process. His reminder that 'men are foolish to forget the truth that lives in power' rings ominously through the history of 19th- and 20th-century Germany.

Two generations of thought thus made nationalism in Germany a doctrine centred upon a sense of cultural superiority, a sense of duty to the national state and an unhealthy admiration of power. Such features were not unique to Germany in the 19th century. Pan-slavism, in particular, imitated some of them (*see* Chapter 6). The combination of these philosophical convictions, however, with the growing political and economic power of Prussia was to make this German nationalism a particularly potent and dynamic force in the history of the next century.

E The fate of the settlement

The principle of the balance of power

In assessing the long-term success of the Vienna settlement, one is confronted with conflicting evidence. If its primary aim was to achieve ideological unity among the governors of Europe, then the settlement failed. Britain never accepted the validity of nor the necessity for conservatism of the Russian or Austrian variety. Unanimity was further undermined by the triumph of the principle of popular sovereignty in France in 1830. Yet the practice of balancing roughly equal power blocs against one another, so that no one power could achieve the supremacy that France had achieved before 1812, proved remarkably durable. This 'Balance of Power' proved to be the greatest achievement of the Vienna statesmen, and the most prominent diplomatic feature of the years 1815–48.

The Holy Alliance

At first, repression played a significant role in the preservation of this stability. The Holy Alliance, contracted between the rulers of Russia, Austria and Prussia in September 1815, was a remarkably abstract entity, 'perhaps the vaguest document ever to trouble European diplomacy' (Alan Sked). It was subsequently subscribed to by most other European monarchs, but rejected on grounds of political principle, religion or fear by the king of England, the Pope and the Sultan of Turkey. The Alliance was ostensibly an agreement to renounce war and to commit the rulers of Europe to friendly co-existence as Christian brothers. It derived this nature from the unstable mysticism of its founder, Tsar Alexander I. To a more hard-headed conservative, such as the Austrian Chancellor, Klemens von Metternich, the scheme was a 'high-sounding nothing'.

Metternich, nevertheless, was to give the Alliance a more practical application. Through him it became a weapon for direct military intervention in the affairs of the lesser states, in the interests of political counter-revolution and of legitimate monarchy. The principle of armed intervention was laid down, despite British opposition, at the Congress of Troppau (1820). It was successfully applied against liberal uprisings in Naples, Piedmont (1821) and Spain (1822). Thus, the Holy Alliance and its interventionist policy destroyed the ideological unity of the five major powers, yet preserved the territorial settlement established in 1815.

The resurgence of liberal nationalism

The policy of intervention did not long survive its early triumphs. By the mid-1820s, old territorial differences between the major powers had resurfaced sufficiently to make the prospect of Austrian armies marching into southern Italy, or of Russian forces entering the Turkish empire, too unattractive to be tolerated as a general principle. Instead, the major powers fell back upon the principle of consultation and co-operation that had been established at the Congress of Vienna.

From 1820 onwards, the causes of nationalism and liberalism won some notable victories. These successes came only with the co-operation of the major powers, in cases where they were convinced that the triumph would not endanger the general European equilibrium. Thus the rebellion of some of Spain's South American colonies in 1822 succeeded because the economic interests of Great Britain, and the desire of the United States for domestic security, made these great maritime powers hostile to the idea of counter-revolutionary intervention by the more conservative powers.

The revolt of the Greeks nationalists against their Turkish overlords (1821–29) was ultimately successful because powerful emotions and influential opinions made it impossible for the European powers to maintain their initial pro-Turkish stance. Metternich's view that massacred Greek rebels 'hanged, impaled or with their throats cut, hardly count' as long as the Turkish bloc was maintained, was widely countered by other forces. In Russia, the Orthodox Church urged support for their co-religionists, and some politicians failed to resist the tempting vision of a pro-Russian Greek satellite on the Mediterranean. In the west, an influential pro-Greek (Philhellenist) movement grew up among the educated classes raised on the glories of classical Greece. Western governments, furthermore, could not tolerate the risks involved if Russia intervened single-handed. A complicated combination of diplomacy and anti-Turkish force brought about a settlement whereby Greece not only became independent from Turkey, but was committed to a position of neutrality.

The Belgian revolt against Dutch rule (1830), which eventually brought about the only major change in the state boundaries of western Europe during this period, succeeded for similar reasons. Great Britain traditionally disliked the prospect of a large stretch of Channel coastline controlled by one state. Therefore Belgian independence, together with an international guarantee of neutrality (1839) suited the interests of Britain, and ultimately those of France. As was to be demonstrated in 1914, Belgian neutrality ensured that no power could henceforth attack France's northern borders without the most severe international implications.

The Eastern Question

The most severe threat both to the balance of power and to the peaceful co-operation of the major powers came from the reopening of the 'Eastern Question', of which the Greek War of Independence was part. At the root of this problem was the obvious decline of the Turkish empire. Britain, France and Austria all had their own reasons to fear that Russia might fill the vacuum caused by such a decline. Having failed to secure any material advantage from the Greek question, Russia made more blatant attempts to strengthen her position in the eastern Mediterranean following the attack upon the Sultan (1832) by his nominal vassal, the Khedive of Egypt, Mehemet Ali. In return for Russian support the Sultan agreed to the Treaty of Unkiar Skelessi, whereby Russia gained greater security behind the closed Dardanelles, and effectively established a form of unofficial protectorate over the Sultan.

Russia's advantage was challenged only in 1839, when the death of the Sultan Mahmud left the Ottoman empire exposed once more to the power of the Khedive, now openly backed by the French. The dual threat of Russian intervention and of the domination of the Turkish empire by a friend of France was sufficient to drive the powers back to the conference table.

There the isolation of France eventually produced the Straits Convention (1841), which preserved the integrity of the Ottoman empire and the existing Middle Eastern interests of the great powers. That it had not definitively solved the Eastern Question was to be proved a decade later by the outbreak of the Crimean War.

Great power relations in 1848

By 1848, rivalry between the great powers was firmly re-established. Russia's ambitions in eastern Europe distanced her even from her Austrian neighbour, and her governmental ideology distanced her from increasingly liberal regimes in Britain and France. Colonial rivalry, and British distrust of French actions in Belgium and Spain guaranteed that the *Entente Cordiale* reached between the two states in the 1830s would never develop into a firm, liberal alliance.

Yet the territorial system established at Vienna, and the balance of power, survived with only minor modifications. Initially war-weariness and the absence of any great, outstanding territorial issues explain this stability. Subsequently, fear of the social and political forces, nationalism, liberalism and socialism, that might surface if the diplomatic mud were stirred too vigorously, caused the leaders of the powers to desist from any such action. This consistent restraint is one of the most striking features of the years 1815–48. The abandonment of such restraint in the era of Napoleon III, of Bismarck and of Cavour sets the years that followed 1848 firmly apart from the preceding epoch.

F   The fate of the Vienna settlement: France

The constitutional monarchy under Louis XVIII

Perhaps the greatest failure of the European settlement of 1815 concerned France. There the Vienna statesmen had sought to guarantee future political stability and to provide a regime that would 'heal the wounds of the revolution' without recourse to the international adventures of the Napoleonic era. The restoration of the Bourbon dynasty was, in theory, a substantial compromise. Louis XVIII was restored as a constitutional monarch. He was committed by the 'Charter' to maintain such fundamental elements of the revolutionary and Napoleonic period as the Civil Code, the sale and redistribution of noble and ecclesiastical estates, and the principles of equality before the law, equality of taxation and careers open to talent. The preamble added by Louis himself, however, made it abundantly clear that he viewed these freedoms, not as natural rights of the people, but as gifts granted by a monarch whose only superior was God.

Although Louis' personal feeling was that the Charter was a reasonable price to pay for his restoration, the compromise was subjected to the most severe strains between 1815–30. The government proved unable, and probably unwilling, to prevent an epidemic of counter-revolutionary vengeance. Its common name, the 'white terror', recalled the unbridgeable gap created between the social classes by the earlier, revolutionary terror. In public life, too, a strong 'Ultra' royalist party enjoyed sympathy at the highest political levels, notably from Louis' brother and heir, Charles, Duc d'Artois. Although such politicians as the Duc de Richelieu sought to maintain the spirit of the constitution, it is generally agreed that the murder of Artois' son, the Duc de Berry (February 1820), started a steady descent into reaction. The succession of Artois as Charles X (1824) merely turned that descent into official government policy.

The constitutional monarchy under Charles X

The measures of Charles' reign included the restoration of clerical influence, especially in education, and the re-institution of press censorship. In addition, the National Guard, cherished by the bourgeoisie as their safeguard against the forces of the monarchy, was disbanded. In 1829 and 1830 elections showed the level of discontent among the enfranchised classes by returning large liberal majorities. Charles responded by attempting to return to personal government in defiance of what most conceived to be the spirit of the Charter. Attempts to dissolve the Chamber, and to influence the election of its replacement by a further reduction of the electorate, precipitated the outbursts of July 1830, which ended the Bourbon monarchy in France for ever.

The popular disturbances which shook Paris at this time also proved that discontent was not limited to the enfranchised classes. They threatened a return to the republican excesses of 40 years earlier, which would have undermined the whole work of the Vienna statesmen. Louis Philippe, Duc d'Orleans, was rapidly elevated to the position of 'King of the French' (a significant acknowledgement of popular sovereignty) by prominent members of the bourgeoisie and of the Assembly. He owed this to the fear of what the alternatives might be if revolutionary action were allowed to continue. Similar motives lay behind his general recognition by the European powers, which foreshadowed their recognition of Louis Napoleon Bonaparte two decades later. Constitutionally, Louis Philippe was to govern France until the great economic crises of the late 1840s under much the same terms as Louis XVIII. The revived Charter of 1830 differed in only a few respects from its prototype of 1815. The major difference was that the king now recognised it as representing the inalienable natural rights of the people and, in public at least, did not balk at the idea of a throne 'surrounded by republican institutions'.

The lessons of the Bourbon restoration

The experience of the French governments between 1815 and 1830 made it clear once more that the major advances of the revolutionary and Napoleonic periods were irreversible. No subsequent French administration seriously considered governing without reference to the interests of those conservative classes, notably the bourgeoisie and the peasantry, that had benefited most from the revolution. The events of 1830 also provided a potent reminder of another force in French politics. 'We did not know the people of Paris,' Remusat was to write, 'and we did not realise what they could do.' The potential for proletarian revolt was not only to be an occasional inspiration to radical leaders until the Commune of 1871 and beyond, but also a powerful agent for the co-operation of conservatives and moderate reformers in France throughout the rest of the century.

Unlike many of his contemporaries, Louis Philippe was confronted by a problem that they could still evade: how to adapt to social and economic developments without harming the fundamental propertied interests upon which his regime rested. His answer was to make his government a 'bourgeois monarchy', a 'government of the élite, and a meeting place of all the aristocracies, whether or birth, wealth or intelligence' (Jacques Droz). Ultimately that basis, although wider than the basis upon which the Bourbon monarchy had rested, was to prove too narrow. His successors, both imperial and republican, would have to seek ways of extending the popular foundations of their authority. For all that, the questions of French domestic stability, and of France's place in the European balance of power, would continue to haunt the statesmen of Europe for years to come.

G The fate of the Vienna settlement: Central Europe

The conservatism of Metternich

It has long been fashionable to refer to 1815–48 as the 'Age of Metternich'. Against this has been raised the objection that the control of the great Austrian diplomat over the European events of this era was extremely limited, that Russia, Britain and, after 1830, France, went very much their own way. Nevertheless, across a great swath of territory in central Europe, across the Austrian empire itself, across the neighbouring Italian states, and across the German Confederation, the principles of Metternich remained dominant. These principles had been formed in direct reaction to the liberal ideas of the early phases of the French Revolution, which had degenerated into domestic terror and into two generations of international conflict. From this degeneration Metternich concluded that monarchical government alone guaranteed the security of the continent. Monarchy alone, based upon the consent of the aristocracy and of the other estates of the realm, ensured authority and stability. Any departure from this time-honoured format, however moderate and reasonable it might appear, was in fact the thin end of the revolutionary wedge.

Metternich's own conservatism fell somewhere between that of de Maistre and that of Burke (*see* section **B**). He was an intensely practical politician, unimpressed by romantic notions of 'divine right', but strictly opposed to any gradual concessions to modernism. Liberalism, to him, was a manifestation of the selfish interests of the 'agitated classes' rather than an enlightened ideal. It was thus to be resisted by direct attacks upon the media most frequently used by the liberals, by censorship of the press, by resistance to demands for direct political representation, and by a complex system of surveillance and other police activity.

Opposition to Metternich in Germany and Austria

In opposition to these principles, the receding tide of the Napoleonic invasions left behind in central Europe many substantial pools of liberal and nationalist sentiment. Within the Austrian empire itself the greatest obstacle to monarchical centralisation lay in the historical separatism of Hungary, and particularly in the powers of the Hungarian Diet. Without the consent of the Diet, laws made in Vienna had no validity in Budapest. As is shown elsewhere (*see* Chapter 2), Hungarian ambitions represented only the most striking element in a bewildering variety of national aspirations.

In Italy, too, although the Austrian-controlled provinces of Lombardy and Venetia were less troubled than most of the other states, Austrian ideals were constantly challenged by radical movements drawing their inspiration from the days of the French occupation.

Similarly, in Germany, the undercurrent of liberal and national demands was persistent. In the years immediately after the defeat of Napoleon it manifested itself mainly in the restricted, but noisy context of the student organisations, the *Burschenschaften*. These were generally given to romantic, but sterile gestures such as the 'Wartburg Festival' (October 1817), celebrating the 300th anniversary of Martin Luther's stand against foreign religious forces. They occasionally descended into violence and even, in the case of the reactionary poet Kotzebue to political assassination (1819). In the ensuing decades the liberalism of the students tended to give way to the liberalism of the professors. By the 1840s the political theorists of the south German universities shared the leading role with the merchants of the Rhineland in voicing demands for the recognition of the great liberal freedoms in the government of the German states.

The Metternich 'system'

Metternich faced these challenges less with a reactionary 'system', as most contemporaries and most subsequent historians have seen it, than with a formidable array of expedients. In Germany he benefited from the conservatism of the princes, and from the willingness of those such as the king of Prussia to be guided by him on constitutional problems. More important still, Austria's presidency of the German Confederation put the machinery of that body at the disposal of his cause. Thus Metternich was able to answer the disruption of the *Burschenschaften* with the Karlsbad Decrees (1819), and the disturbances inspired by the events of 1830 in France by the Six Articles (1832). The combined effect was to gag the liberal press, to impose controls over academic syllabuses, to remove unreliable teachers and to strangle 'progressive' ideas at their source. Perhaps the greatest success of the conservative cause was the cancellation of the Hanoverian constitution in 1837. In Italy, similarly, Metternich could operate through Austria's direct control of Lombardy and Venetia, through her dynastic links with the duchies of Modena, Parma and Tuscany, and through the habitual reliance of other Italian rulers upon Austrian aid *in extremis.*

Paradoxically, it was within the Austrian empire itself that Metternich had to improvise most. His projects for administrative and financial reform to streamline the government of this vast conglomerate were consistently frustrated by an emperor who took his role as an autocrat too literally. He insisted that all major issues should receive his personal attention, which frequently reduced administration to chaos. The succession of the weak-minded Ferdinand in 1835 merely substituted court intrigue for personal interference.

Increasingly, Metternich came to rely upon the most disreputable methods to contain problems that he could not solve. He dominated the state police system, exercised direct control over press censorship, maintained a complex spy network, and distributed bribes and subsidies where they might aid his work. Few major Hungarian leaders escaped substantial periods of imprisonment. All possible allies were exploited. The Catholic Church received enthusiastic backing. The literary and cultural aspirations of lesser nationalities who regarded the Hungarians as a threat were sometimes tolerated and encouraged. Even Austria's economic backwardness was seen as an advantage, for 'the labours to which [the peasants] are obliged to devote themselves are too continuous and too positive to allow them to throw themselves into vague abstractions and ambitions'.

Metternich: success or failure?

Yet, how successful was this great conservative, this 'rock of order'? It is easy to construct a list of failings. In Italy, although he preserved the native rulers from the wrath of their liberal and nationalist subjects, he himself bemoaned his failure to persuade them to undertake such administrative reforms as might strengthen their rule in the long term. In Germany, Austria's leadership failed on two important counts. Her economy was unable to provide adequate commercial leadership. Thus it was Prussia which headed the Customs Union

(*Zollverein*) formed in 1834. Metternich accurately foresaw that 'the links that bind Austria to the other states of the German Confederation would gradually become loosened, and in the end break entirely, thanks to this barrier'. Secondly, Austria's financial degeneracy left her army 'so run-down, demoralised and ill-led that it could scarcely be described as battle-worthy' (Alan Sked). Austria's failure to provide Germany with decisive military leadership in the international crises of 1830 and 1840 foreshadowed her ultimate failure in this respect in the next two decades.

Yet, if Metternich could not defeat nationalism in Hungary, Germany and Italy, and if he could not definitively silence constitutional demands, he prevented these forces from making any significant progress in central Europe for three decades. It was a colossal conservative achievement, and the force of the outburst in 1848 bore witness to the frustration caused by his success. More important, Metternich created one of the distinctive international features of the 1815–48 period. He was in large part responsible for the essential governmental stability of the great territorial mass of central Europe, which served as a barrier to the ambitions of France and Russia alike. Able to resist foreign encroachment, yet too incoherent ever to take the offensive, this bloc thus made a fundamental contribution to the maintenance of the balance of power and of international peace. At the centre, both literally and figuratively, of the international history of the period 1848–1945 is the fact of Austrian decline and disintegration, and the attempts of France, Prussia, Piedmont, unified Germany and Italy, and ultimately of Soviet Russia, to take advantage of that fact. The watershed of 1848, between an 'Age of Metternich' and a 'Post-Metternich Europe' is thus a real and significant one.

H The economic context

Population

Important as the ideological and material disputes created or amplified by the French Revolution were, the development of Europe in the early 19th century was as much the result of a second revolution. The British industrial revolution is often spoken of as an 18th-century phenomenon, but the achievement of that century was really only to produce a firm basis, in terms of technological development and the reorganisation of production, for the great economic 'take-off' that occurred in the three decades after the Napoleonic wars. The revolutionary modifications made to the steam engine by James Watt and their application to the manufacture of textiles, the development of new techniques for iron smelting and coal mining, and the foundation of railway technology, not only provided Britain with a formidable power base, but blazed an experimental trail for continental Europe to follow.

Perhaps the real revolution in continental terms was the population revolution. Between 1750 and 1850, the population of Europe nearly doubled, from 140 million to about 266 million. The staggering impact of this increase may be gauged from the estimate that the previous doubling of the continent's population had taken nearly 12 centuries, while the increase between 1650 and 1750 had been a mere 3 per cent. The rate of increase was, of course, uneven. France experienced only a 30 per cent increase in the 75 years after Waterloo, while the number of Germans and British doubled. Russia felt the pressure most keenly of all, doubling her population in the first half of the century alone.

The main explanation for this lies in a sharp fall in the death rate, attributable to the considerable advances made in medical science, especially the fall in infant mortality, the growth of public order and stability, and the improvements in food production throughout this period. David Thomson is not alone in seeing this population 'explosion' as a prime cause of the discontent, instability and international competition that characterised the 19th and 20th centuries. 'Against this tide,' he wrote, 'no social and political order could stand intact.'

Industrialisation

The effects of technical and social change were felt unevenly across the continent, generally spreading eastwards from their origins in the west. Belgium, fortunate in her natural resources and in the enlightened and coherent policy of her government after independence, was an early imitator of Britain's example. A national railway system was completed between 1834 and 1844 and Liège and southern Hainault became leading areas of coal and iron production. France made a slower start, but the reign of Louis Philippe (1830–48), with its

deliberate identification with bourgeois interests, brought consistent government support for industrial development. Over 3,000 km of railway track were laid in 1837–48 (compared with a 9,600 km system in Britain by 1850) and an important law concerning road improvements was passed in 1836. Industrial areas developed in Alsace, Normandy and in the Nord, where textiles predominated, and in Lorraine, where an important metallurgical industry was growing. Two qualifications must be noted, however. Firstly, technology remained relatively primitive, with nine blast furnaces out of ten still fuelled by charcoal rather than by coke. Secondly, it must not be forgotten that, with only 400,000 Frenchmen employed in factories in 1848, France remained both economically and culturally a predominantly agricultural nation.

Beyond the Rhine, industrialisation was less advanced by 1848. In Germany, political diversity was a major factor in slower and more piecemeal growth, but the foundations had been established. Prussia in 1848 was only 25 per cent behind France in terms of railway mileage. Heavy industry, however, remained scattered, and was operated mainly by small plants relying upon traditional means of production. Even the Krupp works at Essen, the industrial giant of the later 19th century, employed only 140 workers in 1846. German iron output, at 200,000 tons per annum, was only 10 per cent of Britain's total in 1850. As in France, the agricultural basis of German society was strong. Not until 1900 could 50 per cent of Germans be classified as town dwellers.

Nevertheless, the 1830s saw one major step taken towards the future economic strength of Germany. Based in part upon the foresight of such economists as Friedrich List, and partly upon the desire of the Prussian state for economic predominance in Germany, a customs union (*Zollverein*) was established in 1834. It united a number of smaller free-trade unions and comprised all the major German states except Austria. In Russia and in much of the Habsburg Empire, the beginnings of true industrialisation still lay some way in the future.

The urban and rural poor

A major result of this industrial growth was the development of large concentrations of urban population. The French textile town of Roubaix experienced a population increase from 8,000 to 34,000 in 1831–41 alone. The population of Paris rose from 550,000 to just over one million between 1800 and 1850, and the total number of European cities with a population of more than 100,000 rose from 22 to 47 in that same period. Nor were the new industrial cities of the continent spared the dreadful problems of disease and overcrowding that characterised the industrial revolution in Britain. Nine out of every ten young Frenchmen conscripted into the army from urban areas in 1840 were rejected as physically unfit, and the spectacular cholera epidemic in Paris in 1831–32 killed 18,400 victims in six months. With a working day of 13 hours standard in Germany, and 14–15 hours common in France, outbreaks of urban violence were frequent.

While these problems predominated in the towns, the rural population also felt the effects of the technological and demographic upheavals. In the countryside, too, a society relatively stable for centuries was reshaped by the pressure of population increase, the pressure upon food supplies, and increased competition for suitable farming land. A measure of this pressure may be gained from the fact that 236,000 Germans emigrated from their homeland between 1841 and 1850. Although details obviously differed from state to state, and from locality to locality, the 1830s and 1840s were characterised generally for large numbers of peasants and artisans by the uprooting of their traditional ways of life and livelihood, and by their transplantation to unfamiliar environments with unfamiliar problems.

The urban middle class

Lastly, alongside the growth of a new form of urban proletariat, industrialisation also encouraged the transformation of the urban middle class, nourished by the profits from the new forms of production. As the pace of development varied from country to country, so the development of this class varied. In Russia the pace of modernisation was so slow as to make a minimal impact upon the influence of the old governing class until the end of the century, while in Berlin, in 1848, only 700 out of a population of 400,000 were classified as belonging to the capitalist mercantile class.

In France, however, the potential development of that class was already clear. There the prosperity of the middle class is indicated by the fact that, although the wealth qualification for the vote remained at the same high level throughout the reign of Louis Philippe, the number thus qualified to vote increased from 160,000 in 1830 to 240,000 in 1846. Embryonic though they might still be in many parts of the continent, it was clear that powerful rivals to the existing governing classes were emerging.

I Socialism: the utopians

The socialist case

The newest challenge of the 19th century, both to the old hierarchy of the landowner, and to the new one which the bourgeoisie sought to construct, came from that scattered group of intellectuals who called themselves 'socialists'. Socialism, even in 1848, was not widely influential. It was little known among the working classes that it sought to serve, especially among the peasantry, and lacked any true consensus of means and aims. However, the basis had already been laid by then for movements that were to transform European politics and society in the subsequent decades.

Diverse as the term 'socialism' undoubtedly was, those movements that claimed it as their title had certain common bases for their views. One was their common dissatisfaction with the system of industrial production currently developing in Europe. Its main fault was, as Robert Owen put it, that it laid too great a stress upon the production of goods, and too little upon their distribution. The result was that, despite the vast industrial resources and agricultural fertility of the continent, millions of its population 'are but imperfectly supplied with some, and are entirely destitute of most, of the necessities and comforts of life'. Secondly, socialists shared a highly optimistic view of human nature and of humanity's capacity for virtue and co-operation in its social existence. They rejected the opinion of conservative thinkers, such as de Maistre, that people were necessarily sinful, and in many cases they had, as Proudhon put it, 'lost faith in God and found it in humanity'.

From these bases arose the conclusion reached by a number of socialist writers in the 19th century that the reformation of society was possible only by turning one's back upon societies formed for

Marxism

History and influence

The year 1848 saw the greatest single development in the history of socialism with the publication in London of a concise work entitled *The Communist Manifesto*. One of its authors was Friedrich Engels (1820–95), son of a prosperous manufacturer with interests in Manchester and in the Rhineland. His co-author was the greatest and most influential thinker that socialism ever produced. Karl Marx (1818–83) was a Rhinelander by birth, and thus much more closely associated than the utopians with industrial society. He was also a member of a family converted from Judaism, and thus directly acquainted both with oppression and with messianic philosophy. Marx and Engels, both deeply influenced by the dialectical philosophy of Hegel, had already engineered (1846–47) the foundation of the Communist League. Now they presented the outline of communist economic and political philosophy, which Marx was subsequently to expand in such major works as *Capital* (*Das Kapital*, 1867).

The starting point of the Marxist argument was that history consists of a constant struggle between the socio-economic classes, with political power and control of the state lying at any given time with the class that controls the means of economic production. The latest stage of this struggle had seen the steady triumph of the merchant and industrial class, the bourgeoisie. Their victory over the landowning aristocracy was marked out by such great events as the English Civil War and the French Revolution.

Yet, by the very growth of its industrially based power, the economic system of the bourgeosie, capitalism, created the tools of its own destruction. Firstly, capitalism strove towards monopoly, so that competition and the defeat of one company by another became essential, self-destructive features of the system. Secondly, it transformed the working classes by concentrating them in large numbers, by exploiting their labour in a naked and obvious fashion, and by provoking them to unite against these abuses.

He summarised this exploitation in his 'theory of surplus value'. This stated that the value of a product derived largely from the value of the resources, including labour, expended on its production. Yet the wages received by the worker were always lower than the market value of the finished product, the balance passing to the capitalist in the form of profit. In effect, therefore, the profit of the capitalist amounted to the theft of the fruits of the worker's labour.

The development of capitalism also had important international implications. Competition between company and company for limited resources and markets would be reflected in similar competition between state and state. Thus capitalism, which appeared to be so strong in Marx's own day, would steadily manufacture the crisis that would destroy it.

Marx's other great contribution to the development of socialism was to stress the importance of working-class organisation in order to ferment and to exploit this crisis of capitalism, and to promote class-consciousness among fellow workers. In his view, only the Communist Party could fulfil this role, by virtue of its more comprehensive historical view, and its more logical grasp of social and economic realities. The victory of the working class in the resultant revolutionary struggle would be followed by the historical stage referred to as the 'dictatorship of the proletariat'. The machinery of the state, now controlled by the workers, would be turned against the defeated classes, to eliminate them.

Only when this stage was completed could a truly 'communist' society, with public ownership of land and all other means of production, with a heavy and progressive income tax, and with public control of all public resources, come into being. The machinery of the state, since its sole purpose was class exploitation and repression, would have no part to play in a classless society, and would 'wither away'.

personal profit, and by constructing instead communities based upon co-operation and mutual respect. Such projects were generally called 'utopian' by their critics, in reference to Sir Thomas More's great 16th-century social fantasy, *Utopia*.

Robert Owen

Perhaps the most famous of these utopian experiments was that of the Welsh socialist, Robert Owen (1771–1858). Owen believed strongly in the corrupting nature of the modern industrial environment, and sought to demonstrate in his mills at

New Lanark in Scotland that industry could function without exploitation or squalor, and that co-operation could replace competition in society. The success of the New Lanark venture was insufficient to encourage other manufacturers to follow Owen's example, however, and subsequent ventures in America ended in failure. Nevertheless, Owen's views on the potential of human nature, and on the importance of environment and education, exercised a substantial influence on several of the future mainstreams of socialism, especially trade unionism and the co-operative movement.

Saint-Simon and Fourier

With the exception of Owen, utopian socialism had its strongest roots in French thought. Henri de Saint-Simon (1760–1825) possesses a strong claim to be considered the first modern socialist. Saint-Simon did not reject the concept of a hierarchical society, but wished to see it adjusted so that society should reflect the importance of scientific and industrial advance and its potential for improving the lot of the masses. Prominent in the new hierarchy would be, not the decorative but useless courtiers of the *ancien regime*, but the intellectual elite and the captains of industry, capable of providing for the needs of the unpropertied classes. It should become the purpose of the state to serve the interests of the population in general, and not merely those of a privileged minority. Saint-Simon's tolerance of the principle of private property made his views relatively widely acceptable in France in the 1830s and the 1840s, and he had considerable influence over some of those surrounding the throne during the Second Empire.

Like Owen, Charles Fourier (1772–1837) believed that people's future happiness depended upon a radical reorganisation of capitalist methods of labour and production. Human 'passions' or instincts, he believed, were presently misdirected and corrupted by the faults in people's living and working environment. His hope was to create a number of small, self-contained communities (*phalanges*), in which labour would be shared and distributed according to the individual talents and interests of the workers. Frequent rotation of tasks would ensure variety and maintain enthusiasm. Like Saint-Simon, Fourier saw no cause to attack the concept of private property, his principal concern being to increase the satisfaction of the working life, not to redistribute wealth.

Economic restrictions, and his own eccentricity, meant that Fourier's new communities remained a dream. His writings exercised a substantial influence, however, as a comprehensive exposure of the faults and the abuses within the existing capitalist system.

Blanc and Proudhon

The next generation of French socialists was dominated by Louis Blanc (1811–82) and Pierre-Joseph Proudhon (1809–65). Blanc differed from his predecessors mainly in the importance that he attached to the state. He felt that only when governmental power was in the hands of those sympathetic to the working classes could the worker be freed from the curse of periodic depression and unemployment, and enjoy his basic right, the right to work. His view that such a government should establish what he called 'social workshops', co-operative units of production, was seen as the key to wider social co-operation and harmony. Blanc was to play a key role in the events of 1848.

Proudhon's main point of departure from earlier writers lay in his attitude towards private property. In his best known work, *What is Property?* (1840), he answered his own question with the famous phrase that 'property is theft'. The abolition of capitalist property, and the gradual replacement of the state by a system in which universal, fraternal co-operation replaced monolithic authority, lay at the basis of his socialism. 'In him,' Massimo Salvadori has concluded, 'the anarchist component of socialism prevailed over the collectivist.'

In the work of Blanc and Proudhon, therefore, it is possible to discern important points of contact with later trends in socialist thought. Proudhon's anarchism can be detected in the establishment of the Paris Commune in 1871 and, thereby, in the Russian Soviets of 1905 and 1917. Both still apparently failed to grasp some of the fundamental realities of industrial and political power. It was by incorporating these realities into socialist thought that the leading figure of German socialism in the 19th century, Karl Marx, was to make his impact (see page 16).

2

The revolutions of 1848

A contemporary illustration showing French troops attacking a rebel position in the centre of Paris, June 1848.

In the light of this illustration, what were the advantages and disadvantages facing government troops in 1848 when they sought to suppress urban insurrection?

The Historical Debate

The most striking feature of the revolutions of 1848–49 is their great complexity. Each national rebellion raises its own set of historiographical problems. Questions such as the role of Piedmont in the events in Italy, or the achievement of the German liberals, are investigated in the relevant sections of this chapter. Here we are primarily concerned with the views taken of the 1848 phenomenon as a whole.

What justification is there for regarding the outbursts in various states as parts of one great event? For much of the 19th century they were not thought of as such. They were regarded from a national viewpoint, as part of that state's history or development. The tendency to view these events as part of a general European crisis has arisen from the work of two main groups of historians. Those interested in liberal and liberal-national ideas traced many common features in the events of 1848–49. Within a decade of the revolutions an English commentator, E. Shillingfleet Cayley (*The European Revolutions of 1848*, 1859), had noted these similarities.

Many historians have since agreed with the great Italian, Benedetto Croce, that 'it seemed as though one and the same daemon were agitating the entire mass of Europe'. The distinguished list of authorities who have seen in 1848 primarily the clash between liberal ideas and those of the conservative restoration of 1815 has included Veit Valentin (*1848: Chapters of German History*, 1940), Friedrich Meinecke (*The Year 1848 in German History*, 1948), and G. P. Gooch (*The Centenary of 1848 in Germany and Austria*, 1948). Sir

Lewis Namier produced an important variation on this theme when he stressed (*1848: Revolution of the Intellectuals*, 1944) how liberal principles were actually subordinated to nationalist ambitions by the so-called 'liberals' of 1848.

The main alternative to this liberal interpretation also has a pedigree reaching back to the middle of the 19th century. To Karl Marx (*The Class Struggles in France*, 1850) and to Friedrich Engels (*Revolution and Counter Revolution in Germany*, 1851–52), the true meaning of the events of 1848 was as the beginning of the great proletarian revolution. The social and economic factors behind the revolts were thus of far greater importance than the theories of such 'old women' and 'humbugs' as the Frankfurt liberals. Despite, or perhaps because of, these claims, these social and economic factors remained largely disregarded for a century. New respectability was given to these elements by C.E. Labrousse (*1848–1830–1789. How Revolutions are Born*, 1949) with his conclusion that the upheavals of 1848–49 resulted from the coincidence of several crises, political and economic. Since then, important work has been done on social questions in individual states, such as that by G. Quazza (*Social Struggle in the Risorgimento*, 1951) and Jacques Droz (*The German Revolutions*, 1957). It would now be widely accepted that, for a full explanation, political, social, ideological and economic factors

must all be taken into account. As T. Hamerow (*Restoration, Reaction, Revolution*, 1958) has written, 'the revolution was the expression not only of ideological forces like nationalism and liberalism, but also of deep-seated popular dissatisfactions engendered by the transition from agrarian manorialism to industrial capitalism'. Modern historians still differ, however, in the stress that they lay upon any one of these factors.

Secondly, what if anything did the revolutions of 1848 achieve? Probably the most famous judgement upon them is that of G.M. Trevelyan that '1848 was the turning point at which modern history failed to turn'. More recent commentators have often agreed that the 'Year of Revolutions' produced no worthwhile social or political change, but such a judgement is only valid if the events are regarded from a liberal viewpoint. The same is not true of nationalism, however. In the cases of Italy and Germany, the events of 1848 did much to encourage forces that were eventually to influence the unification of those states most profoundly, the power of Piedmont, the power of Prussia, and the ambitions of Louis Napoleon.

In fact, the greatest transformation wrought by the events of 1848 was wrought upon European conservatives. These men now clearly observed the weaknesses and divisions within those political forces that they had feared for decades. The age of Metternich gave way to the age of Bismarck. Confident conservatives were now certain that, with a strong army and a prosperous economy behind them, they could not be harmed by mere ideas.

A The general crisis

A conjunction of crises

The traditional forms of European society had been under pressure from economic and demographic changes as well as from political opposition for some time before 1840. The years between 1845 and 1847, however, formed a particularly severe phase of this crisis. Indeed, one of the most helpful contributions to the understanding of the events of 1848 was that made by the French historian, C. E. Labrousse, when he explained that the revolts resulted not from one crisis, but from a conjunction of several. A particularly acute agricultural crisis coincided with a newer kind of crisis, an industrial slump. The infant industrial economies of Europe had less experience of this and it gave special urgency to the longer lived political problems of the individual European states.

Agricultural crisis

The agricultural crisis became acute in 1845. The potato blight of that year had its most dramatic manifestations in Ireland, where it eventually accounted for the loss of up to a million human lives, but the failure of the crop also cut a swath of hunger and suffering across Europe, in Belgium, Holland, Germany and Poland. The following year the unusually hot, dry weather caused the failure of the grain harvest, and as the failures continued it became impossible to make good the shortfall from the surplus of the previous harvest.

Throughout Europe there were sudden and steep price rises. In Hamburg the price of wheat rose 51.8 per cent between 1841 and 1847, 70 per cent of that increase occurring in the period 1845–47. In Switzerland the price of rye doubled in the same two years, and bread prices doubled in the single year 1846–47. Lastly, it should be remembered that, even when imports of foreign grain were feasible, the incomplete state of most European railway systems made its passage to many parts of the continent impossible.

Industrial crisis

The same years, 1845–47, saw the most severe of the industrial crises that had hit Europe at intervals of roughly ten years since the end of the Napoleonic wars. Partly it was a crisis of overproduction, in which producers, finding that they had saturated the markets available to them, cut back production and thus created unemployment or wage reductions. In France production in the iron and coal industries fell by 30 per cent and 20 per cent respectively in 1847. Similarly in Germany, the amount of spun yarn exported by the member states of the *Zollverein* fell by 40 per cent in 1844–47.

The crisis also resulted from the impact of factory production in some parts of Europe upon older forms of production in other areas. The hostility shown by skilled craftsmen and artisans to factories, mills, railways and their owners in 1848 clearly indicated what they thought to be the origins of their suffering. The industrial crisis was also linked to the agricultural crisis, for in many localities the need to use government and bankers' funds to buy large quantities of foreign corn left little or nothing available for investment in industry. Bankruptcies multiplied and business confidence reached a new low ebb. The impact of all this upon living conditions was naturally most severe. The coincidence of high food prices with declining wages caused great and widespread hardship, especially in the towns. Here, three elements of discontent came together; the unemployed and hungry artisans, the peasants fleeing from the rural ills of land-hunger and semi-feudal oppression, and the middle classes with their liberal and nationalist opposition to the existing regimes.

The relationship between crisis and revolt

The violence of 1848 occurred, not at the height of the European crisis, but during the steady improvement after it. It thus resulted from the steady accumulation of frustration during the previous two and a half years of hardship. 'The wave of high prices,' wrote Labrousse, 'had spread over the country like a flood, and, like a receding tide, it left behind it a ruined population.' Nevertheless, the increasing prosperity of 1848–49 goes far to explain the withering of rebellion in most European states after such promising beginnings. The immediate trigger to the outbursts of February and March 1848 must therefore be sought in the political circumstances and disputes of the various European states. In describing these it is important not to generalise, for the resemblance between the affairs of one state and those of its neighbour was merely superficial. The views of the revolutionary leaders were usually much more diverse than the common distress that briefly provided them with a rank-and-file following. As a whole, wrote C. Pouthas of these leaders, 'the same vocabulary, the same programme, concealed dissimilar situations'.

B France: the crisis

Economic factors

Substantially agricultural, yet experiencing the stirrings of industrialisation, especially in northern and some central regions, France provided a classic example of the conjunction of economic crises. A dreadful harvest in 1846 sent corn prices soaring. In Normandy they more than doubled between mid-1846 and mid-1847. A better harvest in 1847 did not fully counteract the rise, and the year went down in folklore as 'the year of dear bread'. Already that year there were cases of rural unrest in western France. Peasants tried to prevent the transport of scarce grain to the towns, and elsewhere rioters sought suspected hoards of grain from earlier harvests. The fall in the purchasing power of the peasantry combined with the wider recession to produce a spectacular industrial slump. In 1847 one-third of the working population of Paris was supported by charity. Railway building, after rapid progress in the previous few years, slowed almost to a halt, and the gold reserves of the Bank of France sank so low that the Bank was forced to negotiate a £1 million loan from the Bank of England.

The government of Louis Philippe

On the face of it these crises assaulted a government with a better claim to public support than any other in continental Europe. Louis Philippe had ascended the throne as the result of popular revolution in 1830, he governed with the aid of a constitution and an elected assembly, and he claimed the middle classes as his main source of support. His, in short, was a government such as would have delighted most German or Italian liberals. Such an appearance, however, was deceptive. The government of Louis Philippe was not based upon the semi-religious claims that supported the Bourbons, nor upon the glamorous conquests of a Bonaparte. It was based upon the principle that Guizot, first minister in 1847, had recently defined.

'Let us not talk about our country having to conquer territory, to wage great wars, to undertake bold deeds of vengeance. If France is prosperous, if she remains free, rich, peaceful and wise, we need not complain.' When suddenly France was no longer prosperous, the faults of her government became more obvious.

In foreign affairs the government's record provided a sorry contrast with past glories. In the 1830s France had abandoned advantageous policies in Belgium and in the Near East in the face of pressure from other powers. By 1846 she found herself isolated by a rift with Britain over the marriage of one of Louis Philippe's sons into the royal house of Spain. Social policy had failed to meet the needs of embryonic industrialisation. A Factory Act (1841) restricting child labour in larger enterprises stood alone on the statute book, and even that was badly enforced. Meanwhile, those well enough informed could read convincing arguments on social improvement in the works of Louis Blanc (*see* Chapter 1, section I) or of Louis Napoleon Bonaparte (*see* section D and page 24). Persistent demands for the extension of the electoral franchise had been rejected. While Louis Philippe was willing to acknowledge, to an extent, the principle of government for the people, he remained unwilling actually to allow the people to govern. As a result, only about 240,000 of France's population of 32 million were entitled to vote under the electoral law introduced in 1831. 'The feeling of instability,' as de Tocqueville remarked to the Assembly in the last weeks of 1847, 'the feeling that is the precursor of revolutions, exists to a remarkable degree in this country.'

C France: success

The king's abdication

For all this accumulation of tension and discontent, the fall of the French government in February 1848 occurred almost by accident. The moderate opposition in the Assembly was led by Adolphe Thiers. In order to stay strictly within the law at a time when political meetings were banned, the opposition chose the tactic of holding a series of banquets at which after-dinner speakers could, under the thin veil of legality, put forward their views on political reform. The government's decision (20 February) to ban even this essentially middle-class form of protest precipitated demonstrations in the streets of Paris. Louis Philippe's nerve was already sufficiently shaken for him to dismiss Guizot, when a clash with troops (23 February) led to the shooting of between 40 and 50 demonstrators. The following day, with much of the population of Paris in outraged rebellion, and with the National Guard refusing to perform its peacekeeping duties, Louis Philippe abdicated and made his way in confusion to exile in England.

The Provisional Government

The monarchy had not been toppled by a coherent opposition party or coalition. Indeed, it had not been toppled at all. Its forces had not been defeated, so much as abandoned by their commander. The events in Paris found an echo in a few provincial outbursts, as in Lyon, Limoges and Rouen. In the rest of France, as Roger Price has written, 'the revolution must have presented a somewhat artificial and imposed character, accepted because there was no agreed alternative'. The Provisional Government formed on 25 February to fill the vacuum was, like the king it replaced, a compromise. The essentially liberal body envisaged by the poet-cum-politician, Alphonse de Lamartine, was expanded to include more radical elements in order to avoid the risk of the Parisian insurgents forming a rival administration. The uneasy coalition between the intellectuals who had spearheaded the ideological struggle and the workers who had risked their lives on the barricades produced an odd mix of a government. Lamartine was its foreign minister, with Garnier-Pagès in control of the nation's finances, while radicals such as Crémieux and Ledru-Rollin held office as minister of justice and minister of the interior respectively.

Radicalism or reassurance

In policies this administration struggled to reach a compromise between satisfying the radicals' demands and reassuring the bourgeoisie. In foreign policy its priority was to reassure the powers of Europe that the events of 1848 would not have the international repercussions of 1792. Lamartine's grandiose 'Manifesto to Europe' sought to convince them that they were dealing with a much more peaceful France than that which had given way to the temptations of conquest under Napoleon. All the same Europe's sense of reassurance must have been undermined by the statement that France no longer felt bound by the treaties that the Bourbons had concluded in 1815. Within a few days, however, most of the powers had more pressing problems on their hands than the question of revolution in France.

The financial policy of the Provisional Government was mainly conciliatory. In an attempt to maintain business confidence, no attack was made upon the Bank of France and all the debts of the monarchy were officially honoured. This moderate policy represented one of the administration's greatest failures. It failed to arrest the slide in share prices and the drain in gold reserves of the previous two years. The government's attempt to strengthen its financial position by imposing a 45 per cent tax on direct income caused widespread resentment. It was especially objectionable to the many small farmers to whom, given that the last remnants of the feudal system had been swept away in France a generation earlier, the government had very little to offer.

The Luxembourg Commission

The Provisional Government did, however, break radical new ground in terms of domestic political reform. The very decision to found a republic, rather than to accept the regency that Louis Philippe had envisaged, recalled the more extreme phases of the 'Great' revolution. It owed much, like the other domestic reforms, to the pressure of Parisian radicalism. It was followed (2 March) by the introduction of universal manhood suffrage, which instantly raised the electorate from about 240,000 to some nine million.

Most controversial were the measures taken by the administration to alleviate the prevailing social distress. The establishment of the Luxembourg Commission, an assembly of workers' delegates charged with the task of surveying social problems and suggesting solutions, was an eloquent gesture. The establishment of 'National Workshops' to provide work for the substantial number of unemployed could have been more. Ostensibly, the workshops were the embodiment of Louis Blanc's theories on state intervention to guarantee the 'right to work', but they turned out to be a poor imitation. Few projects of importance were entrusted to the workshops for fear of the damage that they might do, with their cheap labour, to private businesses. They achieved little other than minor public works such as the levelling of the Champs de Mars in Paris. Nevertheless, they attracted the bitter opposition and resentment of middle-class opinion because they represented a dangerous alternative to normal employment relationships and seemed to be consuming inordinate amounts of public money without obvious results.

D France: failure

Electoral conservatism

The elections to the Constituent Assembly of the republic, held on 23 April 1848, provided the mass of Frenchmen with their first opportunity to comment upon the events of the last two months. Their response was an unmistakably conservative one. Of 880 seats, radical and socialist candidates secured about 100. Candidates supporting the ideal of monarchy secured three times that number. Why was counter-revolution succeeding revolution so rapidly? Certainly, the influence of the conservative clergy was far stronger in the regions, as the radicals rightly complained, than that of the Provisional Government. However, it is unlikely that they persuaded many to vote against their better judgement.

Karl Marx's classic explanation of the collapse of the revolution was couched in terms of class warfare. February 1848, he explained, saw a temporary alliance of middle- and working-class interests against a common enemy, which soon began to disintegrate once that enemy had fled. Although happy to see the back of Louis Philippe, the bourgeoisie had no desire to see the end of the society that he represented.

More recent writers, although agreeing that the February coalition quickly fell apart, have not seen the causes in such clear-cut terms. G. Duveau has stressed the diversity that existed in the political views of the Parisian working classes, and has warned against treating them as a single unit. P. Amann saw the violence of early 1848, not as a statement of coherent class interests, but as a general outburst of anger that had many causes. The 'banquet crisis,' he states, 'unleashed a wave of violence that sought to redress social grievances, which had nothing to do with revolutionary ideology.' Common to all of these interpretations is the picture of the French merchant and peasant proprietor, aware of the sudden danger to their material interests, salvaging what they could from the wreck of the monarchy.

The 'June Days'

A major clash between radicals and conservatives loomed closer throughout April and May. After a number of demonstrations against the elections to the Assembly, which many of the radicals felt were being held before the electorate had been sufficiently 'educated', a mob demanding French support for the rebels in Poland invaded the Assembly on 15 May. The decisive confrontation came with the outbreak of violence in Paris known as the 'June Days'.

The immediate cause of the outburst was the decision of the government (21 June) to expel unmarried men from the National Workshops and to make plans for their closure. In response to a blatant attempt to 'pervert' the revolution, barricades were raised in many parts of Paris. Four days of bitter fighting (23–26 June) raged between insurgents and their opponents before troops under General Cavaignac won the first great conservative victory of this French revolution. The rebellious quarters of Paris were reduced street by street, with the loss of about 1,500 lives. The defeat of the insurgents represented the defeat of the radical element in the revolution. Over 11,000 people were prosecuted, and Paris remained under martial law until mid-October. Much of the work of the February revolution was undone. The National Workshops and all political clubs were dissolved, censorship of the press was reimposed, and such clauses as that concerning the 'right to work' were deleted from the existing draft of the constitution.

The election of Louis Napoleon Bonaparte

The triumph of conservatism in France was confirmed in December in the elections for the republic's first president. Five of the six candidates had played some role in the events of the year, and their electoral performances clearly showed the limitations of their achievements. General Changarnier received 5,000 of the 7.5 million votes cast. Lamartine, whose tenure of the foreign ministry had lasted little more than a month, achieved

Louis Napoleon

Personality and aims

The most obvious asset of Louis Napoleon Bonaparte was his name. Born (20 April 1808) the son of Louis Bonaparte, the Emperor's brother, he was thus a nephew of the great Napoleon. Superficially there did not seem to be a great deal else to recommend him for the high office he achieved in 1848. He had lived much of his earlier life in Italy where he was possibly involved in the conspiracies of radical political societies, although it has never been conclusively proved.

With the death of Napoleon's only legitimate son, the Duc de Reichstadt (1832), he assumed the leadership of the Bonaparte dynasty. Attempts to pursue what he clearly believed to be his and France's destiny ended in humiliating failure. Attempts to raise revolt at Strasbourg (October 1836) and Boulogne (August 1840) led, first to flight, then to imprisonment in the fortress of Ham on the Belgian border, and finally (1846) to further exile in England.

His image, when he returned to his native city upon the fall of Louis Philippe, was not an attractive one. Yet the mediocrity of his earlier career was one of the factors that aided him at this fateful moment. His success in 1848 owed much to the support of established politicians who felt that they had little to fear from this 'mini-Napoleon', but that they might exploit his name for their own ends. 'He is a cretin,' commented Thiers both unkindly and inaccurately, 'whom we will manage.' His very lack of any successful connection with the politics of the mid-1840s was, at this time, a recommendation. Louis Napoleon's hands were clean.

If he had achieved little by direct action Louis Napoleon had shown his worth as a propagandist. Two works written in exile had already sold some half a million copies in France by 1848. *The Napoleonic Ideals* (*Des Idées Napoléoniennes*) written in 1839 and *The Extinction of Pauperism* (1844) jointly propounded the theory that the social and political problems of France, her economy, her international status and her domestic divisions had only been effectively tackled in the last half century by one regime, that of the Emperor. Only he had been able to reconcile the just principles of the revolution with the national desire for stability and order.

The Napoleonic Ideals, he proclaimed, meant 'to reconstitute French society, overthrown by fifty years of revolution, to conciliate order and liberty, the right of the people, and the principles of law. It replaces the hereditary system of the old aristocracies by a hierarchical system, which, while securing equality, rewards merit and secures order. It disciplines democracy, and renders her an element of strength and stability.'

An electoral manifesto in December 1848 that pledged Louis Napoleon to the reduction of taxation, the increase of employment, the expansion of private economic enterprise, the freedom of the press, and the protection of the educational rights of the Church drew largely upon *The Napoleonic Ideals* and had the widest possible appeal to the new electorate.

18,000 votes. F. Raspail (37,000 votes) and A. Ledru-Rollin (370,000) were both too tainted in the public view by their contact with radicalism to attract many votes outside the capital. Cavaignac, who was second in the election with 1,448,107 votes, appealed to many as the champion of public order, yet in general, attitudes to the 'butcher of June' were ambiguous.

Another man, who had not even been present in France for the first four months of the revolution, had the dual advantages of being free from association with either radical or reactionary events earlier in the year. He also bore a name automatically linked in the minds of many Frenchmen with domestic stability and international prestige. Louis Napoleon Bonaparte had already been elected to the Assembly by four *départements* in June upon his return to France. Now he polled an overall majority by receiving 5,434,226 votes to become the first and only President of the Second Republic.

Conservatism in action

The brief political history of the Second Republic further illustrates the triumph of social conservatism in France. At home the new elections to the Assembly (May 1849) returned some 500 conservatives against some 250 republicans. The most notable domestic legislation of Louis Napoleon's presidency was the so-called Falloux Law (March 1850), giving the Church powers of supervision over education in the localities. This concession to conservative, Catholic opinion had a notable parallel in foreign policy in the military expedition that overthrew the radical Roman Republic (*see* section **M**), restored the Pope to his capital, and left a French garrison as his guardian. Such measures were merely the prelude to a more lasting form of conservatism, that of the Second Empire.

E Germany: the crisis

Hunger and the impact of industrialisation

The complex of states that made up Germany felt the impact of the economic crises of 1846-47 to an even greater extent than France because their own economies were less advanced. Agrarian discontent in the months before March 1848 took different forms in states that had not yet made the advance from feudalism accomplished in France in 1789–92. Land hunger and the persistence of semi-feudal oppression gave rise to demands for the abolition of feudal dues, for the curbing of the social privileges of the nobility and, where possible, for the division of the large feudal estates among the peasantry.

The economic crisis in the German towns displayed two distinct characteristics. The first was the material distress that resulted from the failure of the harvest in the countryside. In 1847 there were bread riots in Stuttgart and in Ulm, and substantial violence in Berlin triggered by the shortage of potatoes. Secondly, German urban revolt was fuelled by the distress of traditional artisans, already under pressure from the growth of mechanised production before the depression of 1846–47 hit them. The early months of 1848 witnessed such acts of 'Luddism' as the burning of mills in Dusseldorf, demonstrations by weavers in Chemnitz, and assaults by wagoners in Nassau upon the newly constructed railways. Factory production, too, experienced severe difficulties as investment and demand declined, and there were strikes for higher pay and shorter hours in Berlin, Leipzig and Dresden. The combination of all these economic factors was in some cases catastrophic.

Political authority in the German states

Politically, too, much remained to be done in the German states that had been achieved in France a generation earlier. Agatha Ramm reminds us that Germany before 1848 'was a country where to have a political opinion was difficult, to express it almost impossible, and to join with others to promote it, conspiracy punishable by the heaviest prison sentences'.

A. J. P. Taylor's view of the personal unfitness of the rulers of many of the German principalities is only slightly exaggerated: 'Ceaseless inbreeding, power territorially circumscribed, but within those limits limitless, produced mad princes as a normal event; and of the utterly petty princes hardly one was sane.' It is certainly true in this context that one of the immediate causes of discontent in Bavaria, second largest of the German states, was the irresponsible infatuation of the unbalanced King Ludwig for an exotic dancer with the stage name of Lola Montez.

Prussia in the 1840s

As so much of the fate of Germany during and after 1848 was to hinge upon the kingdom of Prussia we need to consider the political crisis of the 1840s in that state in greater detail. Superficially, Prussia seemed to conform to A. J. P. Taylor's general pattern. The accession of Friedrich Wilhelm IV in 1840 had brought to the throne a vague romantic, ostensibly interested in the cause of German unity. In reality he never yielded an inch on the principle of the divine right of kings, and was only truly interested in leading Germany himself in the fashion of a paternalistic medieval emperor. In 1847 he had temporarily raised the hopes of German liberals by summoning the Prussian assembly (*Landtag*). He then went on to show that he viewed that body much as a medieval king viewed his Estates-General, meeting not to govern, but to advise and co-operate with their lord.

The other mainstay of Prussian conservatism, the landowning Junker class, also found itself in an unaccustomed position in the years immediately before 1848. Their desire for the construction of an eastern railway (*Ostbahn*), linking their agricultural estates in East Prussia with markets in the major cities, had temporarily placed them in the unusual position of supporting the decision to summon an assembly which alone could grant the necessary funds. Strange and perturbed as the political scene in Prussia seemed in 1846–47, and real as the economic distress was, it must be stressed that no genuine governmental crisis existed. The administration was soundly organised and in many cases, in economic matters for instance, it was pursuing far-sighted and logical policies. The finances of the state were sound, far sounder than those of the Austrian Empire. The army was well-trained, well-equipped and wholly loyal. In the context of the improving harvests and falling food prices in 1848, it was likely to take more than a temporary loss of nerve on the part of the government to achieve any permanent revolution in Prussia.

F   Germany: success

The first wave of reforms

In the German states, as in much of central Europe, the news of the February revolution in Paris was the trigger that turned long-term resentment into actual political confrontation. 'It is impossible,' declared a leading Berlin newspaper, 'to describe the amazement, the terror, the confusion aroused here by the latest reports from Paris crowding on each other almost hourly.' And if the political society of Prussia's capital seemed shaken, what hope was there for such minor entities as Mecklenburg-Strelitz?

By the second week of March the leaders of most German states had despaired of surviving where the king of the French had perished, and had begun the wholesale granting of constitutional demands. In Bavaria, King Ludwig abdicated and saw his successor, Maximilian II, accept the principles of a constitutional assembly, ministerial responsibility, a jury system and a free press (9 March). In Baden all feudal obligations were abolished (10 March) and in Württemberg the king renounced his hunting rights.

Even Prussia could not escape. At first Friedrich Wilhelm seemed to preserve his political position by ordering his troops not to fire upon demonstrating crowds, and by putting his name to the usual list of concessions. An outbreak of street fighting on 18 March broke his nerve and he sought to save himself by ordering the withdrawal of the army from Berlin. As a virtual prisoner of his people, he then appointed a liberal ministry led by Rhineland businessmen, Ludolf Camphausen and David Hansemann.

The Frankfurt Parliament

Liberal reforms were only one of the elements in what seemed a remarkable victory for the insurgents. On the face of it, the most spectacular concession of the rulers of Prussia, Bavaria, Baden and Württemberg was their agreement to participate in the organisation of a German national parliament, a vehicle for the unification of the nation. At the height of the liberal success, the first steps towards such a body were already being taken. A group of enthusiasts, mainly academics and predominantly from the southern states, resolved at a meeting in Heidelberg (5 March) to summon a Preliminary Parliament (*Vorparlament*) which would in turn supervise elections to a German Representative Assembly. Thus this assembly had its origins not in the exercise of any state's power, but in the absence of power, in a vacuum characteristic of March 1848. The *Vorparlament* in its five-day session decided that elections should be by universal male suffrage and proportional representation, with one delegate for every 50,000 Germans.

The assembly that finally gathered in St Paul's Church in Frankfurt (18 May) was predominantly elected by those middle classes preoccupied with constitutions and parliaments, and was a classic illustration of Namier's characterisation of 1848 as 'the revolution of the intellectuals'. Of 830 delegates who sat there at one time or another 275 were state officials, 66 were lawyers, 50 were university professors and another 50 were schoolmasters. Only one came from a truly peasant background, and only four from the artisan classes. Relatively united in social origins and in their view of the Germany that they did not want, they were to discover like most revolutionaries that the construction of a new state and society is a process fraught with difficulties.

G   Germany: failure

The failure of the Frankfurt Parliament

The German liberals who dominated the Frankfurt Parliament have perhaps been more harshly dealt with by historians than any comparable group in the 19th century. Historians of the left have followed Marx and Engels in condemning them for not taking violent action to overthrow existing power structures. In the decades immediately following unification such 'Prussian' historians as von Treitschke blamed them for their opposition to Germany's 'best hope', the Prussian monarchy. Foreign commentators, such as Namier and Taylor, have seen them as ideological frauds, ultimately interested only in German power. Indeed, the failure of the Frankfurt Parliament was almost total, not because it failed to use its opportunities, but because the opportunities of 1848 were illusory.

The problem of national unity

The first set of difficulties faced by the Frankfurt delegates concerned the eventual nature of the state that they hoped to create. What would be the constitutional framework of the united Germany? The majority of deputies felt it was of great importance to recruit the princes as supporters of a monarchical Germany, rather than risk the radical politics that accompanied republicanism. From this two other issues followed. Which of Germany's royal houses should predominate, and what should be the relationship of the Parliament with the older authorities within Germany? Conservatives preferred to see the constitutional decisions of the Parliament implemented by the princes in their individual states, while more radical spirits wished to see princely authority overridden by that of the Parliament.

In June, under the influence of its president, von Gagern, the Parliament took the decision to claim executive power, superior to that of any state or to that of the Federal Diet. They also decided to entrust the leadership of Germany to the greatest of the German families, the Habsburgs, in the person of the Archduke John. The Parliament was thus moving towards a 'Greater Germany' (*Grossdeutschland*) including all German speakers, rather than a 'Lesser Germany' (*Kleindeutschland*) without the Germans of the Habsburg territories. That ambition was to be thwarted by the recovery of Habsburg authority in the Austrian Empire in October and November 1848.

The challenge of non-German nationalism

A second set of problems arose from the fundamental weakness of the Frankfurt Parliament, its total lack of material power. Lacking an army of its own, it was bound to depend upon the goodwill of the major German princes for the most basic functions of government, such as the collection of taxation. Like other constitutional bodies set up in 1848, this assembly was only ultimately able to survive if the regimes that it sought to replace voluntarily handed over their power.

In particular, the Parliament was helpless in the face of two challenges. Firstly, various nationalities laid claim to territory seen by the Parliament as part of the Fatherland. In March 1848 Denmark occupied Schleswig and Holstein, an event closely followed by Palacky's declaration that Bohemia belonged to the Czech nation, and by a rising by Polish nationalists in Posen. The initial sympathy of the assembly for the aspirations of other nationalists evaporated when those aspirations seemed to threaten German power. Seeing no other alternative to the diminution of Germany, the assembly applauded many of the selfish acts of their erstwhile enemies. The victory of the Austrian army in Prague, and the suppression of the Poles by the Prussian army both received widespread applause. When foreign pressure forced the Prussian army, in action against the Danes, to accept a disadvantageous armistice (August 1848), the assembly, for all its harsh words, could only confirm its impotence by accepting the settlement.

The challenge of working-class radicalism

The other challenge came from the embryonic and relatively incoherent working-class movement. In the last months of 1848, German workers' organisations were beginning to react to the failure of the Frankfurt Parliament to solve working-class problems. While the Frankfurt liberals devoted themselves to the abstract task of drawing up a constitution, separate and independent workers' assemblies met in Hamburg and in Frankfurt itself, making economic demands quite against the middle-class interests of the delegates in St Paul's Church. They requested the limitation of factory production, restrictions upon free economic and industrial growth, and the protection of the privileges of the old artisan guilds. When barricades went up in Frankfurt (18 September) and disturbances followed in Baden, Hesse-Cassel and Saxony, the Parliament's only recourse was once more to use Prussian and Austrian troops.

The recovery of Prussia

The emergence of the national issue and the

growing fear of working-class violence were two of the factors that paved the way for the triumph of conservatism in Germany. The third factor was the steady recovery of nerve by the king of Prussia. By August Prussia's own parliament had demonstrated its radicalism by seeking to abolish the feudal, legal and financial privileges of the Junker class. This had brought the Junkers into open opposition to the liberals. Encouraged by their support and by increasing evidence of the reliability of the army, Friedrich Wilhelm dismissed his liberal ministers and ordered his troops back into Berlin. In December he first banished and then dissolved the Prussian parliament. The anti-nationalist stance of the Austrian Habsburgs in March 1849 gave the Frankfurt assembly little alternative but to offer the crown of Germany to the only other German powerful enough to wear it. Friedrich Wilhelm's refusal to 'pick up a crown from the gutter' sealed Frankfurt's failure.

Much has been written about the Prussian king's motives. Certainly his distaste for constitutional monarchy was genuine, but there is also evidence that he harboured a neo-medieval belief in Austria's divinely ordained leadership of Germany and her princes. With the withdrawal of Prussian and Austrian delegates from Frankfurt, the Parliament was already a shell when it moved to Stuttgart to await its dispersal by Prussian troops (June 1849). Although permanent agrarian reforms survived from the events of 1848–49, the liberal, constitutional revolution had achieved nothing. Indeed, we may even accept the judgement of A. J. P. Taylor, that was in no realistic sense a political revolution in Germany at all in 1848. 'There was merely a vacuum in which the liberals postured until the vacuum was filled.'

H Austria: the crisis

Political and economic weaknesses
Nowhere was the conjunction of different economic and political crises so dangerous as in the Austrian Empire, for in 1848–49 the Empire was threatened not merely with radical constitutional change, but with the very collapse of its complex multinational structure. The period of Austrian history between 1815 and 1848 has been described by H. Kohn as 'an era of stagnation'. Those years had witnessed some half-hearted attempts by Metternich at political and fiscal reform, thwarted by the conservatism of the Emperor. Latterly the political scene had been dominated by rivalry and jealousy, notably between Metternich and his rival, Count Kolowrat. The accession in 1835 of the Emperor Ferdinand, physically sick and mentally abnormal, merely ensured that the political malaise spread to the very pinnacle of the state system.

Economically, the Austrian Empire had produced nothing to rival Prussia's policy of tariff reform and industrial modernisation. Austria and Hungary together produced 710,000 tons of coal in 1845, compared with 5.6 million tons produced by the member states of the *Zollverein*, and had made only modest and halting progress in railway construction. Although Austrian cities were as yet spared the horrors of industrialisation, they had little to offer the peasants driven from the countryside by agrarian depression. Urban unrest in Vienna or Budapest owed more to the lack of industrial employment than to the hardships that such employment entailed. Thirdly, the government imposed, or attempted to impose, an intellectual straitjacket upon the Empire. 'I do not need scholars,' an earlier Emperor had informed his schoolteachers in 1821, 'but obedient citizens. Whosoever serves me must teach what I command.'

The challenge of nationalism within the Empire
The rise of nationalism gave the Austrian crisis a distinctive flavour of its own, for in a state of such racial diversity, such doctrines were always likely to be explosive. Although Germans dominated the politics and commerce of the Empire, they constituted only a little less than a quarter of its population. Of the total, nearly 20 per cent were Hungarians, about 7 per cent were Italians, 6 per cent Rumanians, and 45 per cent Slavs. This last section then subdivided into a bewildering variety that included Czechs, Slovaks, Serbs, Ukrainians, Poles and Croats.

The question of national identity and the awareness of national cultures had come to prominence only relatively recently. At the beginning of the century vernacular languages were largely confined to the peasant populations, with the business of the provincial assemblies, or Diets, conducted in Latin. In 1840 Hungarian nationalists succeeded in

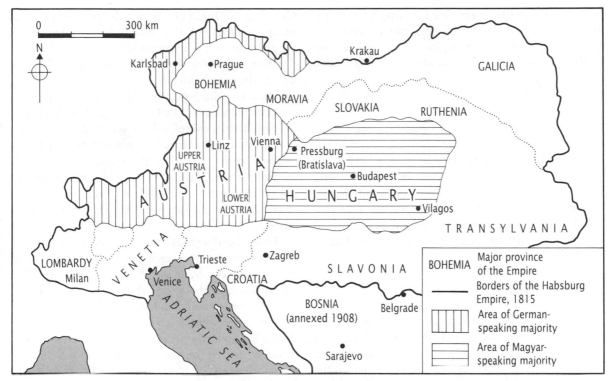

The Habsburg Empire

replacing Latin by Magyar as the official language of their Diet, and over the next four years Magyar also became established in legal and educational usage. Other languages made headway in literary contexts, as in the publication of Jungmann's Czech dictionary, Palacky's history of the Czechs and Preseren's Slovene poetry. Otherwise, the aims of these national minorities varied. Some, such as the Czechs, aimed for improved status within the Empire. Others, such as the Italian nationalists, hoped to secede from the Empire to form part of a larger, independent nation.

In Hungary there was a significant increase in political tension in the late 1830s and early 1840s with the rise of a radical, nationalist journalist, Lajos Kossuth. Where moderate nationalism, under Count Szechenyi, had previously aimed at cultural and economic advance within the Empire, Kossuth demanded far more. His aims were administrative autonomy and parliamentary rule for Hungary. His method was to win the support of the Hungarian gentry for the revival of the old Hungarian state by appealing to their anti-Slav interests and prejudices.

I Austria: success

The fall of Metternich

As was the case in Germany, the news of the February revolution in Paris ignited the tinder of political revolt in Austria. Middle-class liberals, student radicals and elements of the Viennese working class joined together in street demonstrations and the presentation of petitions to the Emperor in the first weeks of March. On 13 March clashes with regular troops led to loss of life, and the Emperor, who had already lost his wits, now lost his nerve. Later that day, the 1848 revolutions gained their most notable 'scalp' with the resignation of the Imperial Chancellor, Klemens von Metternich. Two elements seem to have combined in the fall of the great champion of European conservatism. Some historians, such as the Frenchman M. Pouthas, have seen fear as the main motive within the Austrian court. They portray Metternich, like Guizot in Paris, as a victim sacrificed to save the rest of the establishment. For the Austrian, G. von Poelnitz, the personal antipathy of such rivals as Kolowrat played a greater role, and the popular disturbances provided an opportunity for the pursuit of personal vendettas. The difference in interpretation is important, for what could be seen as the most sensational event of early 1848 takes on far less significance if it was merely the result of temporary divisions within the governing élite of the Empire.

With the departure of Metternich into exile Ferdinand, like Friedrich Wilhelm, preferred concessions to flight. In April he conceded freedom of the press, and gave permission for a constitution for the German-speaking areas of the Empire. The following month he promised a constituent assembly based upon universal manhood suffrage and accepted the arming of a volunteer National Guard in Vienna.

Reform in Hungary

It was inevitable that the collapse of Imperial willpower would encourage opposition in the provinces of the Empire. Indeed, the Hungarian Diet meeting at Pressburg (Bratislava), had begun the formulation of its demands ten days before the fall of Metternich. These demands crystallised into the so-called March Laws, a mixture of classic liberal demands with more specifically nationalist ones. Freedom of the press, equality of taxation, equality before the law, and freedom of religion stood alongside the demand for the removal of all non-Hungarian troops from Hungarian territory. In the countryside all remnants of serfdom were to be abolished, as was the practice of *robot*, the compulsory labour due owed by many peasants to their landlords.

Further, it must be understood that when Kossuth and his supporters spoke of 'Hungary' they envisaged, not merely a state embracing those areas when Magyar was spoken, but all those territories that had been part of the medieval Kingdom of Hungary. Transylvania, Croatia and Ruthenia could thus expect no Hungarian sympathy for their own cultural or national aspirations. On 11 April Ferdinand conceded all the demands of the Hungarian Diet and effectively accepted the establishment of an independent Hungarian state.

Bohemia and austro-slavism

In Prague, the second great centre of nationalist unrest, confidence in national strength was less pronounced. The Pan-Slav Congress which assembled there (2 June) chose, not the path of national independence, but that which became known as 'austro-slavism'. This centred upon the view that the best course for the Slav peoples of the Empire lay within a reformed, yet intact, Habsburg Empire. Outside, they would merely fall prey to the selfish desires of the Germans and the Russians. Indeed, Palacky's refusal to accept a seat at the Pan-German Frankfurt Parliament was a landmark in the Czechs' claim for the recognition of their own national identity. 'If the Austrian Empire did not exist', he had concluded, 'it would be necessary to create it' for the safety of the minor Slav nationalities.

Thus the demands from Prague were for linguistic equality of Czech with German, for the abolition of the *robot*, and for what Palacky called the 'peace, the liberty and the right of my nation', but not for an independent Czech state. Austro-slavism represented an impossible paradox. It depended upon the weakness of the Viennese government for its success, and upon the voluntary dismantlement of absolutism by the Habsburgs. Yet it trusted in Habsburg strength for protection against German or Russian domination. While it illustrates the high hopes of 1848, it also provides a classic example of the chronically weak foundations upon which these hopes rested.

J   Austria: failure

The fall of Prague

The first major success of the counter revolution in 1848 occurred in Prague. As even the Czechs seemed convinced of their own weakness it is scarcely surprising that those commanding the undefeated Austrian forces in the north moved towards the same conclusion. In reaction to renewed radical and student violence in the city (13 June), General Windischgrätz, Imperial governor of Moravia, took the decision to bombard Prague. Within three days the city was in his hands. Not only was the resistance of the insurgents ineffectual, but they found themselves largely without sympathy in the outside world. The hostility of the Frankfurt Parliament was repeated in the violent language of radicals in Vienna. 'The victory over the Czech party in Prague,' rejoiced the journal *Friend of the People*, 'is and remains a joyful event.' The events in Prague serve well to illustrate the fatal isolation of each of the 1848 risings from all of the others.

Reaction in Vienna

The revolution in Vienna suffered from a steady decline rather than from a sudden collapse. By the time of Windischgrätz's triumph, the Viennese radicals had achieved some notable triumphs of their own. They had formed a constituent assembly and a National Guard, and there was more to come. In September the assembly struck at the social basis of rural Austria by abolishing the *robot* and the hereditary rights of the nobility in local administration. These should perhaps be seen as the major lasting changes wrought by the 'Year of Revolutions' in the Empire. The end of the practice of *robot* had a ruinous effect on the lesser gentry who lost a valuable source of cheap labour. This breaking of the power of the local landlords, although it was not the direct aim of the assembly, was to confirm the subsequent dominance of the central authority of the Imperial government.

Fatal weaknesses were already becoming evident in the position of the revolutionaries. The dynasty remained in power and continued to be served by ministers of the 'old school'. The Imperial army was not only undefeated, but actually victorious in the provinces. Worse, divisions began to appear in the ranks of the revolutionaries themselves. Some elements among the German-speaking radicals favoured the cutting of links with the non-German provinces of the Empire, and aimed at a form of *Grossdeutsch* unity with other states represented at the Frankfurt Parliament. Others wished to see the territorial preservation of the Empire and applauded the victories of Windischgrätz and Radetzky.

The discussion of a constitutional settlement aggravated the divisions. Many liberals remained content with a constitutional monarchy of the sort recently overthrown in Paris, while stricter radicals sought a republic. The emergence of workers' organisations in Vienna revived memories of the 'June Days' in Paris, and in August demonstrations were broken up by the middle-class National Guard. The government's decision (3 October) to declare war on the Hungarian rebels brought matters to a head. Radical demonstrations in favour of Hungary, in which the minister of war was lynched, emboldened the conservatives to treat

Vienna as Prague had been treated. The task was harder and bloodier, but by the end of the month and at a cost of 3,000 to 5,000 lives, Generals Windischgrätz and Jellacic had reconquered Austria's capital.

The re-establishment of imperial government

The regeneration of conservative government was steadily consolidated. In November a new government under Count Schwarzenberg took office. In December, as the living symbol of regeneration, the 18-year-old Franz Josef ascended the Imperial throne upon his uncle's abdication. The new administration was firmly based upon realism and upon power politics for, in A. J. P. Taylor's words, 'Schwarzenberg was too clever to have principles, Franz Josef too blinkered to understand them.'

The fate of the constituent assembly well illustrates the methods of Austria's new masters. Since October it had lingered in exile in the Moravian town of Kremsier deliberating over an Austrian constitution. By the completion of its task (1 March 1849), Schwarzenberg felt strong enough to do without an assembly, but not without a constitution. Within three days of the formulation of the 'Kremsier Constitution' he had dissolved the assembly and allowed the minister of the interior, Count Stadion, to introduce an Imperial constitution of quite a different tenor. While it permitted a parliament based upon universal manhood suffrage, it stressed strongly the indivisible nature of the Empire. Although Hungary received recognition of its linguistic separatism, it and all other regions of the Empire could now expect only direct government from Vienna.

Schwarzenberg's reaction to the events of 1848–49 has much significance for the history of the Habsburg Empire in the latter part of the 19th century. It suggests that he had learned much of the weaknesses of the nationalist movements, but little of the weaknesses of his own state. Therefore, while the 1850s were a decade of economic modernisation and reform in France, in Prussia and in Piedmont, they witnessed only the consolidation of political conservatism in Austria. There was to be no Austrian Cavour, and not even an Austrian equivalent of Louis Napoleon. By the end of the century, as Peter Jones has suggested, Austria was to have paid a heavy price for that fact. 'Austria's revival was illusory. The survival of the Habsburg monarchy owed more to individuals – Radetzky, Windischgrätz, Schwarzenberg, Franz Josef – than to any revitalisation of the system of government.'

The reconquest of Hungary

The most important factor leading the government to grant constitutional concessions was the need to maintain a degree of general support while Hungary remained undefeated. From October 1848 the policy of the Imperial government towards Hungarian autonomy had been one of open hostility. Three methods of attack suggested themselves. Firstly, tacit support for the Slav minorities alienated by Kossuth's 'March Laws' became active and overt. The advance of the Croat General Jellacic into southern Hungary was, however, short-lived (September 1848) and unsuccessful. Secondly, the hope that Windischgrätz might win a third counter-revolutionary success with Austrian troops proved ill-founded. He moved slowly against a divided Hungarian leadership and was eventually defeated at Isaszeg in early April 1849. A week later, in response to Schwarzenberg's constitution, an Hungarian republic was proclaimed, and the Viennese government was forced into the extreme measure of appealing for foreign aid. Russia's response to the Austrian appeal owed as much to fears that the Hungarian example would be imitated in Poland as it did to conservative principles, but it proved decisive. The three-pronged attack of Jellacic, Windischgrätz and 140,000 Russians ended the life of the Hungarian republic at Vilagos (13 August 1849) and opened a period of bloody repression and retribution. The official annulment of the Hungarian constitution in 1851 put the final touch to the conservative triumph in the Austrian Empire.

K Italy: the crisis

The economic state of Italy

If the initial outbreak of violence in France came as a surprise, the disturbances in Italy were wholly predictable. The political and economic crises in the Italian states had roots going back to the restoration of 1815 and, in many cases, far beyond. Economic hardship in Italy was the result, not merely of a temporary, cyclical crisis, but of long-standing backwardness. The commerce for which the city states of the Renaissance had been noted had long ago given way to ownership of land as the main source of wealth and prestige, and the handicaps in the way of trade in the early 19th century were enormous. Customs barriers proliferated not only between states, but within states. Piedmont alone had nearly 500 such barriers before the French Revolution. Italy's major navigable river, the Po, was cut into 22 sections by customs barriers. Travel between states was unwelcome to most rulers, many of whom would have shared the view of the Duke of Modena, who declared that 'all travellers are Jacobins', and forbade stage-coaches to cross his territories.

Some 90 per cent of Italy's population was dependent upon the land. Agricultural production was primitive and inefficient. About half the peasantry in the north still owed contractual labour to their landlords and the proportion was much higher in the south. Such semi-feudal conditions made Italian corn subject to huge fluctuations in price, and the abnormal shortages of 1846–47 were already contributing to urban rioting in Rome and Livorno as early as February and March 1847.

Political reaction in Italy since 1815

The restoration of Italy's political divisions in 1815 meant that the peninsula suffered not from one political crisis, but from a whole collection of them. Between them the restored princes represented all that was worst in European conservatism. In Piedmont, also sometimes referred to as the Kingdom of Sardinia, Victor Emmanuel I had marked his return to power by the abolition of both the civil and commercial codes of law, and by the systematic rejection of all innovations, such as vaccination and street-lighting, introduced by the French. In Naples, where tension continued unabated between the mainland territories and the island of Sicily, the constitution of 1812 was revoked and personal government was restored.

The Pope, restored to his temporal rule in central Italy, continued to limit participation in the administration of the Papal States to members of the clergy, and maintained a form of government that even such a conservative as Metternich - considered to be 'both detested and detestable'. Throughout Italy, the conservative influence of the Catholic Church stifled economic enterprise and political or philosophical change.

The influence of Austria and of localism

The direct influence exercised by Austria through her control of Lombardy and Venetia, and her indirect influence over Parma, Modena and Tuscany was essential to the whole conservative structure. To protect her vested political interests and for ideological reasons, Austrian policy was consistently, as Metternich put it, 'to extinguish the spirit of Italian unity and ideas about constitutions'. Worse still for Italian liberals and nationalists, Austrian territorial possessions in Italy made the maintenance of the Italian status quo a central part of the whole European settlement established at Vienna in 1815.

Conservatism also derived strength from the lower levels of society, from the differences of dialect that hindered communication between Italians, from the parochialism of most Italians, and from their preoccupation with local affairs. As a Neapolitan historian explained in the 1850s, 'the patriotism of the Italians is like that of the ancient Greeks, and is the love of a single town, not of a country; it is the feeling of a tribe, not of a nation'. The map of Italy, therefore, remained frozen by a formidable combination of economic backwardness, political apathy, Austrian power, the acquiescence of the major powers, and the authority of the Catholic Church.

The beginnings of conservative reform?

It is tempting to conclude that Italy's political regimes remained similarly frozen. That traditional interpretation, however, is being slowly modified by recent research, which suggests that reactionary regimes were gradually coming to realise the advantages of modernisation and efficiency as the mid-century approached. Metternich himself seems to have realised the advantages of combining legitimist principles with the greater efficiency that the Napoleonic administrations had achieved. Fossombroni in Tuscany and Medici in Naples provide examples of ministers who attempted to implement such policies. Above all, a revisionist study by Narcisso Nada has emphasised the extent of the legal, administrative, financial and military reforms brought about by Charles Albert in Piedmont long before he placed himself at the head of the national cause. Seen in this light, 1848 does not represent a clean break with past Italian history, and the actions of both Charles Albert and Pius IX may be seen as part of a longer process of 'conservative reform'. Considered in this light, the reformist policies of Cavour (*see* Chapter 4) may be seen to have had a much older pedigree.

Italian radicalism: Carbonarism

Against these obstacles, in the 30 years before 1848, was ranged a variety of liberal and nationalist movements, differing in their methods, their aims and the measure of their success. Between 1815 and 1831 the radical stage belonged to those groups, of which the so-called *Carbonari* were the most prominent, who viewed conspiracy and selective revolt as the best means of provoking general rebellion. In 1820–21, in Parma, Modena and the Papal States, the *Carbonari* engineered radical risings and army mutinies. The aims of the rebels were parochial, concerned only with changes in their own state. In each case they encountered considerable popular apathy, or else fought shy of courting popular support, and they found no answer to the might of the Austrian army. By 1831, five of the six main rulers in Italy, Piedmont being the exception, had called in Austrian troops to support them. This was a further indication of how essential the defeat of the Habsburg forces would be to the advancement of the Italian national cause.

Italian radicalism: the influence of Mazzini

Giuseppe Mazzini and the 'Young Italy' movement swept away the parochialism of the *Carbonari*. Mazzini's views, methods and weaknesses are described in more detail on page 35. It is sufficient here to stress his insistence upon a unitary state, rather than a federal arrangement, his preference for a republican form of government and his tireless propaganda work. It was a combination which naturally rendered his policy utterly unacceptable to all crowned heads in Italy and throughout Europe. In practical terms, therefore, Mazzini's career by 1848 was a catalogue of disappointments. He was banished for life from his Piedmontese homeland after an appeal to Charles Albert (1831) to take the leadership of the national cause, and an attempted invasion of Savoy three years later was a total failure. By 1837 he had been further banished from France and Switzerland, and was in exile in London. Later attempted risings, in Mantua (1852), Milan (1853) and Genoa (1857) were no more successful.

Mazzini achieved little in the 1830s and the 1840s, but it is due to him more than to any other Italian leader that an Italian cause in any form still existed in 1848. Like Louis Napoleon his practical failures were offset by a successful career as a propagandist, and his *Duties of Man* and *Thoughts Upon Democracy in Europe* were enthusiastically received in European radical circles. Excessively romantic as his political views undoubtedly were, he succeeded, in the words of Denis Mack Smith, in 'defining the goal and arousing enthusiasm among practised soldiers and statesmen'.

The moderate nationalists

Mazzini's radicalism and republicanism were also unacceptable to a more moderate school of reformers and nationalists who began to put forward their views in literary form in the 1840s. Cesare Balbo, in his work *Of the Aspirations of Italy* (*Delle Speranze d'Italia*) and Massimo d'Azeglio, in his account *Of the Recent Events in the Romagna* (*Degli Ultimi Casi di Romagna*), written in 1844 and 1846 respectively, both recognised the need for political force at the head of the Italian cause. They both viewed the king of Piedmont as their best hope. Practically, many moderates also laid great stress upon the promotion of social amenities, such as savings banks and schools, and upon the encouragement of industry. The cheese industry at Gorgonzola and the Chianti wine industry are largely the results of this interest.

For the churchman Vincenzo Gioberti, however, the future of Italy lay, not with Piedmont, but with the Papacy and abruptly, in 1846, it seemed that Gioberti might have hit upon the right path. Gioberti, in his work *Of the Moral and Civil Primacy of the Italians* (*Del Primato Morale e Civile degli Italiani*), had portrayed the Papacy and the Catholic Church as the chosen agents of Italian national revival. He condemned revolutionary means towards unity, made no specific mention of the expulsion of the Austrians from the peninsula, and advocated a confederation of Italian states under the presidency of the Pope. The scheme certainly had the merits of preserving the local status of the individual princes and of placing the Austrians in the potentially embarrassing position of opposing the head of their own Church. On the other hand, up to 1846, there seemed little prospect of finding a Pope willing to play the role

designed for him by Gioberti and his 'Neo-Guelph' supporters.

L Italy: success

The election of Pius IX

It is perhaps misleading to refer to the events in Italy as part of 'the revolutions of 1848' for that particular phase of Italian history had begun in 1846 with the sensational election of Cardinal Giovanni Mastai-Ferretti as Pope. Under his chosen title of Pius IX he was to be one of the key figures in the events of the next two years.

The election of Pope Pius IX appeared to transform overnight the prospects of neo-guelphism. In his initial burst of political reform Pius amnestied political prisoners and accepted a measure of non-clerical participation in government. In 1847 he put forward the suggestion of an Italian customs union. When Austria, thrown off balance by this 'liberal' Pope, dropped the broad hint of establishing a garrison at Ferrara (July 1847) within Papal territory, Pius protested so vigorously that he became a national hero for such an anti-Austrian gesture. For all his subsequent failure to lead the Italian cause to success (*see* section **M**), the election of Pius had an enormously stimulating effect upon Italian politics. 'It must have seemed,' wrote G. Berkeley, 'as if the chief anti-nationalist stronghold of [the nationalists'] opponents had suddenly hoisted their own tricolour.'

Charles Albert and Piedmont

The second key figure of these years in Italy was Charles Albert, King of Piedmont since 1831. Nationalist historians in the intervening century have created a 'legend of Charles Albert', gallantly sacrificing his own interests, even his own throne, in the national cause. Today it is more acceptable to view him either as 'a romantic without the willpower to transform his vision into reality', as does the Italian A. Omodeo, or like Derek. Beales, as a thorough conservative, opportunist enough to take advantage of European chaos to increase the power of Piedmont, to 'use, but not surrender to ideology'.

Certainly, even before the rising in Paris, events seemed to be running against Italian conservatism. In January 1848, patriotic middle-class Italians

Guiseppe Mazzini

Personality and aims

Born in Genoa (1805) of prosperous, intellectual parents, Mazzini was committed from his teens to the twin causes of Italian unity and liberty. From 1827 he was a member of the conspiratorial society, the *Carbonari*, but was sufficiently aware of their shortcomings by the early 1830s to develop a movement of his own. He drew its ideas and its name from the clandestine journal *Young Italy* (*La Giovine Italia*). Central to the principles of Young Italy was the conviction that the binding together of the shattered Italian people would be the means of that people's moral and religious regeneration. Mazzini, like all Romantic thinkers, accepted Rousseau's argument of the natural goodness of man, and of his corruption by an evil and selfish environment.

The second essential element in the Mazzini's beliefs concerned the relationship between the 'new' Italy and the other nations of Europe. 'Nations,' as he vividly expressed it, 'are the citizens of humanity as individuals are the citizens of the nation.' The achievement of Young Italy would, by its imitation throughout the continent, lead to a 'Young Europe' in which nations would become morally and spiritually enriched. Europe had received from the 'old' Italy the cultural stimulus of the Roman

Empire and the spiritual stimulus of the Catholic Church. Now it would receive from Young Italy the example of the destruction of clerical and feudal privilege, and of all restrictions upon the fulfilment of human potential.

Such ambitions, of course, remained completely unrealistic and entirely unrealised. Mazzini's dependence upon conspiracy, insurrection and guerrilla warfare proved utterly ill-founded. He could not conceive that apathy or ignorance might blind the Italian peasant to his appeal, and he had no means of overcoming the powerful vested interests among the governing élites that felt seriously threatened by his idealism.

Between the time of the Roman Republic and the momentous events of 1860, Mazzini's life was spent entirely in hiding or in exile. Yet in some circles, among British liberals and radicals, for instance, he was accounted one of the greatest men of his time. Thomas Carlyle found him 'a man of genius and virtue, a man of sterling veracity, humanity and nobleness of mind'. 'No man,' concluded *The*

Spectator at the end of his life, 'has ever performed such a feat and made so deep a personal impression on the history of mankind.'

So what was this feat, and what did Mazzini achieve? Clearly he did not unify Italy, and most of those who did so acted through different motives. On the other hand, Mazzini might reasonably claim that it was his principles, put into action by Garibaldi, that forced the Piedmontese government to go further and faster towards unity than it would ideally have wished. He was not far from the truth when he wrote in 1860 that 'we have constantly acted as the spur: we worked, fought and bled for Italy, the Cavour cabinet constantly opposing, then reaping the results as soon as won or unavoidable'.

It is also notable that, for all his initial reliance upon the foreign intervention that Mazzini abhored, Cavour in the end came to rely upon the 'insurrectionist' methods that the radicals had always favoured. In the Central Duchies in 1859 and in the Papal States a year later (*see* Chapter 4) Cavour undertook, according to Denis Mack Smith, 'a Mazzini-style war without the unwelcome presence of Mazzini himself'. In the end, therefore, Mazzini's admirers might claim that he achieved as much of his political programme as was compatible with political reality.

staged a 'tobacco strike' by giving up smoking in order to deprive the Austrians of the revenue from their tobacco duty. On 12 January Palermo, in Sicily, rose in revolt against government from Naples. In February and March the rash of new constitutions began to affect Italy too. Tuscany received one from its grand duke (11 February), and Naples from its king. Even the Pope could not avoid the fashion (4 March). Also in March Austri-

an troops were expelled from Milan and Venice after several days of street-fighting.

Charles Albert did not stop at the granting of a constitution. Less than three weeks later he committed Piedmont to war against the apparently disintegrating Austrians, in support of the risings in Lombardy and Venetia. With reluctant initial support from Naples and the Papacy, Charles Albert had at least the superficial appearance of leading the greatest bid in modern Italian history for freedom and nationhood.

M Italy: failure

The defeat of Piedmont

For all the themes and theories of the previous years, the chance for nationalist action in Italy had been provided by the disruption of the European status quo, and especially by the distraction of the Austrian armed forces. The return of European stability, and the recovery of the Austrian government spelled the doom of Italian freedom. A month after the triumph of Windischgrätz in Prague, the Piedmontese army met the forces of Marshal Radetzky at Custoza (25 July 1848). The Papacy and the king of Naples had already withdrawn their contingents of troops, and defeat badly undermined Piedmontese morale. Although the army survived substantially intact, the pessimism of the generals and Charles Albert's own fear of radical activity at home led to a precipitate retreat from Lombardy.

Renewed pressures upon the king only led to another defeat at Austrian hands at Novara (23 March 1849). The price paid this time was the permanent removal of Charles Albert from political life through his abdication in favour of his son, Victor Emmanuel. In addition, Austria imposed an indemnity of 75 million lire upon Piedmont. That she retained her territorial integrity was due mainly to the European objections that would have been raised to any tampering with this important 'buffer' zone on France's borders. Charles Albert's proud boast that 'Italy will do it herself' (*Italia farà da se*) had proved altogether empty.

The flight of Pius IX

The war had also served to demonstrate the limitations of Pius IX as a leader of the national cause. Leading a confederation of Italian states was one thing. To lead one Catholic state against another was quite a different matter. Pius's confidante, G. Montanelli, put the kindest interpretation upon the Pope's motives. 'As an Italian he wanted to see the foreign invaders driven out of the country, but as Pope – as the universal Father he could never declare a war of independence against Austria.' A more recent historian, E. L. Woodward, has inter-preted the whole pretence of liberal-national leadership as a piece of confused thinking. 'How could the Sovereign Pontiff become a constitutional ruler? Who could be responsible for the actions of the Vicar of God on earth?' Nevertheless, Pius continued to work with his constitutional government until November. Then he fled Rome for the safety of Naples. With his flight died the last hope of the Papacy fulfiling the role that Gioberti had mapped out for it.

The defeat of radicalism

'The royal war is over,' declared Mazzini in a national appeal in August 1848; 'the war of the people begins.' The flight of the Pope paved the way for a second, equally unsuccessful phase in the struggles of 1848–49, the republican phase. In February 1849 a Roman Republic was proclaimed to fill the vacuum left by Pius. With Mazzini providing its political inspiration, and Giuseppe Garibaldi conducting its military defence, the republic represented the pinnacle of radical aspirations. Its decrees calling for the distribution of Church lands to the peasantry, and for the public housing of the poor, could not offset its weaknesses. It was ravaged by inflation, starved of support from other quarters of Italy, and subjected to the combined hostility of France and Austria. After a heroic defence, the Republic was defeated in June 1849, and the presence thereafter of a French garrison strengthened foreign interest in Italy's future.

Meanwhile, with the defeat of Piedmont, Venice and Tuscany had gone their respective ways. Under the leadership of Daniele Manin, Venice once more declared herself a republic, as she had been until the Napoleonic invasion. She resisted Austrian siege warfare, with its horrors of bombardment, cholera and starvation, until late August 1849. Tuscan radicals expelled their grand duke in February 1849, but could not do the same to the Austrian forces that came to restore him in April.

The combination of circumstances in Italy in 1848–49 made those years seem particularly auspicious for the cause of Italian freedom. Yet what did it all achieve? Firstly we find the famous judgement of G. M. Trevelyan that 1848 was 'the turning point at which modern history failed to turn'. Then we have the judgement of the patriot, Settembrini, that 'this generation made Italy', that the example of 1848 was 'the point at which we became Italians, felt ourselves united and gathered together under a single standard'. We must conclude that, although the rebels of 1848 achieved nothing material in Italy, except for the Piedmontese constitution, the future course of Italian history was significantly altered. The refusal of Pius IX to put himself at the head of the national cause, and his conservative response to the events in Rome, killed the hopes of Gioberti and the neo-guelphs. The author himself renounced them and exhorted patriots to look instead to Piedmont.

The failure of radical republicanism demonstrated once more its various faults; the failure of its various advocates to co-operate with one another, and its impotence in the face of opposition from a major power. Leopold II, Grand Duke of Tuscany, and Ferdinand of Naples had shown their true colours by refusing to co-operate with Charles Albert, and much of northern Italy was more firmly than ever under the control of Austria.

The one exception to this catalogue of gloom was the state of Piedmont, whose king had embraced a constitution and staked his soldiers' lives and his own crown upon the Italian cause. Italian nationalists were not likely to forget these actions. The future of Italy, as the next two decades were to prove, lay with Piedmont.

Questions

Essay questions

1 Did the revolutions of 1848 share any common principles or aims? (Oxford entrance)

2 For what reasons did the revolution in France in 1848 trigger other uprisings in other European states? (WJEC)

3 Why did the Austrian Empire, which Metternich described as a 'mouldering edifice', survive the revolutions of 1848–49? (UCLES)

4 'Social and economic factors, rather than political ones, were responsible for the outbreak of revolution in 1848.' To what extent do you agree with this opinion? (JMB/NEAB)

5 Why did the revolutionaries in the years 1848–49 achieve so little in either the German Confederation or the Habsburg Empire? (ULEAC)

6 'A revolution by intellectuals and for intellectuals': to what extent is this a satisfactory explanation of the causes and consequences of the 1848 revolutions in the Habsburg Empire? (ULEAC)

Document question

Study the following source carefully, and then answer the questions based upon it.

DECLARATION OF THE HUNGARIAN PEOPLE, 15th March 1849.
1. Freedom of the press; abolition of <u>censorship</u>.
2. A responsible ministry with its seat in the capital.
3. An annual parliament in Budapest.
4. Political and religious equality before the law.
5. A national guard.
6. Taxes to be paid by all.
7. Abolition of <u>serfdom</u>.
8. Jury system. Equality of representation.
9. A national bank.
10. The military to take an oath to the constitution. Hungarian soldiers not to be stationed abroad, foreign soldiers to be removed.
11. Political prisoners to be freed.
12. Union with Transylvania.
The speaking of Magyar was to be a qualification for members of parliament.

---

a
  i Explain the meaning of the underlined words. [2]
  ii What did the Hungarians mean by 'a responsible ministry' (declaration 2)? [3]
b
  i What underlying themes can you detect in this list of declarations? [3]
  ii How many of these demands were unique to Hungary, and which were to be found elsewhere in Europe in 1848–49? [4]
c In what ways does this source contribute to an understanding of the 1848 revolutions in the Habsburg Empire? [8]

(WJEC)

3

The French Second Empire

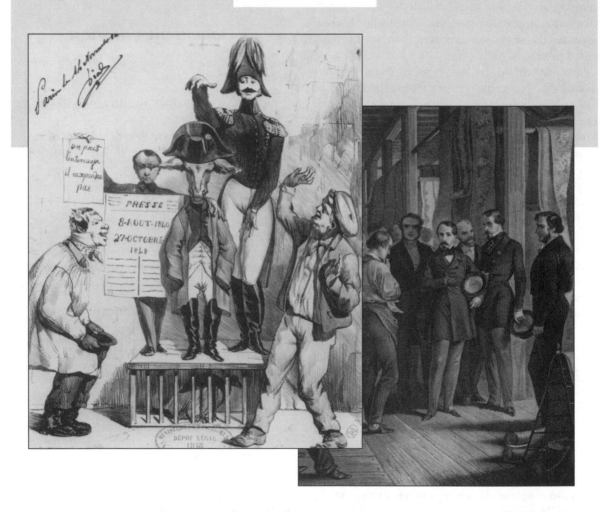

Two views of Louis Napoleon Bonaparte which appeared in the French press in December 1848. One shows the presentation of Louis Napoleon to the electorate, while the other shows him visiting workshops in the Faubourg St Antoine district of Paris.

Summarise in your own words the image of Louis Napoleon that each portrayal seeks to convey.

With which sections of the electorate might either portrayal have found favour?

The Historical Debate

The circumstances of the fall of Napoleon III, amid national humiliation and the distrust of all major European powers, ensured that immediate historical judgements upon him and upon his regime would be harsh ones. The tone was set during the Second Empire itself by two brilliant polemicists with fundamental political objections to the Napoleonic regime, Victor Hugo and Karl Marx. Their chief weapon, as put forward by Hugo in *Napoleon Le Petit* (1852) and by Marx in *The 18th Brumaire of Louis Napoleon* (1852), was ridicule. They claimed that Louis Napoleon was a petty adventurer, rising on the reputation of a man whom he could not hope to emulate. Although great in other fields, neither man could pretend to be an objective historian, and their judgements were judgements upon the political ideology of the Second Empire, and not upon its record of achievement.

Equally, the judgements of many French commentators upon the Second Empire have tasted of political outrage. Given that his own country has been a parliamentary republic for all but five years since 1870, it is unsurprising that Napoleon III's historical reputation has been adversely affected by the 'guilt' of his destruction of the Second Republic. Taxile Delord (*History of the Second Empire,* 1869–75) set the republican trend with a violent indictment in the early days of the Third Republic, and Albert Thomas (*The Second Empire,* 1906) contributed a socialist interpretation and condemnation. Abroad, an Englishman, Arthur Kinglake (*The Invasion of the Crimea,*1863–80) and a German, Hermann Oncken (*The Rhine Policy of Napoleon III,* 1926), established the view that the Emperor was an irresponsible and dangerous expansionist in his foreign policy.

Time and distance have tended to soften judgements on the Second Empire. The major works of the 'revisionist' school have been written by British and American historians, less concerned with the ideological preoccupations of French republican politics. F. A. Simpson, in *Louis Napoleon and the Recovery of France* (1923), stressed that, especially in terms of domestic achievements, the Second Empire was more important than the First, and considerably more fruitful than the regimes that immediately preceded it. Albert Guerard (*Napoleon III,* 1943) extended this understanding to what he saw as the farsighted conception of his foreign policy. Lynn M. Case, in his important work on French public opinion, and the government's means of keeping in touch with it (*French Opinion on War and Diplomacy during the Second Empire,* 1954), demonstrated the very real influence that public opinion exercised upon policy making under Napoleon III. Perhaps the most valuable recent contribution to this school has been the work of Theodore Zeldin, whose books on *The Political System of Napoleon III* (1958) and on *Emile Ollivier and the Liberal Empire of Napoleon III* (1963) have largely illuminated the internal workings of the French government, and revised views on the nature and origins of the liberal phase of the Empire.

The lines of historical interpretation, however, are no longer as clearly defined as once they were. For some time now the ideas of the 'revisionist' school have been reflected in the work of French writers. The process was begun, perhaps, by Pierre de la Gorce. He was not kind to the Emperor in his monumental *History of the Second Empire* (1894–1905) but, in his old age, in *Napoleon III and his Policy* (1934), he began to revise his verdict. 'He was indeed nefarious. But no sooner have I written this, than I would wish to soften this judgement; for he was also good, and at times, enlightened.' Among the most recent French authorities, such as A. Plessis (*The Rise and Fall of the Second Empire, 1852–1871,* 1985) and L. Girard (*Napoleon III,* 1986), there is a tendency to concentrate less upon the political ideology of the reign than upon the significant and lasting progress that was made in social and economic terms, and upon the role played by the Empire in the emergence of modern French society.

Among recent English writers, on the other hand, J.M. Thompson has taken an approach notably critical of Napoleon III. His *Louis Napoleon and the Second Empire* (1954) draws parallels between the Emperor and Hamlet, both men not great enough for the tasks that they set themselves. J.P.T. Bury (*Napoleon III and the Second Empire,* 1964) and James McMillan (*Napoleon III,* 1991) both maintain the Anglo-Saxon tradition of greater sympathy for the Emperor, dwelling upon the consistency with which he applied original and imaginative policies.

A The weakness of the Second Republic

The strength of French conservatism

The essential weakness of the Second Republic in France lay in the incompatibility between the nature of its President and the nature of the constitution by which he was bound to govern. The vast majority of the votes cast for Louis Napoleon Bonaparte in 1848 were votes for permanence, for stability and for order (*see* Chapter 2, section **D**). By 1851 Louis Napoleon had set himself at the centre of a formidable conservative coalition. The elections of May 1849 had returned an Assembly in which the 'Party of Order', the coalition of Legitimists, Orleanists and Bonapartists, held 64 per cent of the seats, as opposed to 34 per cent previously. The support of the French Catholics was assured, not only by their fear of the 'Reds', but by their approval of the French military intervention in Italy in support of the Papacy, and of the Falloux Law passed in 1850. The position of this coalition was further consolidated by the introduction of a new Electoral Law (May 1850), which reduced the electorate by some three million voters.

The position of the President

On the other hand, the President remained saddled with a constitution specifically designed by its authors in 1848 to prevent the emergence of a dominant Imperial figure. The President was limited to a tenure of office of only four years, and he was not thereafter eligible for re-election to that office.

Such an arrangement posed problems both for Louis Napoleon himself and for a large proportion of the French electorate. The strength of the conservative coalition did not necessarily reflect the personal strength of the President himself, and it seemed increasingly likely that the 'Party of Order' would replace him with an Orleanist candidate when the presidency was next contested in 1852. After the experiences of 1848, however, the bulk of the propertied electorate would not necessarily welcome such renewed political contests. The year 1852, therefore, held the twin prospects of a return to political oblivion for the President, and for the propertied electorate of a return to the political battles, and perhaps to the street fighting of 1848.

B The *coup d'état*

The search for a legal solution

Clearly, Louis Napoleon never seriously considered relinquishing power in order to return to obscurity at the end of his four-year term. There is some truth in the charges of his enemies that his personal debts made it impossible for him to turn his back upon the fruits of office. More important was the mission of the restoration of stability and prosperity in France, set down in *The Napoleonic Ideals*, which would have to be abandoned with the loss of office. There is only rough justice in the view propagated by Victor Hugo that Louis Napoleon had cynically sworn his oath to the Republican constitution the better to destroy it, and the better to plunder the state.

Although the President undoubtedly desired the extension of his powers, he originally hoped to achieve this by working within the constitution that he had sworn to implement. Forceful action was very much the last resort of a man who had consistently resisted the suggestions of those who had tried to tempt him into a *coup d'état* earlier in his term of office. Besides, Louis Napoleon had no desire to repeat the experience of his earlier coups. Ignoring the advice of bolder spirits such as Persigny, Louis Napoleon attempted to persuade the Assembly to amend the constitution by legal means to allow the re-election of the President. Such a change, however, required a 75 per cent majority, the support of some 540 deputies. By July 1851 it was clear that Louis Napoleon would not overcome this constitutional obstacle, and by the last month of that year his choice lay between yielding to the letter of the constitution and overthrowing it.

The conduct of the coup

The groundwork for the eventual coup and the preparation of public opinion were thorough. Louis Napoleon had used his presidential powers to remove potential opponents, such as the commander of the Paris garrison, and had replaced them with reliable allies. Saint Arnaud now commanded the troops in Paris, Maupas was Prefect of Police, and Morny, the President's illegitimate half-brother, was minister of the interior. A series of provincial tours in the late summer and autumn allowed Louis Napoleon to gauge public support.

The date chosen was 2 December, a great 'Napoleonic' date, for it was the anniversary of the great victory at Austerlitz in 1805. The code name, 'Operation Rubicon', also had Imperial overtones. Seventy-eight police officers, unaware that they were part of a concerted plot, each arrested a prominent member of the opposition. The dissolution of the Assembly was announced, and was enforced next day by Saint Arnaud's troops. The casualty list by 4 December stood at 215, and 27,000 arrests had been made, of whom some 9,000 were eventually sentenced to deportation, mainly to Algeria.

The effect of the *coup*

The effect of the *coup d'état*, therefore, was twofold. In general, it went smoothly, and was easily accepted. 'If the *coup d'état* of December 2nd was a crime,' F. A. Simpson has concluded, 'then France was its accomplice rather than its victim.' This was borne out by the results of the plebiscite held on 21 December, when 7.5 million out of 8 million voters cast a 'Yes' vote in approbation of Louis Napoleon's action. Louis was delighted and relieved. 'More than 7 million votes have just absolved me,' he told the committee that had organised the plebiscite, 'by justifying an act that had no other aim than to spare our country, and perhaps Europe, from years of trouble and misfortune.' In Paris, however, the figures proved that a centre of opposition had been created that Louis Napoleon would never overcome. There, the margin in favour of the President was only 133,000 with 80,000 abstaining.

C The authoritarian constitution

Presidential powers and political institutions

The first concern of the transformed President, having destroyed the constitution of the Second Republic, was to dictate to the French a new constitution free from the obstructions of 'parliamentarians'. It was indeed a Napoleonic constitution, as Louis Napoleon himself explained. 'I have taken as a model the political institutions which have, since the beginning of the century, and in similar circumstances, consolidated a society which has been disrupted, and raised France to a high degree of prosperity and greatness. . . .Why

should we not adopt the political institutions of that period?'

The constitution granted the President absolute power for a period of ten years. Although he was 'responsible before the French people', and therefore not 'absolute' in the old monarchical sense, he alone could initiate legislation, or conclude treaties of peace or war. He commanded the armed forces and the civil service, and could, if the occasion demanded, govern by decree. He also appointed or dismissed ministers, and these ministers had no collective responsibility to the legislature. The latter consisted of three bodies, all effectively subject to the authority of the President. The Council of State (*Conseil d'Etat*) was directly appointed by the President from among the ranks of the senior civil servants. Its main task was the drafting of legislation, although it had, of course, no powers to initiate any such legislation.

The Senate, the upper house of the Assembly, consisted of 'notables', perhaps generals or retired administrators, appointed for life by the President. They were the prime illustration of Louis Napoleon's claim that he did not 'mind being baptised with the water of universal suffrage', but 'refused to live with his feet in it'. The Legislative Body (*Corps Legislative*) was indeed elected, for a period of six years, by universal male suffrage, but the 260 deputies were limited to the role of accepting or rejecting legislation proposed by the government. They could not initiate their own projects, and could not question ministers on points of their policies. Their debates, furthermore, could not be attended by the public.

This stifling of public political life, a basic principle of the new regime, was further reflected outside the Assembly. Political parties and the political press, already severely handicapped by the deportations and arrests that followed the *coup d'état*, were further shackled. Political meetings could now only be held in the presence of government officials, and the Press Decree of 1852 gave the government extensive powers to suspend and suppress publications. In Paris, for example, only four political journals survived the year.

The establishment of the Empire

This was effectively an Imperial constitution, and Louis Napoleon made little attempt to conceal the fact. It needed but a short step to transform the authoritarian President into an Emperor and, emboldened by the popularity of his moves in 1851, Louis Napoleon began once more to 'test the water' of popular opinion by a series of provincial tours in the autumn of 1852. Upon his return the Senate dutifully produced the legislation necessary to create an Empire in name as well as in form. Appealing to the people once again by plebiscite, Louis Napoleon received another overwhelming popular ratification, this time by eight million votes in favour of the Empire, with a mere 250,000 standing out against it.

Upon this evidence of popular support Louis Napoleon claimed to base his Second Empire. Yet it was noted that he chose as his Imperial title 'Napoleon III', as though the Duc de Reichstadt, the only legitimate son of the first Napoleon, had succeeded his father in spirit, and as though his own claim to power was at least as much dynastic as it was democratic.

D   Enforcing the constitution

The Emperor and his ministers

Popular though it undoubtedly was at the time of its creation, the strength of the Second Empire lay in the effective administrative machine that it operated. The ministers, firstly, depended very much upon the approval and support of the Emperor. Napoleon III drew his ministers from three main sources.

Some were members of the dynasty. Prince Jerome was his cousin, and Morny (minister of the interior and later President of the Legislative Body) was his half-brother, the illegitimate offspring of one of his mother's extra-marital relationships. Walewski (ambassador to London 1851–55, and foreign minister 1855–60) was an illegitimate son of Napoleon I. Others, like Persigny (minister of the interior, and then ambassador to London) had served the dynasty faithfully in exile. Most were survivors of the previous regimes. Morny himself had served under Guizot, but without reaching the highest ranks and unduly dirtying his hands.

Many others, such as Fould, Magne, Billaut and Rouher, had similar histories. This helps us to conclude that, although the principles of the regime were Bonapartist, the personnel was not. Nor

could it have been, for no Bonapartist party or hierarchy had developed in France during the 1830s and 1840s. 'The change,' wrote Lhomme, 'was not in the governing class, but in the governing team.'

Enforcement in the provinces

In the country at large, the influence of the government operated through the prefects and the mayors, themselves creations of the First Empire. The major tasks of the prefects were to keep the Emperor informed of the state of public opinion in the *départements* and to serve the Emperor's interests in local affairs. At elections, in particular, they were under specific instructions to aid government candidates and to do all that they could to hinder those of the opposition. Their efficiency in this task is reflected in the fact that only nine opposition candidates were successful in the 1852 elections.

Although the Second Empire was a distinctly centralised and authoritarian state, it was not in any real sense a military or a police state. J. P. T. Bury points out that although the Emperor made many concessions to the army to retain its support, such as the reconstruction of the Imperial Guard, the institution of decorations for gallantry, and of improved pensions, it was at no stage after the *coup d'état* used as an instrument of government. The police, too, seem to have played the role of tools in the hands of the prefects.

The Church was a much closer and more direct ally, able to exercise a more subtle influence over the populace, and gaining more important concessions in return, such as an increase in government aid for the repair of churches and for the payment of clerical stipends, greater control over education, after the precedent of the Falloux Law of 1850, and the presence of the religious orders in France.

Two points must be emphasised, however, if we are to have a clear understanding of the workings of the Second Empire. One point is that stressed by W. H. C. Smith when he wrote that 'to describe the Second Empire as a dictatorship is to miss the point. The government was authoritarian but at no time, except for the immediate aftermath of December 1852, was France without representative institutions or a code of law.' The other point is that, although Napoleon III stood at the head of a formidable conservative coalition, he was the representative rather than the absolute master of those conservative interests. At no time during his tenure of power could he afford to ignore those interests, nor ignore the possibility that those interests might attempt to replace him with another representative. Such considerations are especially important when seeking to understand the policy changes undertaken during the 1860s (*see* sections **L** and **M**).

E First domestic measures

The first moves of the new regime aimed to consolidate its power and to remove all alternative sources of influence and authority. The National Guard, for example, was suppressed. It had long been regarded as the safeguard of the bourgeoisie against the military tyranny of the monarchy. A good case could now be made for regarding it as redundant now that the champion of the bourgeoisie was firmly in power. Similarly, in a measure that anticipated the actions of future dictators, the Emperor demanded an oath of allegiance from all government servants and officials. The oath was taken, not to the state or to the nation, but to the head of state in person.

The most controversial of these early measures was contained in a decree of January 1852, which confiscated the estates and possessions of the Orleans family. Many, led by Victor Hugo, saw this as a greedy and spiteful act by one whose life the Orleans had spared, and others looked askance at the seizure of private property by one who posed as its protector.

F The Empire's economic aims

The most important and lasting achievements of the Second Empire were those in the related spheres of French commerce and industry. Hostile commentators, nevertheless, have tended to claim that these achievements were overshadowed and devalued by the Emperor's destruction of personal liberty. As recently as the 1950s J. M. Thompson passed the judgement that Napoleon III aimed 'to award economic prosperity as a consolation prize for loss of political liberty'. Others have been more inclined to reverse this judgement, and to see political authoritarianism as a means to the real domestic end of the reign, the drive to realise France's true economic potential.

Much has been made of the similarity between the policy of Napoleon III and the principles of the Saint Simonians. The followers of Comte Henri de Saint Simon (1760–1825) stressed the primary importance of economic production, and the primacy of those involved in this vital area (*see* Chapter 1, section **I**). There is little evidence that the Emperor ever aimed systematically to implement such a philosophy. He was not a sophisticated thinker in either philosophical or economic terms, but the philosophy accorded well enough with the policies of his uncle's regime. The new Emperor was well enough read in contemporary economic and political thought to give a wide freedom to men, such as the Pereire brothers, de Lesseps and Chevalier, who can be shown to have been more directly influenced by Saint Simon.

G The commercial revolution

The economic context of the Second Empire
The Second Empire opened under the most favourable economic circumstances. The steady decline in world prices that had prevailed from 1815 to 1850, and which had exercised a generally depressing effect upon trade, was sharply reversed by a dramatic increase in the gold supply. The major 'strike' in California in 1849 was followed by the equally spectacular 'gold rush' in Australia two years later. Together, the two roughly doubled the world's gold supply. The Emperor's detractors made much of these circumstances to belittle the economic achievement of the Second Empire. Nevertheless, the French derive credit from the fact that no other European country made comparable advances in the 1850s under such favourable circumstances.

Reform of the banking system
The major obstacle to the modernisation of the French economy was the conservatism of the French banking system. Wealthy and highly developed though it was, it lay largely in the hands of such families as the Rothschilds, old established bankers with strong links with conservative dynasties, and with equally conservative economic policies. With the aid of the more progressive Pereire family, the government began to outflank these staid bastions of finance. The Crédit Foncier,

a mortgage bank, was established in 1852, and the Crédit Mobilier, an industrial credit institution, was founded in the same year. Both offered shares for sale to the public. They thus tapped the vast private wealth that was perhaps France's greatest economic advantage. With these huge funds, they could make loans to finance public works undertaken by private contractors, without placing an undue burden upon government finances. Thus outmanoeuvred, the older establishments had little choice but to extend their own range of investments to engage themselves more deeply in industrial finance.

The appearance of the Société Génerale de Crédit Industriel et Commercial (1859), and of the Crédit Lyonnais deposit bank (1863) completed what J. M. Thompson has termed 'a financial revolution'. Whatever difficulties were to be experienced by the new institutions in the less favourable climate of the 1860s, the 'revolution' was not to be reversed.

H An industrial revolution

The development of the railway system

French industrialisation was a long and continuous process, and its foundations existed before the advent of the Second Empire. The progress made in the course of the empire's 20-year life span was, nevertheless, most striking. Communications constituted a priority, for no other industry could thrive without ready access to its sources of raw materials and to its markets.

Work on French railway construction had begun under Louis Philippe but, consisting mainly of short stretches of track dictated by local needs, it scarcely formed a viable basis for a national system. Under the Second Empire public and private finance combined to encourage and to fund further, more comprehensive development. By 1870, the state had invested some 634 million francs in railways, usually by paying for the 'infrastructure', the necessary land and so forth, and for shares with which to maintain their interest in the companies. The companies themselves paid for the 'superstructure' of the lines, for the buildings, rolling-stock and so on, and were granted long-term concessions, up to 99 years, for the exploitation of their new investments.

The impact of the railway system

With the consolidation and rationalisation of the system from 42 smaller enterprises into six main companies, the railways effectively transformed the social and economic life of France. The average cost of transporting a ton of produce dropped from 25 centimes to five in the course of 20 years. Thus total traffic increased, from 6.2 billion km/tons in 1852 to 11.82 billion in 1869, while prices dropped.

By linking the major economic centres of France with Belgium, Spain, Germany and Italy, the railway system was also the key to French international commerce. Lastly, not only did the railway 'boom' provide a new demand for the products of heavy industry, consuming 7.2 per cent of their total production in 1855–64, but it opened the way to new markets and new sources of raw materials. Table 3.1 illustrates both the growth of the French railways and also the related growth of other areas of French heavy industry. The telegraph network, a vital tool of the centralised administration, grew from 2,000 to over 70,000 km in the course of the reign.

Table 3.1 French industrial development, 1845–70

	1845	1848	1855	1860	1865	1870
Railway track ('000 km)	–	2.2	5.5	10.0	13.6	16.9
Freight carried (million tons)	–	2.9	10.6	27.9	34.0	44.0
Mineral fuels (million tons)	4.2	–	7.5	8.3	11.6	13.3
Miners employed ('000)	34.8	–	54.3	65.6	77.9	82.7
Iron ore (million tons)	2.5	–	3.9	3.0	3.0	2.6

I Agriculture

Nevertheless, France, the land of the peasant smallholder, remained a country where agricultural interests continued to play a major role. In 1866, 51.5 per cent of the population derived its livelihood from the land. The improvement of agricultural production in France was a vital area of government concern in which, although similar methods were applied, the results were less uniformly striking. Some impressive figures, nevertheless, can be quoted. By irrigation and drainage, 1.5 million hectares of new land came under cultivation, making the total area of cultivated land in France at the end of the Second Empire 26.5 million hectares, the highest figure in the country's history. The area given over to the cultivation of wheat was 33 per cent greater in 1862 than in 1840, and the increase in the area of sugar beet production stood at a huge 137 per cent. Spectacular improvements, however, tended to be local rather than national, and 'success stories' are offset by cases where no substantial change in production or agricultural methods took place at all. Modernisation occurred, but irregularly, and most frequently upon the large estates. France boasted 9,000 mechanical harvesters in 1862, but they were spread between 3.6 million cultivators of the land.

J The transformation of Paris

The clearest physical imprint of the Second Empire was that left upon the fabric of its capital city. In the first year of his reign Napoleon III had made clear his concern with the material state of Paris by completing his uncle's great avenue, the rue de Rivoli, and by the construction of Les Halles as a central market for the city. The following year, the appointment of Baron Haussmann as Prefect of Paris provided a man of sufficient energy and determination to cut through the web of vested interests and allied complications that stood in the way of the transformation of the medieval city into an Imperial showpiece on the scale of London, Vienna or St Petersburg. The process was long and difficult. The debts incurred were not finally paid off until 1929, and Haussmann made many enemies for himself and for the regime through his cavalier attitude to finance. Enemies claimed that the main purpose of the Emperor and his Prefect was to replace the easily barricaded, revolutionary rabbit-warren of 1848 with vistas that were as suitable for artillery fire as they were pleasant to the visitor's eye. Doubtless, the strategic advantages were not lost upon Napoleon III, but nor do they seem to have been uppermost in his mind. The records of his intense personal interest in the project bear out Persigny's judgement that 'his main aim throughout was to carry out great works

in Paris, and improve the living conditions of the working classes, to destroy unhealthy districts, and to make the capital the most beautiful city in the world'.

Most aspects of modern Paris bear witness to the 'great works' of the Second Empire. The modern boulevards, the railway stations, the open spaces at the Parc Monceau and the Bois de Boulogne, all date from this period. Gas lighting was introduced throughout the city, and a vast new system of sewers was constructed, although these failed to save the city from further outbreaks of cholera in 1866 and 1867. The second stage of the project saw the construction of residential suburbs for those workers displaced from the centre. Numerous other towns, among them Lyon, Rouen, Le Havre, Bordeaux and Marseilles, experienced similar public works schemes upon a smaller scale.

K The Empire and its people

Urban poverty and political opposition

By the mid-1860s, however, substantial sections of the French population were clearly reacting with little gratitude or enthusiasm towards the Emperor's reforms. Was this merely ingratitude, or did it reflect a deep-rooted failure on the part of the government to transform society as the Emperor's early writings had promised? Once more the answer is complicated by vast diversity between region and region, and between industry and industry. It is by no means possible in the 1850s and the 1860s to speak of a homogeneous working class in France with a single set of interests and reactions.

The Parisian worker remained the steadfast opponent of the regime, from the plebiscite of 1851 to the legislative elections of 1863, when the opposition made a clean sweep of the Parisian constituencies, and beyond. The discontent was partly ideological, partly material. The problem of poverty in the first years of the Second Empire was enormous. Research based upon the wills of urban workers suggests that in 1847 between 70 and 80 per cent of the population of Paris was too poor to bequeath any property. The figure scarcely descended below 70 per cent over the next two decades.

The rebuilding of Paris, impressive as it was in the eyes of visitors, in the long run merely changed the location of the slums. The worker found it impossible to return to the rebuilt centre of the city, where rents had advanced far beyond his capacity to pay. He now had to be content with the new suburbs where, in the phrase of L. Lasare, higher rents and immigration from the provinces had created 'a red belt enclosing, besieging the centre of the city'.

Conditions in the textile industry

The French textile industry also provides evidence that causes the historian to question the impressive statistics of the Empire's economic growth. Not only did it suffer badly from increased competition from Britain after 1861 (*see* section **L**), but it was then savagely hit by the 'cotton famine' that resulted from the American Civil War. In 1860, 365,000 bales of cotton entered France through Le Havre, compared with only 31,000 bales in 1862. Thus, although 'real' wages showed a distinct increase under the Second Empire, factors such as these, and price fluctuations beyond the control of any government (such as those caused by bad cereal harvests in 1853, 1855, 1861 and 1867) meant that in local cases no real improvement in living conditions would be noticed.

Consumption and education

Nevertheless, statistics can be quoted to suggest some substantial improvements in the lot of the 'average' Frenchman. Consumption per head of all major foodstuffs was higher in the decade 1865–74 than in the decade 1845–54, sometimes, as Table 3.2 shows, by a substantial margin.

Table 3.2 Consumption per head (in grams per week)

	Bread	Potatoes	Fruit/Veg	Sugar
1845–54	714	107	245	0
1865–74	763	254	265	20
	Meat/Fish		Milk/Cheese	Butter
1845–54	78		168	17
1865–74	100		208	21

Perhaps the most spectacular social developments were in education. The work of Rouland (1856–63) and Duruy (1863–69) at the Ministry of Education made great inroads into the problems of illiteracy and lack of instruction, leaving only 312 French communities without a school in 1867, compared to 2,690 in 1850. By 1866, 68 per cent of French children between five and 14 years of age were attending school, compared to 51 per cent in 1851. Between 1856 and 1881 the estimated rate of illiteracy fell from 31 per cent to 15 per cent. J. Rougerie has concluded that 'there was still real misery, but there is no doubt that the worker of the 50s and 60s lived better than his predecessor of the 40s.'

L   Liberalisation: commerce

A policy of economic liberalisation had been advocated by the Emperor since 1853, but had been strenuously resisted by the Legislative Body. Napoleon III still regarded the principle of freer trade as essential, both as a foundation of the future economic expansion of France, and as the cornerstone of the understanding with Great Britain which he considered a vital element of foreign policy.

British suspicion of French policy in Italy in 1859 made rapprochement more urgent than ever. The free-trade treaty signed with Britain in 1860 known, after the chief negotiators as the Cobden–Chevalier Treaty, had such distinct political overtones that Cobden described it as 'nine-tenths political rather than politico-economical, with a view to cement the alliance with this country'. All the same, its economic consequences were far reaching. Import duties on British coal, textiles, iron and steel were to be lowered by 25 per cent over five years, and French wines, silks and fancy goods would enter Britain at substantially reduced rates. It was the tip of a *laissez faire* iceberg, being followed by reciprocal trade treaties with Belgium (1861), the *Zollverein* (1862), Italy (1863), Switzerland (1864), Spain and the Netherlands (1865), and Austria and Portugal (1866).

This was not, however, a policy guaranteed to bring calm and stability. The beneficial effects of free trade were always envisaged as being in the long term. In the present lay mainly the opposition of conservative businessmen and financiers, and the unrest of workers whose industries suffered from the immediate competition with the industrial might of Great Britain.

M Liberalisation: the constitution

The Emperor's motives for liberalisation

The most important factor in reaching a conclusion as to the nature of the Second Empire is, as Theodore Zeldin has emphasised, the interpretation that one gives to the liberalisation of the government of France in the last ten years of Napoleon III's regime. To the enemies of the Emperor the explanation was simple. He was forced into concessions by mounting opposition, in an attempt to retain his power against the persistent hostility of the republicans. Napoleon III had always spoken of authoritarian government, however, purely as a temporary expedient. In *The Napoleonic Ideals* he had used the comparison that 'liberty is like a river; in order that it may bring fertility and not devastation, its bed must be hollowed out deep and wide'. Indeed, in 1851 he had given himself ten years of absolute power for the accomplishment of this task. More sympathetic commentators have found it reasonable to accept the argument that pressures such as those provided by the economic recession of 1857–58, and by the limited success of the Italian campaign in 1859, did not create the policy of liberalisation, but merely dictated its timing.

It becomes much easier to understand the liberalising reforms of the 1860s if they are viewed in practical terms of political realism, rather than in terms of political ideology. James McMillan takes this view when he writes that 'Napoleon III remained neither a traditional conservative nor an orthodox liberal, but a *politique* who manoeuvred with immense skill to maintain himself in power. ... Before it was "authoritarian" or "liberal", the Empire was a "personalist" regime. At its centre was a lonely figure, wielding power through men who often did not share his vision of politics.'

There is much evidence to suggest that the main threat to the position of the Emperor in the late 1850s did not come from republicans or from political radicals, but rather from Orleanists and other conservatives, who saw less need for this Napoleonic figure now that the main work for stabilisation and for the preservation of property had been completed. James McMillan and other recent writers therefore see the liberal reforms of this period, not as a form of surrender to the pressures of French radicalism, but as a piece of inspired *realpolitik*, aimed at the establishment of new political alliances which might thwart conservative designs.

The reforms of 1860

There is little doubt that the first package of constitutional reforms was proposed by the Emperor himself, and that it met with considerable opposition from the conservative ministers that surrounded him. In 1860 came the grant to the Legislative Body of a package of concessions in the vital area of finance. The Emperor renounced the right to borrow money elsewhere when the Legislative Body was in recess. He also agreed that the budget should be voted in sections rather than as a whole, thus giving the deputies more chance to attack any unpopular section. For the first time, furthermore, their debates could be observed and reported by journalists.

Concessions to the working classes

The first concessions towards the radical opponents of the regime, and towards the urban proletariat predated the initial batch of parliamentary reforms by a year. In 1859 an amnesty was offered by the government to all political exiles. Only Ledru Rollin, the extreme republican, was excluded from the general amnesty, although a number of others refused the conciliatory gesture.

In 1862, the government subsidised the visit of a workers' delegation to the International Exhibition in London, allowing a degree of contact with foreign workers that would have seemed highly dangerous a few years earlier. Thereafter, reform proceeded with great rapidity. Peaceful strikes were legalised in 1864, and the theory of the equality of employer and worker before the law was recognised. The legality of trades unions was fully established by 1868, and proposals to abolish the *livret*, a form of workers' passport without which a man could not be employed, were before the legislature when war broke out in 1870.

The elections of 1863 and their impact

The legislative elections of 1863 saw the return of 32 opposition candidates, a combination of republicans, Orleanists and others, where there had been only five before. It would have been a compliment to the freer political atmosphere in France had not Napoleon subsequently dismissed Persigny from his post as minister of the interior for his failure to secure better results. Thus the government contradicted itself by granting greater freedoms and then reacting uneasily when those freedoms revealed opposition to the regime. Why? One reason seems to have been that the ministers generally found it hard to accept the new course chosen by the Emperor. The limited political activity of the 1850s left the Emperor with a very limited range of politically experienced men from whom to choose a new generation of ministers. Of the older generation most, like Rouher, who was christened the 'Vice-Emperor' for his domination of domestic politics from 1863–69, were bitterly opposed to any relaxation of Imperial control.

Lastly, no account of the last years of the Second Empire makes consistent sense without the knowledge that, at least from the middle of 1865, when a stone in the bladder was diagnosed, the Emperor was acutely ill and often in severe pain. 'I find a sick man,' commented the Empress in 1866, 'irresolute, exhausted. . . . He can no longer walk, no longer sleep, and scarcely eat.'

The limits of reform

The reforming zeal that existed in some quarters in the 1860s, and the range of interests that opposed reform, may be appreciated by considering two areas in which reform failed. One was education. Victor Duruy, for all his achievements at the Ministry of Education (*see* section **K**), attempted a far more radical advance when he proposed free, compulsory, primary education, with a great reduction in clerical control. His statement that 'we have left this education in the hands of people who are neither of their time nor of their country' anticipated the campaigns of Jules Ferry (*see* Chapter 8) by two decades. Clerical influence was not yet ready to yield, however, and opposition to these proposed reforms forced Duruy's resignation in July 1869.

A more damaging defeat was that which the government suffered over the projected army reforms proposed by Marshal Niel, minister of war, in 1867. Niel aimed to increase the size of the army and to make provision for a substantial reserve force, while overhauling the system of conscription to eliminate the inequalities and injustices in it. A set of proposals that would have left the French

army in a far better position to resist the Prussians in 1870 provoked a storm of opposition from a variety of sources. Republicans with an ideological objection to a standing army joined with prosperous bourgeoises and with peasants who had no desire to see their sons dragged into the army where they might earlier have found it easy to avoid conscription. The opposition in the Legislative Body so reduced the effectiveness of the proposals, that the measures passed in January 1868 constituted little more than an impotent compromise, which was to serve France badly in the crisis that was soon to overtake her.

The emergence of the 'Third Party'

Perhaps the decisive domestic stimulus to reform was the formation, in 1863, of the 'Third Party'. Its origins lay in a group of 40 members of the government majority in the Legislative Body who broke away, not to oppose the government outright, but to press for further reform within a constitutional framework. They were joined by others from different political backgrounds, by Orleanists and by former republicans, such as Emile Ollivier. Adolphe Thiers collaborated with the group, although he was never formally a member. The amendment proposed by Ollivier in March 1866 to the Emperor's address from the throne summarised the attitude of much of the apparent opposition at this time. 'France, firmly attached to the dynasty that guarantees order, is no less attached to the liberty that she believes to be necessary for the fulfilment of her destinies.' Other pressures for reform, such as those caused by the failure of the Mexican expedition (*see* section **R**) and the virtual collapse of the Pereire banking empire, came from further afield.

The new elections of 1869 finally galvanised the government into action at a realistic pace. To the government's credit they were the freest held under the Second Empire, and they were the closest. The margin in the government's favour was now 4.5 million votes to 3.3 million. J. M. Thompson regards this as the crisis point for the Empire, remarking that 'perhaps even France never so closely resembled a people in disintegration'. The situation seems rather less dramatic, however, if one considers that, of the 270 opposition deputies, 116 belonged to the essentially loyal 'Third Party'.

The completion of the 'Liberal Empire'

The mandate for substantial reform was clear, and Napoleon III chose the moment to establish the 'Liberal Empire' at which his policies had been hinting. Accepting the resignation of Rouher, he called to office Emile Ollivier, a prominent member of the 'Third Party' and a representative of just that new generation of politicians which until very recently had been conspicuous by its absence. The Emperor then, in the words of J. P. T. Bury, 'adopted the reforming programme of the 116 as his own'. Under the new laws of September 1869 the Legislative Body could propose legislation, elect its own officers, and debate and vote on the budget. At last the Emperor had touched the pulse of the nation. Share prices rose and journals previously hostile to the regime acclaimed its transformation. The plebiscite held in May 1870 to ratify the measures returned a favourable majority, with 7.3 million saying 'Yes', 1.57 million 'No', with 1.9 million abstentions. The popularity of the Empire seemed to have returned.

It can never be clearly established whether this was a temporary expedient which the Emperor aimed to reverse at the earliest opportunity or whether, as Zeldin claims, it was a genuine 'attempt to break the vicious circle of revolution and reaction in which France had been caught since Louis XVI'. Before that question could be answered, the Second Empire had been destroyed by quite different factors. What may be safely concluded is that, by May 1870, the Empire was quite safe from internal disintegration. Perhaps it always had been, for what opposition there was, was much more opposition to the 'authoritarian' Empire than to the idea of Empire itself. Thus the causes of its sudden collapse must be sought further afield.

N Foreign policy: aims

Revision of the Vienna settlement

The ideas laid down in *The Napoleonic Ideals* on the subject of foreign policy were considerably vaguer than those on domestic policy. His uncle, Louis Napoleon had declared, had aimed 'to substitute, among the nations of Europe, the social state for the state of nature, . . .to found a solid European association, by resting his system upon completed nationalities and satisfied general interests'. Did this mean that the foreign policy of the Second Empire was to be a pursuit of the romantic doctrine of nationalities, or was that merely a cover for a general attack upon the autocratic interests that upheld the Vienna Settlement?

The limits of Napoleonic expansionism

The best answer is perhaps provided by a rare moment of honesty in diplomacy. In February 1863, at the height of the Polish revolt, the Empress Eugenie discussed with the Austrian ambassador a far-reaching plan for the settlement of current European disputes, and for the logical resettlement of the map of Europe. She did this possibly to test his reactions and those of his government. The Polish question would be settled by the creation of an independent state and, as compensation, Russia would be free to expand into Armenia and the Caucasus at the expense of the Turkish Empire. The other great questions, those of Italy and Germany, would be dealt with by similar 'give and take'. Austria would surrender Venetia to Italy, thus completing the business of 1859, and would find compensation in the annexation of Silesia, and in influence over that part of Germany south of the River Main. The acquisition of Hanover, and hegemony over Germany north of the Main would make this palatable to the other great German power, Prussia. She would thus be able to release the Rhineland, which could form an independent 'buffer state' under the rule of the King of the Belgians. His obsolete kingdom could then be partitioned between France and the Dutch.

Of course, the scheme was far too grandiose, and touched upon far too many sensitive areas to get further than the theoretical stage. Yet in the light of previous and subsequent events it is not fanciful to see it as a statement of the 'ideal' outcome of Second Empire foreign policy. It incorporated the realisation of national ideals, but only to the extent that best served French interests. Thus there would be two Germanies and three Italian states, where full unification would create powerful neighbours on France's borders. It also betrays the ideal extent of desired French expansion. France might expand to her 'natural frontiers' of the Scheldt, the Alps, and perhaps the Rhine, with friendly and relatively weak 'client' states beyond those borders. Potential enemies, such as

Austria, Russia, and perhaps Prussia, could now be kept at a safe distance.

The place of Britain in French foreign policy

The one element that is not shown clearly enough in the plan of 1863 is the element that Napoleon III undoubtedly regarded as the cornerstone of his policy. Above all he felt that it was the opposition of Great Britain that had defeated his uncle. As in the case of the 1860 commercial treaty, the friendship of Britain was to be retained at all costs. Initially, however, the distrust of all the powers, not least of all that of Great Britain, limited Napoleon III's freedom of diplomatic action. The editor of *The Times* in 1853 was convinced 'that in order to retain his precarious hold upon the French people, and especially upon the army, Louis Napoleon was resolved upon a forward policy'.

0   The Crimean War

France and the 'Eastern Question'

For ten years after the foundation of the Second Empire, the attention of French foreign policy centred upon the Mediterranean. Firstly, attention was concentrated, as so often in the past, upon the 'Eastern Question'. The factors that led to this latest revival of an old controversy were ostensibly religious. Having recently (December 1852) secured the restoration of the rights of the Catholic Church in the Holy Places of Palestine, Napoleon III now saw those rights withdrawn again as a result of the mission of Prince Menshikov, the envoy of the Tsar, to Constantinople in March 1853. Palmerston was correct when he observed that 'the Greek and Catholic Churches are merely other names for Russian and French influence'. The Menshikov mission put forward further significant demands, such as that for a Russo–Turkish defensive alliance, and for Turkish recognition of Russia's right to act as the protector of all Orthodox Christians within Turkish territories.

The search for a diplomatic solution

The contemporary English historian of the Crimean War, A. L. Kinglake, was the founder of the once traditional thesis that from this stage Napoleon III aimed for war with Russia. This reading of events was based upon traditional English mistrust of the French in general and of the Bonapartes in particular. Certainly, a variety of tempting motives must have presented themselves to Napoleon III: the chance to cement his popularity with the Catholic voters in France; the chance to erase the 'blot' of 1812 from the Napoleonic record; the chance to protect important commercial interests in the Levant; the chance to work in harness with Great Britain, and thus to consolidate an important friendship.

All of these objectives, however, could be equally well secured by diplomacy. Thus, the Russian occupation of Moldavia and Wallachia in July 1853, to exert a protective influence over the local Christians, was met by the so-called Vienna Note, rather than by war. In this initiative France joined Austria and Britain in attempting to pacify the Tsar by confirming the Treaty of Kutchuk-Kainardji, while the Turks added a guarantee of goodwill towards Christians within their territories. As late as January 1854, Napoleon III was still proposing a four-power conference to steer events towards a peaceful solution. That war ultimately broke out was the responsibility of the Turkish Sultan. Emboldened by this evidence of widespread international support, he decided upon military action against the invaders of his northern territories. His land victory at Oltenitza was offset by the destruction of his fleet at Sinope, which confronted Britain and France with the prospect of Russian naval domination of the Levant.

War

In a war fought by inexperienced generals and untried troops in unfamiliar terrain, it was difficult for any country to emerge with honour. France, however, probably had more cause for satisfaction than any of the other major powers involved. The campaign centred upon the naval base of Sevastopol, without which the Russians would be unable to maintain a significant fleet in the Black Sea. The Russians finally evacuated their positions there at the end of a siege of exactly one year, and the French contingent could claim to have struck the two most important blows that encouraged them to do so. The destruction of the Russian supplies at Kertch, and the successful assault upon the Malakoff fortress in early September 1855, supplied the allies with the 'great success' that Napoleon III had promised them. The cost, however, was high. Combined allied casualties totalled 115,000 by the time Sevastopol fell, and the siege was estimated in its last stages to be costing the equivalent of £2.75 million per week. With all the major French interests already served, and with Russophobia never so high in France as it was in Britain, it was time to resort to diplomacy again.

The restoration of French prestige

There can be little doubt that the Treaty of Paris, which concluded the war in 1856, marked the high point of Napoleon III's diplomacy. It achieved most of the aims that France could ever seriously have hoped for. The independence and integrity of the Turkish Empire were guaranteed by the contracting powers. Russia's influence in the region was restricted by the clauses that forbade her to build fortifications on the shores of the Black Sea, and which reaffirmed the Straits Convention of 1841. For the satisfaction of Catholic interests, the Sultan acknowledged that his Muslim and Christian subjects enjoyed equal rights, and Russia's claim to protect Greek Orthodox subjects was rejected. Perhaps most important of all, in contrast to decades of isolation and diplomatic impotence, Paris had become the centre of the first major resettlement of Europe since 1815, and her Emperor could with justification pose as the arbiter of Europe. If anyone could claim truly to have won the Crimean War it was surely France.

P Italy

France and the Italian question

It was equally clear that the real loser in the Crimean War was the major non-combatant, Austria. By refusing to extend help, or even sympathy to Russia so soon after Russia's important intervention in Hungary in 1849, she had lost her major ally, and had found no substitute. 'You did not conciliate Russia,' Eugenie criticised the Austrian ambassador to Paris. 'You did not regain your influence over Germany, and you cannot count upon the gratitude of France and England.'

The main factor that denied French and British gratitude to Austria was the Italian question. The Piedmontese delegation to the peace conference had left Paris, nevertheless, despondent and disappointed. For all his past experience of Italian romantic conspiracy, it scarcely seemed possible in 1856 for the French Emperor to free his hands in order to 'do something for Italy'. The concern of French Catholics for the temporal powers of the Pope; the general unpopularity of war in France, even a victorious one; the inadvisability of causing further offence to the legitimist powers so soon after the Russian war; all these were factors that seemed to prove in 1856 that the opportunity had not yet arisen.

The Orsini plot

The turning point came in one of the most bizarre episodes even of Napoleon III's colourful administration. In January 1858 an assassination attempt was made upon the imperial couple by an Italian patriot, Felice Orsini. Innocent bystanders were killed and injured, but Napoleon and Eugenie emerged unharmed. Orsini was captured and condemned to death. Surprisingly, however, the Emperor allowed his would-be murderer to transform his outrage into a martyrdom. From the death cell Orsini was allowed to launch a final appeal to the Emperor to act in support of the Italian cause, his neglect of which had caused Orsini to seek his death. 'The present state of Europe makes you the arbiter of whether Italy is free or the slave of Austria and other foreigners . . . . The happiness or unhappiness of my country depends on you.'. Recent writers have differed in their interpretation of Napoleon III's actions in the case of Orsini. W. H. C. Smith is one who sees more controlled opportunism in the affairs of 1858–59, and interprets the Imperial attitude to Orsini as the calculated exploitation of a most welcome opportunity.

The Pact of Plombières

1858 was a year of careful cultivation of Franco–Piedmontese relations, with one unmistakable aim. The key meeting took place on 20 July between the Emperor and Cavour, at the fashionable spa resort of Plombières in the Vosges. Negotiations were secret and personal, and lasted only four hours, but a clear programme for French intervention in Italy emerged.

It was imperative that France should appear to enter Italy as a protector, rather than as an aggressor, and it was proposed that a union between the tiny principality of Massa-Carrara and Piedmont be used as the bait to provoke Austria into a belligerent ultimatum to Piedmont. The French force of 200,000 men would supplement 100,000 Piedmontese, and this joint force was committed to sweep the Austrian presence from Lombardy and Venetia. It would, however, limit its operations to northern Italy, leaving the Pope undisturbed. The result would be an Italy of four separate, independent sections, the enlarged Piedmont, a Kingdom of Central Italy headed by the Duchess of Parma, the Papal territories, and the Kingdom of Naples. In return, France would be enlarged by the transfer of Savoy, and perhaps Nice, from Piedmont. In the first month of 1859 a formal military alliance between France and Piedmont demonstrated to the world the closeness of serious action by the French against Austria.

Nevertheless, war was not inevitable. As late as April 1859 it seemed that British pressure might bring the powers involved to the conference table. The immediate cause of the war was Austria's blunder in presenting Piedmont with an ultimatum (19 April) demanding unilateral disarmament or war. This occurred just as international negotiations seemed to be stripping France of any credible pretext for intervention. Austria's declaration of war three days later thus enabled Cavour and Napoleon III to play precisely the roles that they had envisaged at Plombières.

The war of 1859

The French campaigns of May and June 1859 lacked the dash and romance of those of the first Napoleon, but they achieved results. The battle at Magenta (4 June) was 'a battle without plan or co-ordination' (J. M. Thompson), but it left the road to Milan open to the French. The Battle of Solferino (24 June) was equally confused and twice as costly. The two engagements cost the French 2,300 casualties to add to the 4,500 who had died of disease. These were considerations serious enough for a humane Emperor reduced by the sight of the field of Solferino to 'a half fainting, half vomiting mass of misery' (L. C. B. Seaman). Other considerations were more serious still. A further advance into Venetia would involve a campaign against the Quadrilateral, a formidable formation of Austrian fortresses, and Cavour's occupation of Tuscany (*see* Chapter 4, section **F**) left many French Catholics

concerned about the Pope's prospects in this new Italy. Most serious of all, Prussia's mobilisation in the Rhineland left France exposed and vulnerable with her main forces committed to a lengthy campaign in the south.

The results of the war

It was no surprise that Napoleon III chose this moment to meet the Austrian Emperor at the conference table at Villafranca (11 July 1859). By the armistice concluded there, and ratified at Zurich in November, Austria surrendered Lombardy to France (a much less embarrassing expedient than surrendering it to Piedmont) and retained Venetia. Only in the short term, and from a strictly French point of view, was Napoleon III's Italian venture a success. The Emperor had shown energy and industry, if little military skill, and had withdrawn 'as soon as the destiny of his country seemed to be imperilled'. He had added the names of two new victories to the Napoleonic Canon. Eventually, in March 1860, he succeeded in negotiating the acquisition of Nice and Savoy, thus completing the first substantial push towards France's 'natural frontiers'. He had left many loose ends, however, and these were to form a complex knot. The Italian question remained unresolved, with an Austrian presence maintained in Venetia. Villafranca ensured the future suspicion of Italy towards France, without disposing of Austria's resentment. Prussian and British suspicions of Napoleonic ambitions were revived so that, in effect, France was as isolated in 1860 as Austria had been in 1859. Lastly, the continued instability of Italian politics gave Napoleon III no chance to withdraw from the thankless, expensive and dangerous task of protecting the Pope from his radical enemies.

Q Colonial expansion

The inheritance and motives of the Second Empire

In many respects the Second Empire presided over the regeneration of French imperialism. The colonial empire of 1850 was a scattered and shabby affair. It consisted largely of pieces of the 18th-century empire that had been preserved from British annexation, and its total population amounted to little more than 659,000. The Emperor's motives in encouraging colonial expansion ran, as J. P. T. Bury points out, parallel to his motives in domestic politics and economics. Economic concerns held a narrow lead over the hope of gratifying the army by presenting them with easy conquests, and the Catholics by conversions to the faith.

North Africa
In keeping with the general Mediterranean orientation of French foreign policy in the 1850s, the most striking colonial efforts were made in North Africa. Building upon firm foundations laid by the July Monarchy, the development of Algeria was impressive both in terms of physical extent and of modernisation. By 1857, French control extended as far inland as the edge of the Sahara, and even the traditionally troublesome Berber tribesmen were effectively tamed. As in metropolitan France, while political liberties were suppressed, especially in view of the republican exiles deported there in 1851–52, railways and telegraphs proliferated. The Emperor's cherished ideal of humane civilian government, however, came to nothing. Partly this was the result of factors beyond his control, such as the locust plague of 1866, the drought of 1867 and the cholera epidemic of the following year. Partly it was due to the later apathy of an Emperor increasingly beset by European problems.

French colonialism had its successes in other parts of Africa. In Senegal, the appointment of the enlightened and energetic General Faidherbe as governor (1854) was to be a guarantee of success. Not only did it mark the beginning of a systematic penetration inland, but also of successful and peaceful economic development, typified by the creation of the port of Dakar (1857) as a base for the export of local goods.

The Suez Canal
Further east, the limitations of French ambitions to 'informal empire' ensured that Egypt would provide one of the great successes of the Second Empire. French strategic ambitions in the Mediterranean joined with Saint-Simonian economic ideals in the project of Ferdinand de Lesseps, a cousin of the Empress, for the construction of a canal linking the Mediterranean and the Red Sea through the isthmus of Suez. The opening of the Suez Canal in 1869, after ten years' work, was a monument to the vision and industry of the Second Empire. Yet in practical terms it badly damaged relations with Turkey and with Great Britain, both of whom naturally saw the project as a serious threat to their interests in a most sensitive area.

The Far East
In the Far East, too, 'formal' and 'informal' empire went hand in hand. In China there was substantial co-operation with the British to secure further European trading rights, but it was that very British presence that frustrated French hopes of the establishment of a major economic base such as the British enjoyed at Hong Kong. In Indo-China, on the other hand, Napoleon III allowed himself to be influenced by the reports of French missionaries, which assured him that direct intervention against the unpopular ruler of Annam, Tu-Duc, would bring rich benefits to the Church and to France alike. As has so often proved to be the case since then, especially in Indo-China, the ruler proved to be more popular and able than expected. France found herself engaged in a lengthy and distant conflict between 1857 and 1860, before the capture of Saigon finally wrung concessions from Tu-Duc. France then gained, by the Treaty of Saigon, control over the three eastern provinces of Cochin China, and guarantees for the free exercise of the Catholic faith over all Annam.

By then, however, the French government was becoming far too preoccupied with its involvement in Mexico to be able effectively to exploit its advantages on the opposite side of the globe. Only by the energy of local French administrators did French influence penetrate to Cambodia (1863) and to the Mekong Valley (1870). Generally, French colonial expansion demonstrated the same tendencies as her political and economic record in Europe. The dynamism and impressive achievement of the 1850s gave way to a slowing pace, and sometimes to confusion and stagnation in the 1860s.

R Mexico

The background to the Mexican venture
The limitations upon French success in Asia and Africa paled by comparison with the spectacular failure of the Emperor's daring intervention in the New World. In terms of results the Mexican venture was Napoleon III's most misbegotten piece of opportunism in a career characterised by

opportunism. The original plan, however, was no worse than dozens of 19th- and 20th-century interventions by European countries undertaken in order to protect their threatened financial interests. It could even be seen as a visionary attempt to revise radically the balance of power in the Americas in France's favour.

The independence of Spain's South American colonies in the 1820s had benefited two major powers in particular. The United States was able to reserve to herself almost total political influence in the continent, and Great Britain alone possessed the naval strength effectively to exploit the economic potential of the region. Other powers traded with and invested in the former colonies very much as 'poor relations'.

The events of 1856–61 created a situation ripe for the revision of this state of affairs. Firstly, Mexican politics plunged into a period of renewed anarchy. Having had 46 heads of state in its 29 years of independence (1821–50), renewed civil war now broke out between the forces of Benito Juárez, an economic liberal and anti-cleric, and the conservative president Miramon. Established in office in 1861, Juárez suspended the payment of interest on all Mexico's international debts. This came at a time when the civil war in the United States dimmed any prospect of American intervention in Mexican affairs. The dual prospect of bringing relief to the Catholic Church and to French investors was attractive enough to Napoleon III. The additional attraction of breaking the hegemony of the United States in the American continents was perhaps the final factor in persuading the Emperor to launch his scheme for a European expedition to oust Juárez and to restore European interests in Mexico.

French intervention

However sound in conception, the expedition soon got out of hand in practice. Firstly, what was to have been an international intervention became a purely French one in 1862 when Spain and Britain developed severe reservations about the possible American reaction. Then, in May 1863, the defeat of a French column at Puebla stung France into a deeper and more costly commitment involving 30,000 troops.

The true tragedy of the scheme, however, sprang from that part of it which was entirely of the Emperor's conception. Possibly under the influence of the Empress, he proposed cementing Mexican stability by establishing a European dynasty there. The choice fell upon the Archduke Maximilian, brother of the Emperor of Austria, and thus the project had the agreeable side-effect of repairing relations between France and Austria. By the Convention of Miramar in 1864 Maximilian accepted the proposal and agreed to pay France 270 million francs once he was established, as repayment of Mexico's original debt and to cover French military expenses.

The extent of French failure

The expedition was, in the words of the new Empress of Mexico, not only 'a gigantic experiment', but it was being carried out at the worst possible time. By 1864 the Civil War in the USA was drawing to a close and the United States was extending encouragement and aid to Juárez to repel the unwelcome European intervention. By 1866 France had far more urgent need in Europe for the forces tied down in Mexico. Long before Maximilian had had the time to win the hearts and minds of his new subjects, his French forces began to be evacuated. The process was complete by February 1867 and within four months the capital was once more in the hands of Juárez. Gallantly refusing to flee his adopted country, Maximilian was executed by firing squad (19 June). 'None,' observed Rouher to the Legislative Body, 'could calculate the passions of the Mexican nation.' It was a pretty poor excuse for a failure that had cost France 6,000 men and the equivalent of £45 million.

S The growth of diplomatic isolation

Between the conception of the Mexican expedition and its final fiasco, a series of events had begun to work a revolution in European diplomacy. For a decade the Mediterranean had been the focus of diplomatic attention. Now a succession of crises turned this attention almost totally towards the north. The details of the revolt in Poland (Chapter 6, section **H**), of the Schleswig-Holstein affair (Chapter 5, section **G**) and of the general collapse of Austro–Prussian relations (*see* Chapter 5) are described elsewhere. What concerns us here is their impact upon French diplomacy.

No French interests were involved directly either in Poland or in Schleswig-Holstein. Domestic tension, and the diversion of a substantial force to Mexico would have made intervention difficult in any case. Such sympathy as existed in France for the 'underdog' did not go as far, as the Emperor was constantly reminded by his agents in the provinces, as a demand for war. Denmark could not even appeal to the liberal traditions of *The Napoleonic Ideals*. Thus Schleswig-Holstein was also 'a question that did not touch the dignity of France'. Reasonable as such an attitude was, the most ominous feature of the events of 1863 and 1864 was the wall of distrust that met the Emperor's attempts to organise a diplomatic solution to the Polish question.

These efforts have been interpreted by the Anglo-American historian A. L. Guerard in the most favourable light. 'In 1863 he was perhaps the last genuine European who stood in a place of authority, a successor to Metternich, a precursor to Woodrow Wilson.' Intervention in Italy and in Mexico merely served to encourage the conviction that French projects for conciliation were designed so that France could pick up further pieces from European collisions. From being the focal point of Europe in 1856 the Emperor found himself isolated and burdened with embarrassing commitments as the greatest threats emerged to the interests of his state.

T Biarritz and the Austro–Prussian War

The decision for French neutrality

The Convention of Gastein (August 1865) that seemed to patch up relations between Austria and Prussia (*see* Chapter 5, section **H**) also appeared to push France further along the path towards diplomatic isolation. It must have been with great relief that Napoleon III heard of Bismarck's willingness to meet him privately at Biarritz in October 1865.

The secrecy that surrounded the Biarritz interview makes it impossible to this day to state with certainty what took place between the two great opportunists. J. M. Thompson states that Bismarck revealed his plans for an armed confrontation with Austria, and secured French neutrality with vague promises of compensation in the Rhineland. J. P. T. Bury maintains that, throughout, Napoleon III's prime concern was with Venetia, which would, in the event of any future hostility, be prised away from Austria to complete France's 1859 undertaking to Piedmont.

As Austro–Prussian relations deteriorated, French policy was based upon the assumption that any future war between them would be long and evenly-matched, leaving France perhaps as arbiter, or as holder of the balance of power in Europe. Perhaps she would even be able to present a bill for her services in either case. France settled her stance by an agreement with Austria (June 1866) that she would maintain her neutrality in return for Austria's promise to surrender Venetia whatever the outcome of the war. At the beginning of July 1866 it seemed highly unlikely that the German question could be resolved without the co-operation and blessing of France.

The impact of Sadowa

On 3 July that view was totally discredited by the engagement at Sadowa in Bohemia where the Austrian army was routed. The initial response to the news in Paris was one of satisfaction at the discomfiture of autocracy and at the liberation of Venetia. This was quickly soured by the realisation of the wider implications of Prussia's triumph. 'We felt,' reported La Gorce, 'that something in the soil of old Europe had just crumbled. Among the people, uneasiness. In the sovereign's circle, bitter complexity.'

The situation might still have been saved, however. It is possible that the real error in French policy was not committed at Biarritz, but at the meeting of the Council of State at St Cloud on 5 July. At the very last minute the proposals of the foreign minister and of the minister of war to mobilise 50,000 men with a view to action against the Rhineland were reversed by the Emperor. Why did France remain inactive? The strongest argument against military demonstrations had been that they would imply support for Austria, and would thus ruin France's long-term cultivation of her relations with Italy. Furthermore, the agricultural depression, the policy of the ministry of finance for greater economy in the military budget, and the knowledge that war was not popular with the people, were all inhibiting factors.

U   The policy of compensation

French options in 1866

The official reaction of the French government remained calm, stressing that the 1815 settlement had been overturned, Venetia had been liberated and the cause of national self-determination had been advanced 'without the movement of a single French soldier'. Unofficially it was clear that French prestige, too, had been mauled at Sadowa and that Prussia could overturn the present balance of power in central Europe whenever she wished to do so. The Empress Eugenie spoke for many when she remarked that 'with such a nation as a neighbour, we run the risk of seeing you at the gates of Paris one fine day before we scarcely realise it. I shall go to bed French and wake up Prussian.' Napoleon III's government was left with two possible means by which to redress the balance. It could accept the growth of Prussian power and use conciliatory diplomacy to build up a system of alliances that might guarantee French security. On the other hand it could search unilaterally for territorial compensation to re-establish national prestige. The two courses were incompatible yet, in the years that remained to the Second Empire, French policy was to pursue them both.

The Luxemburg question

From July 1866 the French ambassador in Berlin was pressing Bismarck on the subject of compensation, mentioning the frontier of 1814, Luxemburg and the Rhineland. Early the following year the Emperor broached the project that came closest to success. His approach to the King of the Netherlands with the offer to purchase from him the Grand Duchy of Luxemburg contained many promising elements. Not least of these was the financial embarrassment of the Dutch monarch. Dutch agreement to the deal was conditional, however, upon the agreement of Prussia, who maintained a garrison in the Duchy. Bismarck raised no official objection to the transaction but German national reaction to the Luxemburg proposals was predictably hostile. In early April, Bismarck replied to a parliamentary question that he was officially committed to the maintenance of all 'German' territories. The Luxemburg deal was dead. This fact was confirmed in May 1867 when an international conference in London, although depriving Prussia of her rights to garrison the Duchy, declared Luxemburg a neutral and independent state.

The failure of the 'policy of tips'

The failure of what Bismarck dismissed as a 'policy of tips' increased the pressure on the French government. The icy response of the Legislative Body to the news of the Luxemburg check confirmed that it could ill afford any further fall in its stock. If the government continued to speak of peace, it showed that it recognised the possibility of war by attempting to construct an anti-Prussian alliance. Austrian and Italian responses in the course of 1867 were, however, most cautious. Austria was understandably reluctant to suffer further defeats, and the price demanded by Italy, the withdrawal of French troops from Rome, was too high. The year 1868 opened, therefore with France still in a position of total diplomatic isolation.

V   The Hohenzollern candidature

Diplomatic success over the Spanish question

The new challenge to France's international prestige that arose in 1868–70 came from an unexpected source. The circumstances whereby the throne of Spain came to be offered to a branch of the Hohenzollern family, the ruling house of Prussia, are described elsewhere (*see* Chapter 5, section **N**). Our prime concern here is with the French reaction when, on 2 July 1870, the French foreign office received official confirmation of the move that would threaten them with diplomatic encirclement. Feeling that justice was wholly on the side of France this time it was made clear, especially through a fiery speech by Gramont, the Foreign Minister, that this was considered sufficient grounds for war with Prussia. In the face of such threats the Prussians rapidly denied any knowledge of, and of course any support for, the candidature. By 12 July Hohenzollern hopes of the throne of Spain were as dead as those of Napoleon III for Luxemburg.

The blunder at Ems

No sooner had the French government ensured

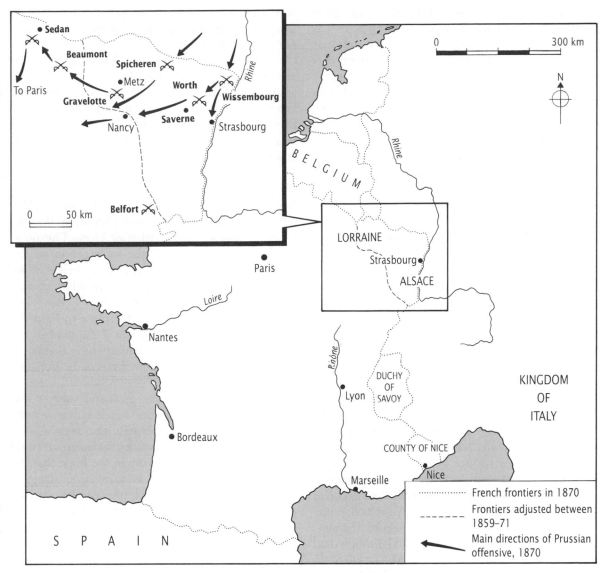

France and the Franco–Prussian War, 1870

that the mistake of 1866 would not be repeated than it committed a new one. The day after the withdrawal of the candidature the French ambassador 'buttonholed' King Wilhelm at the spa resort of Bad Ems 'to ask me in an importunate way that I pledge myself never again for the future to give my consent if the Hohenzollern renewed their candidature'. The implied lack of faith in the Prussian monarch and the attempt to rub Prussia's nose in her own diplomatic defeat were ill-timed and far more likely to cause offence in Germany than the remote diplomatic defeat itself. Bismarck's release

to the press of the skilfully edited text of the king's telegram about the incident, the 'Ems Telegram', created the desired uproar in both countries and acted as Bismarck intended it to, as 'a red rag upon the Gallic bull'.

The last steps to war

France now had to gauge her reaction to the outcry. At first a plan was produced for another international conference but, as public opinion in 1864 or 1866 had not been ready for war, so now it was not ready for conciliation. The wife of the

Austrian ambassador observed that 'Paris was given over to unrestrained enthusiasm, and cries of "On to Berlin!" Don't let them try to tell me today, as they like to do, that nobody in France wanted war; everybody wanted it.' Just as, in domestic policy, the Emperor's 'Napoleonic Ideal' combined with public pressure to produce the 'Liberal Empire', so in foreign policy the same factors combined to produce the Franco–Prussian war. War credits were voted on 15 July, the French ambassador was withdrawn from Berlin the following day and on 19 July France declared war.

W The Franco–Prussian War

French readiness for war

How well was the French army prepared for this, its greatest trial? Some improvements had been made since the 1859 campaigns. Even in its curtailed form, Niel's recruitment law (*see* section **M**) had increased the number of men with military training. By 1870 most of these man were equipped with the Chassepot rifle, a splendid weapon with a range double that of the German Needle Gun. Even so, the weaponry did not necessarily compensate for other defects. 'I am afraid,' commented the writer Mérimée, upon hearing the news of war, 'that the generals are not geniuses.' Nor had they the experience of European wars that the Prussian commanders had recently acquired. Bourbaki had seen successful action, but only in Algeria. Bazaine, in Mexico, had not even enjoyed a record of unambiguous success. MacMahon and Canrobert had yet to be weighed in the balance. Most ominously the French mobilisation was disjointed and at times downright chaotic. Finally, the French were outnumbered, with 275,000 troops covering a front of 250 km, while 450,000 Germans held a narrower 160 km line.

The campaigns

Within three weeks the shape of the war had been established by a series of German attacks in Alsace (see the map on page 57). At Spicheren (4 August) and at Forbach and Froeschwiller (6 August) the forces of Bazaine and MacMahon were surprised and forced into a retreat. Bazaine's retreat took him towards the fortress town of Metz. His fate was sealed by a major engagement between the villages of Gravelotte and St Privat (18 August). There, from good defensive positions, with their Chassepot rifles, the French inflicted heavy casualties. One Prussian regiment lost 8,000 men in 20 minutes at one point, but Bazaine failed to take advantage of the situation by means of a counterattack. Instead the timid commander chose to fall back on the supposed safety of Metz, where he was besieged by the reinforced enemy, and was able to emerge only at the end of October to surrender.

The collapse of the Second Empire

The second French army, commanded by MacMahon and accompanied, or encumbered, by the sick Emperor, moved to the relief of Metz. The slowness of its progress and the indiscretion of the French press, from whom the enemy learned of the army's whereabouts, allowed the invaders to surprise MacMahon some 25 km from Sedan. The French then fell back upon that town to fight the decisive action of the war. On 3 September the French were subjected to a murderous bombardment, ended only by the Emperor's personal decision to surrender.

One hundred and four thousand men, 6,000 horses and 419 guns were handed over to the German forces and, although the war was to survive Sedan by some months, its outcome could no longer be in doubt. Partly in the hope that the war could be passed off as a dynastic struggle, decided by the collapse of one of the warring dynasties, the Legislative Body declared the Second Empire at an end (4 September 1870) and the Republic re-established. For the second time the Bonaparte dynasty, which offered France glory in many different fields, failed to survive a major reverse on the field of battle.

Questions

Essay questions

1   How and why was the French Second Republic transformed into the Second Empire? (WJEC)

2   'Napoleon III had a dynamic personality, pursued forceful policies and engaged in militant diplomacy'. Why then did he fail? (UCLES)

3 'His achievement is easily summarised: all he did was to give Paris an impressive facelift'. To what extent does Napoleon III deserve such condemnation? (JMB)

4 In what ways did Napoleon III's conduct of foreign policy encourage the unifications of Italy and of Germany? (WJEC)

5 What did Louis Napoleon's Bonapartism represent? (Oxford entrance)

6 Is it more apt to describe Napoleon III as a 'dictator' or as a 'liberal'? (ULEAC)

The Plebiscite of 1851

SOURCE A

The counting of the votes was no more than a formality, it was so well known in advance what the splendid result would be. The result still surpassed all expectations, all hopes. Among the 640,000 opponents could be found intransigent legitimists, worth respecting for their inflexible convictions, militant Orleanists and honest republicans; but the dominant element was that of those involved in the rising, from which must of course be deducted those who were in safe custody, those who had thought it prudent to cross the frontier, and finally those who, having had a bone to pick with the law for robbery, bankruptcy, arson, or murder, had been deprived of their civil and political rights.

de Maupas, Mémoires sur le Second Empire, *published in 1885.*

SOURCE B

Might we be said to claim that no one really voted for M Bonaparte? That no one freely and knowingly accepted this man?

Far from it.

M Bonaparte had to support him the rabble of officials, the twelve hundred parasites supported by the budget, and their hangers-on; the venal, the compromised, the shifty, and following them, the half-witted, a notable crowd. He had to support him MM [messieurs] the cardinals, MM the bishops, MM the canons, MM the curés, MM the curates, MM the archdeacons, deacons and sub-deacons, and what are called 'religious' persons, who pray in these terms: O God, put up the price of Lyon shares! Sweet Saviour Jesus, let me get twenty five per cent on my Naples-Rothschild scrip! Holy apostles, sell my wine! Blessed martyrs, double my rents! Holy Mary, Mother of God, immaculate virgin, Star of the Sea, deign to look favourably on my little business on the corner of Tire-Chape street and Quincampoix street! Ivory tower, see to it that the shop opposite does badly!

The following really and undoubtedly voted for M Bonaparte: category one, officials; category two, the ignorant; category three, the Voltairean-landowner-industrialist-believer.

Victor Hugo, Napoleon le Petit, *published 1852.*

SOURCE C

The Bonaparte dynasty does not represent the revolutionary peasant, but the conservative peasant. It does not represent those among the peasantry who wish to escape from the narrow conditions of their farming life; it represents those who wish to perpetuate and consolidate those conditions. It does not represent the enlightenment of the peasantry, but their superstition; not their future, but their past.

The three years' rule of the parliamentary republic had freed some of the French peasants from the Napoleonic illusion, and had even revolutionised them, though superficially; but the bourgeoisie had forcibly repressed any attempt on their part to advance.

In the risings that followed the coup d'état, some of the peasants were making an armed protest against their own votes on 10 December 1848. Their schooling since then had taught them sense. But most of the peasants were so steeped in prejudice that in the reddest of the departments they were most frank and enthusiastic in their support for Bonaparte. In their view the National Assembly had restricted their freedom of movement, and now they were merely breaking the fetters which the towns had imposed on the will of the countryside.

Karl Marx, The 18 Brumaire of Louis Napoleon, *published 1852.*

---

a Explain the following phrases that occur in the sources:
  i 'intransigent legitimists [and] militant Orleanists' (Source A)
  ii 'those involved in the rising' (Source A)
  iii 'their own votes on 10 December 1848' (Source C)
b Compare the explanations given in Source B and Source C for the success of Louis Napoleon in the 1851 plebiscite.
c What are the strengths and weaknesses of these sources from the viewpoint of the historian who wishes to understand the reasons for Louis Napoleon's success in the 1851 plebiscite?
d 'Louis Napoleon was able to overthrow the republican constitution in 1851 simply because he enjoyed the support of a small ruling élite'. How far do these sources, and any other evidence known to you, lead you to accept this conclusion?

4
The unification of Italy

A cartoon which appeared in an Italian political magazine in May 1860, under the title 'A forbidden fruit'. Eve (Cavour) and the serpent (Garibaldi) discuss which of them shall pluck the apple (Sicily).

Why should the artist portray 'Europa' as blindfolded and oblivious to the dispute over Sicily?

How accurate were the artist's ideas of the aims of Garibaldi and Cavour at this time?

The Historical Debate

The historiography of the Risorgimento has been affected by problems just the opposite of those posed by the study of Napoleon III (see page 39). Whereas the failures of the French Emperor prejudiced many earlier and some later accounts of his reign, the success of the movements for the unification of Italy obscured many of the less palatable aspects of the story, and resulted in the undue glorification of other aspects and individuals. On the other hand, like the French Second Empire, the Risorgimento has also been 'borrowed' and reinterpreted to serve the purposes of groups involved in more recent political struggles in Italy. Within Italy, three main schools of interpretation may be identified, each reflecting a major contemporary political interest.

The first of these was the 'official' or nationalist school . Obviously this was a school of thought whose nationalist interpretation was equally acceptable under the fascist regime of Mussolini. For D. Zanichelli the Risorgimento was 'the most important fact of the 19th century', while Victor Emmanuel received special adulation, being hailed by A. Oriani as 'the grandest and most glorious sovereign in the history of Christian Europe'. A second very sympathetic school consisted of those 'liberal' historians who saw in the Risorgimento the defeat of autocracy and reaction and the triumph of modernism in Italy. Within Italy this tradition has been best represented by an outstanding historian, Benedetto Croce (*A History of Italy, 1871–1915*, 1929). For Croce, the methods and tactics of Cavour and other essentially conservative Italian leaders were fully justified by the end product of

the Risorgimento, a successful and modern Italian state. The fascist state under which he was living and writing was an aberration, which owed little to Italian development in the 19th century. This view of the Risorgimento as part of the broader development of 'liberal' Europe was a popular one among English-speaking historians. G. M. Trevelyan (*Garibaldi and the Making of Italy*, 1911) was as prominent as Croce in expounding this view. While he concentrated in particular upon the role of Garibaldi in the process of unification, A. J. Whyte (*The Political Life and Letters of Cavour*, 1930) and the American, W. R. Thayer (*The Life and Times of Cavour*, 1911) emphasised the positive role played by the great Piedmontese statesman.

Left-wing writing has been consistently less sympathetic to the Risorgimento and has been dominated by the prominent communist thinker of the inter-war years, Antonio Gramsci (*The Risorgimento*, 1949, and *Selections from the Prison Notebooks of Antonio Gramsci*, 1971). Gramsci saw the Risorgimento as a 'failed revolution', which had been 'hi-jacked' by clever, right-wing politicians, who had outflanked and ignored the genuine, class-based tensions that existed within Italian society. The Italian state created by the Risorgimento remained, therefore, riddled with class conflicts and with political instability, which in turn contributed to the emergence of fascism.

Non-Italian writing on the Risorgimento in recent years has been dominated by the English historian Denis Mack Smith. Mack Smith has caused controversy of his own by challenging the traditional reputations of many of the Italians prominent in the movement. Cavour in particular (*Cavour and Garibaldi, 1860*, 1954, and *Cavour*, 1985) emerges as a cunning, pragmatic politician, without any ideological attachment to the principle of unification and primarily concerned with the aggrandisement of Piedmont. Similarly, Mack Smith shows little sympathy towards the view of Victor Emmanuel as an idealistic patriot and father of his country (*Victor Emmanuel, Cavour and the Risorgimento*, 1971). His recent work on Guiseppe Mazzini (*Mazzini*, 1994), on the other hand, portrays the great radical as a man of honour and integrity, far more willing to compromise with the interests of monarchical Piedmont than they were with him.

Most historical writing on 19th-century Italy has been dominated by arguments about political principles, and about the leading political figures of the period. Only in the last decade or so has serious research been undertaken into the social and economic context in which the Risorgimento developed. Recent work has concentrated upon the socio-economic structure of society in both northern and southern Italy, and upon the Austrian administration in Lombardy and Venetia in the earlier part of the 19th century. This represents the beginning of a long process in the course of which interpretations of the Risorgimento will undoubtedly undergo further substantial transformation.

A Piedmont and Victor Emmanuel II

Italy in 1850

After the nationalist failures of 1848–49, Italy presented a panorama of military occupation, restored political reaction and suppressed constitutions. There was one exception to this rule. This was the buffer state of Piedmont in the north-west corner of Italy. Although decisively defeated at Custoza and at Novara, she retained her constitution, the integrity of her territory and her freedom from Austrian occupation. Her monarchy had effectively usurped the place previously held by Pius IX in the hearts of Italian patriots by its willingness to lead the cause in 1848. The ruler to whom Gioberti and others now looked after the abdication of Charles Albert in the aftermath of Novara was his son, the 29-year-old Victor Emmanuel II.

The D'Azeglio ministry in Piedmont, 1849–52

Like his first essay in foreign relations, Victor Emmanuel's first domestic actions were not exactly those of a liberal. His first task was to ensure his control of the kingdom by means that included the shelling of Genoa to win it back from the radicals who remained entrenched there. His first administration included several of the 25 military men who were to hold ministerial office during his reign, although by the end of 1849 the administration was in the hands of a group of moderate conservatives under the leadership of Massimo D'Azeglio.

The first major policy of the ministry, nevertheless, concerned one of the great liberal principles of the 19th century, the contest for power and influence between the church and the state. Neither king nor minister wished to tolerate the considerable influence of a body that had set its face so firmly against them both in 1848. The batch of measures produced in 1850, known as the Siccardi Laws, was a substantial first move in a decade of Piedmontese anti-clericalism. Church courts and other ecclesiastical privileges incompatible with parliamentarianism were abolished, the number of holy days was limited, and the senior Piedmontese churchman, Archbishop Fransoni, was imprisoned when he ordered his clergy to ignore these measures.

Such determined measures were rare from D'Azeglio, whom Mack Smith describes as 'an amateur in politics, a painter and a novelist by profession, and a statesman only by accident'. Having found a parliamentary majority hard to come by in the first place, he found it undermined in 1852 by an opportunistic alliance between the leader of the 'middle-class party', Rattazzi, and his own finance minister, Camillo di Cavour. The fall of his ministry was assured when the king refused to accept the next stage of D'Azeglio's anti-clerical legislation, a bill enforcing civil marriage (May 1852), and he was replaced by the most influential figure in the history of 19th-century Italy.

B Cavour's domestic policy

Political authority

Cavour's domestic administration of Piedmont between 1852 and 1859 had as its aim the creation of a state stable and prosperous enough to dominate Italy. In some respects stability was achieved by methods that would not have been approved by the English liberals he so much admired. Mazzinian democrats were persecuted, the Mazzinian press was suppressed, and parliament was blatantly overridden when it did not serve the purposes of the prime minister. For example, in 1857 when the elections returned an unexpected right-wing majority, Cavour seized upon a series of dubious technicalities to unseat a number of the successful candidates and reduce the right wing to manageable proportions. In January 1855 Cavour held all three of the main posts in the administration: prime minister, foreign minister and finance minister. Other policies for creating stability were more liberal. A string of administrative reforms, in the financial departments (1852), in the foreign office (1853), and those of La Marmora in the army, increased efficiency and removed those conservative elements hostile to Cavour. Further anti-clerical measures, notably the suppression of 152 monasteries and 1,700 benefices in 1855, further restricted the influence of the Church, but also added the equivalent of an extra £145,640 to the state's income.

Economic modernisation

The most spectacular achievement of the decade was the laying down of the foundations for

Camillo di Cavour

Personality and aims

Born in August 1810 into a family of the Piedmontese nobility, Cavour's personal background was as much French as it was Italian, and wide open to the broader influences of western Europe. His father served as an official in the Napoleonic administration, and his mother was born in Geneva and brought up a Calvinist. The young Cavour read many of the most progressive names in political and economic theory, including Smith, Bentham and Ricardo. The conventional army career of a young nobleman proved unfulfilling. The years between 1831 and 1847 were spent largely in three types of pursuit. His foreign travels, in France, Britain and Switzerland shaped both his political and economic views. Indirect contact with the men who were dictating the shape of industrial Britain helped to turn him into a broad-minded conservative with views broadly comparable to those of his greatest political 'hero', Sir Robert Peel. Secondly, in his administration of the family estates and business interests in Piedmont, he put into practice the policy of modernisation and development that he had learned abroad. His ventures included the formation of the Lake Maggiore Steamboat Co. and the foundation with others of the Bank of Genoa and the Bank of Turin. Thirdly, he turned to journalism, a natural means for the propagation of his ideas. Writing predominantly on social, economic and scientific questions, he made his greatest journalistic impact in 1847 with the foundation of *Il Risorgimento* (Resurgence). This was a liberal journal immediately popular in Piedmont and with the Italian refugees who flocked into Piedmont from other parts of the peninsula. Only with the first Piedmontese constitutional elections (June 1848) did the chance present itself to take an active part in politics. Elected to the Assembly, Cavour supported D'Azeglio in the conclusion of an armistice with Austria and served as minister of industry and commerce from the summer of 1850, before succeeding him as prime minister in 1852.

Cavour has received a consistent good press since his death, as the most influential figure in the modernisation, liberation and unification of Italy. It is extremely important, therefore, to understand the nature of his 'liberalism' and his 'nationalism' correctly. Of the former M. Salvadori writes as follows: 'Cavour believed in liberty, in responsibility, and in the ability of the educated individual to act responsibly on the basis of his own decisions.' Yet this man achieved his aims in part by bribing newspapers, betraying colleagues like D'Azeglio, and rigging elections. Every major step of his diplomatic career was taken without consultation with parliament. It is perhaps easier to consider what Cavour did not want. As early as 1835 he had written that 'I am persuaded that the *juste milieu* is the only policy right in the circumstances, capable of saving society from the two rocks which threaten to break it – anarchy and despotism'. We shall understand his 'liberal' policies better if we see them as a means of avoiding the main dangers that he felt threatened Piedmont, and perhaps Italy. These were the tyranny of the traditionalist, autocratic state and the dogmatism of a reactionary Church, and on the other hand, the dangerous extremism of Mazzini and the other left-wing radicals active in Italian politics.

The question of Cavour's nationalism has produced even greater controversy. Historians have claimed on the one hand that the unification of Italy was his aim from the beginning of his career, and on the other that he was primarily, perhaps exclusively interested in the expansion and consolidation of his own Piedmontese state. Mack Smith has maintained that, as late as 1858, 'he still could not accept Mazzini's idea of a united Italy. So long as he obtained Lombardy and Venice he would dominate the peninsula, and that was enough.' The answer is perhaps that it is wrong to see Cavour's attitude as being rigid and consistent throughout his career, and we perhaps find a clue in the letter written by Manin to Pallavicino (September 1856). 'We must work incessantly to form public opinion, because as soon as opinion is clear and forceful, Cavour I am sure will follow it. I think Cavour to be too intelligent and too ambitious to refuse the Italian enterprise if public opinion demands it strongly enough'. Thus we may best understand the attitude of Cavour to the question of Italian national unity if we view him not as a man in control of events, directing them towards his preconceived goal, but as a practical politician with aims, originally limited, but modified and expanded by the development of factors over which he had little control.

Piedmontese commercial and industrial prosperity. Already, as minister of finance and commerce, Cavour had concluded a string of free-trade treaties. Treaties were reached with Belgium, with France and with Britain, and had the dual purpose of forging international links with the more advanced states of western Europe, and of attracting into Piedmont the raw materials and machinery necessary for her development. In the same capacity he had floated large internal and foreign loans to pay off the war indemnity owed to the Austrians and to finance the industrial projects of the government. The level of government expenditure on such projects, as well as the long-term effects of the policy, may be judged from the fact that the public debt of Piedmont rose between 1847–59 from 120 million lire to 725 million.

It would, of course, be misleading to refer to Piedmont in 1859 as a 'modern industrial power', but she had produced a number of impressive projects to advertise her status at the head of the Italian states. Of Italy's 1,798 km of railway track in 1859, Piedmont had 819 km. Italy's first steamship, the *Sicilia*, was produced in Genoa in 1855, and Italy's first home-produced railway locomotives were built in the same year. Further schemes were in progress for the construction of the Mont Cenis tunnel through the Alps, and for the modernisation of the port of Genoa. In the course of the 1850s, Piedmont's trade trebled in value. By the end of the 1850s, therefore, Piedmont had effectively claimed the first place in Italy, not only in terms of constitutions and of military leadership, but in material terms as well.

C Piedmont and the Crimean War

Piedmontese motives

Cavour's most important contribution to the liberation of Italy was that he was able to place the 'Italian question' firmly into the general context of European diplomacy. This was the forum in which the 1815 settlement had been shaped, and the only forum in which that settlement could be revised. It was not until the outbreak of the Crimean War in 1854, however, that a real opportunity presented itself. It was a bold step for a minor power such as Piedmont to intervene in a European conflict such

as this, and it is not surprising that some historians have seen this as a masterstroke by Cavour, supported by Victor Emmanuel.

M. Salvadori and Derek Beales have laid the stress rather differently, seeing much of the initiative coming from the allies who felt that Austria would be more likely to send troops to the Crimea if she were assured that Piedmont would be committed there too, and thus unable to attack her in the rear. Characteristically, Denis Mack Smith moves even further from the traditional interpretation, viewing the plan for intervention primarily as the brainchild of Victor Emmanuel who, fretting at the constitutional restraints imposed upon him, saw war as a good opportunity to reassert his royal authority.

The Piedmontese contribution

Whatever the process by which the decision was reached, by the end of 1854 Piedmont had concluded an agreement with the allies by which 18,000 Piedmontese troops would travel to the Crimea and by which Piedmont would, of course, be entitled to a place at the congress at which peace would eventually be made. Neither the military intervention nor the Congress of Paris was the success for the Italian cause that Italian historians have sometimes imagined them to have been.

La Marmora's troops gave a good account of themselves at the Battle of the Chornaya (August 1855), and in their own eyes did something to restore the prestige lost at Custoza and Novara, but the official line that 'about 2,000 of them were killed or died of disease' conceals the fact that not more than 30 of that number actually died of their wounds.

Success or failure

Similarly, Cavour travelled to Paris for the peace conference in 1856 still greatly inexperienced in the ways of 'great power' diplomacy, and with hopes that were never likely to be realised. His first aim was for territorial compensation for Piedmont's efforts, possibly in the shape of the Duchy of Parma. Such a measure never seems to have been seriously considered by the congress. Secondly, he hoped to obtain some commitment from the powers on the subject of the Austrian presence in Italy. He could not hope to obtain this from France which had troops of its own in Rome, and who could not contemplate renewed war so soon after the campaigns against Russia.

On the other hand, the British representative, Lord Clarendon, attacked Austrian excesses and Papal and Neapolitan misgovernment in far harsher terms than Cavour could have used. It was a measure of Cavour's inexperience, however, that he imagined that Clarendon might be speaking for his government. The British were soon to make it clear that they had no intention of intervening actively in so controversial a continental matter. In the context of 1856 Cavour had failed to achieve a diplomatic initiative and had not created the conditions necessary for a military solution to the problem of the Austrian presence.

D Forging foreign alliances

Piedmont and Austria, 1856–59
One result of the events in Paris in 1856 was a significant increase in Piedmontese confidence in her dealings with Austria. Cavour's no doubt felt that the sympathy of Britain and France would at least be sufficient to deter Austria from any threatening ambitions. So it seemed, for Austrian policy in her provinces of Lombardy and Venetia from 1856 was much more conciliatory. The policy of confiscating the property of exiles was relaxed, and an amnesty for political prisoners was announced in 1857. Victor Emmanuel's famous speech of January 1859, in which he declared that he could not stop his ears to the 'cry of grief' (*grido di dolore*) that came from the neighbouring provinces, must have tested Austrian nerves to breaking point. It may have been instrumental in making them blunder into war later that year.

Piedmont and the nationalists
Another undoubted effect of the *grido di dolore* speech was to cement relations between the Piedmontese government and the nationalist exiles within Piedmont.

Relations between Cavour and the exiled nationalists had been ambiguous since the Crimean War. The latter had formed the National Society in 1857, which boasted a membership of some 8,000 and whose main figures were La Farina, Pallavicino and Manin, the hero of the former Venetian Republic. They were further convinced by the intervention in the Crimean War that Piedmont represented Italy's best hope, but still entertained severe reservations about the sincerity of the state's leadership, and especially about that of Cavour. 'Convinced,' Manin had written in 1855, 'that above all Italy must be made, that this is the first and most important question, we say to the house of Savoy: "Make Italy and we are with you. If not, we are not".'

The Orsini affair and the Pact of Plombières
On the other hand, nothing was more likely to damage relations with France, certainly the most important factor in Cavour's calculations, than the assumption by Napoleon III that Piedmont was really serving the interests of a band of radicals. Although Cavour tried hard to consolidate the friendship of the Crimea, all was very nearly ruined by Orsini's terrorist attack of January 1858. As was shown in Chapter 3, the Orsini affair was an obscure and mysterious business, but there seems little doubt that Napoleon III's first reaction was one of great bitterness towards a Piedmontese government that had allowed Orsini to avoid arrest and to reach France.

At this stage it seems to have been Victor Emmanuel, rather than Cavour, who performed one of his periodic services to Italy. In presenting a brave reply to the attacks of the Emperor, he presented Piedmont as the best guarantee in Italy against the excesses of the radicals. These claims, combined with Napoleon's long-standing, if somewhat vague desire to 'do something for Italy', calmed the Emperor. A visit by his confidante, Dr Conneau, to Turin (June 1858) raised hopes of direct co-operation between the two states against Austria. Thereafter progress was rapid, culminating in the secret meeting between Cavour and Napoleon III at Plombières in July, where plans for a four-part confederacy of Italy under the presidency of the Pope were agreed (*see* Chapter 3, section **P**).

It is impossible to escape the conclusion that the terms of the Plombières agreement represent the views of Napoleon III rather than those of the anti-clerical Cavour. One is led once more to the view of Cavour as an opportunist willing to accept conditions of this sort to achieve what he had long known to be an essential precondition of the liberation of northern Italy, namely the military intervention of France.

The political divisions of Italy

E The War of 1859

The Piedmontese war effort

The war which first undermined Austrian authority in northern Italy has already been examined from the viewpoint of the French Empire (*see* Chapter 3, section **P**). For many years the traditional view from the Italian side was of a war of national liberation, cunningly contrived by dedicated Italians and finally betrayed at Villafranca by a cynical foreigner. Instead, study of the Piedmontese and Austrian war efforts should show how absolutely essential the part played by the French forces was to the achievement of even the limited success of 1859.

Italian reaction to the outbreak of war sheds some interesting light upon the extent of Italian enthusiasm. The Piedmontese mobilisation was half-hearted. Not only was there a tendency to leave the hard work to the French, but also a distinct reluctance on the part of the conservative army officers to arm large numbers of men at a time when Piedmont was full of dangerous radical exiles. Where there was enthusiasm it was not always nationalist. Victor Emmanuel felt himself, writes Mack Smith, 'a new man, powerful again, and free from interfering civilians'. Indeed, relations between king and prime minister were rarely worse than at this time when Victor Emmanuel directed affairs in Turin.

For one reason or another, the numbers of the Piedmontese army fell 405 short of the figure agreed at Plombières, and they were not supplemented by a flood of patriotic volunteers from other parts of Italy. Victor Emmanuel had boasted of 200,000 such volunteers rallying to his cause, but only about 10 per cent of that total materialised.

The Austrian war effort

Fortunately for Piedmont the Austrian campaign was also faulty. The command of their forces was left by the Emperor to the 'courtier soldiers' Grunne and Gyulai, rather than to the more able Benedek or Hess. Their mobilisation was carried out at the pace of the Napoleonic Wars, allowing the French ten days to move their troops into Piedmont by rail. The mobilisation could not be more than partial, given the need to leave substantial bodies of troops in other parts of the Empire, especially in Hungary, in anticipation of possible trouble there. The force of 90,000 that eventually assembled in Italy was considerably smaller than the Franco-Piedmontese force that faced it.

The main engagements of the campaign that followed, at Magenta (4 June) and at Solferino (24 June), were predominantly French engagements. Indeed, not a single Piedmontese soldier lost his life at Magenta, although on the day of Solferino the Piedmontese army was involved nearby in a significant subsidiary engagement at San Martino. It was, therefore, logical and perfectly in keeping with the previous history of the 'Italian question' that peace should be made when and how the convenience of the intervening power dictated.

Villafranca and the resignation of Cavour

The armistice concluded at Villafranca on 11 July 1859 emphasises once more the extent to which the fate of Italy was dependent upon wider European considerations. Not only were the negotiations limited to the rulers of France and Austria, but the main factors motivating Napoleon III were distinctly non-Italian (*see* Chapter 3, section **P**). It seems very likely, however, that he was also motivated to an extent by perfectly logical misgivings about Piedmont's conduct of the war. It seemed unlikely that the small kingdom would be able to fulfil her promise to pay France's campaign expenses if the war continued for much longer. Piedmont's commanders had virtually no plans nor much equipment for the prolonged siege warfare that would now be necessary if the line of Austrian fortresses on the borders of Venetia were to be attacked. Finally, it was becoming increasingly clear that Cavour had plans for the central Italian duchies that went far beyond the terms of the Plombières agreement.

The terms of the armistice transferred Lombardy, minus the important border fortresses of Peschiera and Mantua, to France on the assumption that she would transfer the territories in turn to Piedmont. The rulers of Tuscany and Modena, who had fled at the news of Magenta, were to be restored, and the principle of a confederacy under Papal leadership was reaffirmed. Venetia, of course, remained in Austrian hands. The attitude of Victor Emmanuel to the settlement was ambiguous; that of Cavour was not. Meeting his monarch for the first time in weeks, he railed against the terms of the armistice, called the king '"traitor" and worse', and in absolute desperation advised that Piedmont should fight on alone. When the king wisely rejected the foolish advice, Cavour resigned his office.

F The issue of the central duchies

Cavour and the National Society

Even as these events were taking place, however, it was becoming increasingly clear that the terms of Villafranca could never be implemented in full. The major difficulty would be the restoration of the rulers of central Italy. In his main piece of direct co-operation with the National Society, Cavour had connived at the establishment of provisional administrations in the central Italian territories, in the name of 'Italy and Victor Emmanuel'. By taking such action in an area designated at Plombières as strictly beyond Piedmontese control Cavour was already violating the agreement and reinterpreting it in a fashion much more favourable to his own state. The king seems to have had no prior knowledge of the operation and regarded it as madness to risk the alienation of his ally at such a vital stage in the campaign.

Cavour's resignation after Villafranca left his 'commissioners' in Tuscany, Parma and Modena in an awkward position. Faced with the alternatives of acting on their own initiatives, or abandoning their positions, they did the former. Luigi Farini had himself elected dictator in Parma, Modena and Bologna, which he declared united under their old Latin title of Emilia. In Florence, the capital of Tuscany, a provisional government under Ricasoli played the same role. It declared that it would never tolerate the return of the former rulers and that its intention was to become 'part of a strong Italian kingdom under the constitutional sceptre of King Victor Emmanuel'. Further reforms in both Emilia and Tuscany brought the currencies and customs duties of those territories into line with those of Piedmont. A. J. Whyte declares of Farini and Ricasoli that 'these two men saved Italy'.

The plebiscites of 1860

The actions of Farini and Ricasoli were indeed brave and valuable for the Italian cause, but the judgement once again does scant justice to Napoleon III. Not only were his armies indirectly responsible for the original flight of the rulers of Tuscany, Parma and Modena, but it was he, in the negotiations at Zurich to formalise the terms of Villafranca, who insisted that no force should be used to implement the terms relating to central Italy. This ruled out the dangers of Austrian or French intervention on behalf of the former rulers, but made it hard for Piedmont to enforce her own union with the territories. The answer lay in the combination of this piece of unfinished business with another.

The section of the Plombières agreement whereby France would receive Nice and Savoy as repayment for her military aid had been ignored at Villafranca as France's obligations, to clear the Austrians from Lombardy and Venetia, remained unfulfilled. Now it was resurrected in a Franco–Piedmontese agreement concluded in Turin in March 1860. It was decided that Savoy and Nice on the one hand, and Emilia and Tuscany on the other, should hold plebiscites to decide their future allegiances. In both cases the result was emphatic. In Emilia the voting was 426,000 to 1,506 in favour of annexation by Piedmont, and in Tuscany the margin was 366,571 to 14,925, although a total of 153,000 abstentions served as a reminder that Tuscans remained attached to their separate historical and cultural traditions.

The events of 1859–60 therefore represented neither complete success nor complete disappointment for Piedmont. Her area and population were doubled as a result of war and diplomacy. Both of these methods of expansion, however, had depended crucially upon the aid of France, and Piedmont now faced the task of defending and consolidating her gains without the direct protection of her ally.

G The Sicilian Expedition

The Sicilian revolt

No event in the 11-year period (1859–70) during which the modern Italian state was effectively created has so caught the imagination as Garibaldi's invasion of Sicily and the subsequent overthrow of the Neapolitan state. Certainly his tactical expertise and personal charisma were major factors in the success of the Sicilian adventure but the roots of this success were more complicated.

Guiseppe Garibaldi

Personality and aims

The rapid progress of the Italian cause from the apparent deadlock of early 1860 was very largely the responsibility of one remarkable man. Giuseppe Garibaldi was born in Nice (4 July 1807) and was associated from about 1834 with the romantic and conspiratorial nationalism of Mazzini's 'Young Italy'. His first efforts in the Italian cause, participation in an unsuccessful rising in Genoa, were rewarded with a death sentence passed in his absence and with flight to South America, where he established his reputation as a guerrilla fighter and leader of genius. In 1848 he found the Piedmontese wary of employing a known radical, but made an international reputation by his defence of Mazzini's Roman Republic. After further exile in America, and on his island home of Caprera off the coast of Sardinia, he fought in 1859 for Piedmont or, as he saw it, for Italy against Austria.

His aims for Italy were simple. With a fine disregard for the constraints imposed by international diplomacy or by economic backwardness, he worked for a free and unified state, preferably a republic, but a constitutional monarchy if necessary. His political views were confused, so confused that men as far apart as the great English Liberal W. E. Gladstone and the fascist dictator Benito Mussolini could claim him as a kindred spirit. The obituary of Garibaldi published in *The Times* (5 June 1882) passed an accurate judgement upon him. 'In politics, as in arms, his mind lacked the basis of a rudimentary education. He rushed to conclusions without troubling his head about arguments. His crude notions of democracy, of communism, of cosmopolitanism, or positivism, were jumbled together in his brain and jostled one another in hopeless confusion.'

His fame and achievement, however, rest upon his actions rather than his thought. His fame in Italy and abroad rests upon the fact that his contribution to the unification falls halfway between those of the other two great Italian figures, Mazzini and Cavour. Mazzini kept the flame of Italian nationalism burning at the time of greatest adversity, but in material terms achieved very little. Cavour achieved much, but had to dirty himself and his reputation in the murky waters of European politics to do it. Garibaldi seemed to many to have avoided both of these traps. His greatest admirer among historians, G. M. Trevelyan, wrote that his work should be 'an encouragement to all high endeavour amongst us in a later age, who, with our eyes fixed on realism and the doctrine of evolution, are in danger of losing faith in ideals, and of forgetting the power that a few fearless and utterly disinterested men may have in a world where the proportion of cowards and egoists is not small'.

Garibaldi did not initiate events in Sicily. The rising that took place on 4 April in Palermo, the chief city of the island, owed nothing to him or to Cavour. It was the work of a group of Mazzinian republicans led by Francesco Crispi and Rosalino Pilo. As republicans they had refused to identify with the Piedmontese monarchy's war in the previous year, and now Cavour returned the compliment by virtually ignoring their approaches to him. The support that the rising received in Palermo was due to a combination of national and local factors. It was partly a result of the excitement generated by the events of 1859, but more important was the disappointment felt at the continued conservatism of the young King Francis II, newly succeeded to the throne of Naples.

The major difference between this outburst and its Mazzinian forerunners was that the Palermo revolt was quickly taken up in the countryside by the peasantry. Their motives derived entirely from local affairs, and their violent protests were directed as much against the landlords who raised their rents and charged them for the privilege of grinding their own corn, as against the Neapolitan troops who were sent to restore order.

Encouraged by these circumstances, Garibaldi began to prepare for the passage to Sicily. With just over 1,000 volunteers, mainly of middle-class and professional origin and very few of them from further south than Tuscany, he sailed from Genoa in two ancient steamers and landed at Marsala on 11 May. He was greatly aided by the presence of a squadron of ships of the Royal Navy, actually concerned with the safety of local British property, but wrongly supposed by the patrolling Neapolitan navy to be allies of Garibaldi. The arrival of these forces proved to be too much for the harassed Neapolitan troops. On 15 May, Garibaldi had a substantial success at Calatafimi. Palermo fell to him on 30 May, and shortly afterwards agreement was reached with the Neapolitan commanders for the withdrawal of their troops across the straits to the mainland.

H The conquest of Naples

Cavour and Garibaldi

The gallant and romantic Sicilian adventure now took on a succession of more sinister international implications. If Garibaldi followed the fleeing troops on to the Neapolitan mainland, why should he not beat them again? If he did so, what was to prevent him from crossing the border from Naples into the Papal States? If he did that, what could prevent a major international crisis involving the French garrison in Rome and possibly other Catholic powers?

None of these considerations was very attractive to the government of Piedmont, whose attitude to the Sicilian expedition as a whole has been the subject of fierce controversy. Naturally, the 'nationalist' interpretation has been that Cavour and his government gave to Garibaldi all the help they reasonably could without raising a storm of international, diplomatic protest. As Mack Smith stresses, nothing would seem to be further from the truth. Garibaldi received so little help from the government that some would-be volunteers had to be sent home for lack of funds to feed them, and the ships that transported the 'thousand' to Sicily had to be stolen. The government even refused the release of 12,000 of Garibaldi's own guns stored in a police arsenal in Milan.

Victor Emmanuel in 1860

The role of Victor Emmanuel in this confused period of the Risorgimento was crucial, yet is difficult to pin down. He undoubtedly felt dissatisfied with the limits imposed upon his Italian authority and influence at Villafranca, and by France's disapproving attitude over the central duchies. The British ambassador in Turin probably captured the king's state of mind when he wrote that he 'has no head for anything but the sword and the horse, looks forward with glee to drawing the one and riding the other, no matter where'. There is clear evidence that Victor Emmanuel was in contact during this period with Garibaldi and even with Mazzini, and he seems also to have toyed with the idea of obtaining Venetia either by war or by purchase. It is hard to resist the conclusion that he did all this, not through any preconceived principles of unification, but rather through a restless desire to continue the extension and enlargement of his political influence in Italy.

Cavour's policy in 1860

Why then, if it did not support Garibaldi, did the government allow the expedition to gather on Piedmontese soil and to sail from a Piedmontese port? The answer seems to be provided by Cavour in a letter to Nigra the day after the expedition had landed in Sicily. 'I could not stop his going, for force would have been necessary. And the ministry is in no position to face the immense unpopularity which would have been drawn upon it had Garibaldi been prevented.' Cavour's ministry did, indeed, face a major cabinet revolt at that time in protest against the cession of Nice and Savoy to France. Thus, torn between his dislike for Garibaldi's radicalism and the dangers of international objections, and the alternative danger of offending the many Italians who loved and admired Garibaldi, the pragmatic Cavour kept his mouth shut and his options open and waited upon the outcome.

The astonishing success of the 'thousand' forced Cavour's hand. A successful *Garibaldini* invasion of Naples would at best lead to a prestigious, radical regime in the south, disputing the leadership of Italy with Piedmont. At worst, it might precipitate a further international war in Italy over the status of the Papacy. Writing to Nigra once more, Cavour clearly outlined the dangers of the moment. 'If Garibaldi passes over to the mainland and seizes the kingdom of Naples and its capital, as he has done with Sicily and Palermo, he becomes absolute master of the situation. King Victor Emmanuel loses more or less all his prestige; in the eyes of the great majority of Italians he is no more than Garibaldi's friend. With the resources of a kingdom of nine million inhabitants at his disposal, surrounded as he is by irresistible popular prestige, it is impossible for us to struggle against him'.

The union of Naples with Italy

Cavour's first attempts to avert such disaster went sadly wrong. Agents were sent into the Kingdom of Naples to stir up a pro-Piedmontese revolt that would pre-empt Garibaldi, but they only encountered the general apathy that bedevilled generations of Italian revolutionaries. On 22 August 1860, Garibaldi finally crossed the Straits of Messina and landed on mainland Neapolitan territory. With the general population showing no serious inclination to protect him against the invaders, Francis II abandoned Naples on 6 September and the city was occupied by *Garibaldini* the following day. Cavour rose to the occasion with probably the greatest piece of opportunism of his career. On 12 September he informed the European powers that Piedmont had no option but to intervene in the Papal territories to restore order. Opposition from Papal forces was brushed aside six days later at Castelfidardo, and by 1 October the Neapolitan forces between the two sets of invaders had ceased to resist.

At a dramatic meeting at Teano, north of the city of Naples (26 October), Garibaldi faced the choice of acknowledging the precedence of the King of Piedmont, or fighting him. He chose to hand over his conquests to Victor Emmanuel and to retire voluntarily to his island home of Caprera. Plebiscites were held with the now customary haste and by the end of 1860 these had sanctioned the union, not only of the kingdom of Naples, but also of the Papal territories of Umbria and the Marches, with Piedmont, now dignified by the new title of the kingdom of Italy.

I Economic difficulties of the new kingdom

The death of Cavour and its aftermath

The new kingdom of Italy, officially in existence from March 1861, had to face the future without the talents of the man who had done more than anyone else to establish it. Cavour died unexpectedly on 6 June 1861, exhausted by the problems and tensions of the last few years. His aims had undoubtedly been very different from those of Mazzini and Garibaldi, and his relations with his king had rarely been better than cool and suspicious. By his masterly flexibility, however, in the face of great political and emotional forces that he could not directly control, he fully deserved the place with which he was credited by the English poet George Meredith in the creation of Italy:

'We think of those
Who blew the breath of life into her frame:
Cavour, Mazzini, Garibaldi: Three:
Her Brain, her Soul, her Sword; and set her free
From ruinous discords'.

Unfortunately, Italy was very far from being 'free from ruinous discords'. She had been formed hastily, imperfectly and against the will of many, and now had to face the cost of Cavour's policies. In Cavour's place followed a succession of men; Ricasoli (1861–62), Rattazzi (March–December 1862), Farini (1862–63), Minghetti (1863–64) and La Marmora (1864–66). None of these was of the calibre of their great predecessor, and most of them had been kept relatively ignorant of the details of government by Cavour's virtual monopoly of the major cabinet posts.

The cost of unity

Of the three main problems that faced these men, the most glaring was the state of the Italian economy. Not only did the new kingdom have to cope with the huge deficit of 2,450 million lire incurred by Cavour to carry through his policies of 1856 (which cost 50 million lire) and 1859 (which cost a further 250 million), but it also inherited the debts of the smaller regimes that it had helped to oust from other parts of Italy. It was further assumed that a modern state would need certain trappings, such as new roads, railways and military equipment. The construction of a sizeable modern navy, in particular, was a foolish luxury when Italy's most likely enemy, Austria, was predominantly a land power. The result was heavy and unpopular taxation, such as Sella's flour tax proposed in 1865, and the negotiation of large foreign loans often on humiliating terms. By the middle of the 1860s more than a third of Italian government bonds were in foreign hands and most Italian railway shares were owned by non-Italians.

Agrarian and industrial backwardness

Italy faced these problems with its main economic activity, agriculture, so deeply in debt that 30 per cent of each year's product was estimated to be eaten up in repayments, and so archaic in its methods that the economist Nassau Senior considered that cereal production in the south had scarcely increased its output since the days of the Roman Empire. Furthermore, it proved impossible to extend Cavour's principles of financial and industrial modernisation to the rest of Italy. Conservative attitudes in central and southern Italy included a distrust of paper money and a condemnation of financial borrowing and lending as immoral.

Agriculture so dominated the lives of the working classes that the census of 1861 showed only three million people employed in industrial production, of whom 80 per cent were women or children sharing their time between this and agriculture. The textile industry and the production of some chemicals, such as sulphur, had potential, but in an age dominated by coal Italy lacked sources of energy until the development of hydro-electric power enabled her to exploit her considerable water resources.

J   The southern question

The rejection of federalism

The greatest rival in severity to Italy's economic difficulties was the 'southern question': the difficulties that arose from the social, economic and political diversity of the Italian regions. The huge majorities recorded in favour of unity in 1860–61 conveyed a dangerously misleading impression. They constituted a vote against a number of things, the tyranny and incompetence of the previous rulers and the lawlessness of rebellious peasants, for example. They probably also represented a considerable degree of electoral malpractice. An observer of the Nice plebiscite, for instance, noted that the slips necessary for a 'no' vote were often in short supply and sometimes missing altogether, and this was probably true in many cases in the south. What those who voted 'yes' were actually voting for was not absolutely clear.

United Italy could take one of at least two forms; a federal state, in which the regions retained much of their local autonomy, or a centralised one, wholly governed from one national capital. Cavour seems to have considered both options, but in the last months of his life he had firmly set his face against the federal solution. The reasons are not altogether clear. It is true that at that time federalism seemed to have failed in the world's greatest federal state, the USA, which stood on the verge of civil war in 1861. It is difficult to avoid the conclusion, however, that federalism was seen to threaten the dominant position of Piedmont within Italy, and that Cavour's decision was taken to impose a rapid solution upon a problem that he had not expected to arise so suddenly.

The policy of 'piedmontisation'

Italy thus became 'piedmontised' at an almost indecent rate. The legal system of Naples, for example, was revolutionised by the passage of 53 decrees in only two days in February 1861. 'Piedmontisation' involved the division of the new kingdom into 53 provinces on the model of the French *départements*, each governed by a prefect. Customs, coinage, weights and measures were standardised in theory, although the illegal use of old coinage and measures persisted at least until the end of the century. The Italian constitution was, in effect, an expanded version of the Piedmontese constitution. The new assembly comprised 443 members, elected by a mere 150,000 voters who fulfilled the dual qualification of paying 40 lire per year in taxes, and being literate. Thus, on average, each deputy was elected by about 300 voters.

The problems of 'piedmontisation'

'Piedmontisation' had two great drawbacks. One was the daunting degree of ignorance that existed in all parts of Italy about the other parts. In particular, the ignorance of the north about conditions in Naples and Sicily extended to all levels of government. Cavour himself, although he had visited France, Britain and Switzerland, never travelled further south than Tuscany. The policy thus resulted in a bizarre series of misconceptions and mistakes. Compulsory education was prescribed for southern Italy, where 90 per cent of the population was illiterate, but it could not be paid for without attacking the property of the Church.

The dissolution of 2,382 monasteries and convents by 1866 provided some funds, but outraged local religious feelings and deprived the localities of charitable institutions run by the monks and nuns long before the state could afford to replace them. The jury system was introduced throughout the south despite the protests of local authorities that Mafia activity would make the corruption and intimidation of juries a simple matter.

Allied to ignorance, the second drawback was a simple lack of resources, both financial and human. The south, it was fondly imagined by men who had never been there, was rich in minerals. Instead it proved a drain upon the resources of the north, and Piedmont, unlike Prussia in the case of German unification, had neither the income nor the trained manpower effectively to administer her new territories.

The imposition of 'piedmontisation'

'The imposition of the Piedmontese administrative system,' concludes D. Mack Smith, 'reinforced the impression that one region had virtually conquered the rest.' Predictably, the southern regions reacted as they had done against earlier injustices. What the national government referred to as 'campaigns for the suppression of brigandage' amounted in fact to a full-scale civil war in the south. The issue was not effectively settled in the central government's favour until 1865, and the struggle claimed more Italian lives than all the battles of the Risorgimento put together. In 1863 alone the government committed 90,000 troops to peacekeeping operations in the south, far more than had ever taken the field against the Austrians.

It was not realistic to expect that such deep-rooted difficulties would be solved within a decade. The processes of road building, agricultural reform and educational improvement were still far from complete by the outbreak of the First World War. It is not surprising, therefore, that the official utterances of the Italian government sought to concentrate public attention as far as possible upon the third of the new kingdom's outstanding problems.

K The Venetian question

Venetia and the 'party of action'

The government of Victor Emmanuel owed much of its continued prestige in 1861 to the opportunism that had enabled it to be identified with the national cause through its intervention in Naples. It was thus very difficult for the government, especially at a time of such extreme domestic difficulties, to ignore the fact that in the eyes of the nationalists there were still two very important pieces missing from the Italian 'jigsaw'. Upon taking office, Ricasoli was quick to reassure Italians that 'we claim Rome as our natural capital and Venetia as an integral part of our national soil'. Rome and Venice, however, were not Naples. To gain either of them would mean dealing with one or more of the great powers at a time when nearly half of the Italian army was fighting its reluctant compatriots in the south.

The first moves towards a solution to the 'Venetian question' were thus made by men to whom such diplomatic niceties were of little concern, by Garibaldi and his 'party of action'. Assuming that what had worked in Naples would work in Venetia, they were active in 1862 attempting to engineer an armed rising, and again in 1864 pinning their hopes this time upon risings elsewhere in the Habsburg Empire which would draw Austrian troops out of Italy. In both cases news leaked out, and the protests of foreign diplomats caused the Italian government to intervene to scotch Garibaldi's plans.

Alliance with Prussia, 1864–66

Instead, like all the other component parts of the 'Italian question' except Naples, the Venetian question had to wait for a solution until the general mood of European politics was ready. The decline of Austria's relations with Prussia in the course of the Schleswig-Holstein affair in 1864 alerted both Prussians and Italians to the common ground in their foreign policies, and to the common benefits that might result from action against Austria. Italian enthusiasm was not absolute. Victor Emmanuel continued to believe, in Mack Smith's words, that 'the important thing was to have a war, and as soon as possible'. To his anti-constitutional motives of 1859 he now added the desire to distract attention from the problems in the south.

La Marmora, however, recalled the pitfalls involved in playing the role of junior partner to a major power. Hence his offer to purchase Venetia from an anxious Austrian government for 1,000 million lire. When the initial enthusiasm of the Emperor was overridden by the military faction in Vienna, the Italian government had little option but to enter into closer negotiations with Prussia. By April 1866 General Govone's mission to Berlin had concluded a military agreement by which both sides undertook not to conclude a separate peace, thus hoping to avoid another Villafranca, and by which Italy was to receive Venetia as the reward for her role. On 20 June, four days after Prussia, Italy formally declared herself at war with Austria once more.

L   The war of 1866

Military preparedness

After the great gains of 1859–60, Italian expectations were high and the king himself was, according to one of his ministers, 'quite drunk with overconfidence'. In theory, the confidence was quite justified. Italy could expect to put some 250,000 men into the field against the 130,000 that the divided Austrian army could spare for its southern front. The fleet too, after the recent spending 'spree', could count twelve ironclad battleships of the most modern design, to Austria's seven. In reality these advantages were to be outweighed by other factors. The Italian general staff 'was not notable for military skill and experience' (Mack Smith) and many, like the fleet's commander, Admiral Persano, owed their positions primarily to influence and corruption at court.

In any case, it was conveniently overlooked that it was not these men, but guerrillas and Frenchmen who had won the great battles of the Risorgimento. Even below the highest levels of command, organisation was so bad and planning so rudimentary that only about 25 per cent of the army ever reached the front. Once there, the unfortunate troops found strategy paralysed by bitter personal rivalries between prominent officers, and by the presence of a monarch who insisted upon taking overall personal command despite the opinion of General Cialdini that 'the king is wholly ignorant and incompetent'.

Military disaster

The confidence did not last long. On 24 June, La Marmora's and Cialdini's forces fought an indecisive action against a strong Austrian defensive position at Custoza, close to the 1848 battlefield, and then disintegrated due to panic and to confused orders. The confusion seemed in no small part the fault of Victor Emmanuel himself. The engagement wrecked the reputations of La Marmora and Cialdini and burst the 'bubble' of Italian military pride. A month later Persano's fleet engaged the Austrian fleet off the island of Lissa in the Adriatic, and in the midst of similar confusion lost three major ships including the *Re d'Italia*, the pride of the Italian navy. It was claimed at Persano's court martial that the fleet had fired 1,450 shells without scoring a major hit on the enemy. Neither battle was a serious defeat in military terms and casualties were low, 750 at Custoza and 600 at Lissa.

In subsequent years these factors allowed nationalist and monarchist historians such as Volpi and Monti almost to represent the war as a success. Indeed, the crushing defeat inflicted by the Prussians upon the Austrians at Sadowa (3 July) brought about an armistice (23 July) by which Italy gained Venetia after all. At the time, however, it was impossible to see the war as anything other than a miserable failure. Almost all the aims of the government had been frustrated. It had brought none of the heroism or glory necessary to weld the disparate parts of the country into a nationally conscious whole. It had done great harm to the prestige of both the army and the monarchy, and Venetia had come into Italian hands, just as Lombardy had done in 1859, through the triumph of a foreign army. There had been no Venetian uprising in support of the Italian forces and the blindest of patriots could hardly have failed to notice that the huge majority recorded in the subsequent plebiscite in favour of union with the rest of Italy hardly squared with the apathy that Venetians had shown during the war itself.

M   The problem of Rome

Rome and the 'party of action'

The failures of 1866 rendered even bleaker the Italian government's prospects of establishing its capital in Rome. In the five years since Garibaldi had been checked on the Pope's frontiers, two main methods had been pursued for gaining access to Rome, but with little success.

The first solution, of course, had been that of the 'party of action'. Dismissing the power of the Papacy as a 'tottering shanty', Garibaldi seems to have regarded Rome as an easier target than Naples. He was wrong on three counts. Firstly, he would be forced to confront the French garrison as well as the small Papal army. Secondly, he would have to face the army of his own government, who could not permit 'banditry' to prejudice their diplomatic relations with France, and could not contemplate the humiliation of acquiring their capital city from the hands of a revolutionary. Thirdly, he was once more badly mistaken in hoping that his actions might spark off a popular revolt within the Papal territories. The Church, as A. J. Whyte has observed, was at the heart of the region's economy, and was unlikely to be attacked by the populace that it supported. 'The Church amused them, employed them and fed them, and to her they looked alike for consolation in trouble and material help in times of stress'.

Nevertheless, the idealism of Garibaldi and the highly ambiguous attitude of the king and some of his ministers twice tempted the 'party of action' into projects that caused the government acute embarrassment. Firstly, in August 1862, an expedition that could easily have been intercepted had the Italian fleet had clearer orders, landed at Aspromonte in Calabria. It had to be checked by government troops. Five years later, in October 1867, the provisional withdrawal of the French troops gave Garibaldi another opportunity. At Mentana (3 November), however, his forces were defeated by Papal troops, reinforced at the last moment by the hastily returning Frenchmen.

The search for a diplomatic solution

The second possible solution was by means of diplomacy. It seemed unlikely, however, that the Italian government, after a decade of pronounced anti-clericalism, would achieve much by direct negotiation with the Church. Throughout the Risorgimento the reaction of the Papacy to changing social and political circumstances was, in the words of A. J. Whyte, 'to bind her medieval robe more closely about her'. This process of restating an inflexible position culminated in the publication in December 1864 of the encyclical *Quanta Cura*, which listed a 'Syllabus of Errors' of 80 points.

Among the 'errors' were the principles of liberty of conscience, state education, liberalism, constitutional government, and opposition to the temporal power of the Pope. It was an attack upon most of the progressive ideas of western Europe in the 19th century, and as such was an embarrassment to all progressive Catholics. It was also a manifesto of opposition to most of the professed ideas of the Italian government.

Negotiations with France were rather more fruitful. Napoleon III had long regretted the expense and political inconvenience involved in protecting a stubborn and reactionary Pope, but could not agree to abandon him to the 'bandits' who had set up the Roman Republic of 1849. After 1862, and the encounter at Aspromonte, it was possible to claim that the responsible Italian government effectively had Garibaldi under its control.

By 1864, therefore, the French were willing to enter into highly secret negotiations which resulted in the so-called Convention of September. France consented to remove her garrison from Rome in return for an Italian undertaking to protect Papal territory from all external attack. A number of sympathetic commentators have been tempted to admire a move by which, in A. J. Whyte's words, 'the wolves were set to guard the fold'. Denis Mack Smith opposes that view, too, by pointing out that the Italian diplomats must either have been lying deliberately to the French, or else deliberately breaking their promises to the Italian electors concerning the acquisition of Rome.

N The acquisition of Rome

French withdrawal

Whatever the motives behind it, the Convention of September did not bring the Italians any closer to making their capital in Rome. The withdrawal of French troops in December 1866 was reversed by the Mentana fiasco less than a year later, and the situation remained one of stalemate and confrontation until 1870. Then, as usual, Italy's problems were resolved by European factors quite beyond Italy's control. The drift of France towards war with Prussia offered two openings to Italy. The first was diplomatic when, in May 1870, Napoleon III sought a basis for an anti-Prussian alliance. For all her doubts about fighting against her most recent ally, Italy still suggested Rome as the price of her co-operation.

For the French Catholics, that price remained too high. The outbreak of war, however, presented Italy with an opportunity that public opinion would not allow her to miss. France's Roman garrison could no longer be spared and by 19 August the evacuation was complete. The prime minister, Giovanni Lanza, still acted with great caution, waiting until the defeat of France at Sedan. The formal agreement of Spain, Austria and the Catholic German states, and the arrest of Mazzini, ensured that there would be no unfortunate side-effects. The modest Papal army was overcome in a brief engagement on 19 September 1870, as a result of which Rome was at last occupied by the Italian army.

Annexation and relations with the Papacy

The usual plebiscite (2 October) produced the usual result, a huge majority in favour of union with the rest of Italy (133,681 to 1,507). Again the result contradicted the previous indifference of the population, and a French officer in the Papal army, the Comte de Beaufort, published a detailed account of alleged dishonesty at the polls. This included the absence of 'no' voting slips, intimidation, plural voting and the introduction of non-qualified voters. His account is, perhaps, a fair representation of the plebiscites of the Risorgimento.

It was one thing to win Rome, and quite another to win the Church's acceptance of the fact. For instance, although stripped of his temporal powers, Pius IX made his supreme act of defiance in July 1870 by declaring the doctrine of Papal Infallibility. In May 1871, by the Law of Guarantees, the Italian government made a further gesture of conciliation as it sought to define the position of the Pope within the kingdom of Italy. The full spiritual jurisdiction of the Pope was recognised, freedom of communication with the Church throughout the world was confirmed, along with the liberty of appointment to all ecclesiastical offices, and liberty of teaching. The Pope received an annual grant equivalent to £129,000, remained free of Italian taxation, and retained the full use of the Vatican and of Castel Gandolfo. Typically, Pius IX chose to remain 'a prisoner in the Vatican', and not until 1929 was the Italian state formally recognised by the Papacy (*see* Chapter 15).

Questions

Essay questions

1　'Cavour was more concerned with the expansion of Piedmont than with the unification of Italy.' Discuss. (ULEAC)

2　To what extent was Italian unification due more to diplomacy than to nationalist fervour and military skill? (NEAB)

3　Why did Piedmont play such a central role in Italian unification? (Oxford entrance)

4　How strong, and how widespread, was opposition to political change in Italy in the period 1815–58? (AEB)

5　Why, and in what ways, was the influence of other European states important to the creation of a united Italy? (UCLES)

6　What lessons were learned for future progress towards national unity from the uprisings in Italy in 1848–49? (WJEC)

Cavour and Garibaldi's Expedition in 1860

SOURCE A

You will see from Fanti's note that the government is very nearly in real trouble. Fanti was not wrong, as Minister of War, to wish to safeguard the pressing needs of defence. It is evident that the treaty could be the subject of very grave censures (on 10 May). In rushing through the cession of Nice and Savoy without the least regard for the just sensibilities of the country, the French government has succeeded in destroying the influence of the government internally as well as externally: by indefinitely prolonging the negotiations over the frontiers, it will make the existence of the government impossible, and will only give more impetus and prestige to the opposition of Rattazzi and Garibaldi. [The French government] must realise that the position in which they have put me is not sustainable. I must have at least some argument to demonstrate that we have not forgotten to safeguard the interests of the country in these unhappy negotiations. Although one might say that Italy is grateful for the power that France has given us, yet a great number of deputies are not at all inclined to forget that the Peace of Villafranca left not only Venice but also Peschiera and Mantua to Austria, and that the annexation of central Italy was made not by France but against her.

If Fanti resigns, the existing government will not last more than a single day. Fanti is the only one among the existing ministers congenial to the King – and I have reason to believe that HM, who always has a weakness for Garibaldi and Rattazzi, is secretly looking to remove me from the direction of affairs. I would be well content to retire to Leri; but I am not the man to leave the country in the middle of the immense dangers which would spring from the rejection of the treaty. I am therefore disposed to carry the burden of power for a little longer – and the unpopularity. I only ask that the Emperor gives me a little help to accomplish the thankless task I have undertaken, or at least not to make it more difficult for me.

Cavour from Turin to Nigra in Paris, 24 April 1860.

SOURCE B

Wednesday 2 May: Scovazzo informed me that Massimo D'Azeglio, Nigra and Hudson, the English Ambassador, were the people who are working with all their strength to keep Cavour Prime Minister. It now seems that serious opposition is being organised in the Senate over the two provinces of Nice and Savoy. The rebellion is spreading in Sicily.

Thursday 3 May: The news from Sicily is still favourable to the insurrection. Nicolari writes to me from Genoa that Garibaldi is going to leave in two days time with an elect band of young men. The Government is behaving rather passively, the clearest sign that the revolution has taken it by surprise. Public opinion in Turin is moving against Count Cavour: he may fall and never regain power.

From the political diary of Senator Asproni, May 1860.

SOURCE C

Garibaldi has landed in Sicily. It is a great piece of luck that he did not pursue his idea of attacking the Pope. We cannot stop him making war against the King of Naples. Whether it turns out for the best or the worst, it was inevitable. He would have become dangerous in internal politics if he had been held back by force. What will happen now? It is impossible to predict. Will England help him? It is possible. Will France stop him? I believe not. And us? We cannot openly support him, neither can we restrain private efforts on his behalf. Therefore we have decided not to allow any new expeditions to be prepared from the ports of Genoa and Livorno, but not to stop the sending of arms and munitions, provided that it is carried out with a degree of prudence. I am not disguising all the inconvenience of this ill-defined line we are following, but I cannot think of an alternative which doesn't present more serious and dangerous prospects.

Cavour to Ricasoli, Royal Governor of Tuscany, 16 May 1860 (sent before Cavour received Source D).

SOURCE D

Just as the royal government ought to stop any attack on the Papal States at the moment, so it should tolerate and even give aid to the Sicilian insurrection, if that can be done covertly, and at least without compromising ourselves too much. We cannot sufficiently proclaim towards Europe the duty that binds Italians to help their compatriots who are subject to evil governments.

Ricasoli to Cavour, 15 May 1860.

SOURCE E

I entirely agree with you about Garibaldi's expedition. I have nothing to add except that we must save appearances so as not to increase our diplomatic difficulties. France has shown less displeasure than I expected.

Cavour to Ricasoli. 23 May 1860.

---

a Explain briefly the following references:
  i 'In rushing through the cession of Nice and Savoy without the least regard for the just sensibilities of the country' (Source A) [2]
 ii 'the Peace of Villafranca' (Source A) [1]
iii 'It is a great piece of luck that he did not pursue his idea of attacking the Pope' (Source C) [2]
b Does Source B provide convincing support for Cavour's profession of weakness (Source A)? [5]
c Compare the trustworthiness of Cavour's remarks in Sources A and C. [7]
d From these sources and any other evidence known to you, discuss the assertion that 'until long after Garibaldi had sailed for Sicily, Cavour had no policy at all towards the expedition'. [8]

(UCLES)

5

German unification

A cartoon published in 1863 in the Prussian liberal magazine *Kladderadatsch***. Bismarck holds the Prussian constitution at arm's length and declares 'I cannot govern with this'.**

How has the cartoonist indicated the nature of the dispute between Bismarck and the liberals?

Suggest how the portrayal of Bismarck in *Kladderadatsch* might have changed by 1870 or 1871.

A 1850: Erfurt to Olmütz

The Union of Erfurt

Viewed in terms of constitutional change, or of lasting social development, the events of 1848–49 made as little lasting impression upon Germany as upon Italy. In the short term, however, the revolutionary events appeared to have one notable consequence. The prestige of the Prussian state was higher than for many years following her role in recent German affairs, while Austria was still engaged elsewhere with the affairs of her empire. In addition, the German Confederation could be regarded as more or less defunct following the recent constitutional eruptions. How could the vacuum in princely German politics be filled without risking the revival of radical, nationalist ideas?

This was the question that Baron Josef von Radowitz, adviser to the king of Prussia on federal reform for more than 20 years, tried to answer in a set of proposals put to a representative assembly of the German states at Erfurt in March 1850. These included a union of the North German states under the presidency of the king of Prussia, and under the protection of the victorious Prussian army. For Friedrich Wilhelm, the great advantage of such a plan was that Prussian influence would be based upon sound monarchical principles and not, as the offer of the German crown had been in 1849, upon any principles of popular sovereignty. In general, Austria would be excluded from this 'Erfurt Union'. Von Radowitz proposed a compromise, however, by which Austria might be linked to the Union by a second, wider union, based upon free trade and perhaps upon a common foreign policy.

The 'Capitulation of Olmütz'

In effect, von Radowitz was moving too far, too fast. The only real basis for the Erfurt Union was the fear of the German princes at the prospect of a renewed liberal onslaught. He and Friedrich Wilhelm, as A. J. P. Taylor put it, 'thought the princes converted [to the idea of a *kleindeutsch* union] when they were merely frightened'. In fact, it was already evident that many of the 'middling' German states feared Prussian hegemony as much as, if not more than, liberal revolt. Hence the refusal of 11 states, including Hanover, Bavaria,

Saxony and Württemberg, to send representatives to Erfurt. The insuperable weakness of the proposals was that they arose from an Austrian withdrawal from German affairs that was only temporary. By late 1850, with the Hungarian and Italian revolts under control, the Austrian premier, von Schwarzenberg, was able to declare that 'we shall not let ourselves be thrown out of Germany', and began to insist upon the reconstruction of the Confederation as it had existed before 1848.

A constitutional conflict in the small duchy of Hesse-Cassel, which formed the vital link between the two blocks of Prussian territory, provided the test of nerves between the two German powers. With the alternatives of seeking aid from the Erfurt Union or from the Confederation, Hesse-Cassel turned to the latter. For a while Prussia seemed prepared to fight to defend her new-found prestige, but Russian support for Austria, as demonstrated against the Hungarians, proved to be the decisive factor. 'Only the Tsar is sovereign,' wrote Karl Marx at the time. 'In the end rebellious Prussia will bow to his command.'

So, indeed, in a meeting at Olmütz (November 1850), Friedrich Wilhelm gave in once more to his doubts, and to the doubts of many Prussian conservatives, and agreed to abandon the Erfurt Union in favour of the revival of the German Confederation under Austrian presidency. By the so-called 'Capitulation of Olmütz', Prussia abandoned the leadership of Germany for a decade and a half. Prussian reactions ranged from conservative satisfaction at the abandonment of a dangerous innovation, to patriotic humiliation. All were aware that German leadership lay beyond Prussia's reach until there was a change in the military balance of Germany, and in the European system of alliances.

B Prussia and Austria, 1850–60

The attempted extension of Austrian hegemony

The political life of Germany in the 1850s has been dismissed by Agatha Ramm as a period of 'sterile parliamentarianism within the states and sterile diplomacy without'. The charge of sterility is certainly true in the sense that all formal initiatives for a further constitutional development of Germany, like those of 1850, came to nothing.

Between 1851 and 1853, Austrian statesmen attempted to consolidate and to exploit the position of supremacy in German affairs manifested at Olmütz. Firstly, Schwarzenberg proposed the extension of the Confederation to include Austria's non-German territories, thus forming an 'Empire of 70 millions'. When this was rejected by the German princes assembled at Dresden in mid-1851, Austrian proposals switched to an economic tack. Alexander von Bach, minister of the interior, and the Baron von Bruck, the former Rhineland liberal now in charge of Austrian finances, proposed the linking of the Prussian-dominated *Zollverein* with the Empire to produce a vast central European (*Mitteleuropa*) economic union.

The Austrians, however, were overplaying their hand. Olmütz had restored the balance between Austrian military power and Prussian economic power upon which the independence of the lesser princes depended. These princes now had no intention of seeing Austria upset that balance, and their independence, again. Austria had to be content, therefore, with a commercial treaty with Prussia, acting as spokesman for the *Zollverein*, signed in February 1853.

The impact of foreign affairs: the Crimea

It cannot be said, however, that this decade was sterile in the sense that no development took place at all. In Germany, as in most of Europe, the Crimean War acted as a great catalyst to political change. Despite the debt that his state owed to the Russians since 1849, the Austrian foreign minister, Count Buol, believed that Austria should conclude an alliance with the western powers as a safeguard against nationalist action in Italy. He also had no desire to see Russia in control of Moldavia, Wallachia and the mouth of the Danube. This policy necessitated an understanding with Prussia to ensure that she would not seek to benefit in Germany from Austria's preoccupation as she had done in 1850. Prussian opinion, however, was bitterly divided, with conservatives following a pro-Russian policy, while the liberals favoured France and Britain.

In the end, Friedrich Wilhelm followed the least controversial line, that of neutrality. Thus neither of the German powers played any military role in the war, although Austria maintained a highly benevolent attitude towards the allies. The events of the Crimea, nevertheless, resulted in a number of subtle changes in the German status quo. Firstly, Austria's concerns had been shown to be purely imperial, rather than German. Her diplomacy had been dominated by thoughts of Moldavia, the Danube and Italy, and her aims had been caricatured by Bismarck as being 'to procure a few stinking Wallachians'. Secondly, her failure to repay her debt to Russia had ruptured forever the 'Holy Alliance' between the two great legitimist powers, leaving Austria isolated in European diplomacy. Prussia, although also neutral, owed Russia no such debt, and her neutrality had at least guaranteed Russia security on her Polish borders.

In German terms, as Agatha Ramm stresses, the Crimean War was a depressing episode for Prussia, proving her remoteness from the great decisions of European politics and confirming her 'international nullity'. Helmut Böhme prefers to view the war in Prussian terms, as a period of great advance in its prestige within Germany, as proportionately Austria's national and international prestige declined.

The impact of foreign affairs: Italy

The Italian war of 1859 continued the process of Austrian humiliation. In Helmut Böhme's words, 'Austria now buried her plans for a customs union, her German policy and her economic policy on the battlefields of northern Italy.' As a legitimist, the Prussian regent Prince Wilhelm inclined towards aid for Austria, but Austria's isolation from all the other European powers made this a dangerous course to take. In the event, Prussia delayed the mobilisation of her forces until Austria's defeat was virtually assured (July 1859). She then mobilised in concert with the South German princes, with a view to protecting the Rhine frontier against any further French expansionism. Thus Prussia appeared to be making a gesture for the protection of Germany at a time when it was becoming increasingly difficult to believe in Austrian protection.

The year 1860, with Napoleon III's annexation of Nice and Savoy, brought further cause for the princes to seek protection against French aggression. When Napoleon visited Baden-Baden in an attempt to dispel this anxiety (June 1860) he found himself faced with a phalanx of rulers, from Bavaria, Hanover, Saxony and Württemberg, united in their apprehension. In general, the

European events of 1859–60 marked the beginning of German confidence in Prussia's military capacity in addition to her undoubted economic capacity.

C The Prussian army

Helmut von Moltke

In 1850, the prospects of far-ranging conquests by the Prussian army seemed remote. That army still rested very heavily upon the tactics and traditions of the Napoleonic wars. Indeed, as W. McElwee has stated, 'to the outward eye the Prussian army in 1859 was as clumsy and antiquated an instrument as any of the others'. The mobilisation of that year seemed to confirm such reservations, but in fact, at that very point, the Prussian military establishment was in the midst of a process of transformation.

The key date in this process was perhaps 1857, the year in which Helmut von Moltke was appointed as Chief of Staff. Moltke was an unusually cultured and humane man to lead a great national army. 'Every war,' he wrote later in his life, 'even one which is victorious, represents a great national misfortune.' Even the great triumph of 1870 was for him 'a step backwards into barbarism'. Politically, his brand of romantic patriotism was closer to that of King Wilhelm than to the realism of Bismarck. He was not primarily, however, a political animal. 'For Moltke,' wrote Gerhard Ritter, 'politics was an acquired interest rather than a congenial preoccupation and he was deeply concerned with it only when it directly touched the military sphere.'

The size and organisation of the army

In terms of numerical strength, the reforms of 1862 (*see* section **E**) put Moltke's army squarely on terms with that of Austria. Thereby 63,000 men were called up each year, for a total period of seven years, three of them in the standing army and four in the front-line reserve, liable to instant recall in an emergency. This gave a standing army of 180,000, with a fully trained reserve of 175,000. In 1866, therefore, Prussia could mobilise 370,000 men, including some *Landwehr* units. As they had fewer security commitments on other frontiers, they were able to outnumber their enemy on the Bohemian front by 278,000 to 271,000.

The superior organisation of the Prussian army was equally important. The Prussian General Staff had its origins in the War Academy founded by the great military theorist Clausewitz in the Napoleonic era. Not only did it produce officers of great expertise and professionalism, but guaranteed a uniformity of practice and doctrine in all branches of the army. At Moltke's insistence, for example, all senior officers devoted much attention to the adaptation of modern transport and industrial methods to military needs.

By comparison, the Austrian army remained dominated by such senior commanders such as Gyulai and Wimpffen, who owed their rank more to influence at court than to proven ability. At lower levels, too, the Austrian army was riddled with inefficiency. Out of a theoretical force of 600,000 men in 1866, bad reserve training and the practice of allowing the wealthy to buy themselves out of military service reduced the fighting force to about 350,000. Furthermore, basic training in the standing army was so bad that it was estimated that two troopers out of three at the start of the Italian campaign in 1859 were unable to load and fire their muskets.

The army and technology

Finally, the Prussian army undoubtedly led Europe in the application of industrial developments to military purposes. Not only were Prussian railways specifically planned for the swift transit of troops from one distant frontier to the other, but the General Staff operated a special department dedicated to the study of transport by rail. In both 1866 and 1870 this swift concentration of troops was a vital factor. In 1866 Prussia's five railway lines assembled her troops on the Bohemian frontier in five days against 45 days taken by the Austrians. In 1870 it proved possible to transport some troops from East Prussia to Lorraine in only 36 hours.

In terms of armament, the Prussian infantry was synonymous for some years with the Dreyse 'needle gun'. First issued in 1848 and in general use by 1864, it fired at five times the rate of the old muzzle-loader, and its effect at Sadowa caused the correspondent of *The Times* to declare that 'the needle gun is king'. Nevertheless, it had its limitations in range and in accuracy, and the victory of 1870 owed more to the Prussian artillery. Equipped by the mid-1860s with a new Krupp breech-loader, with cooled steel barrel and a breech sealed against escaping gases, this branch of the army perfected its techniques in the new School of Gunnery founded in swift response to the superior performance of the Austrian gunners at Sadowa.

D The Prussian economy

Prussian resources and government policy

Two main factors coincided to ensure that Prussia's economy would become predominant among the economies of the German states. Firstly, Prussia was blessed with remarkable natural resources, supplemented in 1814–15 by the gain of the richly endowed territories of the Rhineland. Through the Ruhr valley and west and south-west across the Rhine lay substantial deposits of coal and iron ore. Rich coal resources were also available in the Saar valley, in Prussian Silesia and in Upper Silesia, where zinc and iron deposits were also worked.

Secondly, although private and foreign capital was prominent in the early promotion of these industries, Prussia was remarkable for the degree of government interest and involvement in their subsequent development. Although recent commentators have stressed the haphazard and partial nature of government intervention, it was undoubtedly effective in some important areas. The contribution of von Motz, the finance minister 1825–30, included tax reforms and a road building programme. P. Beuth, head of the Department of Trade and Industry 1815–45, did much to foster technical education. A sound Prussian banking system owed much to von Rother's reorganisation of the Bank of Prussia in 1846.

The *Zollverein*

The greatest monument to this interest was the establishment of the German Customs Union (*Zollverein*) in 1834. This unit, with an area of 415,000 sq km and a population of 23.5 million, was the culmination of the creation of smaller unions throughout the 1820s. Prussia benefited by securing the effective union of her eastern and western territories, and by establishing her economic influence above that of Austria in German affairs. Prussia's leading position in the *Zollverein* was recognised by those clauses in the establishing treaty which accepted her tariffs as the norm for all,

and which recognised the right of the Prussian government to negotiate on behalf of the *Zollverein* as a whole. This leadership was most effective, as witnessed by a dramatic rise in customs revenue from 14.4 million (1834) to 27.4 million thalers (1845). In addition, a string of treaties won favourable trading terms for the *Zollverein* with Piedmont, Holland (both 1851), Belgium (1852) and France (1862).

The development of Prussian heavy industry

Prussia also took the leading role within Germany in the development of those branches of heavy industry vital to the modern and militarised state. Her iron and coal industries benefited substantially from the introduction of new technology. The number of steam engines operative in Prussian industry rose from 419 (1837) to 1,444 (1848) at a time when the next best figure was Saxony's 197 (1846).

Twenty-four new deep-level mines were opened in the Ruhr coalfield between 1841 and 1849, while new sources of zinc (Dortmund and Bonn), lead (Aachen) and blackband iron (Dortmund) were discovered and exploited in the late 1840s and early 1850s. Prussia's output of iron rose sharply from 0.5 million to 1.29 million tons between 1852 and 1857 due also to rapid conversion from charcoal smelting to coke smelting.

Although private capital was once more of prime importance, government legislation again played a helpful role in Prussia. The Mining Laws of 1851 and 1860, for instance, freed mine owners from strict state supervision and halved taxes upon their output. The laws subsequently did much to free mine labour from the old guild restrictions upon mobility.

The growth of the Prussian steel industry may be measured by the rise of its greatest enterprise, the Krupp factories in Essen. Based upon a successful method of producing cast steel, Alfred Krupp's enterprise grew between 1826 and 1861 from a single foundry employing seven men to a vast complex employing 2,000. In the next three years alone, thriving on military orders from the Prussian government, especially for modern artillery, the workforce trebled again. In all Prussian steel production was seven times greater in 1864 than in 1848. The rate of economic growth within the *Zollverein* boundaries may be gauged from Table 5.1.

Table 5.1 Indicators of economic activity in the *Zollverein*, 1820–70

	1820	1840	1850	1870
Railways (km)	—	549	5,821	8,560
Coal (million tons)	1.0	—	6.9	29.4
Pig iron (million tons)	0.046	0.17	0.53	1.4

Railway construction

Both Bavaria (1835) and Saxony (1837) played an earlier role than Prussia in the foundation of German railways, as the Prussian government was initially just as suspicious about the new mode of transport as other states. The 1840s and 1850s, however, saw a rapid change in their attitude. Having appreciated the advantages of east–west communications for economic and strategic purposes, Prussia constructed Germany's second state-owned line (1847), and then sought consistently to extend state influence over the system as a whole. By 1860, 55 per cent of Prussian railways were worked by the state. Quite apart from its economic significance, the growth of the German railway system as a whole played a considerable role in the process of 'shrinking' the country and in stressing the insignificance of the lesser states. At every turn, therefore, in an examination of Prussian and German economic growth in the 1850s and 1860s, one is reminded of the famous judgement of John Maynard Keynes that 'the German Empire was not founded on blood and iron, but on coal and iron'.

The role of economic factors in German unification

The question raised by Keynes concerns the relationship between the economic growth of Germany, and of Prussia in particular, and the political achievement of Bismarck. The traditional view has been to see Bismarck as exploiting the economic advantages of his time to gain the political ends that he sought. More recently, a school of historians led by Helmut Böhme has concluded that the dynamics of the German economy were of greater importance than the political priorities of the Prussian government. In this light, Bismarck might less realistically be seen as the exploiter of these economic forces, than as a politician whose course was largely determined by those forces and by the social forces that arose from them. Geoff Eley reflects this line of thought when he summarises Böhme's views on the reduction of Austrian influence in Germany. 'The struggle for the control of the *Zollverein* was decisive between 1853 and 1868 in destroying Austrian efforts at reducing Prussia to secondary status. Therefore, 1858 and the opening of a 'New Era' in Prussian government becomes less crucial than 1857 and the economic depression, which widened the gap between the Austrian and Prussian-led economies; 1862 is important less for Bismarck's appointment as Minister-President of Prussia, than for the treaty of free trade with France; Austria's defeat in 1866 is less decisive than its exclusion from the *Zollverein* two years before.'

E The Prussian constitutional crisis of 1860–62

The accession of King Wilhelm I

The period 1858–62 saw a transformation of Prussian domestic politics that turned a decade of sterility into a period of crisis that threatened to bring down the monarchy. The first element in this transformation was a change of monarch. In October 1858, the mental illness of Friedrich Wilhelm necessitated the appointment of his brother, Prince Wilhelm, as regent. He succeeded to the throne upon his brother's death in 1860. Wilhelm was already 61 years old in 1858, his first political memories dating from the Napoleonic Wars.

By 1848 he had the reputation of a strict conservative, but that was an oversimplification. He was, indeed, deeply attached to the principle of legitimate monarchy and to the traditions of Prussian military glory, but he had been convinced of the need to adapt in the face of modern forces. As a man of honour, his attitude towards the constitution granted by his brother was one of respect, 'not,' as Golo Mann has written, 'because he liked it, but because a king must stand by his sacred word.'

The resurgence of nationalism and liberalism

The second major development during this period was the revival of the German national movement in the last years of the 1850s. The national question, in Agatha Ramm's words, 'barely retained public interest' in the early 1850s. In a negative sense, the lack of any German influence over events in the Crimea played a role in its revival. More

Otto von Bismarck

Personality and aims

The new Minister-President of Prussia in 1862 was a man of 47 without any ministerial experience, and with extremely limited experience of government administration. Otto von Bismarck, greatly though he stressed his origins among the Prussian feudal aristocracy, was no ordinary Junker. His middle-class mother had insisted upon an education in Berlin and at the University of Göttingen. There he acquired a veneer of student liberalism and literary radicalism, even if his swordsmanship and riotous living were more in line with typical Junker behaviour. A. J. P. Taylor has attached great importance to Bismarck's psychological reaction against the middle-class trappings of his early life. 'He was the highly educated, sophisticated son of a highly educated, sophisticated mother, masquerading as his slow witted father and living down his middle-class origin by an exaggerated emphasis on the privileges of his class.' By nature he was intensely ambitious, rightly convinced of his superiority over the narrow minded conservatives that made up the Junker ranks, and intolerant of criticism to an extent that often brought on physical illness. From the time of his marriage (1847) he professed a simple, personal Protestant faith, but was able totally to divorce personal from political morality.

This strange semi-Junker gained his first political experience almost by accident at the age of 32, sitting in the Prussian *Landtag* in 1847 only as a substitute for a sick member. From this experience, and from the extraordinary events of 1848–49, he derived an intense hostility towards radicalism. This was matched by his disdain for parliamentary 'talking shops' and a contempt for policies based upon abstract romanticism. Having gained a powerful reputation on the extreme right of Prussian politics, he bitterly opposed the Erfurt Union as 'a shameful union with democracy' and rejoiced at the restoration of the status quo.

The 1850s were a crucial period in Bismarck's personal and political development. From 1850 to 1858 he sat as Prussian representative in the federal assembly (*Bundestag*), apparently ideally suited to aid reconciliation between the two great conservative forces in Germany. Indeed, contrary to his later autobiographical claims, his stance remained pro-Austrian until 1854. Many commentators have interpreted the transformation as the result of Austria's attempts to change the German status quo in her favour. For A. J. P. Taylor it was rather that the events surrounding the Crimean War convinced Bismarck that Austria was now unable effectively to protect conservative interests in Germany. Indeed, Bismarck wrote at the time, 'I should be very uneasy if we sought refuge from a possible storm by hitching our trim and sea-worthy frigate to that worm-eaten old Austrian man-of-war.'

By 1859, Bismarck was so out of sympathy with Austria that he could advise General von Alvensleben during the Italian crisis to 'march southwards with our whole army with boundary posts in our soldiers' knapsacks and drive them into the ground either at Lake Constance or where Protestantism ceases to prevail'. His view was so out of keeping with Prince Wilhelm's concern for legitimacy that his reward was to be packed off as ambassador, first to St Petersburg (1859) and then to Paris (1862). Despite this, and despite the outbreak of three wars in his first eight years in power, we should not regard Bismarck as a warmonger. He followed Clausewitz in believing that 'war is the continuation of politics by other means'. Yet generally he regarded those 'other means' as dangerous and to be avoided whenever possible. 'War,' as A. J. P. Taylor defined it, 'deprived him of control and left the decision to generals whose ability he distrusted.'

In conclusion, Bismarck's beliefs and motives may be sorted into three categories. Firstly, his political instincts were conservative, although his intellect taught him that conservative ends could now only be attained by harnessing more modern notions, such as industrialism and nationalism. Secondly, his allegiance was to Prussia. It was not an allegiance to 'the people' or to 'the nation' as that of the German nationalists was, but to the monarchical, Junker-dominated state which he valued as 'an organ of power, a principle of order and authority'. Only when that state became nominally a German state did Bismarck's allegiance become German. Thirdly, Bismarck believed unswervingly in his own superior claim to exercise political power. 'He claimed', wrote A. J. P. Taylor, 'to serve sometimes the king of Prussia, sometimes Germany, sometimes God. All three were cloaks for his own will'.

positively, the partial success of Italian nationalism in 1859 also had an impact north of the Alps. Also important were the consistent efforts of the lesser German princes to reform the Confederation with a view to increasing its influence over foreign affairs. The revival culminated in the formation (1859) of the National Association (*Nationalverein*), directly inspired by the Italian National Society. The Association was banned in all major German states, but continued to look to Prussia for leadership, as Italians had looked to Piedmont. The journalist J. Froebel wrote in 1859 that 'the German nation is sick of principles and doctrines, literary greatness and theoretical existence. What it demands is power, power, power. And to the man who offers it power it will offer honour, more honour than he can imagine.'

Thirdly, whether as a cause or result of the nationalist revival, came a marked resurgence in liberal political activity. In Prussia it manifested itself especially in the emergence of the Progress Party (*Fortschrittpartei*). Raised upon the anti-Austrian, anti-Russian and theoretically anti-militaristic foundations of traditional Prussian liberalism, it enjoyed great success in the first elections of the new decade. In the elections to the *Landtag* in January 1862 it won 83 seats in an assembly that contained only 16 conservatives. Three months later its strength rose to 136 seats, while the conservatives fell to 11 and the 'old' liberals fell from 95 to 47.

Von Roon and military reform

Such was the political temper of the *Landtag* that had to consider the proposals of the king and of his war minister, Albrecht von Roon, for the reform of the Prussian army. These proposals were also in part the result of the crisis of 1859. The government's prime concern was with the size of the army for, while the Prussian population had doubled since 1814, the annual intake of recruits had remained static at 40,000. Von Roon now proposed to increase this to 63,000 and to create 53 new regiments. He also proposed to change the nature of the army by limiting the role played by the reserve militia (*Landwehr*). This was composed of part-time soldiers who had finished their three years' training and who, in his view and on the evidence of the mobilisation in 1859, 'lacked the genuine soldierly spirit and had no firm discipline'. To the

liberal majority, however, the *Landwehr* had the advantage of being freer from the detested spirit of Junker militarism and of costing them far less in taxes. It also recalled fond memories of the 'people's war' against Napoleon in 1813. Thus von Roon was not only fighting a technical battle, but also a class struggle.

The appointment of Otto von Bismarck

By 1862 the dispute was already two years old, and the assembly had twice been deceived by the government into making temporary grants of money for the army. Angry and alienated, they now refused to sanction the national budget, leaving Wilhelm to contemplate the possibility of abdication. Only as a desperate measure, and at the prompting of von Roon, did he take the most important political decision of his life. He summoned to office a man closely identified with the far right of Prussian politics, the ambassador to Paris, Otto von Bismarck-Schönhausen.

Bismarck was not a man to be impressed by abstract principles, whether of legitimism or of constitutionalism. Nevertheless, his first moves aimed at finding ground for compromise with the *Landtag*. Only when that failed did he take the determined course of adjourning their sitting (October 1862) and collecting and spending the national budget whether they liked it or not. As theoretical justification Bismarck exploited the 'gap theory' (*Luckentheorie*). He claimed that the constitution made the budget the joint responsibility of the two houses of the assembly and the monarch, but failed to cater for the eventuality of a dispute between them. In that event, he claimed without much justification, the executive power reverted to the king.

More important than any theory, however, was the knowledge that real power, rather than moral rectitude, lay in the hands of the government, the more so now that it had 53 new regiments at its disposal. 'The great questions of the day', Bismarck told the *Landtag* in the first and most famous speech of his ministerial career, 'will not be decided by speeches and the resolutions of majorities – that was the great mistake of 1848 and 1849 – but by iron and blood.' For four years, and through two wars, Bismarck was to direct Prussian affairs without a constitutionally approved budget, and in the face of continued parliamentary opposition.

F The basis of Bismarckian foreign policy

The British statesman Benjamin Disraeli recounted in later years a conversation that he claimed to have had with Bismarck in 1862. According to Disraeli, Bismarck laid down a clear programme. 'As soon as the army shall be brought into such a condition as to inspire respect, I shall seize the first best pretext to declare war against Austria, dissolve the German Diet and give national unity to Germany under Prussian leadership.' Recent historians have usually reacted to this either by dismissing the conversation, or by minimising it as the barest outline of long-term aims by a man as yet unaware of the complexities of politics at the highest level. The subjection of Austria, at least in northern Germany, and the destruction of the Confederation, probably represent Bismarck's ultimate hopes well enough. In power, however, he found repeatedly that a masterplan was impossible, and that the only means of progress was the piecemeal exploitation of external events. In the 1860s he became the supreme realist and pragmatist, learning to declare in later life that 'man cannot create the current of events. He can only float with it and steer.'

It is also possible, however, to view Bismarck's spectacular foreign policy in the 1860s in a completely different light. Many recent writers on German history have tended to lay their stress upon the importance of domestic politics, and to interpret foreign policy mainly as a means by which politicians sought to achieve domestic ends. Accordingly, Bismarck's policies in the 1860s are now sometimes interpreted primarily as a continuation of his domestic struggle to contain liberal, constitutional trends within Prussia. No sooner had he come to power in 1862 than the conservative *Kreutzzeitung* predicted that he would 'overcome domestic difficulties by a bold foreign policy'. Bismarck himself observed at the same time that 'as long as we gain respect abroad, we can get away with a great deal at home'. His ambiguous attitude towards liberal principles (*see* section **E**) and his bid for a rapprochement with the liberals from a position of great strength after the victory of Sadowa (*see* section **J**) both suggest that there are grounds for viewing the events of the 1860s from this domestic angle.

Prussia and the Polish revolt

Prussia's position with regard to her major European neighbour, Russia, was improved by factors arising from the Polish revolt of January 1863. The reaction of the Prussian government was to send General von Alvensleben to St Petersburg (February 1863) to offer a convention whereby Russian troops would be allowed to pass through Prussian territory in pursuit of Polish rebels. It was not a startling concession, considering what Prussian Junkers stood to lose from a peasants' revolt, but it contrasted favourably with France's pro-Polish stance and with Austria's Crimean 'betrayal'.

Historians have found it hard to agree upon the merits of the so-called Alvensleben Convention. Erich Eyck followed a traditional line in viewing it as a significant diplomatic success, guaranteeing the future goodwill of Russia. D. G. Williamson and others have disagreed, seeing the Convention in the short term as a serious error which alienated Prussian liberals and made it harder to achieve the rapprochement that Bismarck was seeking with France. In the longer term, however, it remains true that Russia was to acquiesce in Prussia's destruction of the central European balance of power. There was to be no Olmütz in the 1860s.

Austria and the *Zollverein*, 1862–65

Two further issues cemented Prussia's position within Germany. By signing a trade agreement with France in 1862, Prussia theoretically violated existing *Zollverein* treaties. This gave Austria the chance, her last as it happened, to make alternative economic proposals to the princes. Their rejection of these overtures, their acceptance of the Franco–Prussian agreement, and their conclusion of a renewed *Zollverein* treaty, excluding Austria (1865), confirmed Prussia's economic leadership of Germany.

Austria seemed to be on firmer ground on political leadership. The Emperor's decision (August 1863) to summon an Assembly of Princes (*Fürstentag*) to discuss reform of the Confederation, seemed likely to confirm her position and the duality of power within Germany. At Bismarck's insistence, Wilhelm refused to acknowledge Austrian leadership by attending, and refused to accept the reform proposals drafted there. As events were to prove, this was the last attempt to unite Germany by princely consent. Thus Austria's

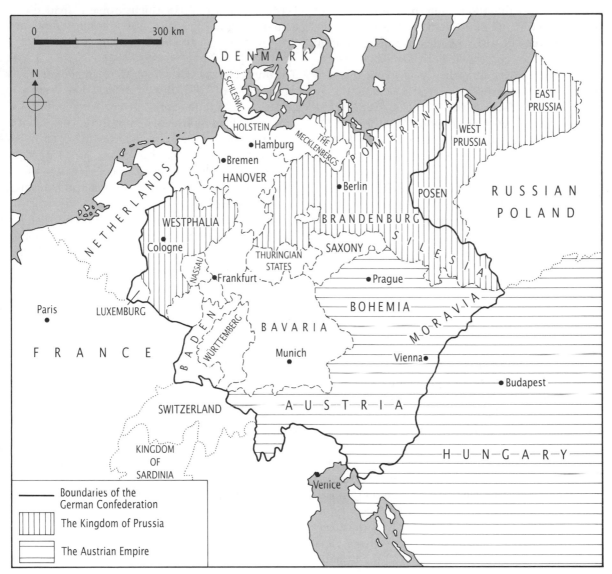

Germany and Central Europe, 1815–66

traditional claim to speak and act for the princes as a whole was open to doubt at the moment when the next crisis of German nationalism erupted.

G Schleswig-Holstein

The crisis and war of 1863–64

The issue of the two duchies on the borders of Germany and Denmark was an old one, and had last come to a head in 1848. The problem arose from a mixed population and from a confusion of dynastic and semi-feudal claims. Schleswig, to the north, was predominantly Danish, while Holstein had a substantial German majority and was actually a member of the German Confederation. The territories were technically subject to the king of Denmark, but enjoyed a large degree of legal and administrative independence. The crisis of 1848 had arisen from the support of the middle-class, nationalist Holsteiners for the Duke of Augustenburg, whose son continued the family's bid for local power in the 1860s. The pre-1848 status of both Schleswig and Holstein was confirmed by the major powers in 1852 by the so-called London Protocol. This confirmed both Danish overlordship and the liberties of the duchies and thus left both parties dissatisfied.

A renewed crisis was precipitated in 1863 by the decision of the new Danish monarch, Christian IX, to regulate the situation in his country's favour. The reaction of German nationalists to this initiative is well illustrated by the declaration of the Prussian liberal, Karl Twesten, that he 'would rather suffer the Bismarck ministry for some years longer than allow a German land to be lost to us'. Bismarck, too, stood to benefit from intervention. In the first place he could not tolerate the increase in the prestige of the German Confederation that would result from an easy victory over Denmark. It seems clear, too, that he always had in mind the ultimate annexation of the duchies. This was not primarily a piece of crude land hunger, but predominantly a means by which to confirm his position in the eyes of King Wilhelm.

At no stage did Bismarck pretend to be acting in the interests of nationalism, writing that 'it is no concern of ours whether the Germans of Holstein are happy'. Nor is it seriously maintained any longer that this was a cynical trap to lure Austria into military commitment and to create the basis for future tensions. The alliance by which the two German powers agreed to joint action (January 1864) was necessary to avoid Austrian jealousy, to prevent her leading a force on behalf of the Confederation, and to minimise the fears and resentments of the other signatories of the London Protocol.

The war itself was a very one-sided affair, concluded by the treaty signed in Vienna in October 1864, whereby King Christian renounced both Schleswig and Holstein. After years of wrangles in which the Confederation had put forward the German viewpoint, that body was now totally excluded from the settlement. The claims of the Duke of Augustenburg were also conveniently ignored, and the newly acquired territories were placed under the joint administration of Austria and Prussia. Their ten months of joint rule were marked by squabbles, accusations and threats of war. Yet rather than precipitate a confrontation, Bismarck accepted the conciliatory Convention of Gastein (August 1865) which formally divided the administration. Prussia took responsibility for Schleswig and Austria for Holstein.

The impact of the crisis upon German politics

At the close of 1865, Bismarck had some cause for satisfaction. Quite apart from influence over Schleswig, his actions had demonstrated once more the impotence of the Confederation. Also, far from opposing him, Austria had been party to that demonstration. For the first time in German political affairs in the 19th century, Prussia had led while Austria followed.

Bismarck was also entitled to suppose that he had done something to lessen the hostility of the liberals towards him within Prussia. Otto Pflanze has claimed that, as a result of the blow apparently struck in the German cause, 'almost overnight the Bismarck cult was born. Its devotees began to reinterpret their hero's actions during the preceding four years. They excused his infringements of the constitution in view of what they presumed to have been his hidden purpose.' Others, such as Golo Mann, do not accept that Prussia's liberals were won over so easily. There is little doubt, however, that within the next year Bismarck was to score remarkable triumphs over all his opponents within Germany.

H The Austro–Prussian War

Diplomatic preparations

The idea that the Gastein Convention was a trap deliberately laid by Bismarck to lure Austria into war is no longer widely believed. It might rather be seen as a semi-satisfactory compromise over a delicate set of problems, which allowed Bismarck to win time. In 1864 and in early 1865, war with Austria still posed too much of a risk. By late 1865 and early 1866, however, several of the outstanding uncertainties had been resolved in a manner satisfactory to Prussia. The first such uncertainty was the attitude of France. Bismarck's meetings with Napoleon III at Biarritz and at St Cloud (October–November 1865) left him confident of French neutrality in the event of an Austro–Prussian conflict. It is far from certain if any promises of territorial compensation were made (*see* Chapter 3, section **T**) and it may be that the most important outcome was Bismarck's realisation that Napoleon's main desire was to remain at peace. Secondly, the attitude of Italy was clarified. A new trade treaty with the *Zollverein* (December 1865) had not fully won Italy over to the Prussian camp, but the failure of her friendly approaches to Austria had decided her course by April 1864 (*see* Chapter 4, section I). By the military alliance then concluded, Italy agreed to fight with Prussia against Austria, with Venetia as her reward. The condition was also laid down that the war should begin within three months. Bismarck had ensured by this diplomacy that he would fight only on one front, while Austria fought on two. He had also ensured that the issue would be decided by war. In May, as a last bid for peace, Austria actually agreed to acknowledge Prussian supremacy in northern Germany, but demanded the retention of Venetia as a condition, forcing Bismarck to reject the offer because of his commitment to Italy.

The war and its outcome

Ostensibly, the war that began with the Prussian invasion of Holstein in June was about the administration of the duchies. Prussia accused the Austrian authorities of violating their mutual agreements by sheltering refugees from the harsh Prussian rule in Schleswig. Clearly, Austria was also in breach of the Gastein Convention when she referred this dispute to the German Confederation. These were obviously convenient excuses. The war was really a trial of Prussian strength, postponed from 1850, against Austria and against the Confederation, which was Austria's main power base within Germany. It was apt that Prussia also went to war with Saxony, Hanover, Bavaria, Württemberg, Baden, Hesse-Darmstadt, Hesse-Cassel and Nassau. In a very real sense this was a war for the conquest at least of northern Germany.

In the war itself the German states proved to be ineffectual allies. Their forces failed to link effectively with those of Austria, and they were eliminated from the conflict in a series of engagements conveniently ignored by subsequent nationalist historians, at Langensalza, Dormbach, Kissingen and Rossbrunn. On the all-important Bohemian front the decisive action was fought at Sadowa (alternatively known as the Battle of Königgrätz) on 3 July. Superior Prussian infantry tactics and armaments ensured heavy Austrian losses (roughly 20,000 to Prussia's 9,000) and left open the road to Vienna. The rapid conclusion of an armistice at Nikolsburg three weeks later was the result of compelling pressures on both sides. The Austrians were motivated by nationalist 'rumblings' in Bohemia and Hungary, while Bismarck had reason to fear the reactions of France and Russia to Prussia's extraordinary triumph. In combating the strong desire of King Wilhelm and his generals for territorial gains, Bismarck was thinking not only of foreign jealousy and the future balance of power, but also of the danger of the conservative Prussian state and administration overreaching itself. 'Our power finds its limits,' he wrote at the time, 'when the supply of Junkers to fill official posts gives out.'

I The Treaty of Prague

Prussia's defeat of Austria, which was enshrined in the Treaty of Prague (23 August 1866), caused a greater disruption to the European state system and to the balance of power than any other event since the defeat of Napoleon. The contemporary German historian Gregorovius captured the importance of the event with only a little exaggeration. 'The entire Prussian campaign has no parallel in the history of the world. The consequences of the Battle of Sadowa are at least as follows: the unification of Germany through Prussia, the consummation of Italian independence, the fall of the temporal power of the Papacy, the deposition of France from the dominion she has usurped over Europe'.

In more sober detail, the treaty allowed Prussia to annex Hanover, Hesse-Cassel, Nassau, Frankfurt and Schleswig-Holstein. By recognition of her right to form all German territories north of the River Main into a new North German Confederation, Prussia achieved the death of the old German Confederation. A seven-week military campaign had thus untied a knot that had defied decades of diplomatic wrangling. Austria suffered no territorial loss, apart from Venetia. Instead, she surrendered to Prussia the only prize that Bismarck really desired, her prestige and status within Germany. Nevertheless, the defeat had profound long-term effects upon the Austrian Empire. At a stroke she was banished from the political affairs of both Germany and Italy. The only direction in which she could now seek prestige and expansion was towards the south-east, towards the Balkans. This was a factor that was to have grave consequences in 1914. For the time being she turned in on herself, reassessing her internal strength and revising her internal organisation. The most important product of these processes was the Compromise (*Ausgleich*) of 1867, by which Hungary was recognised as a constitutional monarchy, free from Austrian interference in her internal affairs and united to her only through the person of her king (*see* Chapter 10, section **M**).

J   The 'surrender' of the Prussian liberals

The Act of Indemnity

The events of 1866 also provided Bismarck with a notable domestic triumph. The Prussian liberal movement had now to decide upon its reactions to this partial unification of Germany. It had sought unification for decades, but had consistently condemned the means by which it had now been achieved. Many were intoxicated by Bismarck's success. 'I bow before the genius of Bismarck,' wrote a previously consistent critic, von Schering. 'I have forgiven the man everything he has done up to now. More, I have convinced myself that it was necessary.' Johannes Miquel insisted that his fellow liberals should now be practical. 'Today more than ever before politicians must ask, not what is desirable, but what is attainable.' In this atmosphere, Bismarck chose the moment perfectly to approach the Reichstag with an admission that he had acted illegally over the past four years, and to request their pardon in the form of an Act of Indemnity. He was duly pardoned by 230 votes to 75. The Progress Party split on the issue and a new political party, the National Liberals, emerged. The new party remained devoted to the principles of free trade and the rule of law, but for the present shared common ground with Bismarck in its enthusiasm for a strong German state.

The relationship between Bismarck and the liberals

Did Prussian liberalism 'sell out' to Bismarck? The answers of historians have tended to reflect the authors' views on liberalism, or on the German state founded by Bismarck. To Heinrich von Sybel, a patriotic contemporary, the Act of Indemnity was an enlightened and moderate compromise. More recently, Otto Pflanze has accused the liberals of surrendering to success. They were the victims, he claims, 'of their own limited ends, their lack of genuine popular support, and their lust for national power'.

It is also important to understand that the relationship between Bismarck and the liberals was more complex than simple confrontation. Although the division between them over constitutional issues was deep, there was scope for genuine co-operation on other, more practical matters. Bismarck retained genuine sympathy for some of the economic priorities of the liberals, and promoted them actively in the aftermath of the constitutional crisis. His succession of trade treaties, for instance, with Belgium, Britain, France and Italy served both parties, catering for the economic principles of the liberals and confirming at the same time Prussia's dominance within the *Zollverein*.

Equally, as the 1860s progressed, both sides could find much to attract them in a policy of *kleindeutsch* national unity. It is not satisfactory to see Bismarck's confrontation with the Prussian liberals in 1862–63 simply as a prelude to the 'real' business of foreign policy. Until the late 1870s, it remained an important priority for Bismarck in domestic politics to maintain some form of working relationship with the liberals. This factor must be borne in mind in assessing what passed between them in 1866.

K   The North German Confederation

The dominance of Prussia

The greatest reality of the new North German Confederation, created by the Treaty of Prague, was that it rested upon military conquest by Prussia. The true nature of Prussian domination was clearly illustrated by the case of Hanover, where a long-established dynasty was deposed and the fortune of its king confiscated. Similarly, in Schleswig-Holstein, Prussia continued to ride roughshod over the Augustenburg claims. Of the 23 states that associated themselves by treaty in the North German Confederation, Prussia supplied five-sixths of the population. The constitution of the Confederation, however, was a compromise. It was a synthesis between Bismarck's original, rigidly conservative ideas, and liberal attempts to preserve some measure of parliamentary liberty. Why, given the power of his position, did Bismarck compromise? Gordon Craig answers that he deliberately attempted to create a viable parliament so as to play it off against the separatist tendencies of the governments of the member states. Perhaps, as Erich Eyck suggests, he also made liberal concessions in the hope that future membership would thus be more inviting to the southern states.

The constitution of the Confederation

As a result of these concessions the North German Parliament (*Norddeutscher Reichstag*) enjoyed voting by secret ballot, election by universal manhood suffrage, freedom of speech and the freedom to publish its debates. The liberals also succeeded in forcing the administration to submit the budget, which was nearly all for military expenditure, for the Reichstag's approval every four (later extended to every seven) years.

On the other hand, Bismarck retained substantial freedom of action. Most taxes were indirect, from *Zollverein* customs and duties, and were therefore beyond the control of the Reichstag. The Federal Chancellor (Bismarck himself) was the only 'responsible' minister, and it was far from clear to whom he was 'responsible'. Indeed, there were no other federal ministers to impede Bismarck. Finally, the initiation of legislation was in the hands of the Federal Council (*Bundesrat*), made up of appointed representatives of the states' governments. This was effectively the old Federal Diet, but now firmly under the presidency and control of Prussia.

L The southern states

Particularism in the south

It is probable that Bismarck had no clear plans for further action at the end of 1866. 'There is nothing more to do in our lifetime,' he had written to his wife. Yet the problem of the southern German states remained, their position problematical and paradoxical. Strong separatist forces survived south of the River Main. Of four southern states, only

Baden, whose Grand Duke was son-in-law to the king of Prussia, showed any real enthusiasm for union with the north. In Hesse, popular enthusiasm for union was offset by the hostility of the government, while in Bavaria and Württemberg opposition to the north was more general. A strong Democratic Party in Württemberg remained hostile to Prussian absolutism, while in Bavaria dynastic jealousy and staunch anti-Protestantism combined with a widespread dislike of Prussian militarism. As late as 1869, the election of a large Catholic majority in the Bavarian assembly seemed to confirm the strength of separatism.

Weaknesses of the southern settlement

Why, then, could the south not be left alone? In part, there was the danger of what allies the southern states might find if they were not the friends of Prussia. The Austrian Emperor, for instance, had given clear notice that he did not necessarily regard the Treaty of Prague as a final and irreversible settlement by appointing the former Saxon premier, Friedrich Ferdinand von Beust, as his foreign minister. France, too, tentatively sought friends south of the Main. Secondly, pressure for further progress came from the liberal nationalists of the north who, like Johannes Miquel, refused to see the River Main as more than 'a preliminary stop where the engine has to refuel and rewater in order to continue the journey'.

Most important was the fact that the separate existence of the southern states was a sham. Mainly because of the mutual jealousy of Württemberg and Bavaria, the southern states were unable to translate the vague phrases of the Treaty of Prague concerning a southern union into any form of reality. As a result they were effectively dependent upon Prussia in both military and economic terms. Members of the *Zollverein* already, the southern states had little choice after 1866 but to accept Prussian proposals for a 'Customs Parliament' that would add political links to existing economic ones. Even so, by electing a majority favourable to separatism, the southern states continued to keep their distance.

The most effective link between the new Confederation and the south was, therefore, the string of military treaties that Bismarck concluded with the southern states in August 1866. These placed Prussia in the position recently vacated by Austria, as their protector. Already, by the end of 1866, war appeared the most likely cause of further German unification.

M Germany and France: the Luxemburg question

Napoleon III and the new German state

The key diplomatic questions raised by the events of 1866 concerned future German relations with France. In the memoirs that he published after his fall from office Bismarck professed to have believed that a conflict with France was an inevitable step along the path to further national unity. In fact, his view at the time was certainly less clear than that. It was based upon the assumption that Napoleon III could not simply accept the changes of 1866, but not upon any clear notion of the form or timing of the Emperor's response. 'Napoleon III,' he wrote at the time, 'has lost more prestige than he can afford. To recover it he will start a dispute with us on some pretext or other. I do not believe that he personally wishes war, but his insecurity will drive him on.'

The Luxemburg project and its failure

After initial probes in the direction of Belgium or the Rhineland, Napoleon's 'policy of compensation' settled upon the Grand Duchy of Luxemburg as its object. The French proposals concerning Luxemburg have already been described (*see* Chapter 3, section **U**). What concerns us here is the German reaction to those proposals. It does not seem possible to maintain any longer that Bismarck trapped or tricked the French Emperor over the Luxemburg question. On the contrary, most recent commentators have agreed that he was quite content to cede the territory and its fortifications to France as the price for placating her and preserving the stability of his new North German creation. What he would not do was to commit himself publicly to that policy when he badly needed the support of the liberal nationalists in the Reichstag.

The insistence of the king of Holland that he would not sell Luxemburg without the specific agreement of Prussia was thus the factor that killed the deal. Bismarck did not initiate the nationalist outcry that now condemned the loss of any 'ancient German land', but he was powerless to act against

it. Prussia effectively gained nothing from the international conference (May 1867) that agreed to the neutralisation of Luxemburg and to the removal of the Prussian garrison. France was not placated, and the strategic position of Germany was not strengthened. Bismarck's only consolation came from the increased unease that now arose in the southern states about French ambitions. When Erich Eyck wrote that 'the Luxemburg affair was the turning point in Bismarck's development from a Prussian to a German statesman', he meant it not in the sense that the Chancellor had undergone a conscious conversion, but in the sense that, for the first time, he had lost the initiative. He had been carried along further than he wished by a force that he had previously exploited with confidence.

N Germany and France: the Hohenzollern candidature

The origins of the candidature

The peace of western Europe survived the Luxemburg crisis with some ease, only to perish three years later over a most unlikely confrontation. In September 1868, revolution in Spain overthrew the ruling house of Bourbon. By the beginning of 1869 the Spanish throne had already been rejected by a number of candidates who placed too high a value upon a quiet life. The candidature was then taken up by Prince Leopold von Hohenzollern-Sigmaringen, a member of the Catholic branch of the Prussian ruling house. By the following February Spanish representatives were busy overcoming the misgivings of the prince, of his father, Prince Karl Anton, and of the Prussians. The Prussian government insisted throughout that the candidature must at no time appear to be official state policy.

With King Wilhelm's permission grudgingly given (June 1870), the project seemed able to go ahead as long as speed and secrecy presented France with a *fait accompli*. Under such circumstances their obvious objections to a monarch with Prussian sympathies on their southern border, would be outflanked. That hope, however, was thwarted by misunderstanding and delay in Madrid. In early July, before the Spanish parliament could formally decide upon their king, the French ambassador received official confirmation of the rumours that he had already heard.

The French response and the Ems Telegram

The reaction of the French foreign ministry (*see* Chapter 3, section **V**) was strong enough, and had sufficient backing elsewhere in Europe, to kill the Hohenzollern candidature. Clumsy French attempts, however, to extract a promise from King Wilhelm that the project would never be renewed, seemed to call into question the royal and the national honour. This gave Bismarck the chance to snatch from the Spanish affair greater advantage than had ever seemed possible. By releasing to the press an edited version of the telegram in which the king reported his conversation with the French ambassador at Bad Ems (the 'Ems Telegram'), Bismarck gave the impression that a blunt exchange of diplomatic insults had taken place. He once more took control of the nationalist forces that had served him so well in the past. Faced with the choice of retreat or further confrontation, France declared war (19 July), initiating a conflict in which a united German state was to be forged.

Bismarck's role in the candidature

In his memoirs, Bismarck was eager to convey the impression of total detachment from the Hohenzollern affair, and to charge the disruption of European peace to the insolence and instability of the French regime. More recent research, especially by G. Bonnin and Erich Eyck, however, has clearly demonstrated Bismarck's close links with the candidature. These range from the initial distribution of bribes, through the difficult process of convincing King Wilhelm of the strategic advantages of the project, to the final affair of the 'Ems Telegram'.

It is difficult to doubt that Bismarck engineered the candidature, but that does not necessarily mean that he did so with a view to precipitating war. Indeed, as Agatha Ramm has pointed out, it was only by accident that the French government found out about the candidature in time to react at all. It is better, therefore, to see Bismarck's aim as being to outmanoeuvre and surround France in such a way as to force her to accept further Prussian aggrandisement without a fight. The thwarting of the plan, rather than the plan itself, left him with no other means than war by which to create stronger links between the northern and southern German states. He could have had unity without war, but only through war could he guarantee that such unity would rest upon a basis of Prussian military domination. This was the only basis acceptable to Bismarck and to those he served.

O 1870: the completion of German unity

The impulse towards unity

The series of military factors by which the Franco–Prussian War was won and lost is described in Chapter 3. Of greater importance here is the series of political developments that accompanied the war, and by which a unified German Empire was formed.

At the outbreak of the war, a powerful combination of factors ensured that the southern states would honour their treaty obligations to Prussia. Not least among these was the popular enthusiasm that Karl Marx dismissed contemptuously as 'south German beer patriotism'. Much pressure also came from the leaders of the National Liberals, especially from Eduard Lasker, who organised persuasive propaganda campaigns south of the Main. The Crown Prince of Prussia, Friedrich, was also a consistent advocate of unity and of the claim of the Hohenzollerns to the Imperial German crown. Although once more events were moving beyond Bismarck's control, he too played his role by the well-timed publication of France's earlier compensation proposals, a frightening revelation for the southerners.

Deciding the form of unity

While the generals, to the chagrin of the Chancellor, kept the conduct of the war closely under their own control, Bismarck's prime concern was to negotiate a settlement with the southern states that would turn a wartime alliance into a permanent union. In this task three main obstacles needed to be overcome: the respective separatisms of Württemberg and Bavaria, and the determination of King Wilhelm not to accept a 'popular' crown, nor to see the Prussian monarchy diminished by becoming a wider, German one.

In the long run, the position of the major southern states was hopeless. They could not rely on each other, could not risk an isolated existence outside an otherwise united Germany, and could scarcely resist growing nationalist enthusiasm inside their own boundaries. Continued separatism, as King Ludwig of Bavaria conceded, 'would be completely impossible politically because of opposition from the army and the people, as a result of which the Crown would lose the support of the country'.

German unity without Austria was assured in November 1870, when a mixture of threats and bribes from Prussian state funds persuaded Ludwig to sign a treaty accepting unification. Bavaria and Württemberg preserved a number of symbols of independence. They retained control over their postal and railway systems, and over their armies in peacetime. This was a small price for Bismarck to pay for an assurance that Wilhelm would now be offered the German crown by the princes, and not by the Reichstag. In the event, that body was merely asked to approve the offer, and did so with enthusiasm. Wilhelm himself had many reservations and regrets about the transformation of his beloved Prussian kingdom. He could at least console himself with the fact that the assembly that proclaimed him 'German Emperor' (not 'Emperor of Germany', for that would have offended Bavarian feelings, and would have raised awkward questions about the extent of 'Germany') at Versailles on 18 January 1871, was an assembly of his fellow monarchs. He had thus remained true to his legitimist philosophy, and had not 'picked up a crown from the gutter'.

Conclusion

Bismarck's great achievement by 1871 was not that he had created a united German state. Many other forces, nationalism and industrialisation, for example, had given him invaluable aid in that process. His great achievement had been to bring about German unity without damaging important conservative elements within the Prussian state. His was a united Germany without true democracy, without parliamentarianism and without Austria. His triumph was a great one. It was a triumph over the radicals, who wanted a different kind of Germany, and over the conservatives, who had been reluctant to take Prussia into any kind of united Germany. Even so, the foundation of the German Empire in this fashion, as T. S. Hamerow has concluded, 'represented the triumph of the mailed fist over the libertarian principle in the life of central Europe'.

Questions

Essay questions

1   'Bismarck's success in enlarging Prussia in the years 1862–71 owed more to "luck" than to "grand design".' Discuss this view. (ULEAC)

2   Why was Bismarck more successful than the liberals of 1848 in unifying Germany? (UCLES)

3   'A masterplanner who pursued the goal of a united Germany'.

   'An opportunist who simply utilised circumstances to create a united Germany'.

   Which of these assessments of Bismarck do you find the more convincing? Give reasons for your choice. (JMB/NEAB)

4   How important was Bismarck to the achievement of the unification of Germany by 1871? (NEAB)

5 a   Explain the attitude of liberal middle-class Germans towards the growth of Prussian power. [7]

   b   Make out a case for the incorporation of the German states south of the River Main (Bavaria, Baden, Württemberg) into the Confederation after 1866. [8]

   c   Would the view that the creation of the Reich was the mere enlargement of Prussia be the one most prevalent in 1871? [10] (WJEC)

6   'Germany united was no more than Prussia enlarged'. Discuss this view of German unification. (Oxford Entrance)

Bismarck, Wilhelm I and the Hohenzollern Candidature

DOCUMENT A
(the numbered notes are referred to in Document B)

Your Majesty,

   Will I trust, graciously permit me with my humble duty to summarise the motives which in my modest opinion speak in favour of the acceptance of the Spanish Crown by His Serene Highness, the Hereditary Prince of Hohenzollern, now that I have already respectfully intimated them by word of mouth.

   For Germany it is desirable to have on the other side of France an ally on whose sympathies (1) we can rely and with whose feelings France is obliged to reckon. During a war between Germany and France it would be necessary to keep at least one French Corps stationed on the Spanish frontier. We have in the long run to look for the preservation of peace not to the good will of France but to the impression created by our position of strength (2).

No danger to the person of the Hereditary Prince need be anticipated. In all the revolutions which have convulsed Spain the idea of an outrage against the person of the Monarch has never arisen, no threat has ever been uttered (3).

I feel a personal need to make it plain by the present humble memorandum that if the outcome is a refusal the responsibility will not lie at my door, especially if in a near or remote future historians and public opinion were to investigate into the grounds which have led to rejection (4).

Von Bismarck (5).

Bismarck to the King of Prussia, 9 March 1870.

DOCUMENT B

(1) How long would these sympathies last?

(2) Agreed.

(3) But the expulsion of the dynasty did take place.

(4) The above marginal notes make it clear that I have strong scruples against the acceptance of the Spanish Crown by the Hereditary Prince of Hohenzollern and would only consent to his acceptance of it if his own conviction told him that it was his duty to mount the Spanish throne, in other words, that he regarded his act as a definite vocation. In these circumstances I am unable to advise the Hereditary Prince to such an act. Wilhelm.

(5) At the discussion which took place in my presence the majority gave adherence to the view put forward by the Minister-President, namely the acceptance of the Spanish throne by the Hereditary Prince. Since, however, the latter upheld his verbal and written declaration that he could only decide on acceptance on my command, the discussion was thereby brought to an end. Wilhelm.

Marginal notes by the King of Prussia to Bismarck's letter (Document A)

DOCUMENT C

When the King heard that the candidature was being further discussed he said that it was 'very extraordinary that this sort of thing was going on without his authorisation'. He wanted to be informed 'of everything that Prim's agent brings either by word of mouth or in writing before any action is taken'.

Report from Thile, Bismarck's principal aide in the Foreign Office, to Bismarck, 19 June 1870.

DOCUMENT D

That beats everything! So his Majesty wants the affair treated with official royal interference? The whole affair is only possible if it remains the limited concern of the Hohenzollern princes. It must not turn into a Prussian concern, the King must be able to say without lying: I know nothing about it.

Bismarck's comments on Thile's report (Document C).

DOCUMENT E

Preparations for war on a large scale are in progress in France. The situation is, therefore, more than serious. Just as I could not bid your son accept the crown, so I cannot bid him withdraw his acceptance. Should he, however, so decide, my 'adherence' will again not be wanting.

King Wilhelm I to Prince Charles Anthony, 10 July 1870.

DOCUMENT F

During dinner at which Moltke and Roon were present, the pronouncement came from the embassy in Paris that the Prince of Hohenzollern had renounced his candidature in order to prevent the war with which France threatened us. My first idea was to retire from the service because I perceived in this extorted submission a humiliation of Germany for which I did not desire to be responsible. I was very distressed for I saw no means of repairing the corroding injury I dreaded to our national position from a timorous policy, unless by picking quarrels clumsily and seeking them artificially. I saw by that time that war was a necessity which we could no longer avoid with honour.

Bismarck discussing 12 July 1870 in his Reflections and Reminiscences, *published 1898.*

---

1   Explain briefly the following references:
a   'it must not turn into a Prussian concern' (Document D)[2]
b   'your son' (Document E) [1]
c   'the corroding injury — — to our national position' (Document F) [2]
2   From a comparison of Documents B,C and E, assess the consistency of the King's attitude to the Hohenzollern candidature. [6]
3   On the evidence of these documents, consider the view that Bismarck treated the opinions of the King with barely concealed contempt. [6]
4   From these documents, and any other evidence known to you, how far would you agree that by 12 July 1870 Bismarck had sustained a major diplomatic defeat entirely of his own making? [8]

(UCLES)

6

The consolidation of Russian conservatism, 1848–94

A work by the Russian artist Vasili Perov, painted between 1865 and 1875 and entitled 'A monastic refectory'.

Where do you think the artist stood in the contemporary debate between westernisers and slavophiles?

What evidence is there in this work of his attitudes towards Russia's past and present?

A The political legacy of Nicholas I

The rejection of liberalism

The reign of Tsar Nicholas I, from 1825 to 1855, represented the highest development of autocratic monarchy in Russia. Yet, like all high points, it contained the main elements that caused its subsequent decline.

The most influential factor in establishing the themes of his reign was the dramatic Decembrist revolt that accompanied his accession. This unsuccessful attempt by liberal intellectuals and army officers in St Petersburg to place his brother Constantine at the head of a constitutional monarchy filled Nicholas with horror. Despite the defeat of France in 1815, and of this blasphemous attempt to undermine the Tsar's god-given authority, he felt revulsion at the spread of radical ideas in Europe. This revulsion was renewed and revivified at intervals, by the deposition of Charles X by the French in 1830, by the Polish revolt of 1831, and by the European revolutions of 1848. His pretension to act as the 'gendarme of Europe' in Wallachia (1848) and in Hungary (1849) typified the role that he felt compelled to play throughout his reign, that of the defender of the old, paternalist discipline against the influences of 'rotten, pagan France'.

Orthodoxy and autocracy

In domestic politics, therefore, Nicholas' reign may be characterised quite accurately by the slogan coined by Uvarov, his minister of education from 1832–49: 'Orthodoxy, Autocracy, Nationality'. Throughout the 19th century the Orthodox Church, with its message of faith in God and unquestioning submission to God's will, was the major support of the Tsarist regime. It endorsed the regime's claim that its power was an expression of the Divine Will. There were numerous other religious groups. Indeed, a commission set up in 1839 reported 9.3 million non-Orthodox Christians in Russia. However, for most of the 19th century it was contended, with varying degrees of coercion, that only members of the Orthodox faith could really be true and reliable subjects of the Tsar.

The autocracy of the Tsar is a more complex concept to grasp. It involved not only authority, but also paternal responsibilities towards his subjects. 'The Tsar is a father', explained a senior police official. 'His subjects are his children, and children ought never to reason about their parents'. To allow children to make decisions about the future of the family would be a dereliction of responsibility by the father. Government in Russia, therefore, remained strictly in the hands of the Tsar, and was exercised through complex and unwieldy machinery. The main tool of government was His Imperial Majesty's Private Chancery. The Third Section of this Chancery was in charge of state security, standing at the centre of a complex web of censorship and surveillance. The work of the censors extended from the strict limitation of any reporting of events in western Europe, to the banning of any criticism of social conditions within Russia. It also involved the control of any careless or dangerous expression in any form of literature. In the reign of Nicholas I the Third Section shadowed some 2,000 persons and dealt with some 15,000 security cases annually.

Westernisers and slavophiles

At the root of the concept of 'nationality' in Uvarov's slogan lay another conviction that dominated the history of Russia in the 19th century. This was the conviction that Russian social organisation, religion, government, culture and philosophy were, by virtue of their very isolation from the mainstreams of western European development, superior. It was thus the duty of all Russians to protect these blessings against all external (i. e. Western) threats. Over the previous century and a half the great philosophical debates in Russia had centred around the struggle between 'westernisers', who desired the spread of some Western technical and philosophical ideas, and 'slavophiles', who wished to preserve and consolidate the essentials of Slav culture, and to spread that culture to non-Slav regions of the Empire. The visible manifestation of this concept of 'nationality' was the general tendency towards the extension of Russian influence over neighbouring territories. To the west, Nicholas made no attempt to imitate Alexander I's grandiose project for a Holy Alliance, yet still showed in 1848 that he shared his brother's deep concern for the political tendencies of neighbouring states. The effect of Western liberalism and nationalism upon Poland was a particular concern. The revolt of 1831 was ruthlessly suppressed and resulted in the abolition of many important elements of Polish national identity. The constitution was withdrawn, the universities closed and the Russian language was more vigorously imposed in Polish public life. To the south, a consistent 19th-century theme was the attempt to convert the declining Turkish Empire into a client of the Russian Empire. Although held in check by the suspicion of the other major powers, Nicholas' continued interest in exerting influence over the Sultan's Orthodox Christian subjects precipitated the Crimean War in 1854 (*see* Chapter 3, section **O**). The most spectacular Russian expansion of the century was to the south and south-east: the acquisition of Persian Armenia (1828), influence over Dagestan and the Caucasus consolidated in the 1830s and 1840s, control over the Uzbeks and the Kazakhs in the same decades, and the establishment of influence in the Far East, typified by the foundation of the aptly named Vladivostok ('Lord of the East') in 1861.

B The social and economic legacy of Nicholas I

Serfdom

The prime social problem of Nicholas' Russia was the institution of serfdom. This legal concept recognised the ownership of one man, woman or family by another, and involved the total subjection of the serf to the will of his or her owner. The moral and practical objections to such a system had been recognised, but swept under the carpet for more than half a century. 'There is no doubt,' Nicholas told the Council of State in 1842, 'that serfdom in its present situation in our country is an evil, palpable and obvious to all, but to attack it now would be something still more harmful.' In 1858, 31 per cent of Russia's population of 74 million, that is some 22.5 million persons, were serfs. In addition over 19 million were 'state peasants', tied to lands owned by the crown. The authority of their owners, sometimes delegated to the elders of the peasant commune (the *mir*), was almost absolute. It extended over the allocation of land, labour dues, taxes and corporal punishment, to the actual sale of the serf to a new master. Under Nicholas I legislation did away with some of the

most inhuman aspects of the institution, forbidding the splitting up of families by the sale of individuals (1833), and banning the auctioning of serfs (1841). The tentative reforms did little to still the peasant discontent that had been a constant feature of Russian politics for a century. There were 712 outbreaks between 1826 and 1854, half of them between 1844 and 1854. Yet two compelling reasons militated against the abolition of serfdom. One was that the monarchy scarcely dared to challenge the vast vested interest of the nobility and landowners, whose financial and social status depended upon the number of 'souls' that they owned. The other was that the monarchy itself derived great benefit, not only as the owner of the 'state peasants', but also because of the allegiance of the serf to the landowner. This was combined with the allegiance of the landowner to the Tsar to constitute the whole political hierarchy upon which the stability of Russia seemed to depend. 'The landowner,' commented Nicholas' Chief of Police, 'is the most faithful, the unsleeping watchdog guarding the state; he is the natural police magistrate.'

Serfdom and industrial backwardness

A further negative result of serfdom, essentially although not exclusively a rural institution, was the restriction that it placed upon the development in Russia of an urban middle class, or of an urban workforce. In 1833 the total urban population was about two million, out of nearly 60 million. Even so, most towns were market and administrative, rather than industrial, centres, and Russia lacked the basis for any serious industrial development on the scale of western Europe. The Soviet historian P. A. Khromov estimated that only 67,000 people were employed in textile manufacture in 1830, and only 20,000 in the iron and steel industries. Russia's cotton industry in 1843 had only 350,000 mechanised spindles to compare with 3.5 million in France and 11 million in Britain. Her share of world iron production dropped, as the industry developed faster abroad, from 12 per cent in 1830 to 4 per cent in 1859. The classic indication of Russia's industrial backwardness was the slow growth of her railways. The first, a short line for the use of the Imperial family from St Petersburg to the summer residence at Tsarskoe Selo, was built in 1837. The first train did not run between St Petersburg and Moscow before 1851.

C Intellectual forces in the mid-19th century

Forces for change

The system of Tsarism survived in Russia for little more than a century after the accession of Nicholas I. It was eventually destroyed, however, by a range of forces that did not exist in 1825. To understand the reigns of Nicholas and of Alexander II, therefore, it is important to appreciate the forces that operated within Russia at that time.

What forces for change existed in the Russia of Nicholas I and how could these forces operate? The Decembrist revolt certainly showed the gap that existed between liberal thinkers and the government, but its failure did not eliminate liberal ideas altogether. Instead such ideas were driven underground and found expression mainly in literature and in the rarified discussions of intellectuals. If those intellectuals were too outspoken in their statements, they might expect severe consequences. Alexander Pushkin, the greatest of Russia's poets, had his work personally censored by the Tsar, and it is possible that his political views contributed to his death in a duel (1837). Pyotr Chaadaev was officially pronounced insane after the publication of an anti-government essay in 1836, and a 'westernising' magazine, *The European*, published by Ivan Kireevski, was close down after only two issues.

Nevertheless, indirect criticism of the existing social system continued to be expressed in more subtle forms. Nikolai Gogol exposed provincial corruption in his play *The Government Inspector* (1836) and satirised the institution of serfdom in his novel *Dead Souls* (1842). The publication of no less than 224 new magazines in the years 1826–54 indicates that ideas continued to circulate in the Russia of Nicholas I, even if the Tsar remained unmoved by most of them. Similarly the number of university students in Russia doubled between 1836 and 1848. This was predominantly due to the government's desire to educate an administrative élite, but inevitably a proportion of this élite would learn to think for themselves. Indeed, one of the most important developments of Nicholas' later years was the emergence of a group identified by W. Bruce Lincoln as the 'enlightened bureaucrats'. These younger officials emerged from the education system into official positions, fully aware of some of the weaknesses of the Russian system, and eager to remedy them if their political masters would permit it. The Milyutin brothers, Dmitri and Nikolai, might fit into this category, and they found influential patrons in such major political figures as Perovski, the minister of internal affairs, and Nicholas' younger son, the Grand Duke Constantine Nikolaevich.

Forces for continuity

The expression of coherent political views was, as we have seen, the preserve of a narrow, educated class élite. The balance of social and political power made it more or less impossible that political change could be brought about by any forces beyond this élite. Even so, it was extremely difficult for members of that élite to express views that conflicted with those of the government.

The greatest weakness of such thinkers was that they had no alternative to Tsarist autocracy, but merely sought to give it a more humane form. They were powerless as long as the Tsar refused to entertain their arguments. The evidence suggests that Nicholas steadfastly refused to do so, not because he rejected change, but because he remained extremely wary about the means of change. As David Saunders has recently concluded, 'the Tsar knew that changes had to be undertaken, but was determined not to allow them to be promoted by any movement or group beyond the control of the government. He believed that reform could be achieved by the government acting alone'. In this respect there was not much difference, after all, between the mentalities of Nicholas I and of Alexander II.

D A crisis for Russian autocracy, 1848–56

Response to the 1848 revolutions

The last years of Nicholas' life were dominated by two great crises: the shock of the revolutions of 1848, and the collapse of much of the regime's prestige in the Crimean War. The main result of the events of 1848–49 was the destruction of any remaining positive elements in Nicholas' paternalism. His plans for intervention in the affairs of other European states were paralleled by stern reaction against any hint of liberalism at home.

Alexander II

Personality and aims

The accession of Alexander II is comparable to the election of Pope Pius IX in terms of the hopes that it raised for an end to blank and sterile political and social reaction. The anarchist Kropotkin recorded that 'at this time in the streets of St Petersburg intellectuals hugged one another, telling each other the good news'. The first actions of the new Tsar, like those of the new Pope in 1846, seemed to justify those hopes. Political prisoners were released, censorship was relaxed, tax arrears were cancelled, and some of the liberties of Poland and of the Catholic Church were restored.

Yet Alexander's motives, like those of Pius, were not liberal in any real sense. Coming to the throne at the age of 36, as undisputed heir, he had been more thoroughly prepared for power than his father had been. He was less of a soldier, less of a disciplinarian, and made more aware by the Crimean War of the faults in the social and governmental systems of Russia. Yet he had no doubts about the institution of autocratic monarchy, and his reforms were motivated by a desire to strengthen autocracy rather than to replace it. We should not imagine that the reforms of the next decade sprang from Alexander's superior political vision. He was not a clever man, and was not at ease in the company of clever men. As a contemporary cruelly noted: 'when the Emperor talks to an intellectual he has the appearance of someone with rheumatism who is standing in a draught'. What then were his motives? Soviet Marxist historians saw emancipation mainly as a means of putting money in the pockets of a regenerated landowning class. Dmitri Milyutin, one of the most prominent of Alexander's reforming ministers, consistently stressed the beneficial impact that emancipation would have upon the army, perhaps because he felt that this was the kind of argument to which his master would be most susceptible.

It may be that Alexander's motives were far less clear-cut than this. As an autocrat, the new ruler recognised it as his duty to rectify a system that had manifestly failed Russia in the Crimea, yet he was uncertain how best to go about the task. Perhaps David Saunders captures the Tsar's state of mind accurately when he concludes that 'the laws which freed the serfs emerged from a process that the Tsar barely understood and over which he had only partial control. Alexander sensed that he was facing a crisis and believed that attack was the best form of defence.' W. E. Mosse and Hugh Seton-Watson both see Alexander II confronting the choice between autocracy and modern constitutional development. Both see him refusing wholly to abandon the former, and failing mainly because he sought to reach an unrealistic compromise between the two. If their analysis is to be questioned, it is only because it is unfair to expect Alexander to have contemplated such a dramatic break with the philosophy of his ancestors. One way or another, therefore, the succession of the new Tsar marked the opening of a period of reform in Russian domestic politics, without any real willingness to recognise the long-term implications of such reforms for the future of Russia.

The campaign against any freedom of thought or expression was typified by the formation of the Buturlin Committee to supervise and regulate the work of the existing censors, and by the attack (April 1849) upon the intellectual circle of M. V. Petrashevsky. This circle was influenced by the works of the French utopian socialists, and included in its ranks the young writer F. M. Dostoevsky. Such a change in governmental attitudes traditionally entailed the appointment of a new minister of education. P. Shirinsky-Shikhmatov duly raised school fees, reduced the number of university students (from 4,600 in 1848 to 3,600 in 1854), and suppressed the study of such dangerous subjects as philosophy and European constitutional law.

Disaster in the Crimea

The justification for such measures was the defence of Slav culture and society from Western infection, so it was inevitable that the conflict in the Crimea should, from a Russian point of view, have wider implications than those directly related to foreign policy. As A. L. Kochan wrote, 'what began as a military trial of strength rapidly developed into a trial of the regime's strength'.

In both trials Russia was found wanting. Allied troops landed on Russian soil at Eupatoria (14 September 1854) and had laid siege to Sevastopol within two weeks, after Menshikov's failure to check their advance at the Battle of the Alma. The year-long siege showed both facets of the Russian military machine. The gallantry of the common soldiers defied all attempts to take the town, but weaknesses of strategy and supply contributed to the defeat of a number of relief operations, at Balaclava (October 1854), at Inkerman (November 1854) and at the Chornaya (August 1855). In the midst of these failures Tsar Nicholas died on 2 March 1855, apologising to his son for the state in which he left his empire.

The implications of the Crimean defeat

A superficial consideration of the peace terms concluded in Paris in 1856 suggests that the results of the defeat were not too severe for Russia. Despite the neutralisation of the Black Sea and the loss of her influence over the Rumanian principalities, Russia was never threatened with the destruction of her 'great power' status as France had been in 1815. The nature and causes of her defeat, however, had more serious implications for the Tsarist regime. Russia's vast military strength had proved to be an illusion. Partly because of the need to maintain forces on other frontiers, but largely because of the lack of a modern system of communications, Russia was never able to muster more than 60,000 of her one million soldiers in the Crimea. Worse still, Russian industry proved largely incapable of equipping these troops properly. It could provide no more than one musket for every two men at the start of the war, and could equip only 4 per cent of Russian troops with the newer, long-range percussion rifle, when 33 per cent of French troops and 50 per cent of British troops used this weapon. As the autocracy justified itself on the grounds that it guaranteed Russian stability and greatness, the defeat in the Crimea seemed to justify comments such as that by the government censor A. V. Nikitenko: 'The main shortcoming of the reign of Nikolai Pavlovich consisted in the fact that it was all a mistake'.

E Emancipation of the serfs

The motives for emancipation

Alexander II remained in essentials an autocrat, but was also responsible for the introduction of the most spectacular social reform of the 19th century. Speaking to the nobility of Moscow in April 1856, and referring both to the Crimean War and to the renewed peasant disturbances, Alexander used the famous phrase that the 'existing order of serfdom cannot remain unchanged. It is better to abolish serfdom from above than to wait for the time when it will begin to abolish itself from below'. It has become clear, however, that this speech did not initiate the discussion of emancipation and that Alexander was reacting to a crisis that was already all too real in Russian politics. The early months of Alexander's reign saw an unparalleled degree of discussion in intellectual, noble and administrative circles, and a remarkable consensus in favour of change. The peasantry too, stirred by the knowledge that wars needed soldiers, and that serf soldiers had traditionally been freed at the end of their military service, was in a state of unusual agitation. Under these pressures Alexander may appear less of a far-sighted reformer than a dutiful ruler with daunting challenges of great complexity.

The process of emancipation

The lapse of five years between Alexander's Moscow speech and the Edict of Emancipation of February 1861 reflected the complexity of the task that the Tsar had undertaken. It also provides some important clues to the forces that shaped the final Edict of Emancipation. Undoubtedly there were those within the government who worked for far-reaching reform that would help to reshape Russian society. Even if, as David Saunders has concluded, 'none of the enlightened bureaucrats of the reign of Alexander II was a social revolutionary, all of them sought greater social fluidity. Like the Tsar, they were determined to maintain order, but they were also anxious to discover new sources of energy.'

Few of the 232,000 serfowners, on the other hand, were sufficiently scared to co-operate unreservedly with the Tsar, and only the Lithuanian nobility accepted his invitation to submit plans for emancipation in their region. The greatest problem was land. To liberate the serfs without land would merely have served to create a vast and dangerous mass of destitute third-class citizens. To grant them land, on the other hand, came dangerously close to accepting the radical doctrine that the land truly belonged to those who worked it.

The terms of the Edict

Ultimately the Edict of Emancipation gave to the serfs their personal freedom over a period of two years, and the land which they had previously worked. Thus 'household serfs', domestic serfs who did not work the land, received no land and constituted a new social problem. For state peasants the period of transition to freedom was five years. The landowners were not expected to surrender land freely, however, and thus to bear the brunt of the measure. In compensation for the land that they transferred to the peasants they received payment in the form of government bonds. To recoup their losses, the government charged the peasants 'redemption dues' in the form of regular repayments over a period of 49 years.

The impact of emancipation

How great a reform was the emancipation? Hugh Seton-Watson stresses its scope and achievement by a valuable comparison with the less peaceful and less successful emancipation of the American negro slaves at the same time. Lionel Kochan, on the other hand, dismisses the emancipation as a 'fraud'. On the one hand, the reform ended an era of Russian social history, and on the other it had a host of implications that detracted from its overall value. In many respects it would be more accurate to say that serfdom was abolished rather than that the serfs had been emancipated. Firstly, the process was slow, dictated by the needs of the individual landowner.

Secondly, the land settlement made upon the ex-serfs was usually unsatisfactory. The areas granted were usually too small, resulting in an average holding of about nine acres, and the landlords rarely hesitated to compensate themselves for the loss of free serf labour by inflating the estimated value of the land. Many peasants thus found themselves saddled with redemption payments far greater than the actual productive value of the land that they farmed.

Thirdly, many peasants were convinced that the land was really theirs in the first place, and thus greatly resented the purchase by redemption payments of their own 'property'. Lastly, although freed from the landowner, the peasant often remained bound to the commune, the *mir*, which continued to exercise many irksome restrictions upon travel and freedom of enterprise.

The persistence of Russia's rural problems

In the shorter run, too, emancipation did not seem to solve the twin problems of rural unrest and industrial backwardness. Nearly 500 outbreaks of violence were recorded in 1861, the worst of which was at Bezdna, in Kazan Province, where 70 peasants were killed by troops. The inadequacy of peasant land holdings ruled out the rapid rise of a prosperous class of peasant consumers. As late as 1878 it was estimated that only 50 per cent of the peasantry farmed allotments large enough for the production of surplus goods, and this proportion failed to increase largely because of a dramatic 50 per cent rise in the rural population of Russia between 1860 and 1897. Nor did the government's reforms help to create a landowning class with the funds for substantial agricultural or industrial investment. The majority of the landowners before emancipation were so deeply in debt that L. Kochan estimates that 248 million of the 543 million roubles paid to them by the government by 1871 was used merely to pay off existing debts and mortgages.

F　Further administrative reform

The *zemstvos*

One inescapable consequence of the emancipation was that the direct government of the localities by serf-owning landlords was broken forever, and needed urgently to be replaced. The intended remedy for this ill was the establishment of the *zemstvos*. These were rural district and provincial assemblies whose functions included the administration of primary education, public health, poor relief, local industry and the maintenance of the highways. Potentially such elected assemblies, supplemented from 1870 by similar urban assemblies, were as radical a measure in an autocracy as the emancipation itself. It is clear, however, that Alexander saw them as props for the autocracy, rather than as a step away from autocracy. Thus the hopes of Russian liberals were dashed almost before they were raised. Both the system of voting and their established local reputations made it easy for the conservative nobility to dominate these assemblies, and at provincial level they occupied 74 per cent of all *zemstvo* seats in 1865–67.

Furthermore, when *zemstvo* bodies had the temerity to suggest that delegates from each assembly should gather to form a central, national body, they were sharply reminded by the Tsar of the limitations upon their powers. This was the point, states Seton-Watson, where Alexander stood at the crossroads between autocracy and liberal reform. Having whetted the appetite for the latter, he remained committed to the former.

Legal, military and educational reforms

The emancipation of the serfs also necessitated substantial reform of the Russian legal system, now that the summary justice of the landlord could no longer be so easily applied in the localities. From 1865 onwards measures were introduced to ensure that legal proceedings were conducted in public, that they were uniform for all classes of society, that a jury system prevailed for the trial of all charges and that judges were independent of the government. These were remarkable reforms, ensuring that, in Seton-Watson's words, 'the court room was the one place in Russia where real freedom of speech prevailed'.

If all these reforms were directly or indirectly a response to the military disasters of the Crimea, then it was only logical that the bases of the Russian military establishment should also be re-examined. Army life, too, had generally reflected the state of Russian society, with privileges for the noble officers and savage penalties for the peasant soldiers. The task of bringing greater equity and efficiency into this system fell to the minister of war, Dmitri Milyutin. He was perhaps the leading liberal figure in Russia in the 1860s, and was hailed by Florinsky and other Russian historians as one of the few outstanding statesmen of imperial Russia. During his tenure of office Milyutin reduced the term of service in the army from the 'life sentence' of 25 years to a period of six years. He also introduced universal military service (1874) to which all males were now liable at 20 years of age, without the loopholes that had frequently allowed the nobility and richer classes to escape the obligation to serve their country. The abolition of more brutal forms of punishment and of military service as a form of punishment for criminal offences went far to humanise conditions in the Russian army. A further victim of Milyutin's reforms were the 'military colonies' to which the sons of long-term recruits had been sent to be trained as the next generation of soldiers.

Lastly, education, always an accurate barometer of the philosophy of Russian governments, was re-liberalised. The minister of education, A. S. Norov, reversed most of the repressive measures of the previous reign. The numbers of university students were allowed to rise again (1855) and lectures were permitted once again on European government (1857) and on philosophy (1860). A new University Statute (1863) gave the universities more autonomy in the conduct of their affairs than at any previous point in their history.

G The growth of radical opposition

Opposition from within the ruling class

Yet the reforms of Alexander II, so far from strengthening and stabilising the regime and earning universal acclaim for the 'Tsar Liberator', drew fierce criticism from most sections of the political spectrum. The Tsar suffered the classic fate of those who try to enjoy the best of both worlds, and became trapped in a crossfire of criticism. Conservatives resented the loss of influence and privilege, while liberals became frustrated at the Tsar's refusal to take his reforms to their logical conclusion. Many governmental departments became the scenes of bitter personal and political rivalries, such as that between Milyutin and P. A. Shuvalov at the ministry of war. The disappointment of conservatives and liberals alike, however, was muted by the need to rally against the more radical and revolutionary forms of opposition that developed as Alexander's reign progressed. This opposition was in some cases fuelled by a fierce ideological hatred of the regime, and encouraged by the freer political atmosphere created by the Tsar's reforms.

From Herzen to nihilism

The most important names on the Russian left in the 1850s and 1860s were those of Alexander Herzen, Nikolai Chernyshevsky and D. I. Pisarev. Herzen, already an exile from Russia by 1848, had moderated his stance as a result of the revolutions of that year and became more willing to accept and applaud reforms, even if they came from the

Tsarist government. His journal *The Bell* (*Kolokol*) was published from London and regularly reached influential persons in Russia by unofficial channels.

Chernyshevsky took the opposite path. Originally part of the literary radicalism of the 1850s and enthusiastic about the emancipation of the serfs, he came to realise that further worthwhile reform was impossible without a fundamental alteration of Russia's political and economic bases. Thus he stands on the threshold of a new generation of Russian radicals who paved the way for the philosophy of the 1917 revolution. Chernyshevsky himself, however, was largely deterred from the further development of his views by the increasing use of violence by those who claimed to be his disciples. Nevertheless his novel *What is to be Done?* (1862) inspired the next generation and provided the title for one of Lenin's most important works.

To a very limited extent Pisarev supplied an answer to Chernyshevsky's famous question. Rejecting revolution as impossible for the present, Pisarev advocated a thorough examination and revision of the moral and material bases of society, in order to provide a better future basis for justice and equality. His followers were advised not to 'accept any single principle on trust, however much respect surrounds that principle'. From this desire to accept nothing of the existing society without question, the novelist Turgenev named this philosophy 'nihilism' (from the Latin *nihil* – nothing). Pisarev liked the term and accepted it.

Populism

Many young radicals were reluctant, however, to wait for revolution as Pisarev thought necessary. Broadly, they envisaged two possible answers to the question 'What is to be done?' One of these was populism, a movement that dominated Russian radicalism in the mid-1870s. The founders of populism, Nikolai Mikhailovsky and Pyotr Lavrov, viewed the Russian peasantry as a force of great revolutionary potential, but as one which needed thorough re-education. Thus in 1874–75 some 3,000 young radicals invaded the countryside to open the eyes of the population to their plight and to the sources of their salvation. This movement 'To the People' was a depressing failure. Hugh Seton-Watson notes that 'some peasants listened with sympathy, many were hostile, and most understood hardly anything of what they heard'.

Over 1,600 of these populists (*narodniki*) were arrested between 1873–77, often handed over to the police by the peasants, blindly loyal to the Tsar, that they sought to help. Learning from these failures, a breakaway group calling itself 'Land and Liberty' (*Zemlya i Volya*) made some progress in the following years with a revised plan that involved living with the peasants for longer periods to learn their mentality better. Perhaps the most lasting legacy of populism was the foundation by members of 'Land and Liberty' of the first unions for Russian industrial workers in Odessa (1875) and in St Petersburg (1878).

The rise of terrorism

For those with equal conviction but less patience, the more attractive alternative was conspiracy and terrorism. The first attempt on the life of the Tsar was in 1866 when a student named Karakozov shot at him in the streets of St Petersburg. The best claim to be the founder of the conspiratorial activism that triumphed in 1917 belongs, however, to Sergei Nechayev. Apparently motivated by a mixture of idealism and ambition, he created a complex system of revolutionary cells up to 1869 by ruthless methods. This system collapsed when internal arguments caused him to murder a fellow conspirator, and the trial that followed gave full publicity to the unsavoury aims and methods of Nechayev. The real 'heyday' of terrorism as a means towards political change followed a split in 1879 in the ranks of 'Land and Liberty'. One wing, led by Georgi Plekhanov and P. B. Axelrod and calling itself the 'Black Partition' (*Chorny Peredyel*), favoured further peaceful work among the peasants. The other, 'The People's Will' (*Narodnaya Volya*), advocated violence as the trigger to general revolution. Although other government officials were among their early victims, their chief target was always the Tsar himself. Within a period of a year Alexander survived another attempt to shoot him (April 1879), an attempt to dynamite the royal train, which blew up the wrong train (December 1879), and an explosion in the banqueting hall of the Winter Palace (February 1880). Although by the end of 1880 the radical opposition within Russia had achieved nothing of worth, many of the methods and preconceptions of the 1917 revolutionaries can be seen in the process of formation during the reign of Alexander II.

H The Polish Revolt, 1863

The nature of the Polish problem

The bitter disillusion felt by Alexander II at the reaction to his role as the 'Tsar Liberator' was not only fed by the troubles that followed the emancipation of the serfs, but also by the revolt of his Polish subjects in 1863. Poland had fallen under the power of the Tsars as a result of a compromise made at the Congress of Vienna in 1815. Rather than allow the former independent kingdom of Poland to become part of the Russian Empire, the allies had preserved her nominal independence, but had allowed the Tsar to rule as King of Poland, thus effectively combining the two states. This special status, and the vague paternalism of Alexander I, had combined to give Poland rather freer institutions than existed anywhere else in eastern Europe. Poland enjoyed a constitution, a parliament, and the use of Polish as an official language. The first Polish rebellion (1830) had resulted, however, in the suppression of many of these liberties by Nicholas I. Nevertheless, Poland like other parts of the Empire, had reason to greet the accession of Alexander II with optimism. His conciliatory gestures included the filling of the vacant Catholic archbishopric of Warsaw (1856) and the formation of a new Agricultural Society (1857) to promote new techniques of cultivation.

The revolt and its consequences

On the surface it appeared that, as in the rest of the Empire, the question of land reform was the most pressing of Poland's problems. Unlike the rest of the Empire, however, the demand for such reform was directly connected with the desire to re-establish Polish nationhood, a desire to which no Tsar could accede. It was nationalist demonstrations in Warsaw that set off a train of events in February 1861. In April the Agricultural Society was dissolved on account of its links with the nationalist unrest, and in the resultant demonstrations up to 200 were killed. In May 1862 the Tsar's brother, Constantine, who had the reputation of a conciliatory liberal, was appointed viceroy in an attempt to defuse the situation. He came close to assassination in his first month in office. A series of further concessions was proposed, including the emancipation of Polish Jews and the opening of a university in Warsaw, but a proposal for the conscription of Poles into the Russian army nullified any calming effect, and armed insurrection broke out in January 1863.

It was largely a rural rebellion, with the majority of the landowners more or less favourable to the rebels, but with the attitude of the peasants remaining highly ambiguous. It took nearly a year to control and was not properly over until August 1864. In that year agrarian reform was at last carried through, giving freehold tenure to 700,000 peasant families, without any redemption payments to the Russian government. Although Hugh Seton-Watson sees the reform mainly as an attempt to separate the peasants from the nationalist landowners, it was in the tradition of relatively liberal treatment used by Russia towards Poland between 1855–63. Its general failure was seen by the Tsar as further evidence of ingratitude and of the futility of conciliatory gestures. In reality the failure demonstrated the impossibility of reconciling such beliefs as Polish nationalism with Tsarist autocracy. Henceforth Russian policy towards all the nationalities of the Empire would be one of russification.

I The death of Alexander II

Alexander's return to reformism

By the beginning of the 1880s Alexander II was, in the words of W. E. Mosse, 'isolated from the Russian people, unpopular with the educated public, and cut off from the bulk of society and the Court. His fate had become a matter of indifference to the majority of his subjects'. This was largely the result of his vacillation between two policies, but even at court he was increasingly unpopular because of his embarrassing passion for the much younger Princess Dolgoruky. She bore Alexander a number of illegitimate children, and he married her with indecent haste upon the death of his first wife in 1880. The passion contributed directly to the further confusion of imperial policy in the last years of Alexander's life. While the Tsar grew more and more disillusioned and conservative, the princess remained the friend and patron of a number of liberal politicians. Thus the government's reaction to the violence of 1879–80 was a mixture once again of repression and concession. Executions took place, but the major political event was the appointment as minister of the interior of Mikhail Loris-Melikov, a member of Princess Dolgoruky's liberal circle.

The Loris-Melikov ministry

Despite the misgivings of the Tsar, Loris-Melikov had, within a year (January 1880– February 1881), abolished the Third Section, replaced the reactionary Dmitri Tolstoy at the Ministry of Education, and steered the Tsar to the verge of the most fundamental reform of his reign. By February 1881 plans were prepared for the calling of a national assembly, partly of nominated members, but partly of elected representatives of the *zemstvos* and the town councils. It was thus a limited body, but a logical and significant step away from total autocracy. The Soviet historian P. A. Zaionchkovsky concedes that 'in the conditions of an increasingly complex situation it might have been the beginning of the establishment of a parliamentary system in Russia'. The Tsar had just given his personal approval to the measure when the luck of the 'People's Will' changed, and on 13 March Alexander was killed by the second of two bombs thrown at his sledge in a St Petersburg street.

J   Alexander III and the return to reaction

The formation of the new Tsar's philosophy

The heir to the throne was Alexander's son by his first marriage, who succeeded as Alexander III. The death of his father did not initiate the conservatism of the son, but the horrible circumstances of that death, and the cruel irony of its timing confirmed it most strongly. 'Alexander III,' wrote Hugh Seton-Watson, 'was a true Russian. He knew his people. He would not sacrifice the truly Russian principle of autocracy.' The greatest influence on the views of the new Tsar came from his former tutor and trusted adviser, Konstantin Pobedonostsev. Pobedonostsev's sympathies lay with autocracy against democracy, with Orthodoxy against all other sects, and with Russians against all other nationalities of the Empire. For him universal suffrage was 'a fatal error'; the principle of the sovereignty of the people was 'among the falsest of political principles'; parliamentarianism was the 'triumph of egoism'; the freedom of the press was

'one of the falsest institutions of our time'. As Pobedonostsev also served the new Tsar as tutor to his eldest son, Nicholas, his influence stretched unbroken from 1881 to the turmoil of 1905.

Pan-slavism

Although of less direct influence, another major 'prophet' of the new temper in Russian thought, and especially in Russian foreign policy, was Nikolai Danilyevski. In his most influential work, *Russia and Europe* (1871), he rejected the enthusiasm of westernisers for Western philosophy and technology, and argued that as Russia had a quite different history and development, she should ignore the Roman and Germanic worlds and concentrate upon her Slav nature and inheritance. This view differed from the old slavophile notions in that it was more aggressive, preaching a union of all Slav nations under Russian leadership stretching from the Baltic to the Adriatic. This regeneration of aggressive, autocratic nationalism was called pan-slavism.

Conservative legislation, 1882–92

It was scarcely surprising that the bomb that destroyed Alexander II also destroyed the careers of his more liberal ministers and the policies that they advocated. Loris-Melikov was replaced as minister of the interior by Nikolai Ignatiev, who later gave way to Dmitri Tolstoy. At the heart of the new policy lay the hope of restoring the Russian nobility to the position of strength and influence that it had held before the emancipation. In July 1889 the office of justice of the peace was abolished in local government and a new office, that of Land Commandant (*Zemsky Nachalnik*) was created. The essential qualification for this office was membership of the nobility, and the holder enjoyed senior administrative and judicial power in the locality, over-riding the authority of the *zemstvos*. The partly elective *zemstvo* became a prime target for the reactionaries. Laws of 1890 and 1892 revised the franchise in rural and urban assembly elections to restrict the popular vote. In St Petersburg the combined effect of the laws was to reduce the electorate from 21,000 to 7,000. Furthermore, the assemblies frequently found their most apolitical proposals obstructed and undermined by the objections of a government fundamentally opposed to the principle of elected assemblies.

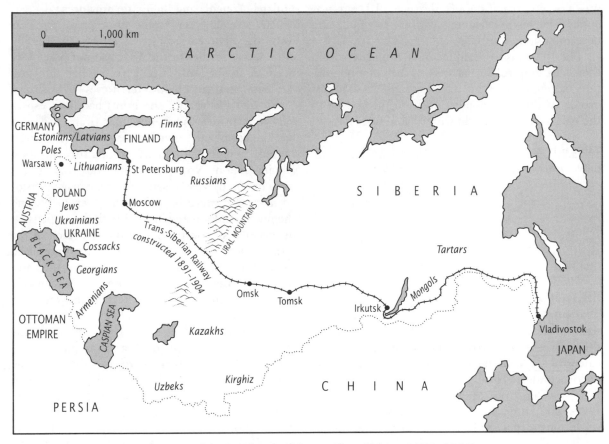

The Russian Empire and its nationalities, 1815–1917

Russian intellectual life in a period of reaction

Naturally, educational policy also felt the impact of this revision of government thinking. The minister of education from 1882 to 1898 was I. V. Delyanov, a man essentially opposed to any 'dangerous' advance in education such as had been proposed in the reforms of Alexander II. Policies towards the universities included the limitation of their administrative autonomy (1884) and the raising of their tuition fees (1887). The raising of fees was also a useful method in primary and secondary education to ensure that the 'children of coachmen, servants, cooks, washerwomen, small shopkeepers, and persons of similar type should not be brought out of the social environment to which they belong'. Only parish elementary schools, safely under the influence of the local clergy, were allowed any real expansion during Delyanov's term of office.

Consequently, by the end of the 19th century Russia presented a bizarre educational paradox.

Her élite contained some of the most famous figures of the century: scientists (Pavlov, Mendeleiev), writers (Chekhov, Tolstoy, Gorky), historians (Klyuchevsky), musicians (Tchaikovsky) of world repute. Yet this brilliant surface of Russian society hid a substructure of rottenness and ignorance represented as late as 1897 by a staggering illiteracy rate of 79 per cent.

K Russification

Nationalism and the Tsarist regime

Referring specifically to Poland, the conservative writer and publicist Y. F. Samarin had described nationalism in the 1860s as 'a dissolving agent as dangerous, in a different way, as the propaganda of Herzen'. The policy of russification, that is of attempting to suppress the local characteristics of various regions within the Empire, and to spread Russian characteristics to all the Tsar's subjects, was not an invention of Alexander III but was applied by his government with fresh vigour and determination.

The Russians were, in fact, in a minority within their vast empire, 55 per cent of the total population belonging to other racial groups. The largest groups within the population were, according to the census of 1897, as shown in Table 6.1.

Table 6.1 Nationalities of the Russian Empire, 1897

Great Russians	55.6 million
Ukrainians	22.4 million
Poles	7.9 million
White Russians	5.8 million
Jews	5.2 million
Tartars	3.4 million
Germans	1.8 million
Armenians	1.2 million
Georgians	0.8 million

'Disloyal' subjects

The total population of the Empire at that time was a little over 125 million. J. N. Westwood has divided these racial groups into three main political categories, which he labels 'mainly loyal, mainly disloyal and the Jews'.

In the 'disloyal' category it was of course the Poles who, after the nationalist outbreak of 1863, could most expect to be the subject of rigid russification. The measures taken by the subsequent governors of defeated Poland, F. F. Berg (1864–74) and P. Kotzebue (1874–80), set the pattern for future policies elsewhere. The property of the Polish Roman Catholic Church was seized (1864) and Warsaw's university was closed (1869). Russian replaced Polish as the administrative language, and more and more Russians replaced Poles in the ranks of the administrators. Similar measures were adopted in the Ukraine, but there, as there had been no comparable nationalist demonstrations, they were mainly directed against a small group of radical intellectuals. The other main components of the 'disloyal' group were the Tartars and the Georgians. In both cases the Orthodox Church played a leading role on behalf of the state, converting an estimated 100,000 Tartars by 1900, and fighting a fierce conflict, that went as far as political assassination in some cases, against the Georgian Church. Islam and the Georgian Church both put up fierce resistance, however, and the problem of separatism among the Tartars and the Georgians was still very much alive in 1917.

Finland, Armenia and the Baltic provinces

Much more damaging to the autocracy of the Tsar were the counter-productive efforts to 'russify' areas whose loyalty to the Tsar had not previously been in doubt. Into this category fell Finland, Armenia and the Baltic territories of Estonia, Latvia and Lithuania. The Finns had been especially well treated under Alexander II and had even had the use of their own language not merely permitted, but actually made compulsory in local administration. Now disadvantageous trade tariffs were imposed, Russians and their language intruded more and more into Finnish government, and the process culminated in 1903 with the suspension of the Finnish constitution, a direct breach of the terms upon which Alexander I had absorbed Finland into the Empire in 1815. The Armenians, too, were essentially well disposed to Russian rule which had done much to protect them from their major enemy, the Turks. Their reward, under Alexander III, included the confiscation of the property of the Armenian Church and the suppression of the Armenian language. Similarly, the Baltic Germans had enjoyed privileged treatment at the hands of the two previous Tsars, who employed several high-ranking ministers from that region. Now, in contrast, the reconstruction of the great Orthodox cathedral in Riga (1885) and the increasing proportion of Russian students at the famous University of Dorpat (now officially known by its Russian name of Yuriev) constituted symbols of uncompromising Russian domination.

The Jews

Characteristically, the worst blows fell upon the shoulders of the Empire's long-suffering Jewish population. Even the Jews had known some relaxation of their conditions under the previous reign. Recruitment of Jews into the army had been put on the same basis as that of Russians and the laws forbidding settlement beyond the 'pale', or official area of Jewish settlement established by Catherine the Great, had been somewhat relaxed. Now, however Alexander III's regime combined in effect the 'official' religious anti-semitism of the Orthodox Church with crude popular hostility that arose from the Jews' economic role. Associating the Jews in propaganda with the Polish rebellion and with the assassination of Alexander II, but also happy to use them as scapegoats on which popular discontent could be vented, the government permitted and even encouraged pogroms. These were riotous attacks on Jews and their property in which robbery, violence and even murder were commonplace. An estimated 215 such disturbances occurred between the first outbreaks in May 1881, in the Ukraine, and the 'great' pogrom of 1905 in Odessa in which nearly 500 Jews were killed. As Minister of the Interior, however, Dmitri Tolstoy was less keen to countenance such actions, not out of any concern for the victims, but out of a general uneasiness at the idea of civil disorder. In their place he instituted a series of less violent, but equally discriminatory measures. No new Jewish settlers were allowed in rural areas, even within the Pale of Settlement. Jews were forbidden to trade on Christian holy days which, as they already closed on Jewish holy days, made it hard for them to compete with non-Jewish rivals. Strict quotas for Jews were set in schools and universities, which never rose above 10 per cent even within the Pale. In 1886 in Kiev, and in 1891 in Moscow all 'illegal' Jews were expelled, which provided a useful opportunity to harass 'legal' settlers as well.

Apart from emigration, two other courses presented themselves for Jews who had had enough of such treatment. One was militant nationalism which took the form of the Zionist movement. The other was revolutionary agitation as seen in the formation of the Jewish socialist *Bund* (1897), which was to play an important part in the development of revolutionary socialism in Russia in the next two decades. Thus, in the long run, the policy of russification proved to be an even more dangerous 'dissolving agent' than the nationalism that it originally set out to combat.

L Foreign policy: Western Europe

Russia and France, 1856–63

Just as the end of the Crimean War signalled a turnabout in domestic policy, with substantial reform taking the place of rigid reaction, so a change of equal proportions came about in the foreign policy of the Russian Empire. The defeat, the evidence that it provided of Russian weakness, and the preoccupation of the government with domestic changes all limited the one-time 'gendarme of Europe' to a largely passive role from 1856 until the early 1870s.

Nevertheless, Russian diplomacy did have one major aim during this period. It was an uncharacteristic one, for the defeat in the Crimea had transformed the greatest conservative power into a revisionist power, eager especially to revise the Black Sea clauses of the Treaty of Paris that placed such humiliating restrictions upon her naval power in that area. Between 1856–63 the best means of achieving this end seemed to be to cultivate the friendship of France with a view to gaining a diplomatic agreement at some future date. Thus at the Paris conference (May–August 1858) which formed Wallachia and Moldavia into an effectively independent Rumanian state, Russia eagerly co-operated with the French 'line'. In March 1859 she even agreed to remain neutral in the event of French action in northern Italy, a very stark contrast to her attitude to disturbances in the Austrian Empire ten years earlier. By the early 1860s, however, the French entente was on its last legs. French interference with the 'legitimate' regimes of Italy was more than Alexander II could tolerate, and the breaking point came with evidence of French sympathy for the liberalism and the Catholicism of the Polish revolt in 1863.

Russia in diplomatic isolation

For ten years from 1863 Russia was almost wholly isolated in European diplomacy. The sole exception was her relations with Prussia which were improved by General von Alvensleben's mission in that year to offer aid against the Polish rebels. It was beneath the Imperial dignity to use the forces of a lesser power to control her own subjects, but the gesture was a friendly one in contrast to French, Austrian and British hostility, and Russia extended benevolent neutrality towards Prussia in her anti-Austrian adventures of the 1860s. Indirectly, Prussia's adventures led to the achievement of Russia's main ambition. With Europe preoccupied with the Franco–Prussian War from July 1870, Russia sensed that this was the moment to renounce the Black Sea clauses. The foreign minister, Alexander Gorchakov, informed the powers in November 1870 that Russia no longer accepted this section of the Treaty of Paris. Although the action was condemned in principle at a conference in London two months later, the powers were content tacitly to recognise that no retaliatory action could be taken.

The League of the Three Emperors

In the longer term the main result of the Franco–Prussian War was that Russian diplomacy had to come to terms with the new German Empire, a more powerful neighbour than she had ever known before. The conclusion of the League of the Three Emperors between the rulers of Russia, Austria and Germany (*see* Chapter 7, section **J**), gave a false air of stability to the politics of eastern Europe. Behind its facade, a series of factors kept alive Russian resentment at rising German power and at Austrian pretensions in the Balkans. The settlement engineered by Bismarck at the Congress of Berlin (*see* Chapter 7, section **K**), which limited Russia's gains from her conflict with Turkey, struck a serious blow to Russo–German relations. Shortly afterwards, in 1883, Rumania formally associated herself by treaty with Germany and Austria. A measure of the tension between Russia and Austria is gained from the refusal of Alexander III (April 1887) to renew the Three Emperors' Alliance, as the League had become in 1881. The Reinsurance Treaty concluded with Germany alone two months later (*see* Chapter 7, section **M**) maintained the facade of stability. It was a dubious piece of opportunism, partially at odds with Germany's undertakings towards Austria, but provided an encouraging indication of Germany's desire to maintain good relations with Russia. Thus the refusal of a new German Kaiser to renew the Reinsurance Treaty in 1890 (*see* Chapter 10, section **E**) seemed to be a specific rejection of Russian friendship, and starkly renewed Russia's international isolation.

The French 'entente'

The result was a revolution in Russian diplomacy whereby she turned towards republican France, different in every important aspect of recent history and culture, but well placed strategically to the west of Germany. The process by which France and Russia passed from financial to military understanding is described elsewhere (*see* Chapter 8, section **P**). Russian approaches to Germany in 1893 have suggested to some historians that the exercise may have been planned as a lever to force Germany into warmer relations. There being no favourable reaction from Berlin, an entente with France became the mainstay of Russian foreign policy *faute de mieux*.

M Foreign policy: the Balkans.

The Balkan crisis of 1875–76

The emergence of a great and concentrated power bloc in central Europe restricted Russian ambitions in two main theatres in the 1870s and the 1880s. The first of these was in the Balkans, where the renunciation of the Black Sea clauses gave Russia a new lease of life. Her policy there continued to be motivated by the familiar blend of concern for national security and the search for prestige in the face of domestic difficulties. This time, extra spice was added by the doctrine of pan-slavism.

In the early 1870s Gorchakov's policies in south-east Europe were conducted more in a spirit of cautious realism than of abstract pan-slavism. In 1875, however, a series of revolts began among the Serbian and Bosnian subjects of the Turkish Sultan, which set off much pan-slav agitation for the dispatch of Russian aid. The brutal suppression of the associated Bulgarian revolt in 1876 further excited both Russian feelings and foreign suspicion. Gorchakov quietened Austrian misgivings by an agreement concluded at Reichstadt (July 1876) whereby Russia would regain southern Bessarabia, lost in 1856, and Austria would receive part of Bosnia and Herzegovina in the event of a successful Russian clash with Turkey. Such a war was brought closer, as it had been in 1854, by the inflexible attitude of Turkey. In the first three months of 1877 the Sultan rejected proposals for reform from several of the major European powers, and Russia formally opened hostilities in April of that year.

The Russo–Turkish War

The war was fought on two fronts. In the Caucasus the Turks used the tactic of stirring up local rebellion to keep the Russian forces occupied, and not until late in the year did the latter gain decisive successes, winning a major victory at Aladja Dag in October and capturing their main objective, the fortified town of Kars, in November. In the European theatre the initial Russian advance was checked at Plevna, which held out against it from mid-July until early December 1877. The fall of that town paved the way to a victory that Russia sealed at the decisive battles of Plovdiv and Shipka (January 1878). It had been, as L. Kochan has noted, 'a war between the one-eyed and the blind – so many errors of strategy and judgement were committed'.

Nevertheless, Russia briefly enjoyed considerable gains. The Treaty of San Stefano (3 March 1878) ignored her Reichstadt undertakings to Austria and created a large Bulgarian state wide open to Russian influence. The diplomatic hostility caused by such success forced Russia, however, to agree to a revision of the treaty formulated at an international congress in Berlin (*see* Chapter 7, section **K**). The size of Bulgaria, and thereby the extent of Russia's influence in the Balkans, was reduced. Russia, nevertheless, was left with southern Bessarabia and the Caucasian gains of Kars and Batum. It was a clever settlement, but left pan-slavs and Russian nationalists bitterly offended, especially with Bismarck whose 'honest broker' stance seemed to them to hide anti-Russian and pro-Austrian intent. In the development of Russian relations with her central European neighbours, therefore, the events of 1877–78 foreshadowed greater conflicts to come.

N   Foreign policy: Asia

If the aftermath of the Crimean War left Russia badly placed to take initiatives in European affairs for several decades, no such restrictions existed along her eastern frontiers. 'These,' L. Kochan had written, 'were the happy hunting-grounds of Russian imperialist adventurers, dubious carpet-baggers, and pseudo-viceroys.' Some voices were indeed raised in St Petersburg against the risks and costs of such unbridled expansion, but they proved unable to check the ambitions of provincial generals and their followers. Motivated by chauvinism, by a sense of a civilising mission, and often by pure greed, Russian control spread steadily into the Caucasus region, across the Caspian Sea, and into Siberia. Turkestan was penetrated by stages that included the taking of Tashkent (1865) and of Samarkand (1868), and the Khanate of Bokhara acknowledged indirect Russian rule in 1875. The integration of these areas into the Empire was slowly effected by settlement by Russian peasants,

especially during Stolypin's period as premier, and by a number of ambitious communications projects, such as the construction of the Transcaspian railway in 1886–98. The spreading of Russian influence in Siberia was a longer process. Substantial areas of territory were gained from China by the treaties of Aigun (1858) and Peking (1860), and the foundation of Vladivostok in 1861 was a tangible symbol of Russian penetration to the shores of the Pacific itself. Here, too, great feats of communication were undertaken. The first work on the Trans-Siberian railway, one of the great engineering feats of the 19th century, was begun in 1892.

The sale of the colony of Alaska to the USA in 1867 defined the limits of Russia's eastward drive, which constituted the most successful example of European territorial expansion in the 19th century.

O   Economic development

Stimuli to industrial expansion

Although the great social reforms of the 1860s did not stimulate general economic growth, the reigns of Alexander II and Alexander III did form a period of overall industrial development. This development was, however, uneven and fluctuating. In the 1860s the difficulties of the emancipation of the serfs, and the 'cotton famine' that resulted from the civil war in America, were retarding factors. In the 1870s, however, the Russian economy benefited from the increase in railway building and from the policy of low tariffs which facilitated the import of raw materials. A. Gerschenkron has written of the former that Russia's 'greatest industrial upswing came when the railway building of the state assumed unprecedented proportions and became the main lever of the rapid industrialisation policy'. The development of Russia's railways was not only substantial in quantitative terms, but also showed much greater economic logic than the earlier lines had displayed. Lines such as those between Moscow–Kursk, Moscow–Voronezh and Moscow–Nizhni Novgorod linked major areas of industrial production to important markets. Similarly, the Kursk–Odessa and Kharkov–Rostov lines linked these, and areas of agricultural production, to the ports of the Black Sea. The Batum–Baku railway (1883) linked the Caspian with the Black Sea, and served greatly to increase oil production.

The steady growth of the Russian railway system is illustrated in Table 6.2.

Following the initial policy of freer trade, tariffs began to rise steadily as it became clear that liberal tariffs were causing a heavy influx of foreign goods and creating a substantial trade imbalance. The first major increase came in 1877, followed by further acts in 1881 and 1882. The policy culminated in the great protective tariffs of 1891, which especially affected iron, industrial machinery and raw cotton. The beneficial effect on domestic coal and pig-iron production is shown in Table 6.3.

Table 6.2 The development of Russia's railway system

Date	Kilometres constructed
1861–65	443 km
1866–70	1,378 km
1871–75	1,660 km
1876–80	767 km
1881–85	632 km
1886–90	914 km

From M. E. Falkus, *Industrialisation of Russia*, Macmillan

Table 6.3 Russian coal and pig-iron production

Date	Coal (poods)	Pig-iron (poods)
1860–64	21.8 million	18.1 million
1865–69	28.4 million	18.9 million
1870–74	61.9 million	22.9 million
1875–79	131.3 million	25.9 million
1880–84	225.4 million	29.2 million
1885–89	302.6 million	37.6 million
1890–94	434.3 million	66.9 million
1895–99	673.3 million	120.9 million

1 pood = 36 lb = 16.3 kg

From M. E. Falkus, *Industrialisation of Russia*, Macmillan

Russia's industrial achievement

In judging the level of Russia's industrial development one certainly sees the truth of the judgement that Lenin passed in 1899: 'If we compare the present rapidity of development with that which could be achieved with the modern level of technique and culture, the present rate of development of capitalism in Russia really must be considered slow.' In the longer term, nevertheless, one can also appreciate the judgement passed by a later economic historian, W. O. Henderson: 'If the Russian economy was still backward in some respects, it was also true that vigorous state action, foreign capital and foreign machinery had given Russia a powerful impetus on the road to industrialisation'.

Questions

Essay questions

1 How profound, and how effective, were the great reforms of the 1860s in Russia? (Oxford Entrance)

2 How effectively did Alexander II cope with the problems that faced him on his accession? (UCLES)

3 Had the reforms of Alexander II strengthened or weakened the Russian monarchy by the end of his reign? (ULEAC)

4 How effective, within the Tsarist Empire, were opposition groups (both Russian and non-Russian) in the period 1855–1904? (AEB)

5 Why did Alexander II attempt to modernise Russia? (WJEC)

6 Comment on the view that Alexander II's reputation as a reformer has been grossly exaggerated. (JMB/NEAB)

The emancipation of the serfs

Read the two documentary extracts carefully and answer the questions that follow.

SOURCE A

Called by Divine Providence and by the sacred right of inheritance to the throne of Our Russian ancestors, We vowed in Our heart to respond to the mission which is entrusted to Us and to surround with Our affection and Our Imperial solicitude all Our faithful subjects of every rank and condition, from the soldier who nobly defends the country to the humble artisan who works in industry; from the career official of the state to the ploughman who tills the soil.

Examining the condition of classes and professions comprising the state, We became convinced that the present state legislation favours the upper and middle classes, but does not equally favour the serfs. Rights of nobles have been hitherto very broad and legally ill-defined, because they stem from tradition, custom and the goodwill of the noblemen. In most cases this has led to the establishment of good patriarchal relations based on the sincere, just concern and benevolence on the part of the nobles, and on affectionate submission on the part of the peasants.

Having invoked Divine assistance, We have resolved to execute this task.

The serfs will receive in time the full rights of free rural inhabitants.

The nobles, while retaining their property rights on

all the lands belonging to them, grant the peasants perpetual use of their domicile in return for a specified obligation; and, to assure their livelihood as well as to guarantee fulfilment of their obligations towards the government [the nobles] grant them a portion of arable land fixed by the said arrangement, as well as other property.

While enjoying these land allotments, the peasants are obliged, in return, to fulfil obligations to the noblemen fixed by the same arrangements. In this state, which is temporary, the peasants are temporarily bound.

At the same time, they are granted the right to purchase their domicile and, with the consent of the nobility, they may acquire in full ownership the arable lands and other properties which are allotted them for permanent use. Following such acquisition of full ownership of land, the peasants will be freed from their obligations to the nobles for the land thus purchased and will become free peasant landowners.

And now We confidently expect that the freed serfs will appreciate and recognise the considerable sacrifices which the nobility has made on their behalf. They should understand that by acquiring property and greater freedom to dispose of their possessions, they have an obligation to society and to themselves to live up to the letter of the new law by a loyal and judicious use of the rights which are now granted to them. Abundance is acquired only through hard work, wise use of strength and resources, strict economy, and above all, through an honest God-fearing life.

And now, Orthodox people, make the sign of the cross, and join with Us to invoke God's blessing upon your free labour, the sure pledge of your personal well being and the public prosperity.

From Alexander II's Decree Emancipating the Serfs, 3 March 1861.

SOURCE B

Governors have called to Our attention that in some settlements peasants of the state and of the nobility, misled by malicious rumours and evil talk, digress from normal order and think that the state peasants will be freed from tax payments, while the peasants of the nobility will be freed from their obligations to their masters.

Feeling sorry about the misleading of these villagers, and wishing to direct them to the truth by means of the kindness natural to Our fatherly mercy, I am ordering announced everywhere:

1. That all talk about freedom of state peasants from the payment of taxes and of the nobility peasants and household people from obligations to their masters is a malicious rumour conceived and spread by ill-intended persons for a profit motive, that is, to enrich themselves at peasant expense.

2. All social strata within the state should fulfil all their obligations according to the law and obey their appointed superiors submissively.

5. And inasmuch as We have received weekly petitions from peasants written on the basis of the above mentioned rumours, to terminate this evil and to preserve safety and order, We decree that the composers or writers of such petitions be brought before the court as disturbers of general peace and punished to the fullest severity of the law,

Nicholas I's Manifesto on Peasant Unrest, 2 May 1826.

---

a On the basis of your background knowledge comment upon the following statements that occur in Source A:

  i 'In most cases this has led to the establishment of good patriarchal relations —- — and — affectionate submission on the part of the peasants'.

  ii 'The freed serfs will appreciate and recognise the considerable sacrifices which the nobility has made on their behalf'.

b To what extent does Source A support the contention that the emancipation of the serfs was a radical political, social and economic measure?

c What similarities exist between the Russian society envisaged in Alexander II's edict and in that of Nicholas I?

7

Germany under Bismarck, 1870–90

A painting by the German court artist, Anton von Werner, showing the acclamation of Wilhelm I as German Emperor by the German princes in the Hall of Mirrors in Versailles, 18 January 1871.

Werner's painting draws attention to specific elements which he suggests were responsible for German unification. Identify them.

In what ways might modern historians consider Werner's portrayal of German unification to be misleading?

Given that it might be regarded as misleading, what is the value of Werner's painting as a historical document?

The

LO

...stion, 1948), German conservatives continued to argue that Bismarck could not be held responsible for later developments. His semi-feudal brand of conservatism, they argued, along with his religion and his 'Little German' views, all distanced him greatly from the principles of Nazism. As Hans Rothfels (*Bismarck and the State*, 1954) put it, 'we may criticise Bismarck for paving the way to some fatal trends of our day, but we cannot very well overlook the fundamental fact that Hitler did precisely what the founder of the Reich had refused to do'.

The most important development in recent decades in the study of Bismarck's Germany has been the move away from the study of 'Grand Policy' (*Grosse Politik*), to diminish the role played by great men such as Bismarck, and to stress instead the wider context in which they operated. W. E. Mosse (*The European Powers and the German Question*, 1958) has stressed the conducive diplomatic circumstances which made Bismarck's task easier. 'If he played his hand with great skill, it was a good one in the first place'.

The most notable work in this area of German studies has been that of Helmut Böhme who, in *Germany's Path Towards Great Power Status* (1966), concentrated upon the social and economic development of contemporary Germany. For Böhme and the writers who have followed his lead, the true current of German greatness in the 19th century lay in the development of her economic life, upon the waves of which Bismarck merely rode and steered.

the ... disposed of. Nee- (*The Franco–Pru...Hidden Consequences*, 1912).

Later many historians, both in Germany and elsewhere, perceived the work of Bismarck as preparing the way for the disastrous era of Nazism. H. Kohn (*Rethinking Recent German History*, 1952) saw Bismarck as bearing direct responsibility for Hitlerism. For other writers, such as Geoffrey Barraclough (*Origins of Modern*

Similarly, the leading British authority of recent times, A. J. P. Taylor (*Bismarck: Man and Statesman*, 1955), has portrayed a much less heroic Bismarck, a brilliant but unstable neurotic, driven less by great principles than by egoism and by overwhelming personal ambition. Led by Gerhard Ritter (*Europe and the German*

A The Treaty of Frankfurt

The outcome of the Franco–Prussian War and the ultimate shape of the German Reich were decided simultaneously by the terms of the treaty signed at Frankfurt on 10 May 1871. France was compelled to pay a war indemnity of 5 billion francs over a period of three years. Territorially, too, France was not to escape as lightly as Austria had done in 1866. German nationalist claims to Alsace had flickered in 1815, among the student societies of the 1820s and in 1848–49. Now that desire was supplemented by power, annexation was perhaps inevitable. 'This territory,' wrote the historian von Treitschke, 'is ours by right of the sword, and annexation follows from the right of the German nation to prevent the loss of any of its sons.'

Northern and eastern Lorraine, with the great fortress of Metz, also became German territory. There was far less justification for regarding these as German lands, and for many years the standard view on this issue was that Bismarck bowed reluctantly to the pressure of the army, the king and the nationalists. More recently, headed by the research of W. Lipgens, it has appeared that Bismarck may have had some role in the formation of this public mood. His motives, however, are unlikely to have been ideological. On a practical level G. A. Craig points out that French bitterness was likely to be just as great, whatever the terms of the surrender, and Bismarck himself wrote in similar vein to his ambassadors abroad. 'We cannot look to the French temper for our guarantees. What the French nation will never forgive is their defeat as such. In German hands Strasbourg and Metz will take on a purely defensive character.'

B The Reich's constitution

The influence of Prussia

In theory, the German Empire created in 1871 was a voluntary association of German states governed by as free a constitution as existed anywhere in Europe. In practice, behind each article of that constitution lurked the power and influence of Prussia. The Empire was a federal state, consisting of the four kingdoms of Prussia, Bavaria, Württemberg and Saxony, 18 lesser states, three free cities, and the Imperial Territory (*Reichsland*) of Alsace-Lorraine. Each of these, with the exception of Alsace-Lorraine, retained substantial autonomy in terms of its own domestic administration. Prussia was by far the largest of the constituent parts, however. It comprised something over 60 per cent of the area of the Reich (134,000 out of 208,000 sq miles) and of its population (24.7 million out of 41 million).

The Reichstag

The basis of the parliamentary constitution was adapted directly from that of the North German Confederation. The Imperial Assembly (*Reichstag*) was elected by universal manhood suffrage, but was beset by a host of limitations which prevented its growth into a true parliamentary body. It had the power to question the Chancellor (which office fell of course to Bismarck) and to initiate debate upon any point of his policy, but neither he nor any other minister was responsible to the assembly for his actions. It had theoretical control over any alteration to the military budget, but largely sacrificed this weapon by agreeing in 1874, largely through fear of precipitating a new constitutional conflict, to approve that budget for a period of seven years. It repeated this process in 1881 and 1887. This 'loss of the full right of budget approval', argues Hajo Holborn, 'blocked the growth of a parliamentary system in Germany'. Furthermore, the bulk of the remainder of the Reich income, from indirect taxation, posts and from the contributions of member states, lay wholly beyond the control of the Reichstag.

The *Bundesrat* and the Emperor

In reality, therefore, political power lay outside the Reichstag. In part it lay with the upper house, the *Bundesrat*, but for the most part it rested with the Prussian hierarchy. The *Bundesrat*, which represented the independent interests of the states, had the power to initiate legislation. Also, with the assent of the Emperor, it had the authority to declare war and to settle disputes between the states. With the interests of the Reich and of the individual states thus balancing each other out, real power lay with the king of Prussia and his ministers. He was by hereditary right German Emperor, with full powers over the appointment and dismissal of ministers, who were responsible only to him. He also had full control over foreign affairs, and the right to the final say in any dispute over the interpretation of the constitution. By virtue of her size, Prussia possessed 17 of the 58 seats in the *Bundesrat* at a time when 14 constituted a veto. The balance of forces in the German constitution indicated very clearly, therefore, that it was designed to block and to prevent any major change or development in the future.

C Parties, philosophies and pressure groups

The parties that competed for seats in the Reichstag, with the varying degrees of success indicated in Table 7.1, were very different organisations from their English counterparts. They were predominantly pressure groups representing the sectional interests of one part or another of the diverse German nation, and they remained in Agatha Ramm's phrase 'social phenomena rather than instruments for winning the struggle for power'.

Table 7.1 Composition of the Reichstag, 1871–1890

	1871	1874	1877	1878	1881	1884	1887	1890
German Conservatives	57	22	40	59	50	78	80	73
Reichspartei	37	33	38	57	28	28	41	20
National Liberals	125	155	141	109	47	51	99	42
Progress Party	46	49	35	26	60	—	—	—
Centre Party	61	91	93	94	100	99	98	106
Social Democrats	2	9	12	9	12	24	11	35
Guelphs	9	4	10	4	10	11	4	11
National groups (Alsatians, Poles, Danes)	14	30	30	30	35	32	29	27

Total seats = 397 (1871: 382)

The conservatives

On the right wing of the Reichstag stood two major groups, the Conservatives (from 1876 the 'German Conservatives') and the Imperial Party (*Reichspartei*). The former had its strength in Prussia itself, among Protestant, aristocratic landowners. Concerned at, and sometimes openly hostile towards Bismarck's flirtations with liberalism and nationalism, it remained a moderate force in the Reichstag, but a major one in the Prussian *Landtag*, which it dominated through local influence. The *Reichspartei* enjoyed a broader geographical basis of support, among landowners and industrialists alike, and its support for the Imperial Chancellor was much more consistent, in admiration of his great achievement in the foundation of the Reich.

The Centre Party

The Centre Party (*Zentrum*), founded in 1870, still tends to be described as the party of Germany's large Roman Catholic minority. In fact it was more than that. Primarily dedicated to the defence of the interests of the Catholic Church, it also attracted others with a partisan objection to the recent work of Bismarck, such as the Protestant Hanoverian 'Guelphs', who were embittered supporters of the deposed King George. Particularly strong in Bavaria and in the Rhineland, the party was led in the Reichstag by a Catholic Hanoverian, Ludwig Windthorst. One of the few great parliamentarians of the 'Bismarck era', greatly respected even by those who loathed his views, Windthorst has been characterised by Golo Mann as 'a sly idealist, a devout fox, a man of principles and a very clever politician, dignified and cunning'.

The liberals and the left

In the 1870s Bismarck had his most enthusiastic supporters in the National Liberals, at one with him in their enthusiasm for a centralised state, if increasingly at odds with him in their support for progressive social and constitutional legislation. To their left stood the Progress Party (*Fortschrittpartei*), diminished but unbowed by the liberal split of 1866, sharing the National Liberals' enthusiasm for free trade and the rule of law, but opposed to the centralism and militarism of the Bismarckian state. In Eugen Richter and Eduard Lasker they too had effective parliamentary leaders, the latter so consistent a critic of the Chancellor as to be described by Bismarck as 'even more of a vile louse than Windthorst'.

Two smaller groupings are also worthy of note. German socialism in 1871 was as yet a modest force, based upon Ferdinand Lassalle's General

Workers' Association (*Allgemeiner Arbeiterverein*) founded in 1863, and the Social Democratic Workers' Party formed by Wilhelm Liebknecht and August Bebel at Eisenach in Saxony in 1869. Its day was, however, soon to come (*see* section **H**).

The 'Great Depression' and its political impact

Neither the political parties of the Reichstag nor Bismarck were able to operate in an ideological vacuum. For much of the so-called 'Bismarck era' the political life of Germany was played out against a background of economic anxiety and depression. The origins of Germany's 'Great Depression' were classical. The economic history of the Reich opened with a short period of financial euphoria, fuelled by over-generous credit policies on the part of German bankers, and by the large amounts of capital pumped into the economy by French war reparations. These stimuli set off a wave of unsound investment projects whose eventual collapse, in the same fashion as the Wall Street Crash, struck a blow to business confidence whose effects could still be felt nearly 20 years later.

It is important to appreciate the exact nature of the impact made by this 'Great Depression'. In terms of production and of economic growth, the German recovery took place relatively quickly (*see* section **O**). The production levels of 1872–73 had been reached again by 1880; urban growth continued unabated, especially in Berlin and in the Ruhr; the development of cartels allowed major industrial enterprises to maintain their stability. After 20 years of uninterrupted economic growth, however, the psychological impact of the slump was considerable, and the effect of the depression on political mentalities was to last well beyond 1880.

Its main political impact was to mobilise and to polarise conservative economic thinking, and above all to create an extremely powerful lobby in favour of economic protection. The rejection of liberal, free-trading policies by the leaders of German industry soon became evident in the formation of such pressure groups as the League of German Iron and Steel Manufacturers (1873) and the Central Association of German Industrialists (1876). When Junker agriculturalists also became convinced that their interests were threatened by free trade, Bismarck was faced by an enormously powerful coalition in favour of protective tariffs (*see* section **G**).

The real impact of the depression, therefore, was that it undermined the political basis upon which Bismarck had founded his power in the early 1870s, and forced him to adapt once more to the prevailing circumstances within Germany. As D. G. Williamson has put it, the economic developments of the later 1870s 'discredited both economic and political liberalism and enabled the conservatives and the survivors of the pre-capitalist era successfully to attack the liberal ethos'.

D The Reich's consolidation

Bismarck and the National Liberals

The first seven years of Bismarck's government of a united Germany, from 1871–78, are frequently described as his 'liberal era'. While Bismarck was by no stretch of the imagination a true liberal, he found it convenient during this period to co-operate in the Reichstag with the National Liberal party. In the first place, they were the dominant party in an assembly where the Chancellor had no party of his own. Secondly, the spirit of conciliation that had motivated the indemnity of 1866 (*see* Chapter 5, section **K**) remained alive. The National Liberals remained broadly sympathetic towards Bismarck as the architect of their major policy aim, national unity. Most important, their immediate aims coincided with Bismarck's in such areas as the consolidation of that national unity and the centralisation of the administration of the Reich.

To conservative critics it often seemed that the alliance with the National Liberals was carrying Bismarck too far to the left, and that he was becoming, in Lothar Gall's phrase, 'the stirrup-holder of liberalism'. In fact it is clear that the Chancellor gave his 'supporters' nothing that involved any immediate political power. The Press Law (May 1874) provided little protection for editors against government prosecution. Attempts in the Reichstag to limit the influence of the Junkers in Prussian local government achieved little of practical value and, as we have seen (*see* section **B**), the Reichstag failed to any serious degree to maintain control over the vital area of government military expenditure.

It is equally important to establish, however, that the measures undertaken in 1871–78 should not merely be written off as 'sops' offered by

Bismarck to 'fool' the National Liberals and to maintain a convenient political understanding in the short term. The economic and administrative legislation of his 'liberal era' was of the greatest importance in the formation of the German state, and illustrates very clearly the complex relationship between Bismarck and the German liberals. The period produced, in the words of Geoff Eley, 'an impressive concentration of forward-looking economic legislation [and] an elaborate framework of capitalist enabling laws'. Although Bismarck refused to grant the liberals the kind of political framework that they desired for Germany, the *kleindeutsch* state of 1875 was, in economic terms, very much what liberal thinkers had always envisaged. Only time would tell whether this delicate balance of socio-economic progressiveness and political conservatism could be maintained.

Administrative and financial consolidation

The state created by Bismarck was a curiously disunited entity. It lacked religious unity and unity of economic interests, and contained national minorities with little or no desire to be part of the German Empire. There is thus much truth in A. J. P. Taylor's description of the Reich in 1871 as merely a 'wartime coalition'. Such were the separatist feelings of the states, for instance, that Germany had no national flag until 1892 and no national anthem until after the First World War. For Bismarck, with his desire for closer political control, and for the National Liberals, with their enthusiasm for national unity, it was vital that this situation be improved. The first session of the Reichstag therefore saw the passage of over 100 acts to this end. The currencies of the states were unified into a national currency, all internal tariffs were abolished, and a uniform body of commercial law was introduced. The Prussian State Bank became the *Reichsbank*, and Germany adopted the gold standard. Uniformity of legal procedures was achieved in 1877. A national appeals court was established by 1879, although the codification of German civil law did not come into effect (January 1900) until long after Bismarck's fall from power.

The problem of the national minorities

After administrative separatism, the second major area of disunity concerned the national minorities within Germany's borders. For nearly 20 years, by a mixture of coercion and conciliation, Bismarck attempted to tie these minorities more closely to the German state, but had no significant degree of success. In Alsace-Lorraine the decision to allow French or pro-French elements to leave the territories resulted in the migration of 400,000 people between 1871 and 1914. The remainder found themselves governed by Prussian civil servants, with the German language imposed in schools and in local administration. From 1874 they were represented in the Reichstag, and the choice of governors for the territories showed some tact and common sense. Von Manteuffel (1879–85) was a humane and conscientious administrator. His successor, Prince Chlodwig von Hohenlohe, was a south German Catholic and had more in common with the Alsatians than with most of his Protestant Prussian underlings. The consistency with which the people of Alsace voted for deputies in favour of separation from the Reich showed, however, that such attempts at conciliation were largely unsuccessful.

In the case of the Poles, conciliation was much less in evidence. The Polish clergy were hard hit during the *Kulturkampf*. Their leader, Cardinal Ledochowski, was imprisoned and his office left vacant for 12 years. The use of the Polish language was outlawed in education and in the law courts. State funds were used to finance the purchase of lands in Polish hands for the purpose of settlement by Germans, although the Poles were rather more successful in raising funds for the reverse purpose. It is scarcely surprising that, given these tactics, the Polish problem remained unsolved.

Finally, the problem of the Schleswig Danes was largely ignored. In 1879, on the eve of the Dual Alliance, Austria agreed to allow Germany to abandon the plebiscite in North Schleswig promised by the Treaty of Prague in 1866. It took a world war to revise the status of North Schleswig and of Alsace-Lorraine, and to resolve the problems of Germany's Polish subjects.

E The *Kulturkampf*: motives

German liberalism and the Catholic church

Much of the first decade of the domestic politics of the Reich was dominated by the clash with the Catholic Church branded at the time as the

'struggle for civilisation' (*Kulturkampf*). It is difficult for us to grasp today, in a generally more
secular age, the feelings aroused by this legal
assault upon Germany's substantial Catholic
minority. We shall miss its significance altogether
unless we accept that, as Erich Eyck tells us, 'in
those years many of the most enlightened and
highly educated men believed that the future of
mankind was at stake'.

The view that Bismarck artificially engineered
this confrontation as a means of uniting various
strands of German opinion against a common
enemy is no longer tenable. The roots of the *Kulturkampf* stretch deep into German history,
certainly back to Prussia's acquisition of the largely
Catholic Rhineland in 1815, and possibly to the
Reformation. A study of Cavour's policy towards
the Catholic Church in Piedmont (*see* Chapter 4)
or of the policies of the French Third Republic (*see*
Chapter 8) reveals that this was not even exclusively a German issue. In the case of Germany in
the early 1870s the struggle was really made up of
two separate clashes. For the German liberals, the
Catholic Church was an old enemy. Even in the
southern states, precursors of the *Kulturkampf* can
be seen, as in the Church Law (1860) and the Elementary School Law (1868) passed in Baden. The
offence of the Catholic Church had been compounded in 1864 with the publication of Pius IX's
Syllabus of Errors (*see* Chapter 4, section **N**). By
condemning as erroneous every major principle for
which German and Italian liberals stood, Pius had
declared moral warfare. For the liberals the battle
was truly one for the future of human thought.

Bismarck and the Catholic Church

For Bismarck the issue was less abstract. Nor,
despite his Protestantism and that of the Prussian
Junkers, was his battle a doctrinal one. 'It is not a
matter of a struggle between belief and unbelief',
he declared, 'it is a matter of the conflict between
monarchy and priesthood. What is at stake is the
defence of the state'. For him the origins of the
Kulturkampf lay in the events of 1866–70, which
had turned tens of thousands of German Catholics
from sympathetic *Grossdeutsch* supporters of the
Habsburg monarchy into reserved followers and
subjects of Prussia. Its origins also lay in the recently declared doctrine of Papal Infallibility (July
1870). By aiming to tie Catholic loyalties directly

to the Papacy, instead of to the national state, the
doctrine was a clear challenge to state power. The
launching of this struggle offered Bismarck certain
other political advantages, such as closer ties with
the anti-clerical Italian government, with Russia,
themselves greatly troubled by Catholic Poles, and
with the National Liberals. His major motive,
however, was probably the desire to combat those
whom he felt quite genuinely to be 'enemies of the
Empire' (*Reichsfeinde*). The Catholics were thus the
first of many minority groups to play this role in
'united' Germany.

F   The *Kulturkampf*: results

The May Laws

The spearhead of the attack upon the Catholic
Church was formed by legislation framed, under
Bismarck's instructions, by Adalbert Falk, the
Prussian minister of religious affairs. Firstly, in
1872, came the severance of diplomatic relations
with the Vatican (May) and the expulsion of the
Jesuit order from German soil (July). In the following year came the main onslaught in the form of
Falk's notorious 'May Laws'. The education of
clergy, clerical appointments and the inspection of
Church schools were all brought under state
control. Appointments to German ecclesiastical
positions were limited to those educated in
Germany, and priests were forbidden to use the
threat of excommunication as a means to coerce
opponents. In a further series of measures civil
marriage, strenuously opposed by Bismarck in
1849, became compulsory in the Reich, and most
religious orders in Germany were dissolved (1875).

The results of the *Kulturkampf*

In 1874–75 Church and state remained locked in
conflict. Eight of the 12 Catholic bishops in Prussia
were deprived of their offices and more than 1,000
priests were suspended from their posts. However,
the desired political effect was not achieved. Spiritually the Church thrived upon its 'martyrdom',
and politically the increase in the representation of
the Centre Party in the Reichstag (*see* section **C**)
frustrated Bismarck's hopes of a quick surrender.
There were also other unhappy side-effects. The
anti-Catholic stance endangered good foreign relations with Austria and the threat of an

Austro–French understanding grew. Prussian conservatives, although staunchly Protestant, disliked the liberals' hostility to all religious instruction in schools and distrusted Bismarck's liberal 'alliance' in general. Indeed, the price demanded by the liberals in terms of free trade and ministerial responsibility for their further support, seemed to Bismarck himself to be becoming unreasonably high.

The death of Pius IX (1878) and the election of the more conciliatory Leo XIII was an opportunity that Bismarck seized with enthusiasm. With the repeal of the bulk of the May Laws (1878) and the symbolic dismissal of Falk (July 1879), the *Kulturkampf* came to an abrupt end. Of the great 'struggle for civilisation', only the laws on civil marriage, state supervision of schools and those against the Jesuits remained.

Did Bismarck, therefore, lose the *Kulturkampf*? Certainly the struggle did much to damage his earlier work of unification, and made the majority of German Catholics more sympathetic to Papal authority than they had been before. On the other hand, reconciliation did at least largely transform the Centre into a purely religious party. If we see Bismarck's aim as the preservation of his state in the longer term, then perhaps we should accept the long-standing verdict of C. Grant Robertson that 'Bismarck deliberately sacrificed victory in the *Kulturkampf* to victory in other issues, more important in his judgement.'

G The move to conservatism

The significance of the reforms of 1878–79

The ending of the *Kulturkampf* cannot be seen, however, merely as a tactical withdrawal, cleverly calculated by a master politician. In 1878–79 Bismarck was faced once again with a crisis of the utmost gravity, which forced him substantially to adapt and revise his policies. The change of direction that he undertook at the end of the 1870s has often been interpreted as political opportunism. More recently, however, historians have come to view this period as a key stage in the development of the German Reich, as significant in its way as the events of 1870–71. Helmut Böhme, for instance, has argued that the Franco–Prussian War established a viable form of unity between the German

states, but did not establish a satisfactory socio–economic balance within the new Reich. It became increasingly clear in the course of the 1870s that Bismarck's alliance with German liberalism failed to meet the interests of many highly influential groups within the Reich. The dramatic switch to economic and political conservatism at the end of the decade, therefore, represented an acceptance on Bismarck's part of conservative social and economic values more closely in keeping with the conservative structure of the state. Agatha Ramm confirms this interpretation in describing these reforms as a 'coherent and systematic revision of policy in relation to the economic, social and financial needs of the Reich'.

The introduction of protectionism

The first of the needs that Bismarck now felt compelled to meet was the growing demand for measures of economic protectionism. While free trade remained an essential principle of the National Liberals, demands for higher protective tariffs increased from other quarters (*see* section **C**). These demands had been heard from the iron and steel industries from the mid-1870s, but now Prussia's Junker landowners added their voices to the argument. Instead of aiming at free access to the markets of Britain and France, they now found themselves vulnerable at home and abroad to the cheap grain arriving from the United States. The adoption of protective tariffs by France, Russia and Austria-Hungary over this same period seemed to make it all the more desirable for Germany to follow suit.

Apart from this impressive array of industrialist and Junker opinion, the government itself had pressing motives. Protection would aid the growth of national self-sufficiency in the event of a future crisis, and tariffs provided the government with a valuable source of income independent both of the Reichstag and of the member states.

From 1876, the path chosen by Bismarck became clearer. In April of that year he accepted the resignation of Rudolf von Delbrück, head of the Chancellor's Office and architect of the earlier free trade policies. In early 1878, the refusal of the liberal leaders to join Bismarck's cabinet unless they were given substantial guarantees over ministerial appointments and policy decisions, sealed their fate in the eyes of the Chancellor. When the new tariff laws were enacted in the Reichstag (July 1879) they imposed duties of between 5 and 7 per cent upon imported foodstuffs, and of 10 to 15 per cent upon imported industrial goods. An amendment proposed by Freiherr zu Frankenstein limited Bismarck's triumph by fixing an upper limit of 180 million marks in tariff income to be retained by the Reich, any surplus being distributed among the states. If this provided those states with some little satisfaction, there was none for German liberalism. A substantial step had been taken back to the path of conservatism, and the 'liberal era' in the history of united Germany was effectively at an end.

H Bismarck and socialism

Bismarck's fear of socialism

The second compelling motive for Bismarck's change of course was his desire to combat what he saw as the menace of socialism within Germany. Although the weakness of the socialists in the Reichstag might have seemed to make them unlikely candidates for the role of *Reichsfeind*, Bismarck, like most European statesmen, was genuinely shaken by recent events such as the Paris Commune (*see* Chapter 8, section **B**). The 'Eisenach' socialists had, after all, refused their support for the war in 1870. Many remembered Bebel's claim in the Reichstag in May 1871 that 'before many decades pass the battle cry of the proletariat of Paris will become that of the whole proletariat of Europe'. It seems probable that if Bismarck's opposition to Catholicism was not primarily ideological, his opposition to socialism was. In A. J. P. Taylor's words, he 'genuinely believed in the turnip-ghost which he conjured up'.

The anti-socialist law

Bismarck's opportunity came in mid-1878 when two attempts upon the life of the Kaiser gave him the chance to raise the cry of 'the Fatherland in danger', to dissolve the Reichstag and to hold fresh elections. Although neither unsuccessful assassin had any clear association with the Social Democratic Party, the mood of the electorate was patriotic and conservative. 'The Emperor has the wounds,' commented a liberal observer, 'the nation the fever.' The Social Democrats themselves had few seats to lose and the real losers of the election were

the National Liberals. A majority was returned in favour of economic protection, the repeal of the 'May Laws', and the passage of Bismarck's anti-socialist measures (*Sozialistengesetz*). The law (19 October 1878) did not directly ban the Social Democratic Party, but savaged their organisation by banning any group or meeting aimed at the spread of socialist doctrine, outlawing trade unions, and closing a total of 45 newspapers. It was originally in operation, thanks to a liberal amendment, for only two and a half years. It was nevertheless renewed regularly until 1890.

'State socialism'

It was clear to Bismarck that socialism could not be conquered by oppression alone. The second string of his anti-socialist policy was thus a programme of 'state socialism'. This involved a series of measures, reminiscent of Junker paternalism, to improve the conditions of the German workers. In 1883, medical insurance and sick pay were introduced. Although these were largely financed by the workers themselves, the employers were responsible for the funding of the scheme of insurance against industrial injuries introduced in the following year. Finally, in 1889, old age pensions were introduced, some two decades before their appearance in Britain.

Historians have differed in their estimates of 'state socialism'. Some, like Erich Eyck, have seen the policy as a fraud, pursued for short-term political advantage. They point out how much more advantageous it would have been to relax the restrictions upon trades unions to allow workers to fight their own battles. They note that old age pensions were paid only to those who reached the age of 70, a ripe old age indeed for an industrial worker. G. A. Craig, however, believes that it is possible to trace such paternalism in Bismarck's policies right back to 1862. 'State socialism', therefore, was based upon genuine conviction.

Was Bismarck more successful against socialism than he had been against Catholicism? Certainly he gained enthusiastic support from 'academic socialists' (*Kathedersozialisten*) such as Brentano and Weber. He horrified some liberals who accused him of attempting to found communism in Germany. Certainly, he failed to check the growth of the Social Democratic Party, whose membership increased from 550,000 in 1884 to 1,427,000 in

1890. The workers, claimed W. M. Simon, saw 'state socialism' as a fraud and gave their support to the left.

A. J. P. Taylor, however, recalls how subservient the German working class was to government policy in the years leading up to 1914 and concludes that Bismarck's policy had at least defused the threat of working-class opposition to the state. 'The workers seemed to have received social security as the price of political subservience, and drew the moral that greater subservience would earn a yet greater reward'.

I The principles of Bismarckian foreign policy

Before 1870 Bismarckian policy had aims, more or less specific, that were pursued and eventually achieved by the skillful exploitation of external circumstances. After 1871 the essential principles of foreign policy underwent a substantial change. In the eyes of Bismarck the 'little German' settlement of that year was final, and Germany was a 'satiated' state, without further territorial ambitions. As he himself remarked, 'when we have arrived in a good harbour, we should be content to cultivate and hold what we have won'. It was now Bismarck's primary aim to prevent external events from disrupting the settlement that he had created. In this undertaking he was to achieve far less success than he had enjoyed in the first decade of his diplomatic career.

J The *Dreikaiserbund*

For some years after 1872 the mainstay of Bismarck's delicate diplomatic balance was the understanding between the rulers of Germany, Russia and Austria-Hungary known as the League of the Three Emperors (*Dreikaiserbund*). First projected at a meeting of the monarchs in 1872, it was confirmed the following year (22 October 1873). It was given more concrete form by a series of bilateral military agreements promising aid to any party attacked by a fourth power.

In concluding this very general and formless agreement, Bismarck probably had three main motives, although authorities disagree as to the placing of the main emphasis. Firstly, the *Dreikaiserbund* represented a natural union of conservative ideals against disruptive forces such as nationalism and the socialism of the Paris Commune. Secondly, as Erich Eyck has stressed, the League ensured that neither Austria-Hungary nor Russia was available as an ally for France.

A. J. P. Taylor, on the other hand, preferred to emphasise the third potential benefit to Germany from the League. 'Its object,' he wrote, 'in so far as it had one, was to prevent a conflict between Austria-Hungary and Russia in the Eastern Question.' In short, preoccupied by domestic issues for much of the decade, Bismarck sought to ensure that Europe remained peaceful by leading a combination of three of Europe's five main powers.

K The crises of 1875 and 1878

The 'war in sight' crisis

Behind the superficial unity of the *Dreikaiserbund* lay self-interest and mutual suspicion that were always likely to undermine it. Two crises in the 1870s demonstrated the instability of the League. The first, the so-called 'war in sight' crisis of 1875, was the result of a major diplomatic miscalculation on the part of Bismarck. He had estimated, since 1871, that his purposes were best served by the survival of a republican government in France, as this would strengthen Russian and Austrian suspicions of France and keep that country in isolation. He even went so far as to dismiss and humiliate his ambassador in Paris, H. von Arnim, when the latter disagreed and promoted royalist interests.

Now, in 1875, political developments in France indicated a rise in royalist support (*see* Chapter 8, section **C**) and displayed disturbing signs of military preparations. Bismarck's reaction was to allow threats of preventative war, which he certainly never intended to fight, to circulate from unofficial sources. These came to a head with an article in the *Berliner Post* (9 April 1875) entitled 'Is war in sight?'. Far from leading to the desired French embarrassment and retreat, the article caused France to appeal to the other powers to prevent a further German assault upon her.

The Eastern Crisis

The second crisis, the Eastern Crisis of 1875–78, was not of Bismarck's making. It arose from the general revolt of the South Slav peoples, with Bulgarian support, against their Turkish overlords in 1875–76. Pan-slavism and practical political interests encouraged successful Russian intervention (*see* Chapter 6, section **M**) and resulted in the Treaty of San Stefano (3 March 1878).

By the terms of this treaty European Turkey was substantially reduced in size by the creation of fairly large Russian client states in Bulgaria, Rumania, Serbia and Montenegro. Bismarck had eloquently disclaimed any interest in the Eastern Question, using the famous phrase that no Balkan issue was 'worth the healthy bones of a single Pomeranian musketeer'. Even so, he could not fail to be concerned at the prospect of a clash between Russia and Austria-Hungary, which now saw its only remaining sphere of influence in the Balkans threatened.

The only alternative to war was a conference of the great powers, and this met in Berlin (June–July 1878) under the presidency of Bismarck. There he played the role of the 'honest broker', not aiming for personal profit, but for a peaceful settlement between his 'clients' Russia and Austria-Hungary. The interests of the other major powers, including Britain, ensured that Russia would not be able to maintain the San Stefano settlement.

The significance of the Congress of Berlin

Superficially, the Congress of Berlin marked a highpoint in Bismarck's diplomatic career. In the short term, he had indeed preserved peace and confirmed Berlin as the centre of European diplomacy. Erich Eyck, on the other hand, was one of those historians who preferred to see the congress as marking the beginning of the end of the Bismarckian system. Russian opinion was bitter at the loss of Slav territory won at the cost of Russian blood, even though they kept their substantial Asian gains from Turkey, and Tsar Alexander II was not alone in seeing the Congress of Berlin as 'a European coalition against Russia under the leadership of Prince Bismarck'.

The introduction of protective tariffs against Russian agriculture in 1879 only confirmed this impression. Quite apart from the chill that entered into Russo-German relations, the *Dreikaiserbund* was further undermined by the installation of Austria-Hungary in Bosnia and Herzegovina against the local population's will.

L The Dual Alliance

German and Austrian motives

Anti-German feeling in Russia arose after the Congress of Berlin as a result of thwarted pan-slav ambitions and of the wounded pride of Gorchakov, rather than as the result of any deliberate reorientation of German policy. It had great long-term importance in that it confirmed the impressions that Bismarck had derived from the events of 1875–78. He felt that the time had come to put Germany's relations with Austria-Hungary on a surer footing. His motives were undoubtedly complex, but were dominated by the desire to avoid diplomatic isolation, and perhaps by the hope of frightening Russia back onto better terms with Germany by the prospect of her own isolation. It was also certain that a clear commitment to Austria would be the most popular of the diplomatic options within Germany, especially at a time when his own domestic policy relied so heavily upon conservative support. As Bismarck wrote to the reluctant Wilhelm, 'German kinship, historical memories, the German language, all that makes an alliance with Austria more popular in Germany than an alliance with Russia'. Nevertheless, it was only with great difficulty that the Emperor's scruples about the 'betrayal' of Russia and of his fellow monarch were overcome. In Austria, on the other hand, the prospect of an alliance was greeted with great enthusiasm.

The Dual Alliance and German diplomacy

In the following years the Dual Alliance became the centre of a system of German diplomacy that has been alternatively interpreted as the salvation of European peace in the 1880s, and as confused and contradictory. In May 1882, the alliance became the Triple Alliance through the association of Italy with Germany and Austria-Hungary. This extension of the Bismarckian system had substantial advantages for Germany in that her mutual undertakings with Italy were specifically anti-French. This provided her for the first time with a committed ally against that country. On the other hand, Bismarck had earlier admitted that Austria's alliances with Serbia (June 1881) and Rumania (October 1882) drew Germany even deeper into areas where she had no direct stake or interest.

M The Reinsurance Treaty

The Reinsurance Treaty and its significance

The crisis that arose over Russia's virtual deposition of Bulgaria's independent-minded King Alexander (August–September 1886) raised the likelihood of an Austro-Russian clash more starkly than at any time since 1878. The resultant collapse of the *Dreikaiserbund* threatened the whole basis of Bismarckian diplomacy. In an attempt to plug the gap and to retain some influence over Russia's actions, the Chancellor was able to conclude (June 1887) a bilateral, completely secret agreement with Russia, known as the Reinsurance Treaty. By its terms both powers agreed to remain neutral in the event of a dispute with a third power. Germany also recognised Russia's preponderant interest in Bulgaria. As these neutrality clauses did not apply in the event of a German attack on France, or of a Russian attack upon Austria-Hungary, Bismarck did in fact gain some means of preventing the latter eventuality. Much controversy has centred upon the question of the compatibility of the Reinsurance Treaty with the Dual Alliance. In fact there was no contradiction in the letter of the two agreements. They placed Germany in the position of having to decide, in the event of a clash between Russia and Austria, who was truly the aggressor and thus which treaty Germany would honour. The achievement of Bismarck in the Reinsurance Treaty was that it maintained Germany's power to arbitrate.

The 'balance sheet' of Bismarckian diplomacy

Unfortunately, within three years, Germany faced the task of maintaining the delicate balance without the services of this consummate diplomat. What, therefore, was Bismarck's diplomatic legacy? J. McManners has concluded that, by his commitment to Austria-Hungary, he bequeathed potential political disaster. This judgement is perhaps too harsh in that it attaches too little importance to the forces driving Bismarck in his decision in 1879, and underestimates the subtlety of the Reinsurance Treaty. It was, after all, Wilhelm II who allowed the treaty to lapse in 1890 when Russian enthusiasm for its renewal remained high. Nor did Bismarck create the eastern European tensions that erupted in 1914.

N The beginnings of German colonisation

The acquisition of colonies

In the mid-1880s the otherwise consistent if complex course of German foreign policy took a quite unprecedented twist. Bismarck gave his government's support to the formation of a far-flung but substantial body of German colonial possessions. This contrasted starkly with the facts that in 1871 he had refused to annex French colonial possessions in place of Alsace-Lorraine, and as late as 1881 had declared that 'so long as I am Chancellor we shall pursue no colonial policy'. Germany's part in the 'scramble for Africa' was concentrated in the years 1884–85, establishing sovereignty in areas where German trading interests had been developed by private firms over the previous decade or so. In April 1884, the state agreed to 'protect' a strip of territory at Angra Pequena, in what is now Namibia. This had been secured from the Nama tribesmen by the Bremen merchant, A. Lüderitz. Within the year, to the deep concern of British interests in southern Africa, this had grown into the colony of South-West Africa.

The reasons for this abrupt departure from tradition have exercised historians ever since, and there is still no general agreement as to Bismarck's motives. The most widely accepted explanation is that, as I. Geiss puts it, 'the German Chancellor had to conform to dominating trends in German society'. German industry, for example, was now powerful enough (*see* section **O**) to seek new outlets and new sources of raw materials abroad. It was perhaps natural that, after the introduction of protective tariffs in 1879, many businessmen should seek similar protection from the state for their interests abroad.

The cost of colonialism

Whatever the rationale behind it, German colonial policy was generally sterile. Bismarck had hoped that colonisation would not become a financial burden upon the Reich, but would be financed by private enterprise. 'I do not wish to found provinces,' he told the Reichstag in 1884, 'but to protect commercial establishments in their development.' These hopes were ill-founded. By 1913 colonisation had cost the German taxpayer over

1,000 million marks in direct government aid. Only Togoland and Samoa had proved to be self-supporting. In almost every respect the results of 30 years of imperialism had been a disappointment. The total German population of the colonies amounted to only 24,000, most of them officials.

O Economic development

The stimulus of unification

The unification of the Reich in 1871 provided a number of direct stimuli to an economy that already possessed a substantial base for prosperity. Alsace-Lorraine, for example, contained Europe's largest deposits of iron ore. Production increased rapidly under German control, from 684,000 tons in 1872 to 1,859,000 tons in 1882. The injection of part of the French indemnity payments into the national economy caused a spectacular if short-lived boom in 1871–73. This was felt especially in the building and railway industries. Lastly, as shown in section D, unity provided the opportunity for a burst of legislation designed further to unify the economic life of the Reich.

Table 7.2 Economic comparisons between Great Britain, France and Germany, 1870–90

	1870	1890
Population		
Germany	41m	49m
Britain	32m	38m
France	36m	38m
Coal (million tons)		
Germany	38	89
Britain	118	184
France	13	26
Steel (million tons)		
Germany	0.3	2.2
Britain	0.6	3.6
France	0.08	0.6
Iron Ore (million tons)		
Germany	2.9	8
Britain	14	14
France	2.6	3.5

In terms simply of output, the 'Bismarck era' provided further dramatic advances for the German economy. Coal production soared, steel production increased by some 700 per cent, and the German merchant marine advanced from virtual non-existence to the position of second largest in the world. Table 7.2, by contrasting German development with that of Great Britain and France, gives an

impression of her advance as a world industrial power. Apart from the doubling of the railway network, it is also important to note the extent of nationalisation that took place during these decades. Twenty-four thousand out of Prussia's 28,000 kilometres of track passed into state ownership between 1879 and 1884.

Banking and finance

In the 1870s and 1880s banking and finance underwent steady and consistent development. What was unique to this period was the development of two important features in the economy. Firstly, the post-war boom provided a considerable stimulus to the German banking industry. By the mid-1870s Germany had a remarkably well-endowed system. Apart from the Reichsbank there were six other banks which dominated commerce and industry with a combined capital of 2,500 million marks.

Industrial cartels

The second distinctive feature of contemporary economic development was the growth of cartels. These were groupings or agreements made between different companies in the same industry to avoid the dangers of competition by such measures as price fixing, agreements on the level of production, and the sharing of markets. There were four such cartels in 1865, and only eight a decade later. Harder times made such arrangements more attractive and Germany boasted 90 in 1885 and 210 five years later.

QUESTIONS

Essay questions

1   In what ways did Bismarck tackle the social and economic problems of Germany, 1871–90? (WJEC)

2   How successful was Bismarck in dealing with internal opposition in the period 1871–1890? (ULEAC)

3   Did Bismarck's foreign policies after 1871 make Europe a safer or a more dangerous continent? (UCLES)

4   What were the limits to Bismarck's power in Germany after 1871? (Oxford Entrance)

5   How far did the domestic and foreign policies pursued by Bismarck between 1871 and 1890

ensure that Wilhelm II's inheritance was a powerful and secure one? (NEAB)

6 How valid is the view that 'the domestic problems facing the rulers of Germany in the period 1878–1914 were primarily the consequences of social and economic change'? (AEB)

Colonial policy under Bismarck

Study Documents I, II, III and IV below and then answer questions (a) to (f) which follow.

DOCUMENT I

22 February 1880. Dinner with Bismarck.
The Chancellor refuses all talk of colonies. He says that we haven't an adequate fleet to protect them, and our bureaucracy is not skillful enough to direct the government of such territories. The Chancellor also alluded to my report on the French plans for Morocco, and thought we could only rejoice if France annexed it. She would then be very occupied, and we could let her expand in Africa as compensation for the loss of Alsace-Lorraine.

Prince Hohenlohe, German Chancellor 1894 to 1900. The Memoirs of Prince Chlodwig von Hohenlohe-Schillingfürst, 1907.

DOCUMENT II

The colonial question may bedevil our relations with England for a considerable period. Should a conflict arise, no other question is so liable to put the future Kaiserin, with her Anglophile tendencies, in a false position vis-à-vis the German nation. For it is precisely the liberals and democrats who want colonies. I am far from supposing that this is the reason why the Chancellor has suddenly made the colonial question a part of his political programme. But if the need arises, he will use it as a means of combating foreign influences.
[Later] The Chancellor is right to pursue a colonial policy. Had he not embarked upon it, it would have remained a slogan for the opposition.

Friedrich von Holstein, Bismarck's subordinate at the Foreign Office, in his diary, 1884.

DOCUMENT III

I begged him to tell me what now, at this moment, he wanted; was it the parts of New Guinea that we were now annexing? Was it Zululand?
The Prince [Bismarck] replied that the understanding he had arrived at with France put it out of his power to take up the question now that he could no longer make any particular target.
The general impression which I derived was that the

Prince does not desire that relations between the two countries [Britain and Germany] should improve at present.

Sir E Malet, British Ambassador in Berlin, 1884-1895, writing to Granville, Foreign Secretary in Gladstone's government, 24 January 1885.

DOCUMENT IV

He [Bismarck] said Mr Gladstone might become Prime Minister again, a man with whom it was impossible to do business. But the policy he had pursued and which had been considered as unfriendly to England was not inspired by any feeling against her. He had sided with France to try and extinguish the animosity of that country against Germany.
He had been following a wild goose chase. France was as ready as ever to seize an opportunity of attacking Germany. There were now no points of difference between England and Germany. He had never favoured the Colonial idea himself, but opinion in Germany ran so strongly in favour of Colonial enterprise that he could not refrain from turning the Colonial stream into the main channel of his Parliamentary policy.

P. H. W. Currie, of the British Foreign Office: notes of a conversation with Prince Bismarck, 28 September 1885.

a In the context of these Documents, explain what is meant by each of the following:
i 'compensation for the loss of Alsace-Lorraine'; and
ii 'the future Kaiserin, with her Anglophile tendencies'. (2)
b According to Documents I and II, what aspects of German home affairs influenced Bismarck's attitude to colonial policy? (3)
c With specific reference to the origins and to the content of Documents I and II, estimate the value and the reliability of memoirs and diaries as evidence for someone studying German diplomatic affairs in the 1880s. (6)
d How far would you agree that Documents III and IV confirm that the author of Document II was correct in asserting that 'The colonial question may bedevil our relations with England for a considerable period'? (4)
e Estimate the strengths and weaknesses of Document IV as evidence for a historian of Bismarck's colonial policy. (4)
f Discuss the view that, from the evidence of these Documents and from your own knowledge, considerations of foreign policy, rather than of domestic policy, were more influential in affecting Bismarck's attitude to colonial questions. (6)

(ULEAC)

8

The French Third Republic to 1914

Two versions of the same symbolic theme: the French Republic distributing rewards and blessings to the people. The first dates from 1848 and the second from 1907.

In what ways have the gifts and the recipients changed?

What reasons might there be for the more jaundiced view of the Republic taken by the artist in 1907?

The Historical Debate

The two most obvious and impressive features of the French Third Republic were its long duration by comparison with other French regimes, and the abject nature of its eventual collapse in 1940. These features, suggesting initial success and gradual stagnation, have imposed an unusual uniformity upon historical interpretations of the period. David Thomson's *Democracy in France since 1870* (1969) may be taken as a statement of the dominant view on the Third Republic. Its success, he claims, was due to the regime's ability to combine conservative political institutions with a set of radical social aims. It was thus 'the first successful attempt to reconcile the conservative and revolutionary traditions of France'.

Its ultimate failure and collapse may be attributed to the unwillingness of subsequent governments to change a formula that had worked in the past. A range of recent French writers have stressed various aspects of this theme. Jean-Pierre Azema and Michel Winock (*La IIIe Republique*, 1970) have concentrated upon the 'narrow, fearful self-interest' of the French bourgeoisie as the main cause of the stagnation of the republican system. Meanwhile F. Goguel (*La Politique des Partis sous la IIIe Republique*, 1946) saw the period as a contest between the policies of 'movement' and those of 'established order'. The gradual triumph of the latter resulted in what Gordon Wright had labelled the 'stalemate society'.

There have been relatively few serious divergences from this central theme, and they have usually reflected a particular political sympathy. J. Chastenet (*History of the Third Republic*, 1952–63) put forward a much more sympathetic view of the 'opportunists' and of the later Radicals, seeing in them not political timidity, but praiseworthy moderation. Marxist writers, on the other hand, have taken their lead directly from Karl Marx himself (*The Civil War in France*, 1871) in viewing the Republic as a wholly conservative institution, springing from the blood of the slaughtered communards. H. Guillemin (*Origins of the Commune*, 1956–60) can be taken as a more recent representative of this viewpoint.

As has been the case with many other historical periods and problems, a recent tendency has been to avoid writing the history of the Third Republic in terms of the development of parties and policies. Eugen Weber, for instance, (*Peasants into Frenchmen: the Modernisation of Rural France*, 1976) has seen the real significance of the Third Republic as being that it witnessed the breakdown of long-standing localism and parochialism. This aided the growth, through developments in communications, education, military service, and so forth, of a true sense of French nationhood.

Meanwhile, the most far-reaching publication on the period has undoubtedly been Theodore Zeldin's monumental *France 1848–1945* (1973–77), which has turned its back upon any attempt at a general, political summary of the era. It concentrates instead upon detailed and intimate examination of the social and psychological roots of the contemporary French society.

A The heritage of the Republic: the war with Germany

The establishment of the Provisional Government
The events of 4 September 1870 in Paris revolutionised the nature of both the French regime and the war with Germany. On that day, undermined by news of the defeat at Sedan and the captivity of Napoleon III, the Empire collapsed and a republic, the third in French history, was proclaimed at the Hotel de Ville. As had happened on the two previous occasions, the provinces generally accepted the *fait accompli* dictated from the capital. The war remained the most pressing business of the Provisional Government that now established itself, with Jules Trochu as its premier and Jules Favre in charge of foreign affairs. Brief hopes that the fall of the Bonaparte dynasty might terminate a conflict largely attributable to dynastic ambitions were quickly disappointed. Encouraged by great popular support in Paris, the government declared itself the Government of the National Defence and announced its intention to wage 'war to the death' (*la guerre à outrance*).

The 'republican' war
The next four months of republican warfare were

to salvage a little of France's self-respect, but were also to poison Franco–German relations for the next 80 years. At the centre of the bitter struggle was the siege of Paris, which lasted from 20 September 1870 to 28 January 1871. In its course Europe's greatest city was bombarded and starved. Elsewhere the Germans were harassed by guerrillas and by three armies raised to relieve the capital. All three had their initial successes, but lacked the reinforcements to make good their casualties. By the time of the surrender of Paris all three had suffered irreparable damage, General Chanzy at Le Mans (13 January), General Bourbaki at Héricourt (17 January) and General Faidherbe at St Quentin (18 January). The unfortunate Bourbaki was even unsuccessful in his subsequent attempt to commit suicide.

The Treaty of Frankfurt

The terms of the Treaty of Frankfurt (10 May 1871) were not as harsh as might have been feared considering the position of France in late January 1871, with no troops to speak of, with war-weariness growing in the provinces, and with revolt imminent in her conquered capital. The loss of the provinces of Alsace and Lorraine was bitterly resented, but predictable. On the other hand, the important border fortress of Belfort, which had survived a siege lasting more than three months, remained in French hands. A reduction of one billion francs was negotiated in the war indemnity charged by Germany, although at five billion francs it remained an enormous sum. Only when it had been paid in full would German forces withdraw from French soil.

It was perhaps one of the greatest achievements of the Republic that it had cleared its territory of the army of occupation by September 1873, and had still managed to balance the national budget by 1875. The administration had achieved this by drawing upon the large reserves of private wealth in France through loans and private investment in government bonds. All the same, the economic heritage of the Third Republic was a millstone of vast proportions. The war had cost France 150,000 lives and the equivalent of £695 million, as well as the mines and the 1.5 million inhabitants of Alsace-Lorraine. By the time of the conclusion of peace the stability and existence of the state were called into question once again.

B The heritage of the Republic: the Commune

The myth of the Commune

Within three weeks of the German entry into Paris, France was further shaken, and further humiliated in the eyes of the world. The cause was the outbreak of civil war that followed the establishment in Paris of the radical administration known as the Commune. The nature of the Commune has been the subject of much controversy among historians. Karl Marx quickly claimed it as the first great proletarian uprising, directed against capitalism by predominantly working-class leaders. This interpretation has dominated the writings of left-wing historians ever since. Most more moderate historians have drawn attention to the other strands of radicalism contained within the Commune, such as anarchism, or the jacobinism of the first French Revolution. They also acknowledge that while 25 of the Commune's elected administrators were workers, the other 65 came from the middle and professional classes. In the views of David Thomson and of Theodore Zeldin, the Commune had its roots in a purely French radical tradition, and has since had a mythology woven around it to serve the purposes of a more modern revolutionary movement. In fact, leaderless and largely incoherent, the Commune was as F. Jellinek describes it, 'fertile in examples of every revolutionary hypothesis'.

The nature of the Commune

In the longer term the origins of the Commune lay in the peculiar urban social problems, and in the tradition of active communal politics that had made Paris a revolutionary battleground in 1789, 1830 and 1848. Its causes in the shorter term may easily be found in the disastrous defeat of 1870–71, and in the severe hardship of the siege by the Prussian army. In the aftermath of their humiliation and suffering, the staunchly republican Parisians saw a largely monarchist Assembly returned in the February elections. Within a month this Assembly confirmed that it would penalise the poorer Parisians despite their earlier heroism. A series of acts in early March suspended the pay of the near mutinous National Guard, and ordered the immediate payment of rents and commercial debts frozen for the duration of the war. Thus, in Sir Dennis Brogan's phrase, 'the Assembly threatened a great part of the population of Paris with bankruptcy or eviction or both'. Still, the Commune was not the result of any general uprising. A government attempt to remove artillery from the city was thwarted by soldiers of the National Guard, and two unpopular generals were lynched (18 March). Thiers and his government responded by withdrawing the administration entirely from Paris to conservative Versailles. The central committee of the National Guard found itself in charge of Paris with neither programme nor tactics not because of any action on its own part, but purely because of the lack of any other government.

The Commune governed Paris for 73 days (18 March–28 May 1871) and for most of that time was doomed to failure, having failed to pursue the government to Versailles and to widen its basis of support. In all, it was far more important for what it was than for what it did. Preoccupied for most of its life with its defence against the Versailles government, the Commune nevertheless passed some laudable legislation. It created co-operative workshops, abolished the system of fines for breaking petty workshop rules, and introduced the principle of free, compulsory education for both sexes, as an antidote to the influence of the Church.

On the other hand, it made little coherent assault upon capitalism, leaving the Bank of France and all forms of private property largely untouched. Its importance lies in the fact that, for the first time since 1792, state power in a European capital lay in the hands of an elected committee composed mainly of working- and middle-class elements. Europe saw no such democracy again until 1917.

The suppression of the Commune

The Commune made its most lasting impression by the nature of its suppression. The entry of government troops into Paris (21 May) began the so-called 'bloody week' in which the city was recaptured street by street. While the communards executed 56 hostages and killed about 1,000 troops, as many as 20,000 citizens died, sometimes in battle, sometimes in summary executions. In the aftermath over 13,000 Parisians were imprisoned and 7,500 were transported to penal settlements in the colonies.

The results of the Commune, like its causes, have been the subject of much dispute. France's international reputation sank to a new low ebb, and the Republic was burdened with a lasting legacy of radical and socialist bitterness. J. P. T. Bury, on the other hand, stresses that the long-standing problem of Parisian insubordination had been tackled deliberately and successfully by Thiers. 'The proscription and exile of so many extremists,' he wrote, 'enabled the new Republic to attain constitutional legality and to develop in a peaceful and orderly fashion during its first formative years.'

Thiers himself has received a mixed press. Theodore Zeldin accuses him of creating the Commune by his evacuation of Paris, with the deliberate aim of crushing Paris as a force in French politics. For David Thomson, Thiers is a more statesman-like figure who, like Abraham Lincoln, had to fight a civil war to preserve the very unity of his country, in France's case already defeated and vulnerable. Whether patriotic or Machiavellian, we must conclude that Thiers' treatment of the crisis of the Commune was energetic, decisive and totally successful.

C The 'Provisional' Republic 1871–77

Thiers and conservative republicanism

For two years after her defeat France lived, in the words of a foreign observer, 'under a provisional government run by an old gentleman of 74'. Adolphe Thiers was the architect of the Orleanist monarchy in 1830, and had been a moderate critic of the Second Empire. He was not even a republican, but rather a supporter of constitutional monarchy. He maintained, as his handling of the Commune had shown, a profound disgust for the politics of the masses.

The government over which he presided as 'Chief of the Executive Power' remained vaguely republican. This was mainly out of a general desire to avoid divisive questions of ideology so soon after the outbreak of civil war, and largely because, in Thiers' own words, 'the Republic divides us least' at a time when the nation seemed to be in genuine danger of disintegration. For all that, the future of the Republic and of the nation remained in severe doubt.

The failure to restore the monarchy

What were the options for the future government of France? Superficially, a restoration of the monarchy seemed most likely, with some 400 monarchists among the 700 deputies returned in the elections of February 1871. They, however, were bitterly divided between the supporters of the houses of Bourbon and of Orleans.

An obvious compromise suggested itself. The Bourbon claimant, the Comte de Chambord, grandson of Charles X, was childless, so might ascend the throne on the understanding that he would be succeeded by the Orleanist claimant, the Comte de Paris, or by the Comte's children. Enmity between the two houses might have thwarted this plan in any case, but the immediate obstacle lay in a bizarre decision by Chambord. Having accepted the principles of parliamentary government and of universal manhood suffrage, he then decided to abandon the tricolour as the national flag and to revert to the royalist white flag. His determination not to let 'the standard of Henri IV, of Francis I, of Jeanne d'Arc be torn from my hands' only served to show how far his 40 years of exile in Austria had distanced him from reality. The attachment of the nation to the flag of the Revolution, and of the Napoleonic victories was so great that Chambord's stubborn repetition of this condition effectively made a restoration impossible.

The attractions of Thiers

With Bonapartism crippled by the death of the former Emperor (1873), popular support for republicanism increased. The original monarchist vote had been a vote for peace and stability. It was steadily undermined by the failure of the monarchists to agree upon a king, and by increasing evidence of the conservatism of Thiers' particular brand of republicanism. In addition to the enormous achievement of paying off the war indemnity, he had pleased the middle classes by refusing proposals for an income tax and by favouring the return to economic protectionism. He had also appealed to the patriotism of the nation through a new Army Law (August 1872) which introduced conscription for a term of five years' service as the basis for the reconstruction of the army. As Sir Dennis Brogan put it, many now asked themselves 'what could a king do that M Thiers could not do as well or better?'

The 'Republic of Dukes'

The resignation of Thiers (July 1873), forced upon him by those who disliked his increasing attachment to republicanism, threw the future of the Republic into renewed doubt. From 1873–77, France was governed by what Daniel Halévy has christened 'the Republic of Dukes'. It was led by Marshal MacMahon, created Duc de Magenta by Napoleon III, and was served in high office by six other dukes, of whom de Broglie and Decazes were the most prominent. The main aim of the administration was to give the government a form and institutions which would guarantee its conservative nature and eventually, if Chambord ever saw sense, could equally form the basis of a constitutional monarchy.

In November 1874, MacMahon's period of office was fixed at seven years. What now was to be his title? The proposal by the deputy, Wallon, that it be 'President of the Republic', was adopted by only one vote (February 1875). The Assembly accepted the status of Republic by only 353 to 352 votes, and then without any guarantee against future change.

The 1875 constitution

The additional laws that made up the so-called 'Constitution of 1875' were designed specifically to strengthen the electoral chances of the conservative parties. The president became eligible for re-election at the end of his term, which had not been the case under the Second Republic, and he retained such important prerogatives as the power to dissolve the Assembly. An upper chamber was instituted, the Senate, with one third of its members chosen for life and the remainder elected for nine years. Lastly, election was to be by single member constituencies (*scrutin d'arrondisement*). This was chosen in preference to the earlier method of electing deputies for a department *en masse* from party lists (*scrutin de liste*), which had always seemed to favour the superior organisation of the left-wing parties. Its main task completed, the 'provisional' Assembly dissolved itself (December 1875) in anticipation of new elections. These frustrated every hope of the conservatives by returning 340 republicans against 200 right wingers and 75 Bonapartists. Even conservative hopes for the Senate proved ill-founded, with 57 of the 75 life members being republicans.

D The consolidation of the Republic, 1877–85

The elections of 1877

The elections of 1875 had created a situation in which the monarchist president found himself faced with a republican Assembly with which co-operation was impossible. The future of the Republic was assured by the crucial election campaign of 1877. Faced with an intolerable political deadlock, MacMahon acted within his constituional powers by appointing an unrepresentative administration under the Duc de Broglie, and by dissolving the Assembly. He stretched those powers to the limit, however, when he dismissed 70 prefects, 226 sub-prefects and 1,743 mayors in an attempt to secure maximum local influence in favour of right-wing candidates. Leading republicans such as Gambetta and Grévy retaliated by fighting one of the most energetic election campaigns of the 19th century, with the death of Thiers in mid-campaign adding an emotional touch. The republican victory by the huge margin of 326 seats to 207 sealed the fate of the 'Republic of Dukes'. MacMahon had failed to impose the authority of the president over that of the Chamber, and had failed to impose the influence of the French aristocracy over the people. He gave way to Jules Grévy, a republican acceptable to the majority of the deputies. 'It was not only a political turning point,' remarked Alfred Cobban, 'it was a more decisive social revolution than anything that had occurred in 1830, 1848 or 1871.'

The rule of the 'opportunists'

Such a judgement can be accepted in the sense that the men who dominated the next decade and a half of republican politics were of a very different social stamp to those who had gone before. Léon Gambetta (Prime Minister 1881–82) was the son of an Italian grocer, dedicated to the replacement of aristocratic influence by what he called the 'new social stratum', meaning the lower middle classes. For Gambetta, states Theodore Zeldin, the Republic 'meant the opening of doors and the breaking down of barriers'. Jules Ferry (prime minister 1880 and 1883–85) came from a more solid legal, bourgeois background, but was equally dedicated to the principle of equal rights and dignity within French society. He attached great importance in this process to universal primary education, and spent a little over four years as minister of education. Thirdly, Charles-Louis Freycinet (Prime Minister 1879, 1882 and 1886) was a Protestant, something still largely unacceptable at the upper levels of French society. His political career was based, not upon the fire and oratory of a Gambetta, but upon his unobtrusive ability as a political manager and conciliator. 'Small, dapper, aloof, subtle, insinuating,' wrote Alfred Cobban, he 'was for a whole generation to run up and down the corridors of the Third Republic like a little white mouse.'

These men, confirmed in power by republican appointments within the army and the judicature, and by great electoral success at a local level, still adhered to the principle of Thiers that 'the Republic will be conservative or it will not be at all'. By abandoning the radicalism by which Gambetta had made his reputation a decade earlier, they became branded as the 'opportunists'.

The reform programme of the 'opportunists'

The early legislation of the 'opportunists' contained much that was predominantly symbolic in nature. For example, the return of the Assembly to Paris from Versailles (1879), the amnesty extended to surviving communards (1879–80), the observance of 14 July – Bastille Day – as a national holiday, and the adoption of the revolutionary *Marseillaise* as the national anthem (1880).

These were closely followed, however, by a series of political reforms of real liberal and democratic content. In 1881 a new Press Law was introduced which removed the possibility of prosecution for the expression of a political opinion. In 1883 all local communities, with the exception of Paris, acquired the right to elect a mayor, rather than having one imposed upon them by the prefect. At the same time the Senate was democratised by the abolition of life membership. 1884 saw the introduction of competitive examinations for offices in the civil service, and the legalisation of trades unions to protect members' economic interests. Simultaneously, the transformed Republic acquired a reputation that rivalled that of the Second Empire in the performance of great public works. The Paris International Exhibition of 1878 was followed by the transformation of Marseilles and Le Havre into modern, international, commercial ports, by the modernisation of France's inland waterways, and by the doubling in size of the French railway network.

E   Politics in the Third Republic

Stability or instability?

The Third Republic presents a startling paradox with contradictory elements of progressiveness and conservatism, and of stability and instability. It triumphed spectacularly over the rule of the aristocracy in 1877, yet made surprisingly few fundamental changes in the social structure thereafter. It saw 108 different ministries installed between 1870 and 1940, with an average life of eight months, yet the 'constitution' of 1875 lasted for 65 years, longer than any other French constitution to date, until it was violently overthrown by foreign aggression.

Limitations upon the executive power

It is easier to resolve this paradox if one realises that this French parliamentary democracy differed greatly from its European counterparts. In the case of French democracy a deliberate attempt was made to ensure that the legislative power (the Chamber) should be considerably more powerful than the executive power (the government). Too often in the past a powerful man or influential group had come to dominate and overthrow republican democracy. The Chamber, therefore, was now dominated, not by the presidents, but by the deputies.

The deputies had at least three main weapons at their disposal to keep the government in check. The practice of 'interpellation', of questioning ministers often on points of minor detail, could delay government business, and often forced the resignation of the government. There might be as many as 4,000 interpellations annually. Secondly, the deputies used their power to initiate legislation to swamp the government with projects. In the parliament of 1893–98, for example, 3,328 bills were proposed, 1,112 of them by private members, often on matters of purely local interest. Lastly, deputies participated in the work of permanent commissions before which all government legislation had to pass. Gambetta, for instance, played a major, if negative role as head of the Commission for Finance between 1877 and 1881.

Elements of stability and continuity

The results of this system were many. The principle of republicanism was rarely backed by coherent programes of reform as governments despaired of ever getting them past the Chamber. Party loyalties, moreover, remained extremely vague and changeable as deputies became preoccupied with their local interests and personal projects for legislation. The deputies, on the other hand, became professionals. They were usually drawn from the professional and middle classes, enjoyed a salary equivalent to that of a colonel or a judge (their British counterparts had to wait until 1912 for a much more moderate salary) and a pension if they served as long as 30 years.

Naturally enough they became primarily concerned, not with great issues of state, but with the relatively minor interests of their constituents, attention to which kept them in their agreeable positions. So agreeable were these positions that elections were frequently marked by various forms of corruption, from falsified registers to the straightforward purchase of votes. Continuity within the regime was also supplied by the civil service, and by the President of the Republic, who was no longer the dominant figure he had been in 1848, but a valuable element of stability. A few major themes, therefore, could run from government to government.

F   Church and state: the policy of Ferry

The French Catholic Church in the 1870s.

Perhaps the most persistent of these themes was the contest between the Republic and the Catholic Church for the hearts and minds of the French people. The Church had flourished during the conservative era of the Second Empire and the 'Republic of Dukes'. From 1851–78 membership of religious orders had soared, from 3,000 to 32,000 for men, and from 34,000 to about 128,000 for women. The total wealth of these orders was estimated at 421 million francs, or £16.8 million in contemporary values. Worst of all, in the eyes of republicans, their future seemed to be assured by the grip upon education allowed to them by the Falloux Law of 1850. In 1878 40 per cent of French education was conducted in Church schools.

Anti-clericalism

The defeat of 1871 polarised views among the anti-clerical opposition to the Church. It was regarded as significant that the defeat had been suffered at the hands of Protestant Prussia, where such an important social role was played by the teachers of the state schools. To many, for example the contemporary historian Edgar Quinet, the defeat of MacMahon at Sedan was the defeat of 'Bonapartism, caesarism, Catholicism, jesuitism', all that was corrupt and sterile within France.

The writings of Auguste Comte were also influential in the formation of intellectual anti-clericalism. In his *Système de Politique Positive* (1852–54) he argued that all aspects of human life and consciousness pass through three stages of development, the theological, the metaphysical, and the highest stage, the scientific or 'positive'. Modern society, now clearly in the third stage in material terms, was thus bound to throw off the constraints of theology and spiritualism. This 'positivism' provided a tempting philosophical basis for the political views of many intellectual republicans.

The reforms of Jules Ferry

In common with the leaders of the German *Kulturkampf* and with the liberals of the Kingdom of Italy, the leaders of the consolidated French Republic felt it impossible to develop the principles by which they hoped to govern while the population remained subject to the enormous pressure and influence, essentially conservative, of the Catholic Church. Indeed, the force of the anti-clerical campaign in France owed much to the fact that it constituted a rare area of agreement between all shades of republican opinion. Its radical attractions were not offset, as in other cases, by the disadvantages of high cost and taxation. 'The most urgent of all reforms,' declared Gambetta, 'must be the liberation of universal suffrage from every sort of tutelage, obstacle, pressure and corruption.' From 1879, therefore, the government waged a far more genuinely ideological 'struggle for civilisation' than Bismarck had attempted. Its key area of attack was education, its primary aim 'to tear away the soul of the youth of France' from the Church. Its key figure was Jules Ferry, minister of education from 1879–83.

By one of the most far-reaching and progressive laws passed under the Third Republic (1882) primary education, from the age of six to thirteen years, became compulsory, and was to be provided free of charge. Equally important to Ferry, it was to be wholly free from the influence of the Church. Teachers in these schools were to be laymen, were employees of the state (1886) and were subject to state examination. To meet the demand created by the disqualification of 40,000 clerical teachers, each department was charged (1879) with the creation of a college for the training of female primary school teachers. The Jesuit order, with others, was first banned from teaching and then (1880) expelled from France. Beyond the primary level, this attack upon clerical influence was part of a wider programme of educational reform. This included the closing of the Catholic universities, the revision of the traditionally classical secondary school syllabus, and the establishment (1880) of the first state secondary school for girls. Beyond the sphere of education altogether, the position of the Church was assaulted by the legalisation of divorce, the introduction of civil marriage (both 1884), and by the repeal of the law of 1814 forbidding Sunday working (1879).

G Church and state: the final separation

The *ralliement*

Between the two spasms of bitter Church–state rivalry in France lay a period of conciliation known as the *ralliement*. The end of the 1880s marked a point of unprecedented strength for the Republic. The centenary of the Revolution was marked in 1889 by the lavish International Exhibition of which the new Eiffel Tower was the 'star', and to which 25 million visitors thronged to be impressed by the wealth and resources of the nation. From such a position of stability the state could afford a more conciliatory attitude towards its clerical enemies, and in 1890, largely at the prompting of Pope Leo XIII, the Church responded. The argument put to French conservatives by Cardinal Lavigerie, the Primate of Algeria, was that, unable to change the political settlement in France, the Church merely suffered unduly from its opposition. After initial conservative resistance to this line, the Pope instructed French Catholics (1891) to accept the authority of the Republic.

The renewal of confrontation

It is true that the *ralliement* had its enemies among Catholics and republicans alike, but it might have survived had not the Dreyfus Affair (*see* section **J**) once more polarised conservative and radical views. When the ministry led by Pierre Waldeck-Rousseau (1899–1902) took office, it had the specific aim of uniting all elements of republican support. It was once again clear that, in J. P. T. Bury's words, 'anti-clericalism was the cement that bound the different elements of the republican bloc together'. The death of Leo XIII in 1903 increased the possibility of a clash, for his successor, Pius X, was of an altogether more dogmatic stamp.

Moderate though he was, Waldeck-Rousseau provided the weapon for the final assault upon the Church. This was the Association Law (July 1901) which forbade the existence in France of any religious body or community without the specific authorisation of the government. In essence, this was a defensive measure, but it was transformed into an offensive one by Waldeck-Rousseau's successor, Émile Combes, a much fiercer anti-clerical. Under his enforcement of the Association Law 54 male and 81 female congregations were banned from France (1902), while the five authorised congregations were ordered to abandon all teaching activities within ten years (1904).

Separation

The year 1904 also witnessed the final crisis of relations between Rome and the Republic. The Pope precipitated the crisis by his protest at the visit of President Loubet to the King of Italy in Rome, the first visit by the head of a Catholic state since the loss of the Pope's temporal power in 1870. The reaction of the French administration was to break off diplomatic relations with the Vatican (November 1904) and to introduce a bill which realised the dreams of generations of anti-clericals by proposing the final separation of Church and state in France. By its passage (9 December 1905), the state guaranteed freedom of worship, but ceased officially to recognise or to subsidise any specific religion or cult. The land and assets of the Church were to be handed over to lay parish corporations (*Associations Cultuelles*), although ultimately all such property was sequestered by the state. This left the clergy simply as tenants of 'buildings needful for worship'.

Bitter as provincial opposition was to so radical a measure, there is much truth in J. P. T. Bury's judgement that 'the momentous separation of 1905 was probably beneficial to both sides'. Although the new and sudden poverty of the Church hit recruitment badly, reducing the annual rate of ordinations from 1,563 in 1905 to 704 in 1914, the same factor probably had a beneficial effect upon the quality of the recruits. Quantity, too, began to recover in the 1920s. Better still, the Church now found itself wholly free from state interference in appointments and other such matters, which had not been the case since the Napoleonic Concordat with the Vatican (1801).

The same could not be said for the Church's conservative ally, the army, whose appointments were so strictly controlled by Louis André, minister of war in 1900–04, as to cause a scandal over his use of spies to enquire into the political views of candidates for promotion. If Bury's opinion is open to doubt it is in the sense that separation removed the best area of common ground between the diverse members of the governmental Radical Bloc. 'Separation,' in the words of Madeleine Rebérioux, 'had marked the end of a common struggle.' From 1905, therefore, the government found itself subjected to a new series of threats from a different point of the political compass (*see* section **M**).

H The Republic in danger: Boulangism

Economic and political tensions in 1885

By the time of the 1885 elections the Republic was about to enter a period of renewed trial. A serious agricultural depression had hit France in the 1880s, the result of cheap corn imports from America. This was compounded by the ravages of the vine disease, phylloxera, which reduced wine production by more than two thirds between 1875 and 1889. In addition, the collapse of a major bank, the Union Générale (1882), ruined many small farmers. Economic hardship coincided with political outrage, especially over the collapse of Ferry's colonial policy at Tonkin (*see* section **O**) in 1885. Already in 1882 the nationalist Paul Déroulède had formed the 'League of Patriots', which had become a powerful right-wing force by 1885 with 182,000 members. In particular, its members protested against a foreign policy which seemed to ignore the question of Alsace-Lorraine.

The 1885 elections were the first under the Third Republic to be conducted by the method of *scrutin de liste* (*see* section **C**). The aim was to improve the standard of elected deputies and to rescue the Republic from the welter of trivial and obstructive interpellations in the Assembly. The surprise result was a dramatic revival of the right-wing vote, increasing its share from 25.9 per cent in 1881 to 43.9 per cent. The reign of the 'oppor-tunists' seemed endangered. The response of the prime minister, Freycinet, was to pass stringent measures against all members of former royal fami-lies, expelling them from France (1886). In addition he appointed to the key post of minister of war a distinguished soldier of proven republican sympathies, General Georges Boulanger.

The emergence of Boulangism

The succeeding months witnessed the transforma-tion of the little-known general into a national cult. His reputation as the long-awaited military saviour of France began with a series of modest but useful army reforms, and continued with the magnificent impression that he made upon the public at the Bastille Day parade at Longchamp. It reached its peak in 1887 with the 'Schnaebele Affair'. The arrest of a French official by Germans on the border of Alsace (April 1887) brought threats of war from the minister, to the horror of the govern-ment, but to the delight of the nationalists. The subsequent release of Schnaebele was interpreted as evidence of Bismarck's fear. Bismarck's use of 'Boulangism' to gain an increased army grant that year only further convinced French chauvinists that they had found 'General Revenge' who would soon win back Alsace and Lorraine for them.

The attempts of a frightened government to rid themselves of an apparently 'Napoleonic' figure failed due to Boulanger's enormous personal popu-larity. Nor was the government helped by a further scandal (November 1887) when the son-in-law of President Grévy was brought to trial for the illegal sale of state honours for private profit. With the resignation of Grévy, with both socialists and nationalists staging huge demonstrations, and with the General winning a string of by-elections, it seemed that France was on the verge of a new *coup d'état* with Boulanger as Louis Napoleon.

That this did not happen was largely due to Boulanger's dramatic refusal to play that role when Paris seemed to be at his feet after his latest elec-toral success (27 January 1889). Instead, he panicked and fled to Brussels to avoid arrest. He committed suicide there after the death of his mistress in 1891.

Boulangism and the Republic

Historical judgements upon Boulanger have varied between harshness and limited sympathy. To J. P. T. Bury he was 'a broken reed, a man who had no real political ideas or political courage'. Alfred Cobban has been a little kinder, however, seeing in his lack of initiative in 1889 some belated common sense and a genuine regard for political legality. However that may be, we have to conclude that the move-ment was of greater importance than the man.

Firstly, it represented the temporary union of all those forces hostile to the Republic. Nationalists, royalists, Bonapartists, and even radical leftists, saw in Boulanger a tool with which to wreck a regime that they hated. The failure of Boulangism, on the other hand, greatly benefited the Republic as it allowed it to reconsolidate its position with an overdue burst of legislation. *Scrutin d'arrondisement* was restored and the practice of standing for several constituencies at once was abolished.

Lastly, Boulangism transformed republicanism into an even more conservative creed, determined now to defend the constitution of 1875 against the sort of extra-parliamentary agitation for which the 'Boulanger Affair' had set a dangerous and lasting precedent.

I   The Panama scandal

The collapse of the Panama Canal Company

To the great frustration of the Boulangists, they had no sooner lost their leader than the Republic was struck by a new scandal. In 1891 the Panama Canal Company, headed by the great engineer Fer-dinand de Lesseps, went bankrupt. It had been formed ten years earlier to repeat the success of Suez, but had run into insurmountable engineering obstacles in Central America that had steadily drained its substantial private capital. Its last hope lay with a grant of public money by the Assembly (1888), secured by the liberal distribution of bribes to deputies, as was common in such business. The grant failed to do more than postpone what was France's worst financial disaster for two centuries. The legal action taken by disappointed shareholders led to a complex variety of charges against public figures. The suspicious death (September 1892) of the Baron de Reinach, a Jewish banker accused by the anti-Semitic press of having distributed the bribes, triggered off a witch-hunt.

The political implications of the scandal

The investigations of the courts and of the hostile press revealed that nearly one-third of the company's capital of 1,000 million francs had been used in bribes. Among those indicted were five former ministers, including a former premier, Floquet, five members of the Senate and a former Governor of Algeria. Although in general the charges could not be made to stick, the suspicions did. The career of Rouvier, the minister of finance, was blighted for a decade, as was that of the controversial Radical leader, Georges Clemenceau.

In a sense there was much that was insubstantial and transient about the Panama scandal. The elections of 1893 indicated no popular outrage against a 'corrupt' Republic. The conservative opposition actually lost a substantial amount of support and a large majority of the suspected deputies were re-elected. In three notable senses, however, the scandal transformed French politics. The prestige of the accused republicans never recovered, and a new generation of younger men like Raymond Poincaré, Louis Barthou and Théophile Delcassé, stepped into their places. They were less marked by the passions that had surrounded the foundation of the Republic, and were more ready to reach working compromises with other political groups.

Secondly, many working-class voters were convinced that a capitalist republic must always be corrupt, so the 1893 elections resulted in the first substantial presence of socialist deputies in the Chamber. There were now 49 instead of 12.

Lastly, the anti-Semitic element in the scandal, fanned by the journalism of Édouard Drumont, the editor of the newspaper *Libre Parole*, and others, established a relatively new factor in French politics that was to persist into the future and which was soon to flourish even more strongly with the emergence of an 'affair' that dwarfed all its predecessors: the 'Dreyfus affair'.

J   The Dreyfus affair

The emergence of the 'affair'

For a decade from 1896, the public life of France was dominated by an issue which divided the politically aware and illustrated starkly that the fundamental divisions within the Republic had survived intact for the first quarter century of its life. In September 1894 a sheet of paper was discovered containing a list of secret documents evidently communicated to the German intelligence service by someone within the French General Staff. On the thin evidence of handwriting, charges were brought against one Alfred Dreyfus, one of the few Jewish officers in the army. He was convicted (December 1894), largely on the evidence of Major Henry of the Intelligence Bureau, and sentenced to life imprisonment on the penal colony of Devil's Island, off the coast of French Guiana.

That the 'Dreyfus affair' arose from such a conviction was largely the responsibility of Lieutenant-Colonel Picquart, appointed head of the intelligence service in March 1896. Alerted by the continued passage of classified material to Germany, and by evidence implicating one Count Esterhazy, a personal friend of Henry, he reopened the case. His suspicions were brushed aside by the army, but by communicating them to the vice-president of the Senate and to the Dreyfus family, he ensured that the matter would become more than a military concern. The two sides in the conflict now became more clearly defined. The army reaffirmed the correctness of its original verdict with the aid of 'conclusive' evidence provided by Henry. This evidence was subsequently proved to be a series of forgeries. At the same time, increasing doubts about the whole conduct of the case erupted with the publication of the famous open letter from the writer Émile Zola to the President of the Republic under the title of *J'Accuse*. In it he made specific allegations of perjury and corruption against individual officers, and was himself tried and sentenced. The case was now a matter of fierce public concern.

What was at stake?

The bitter dispute that now divided politicians, intellectuals and private families was only to a very limited extent about Dreyfus himself. On both sides there were idealists who sincerely wished to see a miscarriage of justice rectified, or who were convinced of Dreyfus' guilt and wished to see him duly punished. Many others were merely fighting on the old battle lines of French politics. Many 'Dreyfusards' saw in the 'affair' only a convenient stick with which to beat the army officers and their allies, the clergy. Among the 'anti-Dreyfusards' were conservatives and monarchists aiming to discredit the Republic. It was also of crucial importance to the nationalists that the honour of the army, the instrument of France's future resurgence, should not be compromised. Anti-Semitism became a force in France more powerful than it had ever been before. Many saw in the attempts to clear the name of Dreyfus the machinations of a Jewish conspiracy against the nation. Incidents ranged from public insults to the President of the Republic, to an attempted *coup d'état* by the nationalist Déroulède in February 1899.

The turning point was reached in late 1898 when a new minister of war, General Cavaignac, reopened the case in an attempt finally to prove Dreyfus' guilt. Instead he came to realise the strength of Picquart's assertions. The arrest, confession and subsequent suicide of Henry, and the flight of Esterhazy, wrecked the case of the 'anti-Dreyfusards'. A retrial of Dreyfus produced another absurd verdict of 'guilty, but with extenuating circumstances' (August 1899), before the government stepped in to issue a full pardon. Not until 1906 was the matter finally settled by the full rehabilitation of Dreyfus into the army and his decoration with the Legion of Honour.

The significance of the 'affair'
What were the results of a decade of scandal and controversy? To a large extent they were negative. Social questions in France had been obscured by what Jules Guesde called a 'civil war of the bourgeoisie'. The rift between state and Church, and between republicans and conservatives, which the *ralliement* had seemed to close (*see* section **G**), now gaped wider than ever. On the other hand, there was a sense in which the Dreyfus affair confirmed the steady advance of republicanism. The forces of the Church and of the army, by stubbornly defending an increasingly hopeless position, had suffered a further major defeat. A purge of the compromised officers made even the army more

sympathetic to the Republic. The administration formed by Waldeck-Rousseau in 1899 thus had as its prime motive the regeneration of the Republic after more than a decade of sterile dispute.

K Economic development

The economic inheritance of the Republic
Economically, as in political and diplomatic terms, the Third Republic inherited a disaster. She had suffered a succession of cruel blows; the cost of the war, the loss of raw materials, especially iron ore in Alsace-Lorraine, and the temporary decline of Paris as a commercial and financial centre during the siege and the Commune. In the short term, they were blows from which France made a remarkable recovery. Writing in 1878 an English commentator, S. Bourne, could declare that 'France is of all the European nations the one of the most growing prosperity. We saw her wealth in the ease with which she provided for the German indemnity and in the rapidity with which she is recovering from disasters enough to have paralysed and destroyed nations even stronger than she.'

In the longer run the 1880s and 1890s were to produce factors (*see* sections **H** and **I**) which were to slow that progress dramatically. France was never again to reach a position higher than fourth among the great industrial powers of the world, significantly inferior to Germany. Domestically, French industry maintained a comfortable and steadily increasing degree of prosperity.

Heavy industry and the 'new' industries
The traditional heavy industries in France made steady progress, although handicapped by comparison with Britain or Germany by a relative lack of resources. They improved their output spectacularly in the years immediately before the outbreak of war. The output of iron ore was especially impressive, based upon the fortunate factor that a substantial part of the Lorraine ironfield, mainly discovered and exploited after 1871, still lay within French territory. In the newer industries, born at the turn of the century, France's performance gave less grounds for satisfaction. Although individual French scientists were responsible for a number of major developments, such as the work of the Curies on radium, and Pasteur in microbiology, the

chemical and electricity industries were slow to grow in France. French investment in electricity in 1913 was only one-third of the equivalent figure in Germany. An exception to this was the French motor industry which, by building more than 107,000 vehicles by 1914, stood second only to that of the USA.

Table 8.1 French industrial growth, 1870–1910

	1870	1880	1890	1900	1910
Coal	13,330	19,362	26,083	33,404	38,350
Iron ore	2,614	2,874	3,472	5,448	14,606
Steel	84	389	683	1,565	3,413

(figures indicate thousands of tons)

From C. Cook and J. Paxton, *European Political Facts*, Macmillan

The move to protectionism

Throughout the period, government economic policy moved away from the *laissez-faire* attitudes of the later years of the Second Empire, to offer greater protection to French industries, which often found themselves at a disadvantage in competition with their neighbours. Freycinet's intervention to modernise railways, inland waterways and harbour installations has already been mentioned (*see* section **D**). There was also the consistent protectionism of Jules Méline as minister of agriculture (1883–85) and as chairman of the Assembly's tariff commission. His work culminated in the so-called Méline Tariff of 1892. This imposed duties of 25 per cent on most agricultural imports and upon most manufactured and semi-manufactured goods, while allowing free entry to those raw materials necessary to French industries.

Living standards under the Republic

In considering the effect of these measures upon the living standards of the average French person, we perhaps find the key to the great paradox of the Third Republic. Its steady survival in the face of almost constant political opposition is perhaps best explained by the fact that the 40 years or so before the First World War were a period of steady improvement in the French standard of living. In the second half of the 19th century the average consumption of wine and potatoes rose by 50 per cent, that of meat and beer by 100 per cent, that of spirits by 200 per cent, and that of sugar and coffee by 300 per cent. The research of M. Lévy-Leboyer

indicates a 300 per cent rise in the gross national product since 1800, with an annual rate of increase in 1900–14 of 1.6 per cent (Britain 2.1 per cent, Germany 2.8 per cent). Whatever abstract and philosophical objections might be raised against the Republic, therefore, its economic performance kept it safe from those most potent agents of political change, hunger and deprivation.

L A cultural golden age

The plastic arts

In Germany after 1870, national victory and solidarity produced very few cultural achievements of lasting value, but an age of defeat and political uncertainty in France coincided with a period of artistic brilliance rarely paralleled in modern times. It would be misleading to speak of this as an achievement of the Third Republic on two counts. Firstly, its roots lay in the period before 1870. 'The fall of the Second Empire,' as Alfred Cobban has noted, 'was not a date in artistic, literary or scientific history.' Secondly, artistic greatness was often achieved in the face of fierce 'official' opposition. The works of those now regarded as France's greatest painters were dismissed by a leading functionary at the time as 'the paintings of democrats, of people who do not change their underwear'. In 1889 the historian Lavisse placed those same artists among the enemies of the Republic along with 'the decadent people, the incoherent people, and General Boulanger'.

Undoubtedly the greatest product of this period was the school of painting known as 'impressionism'. Its roots lay in the realism of such earlier artists as Gustave Courbet and Jean-François Millet, famous for their unsentimental treatment of peasant scenes. The movement advocated that painting should be less concerned with mere outline, and should concentrate instead upon fleeting effects of light and motion, as in Claude Monet's early work *Impression – The Sun Rising*. Add Paul Cézanne, Camille Pissarro, Alfred Sisley, Edgar Degas, Paul Gauguin and Pierre Auguste Renoir, and one still has an incomplete list of the major French artists embraced by the term 'impressionism'. The influence of impressionism was also huge, and is evident in the 20th-century schools known as 'expressionism' and 'cubism'.

Fauvism, which took its name from a critic's insult (*fauve* – wild animal), owes a negative debt to impressionism, by rejecting orthodox treatment of light and perspective. Nor was the influence of the movement limited to painting. The greatest sculptor of the century, Auguste Rodin, also called himself an impressionist in that he tried to catch a moment and a mood rather than merely to reproduce a form, but also suffered from official hostility.

Literature

French literature, too, moved away almost as vigorously from the romantic traditions of the earlier 19th century, producing its own catalogue of immortal names. Literary 'realism', pioneered by Gustave Flaubert in his *Madame Bovary* (1857) and *L'Education Sentimentale* (1869), gave way gradually to its more brutal variety 'naturalism'. Émile Zola's series of Rougon-Macquart novels (1871–93) are a classic example of this form. The same period saw Guy de Maupassant establish himself as the master of the short story, and the flowering of the symbolist school of poets led by Paul Verlaine, Charles Baudelaire and Stéphane Mallarmé.

Music and the birth of the French cinema

French music, like French politics, lived in the shadow of Germany for much of this period. The music of Jacques Offenbach, Georges Bizet and their imitators, popular though it was, was far too frivolous and lightweight to rival the impact of Wagner upon French audiences. Only in 1902, with the appearance of Claude Debussy's opera *Pelléas et Mélisande*, based upon the 'symbolist' play of that name by Maurice Maeterlinck, did a French musical school of comparable stature begin to take shape. It was to be developed further in the succeeding decade by Maurice Ravel, Gabriel Fauré, Paul Dukas and Erik Satie.

As a footnote, not treated so seriously by contemporaries, but of considerable significance in the light of its subsequent development, we should observe the origins of the French cinema in this period. Within ten years of the first projection in Paris by the Lumière brothers (December 1895), the cinema had begun to win acceptance as more than a sideshow. This was largely due to the work of Méliès in the fields of scenery and production techniques. Two other prominent contributors to the French industry before the war are still household names in the modern cinema. Charles Pathé built up France's first major film company between 1903 and 1909, with capital of 35 million francs. Léon Gaumont, builder of a 5,000 seat auditorium in Paris, provided Europe with the prototype of the modern, purpose-built cinema.

M The resurgence of socialism

Guesde and French Marxism

By 1900 French socialism was already deep-rooted. It went back to the traditions of 1848 and beyond, to the ideas of the French utopian socialists (*see* Chapter 1). These ideas had created a broad basis of sympathy, especially among the peasants of the south, long before the advent of widespread industrialisation. The *coup d'état* of 1851, with the punishment of those who opposed it, the conservatism of the Second Empire and the savage repression of the Commune, had all dealt cruel blows to French socialism. That it became a major force once more in the years before 1914 was largely due to the influence of three men.

Jules Guesde (1845–1922) played the greatest role in the introduction of Marxism into France, although in the course of his political career he departed some way from Marxist orthodoxy. He was an unattractive man, and as such was only partly successful as a politician. He was a strict enthusiast, to the extent that his enemies dubbed him 'Pope Guesde' or the 'Red Jesuit'. Nevertheless, he had the great strengths of being, in Theodore Zeldin's words, 'an outstandingly persuasive, enthusiastic and impressive orator, a vigorous, unsuppressible journalist, a tireless organiser'. In 1881 he founded the French Workers' Party (*Parti Ouvrier Français* or POF). It was based mainly upon well-organised pockets of support in the industrial regions of the north, it boasted 16,000 members by 1898 and attracted 294,000 votes in the general election of that year.

Jean Jaurès

Guesde's main rival for the leading place among French socialists during this period was Jean Jaurès (1859–1914). Less impressed than Guesde by the doctrines of Marxism, Jaurès was more independent. He disliked and distrusted Guesde's strict party discipline and the rigidity of his political doctrines. Detesting violence, whether in a national or a class context, he envisaged the achievement of proletarian power 'by the methodical and legal organisation of their own forces under democratic law and universal suffrage'. It was his unswerving faith in the preservation of peace through the co-operation of French and German workers that led to his murder by a crazed nationalist on the eve of the First World War. Nine years earlier, under pressure from the Second Socialist International, these two major forces in French socialism had come together to form the SFIO (*Parti Socialiste, Section Française de l'Internationale Ouvriere*). Its predominantly Marxist manifesto represented a major political defeat for Jaurès.

Sorel and syndicalism

Neither Guesde nor Jaurès could claim as much influence upon the political events of the first decade of the 20th century as Georges Sorel (1847–1922), the founder of syndicalism. His doctrine, propounded in his *Reflections on Violence* (1906), rejected the bourgeois democratic state and advocated direct action by politically motivated trades unions (*syndicat* – union). They were to use the general strike as their main weapon if necessary. There was much in this doctrine that appealed to anarchist and anti-parliamentary traditions in French socialism. The movement had already been deeply divided by the appointment of a socialist, Alexandre Millerand, in Waldeck-Rousseau's cabinet (1899), and had accepted the decision of the Amsterdam Congress of the International (1904) that socialists should withdraw their support from 'bourgeois' administrations. Since the foundation of the CGT (*Conféderation Générale du Travail*) in 1895, French unionism had possessed an organ which could co-ordinate direct action. By 1906, a total of 2,399 unions were affiliated to this central organisation. The acceptance by the CGT of the principle of the general strike as a political weapon in the so-called 'Charter of Amiens' in that year confirmed the tone of French domestic politics during the last decade of European peace.

N The social question

The 'Radical Bloc' under pressure from the left

The period of unusual ministerial stability from 1899 to 1905, when Waldeck-Rousseau and Combes led the so-called Radical Bloc, seemed to promise that the Republic would address the neglected problem of social reform at last. After years of struggle with conservative interests, a French premier could declare that he recognised 'no enemies on the left'. For the first time in European history, he could include a socialist, Alexandre Millerand, in his cabinet. It was not to be. This union of radical and socialist groups could not survive the decision of the socialist Amsterdam Congress to ban co-operation with capitalist governments. The Radicals who now dominated republicanism found themselves forced back into the familar position of fighting to preserve the Republic. This time, however, the threats to social order and stability came from the left.

Strike activity escalated quite suddenly in 1904 to unprecedented levels. The total of 1,026 strikes for that year was twice the total for 1903. The new level of strike action was subsequently maintained, and the strikes often displayed a specifically political content. On May Day 1906, the CGT launched a campaign with the aim of securing an eight-hour working day, which set the tone for a number of disruptions in key sectors of the economy. There were strikes in Marseilles, Paris, Le Havre and other major centres (1907–08). A widespread strike in the south caused disruption in the wine industry (1907), and railway workers (1908) and post office workers (1909) also caused considerable dislocation by their actions.

Clemenceau, Briand and the restoration of order

There was some irony in that the task of dealing with this new threat fell to the ministries of Georges Clemenceau (1906–09), a fierce radical critic of earlier administrations, and Aristide Briand (1909–10), formerly a prominent socialist. Their policies showed the truth of Theodore Zeldin's assertion that the Radicals 'could never work up a fighting enthusiasm for social reform'. Although Clemenceau entered office with a programme of 17 proposed reforms, only one, a measure for a degree of railway nationalisation, was passed. In the last years of peace an act providing for old age pensions (1910) and a codification of labour legislation (1912) were pushed through the Assembly, but an impressive array of proposals were also killed by that body. These included measures for a minimum factory wage, for better factory inspection, and the introduction of income tax. This last innovation was in fact rejected 65 times by parliaments between 1872 and 1907.

Instead, the great achievements of the ministries lay in the vigorous measures that they took to counter the strike agitation. Clemenceau did not hesitate to use the army to oppose the strikers, often on such a scale as actually to outnumber them. Military action frequently led to deaths among the demonstrators, as at Courrières (1906), Raon-l'Étape (1907) and Draveil (1908). The reputation of the premier by the time he left office was of 'Clemenceau the Killer'. Briand proved an apt pupil, breaking a railway strike in 1910 by mobilising the army reservists, a move that put many of the strikers in military uniform and thus subject to military law.

The Republic on the eve of war

By 1914 the greatest positive achievements of the Third Republic lay in the past. Perhaps its major achievement had been to create the broad consensus of support that had enabled the regime so far to survive for 44 years. For all that, the regime still did not seem to preside over a united nation. On the eve of war the General Staff still estimated that as many as 13 per cent of men of military age might refuse to be conscripted. That the eventual figure for refusals was as low as 1.5 per cent shows what success the Republic had achieved against its enemies. In the final analysis, the Third Republic had made great headway with two of its inherited problems. Domestically, it had taken great strides towards the creation of a secular state. In foreign policy it had, belatedly, revolutionised France's status as a European power.

0 Foreign policy: colonialism

The motives behind French colonialism

Colonialism was one of the main themes to run through the history of the Third Republic. Two bursts of colonial activity saw the expansion and consolidation of a French empire that was to outlive the Republic itself. Colonial expansion was by no means universally popular within republican ranks. Its achievement owed as much to private initiative as to concerted government policy.

In his work *Tonkin et la Mère Patrie* (1890), Jules Ferry put forward the view that 'colonial policy is the daughter of industrial policy', that is an industrial country graduated naturally to imperialism to win safe resources and markets. This is likely to have been the justification for an unpopular policy after the event rather than an explanation of original motives, for French industrialists had shown little enthusiasm for colonisation. Even as late as 1914, French industry derived ten times as much of its raw materials from non-colonial as from colonial sources.

It is more likely that colonial ventures represented to many French people the only arena in which France could pursue greatness at a time when the politics of Europe seemed so unfavourable to her. Prévost-Paradol wrote at the time that a Mediterranean empire would be for France 'not only a satisfaction to our pride, but certainly the last resource of our greatness'. There can be no doubt that in this respect Ferry's government received quite explicit support from Bismarck, who saw French colonialism as a valuable distraction from concerns over Alsace-Lorraine. Lastly, Alfred Cobban has stressed the Catholic element in French colonialism, noting that of 4,500 missionaries outside Europe in the 1880s, 75 per cent were French.

Acquisitions in Africa and Asia, 1878–85

For whatever reasons, from 1878, the year of her re-emergence from complete diplomatic isolation at the Congress of Berlin, France began to add in a piecemeal and chaotic fashion to her overseas empire. In May 1881 a military campaign extended French influence in North Africa by forcing the Bey of Tunis to accept a French protectorate in the Treaty of Bardo. Between 1882 and 1885 French representatives established a further protectorate over Madagascar, and created a French territory in the Congo, based upon the explorations of Brazza. In addition, France completed the reconquest of Tonkin and Annam in Indo-China, which de Broglie in 1874 had not thought worth the cost of a garrison.

Ferry and the issue of Tonkin

There were many in the 1880s who shared de Broglie's view. The colonial question bitterly divided French political opinion, and split republicans profoundly. While Ferry saw imperialism as the key to future greatness, socialists saw it as an immoral spin-off of capitalism, while radicals and conservatives joined in condemning it as a waste of men and money that would be better employed seeking revenge against Germany. The nationalist, Paul Déroulède, protested that to offer colonies as a consolation for the loss of Alsace-Lorraine was like offering 20 servants to a couple that had lost two children. Clemenceau went so far as to describe government policy as 'high treason'.

In 1882 these objections led to the sacrifice of French interests in Egypt because the Assembly refused to finance French co-operation with Britain, and they eventually destroyed Ferry's government. A minor reverse at Langson in Tonkin (March 1885) led to a rallying of all Ferry's opponents and those of the Republic to force him out of public life. Some genuinely feared that Tonkin might become another Mexico, but many merely wished to see the back of Ferry. Ferry fell, but Tonkin and the French empire did not. The Assembly granted the reinforcements that it had denied to Ferry to his successor a few weeks later. By 1887, Cochin-China, Cambodia, Annam and Tonkin were united as French Indo-China.

Franco-British rivalry in the 1880s and 1890s

Stimulated perhaps by the knowledge that growing friendship with Russia (*see* section **P**) increased France's European security, French colonialism enjoyed renewed vigour in the 1890s. French influence in Africa was substantially increased by the conquest of Dahomey (1890), the colonisation of the Ivory Coast (1893), the occupation of Timbuctoo (1894) and the annexation of Madagascar (1896).

In European terms this French expansion seemed to be having one of the effects that Bismarck hoped for, in that it promoted jealousy and rivalry between France and Britain. All over the globe agreements were patched up that just about avoided conflict; in the New Hebrides, where a joint administration was agreed in 1887; in Egypt, where the Suez Canal was neutralised by the Constantinople Convention (1888); in the Niger Valley, where spheres of influence were established in 1890.

Tension remained such, however, that the Fashoda crisis of September 1898 nearly brought the two countries to war. A confrontation between a French expeditionary force and Kitchener's British force at Fashoda in the Sudan led to British demands for French withdrawal. Public opinion in France was ready to fight over such an affront, but Delcassé, the foreign minister, was realistic enough to know the strength of the British navy and the damage that a lengthy colonial conflict could do to France's European position. Thus Fashoda decided that France's African influence was to be confined to the west. Anglo–French relations remained bitter and hostile, but only for a relatively short time before other factors worked a transformation upon them.

P Foreign policy: the Russian Alliance

1871–1890: an era of isolation

In 1871 the international status of France was as desperate as at any time in her history. Bordered by a united Germany and by a united Italy, her international isolation was complete. Her eligibility as an ally was at a low ebb, she was humiliated in war and riven by social strife. Nearly two decades later, in 1889, those in charge of her foreign affairs had achieved little improvement. True, foreign reaction to the 'war in sight' crisis of 1875 had reduced the immediate threat of German aggression. French attendance at the Congress of Berlin in 1878 had also marked an overdue return to the diplomatic community, but these events had gained France no reliable friends. By the Triple Alliance and the Reinsurance Treaty, Austria-Hungary, Italy and Russia all remained tied to the Bismarckian system of alliances, which had as its very cornerstone the isolation of France.

The chances of improvement seemed slight. Relations with Russia were soured by the gulf between republican democracy and Tsarist autocracy, and by Russian contempt for French political instability. In the words of Giers, the Tsar's foreign minister, the Republic was merely 'a mass of rottenness'. As regards Italy, her entry into the Triple Alliance (1882) and the declaration of France's protectorate over Tunis, where Italy also had historic ambitions, led to a decade of bitterness. This was fanned by the anti-French economic policies of the then premier, Francesco Crispi.

The creation of the Franco–Russian entente

The remarkable transformation in French foreign relations from 1890 must be explained largely in terms of errors in German diplomacy, although credit is due to two outstanding foreign ministers for their exploitation of these mistakes. Gabriel Hanotaux (1894–95 and 1896) and Théophile Delcassé (1898–1906) dominated the Quai d'Orsay (the French Foreign Ministry) during this period.

The refusal of Wilhelm II to renew the Reinsurance Treaty (*see* Chapter 10, section **E**) compounded Bismarck's uncharacteristic error in 1887 in refusing to sanction German loans to Russia. These factors left Russia herself in a state of isolation. The progress of the two isolated powers towards one another was slow, marked by much Russian reticence, but France had much to offer. An agreement to curtail the activities of Russian nihilists in France was followed by the more important step of opening the French money market to Russian borrowing. This move was worth over £400 million to Russia within a decade. Slowly, between 1891 and 1894, the military understanding all important to France began to take shape. The visit of a French naval squadron to Kronstadt (July 1891) resulted only in a very general agreement to 'consult together on every question that endangers general peace' (August 1891). In the following year, however, meetings between the respective chiefs of staff, Boisdeffre and Obruchev, resulted in an agreement on joint military action. The Tsar finally consented to regard this as the basis of an official Franco–Russian alliance (January 1894). Russia undertook to attack Germany if that country attacked France, or aided Italy in an attack on France. France was similarly committed if Germany attacked Russia, or aided Austria-Hungary in such an attack.

France had achieved one of the great diplomatic coups of the 19th century, overcoming immense dificulties to break the country's crippling isolation. The popularity of the alliance was enormous, and was in stark contrast to public indifference to colonial successes. Public demonstrations on the occasions of the Russian fleet's visit to Toulon (1893), or the visit of the Tsar to Paris (1896) left little doubt that Russia had become 'the first love of the Third Republic'. Only a few detatched voices pointed out that the alliance committed Russia to no action on behalf of Alsace-Lorraine and that it might well embroil France in eastern European questions which had been, hitherto, none of her business.

Foreign policy: Italy and Great Britain

The resolution of differences with Italy

Remarkable as it was, the Russian alliance was only one item among the achievements of French diplomacy at the turn of the century. Within eight years a new relationship had also been forged with Italy. The key to this lay in the fall of the anti-French administration of Francesco Crispi following Italy's catastrophic defeat by Abyssinia at Adowa in 1896. Italian disillusion with African adventures diminished the importance of the dispute over Tunis, and Delcassé was able to conclude a series of agreements on spheres of influence in North Africa. These recognised French rights in Tunis (1896) and those of Italy in Tripolitania (1900). In November 1898 he concluded a new Franco-–Italian trade treaty to replace the one renounced by Crispi in 1887. The significance of these developments should not be exaggerated. Italy was still a member of the Triple Alliance, a status that she confirmed in 1902, while reassuring France at the time that she would never go to war with her under the auspices of that alliance. Clearly then, if Italy remained betrothed to Germany, she was intent upon serious flirtation with other suitors.

Rapprochement with Great Britain

In 1898, for all her diplomatic success elsewhere, France stood on the verge of war with Great Britain over the Fashoda crisis. In subsequent years French hostility to British policy in South Africa, and British hostility to the policy of France's great ally, Russia, in the Far East, scarcely promised warmer relations. This gap, however, was also to be bridged largely by courtesy of errors in German policy. Germany's decision to enter into naval rivalry with Britain, her tactless support for the Boers, and Britain's own increased sense of isolation after the Boer War, all helped to provide a basis for an Anglo–French rapprochement. The keys to improved relations were provided by mutual concessions over influence in North Africa, and by the tactful diplomacy of two men, Paul Cambon, ambassador to London from 1898 to 1920, and Britain's new monarch, Edward VII, whose visit to Paris in 1903 did so much to break down popular antipathy to Britain. April 1904 saw the conclusion of a comprehensive agreement on outstanding colonial questions. France recognised Britain's predominant interest in Egypt, while Britain conceded a 'free hand' to France in Morocco. Lesser disputes concerning Newfoundland, Siam, Madagascar and the New Hebrides were also settled. This so-called *Entente Cordiale* had strict limitations. It contained, for example, absolutely no military commitment by either side. However, it did conclude a remarkably fruitful decade for French diplomacy, at the end of which the Republic could face any political development within Europe with greatly increased confidence.

Questions

Essay questions

1   'The Third French Republic in the years 1871–1914 survived every crisis, but with difficulty and at considerable cost to national unity'. How far do you agree with this view? (JMB/NEAB)

2   Why, by 1914, did the Third Republic enjoy such widespread support in France? (AEB)

3   How seriously did the Dreyfus Affair threaten the stablity of the French Third Republic? (ULEAC)

4   How far had France recovered by 1900 from the effects of the defeat in 1870? (UCLES)

5   Should the history of the Third Republic up to 1914 be regarded as 'more than a series of scandals'? Explain your answer fully. (WJEC)

6   Did the Third French Republic have any significant internal enemies in the period before 1914? (Oxford Entrance)

The Dreyfus Affair

SOURCE A

[Let us consider] on the one hand all those over the last twenty years who have been convicted of treason against the motherland and have, for one reason or another, escaped the death penalty. Marshal Bazaine, convicted of treason, was sentenced to death, but was not shot. Captain Dreyfus, convicted of treason by a unanimous verdict, has not been condemned to death. And, as against these judgements, the whole country sees that they shoot simple soldiers, without mercy or pity, who are guilty of a moment's aberration or violence. (*Applause from the extreme left*)

Such cases as the one for which Marshal Bazaine was prosecuted are not at issue here. Bazaine was condemned to death, and only escaped execution due to one of those presidential pardons, which are not often extended to the soldiers of whom I have just been speaking. (*Very good! Very good! from the extreme left. Interruptions*) But is the Minister of War acting correctly in such cases as that of Captain Dreyfus? Gentlemen, you will understand that I have neither the intention nor the right to discuss such a judgement. But we, Parliament, have the duty to ask ourselves whether justice in this country will not be rendered helpless if such abominable acts as those of Captain Dreyfus are repeated.

Speech by the socialist leader, Jean Jaurès, in the Chamber of Deputies, December 1894.

SOURCE B

As for myself, I formed my opinion in the Dreyfus affair before I knew the facts of the case. I went to Rennes [where the second hearing of the Dreyfus case was held] with the public interest uppermost in my mind. Yet the actual presence of Dreyfus affected me greatly. If I had sensed an innocent man within that human wreck, I would have retired from the struggle immediately. Instead I saw, during those long sessions, that the face of Dreyfus sweated treason.

I told my readers after a fortnight: 'He is certain to be condemned'. Had I got inside information? The judges had spoken to noone. I merely recognised them as good Frenchmen, and the crime was sitting in front of them. Let us rejoice with a free spirit. France has been well served.

Maurice Barrès, a right-wing intellectual, in Scènes et Doctrines du Nationalisme *(1902).*

SOURCE C

It is certain that we can feel pity without contradicting our principles, and without faltering in the class struggle. We can retain our humanitarian instincts while engaged in the revolutionary battle. We are not constrained to turn our backs on humanity in order to remain true to socialism.

By being falsely and criminally judged by the society that we are fighting, Dreyfus himself, whatever his origins may be, becomes a shrill protest against that social order. Through the faults of a society which insists upon using violence, lies and crimes against him, he becomes an element in the revolution. Those socialists who wish to get right to the bottom of the shameful and criminal secrets contained in this affair, may not be concerning themselves with a worker, yet they are concerned with the whole working class. For who is most threatened today by the arbitrariness of the generals, by the violence of military repression? Who? The proletariat. It is thus an issue of the first importance to punish the crimes and the violence of these military tribunals before they become a kind of habit, accepted by everyone.

Because, this time, it is a son of the bourgeoisie to whom the High Command has applied its arbitrary and lying system, bourgeois society is profoundly moved and disturbed. We must take advantage of this disturbance to diminish the moral force and the aggressive power of this retarded General Staff which is a direct threat to the proletariat.

From an article by Jean Jaurès published in 1898 in the socialist magazine Preuves.

SOURCE D

The vast majority of Dreyfusards are motivated by preoccupations that have nothing to do with the issue of innocence.

For some, the important point is to strike a blow at anti-semitism. M. Joseph Reinach [a prominent pro-Dreyfus member of the Assembly] has stated that racial hatred has been greatly stimulated by the Dreyfus Affair, and he seeks to suppress anti-semitic agitation by rehabilitating Dreyfus and, what is more, showing him to be the victim of fanatics.

For others, the important point is to abolish military justice. These gentlemen insist upon a version of events, which they present as fact, whereby false evidence has been put before the military tribunal. In the name of *The Rights of Man and the Citizen*, protestants and liberals deny that the authorities have the power to take special action in the interests of public order, or that special cases should be treated according to special rules.

Such are the men who have been Dreyfusards from the outset. What do they know whether their man is innocent or guilty? They insist upon transforming a judicial fact into a social issue. Why? To promote various obsessions which are close to their hearts, and which have nothing to do with the issues put before the judges at the military tribunal. Thus they say that Dreyfus is a symbol, but let it be understood that these political schemers have taken up this little Jew as a weapon, like an assassin's blade.

Maurice Barrés, Scènes et Doctrines du Nationalisme *(1902).*

a   Explain the references in the documents to:
 i   'Marshal Bazaine' (Source A).
ii   'Dreyfusards' (Source D).
iii   'In the name of *The Rights of Man and the Citizen*' (Source D).
b   What elements of consistency and inconsistency occur in the two speeches by Jean Jaurès (Sources A and C)
c   Comment upon the claims made by Maurice Barrés in Source D
 i   in the light of Sources A and C
ii   in the light of Source B.
d   What evidence do these documents provide of the tensions and divisions within French society at the close of the 19th century?

9

The crisis of Russian autocracy, 1894–1914

A cartoon by the French commentator, Caran d'Ache, which appeared in *Le Figaro* in 1904. It shows the Russian bear impertinently challenged by Japan.

What images of Russia and Japan are projected in this cartoon?

Where would the sympathies of a French commentator be most likely to lie in this matter in 1904?

The Historical Debate

The events that shaped Russian history between 1856 and1917 obviously had an enormous impact and influence upon the history of the 20th century as a whole. This factor has combined with the closed nature of Russian society throughout most of that century to ensure that a large proportion of the historical commentaries on the period have been written from a partisan point of view. Russian writings, in particular, both before and after the revolution, have always clearly reflected an official standpoint. At first this took the form of official court biographies, such as those of Shilder (*The Emperor Nicholas I, His Times and Reign*, 1903) and Tatishchev (*The Emperor Alexander II, His Times and Reign*, 1903). These naturally accepted the Tsarist view of government and society and viewed the events of the reign in that light.

Between the revolution and the recent collapse of Soviet power, Russian historians inevitably interpreted the events of this period in a Marxist sense, stressing the hopelessness of attempts to save a rotten regime by social and economic reforms. Similarly, the period between 1905–17 was treated as one of recurring revolutionary crisis that could have only one logical outcome. Soviet writers were also under much pressure to accept as truths a number of opinions published during this period by Lenin himself. Thus the role of the Bolshevik Party and the correctness of Lenin's interpretation of events between 1905–17 tended to be stressed, while the roles of the Mensheviks, the SRs and, of course, the conservatives were diminished. This is evident in official publications directly sponsored by the government (*History of the Communist Party of the Soviet Union*, 1960), and in more strictly academic works such as those of A. M. Pankratova (*The Revolution of 1905–07 in Russia: Documents and Materials*, 1955–61), Aaron Avrekh (*Stolypin and the Third Duma*, 1968) and A. B. Shapkarin (*The Peasant Movement in Russia, June 1907–July 1914*, 1960).

In general, western historians have not accepted this thesis of 'inevitable' revolution, but have viewed the period immediately before the war as one that was open to many possibilities. This has generated the debate between 'optimists' and 'pessimists' which is referred to in section Q. A. Gerschenkron (*Economic Backwardness in Historical Perspective*, 1962) and Theodore von Laue (*Why Lenin? Why Stalin?* 1964) may be cited as leading representatives of these respective schools. To the 'optimist' school we should also add those liberals, both Russian and foreign, whose sympathy with democracy and with the rule of law convinced them that the Dumas were following the correct road when war intervened. Paul Miliukov, a leading Kadet politician (*History of Russia*, 1932) and S. Pushkarev (*The Emergence of Modern Russia 1801–1917*, 1963) provide good examples of the arguments of the Russian exiles, while Bernard Pares (*Russia and Reform*, 1907 or *My Russian Memoirs*, 1931) provides a classic statement of the problem viewed from a Victorian-liberal bias. Of the many English and American works of recent years, attempting to reach a balanced synthesis of both western and Soviet research on the period, by far the most detailed and authoritative is that by Hugh Seton-Watson (*The Russian Empire, 1801–1917*, 1967).Virtually no serious apology for the Tsarist regime has been attempted, except in the memoirs of certain leading government figures, such as those of Sergei Witte (*The Memoirs of Count Witte*, 1921) and Konstantin Pobedonostsev (*Reflections of a Russian Statesman*, 1898).

A The Russian economy

The peasant problem

The early years of Nicholas' reign brought little respite for the peasantry, or for many of the smaller gentleman landowners, from the problems that had beset them since the emancipation of the serfs. The official government policy of low bread prices meant a low income for the farmers even when harvests were good, and harvest failures were frequent, notably in 1891, 1892, 1898 and 1901. The steady increase in the population of European Russia also increased the pressure upon peasant holdings that had often been inadequate to begin with. It has been estimated that the average peasant holding shrank from 35 acres in 1877 to 28 acres in 1905 due to subdivision within the growing family. The result, quite apart from frequent outbreaks of agrarian violence, was that arrears in taxation and in redemption payments accumulated rapidly.

Government initiatives

Motivated by concern for its own income, and for the future of the landed gentry and nobility, the government attempted two solutions to these problems. One was the formation of an improved Land Bank in 1886. The bank was equipped with funds and with reserves of land, much of it former state land, to encourage the purchase of viable holdings that might satisfy the pressing 'land hunger' of the peasants. Within two years of its formation the interest rates charged by the bank upon its loans were as low as 4 per cent. The second was to exploit a larger proportion of Russia's vast land resources by encouraging settlement on 'virgin' land in the east. In 1896 the government founded its Resettlement Bureau to stimulate migration to Siberia. As a further encouragement, and to improve the public image of Siberia, the shipment of criminals there was suspended in 1900. Neither project was wholly unsuccessful, but neither could hope to do more than scratch the surface of an enormous problem. It is true that the total amount of land in peasant hands increased substantially, by over 26 million hectares between 1877 and 1905, but that in the hands of the nobility declined by nearly 21 million. Equally the fact that 750,000 peasants migrated to Siberia in the last four years of the century needs to be set against the huge total peasant population of nearly 97 million reflected in the census of 1895.

The survival of agrarian problems

By the revolutionary year of 1905 there were still several insuperable obstacles between the peasant and a lasting solution to the land problem. One was the continuing existence of the peasant commune, the *mir*, to which many were still bound by the legislation of 1861. In many cases the *mir* continued to impose restrictions upon travel and freedom of enterprise that rendered government encouragement pointless. Secondly, the consistent lack of direct financial investment in agriculture meant that the Russian peasant was still usually bedevilled by primitive farming methods totally outdated in western Europe. The magnitude of Russian agricultural production was a reflection of her land resources, and not of the efficiency with which they were exploited. In 1898–1902, for example, an average acre of Russian farmland produced 8.8 bushels compared to 13.9 in the USA and 35.4 in Great Britain.

The fact, therefore, that Russia became the world's largest supplier of wheat to foreign markets in 1913 by exporting 3.33 million tons, conceals the truth that much of this was what came to be referred to as 'starvation exports'. The phrase refers to exports made despite domestic demand for the product, to pay for the industrial raw materials and machinery upon which the government, by the late 1890s, was staking the future of Russia.

B Sergei Witte

Witte's view of the future of Russia

For all the political shallowness of Nicholas II, he was served by two ministers who might, given the right circumstances and consistent support, have saved the monarchy. The first of these was Sergei Witte, who became minister of finance in August 1892 and held office until 1903. Witte was of Dutch origin, but his family had achieved noble status by service to the state, and he had risen to his high office by the unusual route of outstanding service in railway administration.

Witte did not regard himself, once in office, as a narrow financial specialist. Self-confident and dynamic, he regarded the ultimate aim of his policies as being the salvation of Russia and the creation of a strong, modern state, but his political views were confused and uncertain. Although he professed himself dedicated to the maintenance of the autocracy, he cannot wholly have failed to foresee the effects that the economic transformation of Russia would have upon that autocracy. This curious mixture of energy and miscalculation naturally made Witte a controversial character among contemporaries and historians alike. Political opponents accused him of extravagance and of unpatriotic concessions to foreign capitalists. A number of more recent historians have criticised him for being insufficiently aware of the need for substantial agricultural reform. Others, nevertheless, have been impressed by the extent of his vision and by his practical political ability. To Theodore von Laue he was attempting 'to rally both government and people to one common, almost superhuman effort'. To Hugh Seton-Watson, similarly, Witte was 'one of the outstanding statesmen of the 19th century'.

Witte's measures

To Witte, the key to Russia's future greatness lay in industrialisation. Russia's only alternative was to become a 'European China', a vast market unable to supply its own needs and thus 'the eternal handmaiden of states that are economically more developed'. His views were not original, being largely those of the previous minister of finance, I. A. Vyshnegradsky (1887–92), and also being influenced by Bismarck's policies in Germany. His real contribution was the coherent programme that he proposed in the 1890s to carry out this desired industrialisation. The basis of the policy was the strengthening of protective tariffs to guard infant Russian industries against the destructive competition of stronger European economies. But how was Russian industry to develop when the vital investment capital was lacking, when the total amount of capital lying in Russian banks amounted to only 200 million roubles? How would foreign powers react if their access to so valuable a market were to be restricted? Witte's solution was to invite these powers to continue to participate in the Russian economy, but by investing capital in it rather than by off-loading their consumer goods on to it. Thus the capital would be provided for the development of Russian industry. Industrial growth would also safeguard the government against social unrest by providing fuller employment, and in the long run higher wages and cheaper goods. Protective tariffs, the attraction of foreign capital and the placing of the Russian currency on the Gold Standard (January 1897) in order to inspire greater foreign confidence, were thus the three prongs of Witte's policy to create a great industrial Russia.

C The Russian economy: industrial development

The development of heavy industries

At the time of the outbreak of the First World War, Russia was still a modest industrial power by comparison with much of Europe and with the USA. For example, she produced in 1912 only 5.6 per cent of the world's pig iron, and only 3.66 per cent of its steel. In 1910 only 30 per cent of Russia's total national production was industrial, compared to 75 per cent in Britain, 70 per cent in Germany, and even 47 per cent in Austria-Hungary. In purely Russian terms, nevertheless, progress had been rapid. An annual industrial output valued at 1,502 million roubles in 1890 had increased to 5,738 million by 1912. It should be remembered that this period included a major economic slump (1899–1902) and very serious foreign and domestic disruptions (1904–06). Development differed from area to area and from industry to industry. Industrial production was largely concentrated in four regions: in St Petersburg and the shores of the Baltic, in Moscow and the provinces of Nizhni Novgorod and Vladimir, in Poland, and in the Donbas and Krivoi Rog regions of the south. Textile production continued to dominate, accounting in 1910 for 40 per cent of Russia's industrial output. Table 9.1 shows that, although they may not have compared so favourably with their more developed world rivals, other industries made impressive advances.

Table 9.1 Russian industrial production ('000 tons)

	Coal	Petroleum	Iron ore	Steel
1880	3,290	382	–	307
1885	4,270	1,966	–	193
1890	6,010	3,864	1,736	378
1895	9,100	6,935	2,851	879
1900	16,160	10,684	6,001	2,216
1905	18,670	8,310	4,976	2,266
1910	25,430	11,283	5,742	3,314

From Cook and Paxton, *European Political Facts, 1848–1918*.

Foreign investment in Russian industry

Certainly, those industries detailed in Table 9.1 were among those that benefited most from the influx of foreign capital stimulated by Witte's policies. There is no recent study of the exact extent to which foreign powers and individuals involved themselves in Russian industry, but older studies show that it was vast. P. Ol, a very early Soviet commentator, showed 214.7 million roubles of foreign capital invested in Russia in 1890, 280.1 million in 1895, and then a very substantial upsurge to reach 911 million in 1900, and 2,000 million before the outbreak of war in 1914. About half of this went into the mining and metallurgical industries of the south, and it is possible that by 1900 as much as 90 per cent of the finance behind these sectors of the economy came from foreign investment. Oil production and banking were the next largest recipients of foreign funds. The greatest financial friend to Russia was her closest political ally, France, whose investment was about 33 per cent of the total in 1914. The other most important suppliers of capital were Great Britain (23 per cent), Germany (20 per cent), Belgium (14 per cent) and the USA (5 per cent).

Railway development and foreign trade

The development of Russian railways also produced some impressive growth statistics, although these also pale by comparison with those of more advanced countries. The rate of railway construction that had produced less than 5,800 km in 1861–90 accelerated to produce a national system of 59,616 km by 1905. The imagination of the world was captured by the vast engineering feat of the construction of the Trans-Siberian Railway, linking European Russia to its most easterly outpost of Vladivostok (1891–1904). The greatest years of industrial expansion, however, coincided with a tailing-off of railway construction. The five years between 1908 and 1913 saw the slowest rate of growth since the 1880s, and although Russia boasted the world's second largest railway network in 1913,there was a substantial gap between Russia and the only state of comparable size. Her network totalled 62,200 km compared to 411,000 km in the USA. Other forms of communication in Russia remained wholly inadequate. Only the major inter-city roads of European Russia matched up to general European standards, and the merchant marine was remarkably small, nearly all of Russia's substantial foreign trade travelling in foreign ships.

The last major feature of Russia's pre-1914 industrialisation was the dramatic increase in her foreign trade. Table 9.2 indicates the steady increase in trade in both directions. It should be remembered, however, that while the balance remained favourable to Russia, her exports were mainly of agricultural produce. The balance in industrial goods, therefore, remained very much to Russia's disadvantage. Russia was most heavily involved with Germany, to whom she exported 453 million roubles' worth of goods in 1913, and from whom she received 652 million roubles' worth. Great Britain held second place in both respects.

Table 9.2 Russia's balance of trade (million roubles)

	Imports	Exports
1904	651.4	1,106.4
1906	800.6	1,094.8
1908	912.6	998.2
1910	1,084.4	1,449.1
1912	1,171.7	1,518.8

D The growth of an urban proletariat

The increase in the scale of industrial production

The steady industrialisation of the Russian economy accentuated the breakdown of the traditional social structures that began in 1861. It combined with Russia's continuing agrarian problems to accelerate the drift of workers from the impoverished countryside to the developing centres of industrial production. In 1900 2.5 million workers were employed in factory or workshop production. Taking into account their families and dependents, this probably meant that between 10 and 13 million Russians were now economically dissociated from the land and were reliant upon an industrial wage. This was a relatively small proportion of Russia's total population of 116.5 million (1895), but was probably three times the figure that had applied in 1880.

Of equal importance was the increase in the size of units of production. Table 9.3, indicating an increase of about 30 per cent in the number of factories while the workforce doubled, makes it clear that the workforce of the average factory grew substantially. Indeed, nearly half of Russia's industrial workforce in 1902 worked in factories employing 1,000 men or more.

Table 9.3 Russia's industrial workforce

	Factories	Workers
1887	30,888	1,318,000
1890	32,254	1,434,700
1897	39,029	2,098,200
1908	39,856	2,609,000

The growth of Russian towns

The results of these changes were typical of the early stages of industrialisation elsewhere in Europe. The dramatic growth rates of the major towns between 1867–97, such as Moscow (197 per cent), Warsaw (253 per cent), Baku (702 per cent) and Lodz (872 per cent), suggest the problems of urban overcrowding that now developed. Living and working conditions are suggested by the trickle of social legislation wrung from a reluctant government by a wave of strikes at the turn of the century. The employment of children under 12 was forbidden (1892). Female labour was banned in mines (1892), and an eleven and a half hour working day was legally instituted (1896), although the law was widely ignored by employers. Factory inspectors were finally introduced in 1903. Nevertheless, major problems persisted, such as overcrowding in factory barracks, and the illegal payment of part of the worker's wages in kind. Strikes, although illegal until 1905, were frequent. Sixty eight were recorded in 1895, 125 in 1900, culminating in 14,000 outbreaks in the revolutionary year of 1905.

E The growth of opposition: Marxism

Plekhanov and the birth of Russian Marxism

The greatest success of Russian populism, the murder of the Tsar in 1881, proved to be its swan-song. The romanticism, the lack of realism, the violence of populism drained much of its public sympathy and created a temporary void which might be filled by other ideas. That the arguments of the German socialist thinker Karl Marx (*see* Chapter 1) came to fill part of that gap was partly due to the enthusiasm of Georgi Plekhanov. It was also due in part to the curious leniency of the Russian censors. Plekhanov was originally a populist prominent in the 'Land and Liberty' movement. Observing the growth of Russian industry, however, he became convinced that Marx, and not those who concentrated upon the Russian peasant and his commune, held the key to Russia's future. Vera Zasulich and P. B. Akselrod were other figures who formed a bridge between populism and Marxism in Russian thought. By 1894 the writings of Plekhanov had given Russian readers their most coherent exposition of Marx's thought. That they were able to read it at all was largely due to censors who admitted Marxist works in the belief that they would weaken the terrorist threat of populism. *Capital* was thus available in a Russian translation as early as 1872.

The limited scale of Russian Marxism in the 1890s

It is only with hindsight that any political importance can be ascribed to the earliest Marxist groups in Russia. A number of very small cells existed from 1889 in St Petersburg, Moscow, Vilna and Kiev. Their only real claim to fame at this point was that one of the St Petersburg groups was joined in August 1893 by a young lawyer from Simbirsk named Vladimir Ilyich Ulyanov. He was later to adopt the 'cover' name of V. I. Lenin. Not until March 1898 did representatives of the various groups meet secretly in Minsk to found the Russian Social Democratic Labour Party (RSDRP). Even then the immediate arrest of eight of the nine delegates rendered Marxism a very modest force in Russian politics at the turn of the century.

As regards tactics, the Russian Marxists rejected the use of terror as counterproductive and chose to concentrate instead upon industrial agitation and propaganda. Marxists were active alongside other opposition groups in the industrial disturbances in St Petersburg in 1895, 1896 and 1897.

F The growth of opposition: other groups

The Socialist Revolutionaries

Given the ultimate success of the Marxists it is easy to understand how a number of western historians, as well as their Soviet counterparts, should have emphasised their importance in the years before 1914, and diminished the importance of other radical groups. Other commentators, however, among them the German E. Oberländer, have tried to dispense with the wisdom that comes from hindsight. They have stressed that in the context of the time at least two other opposition movements had far greater support and played a far more positive role in the events of the years 1900–14.

The first of these was the Socialist Revolutionary Party, founded in 1901. The SRs, as they came to be called, were essentially second-generation populists, their cause revived by severe agrarian distress in 1891 and by the release of some earlier leaders from Siberia. They followed a path recognisable to the earlier generation, but modified to meet changed circumstances, such as the undeniable development of Russian capitalism. It is common for historians to refer to the Socialist

Revolutionaries as 'the party of the peasants'. Lionel Kochan and Hugh Seton-Watson, however, stress the breadth and relative looseness of their views and of their membership. The various groups established in Moscow, in Saratov and in the Ukraine in the 1890s placed a common emphasis upon the need to propagate their views among the urban workers, but they placed varying degrees of confidence in the peasantry and in terrorism as revolutionary weapons. The development, especially in the Ukraine in 1902, of widespread agrarian discontent in which SR agitation was prominent, elevated the role of the peasantry in party theory. When party policy was officially formulated, therefore, the peasantry was placed in the role of the army which would follow the vanguard of the urban proletariat. The main plank of the party's platform was the redistribution of agricultural land to the peasantry on the basis of how much each could profitably use.

The terrorist branch of the SRs also achieved spectacular, if sterile successes. The deaths of the minister of education, Bogolepov (1901), the minister of the interior, Sipyagin (1902), his successor Plehve (1904), and the governor of Moscow (1905), were all the work of its members. The apparent success of peasant agitation and terrorist conspiracy thus made the SRs a party of action, while the Marxists seemed to remain a party of faction and theory. 'More than any other party,' wrote Richard Charques, 'it was the party of youth.' This immediate, superficial appeal made the SRs the most popular of the radical opposition groups until 1917.

Russian liberalism

Secondly came the diverse groups that constituted Russian liberalism. Prominent among these were the *zemstvo* members, some of whom, led by P. N. Shipov, persisted in their hopes for a representative assembly that would provide some form of consultation between the Tsar and his people on the lines of the old *Zemsky Sobor*. Many *zemstvo* politicians, supported by a more radical group known as the 'Third Element', expressed less interest in political institutions than in practical reforms within the existing social system. Among their demands were the abolition of corporal punishment and of the power of the Land Commandants over the peasantry, and the

introduction of universal primary education. In the light of the events of the decade 1905–14 these liberals might claim to have been the most successful of the opposition groups within Russia.

Until 1905, however, the two courses of action proposed by liberals had borne little fruit. For a while it had seemed that direct representations to the government might work. The then minister of the interior, I. L. Goremykin, seemed willing to introduce *zemstvo* institutions into Lithuania, Byelorussia and other areas where none existed. By 1902, however, he had lost both the debate on the subject within the council of ministers and his official post. The other course, common to many opposition groups, was to found a party and a journal in the safety of foreign exile. The establishment of the newspaper *Liberation* (*Osvobozhdeniya*) and the Union of Liberation (*Soyuz Osvobozhdeniya*) was complete by 1903.

The dramatic realisation of several liberal demands was, however, to be brought about by foreign affairs of a quite different nature.

G   The origins of the Russo–Japanese War

The colonial collision in the Far East

The Russo–Japanese War was the direct result of the clash of two sets of imperialist ambitions attempting to expand into the same power vacuum. Russian economic activity in the Far East had a long history. The development of Vladivostok dated from the 1860s but, although important, the port was of limited value as it was closed by ice for three to four months of the year. The decision to begin the Trans-Siberian Railway in 1891 represented a substantial commitment in that area. Between 1891 and the turn of the century, Russia gained substantial advantages from the collapse of the Chinese Empire. The construction of the Chinese Eastern Railway across Manchuria (1897) brought valuable political and economic penetration of that region, and in 1898, to offset German gains in China, Russia demanded and received a 25-year lease on the ice-free port of Port Arthur, together with its hinterland, the Liaotung Peninsula. When Chinese resentment of foreign encroachment made itself felt in the Boxer Rebellion (1900), Russian troops were most prominent in the protection of European lives and interests, creating a dangerous confidence in their ability to defeat any mere oriental foe.

Japan watched Russian progress with apprehension and with resentment. Her recent modernisation and westernisation contrasted starkly with China's decay, and she had taken advantage of that decay to prosecute long-standing territorial claims. The Chinese–Japanese War of 1894–95 had established Japanese control over Korea, Port Arthur and the surrounding Manchurian territory, much of which she had been forced to relinquish by pressure from the European powers established in China. Russia's subsequent acquisition of much of this territory was naturally a source of great nationalist indignation in Japan.

The collapse of Russo–Japanese relations

Two years of effort (1901–03) by Japan to reach an understanding about spheres of influence in Manchuria and Korea failed, largely due to Russian apathy. When, in February 1903, Russia failed to remove her 'temporary' garrison from Manchuria, it looked suspiciously as if she had ambitions to dominate both regions. There is little evidence to suggest a deliberate desire for aggression on Russia's part, but many factors left her inclined to

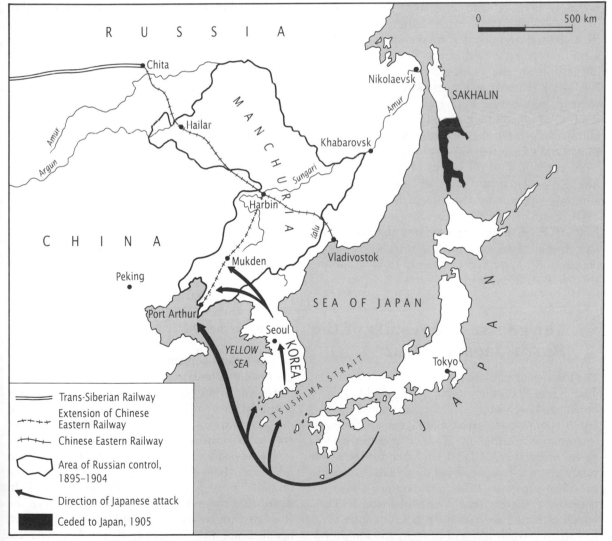

The Far East at the time of the Russo–Japanese War, 1904–05

accept a military solution if the necessity arose. The so-called 'Bezobrasov Theory', or 'Scapegoat Theory', whereby Russian arrogance in the Far East was largely due to the work of an adventurer of that name, is no longer widely held. G. Katkov, for example, has helped to show that the government was more closely connected with eastern financial adventures than was originally thought, and that the blame placed upon Bezobrasov and his like was partly a campaign by prominent politicians, including Witte, to distract attention from their own role. Nevertheless, influential figures did have large financial vested interests in economic ventures such as the Russian Timber Company of the Far East. Furthermore, the Tsar received considerable personal encouragement for adventures in the east from the German Kaiser, happy to see Russian attention diverted from eastern Europe by a cultural 'crusade' against the 'Yellow Peril'. Last, but not least, the domestic political tensions in European Russia made a foreign distraction welcome to the Tsar and his ministers. There were doubtless many in high places who shared Plehve's famous judgement that 'to stem the tide of revolution, we need a successful little war'.

Nevertheless, in the words of Anatole Mazour, 'the Russo–Japanese War was declared by the admirals and not by the diplomats'. In February 1904, their patience exhausted, and aware of the lack of Russian preparation, the Japanese fleet launched an attack on Port Arthur without a formal declaration of war and laid mines to blockade the Russian fleet in the port.

H The course and results of the Russo–Japanese War

The balance of military power
The general assumption that Russia could expect a quick and easy victory over a minor power such as Japan should not survive intelligent and detailed examination. Although Russia's population was three times that of Japan and her territory was vastly greater, Japan enjoyed much easier access to the theatre of war. Russian communications were dependent upon the Trans-Siberian Railway, which operated on a single track for much of its length and which still had a gap of 150 km in it in the region of Lake Baikal. Russian forces in the Far

East totalled only 100,000 men at the beginning of hostilities, which the railway could only reinforce at the rate of 35,000 per month. Political developments in the west made it desirable to keep large numbers of experienced and reliable troops available for action there. Naval reinforcements posed even greater problems with the Black Sea fleet effectively 'locked up' there by the terms of the Straits Convention of 1841.

Lastly, the Russian command structure was crippled by the rivalries between the regular army commanders and the court favourites who directed political affairs in the Far East. Japan, on the other hand, had the capacity to put 180,000 men into the field immediately and to reinforce them by a short sea route. For all the endurance and bravery that they showed, the Russian troops never fought with the nationalistic and semi-religious fanaticism that the Japanese soldiers frequently displayed.

The battle for Port Arthur
On land, the Russian forces quickly found themselves unable to contain the numerically superior Japanese and by May 1904 Port Arthur was cut off. The land campaign then centred upon the respective needs to take or to relieve the port. The eventual surrender of Port Arthur in January 1905 followed a siege of 156 days and cost the Russians 17,200 casualties. Japanese casualties, however, totalled 110,000. As stores and ammunition remained in fair supply, the surrender led to subsequent charges of treason against the Russian commander, General Stoessel. Russian hopes of regaining the vital port faded after the Battle of Mukden (February–March 1905), a larger battle than any in the 19th century.

Japanese naval supremacy
Even so, as Russia still had the potential for reinforcement while Japan's resources were quickly stretched to their limits, the truly decisive factor in the war was in the naval campaign. Without command of the sea Japan would have been unable to supply or to reinforce her troops on the Korean mainland, but Russian attempts to wrest the initiative from her were wholly unsuccessful. In April 1904 the most popular and successful of the Russian commanders, Admiral Makarov, died when his flagship, the *Petropavlovsk*, struck a Japanese mine. Only twice afterwards did the fleet stationed

Nicholas II

Personality and aims

The death of Alexander III from nephritis in October 1894 brought his 29 year-old son, Nicholas, to the throne. As has often been the case, a determined and dominant father had produced a shy and less assertive successor. There is a rare unanimity among historians that the new Tsar was not equal to the tasks that confronted him. He was, in the judgement of Richard Charques, 'a negative character, commonplace in mind, weak of will and fatalistic in temperament, a man transparently immature and of patently insignificant interests'. In an attempt to achieve a balanced assessment, many commentators have drawn attention to his private qualities, especially those as father and husband, but as J. N. Westwood has commented, 'family happiness has never yet saved a dynasty'.

For all this, influences such as the assassination of his grandfather in 1881, and his education at the hands of Konstantin Pobedonostsev, made the new Tsar utterly determined upon one thing. He remained determined to maintain the autocracy of his predecessors. His marriage in the year of his succession, to Princess Alice of Hesse-Darmstadt, only compounded the difficulties of the reign. Alexandra, as she became upon conversion to the Russian Orthodox faith, shared her husband's political ineptitude. Being a stronger character and equally devoted to the principle of autocracy, she was better able to resist the good advice of those who might have saved the monarchy.

The probable course of the reign was indicated at an early stage. Meeting representatives of the *zemstvos* and the town councils in January 1895, Nicholas dismissed their hopes 'for public institutions to express their opinion on questions which concern them' as evidence that they were 'carried away by senseless dreams'. To the horror of those who hoped for some relaxation of the oppression of his father's reign he pledged himself to 'uphold the principle of autocracy as firmly and unflinchingly as my late unforgettable father'. In terms, however, of the social and economic development of Russia, and of the development of foreign affairs, Nicholas was on the verge of a very different world from his father's.

---

at Port Arthur venture out to sea before the surrender of their base.

In May 1905 the powerful Baltic fleet arrived in eastern waters, having completed an epic voyage around the globe, without rest at anchor, and refuelling its huge coal-burning battleships at sea. To reach the theatre of war was a great achievement in itself, but it was the fleet's only achievement. On 27 May 1905, attempting to pass the Straits of Tsushima to reach Vladivostok, it encountered the Japanese battle fleet under Admiral Togo and lost 25 of its 35 ships in battle. Most of the survivors were held in neutral ports for the duration of the war.

The peace settlement and its impact

The Russians had lost largely as a result of numerical and strategic disadvantages. Equally, however, the incompetence of their officers and administrators contrasted, as it had done in the Crimea, with the bravery and sacrifice of the common soldier. The greater effectiveness of Japan's modern equipment has caused J. N. Westwood to ask 'which of the two belligerents was western and which oriental'. Despite these factors, Europeans' convictions of their own racial superiority rendered the outcome of the war stupefying and acutely embarrassing for the Russian state.

On the face of it the peace settlement arrived at through American mediation at Portsmouth, New Hampshire (August 1905), let the Russians off lightly. Port Arthur and the Liaotung Peninsula were ceded, of course, to Japan. Through Witte's tough negotiation, Russia paid no war indemnity, kept half of the island of Sakhalin, and retained her dominance in Manchuria.

The Treaty of Portsmouth, nevertheless, marked a turning point in the foreign policy of Tsarist Russia. Russian interests in the Far East were not ended, but strict limitations were placed upon them. The result was that for the first time in nearly 25 years the foreign prestige of the Russian Empire depended predominantly upon developments in Europe.

I The 1905 Revolution: 'Bloody Sunday'

Military failure and humiliation added to the revolutionary pressure already upon the Tsarist government at the end of 1904. Most of the ingredients for a conflagration were now present. Peasant unrest had recurred sporadically since 1902, industrial strikes had occurred between 1902–04 in most cities, and several explosions of student unrest had taken place in Moscow and St Petersburg in the same years. The spark that set them all off was provided by the 'Bloody Sunday' massacre of 22 January 1905.

'Bloody Sunday' marked the spectacular failure of a daring experiment in the control of revolutionary elements. S. V. Zubatov, the chief of police in Moscow, had proposed the concept known as 'police socialism' in 1902. It consisted of official encouragement of moderate workers' organisations, aiming at genuine improvements in wages and working conditions, in the expectation that members would then refrain from more dangerous political demands. One of the largest of these organisations was the Assembly of Russian Factory Workers, founded in 1903 and boasting 8,000 members within a year. Its leader was the Orthodox priest, G. A. Gapon, a controversial and enigmatic figure.

After 1905, left-wing suspicion of Gapon's motives was so bitter that he was 'executed' by SR agents (1906). Definite evidence of treachery has never been uncovered and it is perhaps more likely, as J. N. Westwood judges, that the misguided man 'rather fancied himself in the role of saviour'. Strict control over the activities of his society was difficult, however, and the plan to present a loyal petition for redress of grievances to the Tsar in St Petersburg on 22 January 1905 carried Gapon along with it.

The demonstration of more than 150,000 people in front of the Winter Palace was perhaps the last occasion on which the Russian people genuinely approached the Tsar in his traditional role as the 'Little Father' of his people. The panic that led the Imperial troops to fire upon the crowd, killing an estimated 1,000, killed 'police socialism', mortally wounded the reputation of the autocracy and triggered the 1905 revolution. 'It did more than perhaps anything else during the whole of the reign,' wrote Richard Charques, 'to undermine the allegiance of the common people to the throne.'

J The 1905 Revolution: spontaneous revolt

The strike movement

Gapon's subsequent denunciation of the Tsar encapsulated the hatred felt by much of the Russian population. 'The innocent blood of workers, their wives and children lies forever between you, the murderer of souls, and the Russian people. May all the blood that must be spilled fall on you, you hangman'. In Russian industry this anger was reflected in an unprecedented strike movement. In February, 400,000 workers went on strike, and the total exceeded 2.7 million by the end of the year. No strike had greater effect than that of the railway workers in October, as a result of which the Russian cities were in imminent danger of starvation and the Russian economy was brought to the verge of collapse. No major city in European Russia escaped the dislocation of its fuel supplies and of its administration.

Peasant unrest

The relatively small size of Russia's urban proletariat made its revolt, although serious, a problem that might be contained. A general revolt of the peasantry, however, was a much more serious prospect.

The first peasant revolt broke out in the Kursk Province in February and by April discontent had spread to most of the prime agricultural regions of European Russia. The peasant unrest was originally spontaneous, but was subsequently exploited by the radical political parties. Thus the All-Russian Peasant Union, formed by regional delegates in May 1905, put forward views very similar to those of the SRs.

At a local level, however, demands and action were far less coherent, inspired by the hatred of past wrongs and by hope of present gain, especially in the form of land. Of these localised disturbances, 3,228 were serious enough to require the intervention of troops, and damage to an estimated value of 29 million roubles was inflicted upon Russian landowners in the course of the year.

The armed forces

The key to the success or failure of the revolution lay in the attitude of the armed forces. Thus a most ominous element in the 1905 disturbances was the sporadic outbreak of mutinies in army units, but more especially in the navy. Rebellions occurred at Kronstadt in the Baltic and at Sevastopol on the Black Sea, but the most famous was the mutiny on board the battleship *Potemkin*, also in the Black Sea in June. Rebelling against the squalor of their conditions of service and the harshness of their officers, the crew seized control of the ship, killed a number of the officers and bombarded Odessa. The prospect of general mutiny posed a grave threat to the survival of the regime, but it did not materialise. The *Potemkin* was forced to seek asylum in a Rumanian port, and mutinies on other ships were suppressed. The larger part of the army remained loyal. Despite a number of cases of fraternisation between troops and rioters, the Imperial manifesto published in December, promising better pay and fairer treatment had the desired effect upon troops mainly of peasant origin. By clever use of non-Russian troops against Russian mutineers, and vice-versa, the government had largely restored military discipline by the end of the year.

K The 1905 Revolution: political crystallisation

Liberal responses

The summer of 1905 encouraged a rapid crystallisation of opposition groups as each came to believe that its hour was at hand. Two main liberal groups emerged. In October the Union of Liberation, supported by some of the *zemstvo* politicians, established the Constitutional Democratic Party, soon known by the abbreviated title of the 'Kadets'. Its demands included an assembly elected by direct and universal suffrage and the restoration of ancient national rights to Poland and Finland. They were thus rather more radical than the Union of Unions formed in February by representatives of a number of professional bodies.

The St Petersburg 'soviet'

The Russian left was caught largely unawares and in a state of disarray by the events of 1905. The emergence in October of a Council (*soviet*) of Workers' Deputies in St Petersburg was not the work of established socialist leaders, but a direct action by politically conscious workers to co-ordinate their strike action. Its 400–500 members represented five trade unions and 96 factories. Once the established leftist groups stirred themselves to tap the potential of the organisation, the Soviet came to represent mainly the Menshevik tendency of the RSDRP, with Bolsheviks and SRs in a distinct minority. Of those who returned from exile, none made a greater impact than Leon Trotsky, an associate of Lenin but more sympathetic at this point to the more democratic Menshevik views. His intellectual and oratorical skills made him one of the leading figures in the political chaos that reigned in the Russian capital.

How much importance should one attach to this first Soviet? To the historians of the USSR its significance was as a 'dress rehearsal' for 1917. On the other hand, the soviet in St Petersburg lasted only 50 days. It was not responsible for the huge strike in October, and the second general strike that it called in November petered out into anti-climax. It is true that its importance outside St Petersburg was negligible, but its significance is in the lead that it gave to later revolutionaries and in the brief influence that it enjoyed in the capital.

L The 1905 Revolution: the Manifestos

Concessions to the liberals

Frightened by his government's loss of control, the possibility of further military disobedience, and the actuality of peasant rebellion which was the oldest fear of the Russian nobility, the Tsar had the choice of two courses of action. In early October he seemed ready to resort to outright military dictatorship but, faced with the objections of most senior ministers and some prominent members of the royal family, he finally recognised the need for concessions. The October manifesto (30 October 1905) was, superficially, an acceptance of most of the classic liberal demands. It granted freedom of person, of speech, of religion, of assembly and of organisation. Above all it confirmed the proposal made in August for the summoning of an elected parliament or 'Duma'.

Concessions to the peasantry

In direct response to the agrarian unrest, a further set of concessions in November cancelled redemption payments and called for the peasants in return 'to preserve peace and order, and not violate the laws and rights of others'. Neither the November nor the October Manifesto really touched upon the true nature of Russia's social and political problems. The former made no concession to the peasants' desperate need for land and the latter set no real limitation upon the autocratic power of the Tsar. Russia faced the last nine years of peace with a liberal facade resting uneasily upon incompatible absolutist foundations. 'A constitution has been given,' remarked Trotsky, 'but the autocracy remains.'

M Stolypin and repression

In another of his characteristically vivid phrases Trotsky described the October Manifesto as 'the whip wrapped in the parchment of a constitution'. Indeed, the government had sufficiently recovered its nerve to set about the restoration of its authority by the dual policy of consistent repression and inconsistent reform. In November both the members of the St Petersburg Soviet and those of the Union of Peasants were arrested. In December, a last desperate insurrection in Moscow was crushed by regular troops with the loss of about 1,000 rebel lives, while loyal troops suppressed mutinous veterans of the eastern war along the route of the Trans-Siberian Railway. The efforts of the government were aided by the activities of extreme right-wing groups hostile to the liberalisation of 1905. A legal political party, the Union of the Russian People (October 1905), was supplemented by terrorist gangs known as the 'Black Hundreds' which attacked known reformists and specialised in anti-Semitic pogroms.

In the course of the next few years, however, counter-terror became a longer-term government weapon in the hands of Pyotr Stolypin. A newcomer to the Council of Ministers in 1906, he was appointed its chairman in 1907. His credentials as a ruthless governor of the province of Saratov during the revolutionary year were perfect for his new task, and he has been widely regarded as the second of the two men, after Sergei Witte, who might have

saved the regime had the Tsar had the wit to listen to his advice. Stolypin's plans for the regeneration of Russia were based on counter terror and reform. He waged an unrelenting war against violent political opposition, a tactic made more necessary than ever by the resurgence of revolutionary violence in the summer of 1906. In 1907, an estimated 1,231 officials and 1,768 private citizens died in terrorist attacks. To this Stolypin replied with terror of his own. His 'field courts martial', operating under Article 87 of the Fundamental Laws, carried out 1,144 death sentences in the nine months preceding May 1907.

The bases of radical politics were also attacked through pressure upon unions and upon the press. Six hundred unions closed between 1906 and 1912, and 1,000 newspapers ceased to publish during the same period. Ostensibly the policy was a success. In 1908 the number of political assassinations dropped to 365. From A. I. Guchkov, leader of the Octobrists in the Duma, was drawn the grudging compliment that 'if we are now witnessing the last convulsions of the revolution, and it is undoubtedly coming to an end, then it is to this man that we owe it'.

N Stolypin and reform

Agrarian reform

Stolypin was not such a reactionary as to imagine that counter terror alone could stabilise the Tsarist regime. Reform, too, was essential, and where Witte had set himself the task of modernising Russian industry, his successor turned to the more deep-rooted problem of the Russian peasantry.

The key to Stolypin's agrarian policy was his belief that the surest basis for the regime was the support of a prosperous and contented peasantry. To achieve this without damaging the interests of the landlords he sought primarily to free the peasant from the communes created by the 1861 emancipation. Acting again through the government's emergency powers he formulated a law (November 1906) whereby any peasant had the right to withdraw himself and his land from the commune. A further law (June 1910) dissolved all those communes where no redistribution of land had taken place since the emancipation. These laws were the culmination of a programme that had also granted equal civil rights in local administration (October 1906) to peasants and had transferred substantial amounts of state land to the Peasants' Bank (September 1906) in an attempt to satisfy 'land hunger'.

The degree of Stolypin's success

The subsequent growth of private peasant ownership was substantial. An estimated 20 per cent of the peasantry enjoyed hereditary ownership of their land in 1905, while the proportion had risen to nearly 50 per cent by 1915. Consolidation of scattered strips of land into viable farms was a slower process, and less than 10 per cent of peasant holdings had been thus improved by 1915. Three million cases, however, were awaiting the attention of land officials when the advent of war slowed their work rate almost to a halt. The lowering of interest rates in the Land Bank and the offering of migration facilities to 3.5 million peasants in Siberia between 1905–15, bear further witness to the concern of the Tsar's senior ministers with the agrarian problem.

The greatest weakness in Stolypin's reforms, like those of Witte, was that they did not enjoy the complete support of the Tsar. Strongly influenced by extreme right-wing factions resentful of any such changes, Nicholas was probably on the verge of dismissing Stolypin when the latter was assassinated in Kiev in September 1911. The murderer, Bogrov, was linked with both the SRs and the secret police and the confusion that has always surrounded Bogrov's motives for the crime is a measure of how Stolypin's 'enlightened conservatism' had attracted the hatred of both political extremes.

0 The Dumas: formation

The Russian constitution in 1906

Outwardly Russia entered 1906 with a radically revised and modernised constitution. In effect, each element in that constitution was little more than a sham. The revived Council of Ministers, presided over at first by Sergei Witte, had the appearance of a cabinet. In fact, the ministers were entirely dependent upon the Tsar for their appointment, direction and dismissal, and thus merely continued to serve the autocracy. The

upper house of the assembly, the Council of State, was half elected, by *zemstvo*, Church, noble and university bodies, but was also half appointed by the Tsar.

The lower house, the State Duma, was wholly elective but from its birth in February 1906 it was tied hand and foot by a series of limitations upon its powers. It had no control over military expenditure, nor over the Tsar's household finances, and in any case an enormous French loan of 2,250 million gold francs (April 1906) rendered the crown financially independent. The Duma had no means of controlling or even of censuring ministers. Most important of all, Article 87 of the Fundamental Laws (April 1906), drawn up without consultation with the Duma, left the Tsar with the power to govern by decree whenever the assembly was not in session.

Table 9.4 Composition of the Dumas, 1906–17

	1st Duma	2nd Duma	3rd Duma	4th Duma
Social Democrats	–	65	14	14
Socialist Revolutionaries	–	34	–	–
Trudoviks	94	101	14	10
Progressives	–	–	39	47
Kadets (also known as the Party of the People's Liberty)	79	92	52	57
Non-Russian national groups	121		26	21
Centre Party	–	–	–	33
Octobrists	17	32	120	99
Nationalists	–	–	76	88
Extreme Right	15	63	53	64

The composition of the Duma

The representative nature of the Duma was further limited by the decision of all major left-wing groups to boycott the first set of elections. Thus the elections in early 1906 were mainly contested by the Kadets and two other groups. The Octobrists were moderate conservatives, taking their name from their acceptance of the October Manifesto. The Labour Group (*Trudoviki*) was a faction largely reflecting the views of the SRs, despite the fact that the SRs were not officially involved in the contest. The relative fortunes of these and other groups in the elections to the four Dumas that met between 1906 and 1917 are reflected in Table 9.4.

The changes in composition from Duma to Duma reflect two factors. One was the eventual decision of groups on both political extremes to participate in elections, if only to change the nature of the assembly. The more important factor was that election was by indirect 'college' voting, whereby communities of differing sizes nominated a delegate to exercise a single vote for them. This has been variously interpreted as an administrative necessity, given Russia's vast size, and as a cynical trick to rig election results. Certainly it gave the government the chance to limit or increase the influence of sections of the population by changing the size of the community exercising one 'college' vote.

P The Dumas: achievement

The failure of the first and second Dumas

The task facing the Duma was nearly impossible. It faced, in G. Fischer's words, 'the dilemma of attaining complex, specifically western objectives in an illiberal, underdeveloped society'. Much compromise would have been needed, and very little was forthcoming. The Tsar was never more than coldly formal towards the Duma, but a number of historians, including G. Fischer and Richard Charques, have laid blame upon the liberal majority in the early Dumas for their inflexibility and their insistence upon unrealistic demands.

The first Duma (April 1906) was unmistakably hostile to the government in its major demands, for land reform and for an amnesty for political prisoners, and it was dissolved after only 73 days. The second Duma (February 1907) suffered from a transfer of influence from the centre to the extremes. The number of Kadets was greatly reduced after their irresponsible and impulsive 'Vyborg Manifesto' (July 1906) in which 120 of their members broke the law and disqualified themselves from future elections by calling for civil disobedience against the government. On the other hand, groups from both the extreme right and the extreme left of Russian politics now decided to participate in the elections and to use the Duma for

their own forms of propaganda. The second Duma, therefore, amounted to three and a half months of continuous uproar.

The third and fourth Dumas

The longer lives of the third and fourth Dumas (November 1907 and November 1912) resulted from Stolypin's dual decision to work with a suitably conservative assembly, and to revise the electoral laws to that end. While the electoral law of 1905 had blatantly favoured the conservative forces of landowners and peasants, the new one (June 1907) even further manipulated the electoral 'colleges'. In effect it left some 50 per cent of the final votes in the hands of the landowners (up from 31 per cent), 23 per cent in the hands of the peasantry (down from 42 per cent), while the growing urban proletariat exercised only 2 per cent of the votes (down from 4 per cent).

The result was the election of two assemblies that 'hovered between two worlds' (Richard Charques), those of reform and reaction. Historians are divided as to whether or not these Dumas should be seen as successes. Certainly the third and fourth Dumas were thwarted on many important reformist issues. Bills for the extension of the *zemstvo* system into Poland and for religious toleration were defeated in the Council of State. When Stolypin used his emergency powers to pass the former measure it was a triumph for the Fundamental Laws rather than for the Duma. On the other hand, the hated Land Commandants (*see* Chapter 6) were replaced by reinstated Justices of the Peace, compulsory health insurance for industrial workers was introduced (June 1912) and, with much local co-operation from the *zemstvos*, much progress was made in Russian education. Universal primary education within ten years was adopted as an official policy (May 1908) and by 1914 it was 50 per cent of the way towards completion, involving 7.2 million children. Figures for attendance at secondary schools (510,000) and at universities (40,000) in 1914 do not, unfortunately, reflect a uniform advance.

As Hugh Seton-Watson has pointed out, however, the achievement of the Dumas should not only be estimated in terms of the measures that they passed. It had not become a truly representative assembly, because the government had never wanted such an assembly, but by 1914 political parties were legally established and, while rebellion was punished, open political discussion was tolerated and was allowed to appear in the press. All of these factors represented advances scarcely dreamed of before 1905.

Q The Russian regime on the eve of war

An assessment of the 'Stolypin years'

Perhaps more than any previous period in Russian history, the 'Stolypin era' has provoked controversy among historians. Two questions predominate. How should Stolypin's work be evaluated, and how far had his reforms, and those of Witte, set Tsarist Russia on a survival course by 1914?

Assessments of Stolypin's work have often followed partisan political lines. Soviet historians, notably Aron Avrekh, have concentrated upon the suppression of revolution, upon the 200,000 political prisoners of 1908, and the 5,000 death sentences passed in 1907–09. To Avrekh the 'Stolypin course' was 'the inescapable situation of reaction, the historic destiny of the rotten regime', for revolution was still the only logical outcome of the social and economic forces at work.

Western appraisals have usually been kinder, ranging through those who excuse his use of terror by reference to the revolutionary terrorism with which he was faced, to the American-Russian emigré Leonid Strakhovsky, who views Stolypin as a most positive reformer and as the brightest hope of the Tsarist regime. Avoiding the bias of both extremes it seems reasonable to view Stolypin as an enlightened and positive conservative, implacably hostile to liberal and revolutionary challenges to the autocracy, but lucidly aware of the inadequacy of mere entrenched reaction.

'Optimists' versus 'pessimists'

On the broader question of the adequacy of Russian modernisation, commentators have divided into 'optimistic' and 'pessimistic' schools, respectively confident and doubtful of Tsarist Russia's prospects had she avoided involvement in the European war. The optimists, for whom the economic historian A. Gerschenkron has been a prominent spokesman, see the increasing economic maturity of Russia, based upon industrial development and sound agrarian reform, as a guarantee of peacetime stability. 'One might surmise,' he concludes, 'that in the absence of war Russia could have continued on the road of progressive westernisation.' This view has been questioned, not only by Soviet historians, but by westerners such as Theodore von Laue, E. H. Carr and W. E. Mosse. They draw attention to the limitations of Stolypin's reforms over Russia in general and stress the possibility that his sacrifice of the weaker peasant to 'the sober and the strong' would, in the end, only have added to the ranks of the revolutionary proletariat.

The survival of the autocratic mentality

Possibly, the decisive factor in the controversy is that stressed by Donald Treadgold who emphasises the implacable hostility towards change of much of the Russian ruling class. This was especially true of the Tsar himself, who regarded good government not as 'an ideal to be sought, but [as] an irrelevance compared to the maintenance of the loyalty of the Russian people to his own person'. It is also important to remember how completely in Russia, even at a time of substantial political reform, the ministers remained the creatures of the Tsar, with no significant scope for personal initiative. This is illustrated by the fact that Nicholas was served between 1905 and 1917 by eight different ministers for trade and industry and by eleven different ministers of the interior.

Hans Rogger describes how 'Sergei Witte, perhaps the ablest man to serve the last two Tsars, at times behaved in their presence like a junior officer – bowing excessively, his hands at the seams of his trousers, and displaying little of his bold and independent mind'. The same author reminds us that 'only an exceptional Tsar could long tolerate an exceptional minister,' and Nicholas, of course, was by no means an exceptional man. Perhaps in the final analysis, therefore, progress towards a more modern Russia might still have been blocked by a narrow–minded and reactionary autocracy.

R Russian science and culture on the eve of war

The sciences

The attention of the optimistic school of historians has not been limited to political and economic affairs. 'Not only the body of Russia but the soul as well,' commented the optimist emigré M. Karpovich, 'was growing stronger in the decade that preceded the World War.' Indeed, considering the narrowness of Russia's educated stratum and the limitations of her facilities for higher education, her contribution to science and technology in the 20 years before 1914 was quite remarkable. In most scientific fields Russia produced men of genius. Ilya Mechnikov was a leading figure in the study of infection and immunisation, running the Pasteur Institute in Paris and winning a Nobel Prize in 1908. An earlier Nobel Prize (1904) went to perhaps the most famous of all Russian scientists, Ivan Pavlov, whose work on digestive enzymes and on conditioned reflexes in dogs still makes him a household name today. In chemistry, Dmitri Mendeleyev evolved the Periodic Table and described a number of new elements, while in agricultural sciences K. A. Timiryazev was the foremost soil scientist of his day.

In applied technology Russia suffered rather more from her material backwardness, but led the world in two important respects. Alexander Popov's work on radio communications ran parallel to, and sometimes ahead of that of Marconi, while Russia's contribution to aerodynamics was of the greatest importance. The work of N. Y. Zhukovsky and of S. A. Chaplygin on airflow, important as it was, gives precedence to that of K. E. Tsiolkovsky whose developments in the fields of design and fuel make him one of the most important figures in the history of rocket technology.

The arts

In most of the arts, a golden age had ended in Russia by 1914. The major exception to this rule was in the performing arts. In ballet, Sergei Diaghilev's *Ballets Russes* (1909) maintained its supremacy for decades. In its choreographer, Mikhail Fokine, its dancers, Vacheslav Nijinsky and Anna Pavlova, and in its primary composer, Igor Stravinsky, it boasted the world's best. The Moscow Arts Theatre, with Konstantin Stanislavsky as its major director, and Russian opera, with Feodor Chaliapin as its leading performer, also raised Russia to a level of unprecedented cultural brilliance. The greatest Russian writers of the age, however, were recently dead, Anton Chekhov in 1904 and Leo Tolstoy in 1910. Although not primarily political writers, both were obsessed in their last works, as in Chekhov's *The Cherry Orchard* and Tolstoy's *Resurrection*, with the stagnation and sterility of Russian society. Their successor was Maxim Peshkov who, writing under the pen-name 'Gorky' ('bitter'), had already produced a stream of novels and plays by 1914. These were more specifically political than those of his predecessors, exposing the squalor and hopelessness of society's 'lower depths'. Lionel Kochan describes Gorky as 'the first consciously proletarian novelist', and these works were to make him the doyen of Soviet literature in the 1920s and early 1930s.

Questions

Essay Questions

1   Why was Nicholas II less successful than Alexander III in maintaining himself in power? (UCLES)

2   How did Tsarism survive the Russian Revolution of 1905? (Oxford Entrance)

3   To what extent was the Revolution of 1905 a significant event in Russia in the reign of Nicholas II? (NEAB)

4   To what extent do the policies pursued by Nicholas II (1894–1917) within Russia reveal that he was determined, as he said, to uphold the principles of autocracy 'firmly and unflinchingly'? (JMB/NEAB)

5   'In July 1914, Tsarist Russia was a time-bomb on a very short fuse'. How accurate is this description? (ULEAC)

6   In what ways did the 1905 Revolution in Russia prepare the groundwork for the overthrow of Nicholas II in 1917? (WJEC)

Nicholas II and the State Dumas

Study documents I, II and III below, and then answer questions (a) to (f) which follow:

DOCUMENT I

The proletariat has risen against Tsarism. The proletariat has been driven to the uprising by the government. Now there is hardly room for doubt that the government deliberately allowed the strike movement to develop and a wide demonstration to be started in order to bring matters to a head, and to have a pretext for calling out the military forces. Its manoeuvre was successful. Thousands killed and wounded – that is the toll of Bloody Sunday, January 22, in St Petersburg.

Lenin writing in the journal 'Vperyod', No 4, 31 January 1905

DOCUMENT II

There are only two ways open: to find an energetic soldier to crush the rebellion by sheer force. There would be time to breathe then, but, as likely as not, one would have to use force again in a few months, and that would mean rivers of blood and in the end we should be where we started.

The other way would be to give the people their civil rights, freedom of speech and press, also to have all the laws confirmed by a State Duma. That of course would be a constitution. Witte defends this energetically. We discussed it for two days, and in the end, invoking God's help, I signed it. My only consolation is that such is the will of God and that this grave decision will lead my dear Russia out of the intolerable chaos she has been in for nearly a year.

Tsar Nicholas II in a letter to his mother, 1905

DOCUMENT III

By Our will, people selected from the population were summoned to legislative work.

Trusting in God's mercy and believing in a great and glowing future for Our people, We expected benefits for the country from their work.

We had intended to make great changes in all areas of the life of the people. Instead of embarking on constructive legislative work, the elected members moved into areas outside their jurisdiction. The peasantry was confused by these irregularities, and as it saw no likelihood of improvement in its conditions through law, in a number of provinces it turned to open robbery.

Our subjects should remember, however, that any improvement in the life of Our peoples is possible only in conditions of complete order and calm. In dissolving the present Duma, we confirm Our unshakeable intention of keeping in force the law. It is with constant faith in God's mercy and in the intelligence of the Russian people that We expect that the new Duma will fulfil Our expectations and will legislate in accordance with the needs of a renewed Russia.

Nicholas II, Manifesto dissolving the First Duma, 8 July 1906

---

a In the context of the Documents:
  i Explain the term 'State Duma', and
  ii identify 'Witte'. [2]
b How convincing is the claim, in Document I, that 'the government deliberately allowed the strike movement to develop [as] a pretext'? [5]
c What do documents II and III reveal about the Tsar's attitude towards the First State Duma? [5]
d What can be deduced from the content of Documents II and III about the nature of Tsarist rule? [4]
e Document II is a private letter from the Tsar; Document III is a public declaration issued by him. What value might each type of source have to historians studying Russia under Nicholas II, and what reservations might such historians have concerning them? [4]
f Using these documents, and your own knowledge of the period, examine the sincerity of the Tsar's wish to 'lead my dear Russia out of the intolerable chaos'. [5]

(ULEAC)

10

Germany and Austria in the Wilhelmine age

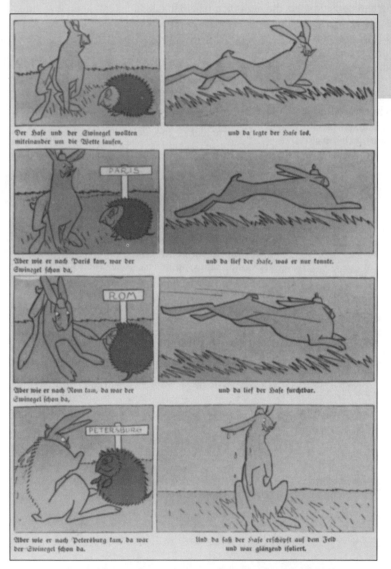

Der Hase und der Swinegel wollten miteinander um die Wette laufen,

und da legte der Hase los.

Aber wie er nach Paris kam, war der Swinegel schon da,

und da lief der Hase, was er nur konnte.

Aber wie er nach Rom kam, da war der Swinegel schon da,

und da lief der Hase furchtbar.

Aber wie er nach Petersburg kam, da war der Swinegel schon da.

Und da saß der Hase erschöpft auf dem Feld und war glänzend isoliert.

A cartoon by O. Gulbransson for the magazine *Simplicissimus* satirises the style and diplomacy of Wilhelm II. Wilhelm is the 'hare', while Edward VII of Great Britain is the 'hedgehog'. When the hare tries to race the hedgehog he finds that the hedgehog has reached Paris, Rome and St Petersburg before him, leaving the hare 'splendidly isolated'.

Explain the image of Wilhelm II that is conveyed by this cartoon.

What judgements does it pass on the Kaiser's diplomatic methods and achievements?

The Historical Debate

'A consensus about Wilhelmine Germany remains elusive,' wrote James Retallack (in G. Martel (ed.), *Modern Germany Reconsidered*, 1992). This, however, was not always the case. Between 1920 and 1960, conservative German historians had established a comfortable consensus, based upon their rejection of the concept of German responsibility for the First World War. According to such distinguished writers as Gerhard Ritter and Hans Rothfels, Germany bore no greater share of responsibility than any other of the major powers. Thus there was little reason to undertake any close analysis of German society and politics in the last years before the catastrophe. Ritter, in particular, saw Wilhelmine Germany as an era of solid, respectable politics, whose sudden disappearance in 1918 created a void which was filled by chaos and radicalism.

This consensus was rudely shattered in 1961 when the German historian Fritz Fischer published his important work *Griff nach der Weltmacht* (Fischer's works published in translation include *From Kaiserreich to Third Reich: Elements of Continuity in German History 1871–1945*, 1986 and *World Power or Decline: The Controversy over Germany's War Aims in the First World War*, 1975). Fischer's central claim was that Germany had carefully formulated expansionist plans before 1914, and that her eagerness for a limited conflict in that year rendered her primarily

responsible for the outbreak of the World War. Sensational as this was in itself, it also had important implications for the writing of Wilhelmine history. Firstly, Fischer claimed that there was a continuity in German history, a series of social attitudes and political weaknesses that left the country consistently vulnerable to authoritarianism and to policies of aggression and expansionism. Secondly, he reversed the traditional view which saw foreign policy as the primary theatre of political activity in the Reich. In the place of a stable society, more or less unified behind its leaders, he portrayed a society in crisis, whose governors sought desperately for policies that might provide a degree of national unity. The wave of work that followed in support of the 'Fischer thesis' was largely synthesised by Hans-Ulrich Wehler in his extremely influential book, *The German Empire* (1973). In it Wehler, too, portrays Wilhelmine Germany as a cynically anti-democratic state, in which élite groups, Junkers, generals, industrialists, sought to protect their self-interests by resorting to demagoguery and nationalism. Volker Berghahn (*Der Tirpitz-Plan: Genesis und Verfall einer innenpolitischen Krisenstrategie*, 1971) also placed the history and

development of the German navy into this interpretation, seeing it as a focus for popular, patriotic emotion, rather than as a strategic military weapon in its own right.

Some modification of this 'new orthodoxy' has emerged in recent years. The most convincing criticisms have come from those such as Richard Evans (ed. *Society and Politics in Wilhelmine Germany*, 1978), David Blackbourn and Geoff Eley (co-authors of *The Peculiarities of German History: Bourgeois Society and Politics in 19th-century Germany*, 1984). Their primary criticism of Wehler and his school is that they have underestimated the complexity of Wilhelmine society, and have thus overestimated the ease with which that society could be manipulated by the government. For these recent writers the diversity of German society and the relative incoherence of its governing élites make it hard to believe in such megalithic concepts as a premeditated and co-ordinated *Sammlungspolitik*. This is the view and the social diversity that James Retallack refers to when he writes that 'the Empire was not entirely bad. It was neither completely urban nor completely rural. It was not populated only by men. Aristocrats did not exclusively set the tone of everyday life – but neither did the Social Democrats. Manipulative strategies to deflect change did not always work as planned [and] often they went disastrously wrong.'

A Kaiser Wilhelm II

The impact of a new Kaiser

The long reign of Wilhelm I ended in March 1888, in the Kaiser's 92nd year. His son, now briefly

Kaiser as Friedrich III, had only months to live. He had suffered for a year from cancer of the throat, which had already deprived him of the faculty of speech, and which ended his life in June. The imperial throne of Germany thus passed to his own

Wilhelm II

Personality and aims

The personality and psychology of the new Kaiser, now 29 years of age, have been a source of unwaning fascination for historians. His relationship with his parents, especially with his English mother, was tense and uneasy, and his personal sensitivity was undoubtedly increased by an accident at birth which left him with a withered arm and partially deaf.

At Bonn University he had shown far less interest in systematic study and learning than in the company of sycophantic student aristocrats, and discovered the true passion of his youth in his years as an officer in the Potsdam Guards. It was an ominous but fair indication of his future character that he gained such satisfaction from the superficial glamour and excitement of military life. Dismissed by his own father as 'inexperienced, immature and presumptuous', Wilhelm has not been much more kindly treated by historians. Some, such as K. S. Pinson, have shown a relatively sympathetic understanding of his weaknesses: 'Under the mask of the proud Emperor there was an essentially sensitive, insecure, timid and nervous individual'. Others, such as G. A. Craig, find more to blame in his personality: 'William had as much intelligence as any European sovereign and more than most, but his lack of discipline, his self-indulgence, his overdeveloped sense of theatre, and his fundamental misreading of history prevented him from putting it to effective use.'

The age of the young Kaiser was also significant. He belonged to a new, confident generation unaware of the dangers that German conservatism had narrowly survived in 1848 and in 1862. As Golo Mann has put it, 'his memories began in 1870. He regarded the position which he owed to brilliant manoeuvres and clever acts of violence as the gift of God, as the natural order of things'.

son, and the 30-year reign of Wilhelm II began. What did the personality of the new Kaiser mean for the conduct of the German government? Firstly, it meant that Wilhelm II would not be content with the passive role played by his grandfather. He believed passionately in the Divine Right of Kings and, from this outmoded thesis, derived a notion of the mystical link between the ruler and his people that resembled the views of Friedrich Wilhelm IV (*see* Chapter 2). Not for him a reign based upon the narrow interest of Junker landowners, or dictated by the advantage of Prussia alone. Wilhelm, in the words of A. J. P. Taylor, 'desired an absurdity – to be Emperor of all of the Germans'. In a state built by Bismarck upon division and confrontation the prospects of harmonious relations between monarch and Chancellor were dim.

Strong though he was on principle, the mode of government of the new Kaiser was hectic, spectacular and shallow. He travelled obsessively, rarely spending as much as half the year in his capital and earning the nickname of *Der Reise-Kaiser* (the travelling Emperor). He had views on everything, but rarely bothered to back his 'inspiration' with hard information. 'He just talks himself into an opinion,' remarked Kiderlen-Wächter in 1891, while Wilhelm's biographer M. Balfour has remarked that 'his fluency in speaking meant that he approached all questions with an open mouth'. It was a fair summary of the man and the monarch that he openly boasted that he read neither the newspapers nor the German constitution. The outcome was a 30-year reign of great spectacle, constant motion, but little positive content. It amounted in the words of the future Weimar minister Walter Rathenau, to a 'dilettante foreign policy, romantic conservative internal policy and bombastic and empty cultural policy'.

B The fall of Bismarck

The collapse of Bismarck's political system

For all the monumental achievements of the past three decades, Bismarck's position as Chancellor of the Reich had remained theoretically dependent upon the goodwill of the monarch. That position had appeared for some years to be threatened by the prospect of the succession of Crown Prince

Friedrich, with his allegedly liberal sympathies, and his English wife, the Crown Princess Victoria. The death of Friedrich saved Bismarck from one challenge to his authority only to confront him with another. The political sympathies of Wilhelm were less liberal, but he differed fundamentally with his Chancellor as to methods of government.

The issues that divided the two men in 1888–90 were, in reality, merely symptoms of their different interpretations of the Reich and of the role of the Kaiser. A strike by miners in the Ruhr (May 1889) gave Wilhelm the chance to display his brand of benevolent paternalism towards the German working class. While he prepared a programme of social reforms, including a ban on Sunday working, Bismarck rejected the principle of conciliation and concession and aimed to continue a policy of hostility and confrontation. Bismarck's plans to make the renewable Anti-Socialist Laws (*see* Chapter 7, section **H**) permanent not only provoked a clash in the royal council (January 1890), but had severe repercussions in the Reichstag elections in the following month. Bismarck's coalition of Conservatives and National Liberals lost 85 of their 220 seats, and the Social Democrats nearly doubled their share of the vote.

Deprived of the support of both monarch and Reichstag, Bismarck had only intrigue to fall back on. His attempts to force through a package of measures to revise the constitution, to facilitate his political control, forced the Kaiser's hand. Wilhelm chose the path of conciliation, demanded Bismarck's resignation, and received it on 18 March 1890.

Bismarck's legacy

For all his earlier achievement, Bismarck bequeathed to Germany a legacy of tension and troubles. The concentration of power in his own hands meant he had consistently obstructed the growth of truly representative institutions in Germany. As Max Weber commented, 'Bismarck left behind him as a political heritage a nation without any political education . . . a nation without any political will, accustomed to allow the great statesman at its head to look after its policy for it'. Undoubtedly, Bismarck had governed with great shrewdness, but the sad result of his political egoism was that his great power now passed into the hands of an irresponsible and unstable

monarch. Wilhelm, furthermore, inherited a variety of thorny problems, especially in colonial and foreign policy, which Bismarck had allowed to develop for reasons of short-term political advantage. Despite his famous announcement upon Bismarck's resignation that 'the ship's course remains the same. "Full steam ahead" is the order', Wilhelm's fundamental misunderstanding of recent German and European history was to guarantee the destruction of most of the essential principles of Bismarckian Germany within the next 30 years.

C German economic growth

Population growth

The years of Wilhelm II's reign to 1914 saw German industry build upon its Bismarckian foundations (*see* Chapter 7, section **O**) to take its place among the foremost industrial economies of the world. In this respect, the character of the country matched that of the Kaiser. It was young, dynamic, and outwardly confident. Underlying Germany's economic acceleration was a continued rapid growth in population, providing native industries with a greater labour force and with more consumers. Between 1870 and 1890 Germany had experienced a population rise of 21 per cent, from 40.9 to 49.5 million. In the next two decades, the rate of increase was half as great again, leading to a population of 65 million.

Heavy industries and communications

The traditional heavy industries of the Reich maintained the direction they had followed in 1870–90, but they did experience a spectacular acceleration in the pace of output. Coal production was challenging that of Britain by the outbreak of the World War, while steel output had surpassed that of Great Britain in 1900, and was nearly double that of her rival by 1910.

The necessary corollary of these increases in German production was the expansion of her communication system. The Wilhelmine period saw a steady continuation of the growth in the railway system that had been a central feature of economic expansion since the foundation of the Reich. A system that extended 19,480 km in 1870, and 41,820 km in 1890, had grown to 59,016 km by 1910. More novel, however, was the spectacular development of a German merchant navy. The total tonnage of steamships registered at Hamburg rose from 99,000 in 1880 to 746,000 in 1900, while the figures for Bremen in the same period were 59,000 and 375,000. Germany's total merchant marine in 1914 amounted to 3 million tons, only a quarter of the British total, but nearly three times that of the USA.

Table 10.1 Key economic indicators, 1890–1913

	Coal & lignite (m tons)	Pig iron (m tons)	Steel (m tons)	Exports (m £)	Imports · (m £)
1890	89.1	4.66	3.16	170.5	213.6
1900	149.8	8.52	7.37	237.6	302.1
1910	192.3	14.79	13.15	373.7	446.7
1913	279.0	-	-	504.8	538.5

The 'new' industries

Nor was German expansion limited to traditional industries. By the outbreak of the World War, she had established a substantial lead over all other European powers in the new chemical and electrical industries. Germany came to produce 75 per cent of world output of chemical dyes by 1914, and played a prominent role in the development of agricultural fertilisers, of pharmaceutical products and of the industrial uses of sulphuric acid, sodium and chlorine.

In electronics Werner von Siemens had already contributed the electric dynamo (1867) and important work on electronic traction (1879 onwards), saw the development of the two biggest electricity combines in Europe, Siemens/Halske, and AEG (*Allgemeine Elektrizitäts Gesellschaft* – General Electricity Company). By 1913 half of the world's electro-technical trade was in German hands. 'Beyond question,' Sir J. Clapham has concluded, 'the creation of this industry was the greatest single achievement of modern Germany.' Such household names as Daimler and Diesel also attest to German achievement in engineering.

National wealth and living standards

The total wealth of the German Reich increased in the peaceful years of the Wilhelmine era, according to the contemporary economist, Karl Helfferich, from 200,000 million marks to 300,000. Table 10.2, produced by Hajo Holborn and relating to Prussia alone, indicates the increase in the number of great personal fortunes in this period. Other

evidence suggests that the increase in German prosperity was more generally felt. Per capita income doubled, for example, in the course of 40 years. It rose from 352 marks per annum (1871–75), through 603 marks per annum (1896–1900) to 728 marks per annum in 1911–13. The dramatic decrease in the rate of emigration, from 134,200 in 1880–89, to 28,000 between 1900 and 1910, also indicates the relative rise in German living standards by the latter decade.

It should be noted, however, that this overall prosperity was not shared by German agriculture. Although scientific methods of cultivation had spread rapidly since 1870, German grain producers could not compete adequately with American imports, especially when large ocean-going steamers and low freight charges cheapened imports further. By 1900, it was cheaper to import grain from America than to transport it 400 km within Germany. Grain prices dropped and heavy internal tariffs were needed to keep the Junker farmers of East Prussia solvent. Economically, therefore, the Germany of Wilhelm II presented a subtly contrasted picture of modern dynamism and embattled conservative interests.

Table 10.2 The rise in incomes

Total fortune of:	1895	1911
Between 100,000 & 500,000 RM	86,552	135,843
Between 500,000 & 1m RM	8,375	13,800
Between 1–2m RM	3,429	5,916
Over 2m RM	1,827	3,425

D Caprivi and the 'New Course': domestic policy

The search for a German consensus

Bismarck's successor as Chancellor of the Reich and as prime minister of Prussia was General Leo von Caprivi. He brought to these offices the prestige of high military rank, personal honesty and modesty, but none of the political experience or deviousness necessary to master the complexities and contradictions of the Bismarckian state. 'The primary problem of the Caprivi Era,' in the opinion of its prime historian, J. Alden Nichols, 'was how to handle a complex political creation that had finally escaped from the control of its creator.' The new Chancellor, like the Kaiser, desired greater conciliation and less confrontation in domestic politics. He refused to regard any political grouping as a *Reichsfeind* and was willing to accept the assistance of any group in furthering his projects. Both men claimed not to be inaugurating a 'new era', an indication of how little they understood of Bismarck's rule.

Reform of the Bismarckian system

In fact, the years 1890–94 saw systematic inroads made into the domestic system established by Bismarck. The Anti-Socialist Laws were allowed to lapse, and attempts were made to win the working classes over to the Reich with a series of reforms that included a ban on Sunday working, the limitation of working hours for women and children, and the establishment of courts for industrial arbitration. Confrontation with national minorities in Posen and in Alsace-Lorraine was eased by the relaxation of rules governing the use of German in administration and education. A moderate reduction was sought in the privileges of Prussia within the Reich. Prussia's independent foreign ministry was abolished, her tax system reformed and a graduated income tax introduced.

Of much more direct offence to the Prussian Junkers was Caprivi's new economic course. In the interests of increased trade and of cheaper food, he abandoned Bismarckian protectionism, that great guarantee of the Junkers' agricultural prosperity. A series of bilateral trade treaties, with Austria-Hungary and Italy in 1892, with Belgium, Switzerland and Rumania in 1893, and with Russia a year later, greatly stimulated Germany's industrial progress but involved as their price the reduction of German agricultural tariffs. The unfortunate coincidence of these measures with the increase in cheap American corn exports drove not only the Junkers, but most farmers into opposition to the government. The Federation of Agriculturalists (*Bund der Landwirte*), founded to organise this opposition (February 1893), boasted 250,000 members within the year and constituted one of several new conservative forces in German politics.

The fall of Caprivi and the return to conservatism

The fate of two pieces of projected legislation illustrated the deterioration of Caprivi's political position. A bill by the Prussian Ministry of Education, proposing religious segregation of schools, and closer control by the Churches of religious education (1892), was defeated by the vociferous opposition of all liberal groups in the Reichstag. The defeat occasioned Caprivi's resignation as prime minister of Prussia, which further weakened his political base. More surprisingly, a new Army Bill, proposing to enlarge the army by a two-year service period instead of three, and to request the renewal of the military budget every five years instead of seven, also ran into severe opposition. Presented to the Reichstag in 1892, it was only passed after a dissolution and new elections in which the conservative parties and the Social Democrats prospered at the expense of the Liberals.

Four years in office served to convince Caprivi that he had underestimated the selfishness of the various political interests in the Reichstag. In the same period, the initial, superficial 'liberalism' of the Kaiser had faded like that of Alexander II or Pius IX. Wilhelm accepted his Chancellor's resignation in October 1894. He was disillusioned at the failure of the workers to desert the Social Democrats and rally to him, perturbed at the resurgence of political violence evident especially in the assassination of the French president by anarchists, and perplexed at the rift between the government and Junker conservatism.

E Foreign policy

The abandonment of the Reinsurance Treaty

It is a more complex matter to decide whether Caprivi departed from the traditional Bismarckian course in handling Germany's foreign affairs. Certainly he presided over the destruction of a central element in the Bismarckian diplomatic system when (March 1890) he refused to renew the Reinsurance Treaty with Russia (*see* Chapter 7). In this, he acted from no essentially anti-Russian motive, and hoped to maintain friendly relations with the great eastern power.

He was influenced, however, by personalities in the foreign office, such as Friedrich von Holstein whose general leanings were anti-Russian. Their convincing arguments concerned the incompatibility of sections of the treaty with German undertakings to Austria and to Rumania, and the undoubted fact that its terms gave far greater advantages to Russia than to Germany. In short, Caprivi acted honestly where greater deviousness might have served better. The result of his action was the almost immediate confirmation of Bismarck's nightmare, a diplomatic understanding between Russia and France (*see* Chapter 8, section **P**). Furthermore, by agreeing to the renewal of the Triple Alliance with Austria and Italy in 1891 he made a substantial contribution to the formation of hostile camps in Europe that eventually undermined the peace.

Attempts to resist *Weltpolitik*

Caprivi remained Bismarckian, however, in the sense that he continued to resist the considerable pressures within Germany for a 'world policy' (*Weltpolitik*). He saw little realistic future in the acquisition of colonies, and the essence of his policy remained European, to consolidate and improve Germany's position in Central Europe. This aim was served by his system of economic agreements with Germany's neighbours (*see* section **D**) and also by the confirmation of the Triple Alliance.

It had its most controversial manifestation, however, in the Anglo–German treaty of July 1890. By this treaty Germany transferred to Great Britain all rights to the island of Zanzibar, and to substantial areas of the adjacent African mainland, in return for the strategic North Sea island of Heligoland. If, however, as Gordon Craig has suggested, the Zanzibar agreement was an opening move in a plan to tempt Britain into closer relations with Germany in place of the Russian alliance, it was a failure. Caprivi underestimated the reluctance of the British to get involved in binding continental commitments.

He also found that his concept of Germany's continental future was not widely popular at home. The Pan-German League (*Alldeutscher Verband*), which took form between 1891–94, was a deliberate attempt to encourage the Reich to pursue a more energetic, prestigious and cosmopolitan foreign policy. Thus, although Caprivi rejected some of the methods most dear to Bismarck, the brief span of his government did represent the last attempt to limit Germany to European commitments before his opponents launched her on the flamboyant and ultimately disastrous course of 'world policy'.

F Wilhelmine Germany: the Chancellors

Hohenlohe

The German Reich was to have three more chancellors between the fall of Caprivi and the outbreak of war in 1914. The first of these was a Catholic, Bavarian aristocrat, Prince Chlodwig von Hohenlohe-Schillingfurst (1894–1900). After a lifetime in state service, he reached the highest office at the age of 75, and was frankly a stop-gap. His conservative views on domestic matters and his pro-Russian sympathies recommended him to the German right, and his lack of any coherent programme of his own fitted in well with Wilhelm's ambitions of personal government. Primarily, in the words of Friedrich Naumann, Hohenlohe was 'an artist in the avoidance of catastrophe', and his years in office constituted in retrospect a lull before the diplomatic storm of the new century.

Bülow

Hohenlohe's resignation in 1900 was precipitated by the Kaiser's persistent failure to consult him on important policy matters. His successor, however, was to be a prime accessory in Wilhelm's irresponsible dilettantism. Bernhard von Bülow (1900–09) was a more cosmopolitan and, it was felt, more modern man than Hohenlohe. Having risen through the Foreign Office, where he had been minister since 1897, he was closely identified with German colonial expansion and seemed to share the Kaiser's enthusiasm for a 'world role'. He had a reputation for brilliance, but superficial polish was not backed by firm principles or broad vision, and he deserved the nickname bestowed upon him by Kiderlen-Wächter of 'the eel'. There was too much of the flattering courtier about Bülow for him to have been a safe moderating influence on the Kaiser as Hohenlohe had been, and Hajo Holborn has laid upon him much of the blame for Germany's diplomatic irresponsibility during the period. The circumstances of Bülow's fall are thus ironic. Although his resignation in June 1909 was ostensibly due to the defeat in the Reichstag of his project for a tax on inherited wealth, the real cause of his downfall was, like Bismarck's, the loss of the monarch's confidence. This arose from Bülow's carelessness the previous year in allowing the publication of an interview given by Wilhelm to the British *Daily Telegraph*. Characteristic irresponsibility on the Kaiser's part led to utterances offensive to Britain and to Russia and highly embarrassing to Germany. An enormous outcry in the Reichstag brought Wilhelm to the verge of a nervous breakdown and ended the 'golden age' of his personal government. In the long run, as many foreign observers have pointed out, the Reichstag missed the opportunity for long-term constitutional change afforded by the *Daily Telegraph* incident, and Bülow alone paid a high price for the affair.

Bethmann-Hollweg

The last peacetime chancellor of Imperial Germany was Theobald von Bethmann-Hollweg (1909–17). A conscientious administrator, and a man of personal courage and honour, he seemed from the point of view of domestic affairs, an ideal choice. However, his crippling disability was his total inexperience in foreign or military affairs. However much this might have recommended him to a Kaiser who desired supremacy in those fields, it was part of Germany's tragedy that such a man led the government at the time when the fate of Europe depended upon such matters.

In an important sense such changes in personnel were of secondary importance. Of greater significance in the years between 1894 and 1914 was the erosion of the overall power of the chancellor, perhaps the most important of all the departures from Bismarck's system of government. In part, this was due to what Ralph Flenley has called an 'invasion from above', to the Kaiser's consistent desire for personal rule. Historians have been divided as to the extent of Wilhelm's personal influence, but J. G. Rohl has made a strong case for regarding 1897 as a crucial stage in its development. Between that time and the crisis of the *Daily Telegraph* interview, he claims, Wilhelm 'dictated policy to an amazing extent . . . all appointments, all bills, all diplomatic moves were made on his orders'. At the same time the power of the chancellor was eroded from below, by the loss of control over various, previously subordinate ministries. Caprivi had allowed far greater freedom to other departments than Bismarck had ever tolerated, and Tirpitz, at the naval ministry, provided a good example of an independence of action inconceivable before 1890.

G The Army

The army in the German mentality

The decline of the chancellor's office, the personal unreliability of the monarch and the failure of the Reichstag to seek fundamental political change, were different elements in the severe weakening of civil government in Germany. The most important result of this was that the German army occupied a status unparalleled in Europe. In part it owed this status to the role that it had played in Germany's growth. In A. J. P. Taylor's phrase, the nation suffered from a 'Sadowa-Sedan complex', based on the memories of the great victories of the past. Glorification of war and virile conquest was commonplace in contemporary German thought and writing. 'The whole nation,' remarked the socialist Bebel, 'is still drunk with military glory and there is nothing to be done until some great disaster has sobered us.'

The Zabern affair

Two illustrations may help to indicate the independence of the army from German government. In November 1913, a series of disturbances broke out in the garrison town of Zabern (Saverne) in Alsace. They were evidently triggered by the arrogant behaviour of garrison troops, and resulted in arbitrary arrests, the use of force to disperse crowds, and the declaration by the military authorities of a state of siege. Fearful for public order, the civil authorities sought to discipline the soldiers involved, but were directly overruled by the Kaiser himself. The 'Zabern Affair' escalated and caused an outcry in the Reichstag comparable with that over the *Daily Telegraph* interview. The vote of censure against the government and its support of the military authorities was carried by 293 votes to 54. Yet the matter ended there. As in 1908, the Reichstag hesitated to take further action, and the Kaiser and his ministers firmly maintained their support of the army. The failure to take any effective action against excesses finely illustrates the virtual immunity of the army from political control.

The Schlieffen Plan

A similar point is made by a study of the contemporary development of military strategy. Under Count von Schlieffen, Chief of the General Staff

1891–1906, the army command had come to terms with the problems of war on two fronts. Their definitive strategy, formulated in 1897, the 'Schlieffen Plan', called for a rapid outflanking movement through Belgium and Luxemburg to eliminate France from the war before Russian mobilisation was completed. Sections of that force could then be transferred to the eastern front to meet the Russians. It was a daring plan militarily, yet was politically indefensible, as Germany was among those nations who guaranteed Belgium's neutrality. Yet, the strategy became the basis of German military planning for the next 15 years. Gerhard Ritter, who saw the growth of unrestrained military independence in Germany as one of the main causes of the disaster of 1914, has outlined the reason for this. 'To raise political objections to a strategic plan worked out by the General Staff would have appeared in the Germany of Wilhelm II unwarranted interference in a foreign sphere'. In the years preceding, and including, 1914, the German military establishment differed from those of other European powers, not in the degree of its preparedness for war, but in the degree of its freedom from civil governmental restraint.

H Domestic politics

The 'primacy of domestic affairs'

For many years after the collapse of the German Reich in 1918, it was usual for historians to conclude that the policies of Wilhelmine Germany had been shaped primarily by foreign aims and ambitions. In recent years, however, a younger 'school' of German historians has insisted upon the 'primacy of domestic affairs'. They argue that domestic struggles were the prime preoccupation of German politicians, and that even the great adventure of *Weltpolitik* was in truth only a foreign means to a domestic end. In the words of Hans-Ulrich Wehler, a leading representative of this school, the true theme of Wilhelmine, and indeed of Bismarckian politics was 'the defence of inherited ruling position by pre-industrial élites against the onslaught of new forces – a defensive struggle which became even sharper with the erosion of the economic foundations of these privileged leading strata.'

Government through repression

Certainly, the years of Caprivi's chancellorship had seen the vested interests of the Junker class threatened by the vaguely benevolent attitude of the Kaiser towards social problems, and by the sympathy of the Chancellor for industrial economic interests. The fall of Caprivi, largely the work of the Junkers themselves, forced future chancellors to seek new tactics against the dual threats of socialism and industrialism. The first tactic was repression. After 1894, the expressed desire of Wilhelm II to be 'King of the Beggars' was rarely in evidence. Instead, the Kaiser pointedly withdrew his original instructions to Lutheran pastors to concern themselves with social questions, and the five years between 1894 and 1899 witnessed a stream of anti-socialist and anti-union legislation proposed in the Reichstag, mostly without success.

Government through national consensus

The refusal of the Reichstag, in which conservative representation dropped 21 per cent between 1893 and 1898, to support a policy of repression, forced a change of tack. Under Bülow's administration, the government embraced a principle defined in 1897 by Johannes Miquel as *Sammlungspolitik*. In other words, it sought to 'gather together' behind a common policy all the major propertied and conservative interests in the Reich. If the antipathy of Junker and industrialist could be bridged, a formidable front could be presented to social democracy. Bülow's policy had two 'prongs'. One was his reorientation of economic policy, evident in 1902 when he abandoned Caprivi's system of trade treaties, to replace them with a set of high tariffs protecting agriculture and certain key German manufactures from foreign competition. Russian corn, incidentally, was largely excluded thereby from the German market, to the relief of the Junkers. The discontent of German heavy industry, meanwhile, was relieved by the inauguration of Germany's massive naval construction programme. Aptly this conciliation of conservative economic interests became known as the 'Alliance of Rye and Steel'. Meanwhile, the wider policy of *Weltpolitik* played the same role. Bülow's explanation of his policy in 1897, while superficially declaring the 'primacy of foreign affairs', in fact betrayed the true nature of *Weltpolitik*. 'I am putting the main emphasis', he declared, 'on foreign policy. Only a successful foreign policy can help to reconcile, pacify, rally, unite.'

Table 10.3 Parties in the Reichstag, 1890–1912

	1890	1893	1898	1903	1907	1912
Conservatives	93	100	79	75	84	57
National Liberals	42	53	46	51	54	45
Left Liberals	76	48	49	39	49	42
Centre	106	96	102	100	105	91
Social Democrats	35	44	56	81	43	110
National minorities (e.g. Poles, Danes, Alsatians)	38	35	34	32	29	33
Anti-Semites	5	16	13	11	21	13

Germany and her minorities

A lesser, but nevertheless significant, feature of the domestic politics of 1894–1914 was the reversal of Caprivi's conciliatory policies towards national minorities within the Reich. In Prussia, for example, Bülow rigorously enforced the laws banning the use of Polish in education, and passed a law in the *Landtag* (1908) allowing the expropriation of Polish estate owners for the settlement of German farmers. It is true that in 1911 Alsace and Lorraine received a new constitution integrating them more closely into the normal political system of the Reich. The 'Zabern Affair' of 1913 (*see* section **G**) showed clearly, however, that the brutal mentality of military occupation still predominated.

The position of Germany's Jewish population during the Wilhelmine years is not easy to define in general terms. Assimilation had produced some impressive success stories. Families such as the Warburgs, the Rothschilds and the Ballins had established themselves with enormous success in banking and in shipping. Middle-class Jews had found little difficulty in carving out successful careers in medicine, science or journalism. More traditional career areas, such as government, the army and the judiciary, on the other hand, remained closed. Wilhelmine Germany also boasted a variety of anti-Semitic political parties, who admittedly won relatively few votes, and provided fertile soil for a growing tradition of pseudo-intellectual anti-Semitism. 1899 saw the publication both of Ernst Haeckel's *Riddle of the*

Universe and of Houston Stewart Chamberlain's *Foundations of the Nineteenth Century*. Both adopted a pseudo-scientific approach to the question of race, 'proving' the superiority of Germanic races, and that this superiority would be undermined if Jews were allowed to 'dilute' German racial characteristics by intermarriage. Even so, recent research has suggested that such 'scholastic' reasoning played relatively little part in the growth of German anti-Semitism. Jack Wertheimer and Egmont Zechlin have both suggested that a more significant role was played by the influx of some 79,000 Jews from eastern Europe who flooded into Germany from Russian territory in the years shortly before the First World War. The element of class threat posed by these poor and unassimilated Jews, they conclude, together with the element of patriotic mistrust generated by the war, formed the true basis of the great anti-Semitic explosion of the 1930s.

I   The Social Democrats

The growth and development of social democracy

If one were to judge merely by the results of Reichstag elections held during the administrations of Bülow and of Bethmann-Hollweg, one would conclude that *Sammlungspolitik* had failed to secure the state against the threat of socialism. As Table 10.3 shows, the temporary lapse of Social Democrat support in 1907 was reversed so effectively that by 1912 the party was the most powerful in the Reichstag. Their triumph certainly had an effect upon the Kaiser and his government. 'The German parliamentarian,' Wilhelm declared in 1913, 'becomes daily more of a swine.' Yet how much of a threat did Social Democracy pose to the Imperial system of government? For all its Marxist origins, the German socialist movement by 1912 was broadly committed to the 'revisionism' proposed by Eduard Bernstein in 1898 in his work, *The Presuppositions of Socialism and the Tasks of Social Democracy*. Bernstein's conclusion was that Marx had been mistaken about the approaching crisis of capitalism, as the rising living standards of German workers proved, and that change should not be sought through revolution. From 1906 onwards, leading Social Democrats were willing to make electoral pacts with the Liberals to forward desirable social policies. They were willing in general to subscribe to an Imperial foreign policy which they interpreted as primarily opposed to reactionary Tsardom, and even supported the financial provisions of the Army Bill in 1913, because they proposed a property tax.

The 'threat' of social democracy

Nevertheless, it is possible to understand the apprehension of the ruling classes at the electoral success of Social Democracy which destroyed the conservative 'Bülow Bloc' of parties, and replaced it with a bloc effectively able to resist any unpopular government legislation. The 1912 elections, wrote W. J. Mommsen, thus created the 'stalemate of the party system'. The Social Democrat party, furthermore, did possess an active left-wing. It was led by Liebknecht, Luxemburg and Mehring, it maintained an orthodox Marxist line, and was to show its mettle in 1918. Lastly, we should not ignore the fact that the prospect of power in the hands of industrial workers appeared outrageous and highly dangerous to many conservatives, quite regardless of the uses to which those workers might turn their power. With or without logical justification, therefore, the election results of 1912 ensured that domestic political tensions were as high as ever as the conservatives of the German government and General Staff approached the international crisis of the last years of peace.

J   *Weltpolitik*: origins

The nature of *Weltpolitik*

In the years that followed the fall of Caprivi, a revolutionary new factor came to dominate the foreign policy of the Reich. That policy departed from the essentially European concerns of Bismarck, and came more and more to demand a world role for Germany. It was by enlarging her interests in non-European affairs that Germany was to claim the status of a 'World-Power' (*Weltmacht*). The reasons for this fundamental change were complex and varied, yet on the whole this 'world policy' (*Weltpolitik*) must be seen as an external reflection of internal German developments.

Firstly, it undoubtedly reflected the mentality and personality of the Kaiser. *Weltpolitik* consisted of a headstrong and incoherent insistence that

Germany should have a say in all major issues, just as Wilhelm intruded his half-formed opinion into all aspects of domestic government. As Imanuel Geiss has put it, 'German foreign policy during this time bore the personal stamp of the Kaiser. He found it more or less congenial and in keeping with his personal ambitions and his style of behaviour.' Certainly, Wilhelm made a direct practical contribution to this policy by his appointment to high office of its enthusiastic supporters. In 1897 alone, the promotions of Johannes von Miquel to the vice-presidency of the Prussian ministry, of Alfred von Tirpitz to the naval ministry and of Bernhard von Bülow to the head of the Foreign Ministry provided the core of the *Weltpolitik* 'crew'.

Weltpolitik and the German economy

Weltpolitik was not merely a result of the Kaiser's whim. The expansion of German industry had renewed and increased the national sense of power, and many leading figures expressed the fear that existing resources and markets would soon prove insufficient and that emigration to the USA might rob Germany of her most dynamic sons. 'Our vigorous national development,' claimed Bülow himself, 'mainly in the industrial sphere, forced us to cross the ocean.' The historian Treitschke and the statesman Delbrück publicised a variation upon this theme. Since German unification the colonial expansion of other powers had cancelled out Germany's advance in status. Germany was faced with the choice of colonial expansion or stagnation as a major power. This theme of world expansion as a logical sequel to unification was most eloquently expressed by the great sociologist Max Weber in his inaugural lecture at Freiburg University in 1895. 'We have to grasp,' he stated, 'that the unification of Germany would have been better dispensed with because of its cost, if it were the end and not the beginning of a German policy of World Power.'

Weltpolitik and domestic government

Lastly, many recent historians concentrating upon the domestic affairs of the Reich have interpreted *Weltpolitik* as essentially an element in the solution of Germany's internal political problems (*see* section **H**). At a time when the apparent factional divisions in German politics were widening, it provided a means of uniting national opinion and neutralising the disruptive opposition of the Social Democrats. The patriotic stance of the Social Democrats in 1914 certainly suggests that *Weltpolitik* succeeded where the reform programmes of Bismarck and of Caprivi had failed. Imanuel Geiss speaks for this school of thought in concluding that '*Weltpolitik* came into existence as a red herring of the ruling classes to distract the middle and working classes from social and political problems at home'. Where Bismarck in 1890 and Wilhelm in 1894 had toyed with the idea of a *coup d'état* as the answer to domestic pressures, Germany now turned to the glamour and excitement of *Weltpolitik*.

K *Weltpolitik*: manifestions

The acquisition of colonies
In the last four years of the 19th century the mentality of *Weltpolitik* manifested itself in all those quarters of the globe subject to European penetration. In Africa it took the form of a pretentious masquerade as protector of the Boers in their confrontation with British imperialism in the Transvaal under President Kruger. After thwarting an ill-organised British-backed coup, Wilhelm dispatched his famous 'Kruger telegram' congratulating the Boers on maintaining their independence 'without having to appeal to friendly powers for assistance'. With German naval power in its infancy, it was an empty and rhetorical gesture, whose only lasting effect could be to cause offence to a potentially friendly European power. The first tangible reward of *Weltpolitik* was reaped in China in 1897. There, alarmed at the extent of Japan's success in her war against China (1894–95), Germany acted in concert with Russia and France to modify the original Japanese gains, and to ensure that China remained open to European penetration. Her own private gain was a 99-year lease of the port of Kiaochow as a trading and naval base. The following year the small groups of Pacific Islands, the Carolines and the Marianas, were purchased from Spain. In 1899, Germany declared dissolved her condominium with Britain and the USA over the islands of Samoa, and assumed possession of the eastern portion of the islands.

Patently trivial as such gains were, the extension of German interests in the Middle East had more serious international implications. As early as 1888,

the Deutsche Bank had agreed with the Turkish government to finance the projected railway from Baghdad to the Persian Gulf. It was clearly a region sensitive to both British and Russian interests. While Bismarck had specified at that time that German money implied no direct German political interest, Wilhelm II showed none of his restraint. In a typically pretentious speech (1898) he referred to himself as 'the protector of 300 million Muslims', and openly referred to 'my railway'. The compensation for strained relations with Britain and Russia was the steady attraction of the Turkish Empire into the German orbit, yet the First World War was to prove Turkey an ally of doubtful worth.

The birth of the German navy
The most spectacular and damaging manifestation of Germany's new ambitions was the growth of her naval power. The development of a mighty battle fleet, like *Weltpolitik* itself, served several purposes. For many, like its founder Admiral von Tirpitz, it was an assertion of the nation's new status. 'The fleet, he declared, 'is necessary to show that Germany is as well born as Britain.' In so saying, he betrayed the essential feature of naval development. It was aimed at, and bound to offend, Great Britain. She was the one major European power with whom Germany had no potential continental argument, and whose friendship might have offset the Franco–Russian alliance. Equally, the decision to develop the fleet provided a huge new outlet for German heavy industry. It was no coincidence that so great an industrialist as Alfred Krupp was a leading member and backer of the Naval League (*Flottenverein*), founded in 1898. To the politically minded middle classes, furthermore, the fleet represented a national weapon relatively free from the influence of the Prussian Junkers. Hence the judgement of Imanuel Geiss that 'the battle fleet was an instrument of the German middle class'. It 'represented the massive economic interests and social aspirations of the most prosperous and dynamic elements of German society'.

The first great Naval Bill, of March 1898, envisaged an eventual force of 19 battleships, 12 heavy cruisers and 30 light cruisers. The launching of the revolutionary British battleship, HMS *Dreadnought* (February 1906), had a double impact upon the naval question. By rendering obsolete all existing battleships, it opened up the real possibility that a German fleet could compete with its British counterpart. At the same time it necessitated an urgent rebuilding of the German fleet. In retrospect, further German bills in 1906, 1907 and 1908 constituted a double misfortune for the German state. They constituted a tremendous financial undertaking, and signalled the beginning of a serious naval arms race between Britain and Germany. It is in these respects that we may accept the verdict of Ian Porter and Ian Armour that 'the whole naval programme was an expensive failure'.

Weltpolitik: the balance sheet

With the exception of the new battle fleet, the physical results of *Weltpolitik* were meagre, even absurd. By 1914, Germany possessed a colonial 'empire' of only about a million square miles. Total German investment in those colonies was only 505 million marks. The colonies were, furthermore, dotted about the globe, almost indefensible and totally vulnerable to the attack of an enemy, as their fates in 1914 were to prove. In terms of Germany's overall diplomatic position, the decision to move towards 'world power' was of enormous negative importance. It completed the destruction of the Bismarckian European balance and prepared the way for Germany's isolation and encirclement. Bernadette Schmitt has summarised the error of *Weltpolitik* as follows: 'A policy of naval expansion, the development of an African empire, commercial and financial penetration of the Near East could each be justified. But to pursue all three courses at the same time was the worst possible policy, for it kept alive the distrust and suspicion of the Entente powers, convinced them of the dangerous reality of German militarism, and made them more anxious than ever to act together.'

L   Germany and Europe 1894–1905

Germany and Russia

The weakening of the Bismarckian system of alliances left Germany's European diplomacy with two central themes in the decade after the fall of Caprivi. The first was the desire to maintain friendly relations with Russia in the hope of detaching her from her new-found friendship with France. 1894 provided two sources of hope in this respect, with the replacement of Caprivi by the more conservative and 'Bismarckian' Hohenlohe, and with the accession of Nicholas II. The new Tsar, a cousin of the Kaiser, enjoyed friendly personal relations with his fellow Emperor, and was susceptible to Wilhelm's entreaties to pursue a civilising mission against the 'Yellow Peril' in eastern Asia. The 1890s saw common action against excessive Japanese gains from China, but the logical outcome of Russian commitment was her embroilment in the Russo–Japanese war of 1904 (*see* Chapter 9, section **G**). Although such distractions suited Germany's purposes well, the conviction in St Petersburg that such a war had always been the German goal merely compounded the damage done by the cancellation of the Reinsurance Treaty. Nevertheless, Wilhelm came close to success in a final effort to separate Russia and France. In a meeting at Björkö (July 1905) he persuaded the Tsar to conclude an agreement whereby both states undertook to aid the other in the event of an attack by another European power in Europe. The success was, however, merely superficial. The Tsar had undertaken more than his ministers would allow him to fulfil. The implications for the loss of French economic aid alone were so serious that they refused to endorse the agreement, and the Treaty of Björkö remained a 'dead letter' from the moment of its signature.

Germany and Britain

A logical response to the growing intimacy of Russia and France would have been to cultivate relations with Great Britain more closely. German attitudes to Britain, nevertheless, remained highly ambiguous. The ambassador to London, von Hatzfeldt, consistently hoped and believed Britain might be drawn into the Triple Alliance and consistently condemned *Weltpolitik* as a tactless means of alienating a valuable ally. The Kaiser himself was certainly attracted to certain elements of British society, but had an intense dislike for others, such as its constitutional monarchy. 'It was a love,' comments Hajo Holborn, 'unfortunately shot through with unruly jealousy.'

Such ambiguity was mirrored in the diplomatic history of the 1890s. The promise of the agreement over Heligoland and Zanzibar contrasted with the lively hostility created by the 'Kruger Telegram'.

Germany's official, and vaguely benevolent, neutrality during the Boer War (1899–1900) was offset by the violently anti-British propaganda of the Pan-German League and the Naval League. Thus, when a Conservative government in Britain abandoned the isolationism of the Liberals and put out feelers for a formal alliance, the opportunity was missed. The first British approach (March 1898) failed because of German fears that a treaty might fail to achieve parliamentary ratification, and that relations with Russia might be strained to no avail. The second approach (January 1901) was killed by a series of miscalculations by the German Foreign Office. In the first place, senior officials remained convinced that a German alliance was Britain's only option. Speaking of British hints of an approach to France, Bülow declared that 'in my opinion we need not worry about such remote possibilities'. Secondly, therefore, Germany set excessively strict conditions upon an understanding with Britain. She was to tie herself, not simply to Germany, but to the Triple Alliance as a whole. Finding the prospect of commitment to the maintenance of Austria-Hungary quite unacceptable, Britain had within three years informally associated herself with the Franco–Russian Entente.

Conclusion

The so-called 'free hand' policy of the German Foreign Office, by rejecting British overtures, and by overestimating the significance of the Björkö agreement, had by 1905 left Germany isolated but for her partners in the Triple Alliance. Given the vacillation of Italy and her closer relations with France (*see* Chapter 8, section **Q**), this effectively meant dependence upon Austria-Hungary as Germany's sole reliable ally. To appreciate more fully the implications of this fact, a brief summary is necessary of the development of Austria-Hungary since her defeat by Prussia in 1866.

M Austria-Hungary: the Compromise and the Dual Monarchy

Hungary's position within the Compromise

The defeat suffered by Austria at the hands of Prussia in 1866 ended the roles played by the Empire as a German power and as an Italian power. It was possible that the defeat would bring about the collapse of her multinational structure and thus end her role as a great European power altogether. That this did not happen was the result of timely concessions granted to the Hungarians, the one nationality capable of destroying the integrity of the Empire, and to the moderate realism of certain Hungarian leaders. 'We must not overrate our strength,' Ferenc Deak warned some of the more headstrong nationalists, 'and must confess that on our own we are not a great state.' Hungarian leaders were thus content to seek concession within the Habsburg Empire, which entered upon a new lease of life as Austria-Hungary, or the Dual Monarchy.

The political form of this entity was laid out in the Compromise (*Ausgleich*) negotiated in March 1867, mainly between Friedrich Ferdinand von Beust, the Empire's Saxon-born foreign minister, and Gyula Andrassy, spokesman for the Magyar nobility. By its terms, Hungary became a separate kingdom, linked to its Austrian neighbour in a variety of ways. In the first place, the Hungarian crown was to be worn by the Austrian Emperor. The unity of the Dual Monarchy was not merely personal, however, for the states were to share a common foreign policy and common armed forces. By paying only 30 per cent of the expenses of the armed forces, Hungary ensured her national security at a remarkably economical rate. Other matters of common interest to the two states, such as customs, the monetary system, and interlinking railway communications, were to be governed by agreements renewed between the two partners at intervals of ten years. The Compromise, therefore, was a unique document, neither an international treaty, nor a confederation.

The position of Franz Josef

At the centre of his new constitutional arrangement stood the Emperor-King, Franz Josef. Having originally come to power in the difficult and dangerous circumstances of 1848, he was a man of many qualities. He tackled his 'God-given' duties with a devotion and Spartan sense of duty that entailed long hours of work and minute attention to the details of government. On the other hand, he lacked the imagination or flexibility to continue the process of constitutional adaptation and development into the 1870s. However, he accepted the Austrian constitution of December 1867, which ended his absolutism by recognising such principles as ministerial responsibility and the independence of the judiciary, and which recognised in theory the equality of the different national groups within the Austrian territories. He also seemed ready between 1868 and 1871 to make concessions to the Czechs in Bohemia that might have established a 'Triple Monarchy'. Dissuaded from this, however, by Magyars and Austrian Germans jealous of their dominant positions in the Dual Monarchy, Franz Josef became content to regard the 1867 Compromise as the definitive and final constitutional settlement to be defended and upheld by any expedient at his disposal. This did not quite make Austria-Hungary, in H. Kohn's phrase, 'an Empire without an idea'. It did ensure, however, that its central idea, the power partnership of Germans and Magyars, would be unacceptable to most of Franz Josef's subjects.

The weaknesses of the Compromise

A principal feature of the Compromise was that it was concluded without reference to any of the other nationalities of the Empire and sacrificed their political and cultural interests to the co-existence of the two leading national groups. Conciliatory gestures were made to the minorities under Austrian rule (*see* section **N**), but the Hungarian constitution offered little consolation to minorities governed from Budapest (*see* section **O**). The aspirations of these national minorities were to be a consistent source of instability and disturbance within the Dual Monarchy.

What judgement, ultimately, is to passed on the Compromise? In the context of 1867, it was a shrewd and successful move which did much to facilitate the survival of the Habsburg Empire as a major power bloc. In R. A. Kann's words, 'the Compromise gave the Danube peoples the chance to live peacefully for nearly two generations and to work hopefully for a longer lasting settlement'. The tragedy of the Compromise was that its initial flexibility gave way to doctrinaire rigidity on the part of the Emperor-King, and to shortsighted egoism on the part of the governing classes of Hungary. In the long run, therefore, it built up a new set of challenges for the Dual Monarchy which it did not ultimately survive.

N The government of Austria

Liberal reform, 1867–79

In the aftermath of the constitutional upheavals of 1867, the Liberal Party, representing in the main German middle-class interests, maintained an ascendancy in the Austrian parliament. Franz Josef thus found himself obliged to co-operate with them, and Austria entered upon a decade of unprecedented liberalisation. As happened in other states, the Catholic Church found itself under attack. It lost control over education and was forced to accept the legalisation of civil marriage (1868). In 1870, in the face of Puis IX's declaration of Papal Infallibility, the Concordat concluded with the Rome in 1855 was cancelled. Other reforms included the provision of free and compulsory elementary education (1869), and various measures to liberalise the civil and legal status of Jews.

It was an impressive programme, but was not matched by the Liberals' record on the question of nationalities. A project to give the Czechs in Bohemia equal footing with Germans and Magyars in a 'Triple Monarchy' was brought to nothing by the vested interest of those two dominant national groups. The conservative Emperor, in any case, was always a reluctant ally of the Liberals and broke with them without regret in 1879 when they opposed the outcome of the Congress of Berlin, and especially Austria's growing control over Bosnia and Herzegovina.

Taafe's ministry

The Emperor now turned to the support of a minister whose conservatism he found much more attractive. Count Edward Taafe, an aristocrat of Irish origins, governed the Empire longer than any other minister between the fall of Metternich and the collapse of the Habsburg regime. His survival was due in part to the bond of trust between himself and the Emperor, but also to the powerful alliance that he established with Polish, Slovene, German and Bohemian conservative landowners. This, he declared, was his 'ring of iron' around the German Liberals. His allies were paid for their support by various national concessions. The Polish language was permitted in various branches of the administration. The Czechs gained a new

The Historical Debate

The historiography of Austria-Hungary during this period has followed a very different course from that of Germany. Historians have investigated, not the groundwork for future aggression and expansion, but the causes of the Dual Monarchy's collapse. In a debate reminiscent of that surrounding the last years of the Russian Empire, the argument has centred upon the question of inevitability. Was the monarchy living on borrowed time since the Compromise, or was its collapse unduly precipitated by the short-term crisis of the World War?

Oscar Jaszi (*The Dissolution of the Habsburg Monarchy*, 1929) was the most influential advocate of the view that the Compromise doomed Austria-Hungary in the long run. By excluding the Slav nationalities from direct participation in government, the arrangement of 1867 created a degree of domestic opposition that could never effectively be overcome. The opposite school of thought might be represented by Edward Crankshaw (*The Fall of the House of Habsburg*, 1963) or by Hugo Hantsch (*The History of Austria*, 1947). These authors stress that, although nationalist feelings undoubtedly ran high, the nationalists often sought the reform of Austria-Hungary, rather than her dissolution.

They conclude that the fate of the monarchy was decided by the short-term crisis of the First World War, and that the monarchy collapsed in the final analysis 'because it lost a war to people who hated dynasties' (Crankshaw). Rather than side with either argument, John Mason (*The Dissolution of the Austro-Hungarian Empire 1867–1918*, 1985) has stressed the need to accept a synthesis of both cases. Characteristically, A. J. P. Taylor (*The Habsburg Monarchy 1809–1918*, 1964) provided just such a synthesis. For Taylor the fate of the Habsburgs had to be seen in the context of their relations with Germany. The events of the year 1866 were thus doubly disastrous, in that they forced the Compromise upon the Austrian government, thus raising the future problem of the Slav nationalities. Worse still, they also began the process whereby the Dual Monarchy became increasingly dependent in foreign affairs upon Germany, a process which ended in disaster.

---

electoral law (1882), that gave them a majority in the Bohemian Diet, and the wider use of Czech in legal administration. Also in 1882, the University of Prague was divided into two sections, one now taught and administered in Czech. In the short term, Taafe's policies enjoyed considerable success, but they aimed merely to preserve an unsatisfactory and problematical 'status quo'. Thus, while A. J. P. Taylor can claim that 'Taafe's system gave Austria a stability and calm such as she had not enjoyed since the days of Francis I', it is equally true to claim, as C. A. Macartney has, that 'Taafe not only did not produce an answer to the riddle of the monarchy, he did not even look for one'.

The growth of political extremes

The relative calm in Austrian domestic politics did not last beyond 1893. There followed a new era of political bitterness and agitation. An important element in this was the emergence in Austria of a vociferous if disorganised Pan-German movement, led by Georg von Schönerer. It was the violent opposition of the Pan-Germans to the policy of concessions to the national minorities that precipitated the fall of Taafe in 1893 amidst controversy so violent that Prague had to be placed under martial law. Four years later, the attempts of his successor, Badeni, to extend the use of the Czech language led to demonstrations and riots that paralysed the functions of parliament and threatened the stability of the state.

Schönerer's organisation was only one element in the new political atmosphere, however. The period also witnessed the rise of the Christian Socialist Party, led by Karl Lueger. The element of paternalist reform in this Catholic party was sincere and, as Mayor of Vienna between 1897 and 1907, Lueger presided over an impressive programme of urban improvement. Equally prominent, however, was the party's anti-Semitism, fed by the economic problems of the bourgeoisie at a time of industrial depression. It is worthy of note that both Schönerer and Lueger exercised some influence over the political development of the young Adolf Hitler. Thirdly, the introduction of universal manhood suffrage (January 1907) furthered the development of an Austrian Social Democratic Party, founded 20 years earlier by Viktor Adler. Like its German counterpart it was Marxist in its theories, but increasingly parliamentarian in its practice. It had made substantial progress in the cities of the Empire by the outbreak of war, winning 87 seats in the election of 1907, to the disquiet of the middle classes.

Elements of stability within the Dual Monarchy

For all these problems and divisions, it is easy to overestimate the weaknesses of the Empire in 1914. The economic coherence of the state, with Hungary supplying agricultural produce to the industrial areas of Austria, was an element of strength. So too was the enduring alliance between crown, Church, army and bureaucracy. Even in the midst of party disputes, and the claims of the nationalities, as A. J. P. Taylor has stated, 'no party on either side seriously desired the break-up of Austria-Hungary'. In the event, for all its apparent weakness, it took four years of fierce, concentrated fighting to bring the Dual Monarchy to its knees.

O The government of Hungary

The Hungarian state

The Compromise of 1867 represented a triumph for the aggressive Hungarian nationalism manifested in 1848–49. It permitted Hungarian domination over the domestic affairs of a territory similar to that of the old kingdom of Hungary, yet still enabled Hungarians to enjoy the security of membership of the Habsburg Empire. Yet only in a very limited sense did it create a Hungarian state. Hungarians, or Magyars, constituted less than half the population, 6 million out of 13.5 million in 1867, and even then political power lay predominantly in the hands of a limited land-owning stratum of Magyar society.

From these factors arose the two dominant features of Hungarian politics: the restriction of the franchise and the policy of Magyarisation. By comparison with its Austrian counterpart, Hungarian

political life rested upon a narrowly restricted franchise. To limit the influence of poorer Magyars and non-Magyars alike, the Electoral Law of 1874 allowed only 800,000 inhabitants to participate in the elections to the Hungarian House of Deputies.

Hungary and its national minorities

Domestic policy was dominated by a strict and thorough policy of Magyarisation, aimed at weakening the national cultures – Rumanian, Slovak, Croat, Serb and Ukrainian – that had threatened Hungarian interests in 1848–49. Ninety-five per cent of all state officials were Magyar, as were 90 per cent of all judges. Eighty per cent of all newspapers were printed in the Magyar language, which also dominated the legal and educational systems, and even the railway timetables. Only the Croats, with a separate Diet, their own schools and police force, and a bloc of 40 representatives in the House of Deputies, effectively maintained an active cultural identity. The fate of the other minority cultures may be represented by the decline in the number of Slovak-speaking schools in the kingdom, from 1,805 in 1875 to 241 in 1905.

It should also be noted that Hungarian nationalism played no small part in determining the foreign attitudes of the Dual Monarchy. The links of Polish and Ukrainian minorities with Poles and Ukrainians in the Russian Empire naturally stimulated Hungarian suspicions of Russian pan-slavism and provided Habsburg foreign policy with a strong anti-Russian impulse. Thus rigid Hungarian attitudes stored up trouble for the future and made a satisfactory settlement of the nationalities problem almost impossible. Nevertheless, under the long premiership of Kalman Tisza (1875–90), official Hungarian enthusiasm for the terms of the Compromise ensured stable and harmonious relations between Austria and Hungary. Tisza, furthermore, presided over the centralisation and improvement of Hungary's communications system, and over a period of modest commercial and industrial prosperity.

The resurgence of Hungarian nationalism

By the late 1880s, however, a new generation of nationalists was proposing a new view of the Compromise. Tisza's Liberal Party found itself challenged by a National Party, under the leadership of Albert Apponyi, and latterly by the

Independence Party of Ferenc Kossuth, son of the great nationalist rebel of 1849. Kossuth's criticisms, in particular, fell upon the limitations imposed upon Hungary's national independence by continued partnership with the Habsburg monarchy. Such nationalist sentiments were fuelled by the death and funeral of Lajos Kossuth (1894), by the millennium of the original Magyar invasion of Hungary (1896), and by a cultural renaissance which produced the composers Bartok and Kodaly as its greatest figures.

Areas of tension between Hungary and Austria

Tension with Austria centred upon two issues: the maintenance of a joint army commanded in German, and Hungarian participation in the Austrian monetary and customs system. Franz Josef's reasonable conviction that a separate military establishment would hinder the military efficiency of the Dual Monarchy precipitated a confrontation with the radical Magyar nationalists in 1905. The defeat in that year's elections of Istvan Tisza, the son of Kalman Tisza and also an enthusiast for the Compromise, led Franz Josef to undertake the forcible dissolution of the House of Deputies, and to propose the introduction of a system of universal manhood suffrage in Hungary. This threatened instantly to put non-Magyars and the Magyar peasantry into a majority in the Hungarian government.

The threat worked, and Kossuth and his followers agreed in 1906 to withdraw their economic and military claims. Unfortunately, it had only been a threat. Franz Josef had had in his hands a weapon for the solution of the nationality problem in Hungary, but had refused to use it. The exclusive partnership between Germans and Magyars was continued.

Under successive premiers Hungary loyally honoured the 1867 Compromise, but made little or no progress on the issues of social reform, or of concessions to the national minorities. On the contrary, 1912 witnessed the suppression of the Croat constitution, while a general strike in the same year showed the level of labour unrest. By solving none of these problems before 1914, the Hungarian governments had, in the judgement of the American commentator A. J. May, 'muffed an opportunity for which they, their Hungary and the Dual Monarchy would one day pay the penalty'.

P   Austria-Hungary: foreign policy and the Balkans

Austria-Hungary and Germany

Between 1859 and 1871 the foreign policy of the Habsburg Empire was reduced to a Balkan policy. In that period Imperial influence was excluded from Italy, while Bismarck's definitive victory over France confirmed that hopes of renewed Austrian influence over Germany were unfounded. In the hands of the Magyar aristocrat, Gyula Andrassy, Austro-Hungarian foreign policy became increasingly pro-German and anti-Russian. Fearing Russian expansion, Andrassy saw the future of the Empire as depending upon economic penetration of the Balkans, and so promoted the construction of important railway links between Austria-Hungary, Constantinople and the Aegean port of Salonika. From the Austro-Hungarian point of view, therefore, it was perfectly logical that the League of the Three Emperors (*see* Chapter 7, section **J**) should eventually develop into a defensive alliance with Germany against Russia, the Dual Alliance (*see* Chapter 7, section **L**). Imperial interests in the Balkans, after all, were not merely a matter of expansion and prestige. Control of the River Danube and access to the Adriatic coast were questions of fundamental economic importance to the Empire, and the rise of Slav nationalism could never be a matter of indifference to a state with so large a Slav population.

Austro-Hungarian ambitions in the Balkans

Three distinct stages may be identified in Austro-Hungarian political involvement in the Balkans. The first of these was begun by the Congress of Berlin (*see* Chapter 7, section **K**), under the provisions of which Austria-Hungary was permitted to occupy and administer the Turkish provinces of Bosnia, Herzegovina and Novibazar. These remained under the nominal suzerainty of the Ottoman Empire, but in reality gave Austria-Hungary a substantial stake and influence in Balkan affairs. This state of affairs survived the crisis of 1885–87, when Russia attempted unsuccessfully to replace King Alexander of Bulgaria with a more amenable monarch, but these years saw a hardening of attitudes and the visible formation of armed camps. Three diplomatic developments provided testimony to Austrian determination to preserve her 'great power' status in the Balkans. Two of these were the renewal of the Triple Alliance (February 1887) with Germany and Italy, and the publication (February 1888) of Germany's commitments to Austria-Hungary under the Dual Alliance. In addition, March 1887 saw the conclusion of a Mediterranean agreement between Austria-Hungary, Italy and Britain, to preserve the status quo around its shores.

Austria-Hungary and Yugoslavism

The second stage was opened by a severe blow to Austro-Hungarian aspirations in the Balkans. In 1903 King Alexander of Serbia, of the pro-Austrian Obrenovic dynasty, was assassinated, and the accession of the pro-Russian Karageorgevich faction signalled a radical change in Serbian policy. King Peter I and his foreign minister, Pasic, quickly made it clear that they favoured a policy of 'South Slavism' (Yugoslavism), whereby Serbia aspired to economic, and perhaps eventually political leadership of the Balkan Slavs, including those under Austrian control. The customs union concluded in 1904 between Serbia and Bulgaria showed that these plans were more than idle rhetoric. Indeed, they badly compromised the ambitions of Austrian 'trialists', who hoped that the Slavs might eventually be admitted to a three-cornered partnership with the Germans and Magyars in running the Empire, and encouraged the view in Vienna that Serbia was 'the Piedmont of the South Slavs'. Furthermore, at the instigation of Hungarian economic interests, the Empire imposed prohibitive tariffs upon Serbian agricultural produce, especially livestock. Between 1904–08, the so-called 'Pig War' helped to maintain an atmosphere of hostility and mistrust between Serbia and the Dual Monarchy. Only at the latter date did the formal annexation by Austria-Hungary of the provinces of Bosnia and Herzegovina (*see* Chapter 11, section **D**) lead her Balkan policy into its third and fatal stage.

Questions

Essay questions

1   'Irresponsibility and a lack of central direction.' Discuss the domestic policy of Kaiser Wilhelm II in the light of this judgement. (UCLES)

2   How valid is the view that 'the domestic problems' facing the rulers of Germany in the period 1878–1914 were primarily the consequences of social and economic change? (AEB)

3   Was German society well served by the governments of the Wilhelmine period? (Oxford Entrance).

4   'A ramshackle Empire': to what extent is this an accurate description of the Habsburg Empire in the period 1867–1914? (ULEAC)

5   Examine the claim that the Ausgleich (1867) worsened political divisions and national disunity in Austria-Hungary. (UCLES)

Documentary Question

Study the information that follows carefully, and then answer the questions below.

SOURCE A *Mineral production within the Kingdom of Austria*

	Coal (thousand tons)	Petroleum (tons)	Iron ore (thousand tons)
1850	877	–	–
1855	1,820	–	599
1860	3,189	–	–
1865	4,450	300	–
1870	7,217	400	835
1875	11,401	600	705
1880	14,311	1,000	697
1885	17,893	2,200	931
1890	24,260	99,000	1,362
1895	28,112	195,000	1,385
1900	32,533	349,000	1,894
1905	35,278	797,000	1,914
1910	38,907	1,768,000	2,628
1915	38,354	578,000	2,547

From C. Cook and J. Paxton, European Political Facts 1848–1918

SOURCE B *Index of overall industrial production in Austria-Hungary. (1900 = 100)*

1880	44	1890	72	1900	100	1910	130
1881	49	1891	77	1901	105	1911	137
1882	51	1892	78	1902	105	1912	150
1883	57	1893	80	1903	106	1913	144
1884	59	1894	86	1904	107		
1885	56	1895	89	1905	113		
1886	60	1896	90	1906	118		
1887	62	1897	91	1907	135		
1888	61	1898	98	1908	132		
1889	66	1899	99	1909	129		

Quoted in J. W. Mason, The Dissolution of the Austro-Hungarian Empire.

SOURCE C Comparative steel production of European powers (thousand tons)

	1891	1901	1911
Austria-Hungary	846	1,142	2,327
Belgium	244	530	2,193
France	744	1,425	3,837
Germany	2,563	6,211	14,556
Great Britain	3,157	4,897	6,565
Russia	429	2,212	3,933

Quoted in J. W. Mason. Ibid.

SOURCE D Division of European and world trade among the European powers.

	European trade (per cent)			World trade (per cent)		
	1860	1870	1880	1885	1895	1908
Austria-Hungary	5.4	6.0	7.2	3.7	3.7	3.3
France	17.5	16.5	17.6	10.4	8.6	8.9
Germany	16.8	15.4	15.4	10.3	11.1	12.3
Great Britain	33.4	33.4	30.4	19.2	17.8	17.2
Russia	4.8	7.3	5.1	5.6	6.0	3.0

Quoted in J. W. Mason. Ibid.

SOURCE E Index of harvest yields in Hungary. (1871–75 = 100)

	Wheat	Rye	Barley	Maize	Potatoes	Turnips
1871–75	100	100	100	100	100	100
1876–80	154	113	126	174	181	247
1881–85	222	141	158	214	301	497
1886–90	261	142	150	201	282	627
1891–95	309	156	184	274	338	852
1896–1900	269	141	180	267	440	1,000
1901–05	315	167	189	229	482	1,123
1906–10	315	163	206	358	555	1,537
1911–15	316	163	227	365	615	1,643

SOURCE F Vienna on the eve of the First World War

Vienna was, from an economic point of view, a staging-post between eastern and western Europe that was hard to avoid. Here were the headquarters of the banks which gathered the capital destined to finance the industry and the commerce of all the territories of the Dual Monarchy. They also had their branches and their associates throughout south-eastern Europe to finance the Ottoman Empire and those states born out of the dislocation of that Empire.

Eventually Vienna became a centre of the first importance for handicrafts and industry. Under the influence of the court, of the nobility, and of long established traditions of elegance and good taste, the production of luxury goods and semi-luxury goods predominated, requiring highly skilled labour. Thanks to the proximity of iron and coal deposits, to the industrial centres of Styria and Bohemia, and to the influence of the German Reich, the capital and its suburbs witnessed the birth of substantial mechanical and electrical industries. Naturally, the population increased, and in 1910 it passed the two million mark. For many years immigrants had arrived mainly from Austrian and German territories. Yet the second half of the 19th century saw the influx of Slavs (whose numbers reached 300,000 before the war) of Galician Poles, but above all of Czechs, who formed a considerable colony.

Report of a French observer, A Tibal, published as Les Communications dans l'Europe danubienne *in 1933.*

a Assess the advantages and the problems for the historian of the types of evidence provided in these documents.

b To what extent does the information provided in these documents support the contention that 'Austria-Hungary, in the twenty years before the First World War, possessed an economy that was backward and stagnant'?

11
The First World War: causes and course

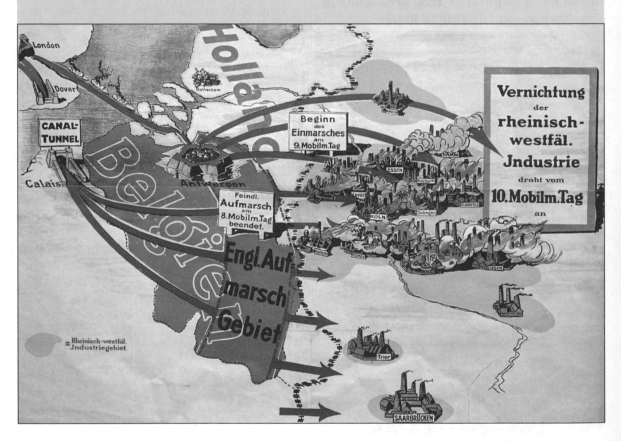

A propaganda poster produced in Germany in 1914 which pretends to show how Britain might launch an attack on Germany through Belgium. It shows how British troops might threaten the industries of the Rhineland on the tenth day after mobilisation.

What impact is the poster supposed to have upon German public opinion?

What elements in the poster would render it unconvincing to well-informed contemporaries?

The Historical Debate

Although 1918 marked the end of the military contest, it marked the beginning of the fierce war of words concerning the causes and nature of the conflict, and the apportioning of 'war guilt'. Clause 231 forced the defeated Germans to admit that they bore the moral responsibility for the carnage by virtue of their aggressive and militaristic policies before 1914. If the politicians of the Weimar Republic were forced publicly to accept that interpretation, her historians were not. The analysis of German documentary evidence from the diplomatic archives, undertaken to substantiate German claims of innocence, culminated in a vast 40-volume work. It was edited by J. Lepsius, A. Mendelsohn-Bartholdy and F. Thimme, and entitled *The Grand Policy of the European Cabinets 1871–1914* (1922–27). This massive piece of scholarship was supported in Germany by interpretative works such as those of H. von Delbrück (*The Peace of Versailles*, 1930) and H. Oncken (*The German Reich and the Prehistory of the First World War*, 1932). These stressed Germany's reasons for fearing encirclement, and sought to lay greater emphasis on French desires to regain Alsace-Lorraine, and Russian designs upon Constantinople. By the early 1930s, however, a number of prominent French writers, among them Pierre Renouvin (*The Immediate Origins of the War*, 1925), J. Isaac (*A Historical Debate, 1914: The Problems of the Origins of the War*, 1933), and A. Fabre-Luce (*The Victory*, 1924), had formulated a compromise that remained the accepted orthodoxy for 30 years. 'The immediate origins', wrote Isaac, '... suffice to tilt the balance [of guilt] to the side of the Central

Empires. Nevertheless, one does not discern in the other camp any miraculous will for peace.'

Such interpretations were not, of course, accepted in Marxist circles. Here the favoured interpretation was that put forward by Lenin himself (*Imperialism, the Highest Form of Capitalism*, 1916). His case was that the war was the inevitable result of the development of capitalism into the monopoly stage, wherein capitalists were bound to compete aggressively for limited resources and markets. The theme still receives wide support in left-wing circles in the west, despite work such as that of Raymond Poidevin (*Finance and International Relations, 1887–1914*, 1970), suggesting links and strong mutual interests between the business communities of the rival belligerent states.

The views widely accepted as orthodox by western historians were dramatically challenged in the 1960s by the work of the German historian, Fritz Fischer. In the first of his two main works, *Germany's Aims in the First World War* (1961), he shifted a great deal of responsibility for the outbreak of war back onto German shoulders with the claim that her leaders had deliberately accepted the risk of war for the furtherance of their political ambitions during the course of the July Crisis of 1914. Fischer later claimed (*The War of Illusions*, 1969) that German actions since 1911 proved a desire, a preparation and a provocation of war. Naturally, such an interpretation provoked

great opposition, especially in Germany. Gerhard Ritter, then completing his masterpiece on German militarism, (*The Sword and the Sceptre*, 1954–68) pointed out that, while it was sadly true that the civil authorities had steadily abdicated their responsibilities in the face of annexationist and military pressures during the reign of Wilhelm II, this did not amount to premeditated aggression. Wilhelmine Germany, he stressed, displayed few of the ideological aberrations of Nazi Germany.

Another of Fischer's prominent critics was Egmont Zechlin (*The Outbreak of War in 1914, and the Problem of War Aims in International Policy*, 1972). He essentially agreed that Germany accepted the apparent inevitability of war in 1914, but sought to acquit her of the charge of provoking it. More recently the Fischer thesis has also been modified by Hartmut Pogge von Strandmann and by H. W. Koch (*The Origins of the First World War: Great Power Rivalry and German War Aims* (ed.) 1984). Strandmann sought to modify the nature of German war guilt by stressing that the error of her leaders was that they anticipated a short war with limited human costs. Koch's emphasis has been upon Germany's fear of isolation, and upon the concern of her leaders with the consequences of staying out of the conflict. Fischer has also been criticised for a line of argument that considers German actions and responsibilities in isolation from those of the other belligerents. In stressing the readiness of the other great powers to use war for the solution of their own immediate political and social problems, others have led the debate back to compromise.

A The status quo in 1905

Sources of tension between the great powers

In retrospect, it is possible to see those armed camps that clashed so violently in the First World War in the process of formation in 1905. In the previous decade and a half, several factors had undermined the stability of the Bismarckian system of alliances. Germany's refusal to renew the Reinsurance Treaty with Russia had meant that Germany was no longer '*a trois* in a Europe of five powers'. Her own decision to pursue a 'world policy', and above all her construction of a battle fleet, resulted in her no longer being able to count upon the benevolent neutrality of Great Britain in continental matters as Bismarck had done. Nor could Germany count upon the isolation of the other powers from each other. Apprehension over German ambitions enabled France and Russia to sink ideological differences, as France and Britain sank their colonial disagreements, in the Entente that formed the embryo of their 1914 wartime alliance.

Over what, however, were the two alignments of European powers to clash? France's cautious new friends were unlikely to back her in a reconquest of Alsace-Lorraine, and a series of international agreements had put the old bugbear of the Eastern Question, in A. J. P. Taylor's phrase, 'on ice'. Two factors between 1903 and 1905, however, suggested that European attention might soon concentrate once more upon the Balkans. Firstly, the advent of a pro-Russian regime in Serbia placed obstacles in the way of Austrian aims in that region. This was the only area, after her diplomatic and military disasters since 1850, in which the Dual Monarchy could still seriously entertain ambitions. Secondly, the defeat of Russia in the war with Japan meant that she too had largely to renounce other ambitions, and concentrate upon an east European role. From 1905, therefore, the Balkans represented the last hope for the 'great power' status of both the decaying 19th-century autocracies.

The limitations of the alliance system

This is not to say that a general European war was in any way inevitable in 1905. On the contrary, many factors stood in the way of such an eventuality. Even within Germany's alliance with Austria-Hungary, the firmest element in European diplomacy, it was far from certain that Germany would back her partner unequivocally in an adventure in the Balkans. Within the Triple Alliance between Germany, Austria-Hungary and Italy the attitude of Italy was extremely ambiguous. The Triple Entente between Russia, France and Great Britain was an extremely loose arrangement. As late as 1911 the relations between the three partners were so uncertain that A. J. P. Taylor has considered that Entente to be virtually 'in the process of disintegration'. The Russo–Japanese war, if it had turned Russian attention more firmly back to European affairs, had also cast severe doubts upon her value as an ally. If her army could not defeat the Japanese, what value could it have in a war with Germany? Colonial disputes, notably in Persia, soured Britain's relations with Russia.

Also, the Franco–British Entente, while representing a great improvement in the relations between the old rivals, contained no element of military commitment whatsoever. On the other hand, the Entente undermined one of the cornerstones of German foreign policy by eliminating the possibility of colonial conflict between Britain and France. If the atmosphere of European diplomacy remained uneasy in 1905, therefore, many more errors and miscalculations were still required to lead the continent to the catastrophe of 1914.

B The 'new imperialism'

The most startling element in international relations in the three or four decades before 1914 was the rebirth of European colonialism. The reasons for this were several (see page 189). This 'new imperialism' was striking for two main reasons. Firstly, it represented the resurrection of a trend that had seemed long dead, killed by the steady decay of earlier empires, such as those established by Britain and Spain in the Americas. Secondly, it surprised contemporaries by its enormous speed and extent.

Although 'new imperialism' was not confined to Africa, the 'scramble' for territory in that continent was its most spectacular manifestation. In 1875, only some 10 per cent of Africa was occupied by European states 20 years later, only 10 per cent remained unoccupied.

The new imperialism

A popular and widely accepted interpretation of 19th-century imperialism has been one that sees it as a natural result of capitalist development in Europe. A pioneer of this view was the English liberal journalist, J. A. Hobson, in *Imperialism: A Study* (1902). The colonies, he argued, satisfied an investment need in capitalists that could not be met by saturated markets nearer home. Imperialism also received support from a variety of capitalist interests, such as shipping companies, armament manufacturers, and the administrative professions, which gained occupation and profit from servicing the colonies.

This interpretation of imperialism was expanded by V. I. Lenin's pamphlet *Imperialism: the Highest Stage of Capitalism* (1916). For Lenin, imperialism was the result of the final stages of monopoly capitalism, when domestic markets have been saturated, and resources of raw materials exhausted, by the earlier process of capitalist competition. Colonies represented new markets and new resources to these advanced capitalists, easily defensible against competition. The First World War, in Lenin's view, had to be seen as a clash between states goaded into confrontation by the selfish interests of their capitalists. Its outcome would inevitably be the final exhaustion of the resources of the capitalist system. Lenin's interpretation was a piece of political invective rather than a reasoned economic or political assessment, and many objections have since been raised to his case and to that of Hobson. In recent years, D. K. Fieldhouse (*The Colonial Empires*, 1966) has led the way in showing how small the extent of investment in the new colonies was. Great Britain, for example, invested far more in the USA than in any new acquisition, and Russia remained far more popular with investors, especially French ones, than any African or Asian territory. Nor is it credible to see certain colonising powers, such as Italy, Russia or Japan, as states that had exhausted their own domestic scope for capital investment. Another line of argument is provided by emerging evidence that the major European powers were by no means locked into cut-throat competition with each other, as Lenin imagined. In particular, R. Poidevin (*Economic and Financial Relations Between France and Germany from 1898 to 1914*, 1969) has shown a remarkable interdependence between the economies of these two arch-rivals. Between 1893 and 1913, French exports doubled, while trade in the opposite direction trebled. Poindevin's picture is one of politicians leading reluctant capitalists into confrontation, rather than the other way around.

The most serious rivals to the economic interpretations of imperialism have been those which see the phenomenon rather as an extension of European nationalism and national rivalries. 'Imperialism', according to Fieldhouse, 'may best be seen as an extension into the periphery of the political struggle in Europe.' In support of such an argument one might note the example of French expansion in the 1880s which was, both for Jules Ferry and for Bismarck, a deliberate attempt to distract attention from the national humiliation of 1870–71.

Although they were undoubtedly secondary, a further set of motives should not be overlooked. The idea of imperialism as a moral and humane duty, as the means of spreading western civilisation and Christian values, undoubtedly spurred on many individuals. Equally certainly, this idea did not motivate many governments. Some 60,000 missionaries, two-thirds of them Roman Catholics, were serving in Africa and Asia in 1900.

In conclusion, some notable individual fortunes were certainly made out of colonial expansion. There are too many obstacles in the way, however, to allow us to accept imperialism as primarily a plot by European capitalists. Instead, we might accept the compromise proposed by David Thomson, when he defines imperialism in the late 19th century as 'the combination of novel economic conditions with anarchic political relations'. Similarly, and of more importance for our present purposes, it is hard to accept colonial movements, for all the tension and ill-will that they occasioned, as primary causes of the war in 1914. Indeed, taking into account Britain's chastening experiences in the Second Boer War (1899–1902), the defeat of the Italians at Adowa in Abyssinia (1896), and the victory of Japan over Russia, one could argue convincingly that the 'new imperialism' was on the wane long before 1914. Referring to one specific European confrontation, R. Poidevin has concluded that 'economic and financial questions are not at the root of Germany's declaration of war on France [in 1914].'

C   The Moroccan crisis, 1905–06

The origins of the crisis

Between 1905 and 1914, tensions between the European powers centred upon two disputed areas: the North African sultanate of Morocco, and the Balkan states that had emerged from the wreckage of the Turkish Empire. Attention was first focused on Morocco by a German initiative that typified the incoherence and illogicality of *Weltpolitik*. In the course of a Mediterranean cruise, the Kaiser was prevailed upon by his chief ministers to land at Tangier (31 March 1905). There, his public speeches and behaviour implied a recognition of the Sultan of Morocco as an independent monarch, and called into question the recent Anglo–French agreements over the colonial status of these territories.

The motives of the Kaiser and his ministers are not altogether clear. They were probably keen to demonstrate, as was now usual, that no international question could be resolved without reference to Germany. They possibly also entertained hopes, by forcing France to give ground, of weakening her credibility as an ally in the eyes of Great Britain and Russia. The Kaiser's coup was followed by the formal demand that the status of Morocco should be referred to an international conference of the major powers.

As that status was formally governed by an international agreement of 1880, Germany looked to be in a strong position, and the prospects of a notable triumph seemed bright. Indeed, when Théophile Delcassé, France's anti-German foreign minister and architect of the Anglo–French Entente counselled resistance to German projects, he failed to win general support and resigned his office. His resignation was, claims A. J. P. Taylor, 'the greatest German victory since Sedan'.

The Algeciras conference

The outcome of the conference convened at Algeciras (January–March 1906) was, however, very different from that anticipated by Germany. Far more impressed by the bullying and peremptory manner of the Germans than by the justice of their case, Spain, Italy, Russia, Great Britain, and even the USA, all supported French rights in Morocco. Isolated but for the faithful support of Austria-Hungary, Germany had to accept confirmation of French predominance in the sultanate, now strengthened by her control over the Moroccan police.

The impact upon international relations

How significant was the outcome of the Algeciras Conference for the future growth of international tension? A. J. P. Taylor went to some lengths to minimise its importance, stressing that no military preparations were made by any power, that British public opinion showed a marked lack of concern over Morocco, and that subsequent Anglo–French military conversations come to nothing. Nevertheless, the impact of diplomatic defeat upon Germany should not be underestimated. It ended Holstein's career and left Bülow in a state of physical collapse. More important, the rebuff did much to confirm German fears that the unreasonable jealously of her neighbours was leading them to pursue a deliberate 'policy of encirclement' (*Einkreisungspolitik*), aimed at stifling her natural growth and vitality. From this point, Imanuel Geiss has claimed, Germany turned her back upon international conferences as a means of settling international disputes.

Lastly, it should be noted that diplomatic co-operation between the French, the British and the Russians at Algeciras also had a number of side-effects. The discussions between the General Staffs of Britain and France were, as has been noted, inconclusive. Colonial discussions between Britain and Russia ended however, with an agreement (August 1907) that solved many of the outstanding disagreements over rival spheres of influence in Persia. That territory was divided into three zones. British control over south-eastern Persia kept Russia at a safe distance from Afghanistan, and thus from India, and thus did much to remove the Asian tensions that had dogged Anglo–Russian relations at the time of the Russo–Japanese War.

D   The Bosnian crisis, 1908–09

The renewal of Austro-Hungarian initiative

By 1908, the Balkans had been free of major political crises for a little more than a decade, despite the emergence of an ambitious and expansionist government in Serbia. In July of that year, however, revolution by the 'Young Turk' movement overthrew the corrupt rule of Sultan Abdul Hamid and offered the prospect to other powers of easy gains in the Balkans while Turkey was preoccupied with domestic upheavals.

The opportunity coincided broadly with the appointment to high office in Austria-Hungary of men eager to re-establish the prestige of the Dual Monarchy. Conrad von Hötzendorf had been Chief of Staff since late 1906, much more confident than his predecessor, Beck, of the Empire's military capacity. At the same time, Aloys von Aehrenthal had succeeded Goluchowski as foreign minister. He came to office envisaging an energetic foreign policy as a useful means of submerging the nationalist tensions within the Dual Monarchy. The joint project of these two men for the re-establishment of Habsburg prestige was the formal annexation of the Turkish provinces of Bosnia and Herzegovina that had been under Austrian administration since 1878. Certainly this was seen as a counter to growing Serbian influence over the Empire's Slav population, and it may even have been envisaged, as Imanuel Geiss has suggested, as the first move in a programme leading ultimately to the eventual partition of Serbia itself.

The annexation of Bosnia-Herzegovina

In September 1908, Aehrenthal sought the compliance of Russia. Meeting her foreign minister, Alexander Izvolski, at Buchlau, he concluded an agreement, whereby Russia would accept the new status of Bosnia and Herzegovina in return for Austro-Hungarian support for Russian designs on the Straits linking the Black Sea and the Mediterranean.

By accepting this agreement, Izvolski perpetrated a diplomatic blunder of the first order. Evidently he had expected the matter to be referred first to an international conference on the lines of 1878. On 5 October, however, Aehrenthal proclaimed unilaterally the annexation of Bosnia and Herzegovina, leaving Izvolski to seek his part of the bargain single-handed. In this, he not only encountered hostile reactions in London and Paris, but had his policy disowned by his own prime minister as outdated and irrelevant to current Russian priorities.

Izvolski's attempts to soften his defeat by demanding that a conference be convened to discuss the annexation, only increased and broadened the international tension. In response, Austria-Hungary sought clarification of the position of its German ally, and received unequivocal assurances of support. 'I shall regard whatever decision you come to as the appropriate one,' wrote Bülow to Aehrenthal at the end of October, while Conrad received assurances from his German opposite number that Germany was prepared to mobilise in support of the Dual Monarchy.

These assurances represented a significant deterioration in the international situation. Motivated primarily by the hope of humiliating Russia, and perhaps of weakening her links with France, Germany was sacrificing another essential Bismarckian principle by involving herself in the Eastern Question where no fundamental German interest was involved, and where Austria-Hungary had acted without any consultation with her ally whatsoever.

The humiliation of Serbia and Russia

Thus emboldened, Germany and Austria-Hungary felt strong enough to rub both Serbia's and Russia's noses in their defeat by demanding from both a formal acknowledgement of Habsburg authority over Bosnia and Herzegovina. In March 1909, both states gave such an acknowledgement, and the crisis was over. Its legacy, nevertheless, was substantial. Russia suffered a humiliation far greater than that suffered by Germany over the Moroccan question. She could ill afford a further reverse if she was to retain any influence in the politics of the Balkans. Aware of her weaknesses in 1908–09, she was now to embark upon a programme of military reconstruction to ensure that a future confrontation would not find her wanting.

Austria's success, and the unconditional nature of German support for her aims, were to embolden her in future Balkan adventures. Serbia's reverse, meanwhile, was to stimulate the growth of nationalist terrorist organisations of the kind responsible for the assassination at Sarajevo in 1914. Although the crisis had given rise to little in the way of serious military preparations, we may accept the logic of Imanuel Geiss's judgement that 'the Bosnian crisis in the East was a kind of dress rehearsal for the First World War'.

E The Agadir crisis, 1911

The occupation of Fez and the German reaction

In May 1911, the focus of European tension switched once more to Morocco. The cause was the French occupation of Fez, the major city of the territory, a move that was widely thought to indicate that France was preparing to establish an overall protectorate. Given that France was exceeding the limits of her agreed role in Morocco, and that relations between her international partners, Britain and Russia, were once again strained, the prospects for German compensation seemed good. It has been argued that Germany's foreign minister, Alfred von Kiderlen-Wächter, was interested in more than compensation. Imanuel Geiss has stressed the enthusiasm of expansionist elements in Germany for the establishment of permanent influence in North Africa, and with Fritz Fischer has attached sinister importance to Kiderlen's apparent willingness to use force to gain Germany's ends. L. C. F. Turner similarly has argued that a great community of interest and aims existed between Kiderlen and the Pan-German League.

Whatever his motives, the German foreign ministry once more acted aggressively and clumsily. The dispatch of the gunboat *Panther* to the Moroccan port of Agadir, ostensibly to protect German interests there, immediately resurrected British fears of a hostile naval presence in the Mediterranean, and of a threat to Gibraltar.

Unequivocal statements of British support for France, such as that contained in Lloyd George's famous Mansion House speech (21 July 1911) weakened the resolve of the less chauvinistic elements in Germany, including that of the Kaiser himself. A compromise settlement in November did grant Germany compensation in the form of territory in the French Congo. However, the maintenance of French influence in Morocco, culminating in the establishment of a formal protectorate (March 1912), clearly demonstrated that German aims in the crisis had failed.

The impact of Agadir upon the alliance system

This second Moroccan crisis was unlikely to lead to a general war, mainly because of the lack of Russian interest in the affair. 'Russian public opinion,' Izvolski informed the French, 'could not see in a colonial dispute the cause for a general conflict.' Nevertheless, the crisis contributed to the likelihood of a future breakdown of international relations in several important ways. Firstly, it worsened relations between Britain and Germany for no good reason, and weakened the support in both countries for reductions in naval building programmes. Indeed, the next two years were to witness the height of the naval 'arms race'. Secondly, French reaction to the compromise settlement destroyed the administration of Joseph Caillaux (January 1912), whose main aim had been to achieve some measure of reconciliation with Germany. 'The events of 1911', in the opinion of E. Weber, 'persuaded many of the pacific, the hesitant and the indifferent that the threat to France was real and that war was only a matter of time'. The succession of the more aggressively patriotic Poincaré can be seen as the beginning of the 'national awakening' that led France into war by 1914.

Thirdly, as a combination of these two factors, especially stimulated by the increased German naval estimates of 1912, the crisis led to a degree of formal military co-operation between Britain and France. This took the form primarily of the naval agreement of March 1912 whereby Britain confined her central Mediterranean interests to the protection of the French fleet, and concentrated her resources in home waters and at Gibraltar. Such an agreement still did not amount to a formal alliance, but indicated very clearly Britain's awareness of the German threat to her interests. Lastly, the Agadir crisis dealt a blow to the prestige of the German government similar to that suffered by the Russians in the Balkans. Germany, too, if faced with a similar crisis, might feel that the cost of further compromise might justify the risk of war.

F The Balkan Wars, 1912–13

The formation of the Balkan League

The Agadir crisis brought European politics to a pitch of tension from which it was not released before the outbreak of general war. Its implications spread eastwards down the Mediterranean. A direct result of the extension of French influence in Morocco was Italy's attempt in 1911 to improve her own standing in North Africa. To this end she launched an unprovoked attack upon the Turkish possession of Tripoli. This stretching of Turkish resources provided an irresistible temptation to the Balkan states to free themselves forever from the influence of Turkey, and from this temptation there emerged in the early months of 1912 the Balkan League of Serbia, Bulgaria, Greece and Montenegro.

The First and Second Balkan Wars

The First Balkan War, between the League and Turkey, began in October 1912. By the end of that month the Turks had suffered a string of defeats and had been driven out of their European possessions, apart from Constantinople, the peninsula of Gallipoli and the fortresses of Scutari, Adrianople and Janina. Renewed hostilities in early 1913, however, transferred those last two strongholds to the Bulgarians and the Greeks respectively. Now tension centred upon the division of the spoils. Already in late 1912, Austria-Hungary had attempted to maintain her prestige and security by insisting upon the establishment of an independent Albanian state, and upon the exclusion of Serbia from the Adriatic coastline. L. C. F. Turner has demonstrated in detail how close Russia came to mobilisation in support of Serbia over this matter.

More immediate tensions arose, however, between the victors. Serbia, thwarted over designs on Albania, and acting in partnership with Greece, occupied territory in Macedonia originally earmarked for Bulgaria. Bulgaria's attempts to clear Macedonia of Serbian and Greek forces in June 1913 precipitated the Second Balkan War. The move was disastrous for Bulgaria. By the Treaty of Bucharest (August 1913) she had to cede territory to Serbia, Greece and Rumania, which had seized the opportunity to intervene. Even Adrianople, won earlier at great cost from the Turks, was now returned to its former masters.

The status of Serbia and Austria-Hungary

The renewed Balkan crisis of 1912–13 contributed to the advent of general war in numerous important respects. Most obviously, Serbia emerged from these events with both her prestige and her power enormously increased. She had added some million and a half people to her population, and could now mobilise an army of some 400,000 men. Conversely, as A. J. P. Taylor put it, 'the victory for Balkan nationalism was a disaster beyond remedy for the Habsburg monarchy'. Even with Serbia preoccupied, her foreign policy had appeared frozen into inactivity. This was partly due to the indecision of the new foreign minister, Count Berchtold, partly to Magyar distrust of actions that might create more Slav subjects for the Dual Monarchy, and partly to uncertainty as to Germany's attitude. By mid-1913, it was clear that the government of Austria-Hungary could not afford further retreat. When, in October, Serbian troops entered Albanian territory to 'mop up' partisan resistance, the Dual Monarchy issued an ultimatum which foreshadowed that of 1914. On this occasion, Serbia yielded and withdrew her troops.

Political attitudes in Germany and in France

The crisis also had its effect upon official attitudes in Germany and France. There is much evidence of increased popular willingness in Germany to accept the prospect of war in 1911–12. The government was attacked from all sides in the Reichstag (November 1911) when the compromise settlement over Morocco was debated. The next year and a half saw substantial increases in military estimates. When General Bernhardi published his book *Germany and the Next War* in 1912, it quickly ran to several editions. He claimed that Germany faced the choice between decline and aggressive expansion. In 1912 the government remained reluctant to become involved in Balkan hostilities. 'I will keep out of it,' wrote the Kaiser in October. 'Let them get on with their war undisturbed.'

The outcome of the Balkan Wars, however, caused a radical reconsideration of Germany's military position and of her relationship with Austria-Hungary. In July 1913, the Reichstag sanctioned the addition of 130,000 men to the army in the biggest army estimate in German history. By October 1913, at the time of Vienna's ultimatum to Serbia over Albanian independence, the Kaiser was urging his ally to take a firm stance, and assuring her of unswerving German support. He informed Berchtold that month, in a famous and fateful phrase, that 'you can be certain that I stand behind you and am ready to draw the sword whenever your action makes it necessary . . . Whatever comes from Vienna is for me a command.'

France, too, had recently ceased to restrain her major ally. During his visit to Russia (August 1912)

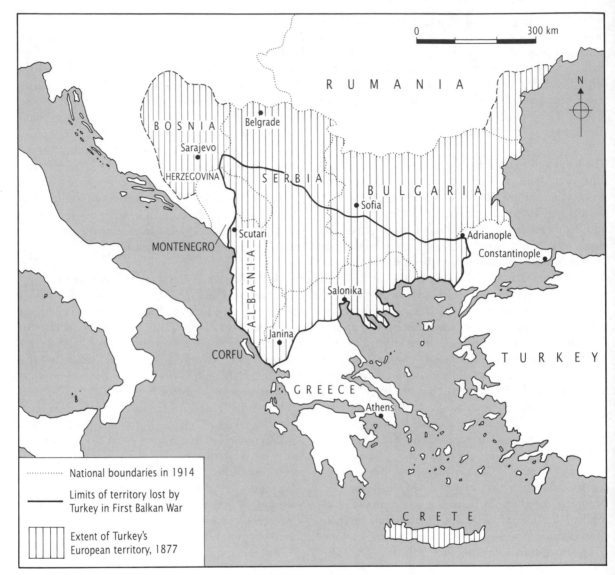

The Balkans in 1914

President Poincaré left Russian ministers in no doubt that, although their formal agreements only committed France to support of Russia if she were attacked by Germany, she could expect French help in the event of a clash with Germany triggered by a confrontation with Austria-Hungary. In the words of E. Helmreich, 'France had virtually given Russia a blank cheque on which she might inscribe whatever she wished'. In short, by October 1913, all the ingredients of the following year's catastrophe were present. Franco–Russian and Austro–German commitments were tighter than ever, the confidence and daring of Serbia were at a

peak, and the prestige of Austria-Hungary and of Russia was at so low an ebb as to make them unable to tolerate any further blow. Only the attitudes of Great Britain and Italy were uncertain.

G The July crisis, 1914

Sarajevo and the response of Austria-Hungary

'Fifty years,' wrote Basil Liddell Hart, 'were spent in the process of making Europe explosive. Five days were enough to detonate it.' On 28 June 1914, the final crisis was triggered by the assassination in the Bosnian town of Sarajevo of the Archduke Franz Ferdinand, nephew of the Austrian Emperor. His murderer was Gavrilo Princip, a member of a Serbian terrorist organisation known as the 'Black Hand'. Although it has proved impossible to establish any clear responsibility on the part of the Serbian government, it is clear that her intelligence chief, Colonel Dimitrievich, played a leading role in the conspiracy, and that her prime minister had some foreknowledge of the attempt. Ironically, as Norman Stone has pointed out, the death of the Archduke removed one of the strongest influences for peace at court.

The opinion was now widespread that Serbian pretensions had to be checked. In this resolution the Dual Monarchy received backing from Berlin, a fact which Fritz Fischer, Imanuel Geiss and others have interpreted as showing the willingness, even the eagerness of the German government to accept the consequences of general war. On the other hand, Germany could hardly accept the further humiliation of her only firm ally, and other authorities have produced evidence to indicate that Germany still hoped that the coming conflict might be confined to the Balkans. Thus encouraged, Austria-Hungary delivered an ultimatum to Serbia (23 July) framed in such extreme terms that it was almost impossible for Serbia to accept. Her government was required, for instance, to suppress all anti-Austrian organisations and propaganda, and to dismiss any officials to whom the Vienna government might object.

The spread of the Balkan crisis

Within a week Europe was at war. The first factor to determine this outcome was the reaction of Russia. Although Serbia's reaction to the ultimatum was conciliatory, it did not satisfy Austria-Hungary's demands, and she declared war on 28 July. For Russia to remain inactive would have stripped her of any influence in the Balkans and could have devalued her as an ally in the eyes of France. Thus she chose to mobilise her forces on her southern borders. Automatically such action triggered the Austro-German alliance, and raised the question of German support for her ally.

The escalation of the crisis caused last-minute hesitations in Berlin, while the generals advised energetic action. Essentially, German military plans obliged her to act rapidly to deal with France before the Russian machine was fully operative. She thus took three fateful steps. On 31 July, she demanded the suspension of all Russian mobilisation and the following day, when mobilisation continued, declared war. Lastly, she demanded from France a formal declaration of neutrality, and the surrender of the border fortresses of Toul and Verdun as guarantees. Acceptance would have been quite incompatible with France's 'great power' status, and her inevitable refusal led to a further declaration of war by Germany (3 August).

Now German diplomacy centred upon attempts to keep Britain out of the war. Bethmann Hollweg had already promised not to annex French territory and to restore the integrity of Belgium after the war. German military strategy, however, depended heavily upon the violation of Belgian neutrality for the purposes of the attack on France. When Germany invaded Belgium on 3 August, Britain's course was decided by her treaty obligations to Belgium, and the following day she, too, entered the war.

Why did the powers go to war?

Although the victors in 1918 were quick to formulate questions of 'war guilt', the outbreak of the conflict makes much more sense if it is seen as a monstrous combination of miscalculations. The government of Austria-Hungary erred in believing that a clash with Serbia could be settled without wider complications. Russia's partial mobilisation on 30 July was undertaken without sufficient awareness of its effect upon German policy. In Berlin there were a whole series of misjudgements: the hope that an Austro–Serbian clash could be localised; the failure to appreciate that the invasion of Belgium would bring Britain into the war; the long-term failure to anticipate foreign reaction to the bullying tone of *Weltpolitik*. The further naive supposition that a brief and successful war might ease domestic difficulties was an error shared with Vienna and St Petersburg.

The course of events in 1914 also serves to confirm A. J. P. Taylor's contention that the conflict arose from feelings of weakness rather than feelings of strength. Russia and Austria-Hungary felt that compromise would destroy their credibility as major powers. France and Germany felt that valuable allies had to be supported lest they themselves be left in isolation.

In the German army, too, the feeling predominated that war in 1914 was preferable to war in two or three years' later, when the Entente powers would be much stronger. Lastly, all the participants misjudged the nature of the conflict to which they were committing themselves. They anticipated campaigns as sharp and decisive as those of the Balkan Wars, or of the wars of 1859, 1866 or 1870. They anticipated no great strain upon society, and would have been horrified to think that four years of trench warfare, technological revolution and economic attrition were about to tear apart the very fabric of European society.

H War aims

Germany and the 'September Programme'

Only one of the great European powers that entered the war in August 1914 had any really clear idea of what they hoped to gain by victory. Austria-Hungary desired to end the challenge of South Slav nationalism, while the other states entered the conflict primarily through fear of the consequences of neutrality. In all other cases, therefore, late 1914 presented the bizarre sight of combatants clumsily formulating war aims after the conflict had begun.

German propaganda portrayed the war as an attempt to escape strangulation by the encirclement policy of jealous and hostile neighbours, and righteously proclaimed that Germany was 'not driven by the lust of conquest'. On 9 September, however, under pressure from industrial and Pan-German interests, and from public opinion inflamed by the early success of German arms, the Chancellor signed the so-called 'September Programme'. This made it clear that the war aim of achieving 'security for the German Reich in west and east for all imaginable time' involved an unparalleled programme of annexations and expansion. Predictably, the 'September Programme' has provided historians who have considered Germany guilty of premeditated aggression in 1914, such as Fritz Fischer and Imanuel Geiss, with their main weapon. Others have preferred to see the programme as a chauvinistic response to early German victories.

Under the Programme's proposals, Germany was to demand the fortress of Belfort, the ore fields of French Lorraine and possibly a strategic coastal strip from Dunkirk to Boulogne from France. In addition, France would have to pay an indemnity, and accept a disadvantageous commercial treaty. Belgium, by losing Liège, Verviers and possibly Antwerp, would become a German satellite. Luxembourg would become a German federal province. No such specific details were outlined for the east, but the general principle of the eventual peace settlement was to push Russia back 'as far as possible from Germany's eastern frontier'. Germany's conception of security consisted, therefore, of domination of Central Europe (*Mitteleuropa*), with Austria-Hungary as a junior partner. Also, important controls would be exercised over her western and eastern neighbours. If the war had not begun as a war of conquest, it became one in September 1914.

British, French and Russian war aims

On the Entente side, the allies were effectively fighting for their survival as major powers, but public opinion demanded the formulation of more appealing war aims than this. As the major threat to their status was the growth of German power, British and French war aims in particular came to concentrate upon the destruction of those forces which made Germany an 'international danger'. Propaganda demanded the elimination of Junker militarism, and of the power of the house of Hohenzollern as essentials for a stable peace, for a Europe 'safe for democracy'. It was not quite consistent with these aims that the provisions upon which Britain was most insistent were the elimination of the German navy and colonial empire. Both were less of a threat to 'democracy' than to British trading interests. The French equivalent was to demand the return of Alsace and Lorraine. It was only indirectly, and over the course of the next year that the dismantling of the Habsburg Empire and the establishment in its place of independent nation-states, also became an article of faith for the allies.

Russia had little to gain by defeating Germany, except for more troublesome Polish subjects, and her official war aims soon came to concentrate upon the old attractions of the Straits and Constantinople. In March–April 1915, Britain and France finally agreed that Russia should have these in the event of victory, as long as they were compensated by gains in Egypt and the Near East. In the event of an Entente victory, therefore, the Ottoman Empire, too, was doomed to disintegration.

The search for allies

In the shorter term, both sides sought to strengthen their alliances by tempting neutrals into their 'camps'. The greatest enigma was Italy, formally linked by the Triple Alliance to Germany and to Austria-Hungary, yet set against the latter by all the precedents of 19th-century history. Only the Entente could offer Italy the Habsburg territories in the Tyrol and down the Adriatic coast that her nationalists demanded to complete the process of unification. Thus Italy finally sided with France, Britain and Russia in May 1915. Her war had little to do with the issues that convulsed the rest of Europe and much to do with the anti-Austrian tradition of the 19th century. Among the Balkan states, Russia's growing ambitions facilitated the task of the Dual Alliance powers, and Turkey (December 1914) and Bulgaria (September 1915) both declared war on the Entente. In her turn, Bulgaria's old rival, Rumania, entered the war on the side of the Entente in August 1916, although she declared war only on Austria-Hungary.

I The western front 1914–16

A war of movement

On both fronts, at the outset of the war, the combatants anticipated campaigns of movement with the accent on offensive strategies and rapid results. In the west, the French pinned their hopes upon 'Plan XVII'. This dictated a thrust into the Saarland and into Lorraine, with decisive encounters close to the battlefields of 1870, and won by the natural *élan* or dash of the French soldier. The German High Command had chosen a different geographical location. Their 'Schlieffen Plan' proposed a bold sweep by seven-eighths of Germany's western armies through Belgium and Luxembourg to envelope the French forces, held in check by the remaining German troops. Victory was expected within about six weeks, after which the bulk of the German forces would be free to confront the threat from Russia.

The failure of the Schlieffen Plan

The German plan had considerable weaknesses. It was liable to dangerous delays by the destruction of bridges and railways, not to mention by enemy action. Yet it was very nearly successful. The German offensive commenced on 4 August, took the border fortress of Liège within two weeks, and entered Brussels on 20 August. Meanwhile, the French offensive ran into stubborn resistance in Lorraine and in the Ardennes and her troops began to retreat with heavy casualties. The British Expeditionary Force, after an initially successful delaying action at Mons (23–24 August), was also forced to fall back to avoid isolation. Now the German commanders departed from the original plan of von Schlieffen. To avoid creating a break in the German line, Generals von Kluck and von Moltke chose to swing east of Paris to finish off Joffre's retreating Frenchmen, instead of surrounding and capturing the French capital.

On 5–9 September the invaders and Joffre's brilliantly regrouped armies fought the Battle of the Marne. This western engagement did indeed determined the future shape of the war, although in a different sense than the combatants had intended. The allied victory ensured that the Schlieffen Plan was a failure, while the Germans' establishment of strong defensive positions along the River Aisne, to check their own retreat, virtually put an end to the 'war of movement' and established the future pattern of trench warfare and siege tactics. The 'war of movement' had one last phase in the west, as both forces attempted outflanking movements to the west of their opponents. When, in mid-November, the rival forces reached the Channel coast, a line of trenches extended unbroken for 720 km from the sea to the Alps.

This stabilisation of the western front was also created by the unprecedented losses of 1914. Some sectors of the front units had lost up to 40 per cent of their strength, and a little over 10 per cent of the French officer corps had been killed. Munitions manufacturers, too, had not foreseen a war of attrition, and stocks of shells had been roughly halved. In the last weeks of 1914 both sides were drawing breath and preparing for a form of warfare that neither had experienced nor anticipated.

Stalemate in 1915

Where strategy had failed to achieve a decisive breakthrough in 1914, the next two years saw the increasing use of new technology in an attempt to break the deadlock. In April 1915, near the Belgian town of Ypres, the Germans used poison gas for the first time. As anticipated, it caused panic and severe losses and knocked the desired hole in the allied lines, but it also handicapped and delayed the subsequent German advance, and the line was closed up in time. Allied offensives in 1915 preferred the new technology of heavy artillery and prefaced their attacks with enormous bombardments using hundreds of thousands of shells. The subsequent assaults usually foundered upon a fully prepared second line of defences, behind the original German trenches. 'The western commanders,' Marc Ferro has concluded, launched attacks not from any real hope of victory, but 'to keep their troops in a state of alert.'

The cost was enormous. The Battles of Artois (May), Loos and Champagne (September) cost 135,000 French dead and killed 140,000 Germans. This contributed to a total for 1915 on the western front of 400,000 killed or captured, and over a million wounded. Survivors, too, suffered unprecedented hardships. A French officer's description of troops returning from the front conveys their suffering. 'Squads came on, their heads bowed; stricken, sad eyes appearing from beneath field caps; rusty, muddy rifles were held suspended by the sling. Caps and faces were coloured alike by the dry mud, and then covered by more mud. The men were now beyond speech; they no longer had strength even to complain; you could see in their eyes an abyss of grief, a petrification through dust and strain. These dumb faces proclaimed a martyrdom of hideous proportions'.

Verdun and the Somme

The year 1916 was dominated in the west by one enormous engagement, the most terrible of the war. The logic behind German strategy at the Battle of Verdun was that if France were 'militarily and economically weakened, almost to the limit of her endurance', then Britain in turn would find herself isolated and be forced to seek peace. To achieve this, a blow would be struck at the place of paramount importance. This would leave France the alternatives of withdrawal, with its disastrous effect on morale, or resistance, in which case German bombardment would bleed her resources white.

The bombardment began on 21 February 1916

and used some two million shells. The subsequent infantry advance captured 3 km of ground in three days, then General Pétain took command of Verdun to conduct one of the great defences of history. French units were rotated regularly so that none would be completely overwhelmed by the dreadful conditions in which it fought. The road from Bar-le-Duc became the 'Sacred Road' (*La Voie Sacrée*), over which lorries passed at intervals of 14 seconds to supply the defences. In June the Germans captured one of the foremost defences, Fort Vaux, and plans were prepared for evacuation, but German resources gave out first and they discontinued their offensive in mid-July. French counter-attacks in October and December regained virtually all their earlier losses.

The massive casualty list of 700,000 dead was evenly divided between the two sides, but it has been argued that the French suffered a further disadvantage in that the widespread experience of the horrors of this battle did much to breed the pacifism that affected France in the 1930s. 'Troops coming up to relieve the soldiers,' writes Marc Ferro, 'were often overwhelmed at the horror of Verdun; they saw an implacable fate before them, of digging a grave to stay alive, and then supporting it with their corpses . . . The only certainty was death – for one, or other, or all.'

Further west, on the Somme, the allies launched their own massive offensive (July–November 1916) in part to deflect German resources from Verdun. Despite a week of preliminary bombardment, the failure of the offensive was evident within minutes of its launch. Failure to admit as much cost 600,000 casualties for no significant gain. Between them the two monumental failures of 1916 brought an end to the 'war of attrition' on the western front.

J   The eastern front, 1914–16

Russian defeats in 1914

The Russians, too, expected early results, although less from rapid strategic thrusts than from the huge numbers of peasant soldiers that they could mobilise. On 17 August, far earlier than the authors of the Schlieffen Plan had envisaged, the Russian 'steam roller' entered German territory in East Prussia. Three days later, General Rennenkampf defeated a German force at Gumbinnen. The

The First World War, 1914–18

defeat, however, merely brought on the scene the two most successful German commanders of the war: Paul von Hindenburg and Erich von Ludendorff.

In the campaign of the next month, by which they sought to defend the Junker heartland of Prussia, they were helped by a variety of Russian shortcomings and errors. The Russian army had attacked before it was fully ready for the task in order to give maximum aid to the French, and the personal hostility between Generals Rennenkampf and Samsonov made co-operation between the two main attacking forces difficult. Furthermore, the generals allowed the two Russian armies to become separated by the 80-km chain of the Masurian Lakes. As a result, Hindenburg and Ludendorff were able to tackle the two forces individually. Samsonov was defeated in the massive engagement christened the Battle of Tannenburg (26–29 August) in memory of and in revenge for the defeat of the Teutonic Knights by the Slavs in 1410. Less then two weeks later Rennenkampf's army was similarly defeated at the Battle of the Masurian Lakes (8–9 September). In the precipitous Russian retreat, the Germans took some 130,000 prisoners.

A war of attrition in the east

These two great battles saved Prussia from Russian invasion and established Hindenburg as the major German folk-hero of the war. Their influence on the war in the east as a whole should not, however, be overestimated. Indeed, by forcing the withdrawal of German troops from the western front, the Russian offensive had made no small contribution to the defeat of the Schlieffen Plan. Farther south, Russia secured some notable successes against her main rival, Austria-Hungary. Lemburg (Lvov), the fourth largest city in the Dual Monarchy, was captured in early September, and the Russians, in B. Tuchman's words, 'accomplished a mutilation of the Austro-Hungarian army, especially in trained officers, from which it was never to recover.'

Hesitant Russian leadership and substantial German intervention in support of the crumbling Habsburg forces then combined to produce two years of fluctuating fortunes on the main eastern fronts. 1915 was marked by a slow and costly rolling back of the Russian forces beyond their frontiers. The long German campaign in Poland, launched in October 1914, finally achieved its purpose with the capture of Warsaw (August 1915), while a combined Austro-German offensive in the Carpathians (May 1915) had recaptured most of Russia's gains of 1914 by late June. By the end of the year, the Russian lines had withdrawn some 450 km, leaving behind a million dead and a further million prisoners.

The Brusilov offensive

1916 witnessed the greatest Russian successes of the war. Remarkably, neither her resources nor her morale had been crushed by the earlier reverses. Norman Stone has emphasised the upswing in Russian military supplies and production by this point in the war, and J. N. Westwood has stressed

that, since 1812, retreat was not necessarily seen as a shameful or dispiriting factor in Russian military circles. Urged on by Russia's allies to relieve pressure on Verdun and on the Italian front, General Brusilov launched a massive offensive over a wide front in June 1916. Its initial success was startling. Three of the four Russian armies involved achieved an immediate breakthrough and within five days Brusilov had taken 70,000 prisoners. By early August however, lack of adequate resources, political jealously at headquarters, and a further influx of German support for the wavering Austrians had all brought the 'Brusilov Offensive' to a halt.

Nevertheless, the 340,000 casualties inflicted upon Austria-Hungary, plus another 400,000 taken prisoner, were more than the Dual Monarchy could stand. The offensive, states A. J. P. Taylor, 'marked the moment when the armies of Austria-Hungary lost their fighting spirit. Unity, cohesion, loyalty vanished; and from this time Austria-Hungary was kept in the war by German power.' It also marked the last great effort of the Russians, and almost achieved its aim of eliminating Austria-Hungary from the conflict. Where victory might possibly have prolonged the life of the Russian monarchy, a further million casualties combined with mounting civilian hardships at home (*see* Chapter 12, section **B**) were to lead the Romanov dynasty into its final crisis.

K The Balkans, Gallipoli and the Italian front

The Central Powers in the Balkans

In the Balkans, meanwhile, the issue that had precipitated the whole conflict was largely decided by late 1915. At first, Austria-Hungary's offensive foundered upon stubborn Serbian resistance and suicidal counter-attack. The invaders held the Serbian capital, Belgrade, for just two weeks in December 1914, and were then flung back with 100,000 casualties. Serbian losses were even higher, and her army was further ravaged by disease. In mid-1915, two factors combined to seal her fate. One was the German decision to intervene in the interests of maintaining safe communications with Turkey, and the second was the entry of Bulgaria into the war. The Serbian army was overwhelmed by a joint Austro–German–Bulgarian offensive in

October 1915, and allied forces planning to come to its aid through Greek territory from Salonika were hopelessly delayed by political and geographical obstacles. The remnants of the Serbian army at least saved face by an epic retreat through Albania to the sea. Thence they were evacuated to Greece to continue the struggle, but without conspicuous success.

The entry of Rumania into the war on the side of the Entente was a brief and unhappy episode. Badly equipped and poorly led, her army was in precipitous retreat within a month of its first campaign (August 1916), and her contribution effectively ended with the fall of her capital city, Bucharest, to German forces in early December.

The failure of the Gallipoli campaign

The most ambitious undertaking in this theatre of war was the assault upon the Gallipoli peninsula, to gain control of the Dardanelles, between February and November 1915. It was motivated primarily by the deadlock on the western front, and was conceived as a combined operation by sea and land forces to capture Constantinople, knock Turkey out of the war, and to re-open secure lines of communication with the hard-pressed Russians. The operation's prospects at the time of the initial naval bombardment of the Turkish defences (February 1915) were bright. The allies had the advantage of surprise, and the Turkish positions were weak. The allied campaign, however, was distinguished, in Basil Liddell-Hart's phrase, by 'shortsighted lethargy'. A landing in strength was not attempted until April, and in the ensuing months the allied cause suffered from lack of co-ordinated command, shortages of supplies, delays and elementary tactical errors. The loss of four allied battleships to Turkish mines further dampened the initial enthusiasm of the naval commanders. When, in November, the operation was finally abandoned, it had cost the allies 250,000 men, dead, wounded or captured, and had served to convince most allied commanders that the war could only be settled on the western front.

The Austro-Italian front

Meanwhile, to the north-west, Italy's entry into the war produced a campaign of attrition grim and fruitless even by the standards established in France. In answer to the Italian strategy of an attack along the line of the river Isonzo in the north-western corner of the country, Austro-Hungarian forces occupied a line of mountainous defensive positions. As P. Pieri had noted, 'the river could not be crossed until the mountains had been seized, and the mountains could not be seized until the river had been crossed'. Thus, between June 1915 and August 1917, 11 separate battles of the Isonzo were fought, costing Italy nearly a third of her original army strength for minimal gains. Even as a diversion the Isonzo front was of little value, tying down only a dozen Austrian divisions.

When a breakthrough finally came (October 1917) it was the Italians who fell back in disorder, handicapped by their own low morale and lack of ammunition, in the face of a combined Austro–German offensive at Caporetto. The Italian army had lost over 300,000 men, many miles of territory, and very nearly the war, before her forces were successfully regrouped on the line of the river Piave in November. But it was an exhausted Austrian army, pressed by allied victories in the Balkans, and disrupted by domestic upheavals, that was finally swept from Italian soil in October 1918 in the Battle of Vittorio Veneto.

L The war at sea

The maintenance of British naval supremacy

Two decades of escalating naval expenditure, and the development of fleets of fast, heavily armed dreadnought battleships, had created the impression by 1914 that the disputes between Britain and Germany would be settled primarily by a major confrontation between their fleets. Ironically, the earliest naval events of the war made it clear that decisive roles would be played by cheaper and less glamorous weapons. On 22 September 1914 the German submarine U9 sank three British cruisers within minutes, and a month later the British battleship HMS *Audacious* was sunk by a mine. It immediately became obvious that battle fleets could not after all range freely in search of each other.

In the early months of the war, therefore, German ships were mainly concerned with raiding missions against British and allied commerce on the high seas. The *Emden* in the Indian Ocean and Admiral von Spee's cruiser squadron in the Pacific did great harm, the latter badly shaking British complacency by destroying a British force off the Chilean coast at Coronel (1 November 1914). Eventually, however, the redisposition of British resources won back the advantage. Von Spee's force was destroyed at the Battle of the Falklands (December 1914) and the sinking of the *Dresden* in March 1915 effectively ended the threat from German surface raiders.

The British navy enjoyed surface supremacy for the rest of the war, a fact of enormous strategic importance. It allowed 8.5 million troops to be mobilised from the Empire without a single loss at sea; it established and maintained the crippling blockade imposed upon Germany; it facilitated the conquest of nearly all German colonies in the first year of the war, and ultimately made possible the convoy system that helped thwart German submarine warfare, and the transport of American men and equipment to play their decisive role in the European conflict.

The Battle of Jutland

Nevertheless, the war did produce two more threats to that British supremacy. The first was the Battle of Jutland (31 May 1916), the only major encounter in naval history between massed fleets of dreadnoughts. Fought in the North Sea, at the mouth of the Skagerrak, the battle resulted from the eagerness of the new German commander, Admiral Scheer, to tempt sections of the Grand Fleet out of their ports into the open sea where they might be attacked by superior German forces. The British ability to decipher German radio signals meant that Scheer had to undertake an engagement involving some 250 ships. The German fleet demonstrated superior gunnery and superior ship design, and lost two capital ships, nine lesser vessels and 2,500 men, compared to the three capital ships, eleven lesser vessels and 6,000 men lost by the British. Both sides claimed victory, both with some justification, but the fact remained that only the outright crippling of the British fleet would have transferred the strategic initiative to the Germans, and this they failed to achieve.

The German submarine campaign

Although the German surface fleet played no further role in the war, her submarines did. Even as the dreadnoughts were failing to impose a strangle-

hold on Britain, there was a dramatic rise in the amount of British shipping sunk by U-boat action. In February 1917, when Germany adopted unrestricted submarine warfare, Britain lost 464,000 tons of shipping. In April she lost 834,000 tons, and between February and June 1917 one ship in every four dealing with British ports was destroyed. British corn supplies dwindled to the equivalent of six weeks' normal consumption and defeat seemed near. The adoption of the system of escorted convoys, in the face of much opposition from the Admiralty, did not eliminate the submarine threat. In the first quarter of 1918 Britain still lost over a million tons of merchant shipping. It reduced losses, however, to a level that could be made good by new vessels leaving the shipyards. By the end of the war, the new counter-technology of mines, depth charges and other devices, had destroyed half of the U-boat fleet. Considering, too, the role that German submarines played in bringing the USA into the conflict on the allied side, it becomes clear that their use, although an extremely dangerous tactic, was also ultimately an unsuccessful one.

M The Home Front

1914: the triumph of patriotism

Quite apart from the new brand of 'total' warfare waged at the front, the First World War was also remarkable for the fact that it was the first to have a substantial impact upon the civilian populations left at home. At first, this impact was wholly unforeseen. The popularity of the conflict in all the participating countries is not in doubt. In France, earlier political differences were submerged in the 'Sacred Union' (*L'Union Sacrée*) for the defence of the country. Where a rate of conscientious objection of 13 per cent had been feared by the security services, the actual level was only 1.5 per cent of those summoned to the colours. Germans, similarly, spoke of the *Burgfriede*, the domestic peace that reigns in a besieged fortress. Speaking of mid-1915, A. J. P. Taylor concluded that 'there was, as yet, hardly a flicker of discontent or discouragement in any belligerent country'.

The development of economic warfare

The first dents to appear in this universal optimism were the results of the rapid spread of economic warfare. Germany's geographical position made her most vulnerable to this form of attack, and her own merchant navy had virtually ceased to function by the end of 1914. Although imports continued to seep in through neutral neighbours, the value of German trade with the USA, for instance, fell from 68 million dollars in December 1914 to 10 million in January 1915.

Germany's recourse to submarine warfare later subjected Britain to similar difficulties, and the German occupation of northern France and of Poland deprived France and Russia respectively of important industrial resources. The entry of Turkey into the war aggravated Russia's problems, with domestic results that are outlined elsewhere (*see* Chapter 12, section **B**).

Food supplies were also hit by the mobilisation of large numbers of men and horses as the war progressed. It has been estimated that in Germany agricultural production fell by 50 to 70 per cent, according to the individual region. The drop in Russia was 50 per cent and in France it ranged between 30 to 50 per cent. Germany was the first to introduce rationing, limiting supplies of bread, meat, potatoes and fats, while Turkey, in particular, suffered an alarming rise in the death rate from such disease as typhus.

Social change: the roles of the state and women

In several respects, the war resulted in the greater subjection of the citizen to central political authority. Germany was the first combatant to take measures to direct and to control resources and production, creating the War Materials Department (*Kriegsrohstoffabteilung* – KDA) in 1914. All combatant countries, however, soon experienced government pressure to push available labour into war industries. By the end of the war, these industries employed 76 per cent of all industrial labour in Russia, and 64 per cent in Italy.

A further notable result of the war was the substantial employment of female labour in order to release men for the forces. In France, by 1917, one in four war workers was a woman, and Joffre could claim that 'if the women in the war factories stopped for twenty minutes, we should lose the war'. Secondly, the citizen felt the influence of central authority in the unparalleled degree of propaganda and censorship. News of military failures, of heavy casualties, and of anything else that could contribute to 'defeatism' was progressively eliminated from publications. Thirdly, the enormous losses of the early campaigns made the citizens in most belligerent countries liable for the first time to military conscription. France introduced conscription at an early stage of the war, and lost men at such a rate that those timetabled for call-up in 1917 were called in December 1915. Even Britain, with her relatively modest contribution to the war on land, abandoned the principle of a volunteer army in January 1916.

Civilians in the firing line

For the first time, the civilian did not need to go to the front to become a casualty of war. The new and developing technology of the conflict produced at least three means of striking at the enemy's resources and population. Paris was shelled at regular intervals, at a range of 126 km, by the massive gun christened by the Germans 'Long Max'. London, meanwhile, suffered her first air-raids. As part of the retaliation demanded by public opinion, British planes in the last year of the war inflicted 24 million marks worth of damage on German factories and towns.

The growth of war-weariness

Eventually the strain of war, at the front and at home, broke down the enthusiastic unanimity of 1914. Isolated socialist and pacifist voices had been raised against the war, and September 1915 had seen the publication of the Zimmerwald Manifesto by international socialists meeting in Switzerland. Even so, discontent was ultimately the result of price rises and declining living standards. Reliable figures are incomplete, but it is possible to state that in England in 1917 food prices were 70 per cent higher than in 1914, while wages were only 18 per cent up. The figures for France were 74 per cent and 30 per cent respectively, while those for Italy were 84 per cent and 38 per cent. The social impact of the war upon Russia is described in detail elsewhere (*see* Chapter 12, section **B**). The contrast between the figures above and the substantial increases in the profits made by most branches of heavy industry began to trigger off militant action by 1917. Table 11.1 shows the initial fall in strike action at the outbreak of war, contrasted with the renewal of industrial unrest as the strains of three years of total war attacked the fabric of society.

Table 11.1 Number of strikes, 1913–18

	1913	1914	1915	1916	1917	1918
Russia	2,404	3,534	928	1,410	1,938	–
Britain	1,459	972	672	532	730	1,165
France	1,073	690	98	314	697	499
Germany	2,127	1,115	137	240	561	531

From Marc Ferro, *The Great War, 1914–18*.

N 1917

The failure to achieve a breakthrough

After the failure of the policy of attrition on the western front in 1916, allied commanders could devise no better plan than a return to the optimistic and unrealistic offensive tactics of 1914. Joffre's replacement at the head of the French forces, General Robert Nivelle, was another firm believer in the *élan* of the French infantryman, and was able to 'sell' the idea of a combined allied offensive to the British. However, as the Germans had withdrawn (March 1917) to prepared positions on the so-called Hindenburg and Siegfried lines, the 'Nivelle Offensive' of April was launched against the best defences that the Germans had so far occupied. Although some objectives were achieved, such as the Chemin des Dames and Vimy Ridge, the casualty list of 118,000 losses on the French side alone told a familiar story of wasted lives.

In May, a disillusioned Nivelle was replaced by Pétain who, returning to the tactics successful at Verdun, declared himself committed to a waiting game: 'I am waiting for Americans and tanks'. For the rest of the year, British troops bore the brunt of the futile offensives on the western front. The Battle of Messines (June) produced some successes, including the spectacular use of mining operations to blow up German positions, but the Third Battle of Ypres, or Passchendaele, (July–November) became a by-word for mud-encumbered deadlock. Three hundred and twenty-four thousand casualties failed to secure any significant advantage.

Only the engagement at Cambrai brought promise of an end to the stalemate. There, on 20 November, a massed force of 381 British tanks broke through the German lines and achieved an advance of 8 km. Success was only partial. The infantry could not keep up with the advance, and there were not enough reserves. Thus German troops were able to largely repair the initial damage within ten days. Nevertheless, the world's first true tank action gave a foretaste of the new 'war of movement' that northern France would witness a generation later.

The entry of the USA into the war

If tanks did not fulfil Pétain's expectations, the year also witnessed a decisive augmentation of allied strength. The isolationism that had so far characterised America's attitude to the war was ultimately overcome by two German errors. The first was the decision to wage unlimited submarine warfare from February 1917, which inevitably involved attacks upon American ships and loss of American lives. The second was the dispatch of the so-called Zimmermann Telegram. In March 1917, the German Secretary of State authorised his minister in Mexico to offer that country German support in an attack upon the USA, for which Mexico would regain those territories lost to her neighbour in the 19th century. Intercepted, the message had a predictable effect upon public opinion in the USA. Several authorities have stressed, however, the extent to which the USA was, in any case, committed to the side of the allies by February 1917. American producers had deals to provide copper, cotton, wheat and other commodities, and her bankers had forwarded substantial loans. Thus German submarines, and the threat of ultimate German victory, put substantial American interests at risk. The fall of the Tsar, in early 1917, also removed the ideological obstacle to American involvement. Having broken off relations with Germany on 2 February over the submarine issue, President Wilson declared war on 6 April.

American war aims: the Fourteen Points

In moral terms, American intervention changed the nature of war. Without any threat to her security, and far removed from the territorial concerns of the European combatants, the USA approached the war as a moral crusade for the preservation of democracy. This was confirmed by Wilson's major statement on his country's war aims in his 'Fourteen Points' (8 January 1918). Some of his demands, for the evacuation of occupied Belgian and Russian territories, the restoration of Alsace-Lorraine to France, the establishment of self-government among the minority peoples of the Habsburg Empire, were fully consistent with earlier allied declarations (*see* section **H**). On the other hand, the calls for the abolition of secret diplomacy, for total freedom of the seas, for the abolition of all trade restrictions, for a general reduction in armaments, and for the 'absolute impartial adjustment of all colonial claims', were not at all what the allies had originally had in mind.

France and Italy hang on

Materially, nevertheless, this intervention was unlikely to make an immediate impact. Time was needed for the mobilisation of men and resources, and thus the American declaration was, in A. J. P. Taylor's phrase, 'a promissory note for the future, provided that the allies held on until it could be cashed'. Several factors in 1917 did indeed cast doubt upon the ability of America's partners to survive long enough to benefit from her assistance. On the western front, 1917 saw the French army shaken by a series of mutinies involving 54 divisions, mainly in protest against the murderous strategy of the commanders. Miraculously, Pétain was able to restore order before the Germans realised their opportunity. Some 23,000 soldiers were charged as a result, and over 430 sentenced to death, although it now seems that only 50–55 were executed.

Meanwhile the Austrian offensive at Caporetto (*see* section **K**) threatened the continued existence of the Italian front. Most serious of all, the aftermath of the Bolshevik revolution in November saw the total withdrawal of Russia's forces from the conflict. Even at the very end of 1917, therefore, it was far from certain that American involvement would decide the war in the allies' favour.

O 1918: Rebellion and collapse

The German spring offensive

1918 opened with the dual prospect for Germany of immediate advantages, in the form of men and supplies transferred from the eastern front, but long-term disadvantage from the influx of American resources and the continued effects of the allied blockade. Ludendorff's strategy was thus to throw everything into a final 'Peace Offensive' (*Friedensturm*) to drive Britain and France out of the war. Three major offensives won the greatest German

successes of the western conflict. In March, 35 divisions on the Somme made gains of about 65 km against the British. In April, in Flanders, a breakthrough was achieved which for a time threatened allied control of the Channel ports. In May, on the Aisne, the French line broke, and German forces once again reached the Marne within 80 km of Paris.

The strategy had not, however, achieved the desired victory. Each advance, as it lost its impetus, left German forces deep in a salient, around which the allies massed their growing forces. Meanwhile Germany struggled to replace her latest 800,000 casualties. Allied forces at last came under co-ordinated control with the appointment of General Foch in April as 'Commander-in-Chief of the Allied Armies in France'. The last German offensive of the war came in July around Rheims. It met stiff opposition and made no significant progress. Instead, the French counter-attack made a breakthrough, and Ludendorff's forces fell back to safer ground.

The allied breakthrough

8 August 1918 marked the beginning of the end for Germany. On what Ludendorff dubbed 'The Black Day', a combined allied offensive made the greatest gains achieved since the stabilisation of the front in 1914. A British tank attack east of Amiens, in particular, broke the German line and advanced some 9 km. Yet the German resistance did not collapse then, nor during the next allied offensive in mid-September. Their morale, however, suffered a fatal blow. The loss of ground, combined with disappointment with the results of their own *Friedensturm*, stated A. J. P. Taylor, 'shattered their faith in victory which, until that moment, carried the Germans forward. They no longer wanted to win. They wanted only to end the war'.

The collapse of Germany's system of alliances

For at least a year, war-weariness had affected all the belligerent capitals. The *Union Sacrée* in France had been strained to breaking point by the decision of the socialists to leave the cabinet in September 1917, and as early as November 1916, the Emperor Karl, succeeding Franz Josef at the head of the Habsburg Empire, had made tentative peace proposals to the allies. While the advent of Clemenceau to power in Paris (November 1917) had strengthened the fight against defeatism in France, morale in Germany and Austria continued to decline. By January 1918, the daily flour ration in Vienna had dropped to 165 grams, food trains from the east were plundered, and the incidence of desertion from the forces rose sharply.

In June the German Secretary of State, Kühlmann, publicly broached the subject of a compromise peace, but was disowned and forced from office by the military leaders. By early October, however, reverses on the western front and the surrender of Bulgaria (29 September) to the east, had changed their minds. Ludendorff acknowledged the need to accept withdrawal from occupied territories, and to accept Social Democrats into the government in order to mollify the democrats among the allies. On 4 October, the new government led by the liberal Prince Max of Baden requested an armistice based upon the 'Fourteen Points'. On 20 October, Germany officially ended submarine warfare.

Meanwhile, although the war effort in the west was maintained, that in the east collapsed. Turkey signed an armistice in late October, broken by highly successful British campaigns in the Middle East. At the same time the Austro-Hungarian Empire quietly disintegrated, with the peaceful declaration of independent nationhood by the Czechs, South Slavs and the Hungarians (31 October). Three days later, the remnants of the Habsburg armies requested an armistice. The sequence of events in Germany, too, made further resistance impossible. On 20 October, naval crews at Kiel began to mutiny in protest against orders to resume operations at sea. On 9 November, a German Republic was proclaimed in Berlin by Social Democrats, and the Kaiser left his throne for exile in Holland.

Armistice and reckoning

The threat of domestic revolution added urgency to the government's quest for peace. Although horrified by the severity of the armistice terms dictated by the allies, the German delegation signed them at Compiègne, in northern France, on 11 November 1918. Germany was to hand over her fleet, and her vast stocks of war material. She was to evacuate all occupied territories on the west and to permit allied occupation of the left bank of the Rhine. She was annul the peace treaties made with defeated Russia and Rumania. As a formal, impotent protest, the leader of the German delegation stated that 'a nation of seventy millions suffers, but does not die'. Foch remarked '*très bien*', and closed the interview that closed the First World War.

The revolutionary nature of the events of the past four years could scarcely be exaggerated. Their most obvious impact is summarised in Table 11.3, showing the human and material cost of the war. Equally sensational was the war's impact upon the future of European politics. With the almost simultaneous collapse of three great empires, Germany, Russia and Austria-Hungary, the major points of reference in a century of European history vanished. The traditional balance of power was destroyed, and the peace settlement failed to put anything substantial in its place. Indeed, with the unparalleled intervention by the United States, the whole role of Europe in the world had been called into question. Although the truth took some little time to sink in, Europe in effect ceased to be the centre of the world in 1918.

Table 11.3 The cost of the First World War

	Dead (millions)	Financial cost (million £)
British Empire	0.947	6,418
French Empire	1.400	5,200
Germany	1.800	8,300
Austria-Hungary	1.200	4,100
Russia	1.700	5,060
USA	0.116	2,600
Italy	0.650	2,400
Serbia	0.048	–

From T. G. Charman, *Modern European History Notes.*

Questions

Essay questions

1   Compare and contrast the motives of the European powers for establishing colonial empires in the period 1880–1914. (UCLES)

2   How important was the Eastern Front to the outcome of the First World War? (ULEAC)

3   Why, and how, did Austria-Hungary contribute to the growth of international tension in the period 1908–14? (JMB/NEAB)

4   Discuss the view that the alliance system made general European war inevitable in 1914. (UCLES)

5 For what reasons was the conduct of warfare, 1914–18, so costly in lives? (WJEC)

6 'The Allies won the First World War in 1918 because the Americans arrived in time'. Discuss this statement. (NEAB)

7 Why did the First World War last as long as it did? (Oxford Entrance)

French and German policy, Morocco, 1904–1905

Study Documents I and II below and then answer questions (a) to (f) which follow:

DOCUMENT I

2 June 1904.

For some time I have been observing the growth of a new mentality in Germany crediting the German race with a special and divine mission to take over the future government of humanity. Its ravages have been manifested in the arrogant resolution passed by the Colonial Union and the Pan-German League 'That Germany feels herself humiliated at not being consulted during the negotiation of the Anglo-French agreement. She considers she has quite as much right as France to develop her commercial interests and political rights in the Empire of the Maghreb'.

31 March 1905

The Hamburg anchored in Tangier harbour. The Kaiser landed. [To the French representative] the Kaiser thundered out, 'I am determined to see that German commercial interests are respected'.

6 June 1905.

Delcassé announced his resignation. He described the discussion with his colleagues. 'Germany', I told them, 'is threatening us. I consider that threat is only bluff. We should therefore resist it'. Rouvier replied 'You must not think that Germany is bluffing. She is both worried and humiliated by the isolation in which you are keeping her. She will, if necessary, stop at nothing'.

G. M .Paléologue, *French diplomat*, The Turning Point. Three Critical Years 1904–1906, *First published c .1935*

DOCUMENT II

[The Anglo-French Treaty of 1904] appeared to be only an attempt to remove a number of old differences between England and France. I replied to opposition from the Pan-Germans that we aspired neither to the whole nor to part of the Sherif's Empire.

But in the winter of 1904 to 1905 Delcassé again showed his claws. The French newspapers demanded the 'Tunisification' of the Moroccan Empire. The French ambassador demanded from the Sultan that he should place the customs duties under the supervision of French officials.

It was not only the extent of our economic and political interest in and about Morocco which decided me to advise the Kaiser to set his face against France. In the interests of peace we must no longer permit such provocations. I do not desire war with France, but I did not hesitate to confront France with the possibility of war. I felt that I could prevent matters coming to a head, cause Delcassé's fall, break the continuity of aggressive French policy, knock the continental dagger out of the hands of Edward VII and the war group in England, and simultaneously ensure peace, preserve German honour, and improve German prestige.

Prince von Bülow, Memoirs, 1903–1909, *1930*

a In the context of these documents, explain what is meant by each of the following:
   i 'Pan-German'
   ii 'Tunisification' [2]
b What possible reasons for German intervention in the Morocco question are mentioned or implied in Document I and Document II? [4]
c How far does the evidence provided in Document II support Delcassé's view in Document I that Germany's 'threat is only bluff'? [4]
d Bearing in mind the origins and authorship of Document I, what points should a historian consider when assessing its reliability as evidence of events in 1904–1905? [5]
e In what ways do the language and tone of Document II suggest that the author intended to appeal to the emotions of his readers and so justify his actions? [3]
f Making use of these documents and of your own knowledge, would you agree that Bülow was successful in the aims he sets out at the end of Document II? [7]

(ULEAC)

12

The Russian revolutions: 1914–24

'Comrade Lenin sweeps away the world's dirt', a propaganda poster produced in 1920.

What elements are emphasised by the poster as those which Lenin was most concerned to defeat in 1920?

Why has the artist chosen to emphasise these elements?

How accurate is the poster as a portrayal of Lenin's priorities in 1920?

The Historical Debate

No series of events in modern history has been written about with so much partisan enthusiasm and with so little detachment as the Russian revolutions. Political views have continued for many years to play a large part in determining historical views on this subject.

Much of the work produced in the west may be broadly classified as belonging to the 'liberal' school of interpretation. That is to say that it sees Russia's political history since the mid-19th century, through the Emancipation, the formation of the *zemstvos*, and then of the Duma, as a promising progression towards liberal institutions. This progress was then shattered by Russia's disastrous involvement in the First World War, which provided the extremists with their opportunity.

Propounded in the beginning by disappointed Russian liberals, such as P. N. Miliukov (*History of the Second Russian Revolution*, 1921) and M. Florinski (*The End of the Russian Empire*, 1931) this line is, with modifications, that taken up more recently by Leonard Schapiro (*The Origins of Communist Autocracy*, 1955) and by the English authority Hugh Seton-Watson (*The Russian Empire, 1801–1917*, 1967).

The 'liberal' school, of course, has been in competition primarily with Marxist interpretations. One must stress the plural here, for it was a feature of Soviet writing to shift the emphasis and interpretation of events in line with political shifts within the Soviet government. The very first Marxist account, that of Trotsky in *The Russian Revolution to Brest-Litovsk* (1918), portrayed the October coup as a measure forced upon the Bolsheviks by the conspiracies of their opponents. The extremely influential account of the American socialist, John Reed (*Ten Days That Shook the World*, 1919), confirmed this view.

Once firmly established in power, however, the Soviet leadership changed its tune. By 1922 Trotsky and Iakovlev (*On the Historical Significance of October*) were portraying the October coup as a political masterstroke, splendidly orchestrated by the Bolshevik leadership, and in sharp contrast to the spontaneous and chaotic events of the February revolution.

The Stalinist era, of course, produced a third version of the same events. In 1939, the official *Short Course of the History of the Russian Communist Party (Bolsheviks)* attributed a leading role to the Bolsheviks in the February revolution and, naturally, either minimised or ignored the roles played by Stalin's political rivals. Stalin himself, meanwhile, emerged as a key figure, at the right hand of Lenin himself. Such interpretations were modified in their turn after the death of Stalin.

Variations upon these Marxist themes have been put forward by socialist commentators unsympathetic to Bolshevism, who claim that Lenin's actions in and after 1917 were premature, and that the revolution was rushed into a socialist phase before a mature bourgeois phase had been attained, in direct defiance of Marxist principles. This view has been argued by exiled Mensheviks such as V. M. Chernov (*The Great Russian Revolution*, 1936) and T. Dan (*The Origins of Bolshevism*, 1964). Trotsky, with an intimate knowledge of the events, saw the revolution (*History of the Russian Revolution*, 1936) as a series of corrections of course by Lenin, each in keeping with Marxist principles, but carried out in the face of excessively doctrinaire Marxism on the part of the party.

Indeed, few western writers have questioned the greatness of Lenin. Most, however, have tempered their praise with an awareness of his role in the formation of subsequent communist dictatorship. This approach can be seen in the work of Daniel Shub (*Lenin: A Biography*, 1948) and A. Ulam (*Lenin and the Bolsheviks*, 1965). Sympathetic English writing on the revolution as a whole, however, continues to be dominated by the massive work of E. H. Carr (*The Bolshevik Revolution*, 1950–54).

The next decade or so will undoubtedly see important developments in this field of historiography. The relaxations that came about as part of the policy of *perestroika*, and in particular the collapse of the Soviet communist party after the failed coup of 1991, have meant that the archives in Russia are no longer under strict government control. Hitherto secret documents are becoming available which cast important light on events of this period. Future historical writing on the subject may be expected, therefore, not only to resolve some of the political problems outlined above, but also to deal more fully with the deeper social and economic problems affecting Russia during the revolutionary years.

A War and the Russian regime

The initial popularity of the war

Despite grim forebodings in some informed circles, the declaration of war in 1914 was undoubtedly popular in Russia. Although the former minister of the interior, P. N. Durnovo, accurately warned that the main burden of fighting would fall on Russia, voices such as his were drowned out in the swell of popular enthusiasm. The immediate voting of war credits by the Duma (8 August), the sacking of the German embassy by patriotic students and the general acceptance of the government's ban on the sale of vodka, all bore witness to the readiness at first to suspend old animosities in defence of 'Mother Russia'. Even the capital city was renamed, the Germanic sound of St Petersburg giving way to the Slav Petrograd. Briefly, the Tsar enjoyed more popularity than at any other point in his reign. For once he could pose convincingly as the personification of all the Russians. Yet, within three years he was Tsar no more, his prestige worn away inexorably in a dismal succession of failures and miscalculations. Three interrelating factors stand out as contributing to this last collapse of Tsarist prestige.

War and the autocracy

Firstly, the patriotic formation of such bodies as the Union of Zemstvos, to provide medical facilities, and the Congress of Representatives of Industry and Trade (August 1914), to co-ordinate production, raised an old and thorny question. How far could representative bodies, and the latter even included representatives of the workers, be allowed to influence the conduct of the war? The attitude of the government was clearly that the autocracy should exercise sole control. A matter of particular controversy was the formation of 'military zones' (July 1914), comprising most of Finland, Poland, the Baltic provinces, the Caucasus and Petrograd. Within them all civil authority was subordinated to that of the military, and every obstacle was put in the way of would-be civilian participation. To many it seemed that political ideology was becoming more important than the effective prosecution of the war. Tsarist apologists laid the blame at the door of 'disloyal' liberals, but modern commentators are more inclined to blame

the Tsar. 'The truth is,' states Hugh Seton-Watson, 'that the insuperable obstacle was his dogmatic devotion to autocracy.'

Secondly, at this tense juncture came the decision of the Tsar to assume personal command as Commander-in-Chief of the armed forces (September 1915) and to take up residence at the front. However understandable in terms of royal duty and military morale, the decision directly identified the Tsar with all future military disasters, and left the government in Petrograd at the mercy of the Empress' infatuations and the schemes of political opportunists.

The role of Rasputin

Most famous, and perhaps most damaging was the increased influence over the Empress, and thus over government policy, of Grigori Rasputin. Rasputin, a Siberian *starets* or holy man, had been known to the Imperial family since 1905. His influence over them dated from 1907 when it began to appear that he was able to control the haemophilia, a blood disease, from which the heir to the throne, Alexis, suffered. The means by which he did this have never been satisfactory explained. With the Tsar at the front, he became the main influence upon the deeply religious Empress.

The view of contemporary opponents such as the prominent Duma politician M. V. Rodzianko that Rasputin was the supreme evil influence on the government is not always accepted today. Some have seen him rather as the tool of self-seeking schemers. At any rate, contemporaries saw his advice to the Empress as the main force behind the 'ministerial leapfrog' that occupied the year beginning in September 1915. Some ministries had as many as three or four chiefs within the year, most of them nonentities. Rasputin's murder in December 1916 by right-wingers came too late. The damage to the government and its reputation was irreparable and many contemporaries, remembering the German origins of the Empress, could not avoid the suspicion of treason.

B War and the Russian people

The organisation and equipment of the army

In the end, the collapse of the Romanov dynasty in Russia was not triggered by ideological arguments, but by the sheer suffering imposed by the war upon the Russian people.

The most immediate hardships, of course, were met by those actually serving in the armed forces. Although Russia only mobilised a little less than 9 per cent of her population during the war, compared to roughly 20 per cent in both Germany and France, the size of the Russian population meant that a very substantial number experienced the horrors of the front. The Russian army totalled 5.3 million men after the initial mobilisation (Germany and France mobilised 3.8 million at this point), and a total of 15.3 million Russians had seen military service by the end of hostilities. Numbers, however, were the Russian soldier's only advantage. Compared to his opposite numbers in other armies he was worse armed, worse treated and worse led. Shortcomings of armament and tactics exposed in the war of 1904–05 were being treated, but had not been overcome by the outbreak of war in 1914. It was still not unusual in 1915 for Russian artillery to be limited to two or three shells a day, and after mobilisation in 1914 the infantry had only two rifles for every three soldiers. Men were sent into battle with instructions to help themselves to the weapons of fallen comrades. Such factors made casualty levels that were in any case horrendous all the harder to bear. By early 1917, Russia had lost 1.6 million dead, 3.9 million wounded and 2.4 million taken prisoner.

The impact upon the civilian population

The civilian population also had increasingly daunting problems to face. 1916 was a comparatively good year for military production, with rifle production doubled and that of heavy artillery quadrupled, but these advances were made at the expense of civilian needs. Locomotive production, for example, was halved between 1913 and 1916 with only 67 new engines completed in 1916. This, together with constant military interference with the railway network for strategic purposes, contributed to the semi-breakdown of communication and distribution systems that was the main cause of urban food shortages.

There were also other factors. Conscription caused a scarcity of both men and horses on the larger country estates, and town populations increased as war industries demanded extra labour, but generally there was enough food. It simply was not getting to those who needed it. Indeed, Norman Stone has shown that military shortages, too, were due less to failures of production than to inefficient distribution. Fuel shortages constituted another consistent problem. After the early loss of the Polish coalfields, total coal production in Russia never reached the same level as was achieved in the last year of peace, and an increasing proportion of what fuel there was was channelled towards military uses. Food prices rose dramatically. On average, and the figures were actually higher for major urban conglomerations such as Petrograd, the price of flour rose by 99 per cent between 1913–16, meat by 232 per cent, butter by 124 per cent and salt by 483 per cent. Money wages, it is true, rose by 133 per cent over the same period, but this figure has to be set against a drop in the value of the rouble to only 56 per cent of its pre-war value.

C The March Revolution

The growth of liberal opposition

If the World War does not fully explain the collapse of the Tsarist regime, it did act, in Lenin's words, as a 'mighty accelerator' in the process of alienating the Russian people from their rulers. By August 1915, the combination of the Kadets, Octobrists and Progressists in the Duma into the so-called Progressive Bloc, demanding a government 'possessing the confidence of the public', indicated that the old wounds were open once more. The government's answer was to dismiss the Duma (15 September 1915). Between that date and January 1916, the dispute centred upon the conduct of the ministers including the premier, I. L. Goremykin, the foreign minister, S. D. Sazonov, and the war minister, A. A. Polivanov. By mid-November 1916, the liberal politicians in the Duma had determined upon a more uncompromising attitude towards the government and its failures. On 15 November the assembly heard a famous denunciation of official incompetence by P. N. Miliukov. Questioning whether government policy represented 'stupidity or treason', he concluded that 'we have lost faith in the ability of this government to achieve victory'. By January 1917 some leading members had even prepared provisional plans to force Nicholas' abdication in favour of his son.

The collapse of civilian and military morale

If some commentators have stressed the role of the liberals in the final discrediting of the monarchy, there is wide agreement that neither they, nor any other organised political groups, bear responsibility for the events that finally brought it down. 'The collapse of the Romanov autocracy,' stated the American commentator William H. Chamberlin, 'was one of the most leaderless, spontaneous, anonymous revolutions of all time.'

The initiative came primarily from the Petrograd workers whose patience with the deprivations of war was nearing exhaustion as 1917 opened. In January, some 150,000 of them had demonstrated on the anniversary of Bloody Sunday, and 80,000 had demonstrated support for the reopened Duma in February. International Women's Day (8 March) brought tens of thousands of women exasperated by months of food shortages on to the streets, and the coincidence of this with a wage strike at the Putilov works raised the number of demonstrators on that day to a new 'high' of perhaps 240,000.

The decisive anti-Tsarist factor, however, was the armed forces. The major difference between the events of 1917 and those of 1905 lay in the attitude of the Petrograd garrison. The shooting of 40 demonstrators on 11 March broke the morale of many of the conscript soldiers, and regiment after regiment fraternised with, and then actively supported the strikers. Even the dreaded Cossack regiments refused to obey their officers. By the end of 12 March, at a cost of an estimated 1,300 civilian and military lives, Petrograd was in the hands of a revolution without recognised leaders. 'Not one party,' wrote the socialist observer N. N. Sukhanov, 'was preparing for the great overturn.'

The abdication of the Tsar

In the task of filling the power vacuum in Petrograd the liberal members of the Duma had the incalculable advantage of being on the spot, but their attitude was highly ambiguous. They half obeyed the Tsar's order to disperse, by transforming themselves into a Provisional Committee (12 March) and most of those members who supported M. V. Rodzianko's advice to Nicholas to abdicate did so only in the hope of salvaging something of the monarchy by crowning a more popular, constitutional Tsar. That these men ended as the Provisional Government of a republic was largely due to the indecision and fatalism of the Tsar himself.

The Tsar, having originally dismissed the Duma's pleas for last-ditch reforms as 'some nonsense from that fatty Rodzianko', then toyed with the idea of a military assault upon his own capital. He was dissuaded by the pleas of his generals, notably Brusilov and Ruzsky, who wanted constitutional reform. However, he was unable to the last to compromise his own autocracy, and agreed to abdicate (15 March). The following day his brother, the Grand Duke Michael, refused the crown, leaving Russia a republic after 304 years of Romanov rule.

D   The Provisional Government and the Soviet

Russia's new leaders

The new republic was in the hands of two powers tolerating, but scarcely supporting each other. The Provisional Committee of the Duma formed itself into a Provisional Government (15 March) containing the most notable Kadet and Octobrist leaders. E. E. Lvov was the first premier, with P. N. Miliukov as foreign minister and A. I. Guchkov as minister of the interior.

Its rival for influence was the Petrograd Soviet, formed on 12 March, after the model of 1905, by the spontaneous action of workers and soldiers. It was at first an unwieldy body of up to 3,000 members, not dominated by any party, but by individuals of various persuasions. Among its leading orators, A. F. Kerensky was a Trudovik member of the Duma, while N. S. Chkeidze and M. I. Skobelev were Mensheviks.

The policy of the Soviet

Lenin was later to accuse the Soviet of a 'voluntary surrender of state power to the bourgeoisie and its Provisional Government'. The charge is not strictly fair in that, while the Duma politicians took on the responsibility of government, the support of workers and of soldiers left the Soviet with most of the practical power. Such was its control over post, railway and telegraph services in Petrograd that virtually nothing could be done without its consent. Guchkov himself wrote that 'the

Provisional Government possesses no real power and its orders are executed only as this is permitted by the Soviet of Workers' and Soldiers' Deputies.'

The Soviet's 'Order Number One' (14 March), moreover, decreed the establishment of soldiers' councils in each regiment of the armed forces, thus extending its influence to the military sector. From May 1917, the Soviet participated more directly in government when six Mensheviks and Trudoviks, including Skobelev (minister of labour) and Kerensky (minister of war), became ministers in the Provisional Government. From July, Kerensky actually led the government as premier, but failed to bridge the gap of mistrust that separated the bourgeois body from that of the Petrograd workers, leading to an uneasy co-existence.

E The Provisional Government: search for a policy

The land question

The first steps towards a policy that would be acceptable to both bodies were easily agreed. On its first day in office the Provisional Government decreed an eight-point programme that included a complete amnesty for all political prisoners, complete political and religious freedom, and the promise of elections to a Constituent Assembly. Poland's right to independence was at last recognised (30 March) and capital punishment was abolished, even in the armed forces.

Thereafter, the problems of policy became more thorny. Two major tasks confronted the government, the more pressing of which was satisfying the peasants' age-old demand for land. Although the government quickly recognised their right to the great landed estates, an official policy of partition was impossible to implement without inviting mutiny and desertion by peasant soldiers 'trapped' at the front while their local estates were distributed among their neighbours.

The peasants, however, were unwilling to wait, and thus disorder spread in the countryside as they took the law into their own hands. The government received nearly 700 complaints about illegal attacks upon landed property in June 1917, and over 1,100 in July. It was the turn of the peasant now, in L. A. Owen's phrase, to pose as 'the autocrat of Russia'.

The maintenance of the war effort

Clearly, a solution to the land problem depended upon a solution to the second problem, that of the war in which Russia was engaged. The revolution raised the question of what war aims she should now pursue. The unanimous conviction of the Provisional Government was that the war should be pursued to a victorious conclusion. Miliukov, for one, saw no reason to abandon the original aims of annexations in eastern Europe and in the Turkish Empire, but was so far out of touch with popular opinion that he was forced to resign (15 May). The attitude of the Soviet was not for immediate peace either, for such a peace might merely put them at the mercy of a monarchist Germany. Instead, they rejected the 'policy of annexations' and refused 'to serve as an instrument of conquest and violence in the hands of kings, landowners and bankers'. Compromising between popular pressure and the need to honour obligations to Russia's allies, the Provisional Government accepted (8 April) the prime war aim of 'the establishment of a stable peace on the basis of the self-determination of nations'.

Collapse of the war effort, and the Kornilov coup

The collapse of the war effort, nevertheless, was the first major failure of the new government. Its July offensive in Galicia, aimed at proving the government's worth to allies and Russians alike, ended in the retreat of demoralised and under-equipped forces over a large area. In the same month came demands for the autonomy of the Ukraine, to which some ministers seemed ready to agree, while the left-wing 'July Rising' led by Bolshevik sympathisers from the Kronstadt naval base further illustrated the precariousness of the government's position. In September, the threat came from the right. General L. G. Kornilov, appointed by the government to head the armed forces, marched on Petrograd. His primary aim was probably to oust the Soviet which he saw as undermining military discipline, but his actions and pronouncements could be seen as attempting to impose a counter-revolutionary regime. His failure, largely due to the refusal of troops to obey his orders, left the prestige of the government at a new low ebb, and strengthened the hand of the Bolshevik extremists in the Soviet.

The attitude of historians to the events of June–September 1917 are, of course, deeply influenced by political sympathies that have not yet cooled. The role of the Bolshevik Party in the July Rising has been played down by Soviet writers who portray the events as spontaneous, while many western commentators follow the line of David Shub, who sees the events as a seriously planned 'coup' from which the Bolshevik leaders retreated at the last moment due to loss of nerve.

The truth of the Kornilov incident has been equally difficult to unravel. Most Soviet sources, and some non-Soviet writers, such as L. I. Strakhovsky, assert that Kerensky was using Kornilov (who in Trotsky's phrase had 'the heart of a lion, but the brains of a lamb') for his own anti-Soviet ends. The charge has never been proven, and has been strenuously denied in Kerensky's own writings, with the more recent support of western authorities such as A. Ascher and W. E. Mosse.

F   Lenin and the Bolsheviks

Bolshevik strengths and weaknesses
The major turning point in the destiny of the revolution was the arrival in Petrograd (16 April) of Vladimir Ilyich Lenin, leader of the Bolshevik wing of the Social Democratic Labour Party (*see* Chapter 9, section **F**). He found the Bolsheviks in Russia in a sad state. They numbered only 26,000 members, were in a minority in the Petrograd Soviet and were severely divided on the issue of co-operation with the Provisional Government. On the other hand, they had so far 'kept their hands clean' by avoiding identification with the administration's failures. The fact that Lenin and his comrades had had their passage from exile in Switzerland arranged for them by the German government was of ambiguous value. It naturally laid the Bolsheviks open to the charge of being German agents. Although Lenin was, of course, serving Germany's purpose by further disruption of the Russia war effort, the charge has not been taken seriously by historians in its literal sense, but the allegation that the Bolsheviks subsequently received large sums of German money to further their cause has better foundation. Soviet historians naturally follow the contemporary lead in denouncing what Trotsky called 'the most gigantic slander in world history'. Others, however, have found the case more convincing, and David Shub for example has produced

evidence of transactions which, if genuine, would have given the Bolsheviks a very substantial economic advantage over their revolutionary rivals.

Lenin's programme
The programme that Lenin pronounced upon his arrival, and published in *Pravda* in the so-called 'April Theses', was a complete rejection of the co-operation between the Soviet and the Provisional Government that was even advocated by a number of Bolsheviks. The ten points included an appeal for an immediate end to the war, total withdrawal of support from the government, socialisation of the economy and the transfer of all state power to the Soviets. Thus Lenin's arrival marked, in the words of the Bolshevik F. Raskolnikov, 'a Rubicon between the tactics of yesterday and today'.

The slogan 'All power to the Soviets' was not necessarily an immediate demand, for the Bolsheviks were far from controlling these bodies. What was immediate was the need for Lenin to impose his will upon his own party, and for constant propaganda to win the support of those alienated by the delays and failures of the Provisional Government. Lenin's contribution to this propaganda was *The State and Revolution* in which he set forth in the Russian context the Marxist doctrine of the need completely to dismember the bourgeois state before a proletarian society could be constructed. This form of persuasion, which was not actually published until 1918, was of course less effective than the simple slogans ('End the War', or 'Bread, Peace, Land') aimed at less sophisticated political thinkers. 'If the peasants had not read Lenin,' Trotsky observed, 'Lenin had clearly read the thoughts of the peasants.'

Strengthening the Bolshevik position
Meanwhile the Bolsheviks generally accepted Lenin's policy of opposition to and separatism from the Provisional Government. At the first Congress of Soviets in June, where only 10 per cent of representatives of 305 Soviets were Bolshevik, Lenin unsuccessfully advocated a break with the government. In July, complicity in the Petrograd rising led to an open attack upon the Bolsheviks, and a government attempt to arrest leaders such as Lenin, G. E. Zinoviev and L. B. Kamenev.

Bolshevik support grew in these months for both negative and positive reasons. Among the

Lenin

Personality and aims

No individual made so radical and influential an impact upon the history of Russia between 1848 and 1945 as did Vladimir Ilyich Ulyanov, known as Lenin. Born in April 1870 in Simbirsk (later renamed Ulyanovsk in his honour), the son of a teacher and school inspector, Lenin's active political life may be divided into three periods.

In the earliest stages of his political life, Lenin presents the classical picture of the intellectual revolutionary, turning his back upon comfortable middle-class origins and accepting a life of imprisonment and exile. The key event of this period was probably the execution of his elder brother, Alexander, in 1887 for his involvement in an attempt to assassinate the Tsar.

The event appears to have triggered latent radical tendencies in the younger Ulyanov, and to have marked him as a radical both in his own mind, and in the view of the authorities. The years between 1887 and 1900, with their mixture of expulsion from university, practice as a radical lawyer, imprisonment in Siberia, and eventual flight to western Europe, present a picture representative of the biographies of many contemporary Russian radicals.

During the second phase of his political life Lenin distinguished himself as a prolific writer and publicist, elucidating Marxist theory and laying down his strong views on

how the future struggle of Russian socialism should be organised. The most important development of these years was perhaps the foundation with Julius Martov in Germany (1900), of the journal *The Spark* (*Iskra*).

In 1902 Lenin published what Hugh Seton-Watson calls 'his greatest contribution to political theory, and perhaps the most significant document in the history of communism'. *What is to be Done?* rejected the arguments of those who would have socialists limit themselves to legal economic activities and of those who continued to place their faith in the peasantry. Instead, Lenin stressed the need for a 'party of a new type'. He envisaged a tight knit, disciplined and dedicated group of professional revolutionaries. By rejecting reliance upon the eventual good sense of workers and peasants, by rejecting the aid of well-meaning but amateurish intellectuals, and by rejecting terrorism, *What is to be Done?* represented a substantial break with the past traditions of the Russian left.

Such an organisation, however, was unacceptable to many who wished for a broader, more popular

basis to the party, and who distrusted Lenin's tendency towards autocratic leadership. At the second congress of the RSDRP in London in 1903, the party split into the 'Men of the Majority' (*Bolsheviki*), favouring the views of Lenin, and the 'Men of the Minority' (*Mensheviki*), favouring the more democratic alternative now championed by Martov. The terms are misleading, as Lenin's group had actually been outvoted by the end of the congress, but the names coined by him stuck firmly to the factions whose differences further weakened the short term effectiveness of the RSDRP.

On the eve of the World War, therefore, Lenin enjoyed a dual reputation within the very narrow circles that constituted Russian Marxism. In addition to being one of the outstanding theorists and revisionists of the movement, he was also an utterly determined political pragmatist, wholly convinced of the correctness of his own interpretation of events, and largely intolerant of opposition from within the movement. His role in the implementation of these interpretations, between 1917 and his death in 1924, belongs to the narrative of this chapter. So too does the historical debate over whether Lenin or Stalin should be held responsible for the excesses committed by the Bolshevik regime in the name of Marxism and of international socialism.

negative reasons were the collapse of the government's military offensive, the reaction of Petrograd workers to the Kornilov coup, and the suspicion that Kerensky might be willing to abandon Petrograd to the advancing Germans. More positive were the Bolshevik promises to tackle the questions of land and of peace and the growing support for the party among Petrograd factory Soviets.

By August the party had 200,000 members, produced 41 different newspapers, and had recruited a striking force of 10,000 'Red Guards' in the factories, whose workers were often, in Lenin's words, 'more Bolshevik than the Bolsheviks'. When the Petrograd Soviet was re-elected in September, the Bolsheviks held a majority of seats for the first time, a success repeated in Moscow and elsewhere.

G The Bolshevik seizure of power

The social and economic background

The circumstances under which the Provisional Government lost power during the 'second revolution' of November 1917 were in direct contrast to those that had brought them to power. True, substantial social and economic problems persisted. Industrial production was badly disrupted. Some plants closed, causing unemployment, and inflation quickly cancelled out any benefit that the workers may have gained in terms of higher wages.

The army, meanwhile, came closer to disintegration, demoralised by continuing failure and by Bolshevik propaganda. 'The soldiers,' recalled N. Sukhanov, 'flowed through the countryside from the rear and the front, recalling a great migration of peoples.' An estimated two million desertions took place in the course of 1917.

The decision for a coup

The events of November, however, owed little to spontaneous discontent, and almost everything to the deliberate actions of a tightly-knit group of revolutionary leaders. By late September, Lenin had decided that the circumstances were right for the Bolsheviks to bid for power. The decision had nothing to do with the feelings of the masses. 'We cannot be guided by the mood of the masses,' he wrote at the time, 'that is changeable and unaccountable . . . The masses have given their confidence to the Bolsheviks and ask from them not words, but deeds'.

It took over a month for him to convince the party as a whole, however, and even then such notable members as Zinoviev and Kamenev stood out against him. His arguments in favour of an immediate insurrection were based not only upon the fear of a 'second Kornilov affair', or of a surrender of Petrograd to the Germans, but especially upon the hopeful signs of unrest in the German forces. This encouraged him to hope for international working-class support for a Communist coup.

It was also essential to have practical control before the meeting of the next Congress of Soviets, which might be more difficult still to convince of the merits of such an adventure.

The execution of the coup

The weapon for insurrection also presented itself with the formation (26 October) of the Military Revolutionary Committee by the Soviet, pledged to protect Petrograd against the Germans. With 48 Bolsheviks among its 66 members, it was capable too of being turned against other enemies.

The 'revolution' of 7–8 November (24–25 October by the existing Julian calendar; hence the more familiar title of 'October Revolution') was, in reality, an extremely skilful military '*coup d'état*' directed predominately by Trotsky. Key positions such as railway stations, telephone exchanges, banks and post offices were seized by 'Red Guards' with a remarkable lack of opposition from their opponents. The body assembled at the Tauride Palace to discuss the formation of a Constituent Assembly was dismissed, and late on 8 November the half-hearted defence of the Winter Palace, now the headquarters of the Provisional Government, was overcome.

The second Congress of Soviets, meeting that same day in Petrograd, now had 390 Bolshevik representatives, only too eager to accept Lenin's *fait accompli*. For Kerensky, there was no immediate alternative to flight, while the Mensheviks and the Social Revolutionaries, with only 80 and 180 seats respectively in the Congress, had little choice but to accept Trotsky's famous dismissal: 'You have played out your role. Go where you belong: to the dust heap of history'.

1917: conclusions

What judgement should be made on the Provisional Government that fell after eight months in office, and on the reasons why it was the Bolsheviks who supplanted them? The programme and theory of the government were admirable, as the most liberal constitution that the continent had yet seen had been created out of Europe's strictest autocracy. 1917, however, was a time for action on pressing problems, not for theory, and 'although noble in intent', as Anatole Mazour has written, 'the programme was ill-defined and poorly enforced'. Kerensky, in his memoirs, lays most of the blame for this upon those who 'betrayed' the government, most notably Kornilov and his supporters. Others, such as Donald Treadgold, are inclined to blame Kerensky himself, for whom 'oratory became a substitute for action'.

As for the Bolsheviks, the official Soviet explanation for their triumph lays great stress upon the party's mastery of Marxist theory, which made it 'a revolutionary party of the proletariat, a party free from opportunism . . . and revolutionary in its attitude towards the bourgeoisie and its state power'. To most western commentators it has been difficult to give this credit to the party as a whole. E. H. Carr represents the view of many in writing that 'the triumph of the party seemed almost exclusively due to Lenin's consistent success in stamping his personality upon it and leading his often reluctant colleagues in his train'.

H The foundation of the Soviet State

The extension of Bolshevik power

Lenin's first speech to the Congress of Soviets consisted of the simple statement, 'We shall now proceed to construct the socialist order'. As D. Mitchell has pointed out, however, the business of ruling Russia was not so simple. 'The Bolsheviks had not captured a Ship of State, they had boarded a derelict.' The priority of the first Soviet government was, therefore, the extension and consolidation of Bolshevik power. In early November, the authority of the administration elected by the Congress extended little beyond Petrograd. Lenin was chairman of the Council of People's Commissars, A. I. Rykov commissar of the interior, and L. D. Trotsky commissar for foreign affairs. In some places, as in Moscow, Kiev, Kazan and Smolensk, Bolsheviks had to overcome stern armed resistance. November, nevertheless, saw 15 main provincial towns fall into their hands, followed by 13 in December and further 15 in January 1918.

Opposition to the Bolsheviks

Within the territory thus secured the main constitutional opposition to the Bolsheviks came from the election of the long-awaited Constituent Assembly, which gathered in Petrograd with 380 SR representatives as against only 168 Bolsheviks. Lenin, however, was in no mood for constitutional games, and the body was dispersed by force after less than two days. It was, declared Lenin, 'a complete and frank liquidation of the idea of democracy by the idea of dictatorship'.

The CHEKA

The Marxist concept of the 'dictatorship of the proletariat' (*see* page 16) also necessitated the formation of two armed forces to destroy the remnants of aristocratic and bourgeois power. A secret police force known as the 'Extraordinary Commission' (but generally known as the CHEKA, from its Russian initials) was formed, in contrast to the leniency of the Provisional Government. Its aim was quite openly proclaimed as the combating of 'counter revolution and sabotage' by means of terror. 'The CHEKA,' claimed one of its leaders, 'does not judge, it strikes.' Its chief was Felix Dzerzhinsky, a dedicated Polish Bolshevik, but contemporary evidence clearly indicates the role played by Lenin himself in enforcing the policy of terror. In July 1918 he urged that 'the energy and mass nature of the terror must be encouraged' and, a month later, called for it to be extended even 'to execute and exterminate hundreds of prostitutes, drunken soldiers, former officers, etc.'. The Imperial family, under arrest at Ekaterinburg, were the most famous victims (July 1918). The official figure for executions in 1918 is 6,300, but this must be regarded as a conservative estimate.

The Red Army

On a more regular basis, the Bolshevik regime, having undermined and dispersed an army upon which it could not depend, now set about the formation of an army of its own. The Red Army was formed in January 1918, open to all 'class-conscious' workers of 18 years of age or more. The bourgeoisie was banned from membership, but 50,000 former Tsarist officers were retained to train the new force. To oversee them and the force as a whole, political commissars were attached to each unit, responsible for indoctrination and for ensuring that the army remained under Bolshevik control. The reforms made since March 1917 were systematically cancelled to ensure reliable discipline. The powers of the regimental councils were curtailed, the practice of electing officers was abolished and the death penalty for deserters was reintroduced.

By August 1919 the Red Army numbered 300,000, and by January 1920 it boasted over 5,000,000 members, under the supreme command of Leon Trotsky.

The first Soviet constitution

Meanwhile, the constitution of the state took shape. A series of decrees in February attacked the Church, separating it from the state and banning religious teaching in schools. Another series between April and June, nationalised banks, mineral resources, industrial concerns and foreign trade, and made the inheritance of property illegal. A formal constitution became law on 10 July 1918. The state was given the name of the Russian Soviet Federated Socialist Republic (RSFSR). It proclaimed itself a classless society, with freedom of worship, no private ownership of property, and based upon the economic principle of 'He who does not work, neither shall he eat'. The electoral system was based upon the unit of the village and city soviets, culminating in the All-Russian Congress of Soviets, the supreme authority in the state. The suffrage was universal, with the exception of former members or agents of the Tsarist government, those who profited from the labour of others, those with unearned income, priests, lunatics and criminals.

I   Soviet policy in 1918

The Treaty of Brest Litovsk

In the first days of Soviet power, as their earlier propaganda had obliged them to do, the Bolsheviks produced a 'Decree on Peace' and a 'Decree on Land'. The former called upon all participants in the war to begin immediate peace negotiations, while the latter abolished all landed proprietorship, but encouraged the peasantry to continue the process of carving up the great estates themselves. The achievement of such ideals was not, however, such an easy matter.

The new regime formally opened peace negotiations with the Central Powers at Brest-Litovsk in late November, confident that the Bolshevik coup would trigger a general European revolution, thus ending the war in any case. When, by early 1918, this had not materialised, and the impatient Germans had pushed deeper into Russian territory, Lenin was eventually able to convince his party that a separate peace was necessary, even at the harshest price. The Treaty of Brest-Litovsk was concluded on 3 March 1918. From a patriotic point of view, its terms were disastrous. Georgia, the Ukraine,

Latvia, Lithuania and Poland came formally under German occupation. This meant that, of her pre-war resources, Russia lost 26 per cent of her population, 32 per cent of her arable land, 33 per cent of her manufacturing industry, and 75 per cent of her coal and iron resources. A variety of motives have been suggested to explain and to justify the Bolshevik sacrifice. Basil Dmytryshyn is quick to point out that most of the lost territory was not under Bolshevik control, while Daniel Shub has cited evidence that the Bolsheviks were still in receipt of German funds, and could not risk the exposure of that fact. Above all, the most pressing motive must be recognised as that stated by Lenin himself in 1920: 'we gained a little time, and sacrificed a great deal of space for it'.

Economic policy

The succession of events of which the Treaty of Brest-Litovsk was part soon demonstrated the inadequacy of edicts such as the 'Decree on Land' and the 'Decree on Workers' Control'. The piecemeal division of land by peasant committees and the direction of factories by workers' committees proved wholly unsatisfactory as Russia was stripped of huge agricultural and industrial resources while faced simultaneously with the likelihood of a large-scale civil conflict. It was soon evident to Lenin that the intended slow progress towards nationalisation of the 'commanding heights' of the economy, such as fuel, transport and banking, was insufficient. The formation of a Supreme Economic Council (*Vesenkha*) in December 1917 can be seen as the first step towards the policy established by the 'Decree on Nationalisation' (June 1918), and now known as War Communism.

War Communism

The main features of War Communism were to be strict centralised control of all forms of economic production and distribution, the virtual outlawing of all private trade, and the near destruction of the money economy by the printing of vast quantities of banknotes. In January 1918 there were 27 billion roubles' worth of notes in circulation, backed by only 1.3 million roubles in gold. Three years later the figures were 1,168 billion and 0.07 million.

In the countryside the main manifestation of the new policy was the large-scale requisitioning of grain in order to feed the towns. In June 1918 the government formed 'Committees of Poor Peasants' to control the richer peasants, or '*kulaks*', but soon had to resort to direct confiscation of supplies by military force. All food distribution was centralised into the hands of a Commissariat of Food and Commissariat of Agriculture. These divided the population into four categories, the food ration of each depending upon its contribution to the economy. The highest category had roughly one-seventh of the calories received by German workers at the height of the allied blockade, while the lowest had rations insufficient to prevent starvation.

The disillusioned peasantry turned, as before, to disorder. Two hundred and forty-nine rural risings were recorded in 1918, and 99 in Bolshevik controlled territory the following year. In the towns the main feature was the wholesale nationalisation, which extended by December 1920 to all enterprises employing ten people or more, a total of about 37,000 enterprises. Accompanying this came the forced mobilisation of unemployed labour to serve essential strategic industries, the outlawing of strikes, and a large-scale desertion of the towns in favour of the countryside where food seemed more easily available. Petrograd, with a population of 2.5 million in 1917, boasted only 0.6 million inhabitants three years later.

J   The Civil War: the Whites

The diversity of the White cause

By early 1918, the events of the 'second revolution' had alienated large sections of the Russian population from the Bolshevik government, but without uniting the aims or motives of these opponents. Whereas the Reds fought in the Civil War for very specific aims and Marxist-Leninist principles, albeit with a strong degree of compulsion at times, the Whites formed no such homogeneous grouping. Broadly, the White forces consisted of three main parts: those attached to other revolutionary groups, hostile to or rejected by the Bolsheviks; former officers of the Imperial army, usually resentful of the 'betrayal' at Brest-Litovsk; and nationalist groups seeking independence for their particular minority.

The administration that established itself in the Don region of southern Russia early in 1918 illustrates this diversity. Its military leaders were Tsarist generals, such as A. I. Denikin, L. G. Kornilov and P. N. Krasnov, who had also held office under the Provisional Government and now claimed to fight 'until the Provisional Government and order in the nation are restored'. The politicians who joined them, however, were a mixture of Kadets such as P. N. Miliukov, and SRs such as V. M. Chernov. Other SRs concentrated their forces further north, along the Volga, where they established an administration based at Samara (June 1918). In the Don region, the nationalist element was represented by the Cossacks, whose local ambitions clashed fundamentally with such White slogans as Alexeyev's 'Russia One and Indivisible'.

The disintegration of the Russian empire

Already other independent republics had declared themselves, in the Ukraine and in Transcaucasia (November 1917) and in Finland (December 1917). With the collapse of the German war effort in the next year, Estonia, Latvia, Lithuania and Poland all pressed their own claims to independence. The Polish claim was especially complicated for, although both the Soviet government and the victorious allies assembled at Versailles recognised Poland's right to independence, it was not clear whether her eastern borders were to be fixed by the so-called Curzon Line, drawn by the allies around the main areas of Polish-speaking populations, or by the historic borders of the old Polish kingdom as it had existed before partition in 1772. The difference was considerable, and involved a Polish claim to much of Lithuania, the Ukraine and Byelorussia. The dispute raised tensions between Poland and her new communist neighbour that were to culminate in war in 1920.

The role of the Czechoslovak Legion

The great catalyst of civil conflict in Russia was the successful revolt of the Czechoslovak Legion. The Legion had been formed in 1917 from Czechs and Slovaks resident in Russia and from prisoners of war, and was dedicated to the fight for independence from the crumbling Austro-Hungarian Empire. After Brest-Litovsk it had placed itself at the disposal of the French, and begun a long journey via Siberia and the USA to continue the fight on the western front. In May 1918, a confrontation with Hungarian prisoners at Cheliabinsk led local Soviet officials to attempt to disarm the

Legion. Instead they themselves were seized, and when Trotsky ordered military retaliation, the well-organised and well-equipped Czechs proceeded to seize and occupy all the main towns along the Trans-Siberian railway in the regions of Cheliabinsk, Omsk and Irkutsk. Although the Legion had no specifically anti-Bolshevik aims, its resounding success against Soviet forces provided enormous encouragement for the White cause. By June representatives of the SRs had combined with the Czechs to form a third centre of White administration at Omsk.

K   The Civil War: allied intervention

An ideological crusade?

The motives that led Russia's former allies to intervene in her internal conflicts have been the subject of considerable controversy. The standard interpretation among Soviet historians has reflected the contemporary view expressed by Lenin. Concerned, as John Bradley has stated, 'with political analysis and success rather than with historical analysis and truth', Lenin portrayed the allied missions as essentially concerned with the suppression of communism. Some sympathetic western commentators have accepted this view. E. H. Carr, for example, describes the allies' declared intention of re-opening the World War in the east against Germany as 'a pretext', and speaks of 'the fear and hatred felt by the western governments for the revolutionary regime'. John Bradley, on the other hand, points to a number of factors that contradict this interpretation. A plan by Marshal Foch for a co-ordinated anti-Bolshevik campaign (January 1919) was rejected by allied leaders at Versailles, and in February 1919, the Americans in particular were proposing negotiations between the Reds and Whites at Prinkipo Island, near Istanbul. It is also true that Britain and the USA had come close, before Brest-Litovsk, to aiding the Red Army, at Trotsky's request, against the Germans.

Intervention and the World War

Thus there is much evidence that, in its early stages, allied intervention in the Russian conflict must be viewed in the context of the World War. The separate peace made by the Bolsheviks at Brest-Litovsk released huge German forces and resources for use on the western front. It thus became imperative for the western allies to attempt to restart the war in the east, or at least, to prevent Germany from making free use of the Russian, Polish and Ukrainian raw materials available to them under the terms of Brest-Litovsk. German success in the east also seemed to threaten large concentrations of allied stores supplied earlier to Russia. It is no coincidence that British forces landed first in Murmansk (March 1918), and that British and Japanese forces also concentrated on the distant port of Vladivostok (April 1918) which was far from the Bolshevik 'heartland', but where substantial allied stores were housed. Britain's seizure of Baku, on the Caspian Sea, was also motivated by the desire to keep local oil resources out of hostile hands.

Allied motives after 1918

The end of the World War did not strip the allies of their reasons for intervention. The French, for instance, continued to have a pressing motive in the form of the vast sum of 16 billion francs invested in Tsarist Russia between 1887 and 1917, in enterprises now nationalised without compensation by the Soviet State. Britain and the USA had lesser investments to defend, and Japan, after the hard-won gains of 1904–05, found the prospect opening up of substantial territorial gains in eastern Asia at Russia's expense. That they failed to realise these ambitions was primarily due to the presence of American troops in Siberia, probably more concerned with checking Japanese annexations in the east than with combating Bolshevism further west. Nevertheless, by late 1918, as many as 70,000 Japanese troops had occupied Vladivostok, northern Sakhalin and much of Siberia east of Lake Baikal. Only when the Third Communist International ('Comintern') began in mid-1919 to proclaim the 'overthrow of capitalism, the establishment of the dictatorship of the proletariat and of the International Soviet republic' did intervention become overtly ideological, and by then allied efforts in Russia had become negligible.

The scale and the achievement of intervention

The scale and scope of the intervention were in any case strictly limited. At the end of 1918 there were only about 150,000 troops in northern Russia and these were affected by acute war-weariness after four years of European conflict. The USA sent only about 6,000 to the Siberian theatre of war, and then with strictly limited objectives. More important were the substantial sums of money and the large quantities of military stores made available to the Whites. Britain and France both allocated the equivalent of 20 million pounds for this purpose, although R. Luckett has stressed that corruption and inefficiency often meant that relatively little of this aid actually reached the front.

Even more limited was the success achieved by the intervention. The number of troops involved was small, and only in the north, around Murmansk and Archangelsk, did foreign troops really predominate in the White war effort. Aims and motives were all too often at odds, as in Siberia, where the political views of Admiral Kolchak's regime were of such an undemocratic nature that the Americans refused all co-operation with him, and the French could only co-operate with the greatest difficulty. In all, the intervention probably gave far greater assistance to the Soviet authorities who could now draw a veil over domestic disagreements by claiming that they were defending Russia against foreign imperialism. At the conclusion of British involvement, Lord Curzon described it as 'a totally discredited affair and a complete failure'. The same judgement could probably extend to the allied intervention as a whole.

L The Civil War: the campaigns

The White armies

In the summer of 1918, the combination of forces ranged against the Soviet government seemed overwhelming. To the south, the Volunteer Army under A. I. Denikin, with French and British support, had cleared the Don and Kuban regions of Bolsheviks, and threatened the food and fuel supplies to Soviet-controlled areas. To the east, the varied forces occupying Siberia and controlling the Trans-Siberian Railway had at length agreed (September 1918) to the formation of a coalition government, the Directory. To the north, White forces under the Tsarist general E. K. Miller, with British support, controlled the ports of Murmansk and Archangelsk. To the west lay the Germans and

a variety of hostile nationalists. Even in Russia, less-organised opposition, especially among the peasants and the SRs, led to risings in some 25 towns and cities. There was a rash of assassination attempts that killed M. S. Uritsky, chief of the Petrograd CHEKA, and the German ambassador, and saw Lenin himself seriously wounded.

The defeat of Kolchak

The first concern of the Soviet government was to tackle the opposition forces centred upon Omsk. Their eventual success on this front owed as much to the shortcomings of their opponents as to the efforts of the Red Army itself. Certainly Trotsky's organisation and the military leadership of commanders as M. V. Frunze were important factors. The Whites, nevertheless, were disunited and quarrelsome. The internal dispute that brought down the Directory (November 1918) resulted in the elevation of A. V. Kolchak, formerly Admiral of the Black Sea Fleet, and a political conservative, to the title of 'Supreme Ruler of All the Russias'. His failure to establish satisfactory understandings with the SRs, the Czechs, or even with some of the allies, contributed to a steady retreat after reaching Perm and Ufa in March 1919. By June, Kolchak's force had been pushed back beyond the Urals, and Soviet forces captured Omsk itself in November. Kolchak suffered the indignity of being handed over to the Red Army by the commander of the local French forces, and was duly shot (7 February 1920).

Bolshevik victory in the south and west

In the south and west, similarly, White forces under Denikin and under N. N. Yudenich initially made rapid progress. In two months (August–October 1919) Denikin's forces advanced from Odessa to within 400 km of Moscow, while Yudenich came within 50 km of Petrograd in mid-October. In both cases, retreat was as rapid as the advance had been. Stubborn defence, organised by Trotsky, thwarted Yudenich before a counter attack drove him back into Estonia. Between October and December, Bolshevik forces pushed Denikin back until most of the Ukraine had been recaptured from the Whites. From April 1920, only the force in the Crimea under P. N. Wrangel stood between the Red Army and victory. Wrangel was probably the most able of the White commanders, exercising strong discipline over his

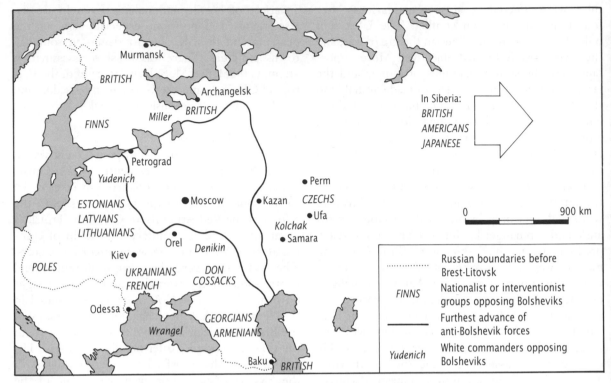

In Siberia:
BRITISH
AMERICANS
JAPANESE

Murmansk

BRITISH

Archangelsk

FINNS   Miller   *BRITISH*

Petrograd

Yudenich

Perm

ESTONIANS   Moscow   Kazan   *CZECHS*
LATVIANS   Ufa
LITHUANIANS   *Kolchak*
              Orel   Denikin   Samara
Kiev   Don
POLES   UKRAINIANS   *COSSACKS*
             FRENCH
Odessa
             GEORGIANS
Wrangel   ARMENIANS
                    Baku   *BRITISH*

0   900 km

....   Russian boundaries before
                 Brest-Litovsk
FINNS   Nationalist or interventionist
                 groups opposing Bolsheviks
———   Furthest advance of
                 anti-Bolshevik forces
Yudenich   White commanders opposing
                 Bolsheviks

The Civil War in European Russia, 1918–21

men and with an intelligent agrarian policy to appeal to the peasantry, but he had come on the scene too late. His army won some notable victories while the Red Army was distracted by the Poles, but in mid-November 1920 he, too, with 135,000 soldiers and civilians, evacuated the Crimea, the last stronghold of the White cause.

Reasons for the Bolshevik success

The defeat of the Whites, like that of the Russians in Korea in 1905, was not as surprising as it might at first have seemed. In the south and in the east their armies fought on very wide fronts, often in areas with poor communications and far from major centres of industry. The aims of the military leaders were sometimes at odds with those of the intervening allies. With the exception of Wrangel, none of the military leaders could sympathise with or even understand the hopes and wishes of the peasantry and the national minorities, and became hopelessly identified with the restoration of the landlords and the old regime.

The political leaders, meanwhile, who identified themselves with the White cause made almost no impact on policy or on international relations at all. 'They failed to recognise,' wrote Anatole Mazour, 'that they were coping with a great revolution and not an isolated plot.' Methods of operation, as well as aims, were defective. 'I think most of us were secretly in sympathy with the Bolsheviks,' wrote a British officer serving with Kolchak's forces, 'after our experiences with the corruption and cowardice of the other side.' The communists, meanwhile, had the benefits of excellent leadership and coherent policy and propaganda. Louis Fischer's description of Lenin as 'a one-man political-military staff' is inaccurate only insofar as it undervalues the dynamic role played by Trotsky, who made his main contribution to the revolution by his brilliant direction of the war on most of the major fronts.

The triumph of Polish independence

One anti-Bolshevik force, however, remained undefeated. In April 1920, Poland and Russia had finally resorted to arms to settle the question of the boundaries of the new Polish state (*see* section J). This was far more of a national war than an affair of Red versus White and it, too, brought varying fortunes for the participants. In May 1920 the Poles under Marshal Pilsudski were in Kiev. Two months later the Red Army was within reach of Warsaw. Finally, by August 1920, with moral and material aid from the allies, Pilsudski's counter attack had driven the Red Army almost back to Minsk.

The Treaty of Riga (18 March 1921), like Brest-Litovsk, was accepted by Lenin because 'a bad peace seemed to me cheaper than the prolongation of the war'. It settled Russia's western borders until 1939 by granting Poland Galicia and parts of Byelorussia, and by confirming the independence of Estonia, Latvia and Lithuania.

M The New Economic Policy

The failure of War Communism

By 1921, social and economic life in Russia had been brought to their knees by an unparalleled series of disasters. The rigours and miscalculations of War Communism combined with the damage caused by the civil war. The number of deaths directly caused by the war has been estimated by Robert Conquest as 'no more than a million', but the economic collapse that accompanied war had far more drastic effects. Urban industry declined disastrously. The Russian coal industry in 1921 produced 27 per cent of its pre-war output, a large proportion compared with steel (5.5 per cent), pig iron (2.5 per cent) or copper (1.7 per cent). Inflation had effectively destroyed the rouble, and some 90 per cent of all wages were paid in kind. This was compounded by disastrous famines. Especially serious in the Ukraine and in other parts of southern Russia, the famines probably caused some 5 million deaths. Taking into account associated diseases, the casualty figure for the years between 1917 and 1921 may be as high as 9 million.

The Kronstadt rebellion

Probably as serious from Lenin's point of view was the evidence of political discontent from within the communists' own ranks. The most spectacular example of widespread refusal to tolerate any further the deprivations of wartime came with the revolt at the Kronstadt naval base (February—March 1921), originally a major source of Bolshevik support. The demands of the sailors included freedom of the press, elections by secret ballot, and the release of political prisoners. The rising was brutally suppressed like similar, lesser peasant risings, but it could not be ignored, 'It illuminated reality,' stated Lenin, 'like a flash of lightning', and perhaps contributed more than any other single factor to the decision of the government to pursue a New Economic Policy (NEP).

Lenin made it very clear that the NEP was another in the series of temporary compromises that communist theory had to make when confronted with adverse circumstances. 'Life has exposed our error,' he told the Party. 'There was a need of a series of transitional stages to communism.' The NEP was thus a sort of economic Brest-Litovsk and, like that treaty, had to be imposed against fierce criticism from communist purists.

The nature of the NEP

The major features of the new policy were concerned with agriculture. Above all, the government decided to abandon the requisitioning of grain supplies from peasants and to demand instead a tax paid in food, set at a lower level. Thus the peasant retained some of his surplus which he was now permitted to sell for private profit, and was thus likely to be encouraged to grow more. Although the land remained the property of the state, the peasant was free to hire labour, machinery, and so forth.

On a secondary level, in industry, freedom of enterprise was restored in a host of small factories and workshops, while the state continued to control the 'dominating heights' of the economy, such as heavy industry, transport and foreign trade. In 1922, 88.5 per cent of all enterprises were privately run, although the smallness of their scale is indicated by the fact that they employed only 12.4 per cent of the workforce. The third main feature of the NEP was the restoration of a stable Soviet currency. In October 1922 the reconstituted State Bank introduced the reconstituted rouble, backed by precious metals and foreign currency. Early in 1923, savings banks were re-opened.

The achievement of the NEP

The path of the NEP was not always smooth. Bad harvests and drought in 1921 nullified most of the benefits to be gained by the peasants, and in 1923 they had to contend with the so-called 'scissors crisis' when declining food prices and the soaring price of industrial goods minimised their gain from free enterprise. The government had to defend itself, right up to the launching of collectivisation in 1928, against the charge that it was defending this 'state capitalism' as a preparation for a return to private capitalism.

Table 12.1 Russian economic indicators, 1913–26

	Factory output (m. new roubles)	Coal (m. tons)	Electricity (m. kW)	Steel ('000 tons)	Grain (m. tons)
1913	10,251	29.0	1,945	4,231	80.1
1920	1,410	8.7	–	–	46.1
1921	2,004	8.9	520	183	37.6
1922	2,619	9.5	775	392	50.3
1923	4,005	13.7	1,146	709	56.6
1924	4,660	16.1	1,562	1,140	51.4
1925	7,739	18.1	2,925	2,135	72.5
1926	11,083	27.6	3,508	3,141	76.8

From Alex Nove, *An Economic History of the USSR*, Pelican.

Indeed, in 1923 it was true that 75 per cent of Russian retail trade was being handled by the 'Nepmen', the private traders who flourished under the NEP. Thus one of the by-products of the NEP was the strengthening of party discipline to eliminate internal friction. Over 30 per cent of the party's membership was expelled between 1921 and 1924, a precedent that was to have grave implications in the 1930s. Eventually the aims of the policy, the restoration of production and of economic stability, were largely achieved. Table 12.1 shows that, in most major industries, production figures by 1926 had nearly regained their pre-war levels.

The death of Lenin

Lenin, however, did not live to see this recovery completed. A series of strokes that began in May 1922 finally killed him in January 1924. His organisational genius and unique blend of determination and flexibility played a greater role than anything else in the creation of Soviet power. Public reaction to his death, represented by the millions who filed past his embalmed body in its mausoleum in Moscow's Red Square, showed that the communists now had a saint to venerate, like the Orthodox Church before them. However, his insistence upon party power and party discipline, and his initiation of the policy of terror as a political weapon, made him the creator of those unacceptable elements in Russian communism that were to dominate its history in the 1930s.

N A cultural revolution?

The 'constructivists'

The period from 1917 to the end of the NEP experiment was one of unparalleled experiment in Russian culture. Although a large number of artists and writers left the country at the outbreak of the revolution, those that remained revelled in the brief freedom from Tsarist censorship. They accepted the Soviet doctrine that they, too, were now freer agents, released from the exploitation of bourgeois and aristocratic patrons.

Immediately, however, the revolution raised new controversy which was eventually resolved by the pressure of the state. Those artists who more keenly supported the new regime, calling themselves 'constructivists', claimed that art should now serve an active social and political purpose. One of the greatest literary figures of the immediate post-revolutionary period was the poet Vladimir Mayakovsky, of whom T. Frankel has written 'his every effort was to unify art and life, to enlist art in the service of society'. His work in this period included slogans for political campaigns and posters as well as pro-Bolshevik poetry. Theatre, too, rallied to the new atmosphere of revolution and liberation. The great producer and designer V. E. Meyerhold teamed up with Mayakovsky and the artist K. Malevich to produce the pageant *Mystery Bouffe* (1918) which showed the proletariat defeating its exploiters. In 1920, N. Yevreinov celebrated the third anniversary of the Revolution with a re-enactment of the storming of the Winter Palace, employing a cast of 8,000, and founding the tradition of May Day parades in Red Square. The group that formed itself around the journal *Proletarian Culture* (*Proletkult*) also enjoyed brief success between 1918–22 in their efforts to found new literary and cultural forms by workers and for workers.

The 'fellow travellers'

A more lasting achievement, however, was made by that group of writers and artists in Russia characterised by Trotsky as the 'fellow travellers'.

In general, these men and women were not communists, but were broadly in sympathy with the ideals of the revolution, and found much fascinating human material in the great events of the revolution and the civil war. Some of the leading writers of this tendency were D. A. Furmanov (*Chapaev*), V. V. Ivanov (*Armoured Train No. 14-69*), and M. A. Sholokhov (*Quiet Flows the Don*). Another, E. I. Zamyatin, produced a political satire, *We* (1920) in which he showed a regimented socialist society whose inhabitants were identified only be numbers: the forerunner both of Huxley's *Brave New World* and Orwell's *1984*. In poetry, Sergei Yesenin rivalled Mayakovsky's popularity with work that was highly personal, almost mystical.

Soviet cinema and Soviet music

'The cinema,' Lenin declared in 1921, 'is for us the most important of all the arts.' Naturally, therefore, the new art form found itself constrained at first to serve largely propagandistic purposes. Nevertheless, in the greater freedom of the NEP period, the Soviet cinema produced more than its fair share of the art's early classics, notable examples being Sergei Eisenstein's *Battleship Potemkin*, A. P. Dovzhenko's *The Land*, and V. I. Pudovkin's *Mother*, a film version of Gorky's novel. Music produced only one immediate heir to the great Russian traditions in Dmitri Shostakovich. He produced his First Symphony in 1926, and the subtitles given to the next two, the October and the May Day symphonies (1927 and 1929) demonstrated the tight rope that he, too, had to walk between artistic expression and official disapproval.

The growth of state control over the arts

The growth of collectivist policies under Stalin (*see* Chapter 13, section E), however, also extended to the arts. Earlier means of artistic control employed during the civil war, such as the state's monopoly over publishing through the State Publishing Organisation (*Gosizdat*) were renewed, and new ones introduced, such as the concentration of artists and writers into official unions. A policy aimed at constraining artists and writers strictly to serve the purposes of government policy saw the collapse of the best elements in the revivified Russian culture. The artists Marc Chagall and Vasili Kandinsky had already chosen in the early 1920s to conduct their experiments in surrealist painting in western Europe. Zamyatin followed them in 1931. In 1930 Mayakovsky, who had recently attacked the bureaucracy and narrow-mindedness of Soviet leadership in *The Bedbug* (1929) and *The Bathhouse* (1930), committed suicide, as Yesenin had done five years earlier. Even Gorky, the greatest of the Soviet writers, had protested against the 'disgraceful attitude' of the Soviet leaders 'towards the freedoms of speech and of person'. His own death in 1935 was surrounded by suspicious circumstances and rumours of poison.

The period between 1928 and 1953 was to be the age of 'Socialist Realism' in art, under which Soviet artists and writers were to concentrate upon subjects conducive to the building of a socialist society. Such subjects were defined by Basil Dmytryshyn as including 'contented cows, dedicated milkmaids, devoted pig breeders, vigilant party members, and young lovers arguing by the light of the moon about the problems of industrial production'.

Questions

Essay questions

1 To what extent does Russia's involvement in the First World War explain the success of the Bolshevik Revolution of October 1917? (NEAB)

2 'The Bolsheviks did not seize power; they simply picked it up.' How accurate is this assessment of the Russian Revolution in 1917? (ULEAC)

3 'Lenin was more responsible than was Stalin for the emergence of totalitarian government in the USSR.' Discuss this view. (ULEAC)

4 By what means, and how effectively, did the Bolsheviks deal with their opponents between 1917 and 1924? (UCLES)

5a Identify the main political parties in Russia in 1917. [4]

b Explain the policies of the Bolsheviks on war and land reform.

c To what extent were Bolshevik policies attractive to the Russian people in 1917? [7]

d Was the weakness of the Whites the main cause of the Bolshevik victory in the Russian Civil War? Explain your answer fully. [9] (WJEC)

6　Why was the Provisional Government in Russia unable to consolidate and maintain its power in 1917? (Oxford Entrance)

The Kronstadt Rebellion

Study Sources 1 to 6 and then answer all parts of the questions that follow.

Source 1: Declaration of the Kronstadt rebels

The glorious arms of labour's state – the sickle and hammer – have actually been replaced by the Communist authorities with the bayonet and the barred window, for the sake of preserving the calm, carefree life of the new bureaucracy of Communist commissars and officials. ... With the aid of militarised trade unions they have bound the workers to their benches. ... To the protests of the peasants, expressed in spontaneous uprisings, and of the workers, who are compelled to strike by the circumstances of their life, they answer with mass executions and bloodthirstiness, in which they are not surpassed by the Tsarist generals. ...

Here the banner of insurrection has been raised for liberation from the three-year violence and oppression of Communist domination. ... The present overturn at last makes it possible for the toilers to have their freely-elected soviets, working without any violent party pressure.

from What We Are Fighting For, *News of the Kronstadt Temporary Revolutionary Committee (8 March 1921)*

Source 2: Lenin on the causes of the Kronstadt Rebellion

The Social Revolutionaries and the bourgeois counter-terrevolutionaries in general resorted in Kronstadt to slogans calling for an insurrection against the Soviet Government of Russia ostensibly in the interests of the Soviet power. ... The Mensheviks took advantage of the disagreements and certain rudiments of factionalism in the Russian Communist Party actually in order to egg on and support the Kronstadt mutineers, the Social Revolutionaries and the White Guards. ...

from Lenin's draft resolution for the Tenth Party Congress (8–16 March 1921)

Source 3: Lenin on the importance of the Rebellion

I believe that there are two kinds of government possible in Russia - a government by the soviets or a government headed by a tsar. ... This Kronstadt affair in itself is a very petty incident. It no more threatens to break up the Soviet state than the Irish disorders are threatening to break up the British Empire. ... There is nobody to take our place save butcher generals and helpless bureaucrats who have already displayed their total incapacity for rule.

from an interview between Lenin and an American reporter, published in the New York Herald Tribune *(15 March 1921)*

Source 4: Trotsky on the Kronstadt Rebellion

The best, most self-sacrificing sailors were completely withdrawn from Kronstadt and played an important role at the fronts and in the local soviets throughout the country. What remained was the grey mass ... without political education and unprepared for revolutionary sacrifice. The country was starving. The Kronstadters demanded privileges. The uprising was dictated by a desire to get privileged food rations. ... All the reactionary elements, both in Russia and abroad, immediately seized upon this uprising. The White emigrés demanded aid for the insurrectionists. The victory of this uprising could bring nothing but the victory of the counterrevolution, entirely independent of that the sailors had in their heads. But the ideas themselves were deeply reactionary. They reflected the hostility of the backward peasantry toward the worker, the self-importance of the soldier or sailor in relation to 'civilian' Petrograd, the hatred of the petty bourgeois for revolutionary discipline.

from a letter written in Mexico by Trotsky (21 August 1937). It was written to a member of the Commission of Enquiry investigating charges made against Trotsky in the Moscow show trials of the 1930s.

Source 5: An analysis of the Communists' strategy at Kronstadt

In 1921 the Russian Revolution stood at the crossroads. The democratic or the dictatorial way, that was the question. By lumping together bourgeois and proletarian democracy the Bolsheviks were in fact condemning both. While waiting for a world revolution that was not round the corner, they built a state capitalist society, where the working class no longer had the right to make the decisions most intimately concerning it. ...

Both he [Lenin] and the Bolsheviks were fully aware that what was at stake was the monopoly of their Party. Kronstadt might have opened the way to a genuine proletarian democracy, incompatible with the Party's monopoly of power. That is why Lenin preferred to destroy Kronstadt. He chose an ignoble but sure way: the calumny that Kronstadt was allied to the bourgeoisie and the agrarian counterrevolution.

from The Kronstadt Uprising *(1971) by I. Mett.*

Source 6: The importance of the Kronstadt Rebellion

The 'triumph' of the Bolsheviks over Kronstadt held within itself the defeat of Bolshevism. It exposed the true character of the Communist dictatorship. The whole Bolshevik economic system was changed as a result of the Kronstadt events. ...

[This 'triumph'] sounded the death knell of Bolshevism with its Party dictatorship, mad centralisation, CHEKA terrorism and bureaucratic castes. ... It demonstrated that the Bolshevik regime is unmitigated tyranny and reaction, and that the Communist State is itself the most potent and dangerous counterrevolution.

Kronstadt fell. But it fell victorious in its idealism and moral purity, its generosity and higher humanity. ...

Kronstadt was the first popular and entirely independent attempt at liberation from the yoke of State Socialism - an attempt made directly by the people, by the workers, soldiers and sailors themselves.

from The Russian Tragedy *(1922) by A. Berkman*

a   Using your own knowledge, explain why a revolt by the Kronstadt sailors was of particular significance to the Bolshevik regime. [4]

b   Compare and contrast Sources 1, 2 and 4 in their interpretation of the causes of the Kronstadt Rebellion. [7]

c
   i   To what extent do Sources 3, 5 and 6 agree in their assessment of the significance of the Kronstadt Rebellion? [7]
   ii How do you account for any differences of interpretation among Sources 3, 5 and 6? [4]

d   Using this collection of Sources 1 to 6, and your own knowledge, explain the difficulty of writing an objective analysis of the causes and consequences of the Kronstadt Rebellion. [8]

(AEB)

13

Russia without Lenin

'Festival at a Collective Farm', a work by the Soviet artist Arkadi Plastov.

At roughly what date, and for what purpose, would this picture have been painted?

What are the major propaganda elements in the painting?

The Historical Debate

In forming so much of the structure of the Soviet Union at the height of its power, Stalin and his government engineered one of the most monumental achievements of the 20th century. This, together with Stalin's complete control over a totalitarian regime, ensured that he would be praised during his tenure of office as the all-wise leader, the natural continuator of the ideology of Marx and Lenin, guiding his country through the various perils of the epoch. Much of the official history of the revolution was rewritten to support this view.

On the other hand, the human cost of that achievement was so enormous as to stimulate bitter criticism from Stalin's surviving opponents. The most violent opposition to Stalin in his lifetime came, not from the west, but from the followers of Leon Trotsky. Trotsky's own works, such as *The Revolution Betrayed* (1937), portray Stalin as a political and intellectual mediocrity, whose whole career in power, the building of the party bureaucracy, the development of personal leadership, the whole concept of 'Socialism in One Country', was a betrayal of the principles of Marx and Lenin. The man responsible for this perversion of the revolution was thus, in Trotsky's famous phrase, the 'gravedigger of the revolution'.

A similar view was put forward in the Soviet Union more recently by Roy Medvedev (*On Stalin and Stalinism*, 1979). An orthodox Leninist, Medvedev consistently condemned Stalin as a perverter of Leninist principles, and as the man primarily responsible for diverting the revolution from its correct and beneficial course. This view is in direct contrast with that of the American writer A. A. Ulam (*Stalin: the Man and his Era*, 1974). For Ulam, Stalin represents a remarkable continuity with earlier Bolshevism. He was forced to deal with problems created by Lenin's opportunism, and solved them by methods quite consistent with earlier Bolshevik practice. He, rather than Lenin, is the greatest and most successful of the Bolsheviks.

Upon Stalin's death in 1953, his successors in power formulated a synthesis that disapproved of Stalin's methods, without fundamentally rejecting the end product of his work. Stalin, it was now declared, had perverted the course of the revolution by allowing the 'cult of personality' to develop in the 1930s and by taking savage and unwarranted actions against other sound communists in the purges. The official view of Stalin during the last 40 years of the life of the Soviet Union was probably close to that stated by Nikita Khrushchev in a speech in 1957. 'It is, of course, a bad thing that Stalin launched into deviations and mistakes which harmed our cause. But even when he committed mistakes and allowed the laws to be broken, he did that with the full conviction that he was defending the gains of the Revolution, the cause of socialism.'

Western commentators upon Stalin since the Second World War might be roughly divided between two 'schools'. The first is that which broadly accepts the middle ground view defined by Khrushchev. E. H. Carr, the most prolific English writer on Soviet history (*A History of Soviet Russia* and *The Russian Revolution from Lenin to Stalin*, 1979) has concentrated less upon the personal rule of Stalin, than upon the dynamic impetus of the original revolution in Russia. Far from diverting those revolutionary forces, therefore, Stalin was borne along by them, and they bestowed a degree of inevitability upon his policies and upon their outcome. David Lane (*Leninism: a Sociological Interpretation*, 1981) and Isaac Deutscher (*Stalin*, 1967) both attempt to view the phenomenon of Stalinism in an even wider Russian context, stressing the peculiarities in Russian social, economic and political development which might help to explain the particular course taken by Soviet socialism under Stalin's leadership.

Lane's stress, like that of Alex Nove (*An Economic History of the USSR*, 1969) and Roger Pethybridge (*The Social Prelude to Stalinism*, 1974), is upon the agricultural and industrial backwardness of post-revolutionary Russia, which faced Stalin with the alternatives of drastic action or ultimate political failure.

The second 'western' school, of course, is that which rejects Stalin and his work as unrelievedly negative. Robert Conquest (*The Great Terror: a Reassessment*, 1990) may be taken as a consistent representative of this view, stressing that the immorality of Stalin's methods was not in fact offset by any remarkable elevation of Russian living standards beyond those of pre-revolutionary years.

With the collapse of the Soviet system, it is no longer easy to view Stalin's excesses as justifiable steps along the road to socialism, and it may be that Robert Conquest's interpretation will enjoy wide acceptance in the years ahead.

A   The succession to Lenin

The uniqueness of Lenin's position

The paralytic stroke that removed Lenin from active politics (26 May 1922), and which finally killed him (21 January 1924), destroyed the undisputed source of leadership in Russia. 'The impact of Lenin's illness on the Bolshevik leadership can hardly be exaggerated,' wrote Isaac Deutscher. 'The whole constellation ceased, almost at once, to shine with the reflected light of its master mind'.

There could be no adequate replacement for Lenin's genius, and the shortcomings of the various candidates had already been aptly summarised in his Testament, composed during his last illness. Trotsky, for all his great intellectual qualities, was guilty of a 'too far-reaching self-confidence and a disposition to be too much attracted by the purely administrative side of affairs'. Zinoviev and Kamenev had shown a disturbing hesitancy in the months before the seizure of power in October 1917, and Bukharin's grasp of theoretical Marxism was regarded as faulty. Josef Stalin, lastly, offset his great practical abilities with an excessive roughness, impatience and lack of caution and of consideration for his colleagues.

The main candidates for the succession

The main feature of the struggle for the succession during the last weeks of Lenin's life was the isolation of Trotsky from the other candidates. In part this was due to his personal arrogance, and in part due to the fact that he never quite lived down the lateness of his conversion to Bolshevism. His achievements at the head of the Red Army, furthermore, were offset by the widespread fear that this military leader might turn against the Russian Revolution as General Bonaparte had turned against the French Revolution. The failure of his campaign between October 1923 and January 1924 for greater democracy in the upper echelons of the party stressed the narrowness of his support, and his absence through illness from Lenin's funeral badly undermined his credibility as a successor in the popular view.

The coalition that opposed him, a triumvirate of Zinoviev, Kamenev and Stalin, on the other hand exerted immense influence. Zinoviev dominated the party organisation in Petrograd (renamed Leningrad in honour of the dead leader in 1924), and was head of the Comintern. Kamenev exercised similar influence in Moscow. Stalin, while occupying the relatively unglamorous post of commissar for nationalities, had spent the past years insinuating himself into an impregnable position in the party bureaucracy. Not only was he, like Zinoviev and Kamenev, a member of the party's inner cabinet (*Politburo*), but he was also prominent in the executive bureau (*Orgburo*) and in the Commissariat of Workers' and Peasants' Inspection, which was responsible for the elimination of economic inefficiency and corruption. Above all, since 1922, he had held the post of general secretary of the party's Central Committee. This enabled him to exert substantial control over party membership. In terms of the range of political weapons available to him, no other Bolshevik was the rival of Stalin.

B   The consolidation of power

Stalin's control over the party machinery

In 1924 it was widely assumed that the death of Lenin would result in a collective leadership of the Soviet Union. The reasons for the steady decline of that form of political authority, and the emergence of Stalin's undisputed leadership are complex. Neither the Stalinist explanation, that he offered the only correct analysis of the future course of the Soviet Union, nor Trotsky's bitter reflection that Stalin rode to power on a wave of war-weariness and reaction, is fully satisfactory. In large part the phenomenon must be explained by Stalin's consummate political skill, and by his shrewd handling of the weapons at his disposal.

Foremost among these was the party machinery over which he exercised such control, and which he could use to assign supporters of his opponents to remote posts, while admitting to high office those upon whose support he could rely. The promotion to the Central Committee of Lazar Kaganovich (1924) and Anastas Mikoyan (1923) and to the Politburo of Vyacheslav Molotov and Mikhail Kalinin (1926) marked the emergence of a new school of 'Stalinist' Bolsheviks. The appointment of Sergei Kirov as head of the party in Leningrad (1926), formerly Zinoviev's stronghold, and of Kliment Voroshilov in Trotsky's former military office (1925), marked the extension of this tactic to

Josef Stalin

Personality and aims

The future dictator of the Soviet Union was not Russian by birth, but from Georgia, the province in the Caucasus mountains. Georgia was absorbed by Russia in the 19th century, but had a long independent culture and history of her own. He was born as Josef Djugashvili, in the small town of Gori (21 January 1879), the son of a shoemaker and the grandson of serfs. He was thus one of the few true proletarians in the leading ranks of the Bolsheviks. The most significant features of his early life were the harshness and occasional brutality of his early upbringing and the unusual fact that the ambition and devotion of his mother secured for him the rare privilege of 11 years of education (1888–99). A boyhood friend later recalled that 'undeserved and frightful beatings made the boy as grim and heartless as the father'. As to his education, it was significant that the theological seminary in Tblisi that Djugashvili attended from 1894 until his expulsion five years later, had a history of student unrest and political disloyalty. 'I became a Marxist,' its most famous student was later to reminisce, 'because of my social position . . . but also . . .

because of the harsh intolerance and Jesuitical discipline that crushed me so mercilessly at the seminary.'

Djugashvili's political stance seems to have developed steadily between 1898, when he joined a social democratic underground group in Tblisi, and 1904 when he clearly identified himself with the Bolshevik faction of the communists. His subsequent career, unlike those of the intellectual Marxists in exile, followed a practical path of strike organisation, agitation and armed robberies for the benefit of party funds, interspersed with periods of imprisonment and Siberian exile. Sheltering behind revolutionary pseudonyms, he used the name 'Koba' from 1902, and signed himself 'Stalin' ('man of steel') for the first time in 1913. The leading traits of his character: distrust, alertness, dissimulation, endurance and, above all, an intense sense of

class hatred that was never for Stalin merely a matter of Marxist theory, can all be traced from his childhood and early career. 'In Djugashvili,' Isaac Deutscher had written, 'class hatred was not his second nature – it was his first.'

Stalin's reputation in local revolutionary circles expanded to a wider stage between 1905, when he travelled abroad for the first time to attend a Bolshevik conference in Finland, and 1912 when he was appointed by Lenin to the Central Committee of the party. Lenin's choice in this, A. Ulam suggested, was determined by his desire to leaven the assembly of theoretical Marxists with a rougher breed of revolutionary, more truly a 'man from the people'. In exile in Siberia at the beginning of 1917, Stalin quickly assumed a number of unobtrusive but influential roles in the revolution. He was editor of the Bolshevik journal *Pravda*, leader of the Petrograd Soviet, and temporary director of Bolshevik strategy until the return of the exiles from abroad. Thus he was, if not a familiar public figure, a man of substantial internal political influence, as the events of the next decade were to demonstrate.

key political areas. At this crucial point in the struggle, the Stalinists also enjoyed the support of the 'Rightist' wing of the party, headed by Nikolai Bukharin, Mikhail Tomsky and Alexei Rykov.

Creating the cult of Lenin

Secondly, Stalin showed great skill, both in the creation of a cult of 'Leninism', and in the formation of his own image as 'the best, the staunchest, the truest comrade-in-arms of Lenin'. His stage-management of Lenin's funeral was, in Isaac Deutscher's words, 'calculated to stir the mind of a primitive, semi-oriental people into a mood of

exaltation for the new Leninist cult'. The effect was compounded by Stalin's foundation of the Lenin Institute (January 1924), and a series of carefully calculated lectures on 'The Foundations of Leninism' delivered at the Communist University in Moscow (April 1924). Given his late conversion to Bolshevism, Trotsky was at a particular disadvantage in terms of Leninist orthodoxy.

Stalin's third great advantage lay in the blameless orthodoxy and simplicity of his former private and political life. His image as the uncomplicated and dedicated peasant, married (1918) to the daughter of an old Bolshevik, contrasted favourably with those of his more sophisticated rivals. As commissar for nationalities, moreover, he could claim the successful merging of the national republics into the Union of Soviet Socialist Republics (1922) as one of the greatest achievements of the revolution to date.

The failure of the opposition

Lastly, Stalin benefited from a string of tactical errors by his most prominent opponents. Trotsky's attack upon such elements of Lenin's policy as the New Economic Policy, in his essays *Lessons of October* (1924) was a serious miscalculation in the prevailing atmosphere of 'Lenin worship'. The refusal of both Trotsky and Zinoviev to publish Lenin's Testament, with its damaging verdict upon Stalin, saved Stalin from the most dangerous threat to his position. Indeed, Roy Medvedev has stressed that in the crucial early stages of the contest, 'Trotsky considered it beneath his dignity to engage actively in a struggle for power'. The belated union of Trotsky, Zinoviev and Kamenev (1926) in the so-called 'United Opposition' to Stalin, was unlikely to increase their credibility in the light of the mutual hostility of a few months earlier.

It is important to remember how ill-equipped most members of the Politburo were to cope with a political opponent of Stalin's talents. As Martin McCauley has explained, 'the Politburo opponents of Stalin had had little practical experience of politics before 1917. They had not mounted the party ladder step by step and had not had to claw their way up; 1917 made them, at a stroke, key political figures. They were singularly ill-equipped to recognise a party climber when they saw one.'

From 1926 onwards, the position of this opposition became more and more hopeless. Isolated and outnumbered, Zinoviev lost his leadership of the Communist International, and all three leaders of the 'United Opposition' were voted from the Politburo by the end of the year. In October 1927, Trotsky and Zinoviev lost their places on the Central Committee, and were expelled altogether from the party a month later, followed by 75 of their supporters. In January 1928, Trotsky began a period of internal exile in Soviet Asia, and was taking the first steps upon a road to banishment from the USSR that was only to end with his murder in Mexico in 1940.

C 'Socialism in one country'

Consolidation or continuation?

The leadership struggle of the late 1920s was certainly in part a clash of powerful personalities. It was also, however, a genuine dispute about the future path of Soviet communism. The candidates, for instance, differed over the issue of democratic decision making within the party, over the pace at which the economic backwardness of the Soviet Union should be tackled, and over the roles allowed to independent merchants, manufacturers and peasants under the New Economic Policy. Above all, the dispute centred around two alternative views of the future of Bolshevism.

Trotsky and his followers held fast to the theory of the 'permanency of revolution'. The revolution in Russia, they claimed, could not be regarded as an end in itself, but only as a vital link in the wider process of European and even world revolution. By its example, and with the continued assistance of the Soviet Union, the revolution would eventually lead to the general destruction of capitalism. Only then could the future of the Soviet system be assured. It was a view closely in accord with the expectations of Lenin right up to his death, but offered a prospect of further struggle that was a bleak one after recent Russian sufferings, and discouraging in the light of recent socialist failures in Germany, Hungary and elsewhere.

Although Stalin seems to have subscribed to this view until late 1924, he thereafter formulated an alternative usually known as the theory of 'socialism in one country'. By this he stressed that, despite the Soviet Union's present state of ruin and exhaustion, her immense resources would be sufficient for the construction of a stable socialist society, without external aid. Within two years, 'Trotskyism' was being officially branded as 'a lack of faith in the strength and capabilities of the Russian revolution and as a negation and repudiation of Lenin's theory of proletarian revolution'. While Stalin left open the possibility of future Soviet participation in a wider revolution, he made consolidation of the Russian achievement an unalterable priority.

The appeal of 'socialism in one country'

By the last two years of the decade Stalin's thesis

had won complete dominance over that of Trotsky as the official view of the Soviet government. Some writers have explained this as the natural consequence of Stalin's political victory within the party. It is now, however, more usual to reverse this reasoning and to see Stalin's political supremacy as the result rather than the cause of the wide acceptance of the theory of 'socialism in one country'. The American researcher S. F. Cohen has argued strongly that Stalin's rise depended in large part upon his acceptance by the 'influentials' within the party, and that a majority of them supported him 'less because of his bureaucratic power than because they preferred his leadership and policies. To some extent their choice doubtless expressed their identification with the General Secretary as a forceful practical politician'.

Why was the principle so widely accepted? Firstly, whatever its unorthodoxy in pure Leninist terms, it was hard to dispute the practical logic of Stalin's approach in the light of contemporary European developments. Secondly, as Isaac Deutscher has stressed, it offered the prospect of a future that lay wholly in Soviet hands, and involved little dependence upon forces beyond Soviet control. 'It gave them,' he stated, 'the soothing theoretical conviction that, barring war, nothing could shake their mastery over Russia.' Lastly, it offered to the Soviet people as a whole the prospect of relief from the enormous suffering and perpetual struggle of the decade between 1914 and 1924. There was perhaps some justification, after all, in Trotsky's later conviction that the unreadiness of the people to undertake a further era of struggle contributed largely to his defeat in the leadership contest.

D Stalin's government

The constitution of 1924

The theoretical heart of Soviet political organisation in 1928 was the constitution introduced in 1924. Confirming the merger of the component national units of the old Empire into the Union of Soviet Socialist Republics (USSR), it left each republic with the theoretical right to secede from the Union if its 'non-Russian working class' so wished, although in reality any such wish would invariably be treated as the counter-revolutionary agitation of nationalist, bourgeois elements.

At the head of the constitutional structure stood the All-Union Congress of Soviets, with its executive Central Committee, and its élite Presidium, in which all major decisions were made. Below stretched a hierarchy of Soviets at republican, provincial, district and local levels. The right to vote belonged to all adults, except those deprived of citizenship. It extended, however, only to the election of local soviet members who, in turn, selected members for each higher soviet. The system thus constituted a complex filter to test the orthodoxy of each aspiring politician.

The Communist Party of the Soviet Union

The articles of the constitution veiled the three main driving forces of Soviet politics. The first of these was the Communist Party of the Soviet Union (Bolshevik), membership of which was an essential qualification for every political aspirant. It was a body that had undergone substantial changes since the heady days of 1917. A series of purges had by 1922 rid the party of any serious ideological diversity, eliminating the last traces of Menshevik or Social Revolutionary opinion. In the later 1920s two more changes took place. The party grew steadily in size, from 1.3 million members in early 1928 to 3.5 million in January 1933, and it also changed its composition. It became less of a party of the workers, who constituted 48.6 per cent of membership in the 1930s, and more a party of a new, Soviet-educated intelligentsia.

The political police

The constitution also failed to indicate the growing importance to the state of the government agencies for internal security. The State Political Administration (GPU or OGPU) was the successor of the CHEKA, the post-revolutionary secret police. It was headed by the CHEKA's founder, Felix Dzerzhinsky, until his death in 1926. Its duties were vaguely defined but, as Leonard Schapiro has noted, 'in practice, it never lacked the power to do whatever it was required to do by the party'. In July 1934, the OGPU was merged into a wider body, the People's Commissariat of Internal Affairs (NKVD). Under the leadership of H. G. Yagoda (1934–36), Nikolai Yezhov (1936–38) and Lavrenti Beria (1938–53), the NKVD was the main tool for the internal policy of the Soviet state. It supervised many of the most important and dangerous projects of the Five-Year Plans, including the Pechora railway and the White Sea Ship Canal, played a central role in the purging of the party, and controlled a labour force perhaps as large as 10 million in the state's prison camps.

The army

The third element in the practical government of the USSR, the army, was also brought under close party control by the end of the 1920s. Trotsky's hopes of a citizen militia, under direct proletarian control, were killed off by the necessities of the Civil War. Trotsky himself was replaced as commissar for war by M. V. Frunze in 1925. A series of reforms in 1924–25 placed the political supervision of the army firmly in the hands of the party's Central Committee, and confirmed the system of dual command whereby the military commanders worked alongside political commissars who took precedence over them in all political decisions. By 1933, all senior commanders and 93 per cent of divisional commanders were party members. The degree of authority enjoyed by the party was illustrated in October 1925 when Frunze was ordered by his political superiors to undergo a dangerous medical operation from which he died. The influence of the party's leaders was, of course, to be confirmed spectacularly during the course of the political purges of the 1930s (*see* section **J**).

E The planned economy

The abandonment of NEP

The most dramatic policy decision of the Stalinist establishment was the abandonment of Lenin's New Economic Policy, with its elements of private enterprise, and of Bukharin's policy of 'the creep at a snail's pace' towards socialism. Apart from the obvious ideological hostility within the party to the NEP, it is also true that it had, by 1926, largely achieved its industrial purpose. The toleration of a degree of private economic activity had restored output in most major areas of the economy to pre-1914 levels, and the level of private trading outside agriculture dropped steadily from 42.5 per cent of the total (1924–25) to 22.5 per cent (1928).

The alternative of rapid, forced industrial growth through centralised planning and control

had been advanced by Trotsky, Kamenev and Zinoviev in the mid-1920s, but had been resisted by Stalin as too great a departure from Leninism. His change of view now involved a predictable break with his former 'rightist' allies within the party. Tomsky's leadership of the Soviet Trades Unions, Bukharin's post at the head of the Comintern, and Rykov's chairmanship of the Council of Commissars (*Sovnarkom*), all passed to Stalinists in June 1929. The public admission by the 'rightists' that their views were erroneous (November 1929) dates the beginning of Stalin's undisputed power in the USSR which was to last until his death in 1953.

The procurement crisis

Why did Stalin now change course so abruptly to embrace the policies of his conquered opponents? Although this has sometimes been seen as a cynical expression of his new-found political security, it is more likely that it was a pragmatic response to the risk of substantial food shortages resulting from the so-called 'procurement crisis' of 1927–28. Despite the decline in private industrial trade, in 1928 the independent peasant continued to cultivate 97.3 per cent of the farmland of the Soviet Union. The difficulty in procuring sufficient grain supplies for the industrial towns arose in part from the inefficiency of many small, private farms, but also from the peasants' reluctance to deliver precious grain at the artificially low prices offered by the state. The result was a shortfall of 2 million tons of grain by 1927, potentially disastrous in view of the role played by urban hunger in the events of 1917. Under such circumstances, the policy of 'socialism in one country' risked falling at the first hurdle thanks, it was felt, to the greed of the richer peasants, the Kulaks.

The principle of the Five-Year Plans

The introduction of the first Five-Year Plan, to run from 1928–33, committed the USSR to the path of planned and centralised economic policy. A second Five-Year Plan followed between 1933 and 1937, while a third (1937–42) was disrupted by the outbreak of war. The overall aim of these plans was to match and to overhaul in the shortest possible time the economies of the advanced capitalist states. 'We are fifty or a hundred years behind the advanced countries,' Stalin declared in 1931. 'We must make good this distance in ten years. Either we do it, or we shall be crushed.' In view of the fate that befell the USSR in 1941, the prediction proved to be uncannily accurate.

The main tool of the government in these tasks was the Central Planning Committee (*Gosplan*). In industry, the planned economy meant an expansion of output, an improvement of communications, the discovery and exploitation of new resources, all to predetermined production quotas. In agriculture it meant, not only the forced grain procurements of 1928–29, but a fundamental change in the agrarian life of the USSR. The way out of Russia's agrarian backwardness, Stalin declared to the party in December 1927, 'is to turn the small and scattered peasant farms into large united farms based upon cultivation of the land in common'. Although it was stressed that the party should proceed with caution, and should frown upon coercion, the statement spelled the end of the brief decade of liberation for the Russian peasant, and marked the beginning of the era of collectivisation.

F Industry

The first Five-Year Plan

The task of the first Five-Year Plan, commenced in 1928, was nothing less than to lay the foundations for the transformation of Soviet society into an industrial force comparable to the United States. Its main emphasis, therefore, fell upon the production of energy and of construction materials, upon coal, oil, electricity, iron, steel and cement. The rate of increase envisaged, averaging an annual rate of 20 per cent, was hugely unrealistic, and the declaration (31 December 1932) that the Plan had been completed in four years, was wholly a propaganda exercise. Detractors might point to significant shortfalls, as in steel production (where only 62 per cent of the quota was completed), in iron (59 per cent), in heavy metallurgy (67.7 per cent) and in consumer goods (73.5 per cent). A more friendly observer might still conclude that the achievement of 1928–32 was substantial. Machinery output increased four times, oil production doubled and electrical output in 1932 was 250 per cent of the 1928 figure. Seventeen new blast furnaces were completed and 20 others modernised. Fifteen new rolling mills came into operation with 12 others reconstructed. The plan

also produced some notable 'show pieces', such as the new centres of iron and steel production at Magnitogorsk in the Urals, and Kuznetsk in central Siberia. Also there was the building of the Dnieprostroi Dam, the biggest in Europe. Stalin's own criticism of the Dnieprostroi project in the mid-1920s, that is was like a poor peasant spending money on a gramophone instead of buying a cow, remained true, but he was now far more appreciative of the propaganda value of such achievements.

Table 13.1 The Five-Year Plans

	1927	1932	(goal)	1937	(goal)
Electricity (million kWh)	505	1,340	(2,200)	3,620	(3,800)
Coal (million tons)	35.4	64.3	(75)	128	(152.5)
Oil (million tons)	11.7	21.4	(22)	28.5	(46.8)
Iron ore (million tons)	5.7	12.1	(19)	?	?
Pig iron (million tons)	3.3	6.2	(10)	14.5	(16)
Steel (million tons)	4.0	5.9	(10.4)	17.7	(17)
Labour force (millions)	11.3	22.8	(15.8)	26.9	(28.9)

The second Five-Year Plan

The second Five-Year Plan, which ran its full course from 1933–37, avoided some of the mistakes of the first. Its average annual target was a rather more reasonable 14 per cent increase, and by virtue of a more experienced and better-trained workforce avoided at least some of the waste and poor quality of 1928–32. Priority continued to be given to heavy industry, but greater emphasis was now placed upon newer metallurgical resources, such as lead, zinc, nickel and tin. The second plan also concentrated more upon the improvement of Soviet communications. Railways were largely double tracked, and this sphere of activity produced many of the 'show pieces' of this plan, such as the Moscow–Volga and Volga–Don Canals and, most famous of all, the palatial Moscow Metro. Before the end of the second Five-Year Plan, the deteriorating international situation called for more and more state investment to be diverted to rearmament and began to interfere with the projections of the planners. Whereas armaments had consumed only 3.4 per cent of total expenditure in 1933, the figure had swollen to 16.1 per cent in 1936, and in 1940, the third year of the third plan, accounted for 32.6 per cent of government investment.

Nevertheless, there can be little doubt that the pre-war Five-Year Plans achieved their primary aims. They may indeed by criticised for lack of realism, for administrative inefficiency, and for the human cost they entailed (*see* section **I**). Yet the goal of making the Soviet Union an industrial power, and able to withstand conflict with a major capitalist state was, within the short space of ten years, undoubtedly achieved as Table 13.1 shows.

G Agriculture

The elimination of the Kulaks
No branch of the Soviet economy was as sensationally affected by the policy of centralisation as agriculture. In the short term, the 'evils' of small-scale farming, inadequate equipment, and low proportions of the harvest reaching the market, were combated by rigorous and often brutal searches for and confiscation of grain stocks by local officials. In the longer term, under the aegis of the Five-Year Plan, they were combated by the forcible collectivisation of peasant production. This was not so much a 'war against the peasant' as Roy Medvedev has described it, as a 'war between peasants'. The government's main weapon against the prosperous Kulaks, just under a million of the total peasantry, was the jealousy of the seven million *Bedniaks*, or poor peasants, those without livestock or modern implements of any kind. With the aid of party officials, police and army, a class war was waged in the countryside between late 1928 and March 1930, involving the dispossession, deportation and often the murder of those designated as Kulaks. By 1930, it was announced that 58 per cent of peasant holdings were 'collectivised', although the term meant little more than the land, livestock and equipment of the Kulaks had been handed over for communal use by the Bedniaks. The middle peasants (*Seredniaks*) were not only scared into the collectives by the fate of the Kulaks, but left with no alternative form of livelihood.

Collectivisation
Briefly, in 1930, even Stalin seems to have taken fright at the 'pandemonium' reigning in rural Russia and, by blaming local officials for overzealousness, and authorising withdrawal from collectives, produced the sharp drop indicated in Table 13.2. In reality, however, policy remained unchanged. The ruthless elimination of the private farmer continued until, in 1938, the Soviet Union boasted 242,000 collective farms. These farms subdivided into two basic types. The state farm (*Sovkhoz*) was entirely state property, on which peasants worked for wages. The collective farm (*Kolkhoz*) was, on the other hand, a 'voluntary' co-operative on which land and equipment was collectively owned by the peasantry. Until 1958, no collective farm possessed its own heavy machinery, but were served instead by 'machine tractor stations' whose state-owned machinery and state-controlled specialists were at the disposal of the peasantry. Each *Kolkhoz* was committed to deliver a substantial proportion of its produce to the state, while on a *Sovkhoz*, the produce was, in any case, state property.

Table 13.2 Collectivisation

Year	Proportion of households collectivised (per cent)
December 1928	1.7
October 1929	4.1
March 1930	58.0
September 1930	21.0
1931	52.7
1932	61.5
1933	65.6
1934	71.4
1935	83.2
1936	90.5

The cost of collectivisation
It is certain that, as Basil Dmytryshyn has written, 'the speed and ferocity with which the mass collectivisation was carried out benefited neither the state, nor the collective farms, nor the peasants'. Destruction by rebellious peasants, the loss of Kulak expertise, and the inexperience of many collective farm managers resulted in a sharp decline in many areas of production. Between 1928–34 the cattle production of the USSR declined from 66.8 million to 33.5 million, the number of sheep and goats fell from 114.6 million to 36.5 million, and the number of horses from 34 million to 16.5

million. Grain shortages, combined with continued forced procurements, led to rural famine. This was especially severe in the Ukraine and northern Caucasus region, where successive census figures between 1933 and 1938 suggest a death toll of around five million people.

Only slowly, as a government confident of victory showed more tolerance towards small-scale private enterprise among the peasantry. did livestock populations and rural living standards rise. Not until 1940 did figures for grain production match those of 1914. What gains there were from collectivisation in the short term were enjoyed by Soviet industry, which benefited from a flow of surplus peasant labour into more attractive factory occupations, and by industrial workers, who gained a reliable, if not always plentiful supply of cheap grain. A crucial part of the basis of Soviet industrial power was thus laid at the cost of the peasantry. Stalin himself would later privately compare this battle with the later struggle for survival against the Germans.

H Living standards

The regimentation of industrial labour

Quite apart from the obvious deprivations suffered by much of the peasantry in the course of collectivisation, the Five-Year Plans also involved considerable sacrifice for many industrial workers. The initial stage of industrialisation rode roughshod over the individual freedom of the Soviet worker. The government's more ambitious projects might involve the mobilisation of labour to remote areas, working with inadequate equipment and without facilities and comforts of their own, closely supervised by NKVD 'shock brigades'. Unrealistic production quotas usually meant the neglect of safety precautions and the ever-present risk of prosecution as a 'saboteur' or 'wrecker', if the targets were not met.

The replacement of Tomsky by N. M. Shvernik as head of Soviet Trades Unions (June 1929) turned these bodies into virtual government departments unresponsive to the interests of the individual workers. Similarly, the worker found himself hedged in by a whole new body of Soviet law. Absenteeism from work without due cause became (November 1932) an offence punishable by

loss of job, food rations and housing. The internal passport system of Tsarist days was reintroduced (December 1932) to prevent the drift of labour from areas of greatest need. It must be extremely doubtful whether the gradual and irregular introduction of such facilities as subsidised canteen meals and free medical attention fully offset these losses.

Prices and wages

Tremendous difficulties confront the historian who tries to make precise judgements about industrial standards of living in this period. The task, writes Alex Nove, 'is rendered almost impossible not only by the existence of rationing, price differences and shortages, but also queues, declines in quality and neglect of consumer requirements'. There can be little doubt, however, that the first years of collectivisation were accompanied by a wave of rises in food prices. In 1933 alone, official Soviet figures showed rises of 80 per cent in the cost of bread and eggs, and of 55 per cent in the cost of butter. Nove has been quite uncompromising in his description of the years 1928–33 as witnessing 'the most precipitous decline in living standards known in recorded history'. Although the subsequent years saw a steady improvement in levels of wages and of consumer goods production, western and Soviet research has agreed that 'real' wages in 1937 were not more than 85 per cent of the 1928 level, an indication of how low the level must have been in 1933.

Such statistics, of course, often veil more immediate problems. While the number of industrial workers doubled in 1927-32, the living space created for them increased by only 16 per cent. Thus 'overcrowding, shared kitchens, frayed nerves, limited sanitation and poorly maintained buildings became a way of life for a whole generation of Soviet people' (Martin McCauley).

Furthermore, the worsening of the international situation after 1938 once more limited the production of consumer goods. It caused a tightening of government control over the workforce, and ended the temporary trend towards better living standards. Renewed labour legislation in 1940 lengthened the working week from five days to six, and made absenteeism, which came to include lateness for work by more than 20 minutes, a criminal offence punishable now by imprisonment.

The Stakhanovites

For a select few, the industrial drive could bring recognition and rewards. The abandonment in 1931 of earlier attempts to level wages paved the way for the privileged treatment of the most skilled and productive workers, which culminated in the 'Stakhanovite' movement. This took its name from a Donbas miner, Alexei Stakhanov, who in September 1935 achieved the (probably contrived) feat of cutting fourteen times his quota of coal. Such workers stood to gain rewards in many forms, such as higher salaries, access to better housing and to scarce consumer goods. For the average worker, however, the 'Stakhanovites' were the cause of greater government pressure for increased production. Thus government decrees of 1936, 1938 and 1939 all demanded the raising of shift production quotas by as much as 50 per cent. In general, it was not until the later 1950s, when the scars of war had been partly erased, that the Soviet government ceased so completely to sacrifice the interests of the individual workers to those of the state.

I   The purges: causes

Precedents for the purges

Between 1934–38, having initiated an economic transformation of revolutionary proportions, Stalin set about the transformation of the Soviet communist party by a series of murderous and far-reaching purges. In seeking to establish his motives we must first realise that purges in themselves were relatively commonplace in Soviet government. In addition to the purges carried out during Lenin's lifetime, 116,000 members had been expelled from the party in April 1929 on charges of 'passivity', 'lack of discipline', or as 'alien elements'. They were followed by another 800,000 in 1933. The Five-Year Plan also brought 'show trials' in its wake, such as the so-called Shakhti trial (1928) in which bourgeois mining specialists and foreign technicians were accused of sabotage. It is with some justification, therefore, that Z. Brzezinski has referred to Soviet government between the wars as the 'permanent purge'. The 'Great Purge', like London's 'Great Plague', was an extreme example of a well-known phenomenon. It was striking in its extent, and also in that is victims were not Whites or Kulaks, but respected communists and comrades of Lenin himself.

Motives for the purges

Nevertheless, Stalin's precise motivation is not easy to establish. The official contemporary claim that the party was infiltrated by 'Trotskyites', 'Zinovievites' and 'Bukharinites' who were all agents of international capitalism, can no longer be taken seriously. Nor does the claim that Stalin sought scapegoats for domestic economic problems explain the eventual scale of the purges. It is true that there was a strong and growing element of opposition within the party to Stalin's ruthless and divisive policies, especially to the pace and consequences of collectivisation. As Trotsky wrote in March 1933, 'within the party and beyond the slogan "Down with Stalin" is heard more and more widely'. His political opponents still retained some influence. Bukharin for instance was now editor of *Isvestya*, and without doubt the emergence of Sergei Kirov, head of the party organisation in Leningrad, seemed to many to offer a capable and popular alternative to Stalin. The fact that five members of the ten-man Politburo in 1934 (Kirov, Kossyar, Kuibyshev, Ordzhonikidze and Rudzutak) died in various circumstances in the years of the purge, suggests that resistance to Stalin may even have been widespread in the top ranks of government. It is difficult to avoid the conclusion that Nikita Khrushchev was close to the truth when he stated in his famous 'Secret Speech' of 1956 that Stalin had committed his excesses to boost and guarantee his own security, the continuation of his supremacy, and the supremacy of his policies within the Soviet Union.

J   The purges: course

The murder of Kirov

The course of the Great Purge may be conveniently divided into three stages. The first stage may be precisely dated from 1 December 1934, when the leader of the Leningrad administration, Sergei Kirov, was assassinated at his office. Whether or not Kirov died at Stalin's orders continues to puzzle historians. Official Soviet sources successively blamed the crime on foreign capitalists, on Soviet rightists, and on Trotskyites, while Robert Conquest speaks for very many western writers in concluding that Stalin was directly responsible for the murder of a potential rival. Isaac Deutscher, on the other hand, suggests that Stalin may have been genuinely shocked by the event, but turned it to his own purposes much as the German Nazis had recently exploited the lucky stroke of the Reichstag fire.

A feature of this first stage was that the senior ranks of the party remained untouched. The fourteen men executed for Kirov's murder were all minor figures and, although Kamenev and Zinoviev were imprisoned for 'opposition', they were not directly accused of the assassination. Nevertheless, the deaths at this time of Politburo member Valerian Kuibyshev (1935) and of the writer Maxim Gorky (1936) have never been satisfactorily explained, and may mark the beginning of the elimination of those who opposed Stalin's chosen path. In retrospect, this early stage also saw the establishment of the machinery and personnel necessary for the succeeding waves of purges. By appointing Andrei Zhdanov in Kirov's place in Leningrad, by inserting Nikita Khrushchev at the head of the party in Moscow, and by subjugating the law courts to the influence of Andrei Vyshinsky as Chief Procurator, Stalin ensured reliable implementation of his orders in several vital areas of the administration.

The elimination of Kamenev and Zinoviev

The second stage was triggered in August 1936 by the arrest and execution of Kamenev, Zinoviev and fourteen others. They were charged with plotting terrorist activities, including the death of Kirov, on behalf of the 'Trotskyite–Zinovievite Counter-Revolutionary Bloc'. Their trials produced several features soon to become familiar, notably the confessions of the accused and the implication in those confessions of other prominent figures. Why did these men confess? The application of torture, and of threats to their families undoubtedly explains much. It has also been argued that many of the victims of the purges saw their deaths as a last service to a party to which they had dedicated their lives, and which they genuinely believed to be under attack. 'The loyalty of these men to the idea of "the party"', Leonard Schapiro has written, 'was in the last resort the main reason for Stalin's victory.' The same writer also stresses the number of accused who refused to confess, and who therefore met their fate under much more obscure circumstances.

The extension of the purges

Nevertheless, Stalin's control of events was not yet complete, as was demonstrated by the acquittal (September 1936) of Bukharin and Rykov on charges arising out of the earlier trials of the 'Sixteen'. This acquittal is often seen as the trigger of the third and greatest wave of purges. Among its first victims was Yagoda, head of the NKVD. One of the first tasks of his successor, Yezhov, was the preparation of renewed charges of treason and espionage against Bukharin and Rykov. The fact that the commander-in-chief of the Red Army, Marshal Tukhachevsky, and several other senior officers, were also tried and shot (June 1937) for plotting with Japan and Germany, indicated that the armed forces too were about to be 'cleansed'.

The last great series of show trials ran into 1938, involving the condemnation of 21 prominent Bolsheviks including Bukharin and Rykov. These, however, were merely the tip of the iceberg of suspicion and implication that involved the friends, families and subordinates of the accused. Suspicion reached into every area of Soviet life. No reliable figures as to the extent of the purges are possible, of course. It is extremely unlikely that the total number of deaths can be estimated at less than hundreds of thousands, while the total population of the USSR's penal camps by 1940 has sometimes been set as high as ten million.

K The purges: results

The establishment of a Stalinist élite

When the great tide of political persecution receded in 1938, ending with the execution of Yezhov and other NKVD functionaries, two major changes in Soviet government were discernible. Firstly, the political position of Stalin himself was almost unchallengeable. All possible sources of opposition, in the party, in the armed forces, among economic and political theorists, had been crushed. 'Every man in the Politburo,' wrote Leonard Schapiro, 'was a tried and proved follower of the leader, who could be relied upon to support him through every twist and turn of policy . . . Below the Politburo nothing counted.' Secondly, the Soviet communist party, which had borne the brunt of the purges, was transformed. It was not just a matter of personnel, a substitution of

Zhdanov, Khrushchev, Voroshilov and Molotov for Zinoviev, Kamenev, Bukharin and Rykov. Stalin had effectively destroyed the revolutionary generation of Russian communists. Over 90 of the 139 Central Committee members in 1934 were shot. In the same year, of 1,961 delegates to the 17th Party Congress, 1,108 were arrested in the purges.

Foreign communists living in Russia also suffered heavily, the Hungarian revolutionary leader Béla Kun figuring among the victims of the NKVD. Of Lenin's Politburo, only Stalin and Trotsky remained alive, the latter under sentence of death passed in his absence. Stalin knew, Deutscher has explained, 'that the older generation of revolutionaries would always look upon him as a falsifier of first truths, and usurper. He now appealed to the young generation which knew little or nothing about the pristine ideas of Bolshevism and was unwilling to be bothered about them'. A generation of officials, in short, replaced a generation of revolutionaries.

The impact of the purges upon Soviet security

Apart from the human cost, the whole security of the Soviet Union was nearly undermined as the price of this transformation. The Red Army in particular paid a terrible price for arousing Stalin's mistrust. Three marshals out of five, and 13 army commanders out of 15 died. Ninety per cent of all Soviet generals, 80 per cent of all colonels, and an estimated 30,000 officers below the rank of colonel lost their posts and often their lives. The difficulties experienced in the 'Winter War' with Finland in 1939–40 may be traced directly to the loss of so much military expertise in the purges.

The foreign relations of the Soviet Union were also bound to be adversely affected, for foreign powers were offered the alternatives of viewing the Soviet Union as a state riddled with treason, if the charges against purge victims were accurate, or as a power led by a madman if the charges were false. Lastly, the less tangible legacy of the purges may be traced today in the insularity and siege mentality natural in people led to believe that their society was under assault from capitalists, fascists, imperialists and renegade communists alike. This legacy also survived for years in 'a grotesque fear of initiative and responsibility in all grades of the administration' (Deutscher). This was a direct result of the personal peril that accompanied any position of responsibility during the years of Stalin's purges.

L The 1936 Constitution

The significance of the new constitution

'Stalin,' Deutscher wrote, 'offered the people a mixed diet of terror and illusion.' Alongside the terror of the purges he created the illusion of a true dawn of socialism by the formulation of a new Soviet constitution in 1936. The theoretical basis of the document was the assumption that victory over the Kulaks had ended the decade and a half of class struggle in Russia and that a truly socialist order had now been constructed.

Although couched in familiar liberal terminology, the Stalin Constitution had very different aims. Primarily, it sought to protect, not the rights of the individual, but the continuity of the Soviet system. Secondly, it sought to impress foreign opinion at a time when democratic institutions in the west were under severe pressure from fascism, and in this it achieved no mean success. Also, as A. Ulam has pointed out, the constitution should be seen as part of Stalin's desire to show that the USSR had emerged from her period of revolutionary buffetings. 'For him the constitution was a welcome proof that the USSR was becoming a "respectable state".' In addition, the purges appeared to discard much of Bolshevism's revolutionary past.

Government and the rights of the individual

By comparison with its predecessor, the 'Stalin Constitution' extended the jurisdiction of the central, federal government. Moscow now exercised control, through All-Union ministries, over all important areas of administration, such as defence and foreign affairs, leaving to the constituent republics responsibility for such relatively minor matters as elementary education. This dominance was confirmed by Moscow's overall control of the budget, and by the pervasive influence of the party. The chief legislative body of the USSR continued to be the Supreme Soviet, whose Presidium continued to exercise all major executive functions of the state. As a further indication of the end of class warfare, clergymen, former Tsarist officials, and so on, now enjoyed full civil rights again.

Among the rights now guaranteed to Soviet citizens were the freedom of speech, of the press and of association, along with the rights to work, to rest and leisure, to education, and to maintenance in old age and in sickness. The constitution stated quite clearly, however, that these rights existed only if exercised 'in conformity with the interests of the working people and in order to strengthen the socialist system'.

M The bases of Soviet society

Soviet educational achievements

Overall, the educational achievement of the Soviet government between the wars was impressive. The introduction of compulsory primary education (July 1930) resulted in the doubling of the Soviet Union's primary school population, from nine million to 18 million, between 1920 and 1933. Meanwhile, the number of secondary pupils rose from 0.5 million (1922) to 3.5 million (1933). In 1941, the total school population of the USSR was around 35 million. The greatest achievement was the victory over the traditional peasant curse of illiteracy. This afflicted 75 per cent of the population in 1917, but was rare by the outbreak of the Second World War, by which time 70,000 public libraries had opened in the Soviet Union.

Who received this education? The drive to educate children of working-class origin to the exclusion of others was abandoned in the early 1930s to meet the demands of the Five-Year Plan. The proportion of women in higher education rose sharply, and by 1940, 58 per cent of all higher education places (40 per cent in engineering and 46 per cent in agriculture) were held by females. The nationalities of the USSR, on the other hand, were not evenly represented, and in the course of the 1930s, Russians, Ukrainians and Jews accounted for 80 per cent of all the places in higher education.

The family

As social stability became the government's priority, the family began to revert to its traditional role. As an institution it had been under severe pressure in the 1920s, from revolutionary notions such as free love, free divorce and legalised abortions. It was also under pressure from the efforts of such party organisations as the Communist League of Youth (*Komsomol*), to divert the allegiance of the young. A fall in the official birthrate, and a rise in crime figures prompted an official change of course. Decrees, such as that which established parental responsibility for the misdemeanours of their children (May 1935), and that which made abortion illegal except upon medical grounds (June 1936), reinstated the family as the basis of society. The role of the mother was also traditionalised by a system of rewards for child-bearing. A mother of five children received the 'medal of motherhood', while the mother of ten became a 'mother heroine'.

Religion and the state

The most serious opposition to the Bolsheviks in their attempts to create a new society had come from established religions, especially from the Orthodox Church. Marxists could not easily tolerate a philosophy that stressed the importance of the next world at the expense of material conditions in this one. On the other hand, the creation of martyrs was counter productive. It was assumed that religious belief, being a feature of the old society, would lose all purpose as the new society took shape. The Soviet compromise was thus to strip the churches of all material possessions and of all state power, but to enshrine in successive constitutions the right to freedom of worship, alongside the right to have no religious beliefs at all. Thus, in 1918, Church and state were formally separated. This involved the confiscation of all Church property, but allowed congregations to lease back buildings from the state, and to maintain priests for their worship. In 1921 public religious instruction was declared illegal for all citizens under 18 years of age, and churchmen were deprived of civil rights as 'non-productive workers'. After an initial period of overt resistance, which saw the imprisonment of religious leaders for anti-communist utterances, and for refusal to surrender Church property. The Orthodox Church and most other communities settled into a period of uneasy co-existence with the Soviet regime. Undoubtedly the political influence of the Orthodox Church was broken. There is much evidence to suggest, however, that its spiritual influence survived, diminished, but unbroken. The Orthodox Church received its reward for its patience during the war years of 1941–45, when the need for national unity caused the government to restore some of its former autonomy.

N Soviet foreign policy aims

The theory of communist foreign policy
In the immediate aftermath of the October Revolution, many Soviet theorists did not anticipate any problems in the formulation of foreign policy. In their view the Russian revolution was the forerunner of the general collapse of capitalism, and the end of international tensions and disputes which were the product of capitalist rivalries. Instead, in the next three years they witnessed the traumas of civil war and of foreign intervention. To this was added the total failure of those communists who, in Germany and in Hungary, attempted to follow the Russian example. By the conclusion of the peace treaties in Paris, Russia's international situation was precarious in the extreme. She was isolated, surrounded by hostile powers, and in great economic difficulties. Thus, the central aim of Soviet foreign policy between the wars was simple and singular: it was survival.

Two principal routes to survival suggested themselves in the 1920s. For Trotsky, and for many others on the left of the Bolshevik party, the favoured foreign policy was collaboration with foreign revolutionaries to undermine the strength of the capitalist regimes. The consolidation of Stalin's power, however, saw an irreversible drift away from this internationalism. In foreign as in domestic policies, Stalin saw the best hope for Soviet survival in the development of material strength. Where normal co-existence with capitalist states served Soviet interests, he was quite willing to countenance it.

Communist foreign policy in practice, 1921–29
The fact remained that the Soviet Union had no natural allies, no states with whom she had an overall community of interests, among the European powers. They remained capitalist powers and, in G. F. Kennan's words, 'the enmity Stalin bore towards the western bourgeois world was no less fierce than that of Lenin'. Thus, Soviet contacts with Britain and with France remained ambiguous. The declaration of G. V. Chicherin, commissar for foreign affairs (October 1921), that Russia was willing to recognise and honour Tsarist debts to other powers, helped to counteract initial hostility. In the years that followed, the Soviet government

secured several important benefits from the victorious powers. A trade agreement was secured with Britain in March 1921, and official recognition of the Soviet regime was forthcoming from Britain, France and Italy in 1924. Mutual suspicion of long-term motives, however, made closer relations impossible. The incident of the so-called 'Zinoviev Letter', purporting to contain instructions to British agitators for political and economic disruption (October 1924) from the prominent Bolshevik and chairman of Comintern, showed the fragility of Soviet credibility. Although it was never proved genuine, many conservatives remained convinced that Russia still harboured ambitions for international revolution. Indeed, between 1927 and 1929, all official relations between Britain and the Soviet Union were severed.

The Treaty of Rapallo
Superficially, the greatest successes for Soviet diplomacy were scored in dealings with Germany. In the short term, the signature of the Treaty of Rapallo (April 1922) seemed a triumph. The establishment of full diplomatic relations with Germany ended Soviet isolation and ensured that Germany would drop claims for the repayment of Tsarist debts. The military and economic advice gained from Germany was invaluable in the post-revolutionary chaos. In the longer term, however, the appearance of triumph was deceptive. Rapallo provided a sharp shock to the allies, and their persistent assumption that it concealed a deeper relationship between Germany and the Soviet Union soured Soviet relations with the west until 1941. Furthermore. Rapallo was not an alliance, but merely an arrangement momentarily useful to two isolated and apprehensive states. Russian relations with Germany continued to see-saw for a decade afterwards. Germany's apparent integration into the Versailles 'system', through the Locarno Pact and the Dawes Plan, could be interpreted in Moscow as evidence of growing capitalist solidarity. Conversely, incidents such as the failed communist rising in Germany in October 1923 served to renew fears of revolutionary internationalism.

Stalin's reaction to Nazism
Although, in retrospect, the rise of Adolf Hitler was a turning point in Soviet–German relations, it does not seem that Stalin was immediately aware of

the fact. Contemporary Japanese expansion in China probably made it unclear whether the greater threat to Soviet territory lay in the west or in the east. 'To him,' Isaac Deutscher has written, 'Hitler was merely one of the many reactionary leaders whom the political see-saw throws up for a moment, another Brüning or Papen, another Baldwin or Harding.' Nazism, in the view of Soviet theorists, was no new phenomenon. It was the inevitable death agony of capitalism caused by the recent economic crisis. To seek allies among the capitalist powers against a purely capitalist threat would thus be absurd. It is not clear at what point Stalin changed his view of Nazism. Several commentators have attached great importance to the non-aggression pact between Germany and Poland in January 1934. This suggested that, whatever the nature of Nazism, it was making common cause with Russia's enemies to threaten the domestic security of the Soviet Union.

Certainly 1934 saw a major change in the tactics of Soviet diplomacy. Firstly, the Soviet Union showed great interest once more in understandings with western states, concluding mutual assistance pacts with Czechoslovakia and France (May 1935). In the course of these negotiations the USSR also undertook to enter the League of Nations (September 1934). We may conclude that Soviet motives included a desire to scare Hitler into a revision of aggressive plans. They also wanted to ensure that, if he did precipitate a conflict, it would be fought on several fronts, and not concentrated against the USSR. Lastly, the nature of Moscow's advice to foreign communist parties changed radically. After a decade in which they had been consistently instructed that socialists and social democrats were capitalist allies and false friends, they now found themselves advised and instructed to form 'popular front' alliances with those parties. This would present more effective opposition to the real enemy, fascism.

Questions

Essay questions

1 'Lenin was more responsible than was Stalin for the emergence of totalitarian government in the USSR.' Discuss this view. (ULEAC)

2 Why, and with what results before 1941, did Stalin adopt a policy of 'terror' in the USSR? (UCLES)

3 To what extent was Stalin's pre-eminence based on violence? (Oxford Entrance)

4 'The Soviet state gained but the Soviet people lost as a consequence of the economic policies pursued by Stalin in the period 1928–1945.' Discuss this statement. (NEAB)

5 Assess (a) the similarities and (b) the differences between Tsarist and Bolshevik rule in Russia in the period c.1900–1929. (AEB)

6a Who were Stalin's rivals for the leadership of the USSR after the death of Lenin? [4]

b Explain the policies of one of these rivals. [5]

c To what extent did Stalin share the policies of his rivals? [7]

d Was the 'Great Terror' of the 1930s really necessary? [9] (WJEC)

The Peasantry in Russia and the Soviet Union, 1918–33

Study Sources 1 to 7 and then answer all the questions that follow.

Source 1. Lenin on the peasantry

Coercion would ruin the whole cause. Prolonged educational work is required. . . . We do encourage communes (collectives) but they must be so organised as to gain the confidence of the peasants. . . . The aim is not to expropriate the middle peasant, but to . . . learn from him methods of transition to a better system, and not to dare to give orders!

From a report by Lenin to the 8th Congress of the Party (March 1919).

Source 2. Peasant discontent

The peasant uprisings develop because of widespread dissatisfaction on the part of small property-owners in the countryside with the dictatorship of the proletariat, which directs at them the cutting edge of implacable compulsion. The Soviet regime is . . . identified with flying visits by commissars. . . . In the countryside the Soviet regime is still predominantly military-administrative rather than economic in character. . . . In the eyes of the peasants it is tyrannical and not a system that, before all else, organises and ministers to the countryside itself.

Report sent to Lenin by the head of the CHEKA in Tambov province (20 July 1921)

Source 3. Bukharin on the peasantry

The Kulak is discontented with us because we are preventing him from accumulating. At the same time, the poor peasants sometimes grumble against us because we do not let them take employment as agricultural workers in the service of that same Kulak. . ... Our policy . .. should develop towards a reduction and partial abolition of the many restrictions which hold back the growth of the farms belonging to the well-to-do peasant. . . . We ought to say to the peasants, to all the peasants: get rich, develop your farms. . . . Paradoxical as it may seem, we must develop the farm of the well-to-do peasant so as to help the poor peasant and the middle peasant.

From a speech by Bukharin printed in Pravda (17 April 1925)

Source 4. Stalin on the peasantry and the Party

Our Party's growth in the countryside is terribly slow. I do not mean to say that it ought to grow by leaps and bounds, but the percentage of the peasantry that we have in the Party is, after all, very insignificant. Our Party is a workers' party. . . . But it is also clear that without an alliance with the peasantry the dictatorship of the proletariat is impossible, that the Party must have a certain percentage of the best people among the peasantry in its ranks.

From a speech by Stalin (1927)

Source 5. Stalin on collectivisation

A great deal of work has still to be done to remould the peasant collective farmer, to set right his individualistic mentality and to transform him into a real working member of a socialist society. And the more rapidly the collective farms are provided with machines, the more rapidly this will be achieved. . . . The greatest importance of the collective farms lies precisely in that they represent the principal base for the employment of machinery and tractors in agriculture, that they constitute the principal base for remoulding the peasant, for changing his mentality in the spirit of socialism.

From Stalin's speech 'Concerning Questions of Agrarian Policy in the USSR' (December 1929)

Source 6. Stalin on the pace of collectivisation

By February this year 50 per cent of the peasant farms throughout the USSR had been collectivised. . . . But successes have their seamy side. . . . People not infrequently become intoxicated by such successes; they become dizzy with success, lose all sense of proportion and the capacity to understand realities. . . . Collective farms must not be established by force. That would be foolish and reactionary. The collective farm movement must rest on the active support of the main mass of the peasantry. . . . In a number of areas of Turkestan there have already been attempts to 'overtake and outstrip' the advanced areas of the USSR by threatening to use armed force. . . . How could there have arisen in our midst such block-headed exercises in 'socialisation', such ludicrous attempts to overleap oneself?

From a speech by Stalin printed in Pravda *(2 March 1930)*

Source 7. A Soviet historian's view of collectivisation

The transition to solid collectivisation signified a radical turn of the bulk of the peasantry toward socialism. The working peasantry was abandoning the old path of development which spontaneously engendered capitalism and led to the enslavement of the poor and middle peasants by the Kulaks. Eventually the Kulaks were completely expropriated. This was the only way to deal with the Kulaks. In this process, however, there were also unhealthy signs; above all, the Leninist voluntary principle of forming collective farms was being violated. The Kulaks and their toadies tried to take advantage of this mistake, and as a result of their hostile actions, animal husbandry in the USSR suffered a heavy loss.

Adapted from History of the Communist Party of the Soviet Union *by B. Ponomaryov (1960)*

---

a　Using Source 2 and your own knowledge, explain the attitudes of the peasantry towards the Soviet regime, as described in Source 2. [5]

b　Using Source 3 and your own knowledge, explain why Bukharin's speech (Source 3) aroused controversy within the Communist Party. [5]

c　Compare the attitudes towards the peasantry expressed in Sources 1,4 and 5. [5]

d　Discuss the value and limitations of Source 6 for an understanding of Stalin's policy towards the peasantry. [6]

e　Using the evidence of Sources 1 to 7, examine the judgement that the problems posed by the peasantry for the Soviet Government between 1918 and 1932 were political rather than economic. [9]

(AEB)

14
Democracy in crisis

'The March of Hunger', a painting by Hans Grundig (1932).

Who is catered for by the 'Republic Cafe' and who is excluded?

Grundig's criticism is aimed specifically at the German Republic. How valid would his criticism be of the republics in France and in Spain?

The belief and hope of the western allies that the defeat and collapse of three autocratic Empires would create a 'world safe for democracy' was soon to prove an illusion. The end of the World War proved to be the opening of two decades in which parliamentary democracy was to be shaken to its foundations.

A   Germany: the birth of the Weimar Republic

Political forces in the Republic

Republican government in Germany was born (9 November 1918) under the most inauspicious circumstances. Quite apart from the imminent collapse of the war effort, and the abdication of the Kaiser, the fleet was in mutiny at Kiel and at Wilhelmshaven. Soldiers' and workers' councils had appeared in Berlin, in Cologne, and in Munich where a Bavarian republic was declared. The very name by which the German republic is commonly known derived from the fact that the dangerous condition of the capital in 1919 obliged the newly elected National Assembly to meet in the small provincial town of Weimar. The earlier failure of successive emergency governments, the desire of many conservatives to present a liberal front to the allies, and the radical nature of much anti-government agitation, all placed the Social Democratic Party (SPD) in the van of events. The shape of the Weimar Republic was to be determined by the state and aims of that party.

The German socialist movement was deeply divided. An Independent Social Democratic Party (USPD) had broken away from the SPD (April 1917), and a more extreme Communist Party (KPD) had been formed in November 1918. While the communists advocated seizure of power and implementation of radical programmes, the SPD followed the lead of its chief, Friedrich Ebert, in preferring peaceful and democratic change through an elected assembly. The non-revolutionary nature of Ebert's government was confirmed on the first day of the republic's life, when he accepted General Groener's offer of army assistance against the forces of the left. His decision undoubtedly strengthened his government by its alliance with such a traditional and respected force. A. J. Nicholls has written that he possibly saved Germany from the intervention of allied troops. Naturally, however, it drew fierce criticism from the left. This criticism increased during the next few weeks when army units, aided by a newly formed Volunteer Corps (*Freikorps*) bloodily suppressed a communist ('Spartacist') rising in Berlin (January 1919) and dispersed the 'Soviet' that had briefly held power in Munich (April 1919). Thus, while the republic came into existence over the corpses of some of its enemies, it owed that passage to a force that was merely a temporary ally. In the light of subsequent events, it was ominous that Groener had made no promise to protect the Republic from the forces of the right.

The Weimar constitution

The elections to the National Assembly (January 1919) placed the SPD at the head of the poll, but without an overall majority. It was thus obliged to enter a coalition with the Centre Party and the Democratic Party (DDP), a move which was to characterise the fragmented political life of the Weimar Republic. The constitution drafted by the Assembly (July 1919) nevertheless represented a considerable democratic advance since 1914. It designated the Reichstag as the sovereign authority of the state, and decreed that it should be elected every four years by proportional representation, by all men and women over twenty-one years of age. The President, elected every seven years, was to be subject to the authority of the Reichstag, although he also possessed special powers for use in a national emergency. A further outstanding break with the principles of the Bismarckian constitution concerned the powers of the upper house (*Reichsrat*). This continued to represent the interests of the component parts of the federal state, but was now subservient in all respects to the Reichstag. These component parts, instead of existing as sovereign kingdoms or duchies, were now designated merely as provinces (*länder*).

A vigorous historical debate has surrounded the events of 1918–19 and their true significance. For A. J. Nicholls they represented a true democratic advance for Germany, bringing peace and a more genuinely representative system in place of the parliamentary 'charades' of Bismarck's time. Yet to Gordon Craig these events constituted an 'aborted revolution' which failed to change basic political attitudes and prejudices, and which thus condemned the Republic to failure in the long run. J. W. Hiden has compromised between the two views, seeing the 1919 constitution, like the preceding events, as 'a synthesis between progressive political and social ideas and the desire to protect traditional institutions'.

B Germany: the Republic and the Versailles Treaty

As imminent defeat in war brought the Republic into being, so its most pressing task was the conclusion of peace. In this task, its freedom of action was virtually nil. The military chiefs advised that continuation of hostilities was impossible, and forced to accept the allies' dictated terms as the only alternative to invasion, the Republic inherited a legacy of bitterness and resentment at its actions. German hopes that peace would be based upon Woodrow Wilson's 'Fourteen Points', and that the replacement of the Kaiser by social democracy would incline the allies to leniency, proved wholly misplaced. The terms (*see* Chapter 17, section **A**) that the Republican ministers Müller and Bell finally accepted caused widespread resentment. Germany would not be accepted into the community of the League of Nations, she lost eastern territories to states that could not pretend to have defeated her, and in future German industry would pass on the fruits of its labours in the form of reparations to foreign capitalists. Worse, it was claimed that the German armies had not been defeated by the enemy, but betrayed by the secret enemy, the socialist and the Jew, at home. The myth of the 'Stab in the Back' (*Dolchstoss*) was born.

Despite the widespread feeling that 'the true basis of the Republic is not the Weimar Constitution but the Treaty of Versailles', it is not fair to imagine that the regime was doomed by the circumstances of its birth. For all its losses, republican Germany still had potentially the strongest economy in Europe, and her recovery was rapid. The political demoralisation caused by Versailles was more serious, for it not only guaranteed a constant right-wing opposition to the Republic, but also undermined the initial enthusiasm of more moderate patriots for the regime. The future of the Weimar Republic, therefore, depended upon surviving long enough for such passions to cool.

C Germany: the enemies of the Weimar Republic

Opponents on the left

The passage of the Weimar Constitution by 262 votes to 75, and the success of the centrist parties in the elections of 1919, should not obscure the substantial hostility in Germany to the new regime. The election result, E. Troeltsch has explained, was not really a vote of confidence, for 'this democracy was in essence an anti-revolutionary system, dedicated to the maintenance of order and opposed to the dictatorship of the proletariat'.

On the left extreme of the Republic's enemies stood the KPD, separated from the regime by a gulf of bitterness formed during the risings of 1919, and by the brutal murders of communist leaders Karl Liebknecht and Rosa Luxemburg by *Freikorps* men. By December 1920, when its decision to join the International (the International Organisation of Communist and Socialist Parties) attracted many converts from the Independent Social Democrats, the KPD could boast a membership of 400,000 with 33 daily newspapers at its disposal. Although closely tied to a pro-Moscow policy by the leadership of Ernst Thälmann (1925–33), the party pursued a cautious policy, preferring the steady consolidation of strength, membership and influence to further adventures on the lines of 1919. Its achievement was, however, unimpressive. It failed to win any great influence among the trades unions, and alienated many potential supporters by its pro-Soviet stance. Nevertheless, the hostility between communists and social democrats continued into the next decade and helps explain the failure of the left in Germany to resist the rise of Nazism.

Opponents on the right

A more daunting array of opponents lay to the right of the Republic. The nationalists, grouped especially around the German National People's Party (DNVP) represented the brand of conservatism that hankered after the principles and institutions of Wilhelmine Germany. The DNVP had especially influential support in the civil service, in the judiciary, among industrialists, and in the Churches. Indeed, the hostility of the legal system towards the Republic, shown in the lenient sentences passed against right-wing terrorists and insurgents, has been described by K. S. Pinson as 'one of the most shameful chapters in the history of that epoch'. The nationalist threat to the regime was, nevertheless, limited by several factors. The leadership of the DNVP was divided over the issue of co-operation with the republican regime, and the whole stress of the party's policies was laid upon principles partly compromised by the defeat of the old Germany in 1914–18.

The Nazi party

In the course of the later 1920s the nationalists began to surrender the leadership of the right-wing opposition to the National Socialist German Workers' Party (NSDAP or 'Nazis'), the most successful of the *völkisch* groups that appeared on the right of German politics. They laid their stress upon the concept of race (*volk)*, preaching the superiority of the German racial characteristics and culture, and the need to protect them against alien influences, especially the insidious influence of the Jews. Founded in 1919 by Anton Drexler, but soon dominated by the determined and brilliant orator Adolf Hitler, the Nazis came close to ruin in their early life by placing their trust in a policy of insurrection (*putschism*). This resulted in public discredit and the imprisonment of their leaders.

Although the subsequent change of emphasis, whereby the NSDAP now sought power by parliamentary means, led to poor results, the party had hidden strengths. Its local organisation, although uneven, was especially strong in Bavaria. Elsewhere it employed some notable local leaders such as Gregor Strasser and Julius Streicher, who ensured tight local discipline.

It also deployed a powerful paramilitary force, the Stormtroopers (*Sturmabteilung* or SA), which proved more than a match for its communist rivals in the street violence that scarred the political life of the Weimar Republic. Lastly, its wide policy appealed to the resentments of the defeated Germans, both 'national' and 'socialist'. Although this policy had little success in the years of republican prosperity, it promised to serve the party well should Germany once more fall upon hard times.

The army

It is open to dispute whether the German Army (*Reichswehr*), in its reduced post-Versailles form,

should be listed among the Republic's enemies. Although it had done much to enable the Weimar government to survive its first weeks, there was much in the principles of the traditional officer class, which still drew 21 per cent of its membership from the nobility, that was at odds with the philosophy of the social-democratic Republic. The view of Hans von Seeckt, chief of Army Command between 1920 and 1926, was that the *Reichswehr* should be an apolitical body, preserving its traditional values above the hurly-burly of party rivalry. Comparison between *Reichswehr* action in 1919, and its refusal to act against army veterans in *Freikorps* units during the Kapp *putsch* (*see* section **D**), clearly showed that its attitude towards the regime was merely lukewarm. In the words of J. W. Hiden, it 'would tolerate the Republic for the time being in its own interests'.

D Germany: the years of crisis, 1920–23

The Kapp *putsch* and the Beerhall *putsch*

In the first months of its life, the Weimar Republic fought for its life against the hostility of the left, surviving by virtue of its temporary allies. In the next four years, however, there was much to maintain the sense of crisis and bitterness. The belated revelation (April 1921) of the magnitude of Germany's commitment in reparation payments to the allies and Matthias Erzberger's plans to strengthen the national economy by taxes upon war profits and upon inherited wealth, combined to stir special resentment on the right. This merged with existing nationalist hostility to subject the Republic to increasing right-wing violence. During those stages of the Republic's life, wrote Gordon Craig, 'its normal state was crisis'.

The first of these violent assaults was the 'Kapp Putsch' (March 1920). Although the attempted *coup d'état* was a symptom of wider right-wing discontent, the immediate trigger was the government's attempt to disband a *Freikorps* unit under Captain Ehrhardt at the request of the allies. Ominously, the *Reichswehr* took up a neutral stance, claiming that 'obviously there can be no talk of letting *Reichswehr* fight against *Reichswehr*'. Kapp's plans were frustrated instead by Berlin workers and civil servants who refused the orders of the insurgents and denied them transport and publicity facilities. Unfortunately, this concerted action was not repeated in later moments of republican peril.

Meanwhile, Germany experienced political violence and assassination unparalleled in her history. The most spectacular examples were the murders of Walter Rathenau, the foreign minister (June 1922) and Matthias Erzberger, former finance minister and one of the leaders of the armistice delegation (August 1921). The final drama of this period of right-wing pressure was played in Munich in November 1923 when Hitler and some Nazi followers attempted to exploit a clash between the reactionary government of Bavaria and the federal authorities to institute a 'March on Berlin' after the style of Mussolini. Resolute police action reduced the so-called 'Beerhall *Putsch*' to fiasco. Taken out of context it would indeed be possible to dismiss the activities of Kapp and Hitler as, in K. S. Pinson's phrase, 'a ludicrous fizzle'. Nevertheless, the derisory sentences passed on the offenders, five years' imprisonment for Hitler and no punishment for any of Ehrhardt's *Freikorps* men, made clear the sympathy in high places for their cause. The Reichstag elections held in June 1920 added further indications of the ascendancy of the right.

Inflation

By the time of Hitler's *putsch*, the Republic had also to confront a more serious threat from another, international, source. The reasons for, and the course of the Franco–Belgian occupation of the Ruhr in January 1923 are described elsewhere (*see* Chapter 17, section **D**). Here we have mainly to consider the domestic effects of that action upon Germany. The most sensational of these was the acceleration of the decline of the Reichsmark that had been in progress since the war. The initial blame lay, not with the French invasion, but with the crippling cost of the war, the pressure of reparation demands, and the sad policy of the Republic of printing money to meet resultant budget deficits. As Table 14.1 shows, the decline now raced out of control. Apart from its role in the origins of the inflation, the government bore some responsibility for not checking it at an early stage. 'Cheap money' had its attractions for the industrialist who now found plant and wages cheap, and for the landowner whose mortgages were easier to pay off. Some enormous fortunes, of which the greatest

was perhaps that of the industrialist Hugo Stinnes, were forged out of the financial chaos. Inflation had no consolations for the small saver or investor whose carefully accumulated sums and guaranteed interest became worthless in a matter of days.

The collapse of the value of pensions and savings ruined many, and the number of recipients of public relief in 1923 was three times that in 1913. 'Millions of Germans', wrote Gordon Craig, 'who had passively accepted the transition from Empire to Republic suffered deprivations that shattered their faith in the democratic process and left them cynical and alienated'. As a further ominous by-product many trades unions, unable in the crisis to protect their members' interests, suffered a sharp drop in their rolls and in their political influence.

Table 14.1 Value of mark against the US dollar

July 1914	4.2
July 1919	14.0
July 1920	39.5
July 1921	76.7
July 1922	493.2
Jan. 1923	17,972.0
July 1923	353,412.0
Aug. 1923	4,620,455.0
Sept. 1923	98,860,000.0
Oct. 1923	25,260,208,000.0
15 Nov. 1923	4,200,000,000,000.0

From: Gordon Craig, *Germany 1866–1945*, Oxford.

E Germany: the prime of the Weimar Republic, 1924–29

Gustav Stresemann and Paul von Hindenburg

The Weimar Republic not only survived, but launched out upon the most successful period of its life, a period when long-term survival at last seemed possible. Two factors contributed greatly to this recovery. For the first time, the Republic had at its head men who commanded substantial respect.

The fall of the broken Chancellor Cuno (August 1923) brought into office the major political figure of the Republic. Gustav Stresemann's political apprenticeship had been served in nationalist and militarist circles but, despite his initial sympathy with the Kapp insurgents in 1920, he had been shocked by the growth of political violence and instability in Germany. He became republican because he was horrified by the alternatives. His political background, nevertheless, made him acceptable to many who could barely tolerate his predecessors. Although Chancellor for only three months, he continued to exert a profound influence upon German politics from the foreign ministry until his death in 1929.

The earlier death (February 1925) of Ebert brought to the presidency of the Republic the wartime hero Field Marshal Paul von Hindenburg, a man of impeccable patriotic credentials. His election was to a large extent a statement of nostalgia for the stability and strength of the 'old' Germany. 'The truth is,' stated Stresemann, 'that Germans want no president in a top hat. He must wear a military uniform and plenty of decorations.' Hindenburg, however, wore both his uniform and his office with tact, and effectively defended the Republic from the worst barbs of its right-wing opponents. The second vital factor in the recovery of the Republic was the urgent desire of the former wartime allies to prevent the collapse or political disintegration of Germany. Foreign co-operation was central to the regime's new lease of life.

The achievement of financial stability

The first achievements of the revivified Republic were the rescue of the German currency and the regularisation of the reparations question. At the end of 1923, thanks to the work of Hans Luther at the Ministry of Finance, the discredited mark was replaced by the so-called 'Rentenmark'. In the absence of sufficient gold reserves, the new currency was backed in theory by Germany's agricultural and industrial resources. It was a novel, and largely fictitious form of security, which relied heavily upon foreign goodwill for its general acceptance. There was enough of this goodwill not only to support the stabilisation of the currency, but also to regulate the question of Germany's reparation payments through the formulation of the Dawes Plan (*see* Chapter 17, section **E**) in 1924.

Outwardly, the German economy presented a picture in the later 1920s of stability and prosperity. The emergence of giant industrial combines such as I. G. Farben and United Steelworks (*Vereinigte Stahlwerke*) in 1926 seemed to testify to the renewed dynamism of German heavy industry, while in 1927 overall production figures at last matched those of 1913.

The achievement of political stability

Financial stability was accompanied by a greater degree of political stability. Apart from the relative acceptability of Stresemann and Hindenburg, the economic recovery blunted nationalist opposition to the Republic by appeasing the industrialists who played a substantial role in the DNVP. The armed forces, too, seemed to be on better terms with the Republic after the resignation of von Seeckt (October 1926) as commander of the *Wehrmacht*. After the appointment of General Groener (December 1927) as defence minister, 1928–29 provided two pieces of electoral comfort for the government. The Reichstag elections in May 1928 provided the worst results for a decade for the parties of the political extremes. Between them the DNVP (14.2 per cent), the NSDAP (2.6 per cent) and the KDP (10.6 per cent) secured less than 30 per cent of the popular vote. In December 1929 there was a referendum forced by a coalition of nationalists and Nazis, trying to condemn the Young Plan and propose treason charges against the government for trafficking with foreign interests. It received only 13.8 per cent of the votes cast.

Surviving weaknesses of the Republic

Yet the Republic still had its weaknesses. It seemed to be winning the public relations battle, but it had established few durable institutions to sustain it in time of crisis. The lukewarm toleration of the regime shown by the *Reichswehr* was not generally imitated by the civil service, the universities or the schools. K. S. Pinson has described in detail the atmosphere of German education in the 1920s. 'The essential control of both lower and higher education remained in the hands of those who had nothing but contempt for the Republic and who therefore made no effort to prepare the German youth for republican citizenship. Not a single school text in Weimar Germany presented the true story of German defeat in 1918. German geography texts still inculcated in the minds of the young the definition that Germany was a country surrounded on all sides by enemies.'

Neither had the Republic developed a system of parliamentary parties strong enough to give stability to its democracy. The classic Weimar coalition parties, the Social Democrats, the Democratic Party and the Centre Party, remained divided on many points of economic, political and religious doctrine. Their lack of cohesion in the face of the rise of a popular anti-democratic movement would play a major role in the disasters of the early 1930s. Lastly, for all the appearances of superficial prosperity, the basis of the German economy was essentially unsound. Industrial investment and government expenses were not adequately financed from German capital or German profits. More than a third of all capital invested in the late 1920s came from foreign loans. Imports, between 1924 and 1930, were always greater than exports. The total deficit on the German budget over those years amounted to nearly 1.3 billion Reichmarks. It is impossible to deny that in 1924–29 the Weimar Republic was progressing and achieving some of the attributes of permanency. In that limited period, however, as Hajo Holborn has put it, 'normalcy was never quite achieved, and even the period when it appeared close at hand proved only a belief interlude between two disasters'.

F   Germany: foreign affairs

German affairs were a central factor in the development of international relations between the world wars, and are thus described in detail elsewhere (*see* Chapter 17). In the context of the Weimar Republic, however, it is useful to establish separately the essential aims of German policy in the 1920s.

The 'policy of fulfilment'

For most Germans,' writes John Hiden, 'foreign policy meant an unremitting effort to revise the terms of the Treaty of Versailles.' In addition to the material deprivation suffered as a result of the Treaty, successive German governments sought also to remedy the dangerous diplomatic isolation that resulted from defeat, and to restore the degree of national independence lost to the allies and their occupation agencies. The first method was the simple tactic of sullen obstruction. Hence the clauses of the Treaty aimed against the Kaiser and other alleged war criminals were never effectively enforced. The disbanding of paramilitary organisations was slow and unreliable, and the clauses relating to disarmament and to reparations were implemented only with constant allied supervision. Such a policy could not long be successful against

opponents with both the determination and the means to enforce the treaty terms, and could only lead to disasters such as the occupation of the Ruhr. German policy thus changed under the chancellorship of Joseph Wirth (May 1921–November 1922) to one of 'fulfilment' (*Erfüllungspolitik*). This apparent co-operation with the allies was one of the greatest causes of bitterness among the right-wing opponents of the regime, and played a direct role in stirring the political violence of the period.

It was, nevertheless, a sensible and realistic policy, based upon the recognition that 'the realities of the European situation made patience, ambiguity and opportunism requirements of Germany foreign policy' (Gordon Craig). It was designed to encourage future allied leniency towards Germany. Its introduction coincided with a successful solution to the problem of diplomatic isolation. The conclusion of the Treaty of Rapallo with the Soviet Union in April 1922 (*see* Chapter 13, section **N**), created investment opportunities for Germany, and opened up substantial prospects for evading the military restrictions imposed at Versailles. It may also be argued that it did much, in combination with the chaos caused by the French occupation of the Ruhr, to frighten the western powers into a more reasonable attitude to Germany.

The achievement of *Erfüllungspolitik*

The greatest successes of *Erfüllungspolitik* were achieved during Gustav Stresemann's tenure of the foreign ministry, during which he combined the broad principles of 'fulfilment' with a distinct attempt to lay the foundations for a revision of the peace treaties. He was portrayed by liberal historians as a 'good European', eager to put co-operation in the place of confrontation, and by historians of the Marxist left as a capitalist joining the Locarno Pact for essentially anti-Soviet reasons. The publication of his official papers has indicated that Stresemann was neither of these things. His primary aim was to rid Germany of foreign restraints, and to regain for her full sovereignty and freedom of political action. Thus the Locarno Pact of 1925 (*see* Chapter 17, section **F**) guaranteed Germany's western borders against further incursions, without committing Germany to acceptance of the hated territorial settlement in the east. It also paved the way for Germany's acceptance into the international community of the League of Nations. The agreement of the Dawes Plan in 1924 and the Young Plan in 1929 (*see* Chapter 17, section **C**) were classic examples of the policy of 'fulfilment'. They reduced Germany's total reparation debt, and gained foreign recognition of her difficulties in paying it at all.

Steadily, from January 1926, Germany began to reap the fruits of this policy. In that month, British withdrawal from Cologne marked the first major reduction of the occupying forces. This was followed in January 1927 by the withdrawal from Germany of the Inter-Allied Control Commission, the major 'watchdog' of the Versailles terms. Before the fall of the Republic, the evacuation of foreign troops was completed by the French withdrawal (August 1929). The continuation of reparation payments had been dealt a near mortal blow by Chancellor Brüning's successful application to the United States for a 'Moratorium' (June 1931). No area of policy under the Weimar Republic could claim to rival the success of its foreign policy. Its tragedy was that it failed consistently to convince the zealots of the political extremes of the constructive good sense of that policy. When international economic crisis undermined the Republic, its foreign policy of restrained national reassertion was to be one of the first casualties of its collapse.

G Germany: the collapse of the Weimar Republic

The economic impact of the Wall Street Crash
'Germany,' Stresemann had warned in 1928, 'is dancing on a volcano. If the short-term credits are called in a large section of our economy would collapse.' Indeed, within days of Stresemann's premature death (3 October 1929), the slump of the Wall Street stock market (24 October 1929) triggered off just such a phenomenon. Germany's foreign capital, which had stood at 5 billion marks in 1928, dropped by half in 1929, and shrank to a mere 700 million marks in 1930. Loans began to be called in and bankruptcies multiplied. With the government consistently reluctant to set off a new inflation of the mark, the crisis manifested itself primarily as massive unemployment. The problem had haunted Germany since the recovery of 1925,

with 2 million out of work in the winter of 1925–26 and 1.5 million jobless a year later. The rise towards the catastrophic figures of the Depression began in the summer of 1928. One and a half million were unemployed in mid-1929 and in the following winter the figures soared out of control. Three million were affected in the winter of 1929–30, 5 million by the end of the following summer and 6 million in both January 1932 and January 1933.

The political impact of the crash
The political effect of the economic slump was a substantial revival of extremism. As Table 14.2 indicates, the elections of 1930–32 were marked by the dramatic growth of those parties offering extreme solutions to the contemporary distress. The KPD achieved greater support than it had ever had before, but above all it was the Nazis that benefited from the economic tragedy.

Table 14.2 Elections to the Reichstag, 1919–32

	Jan 1919	June 1920	May 1924	Dec 1924	May 1928	Sept 1930	July 1932	Nov 1932
NSDAP	–	–	32	14	12	107	230	196
DNVP	44	71	95	103	73	41	37	52
DVP	19	65	45	51	45	30	7	11
Centre	91	85	81	88	78	87	98	90
DDP	75	39	28	32	25	20	4	2
SPD	165	102	100	131	153	143	133	121
USPD	22	84	–	–	–	–	–	–
KPD	–	4	62	45	54	77	89	100

The rise of the Nazis
The general appeal of the NSDAP is analysed elsewhere (*see* Chapter 16, section **C**), but there can be no doubt of the importance of the crisis in its increasing popularity. The research of Martin Broszat, for example, has established that, of all the working-class recruits joining the Nazi party in 1930–33, some 55 per cent were unemployed. As Alan Bullock wrote of Hitler, when 'disaster cast its shadow over the land again, the despised prophet entered into his inheritance'. Nevertheless, there was nothing inevitable about the Nazi advent to power. They never represented a majority in the Reichstag and their electoral fortunes were in fact in decline by late 1932. Their triumph resulted from the degeneration and miscalculations of republican politics in the years of economic crisis.

Brünings's administration

The resignation of Chancellor Müller's cabinet (March 1930), the Republic's last Social Democrat administration, marked the end of majority government in Germany. As the political parties of the centre continued to place sectional interests before national need, the effective government of the state fell into the hands of President Hindenburg and such advisors as General Groener and General von Schleicher. Their primary aim, predictably, was less the protection of democracy and parliamentarianism than the formation of a more authoritative and authoritarian government to face the economic crisis. Their first choice as Chancellor, Heinrich Brüning, had admirable qualifications for office. He was a social, political and economic conservative, a devout Catholic, a decorated war veteran, and suitably hostile to the principles of social democracy. He sought primarily to cement his administration with some foreign success, such as the suspension of reparation payments, and he tackled Germany's domestic crisis by orthodox, deflationary economic tactics. Reductions in social services and in unemployment benefits, at the time of greatest need, were unlikely to rally wide support. They led to Brüning's reputation as the 'Hunger Chancellor'. They also drove many more unemployed into the ranks of the paramilitary organisations. Meanwhile, military expenditure and subsidies to the Junker farmers were maintained.

Brüning's greatest political error, however, was surely the dissolution of the Reichstag (July 1930) in search of a secure majority. Instead, at a time of mounting crisis, he found the political extremism of the streets translated into Reichstag seats. Continued failure to curb economic depression, and to achieve ministerial stability, finally encouraged the President to replace Brüning with Franz von Papen in May 1932. This was the move which, according to the liberal historian Erich Eyck, 'killed not only the German Republic but the peace of Europe'.

Papen, Schleicher and the advent of the Nazis

Papen's responsibility for the advent of Nazism is great. In June, he raised Brüning's ban on the SA. In July he used the resultant street violence, and the spate of deaths in clashes between Nazis and communists as a pretext to dismiss the Social Democrat provincial government in Prussia, one of the last bastions of democratic government in Germany. Like Brüning before him, his decision to hold new elections (July 1932) played into the hands of the Nazis with their increasing support. Papen's efforts to establish an electoral alliance with Hitler as the junior partner were frustrated, both by Hitler's refusal to accept any office less than that of Chancellor, and by the aged President's personal and social antipathy to the Bavarian upstart. The government had only one alternative to Hitler. When von Schleicher failed in his brief chancellorship (December 1932–January 1933) to split the Nazi leadership by negotiating with Gregor Strasser, Hindenburg at last accepted Hitler as the only alternative to political chaos and possible civil war. He thus became Chancellor on 30 January 1933, with a cabinet of three Nazis and ten conservatives, the latter representing the vain hope of the traditional German right that they might still use the dynamic force of Nazism for their own purposes. A seven-hour torchlight parade by the SA in the streets of Berlin formed the funeral celebrations of the Weimar Republic.

H France: the price of victory

The human cost of the war

The Weimar Republic's heavy burden imposed by defeat was hardly as daunting as the price that France had paid for victory. The human cost of the war could not be measured in numbers alone, although the figures of 1,390,000 dead and 740,000 maimed represented the highest proportional loss of any combatant apart from Serbia. The quality of the losses, and their significance for the future, were even more crippling for the vital generation of young Frenchmen had been shattered. Of every ten men aged between 20–40 years in 1914, as Georges Dupeux has expressed it, 'two had been killed, one had become a burden upon his fellow citizens, and three had been handicapped whether in the short term or long term'. The result, it has been estimated, was a further loss of 1.7 million French citizens through the decline in the birthrate, and the highest proportion of elderly citizens of any European country.

The economic impact of the war

A further casualty of the war was France's

proverbial stability. She had to write off the substantial sums invested in pre-revolutionary Russia, yet remained committed to repay 30 billion francs worth of war debts, owed mainly to the USA. This burden was faced with industrial production reduced by 20 per cent by wartime damage, and a chronically unstable currency. Fearful of public reaction to higher taxation, and largely sharing the public view that in the long run German reparations would pay for the recovery of France, successive governments resorted to the printing presses for the necessary finances, with predictable inflationary results. The total amount of currency in circulation had risen between 1913 and 1920 from 6 billion francs to 38 billion. For all her private wealth, France now became in the inter-war years, in Gordon Wright's phrase, 'a wealthy country chronically on the verge of bankruptcy'.

The recovery of Alsace-Lorraine

Even the great territorial and national gain of the war held its disappointments. The citizens of Alsace-Lorraine, instead of rushing joyfully into the arms of their liberators, showed wide resentment at the increased central control that France now intended to exert over them. Alsatians resisted the extension of anti-clerical legislation to the provinces and opposed attempts to replace their German-based dialect with French as the language of education and administration. The development of an Alsatian autonomist movement in the mid-1920s was strong enough to alarm Parisian politicians and to precipitate political arrests and trials. In every important respect, therefore, there was an ominous accuracy in the judgement of Jules Cambon in 1918 that 'France victorious must grow accustomed to being a lesser power than France vanquished'.

I   France: domestic politics 1919–29; *Bloc* versus *Cartel*

The *Bloc National*

Under such unpromising circumstances, the wartime unity of French politics barely survived the armistice. In the words of H. Tint, 'bourgeois France had one supreme ambition: to return to bourgeois comforts', but the French left, active and militant enough in the pre-war decade, was now galvanised by the Russian revolution. They saw the prospect of a real and probable alternative to bourgeois France.

The response of French conservatives to the challenge of communism was the *Bloc National*, a coalition of centre and right-wing political, financial and industrial groups. They were united, as their manifesto declared, by 'the desire to combine in one vigorous group those workers, employers and employees who refuse at all costs to suffer Bolshevik tyranny'. The result of the 1919 elections, 433 seats for the *Bloc*, 86 for the Radicals and 104 for the Socialists, represented the greatest triumph for the French right since 1871. However, the appearance of national unity and purpose was false. A great part was played in the *Bloc* victory by a curious new electoral system which distributed seats in each department according to the proportion of votes cast for each party's list of candidates. It gave all the seats to any party gaining an overall majority. Thus the system favoured such combinations as the *Bloc*. The euphoria of victory in the world war, and the disunity of the left also inflated the *Bloc*'s triumph. Five years later, after a tenure of office dominated by foreign affairs and post-war economic difficulties, the *Bloc* found that the left too had learned the value of electoral alliances. In 1924, in the aftermath of the occupation of the Ruhr (*see* Chapter 17, section **D**), it was the turn of the *Cartel des Gauches*, an alliance of Radicals and Socialists, to benefit from the electoral system. A very moderate swing in votes, which saw the shares of Radicals and Socialists alike increase by only 0.2 per cent, left their coalition with 266 seats to the *Bloc*'s 229.

The *Cartel des Gauches*

Once again, France was to be frustrated in her hopes for stable and successful parliamentary government. The *Cartel des Gauches*, although it could claim that its conciliatory foreign policy was more successful than the confrontation tactics of the *Bloc*, suffered from two insoluble problems. The first arose from the position of the Socialists within the coalition. They had suffered gravely from the emergence of communism in France. At the Congress of Tours (December 1920), the French communists secured a vote to join the Third Communist International. In doing so they had stripped the Socialists of some 140,000 party members, much of its administrative machinery, and its daily journal *L'Humanité*. Although the communists themselves remained divided and on the fringes of parliamentary politics, the Socialist leader Léon Blum, controlled a rump of some 30,000 members. Unable to risk the alienation of their remaining followers by supporting the Radicals too enthusiastically, the Socialists refused positions in Herriot's Radical cabinet and contented themselves with lukewarm parliamentary co-operation.

The crisis of the franc

There could be no co-operation, however, over the second of the *Cartel*'s problems, which was the increasing weakness of the French currency. On this matter, Socialist and Radical philosophies differed fundamentally. The Socialists favoured positive action such as heavy direct taxation. The Radicals, aware of their support among small businessmen, peasant farmers, and so forth, favoured minimal government intervention. This was a recipe for disaster in the economic climate of the mid-1920s. Uncontrolled inflation ravaged the savings of the average Frenchman and undermined the traditional security of the franc. From a value of 90 to the pound (December 1924), the currency slid to 130 to the pound (December 1925), and down to 240 in July 1926. In 1928, price levels were 650 per cent of those in 1914. The impact of this collapse should not be underestimated. 'The collapse of the franc,' wrote D. S. Landes, 'after over one hundred years of stability, was utterly demoralising in a society whose greatest economic virtue was thrift.' A return by Herriot to the outdated policy of anti-clericalism, attempting to break off diplomatic relations with the Vatican and to extend anti-clerical legislation to Alsace-Lorraine, was no longer enough to unite the left. In 1926, the Radicals supported the return of the strong conservative, Raymond Poincaré, to the premiership as a symbol of confidence and stability. From this point the *Cartel* was effectively dead.

Poincaré and the return to stability

The return of Poincaré was at least a financial success. By traditional methods which were largely abhorrent to the left, he had restored the franc to stability by 1928. The currency was revalued at 20 per cent of its pre-war value (1926), and put on the gold standard (1928). The substantial budget deficit was made good by a sinking fund, and by raising an extra six billion francs in indirect taxation. The price paid, however, for three years of apparent prosperity and stability in 1926–29 was the infliction of deep scars upon French parliamentary politics. The advent of Poincaré, with the apparent support of the *Cartel des Gauches*, convinced many voters on the left that their democratic will would always be obstructed by the 'wall of money' (*Mur d'Argent*), and by the vested interests of bankers and industrialists. They felt that other means of political expression might bring better results. In a period of less economic stability it was to become evident that France had all the ingredients of 'veiled civil war' (J. P. T. Bury). Involved were the remnants of wartime nationalism, the rise of communism, the insecurity of small tradesmen and farmers, and the vested interests of financiers.

J France: economic recovery

Post-war reconstruction

While state finance suffered a decade of crisis after the war, the national economy underwent a remarkable recovery that Sir Dennis Brogan has described as 'the greatest economic achievement of post-war Europe'. To an extent, the economy benefited from the very factors that had afflicted the government. The weakness of the franc favoured French exports, and rising prices were an encouragement to manufacturers to produce more. A further industrial benefit was the recovery of the valuable potash and iron-ore deposits of Alsace-Lorraine.

The resurgence of the French economy expressed itself in three main ways. Most spectacular was the successful reconstruction carried out in areas and industries devasted by the war. In 1918, of two million hectares of agricultural land left barren 95 per cent was under cultivation once more in 1925. Meanwhile, the investment of 80 billion francs in the mines and factories of the north provided the opportunity for large-scale modernisation. Secondly, heavy industries, both old and new, made substantial advances in production. Of the old, coal production increased from 40 million tons in 1913 to 55 million in 1929, while steel production doubled. The most impressive of the new developments was the rise of the French motor industry. With the emergence of such giants as Renault, Citroën and Peugeot, the industry led the world by 1929 with an output of 250,000 vehicles. Lastly, France achieved virtually full employment. In fact, due to wartime losses, she actually suffered from a shortage of manpower which necessitated the importation of 1.6 million foreign workers by 1931.

The limits of economic recovery

There were limitations to this economic resurgence, however. Agriculture did not share in the advances of other sectors. Production in 1929 was only 3 per cent higher than in 1913, although considering the wartime loss of 673,000 peasants, that modest figure represented substantially greater efficiency in production methods. The post-war recovery also represented a triumph for the larger industrial and financial combinations, rather than for the smaller producer or tradesman. The years that saw the rise of the giant Kuhlmann and Saint Gobain chemical companies, and of the Monoprix, Prisunic and Uniprix chain stores, still held the prospect of insecurity and low investment for smaller enterprises. Gordon Wright has stressed how the recovery of the French economy accelerated its division 'into two increasingly divergent sectors; the dynamic and the static'. For the dynamic sector, especially, the successes of the 1920s were about to meet an abrupt end.

K France: the economic impact of depression

In October 1929, the collapse of the New York stock market set off the greatest economic crisis experienced by world capitalism. It naturally had its primary effect upon the most industrialised states. France, protected somewhat by the stability and the low value of the franc, enjoyed a period of immunity. By late 1931, however, she too was feeling the effects of the world 'slump'. Depressed foreign markets showed less and less interest in French luxury goods, and home sales too found it hard to compete with cheap foreign goods dumped on the market in a desperate search for sales. Firstly, the slump manifested itself in declining production. Steel production fell by 40 per cent

between 1930 and 1935 and aluminium production by 50 per cent. Overall industrial output in France in 1932 was only 80 per cent of the 1928 figure. Secondly, France felt the pressure of unemployment after a decade of labour shortages. Forty thousand jobs per month were lost in the first half of 1931, and although the official unemployment figures for January 1932 were only 250,000, these took no account of departing foreign workers. Taking the latter into consideration, the number of jobs lost by early 1933 would total some 1,300,000.

If France suffered less than other European states from the economic depression, she also suffered longer. Government reaction to the crisis typified the conservatism and lack of imagination of much of French political thinking at the time. Traumatised by the collapse of the franc in the 1920s, the politicians and economists gave undue importance to the preservation of 'sound money'. The franc was one of only four major currencies to remain on the gold standard, while the government sought salvation instead in tariff barriers and quotas imposed upon foreign imports. Thus in France the deflationary spiral continued for a full three years. The economy did not show signs of a recovery until 1935, and then it was painfully slow.

L France: the political impact of depression

An era of political inexperience

The political handling of the economic crisis was perhaps made all the worse by the fact that the task fell to a new and comparatively inexperienced political generation. The departure through ill-health of Briand and Poincaré had left among their successors, Laval, Tardieu, Daladier and Chautemps, no figure of comparable national stature. The crisis also hit a country bitterly divided by dogma and ideology. Conservatives sought safety in salary reductions and similar measures wholly intolerable to the left, with their visions of extensive and costly programmes of direct aid and relief. Unable to find either policies or personalities to command general support, French politics lurched into one of its worst periods of administrative instability. Eight different cabinets were formed between those of Tardieu (February 1932) and Doumergue (February 1934).

The rise of right-wing extremism

As in Italy and Germany, the weaknesses of French parliamentary politics increased the attraction of extra-parliamentary action. Since the mid-1920s, France had witnessed a proliferation of political 'leagues'. They were determined and often vicious in their opposition to the Republic, and drew support from the same sources as many of the European fascist groupings. The oldest of these was the *Action Française* which enjoyed considerable support among right-wing writers and intellectuals. Ostensibly Catholic, it was in fact repudiated by the Vatican in 1926. Ostensibly monarchist, it was viewed with great suspicion by the current claimant to the French throne. In reality, it was a classic, backward-looking, reactionary movement which attracted, according to Alfred Cobban, 'those who saw themselves as an élite under attack from the forces of egalitarian democracy and unegalitarian finance'. The *Croix de Feu* movement, founded by Colonel de la Rocque (1928), had more direct appeal to ex-servicemen, and put forward a vague and general appeal against socialism and internationalism. Also worthy of note are P. Taittinger's *Jeunesses Patriotes*, with their fascist style in uniforms and their substantial financial backing from the cosmetics millionaire François Coty, and the *Francistes*, founded by M. Bucard with a special line in anti-Semitic propaganda.

Political extremism in action

It seems unlikely that the leagues could seriously have aspired to a seizure of power in France such as Mussolini achieved in Italy. Their total membership in early 1934 was probably not much higher than 150,000, and it is typical of contemporary French politics that the forces which combined elsewhere into substantial right-wing movements were in France divided among half a dozen different factions. If the capacity of the extreme right to take power was limited, their capacity for political disruption was enormous. Firstly, they exercised that power through journalism. Scurrillous, vicious and sometimes obscene defamation of republican and left-wing figures was the speciality of such papers as *Le Matin*, *Candide* and *Je Suis Partout*. Alfred Cobban has stressed that 'the part played by the journalists of the right . . . in sapping the moral fibre and powers of resistance of the Third Republic can hardly be exaggerated'.

The Stavisky affair

Secondly, in a manner reminiscent of the Boulanger affair or the Panama Scandal, the right was able to take advantage of another political/financial scandal to assault the Republic. The 'Stavisky affair' centred around a shady financier, Serge Stavisky, arrested 19 times between 1927 and 1933 in connection with various swindles. He was released each time, it was widely supposed, upon the intervention of influential friends. In January 1934, when he was found dead, many disregarded the verdict of suicide, and preferred to believe that his protectors had killed him to cover their tracks. The government's refusal to mount an enquiry was the trigger of France's most serious civil disturbances since the war. Unassuaged by the resignation of Chautemps' government, the leagues precipitated extensive rioting in Paris in February. The death of 15 people and serious injuries to another 328 further enflamed political tempers. The left remained convinced that the leagues had made a serious bid for power. With the resignation of Daladier's short-lived administration they felt no confidence in the power of the regime to keep them at bay.

Were the riots of 6 February 1934 a serious attempt to seize power? It has been the consistent claim of the French left that they were, and as late as 1947 an official enquiry described the events as 'a genuine insurrection, minutely prepared'. Others have seen them merely as a spontaneous outburst of anger and frustration against the 'invertebrate republic'. In Robert Brasillach's words the events were 'an instinctive and magnificent revolt'. Whatever the case, 6 February 1934 marked a hardening in the political divisions within the nation, and a significant stage in the decline of the Third Republic.

M France: the Popular Front

The formation of the Front

'The most important consequence of the 6th February,' in the judgement of Alfred Cobban, 'was the traumatic effect it had on the French left.' Nevertheless, the startled awareness of the threat of fascism was only one of several reasons for the increased unity of the left between 1934 and 1937. Equally important were the changed tactics of the communists, now instructed by Moscow to co-operate with social-democratic forces against the common enemy (*see* Chapter 13, section **N**). At the same time French suspicions of Russian motives decreased in the light of improved Franco-Soviet relations. Consequently, by July 1934 the Socialist and Communist parties had decided upon a common course of political action for the 1936 elections, drawing the Radical party into their alliance in the following year. The domestic programme of this 'Popular Front' (*Front Populaire*) was based upon a call for the dissolution of the fascist leagues, and for the destruction of the influence of the 'two hundred families', the Regents of the Banque de France, who were traditionally supposed by the left to dominate the economic shape of the nation. In foreign affairs, the Front advocated peace through collective security, and the consolidation of the Franco–Soviet Pact.

The elections (April 1936) took place in an atmosphere of high unemployment, deflationary economics and continued street violence, and the results indicated a widespread desire for a new political departure. A gain of 39 seats for the Socialists and a huge advance by the Communists from 10 seats to 72 gave the Popular Front a total of 380 seats. Nevertheless, the parties of the right still won 43 per cent of the vote. This, and the fact that Léon Blum, France's first Socialist prime minister, was of Jewish origin, did not promise a decrease in political bitterness and division.

The Front in power
In one respect, the short-lived Popular Front administration (April 1936–June 1937) marked an important change of direction in French politics. In two other respects, it represented a sad continuation of the slide towards political disaster. Its greatest achievement was to end the stagnation of French social legislation since the war with a package of important reforms. Prodded into premature action by a wave of strikes and factory occupations with which over a million French workers greeted 'their' electoral victory, the government concluded the Matignon Agreements with representatives of unions and employers in June 1936. The agreements included wage increases of an average of 12 per cent, a 40-hour working week, compulsory collective bargaining with unions over future salary settlements, and two weeks' paid holiday per year. Independently, Blum's government took measures to nationalise arms manufacture, to bring the Banque de France under closer government control, and to stabilise the price of wheat.

The Front in difficulties
The Matignon Agreements, although they went far to remedy the long-standing social backwardness of France, served nevertheless to aggravate the nation's two greatest problems. The cost of the policies, the impact of the 40-hour week upon production, the apparent confirmation of the fears of industrialists and financiers, and the sporadic continuation of strike action, all served to prolong France's economic problems. The left-wing interpretation of the undermining of the Popular Front, by capitalists exporting bullion and refusing investment, obviously has some validity. The continual stagnation of production, at about 86 per cent of the 1929 level, suggests that the government was also let down by the very workers that placed such faith in it. Between May and December 1936 prices rose 17 per cent, eroding the value of salary increases and eliminating the possibility of the increased consumption in which Blum had placed his hopes of recovery.

In October, Blum was forced to devalue the franc after all by 25 per cent. The government's decision (March 1937) to institute a 'pause' in its social programme, for economic reasons, had a predictable effect upon the unity of the coalition. The refusal of the Senate (June 1937) to allow the government special powers to repay its debts effectively ended its existence.

The political legacy of the Popular Front
Secondly, far from bridging the rifts in French political society by the introduction of greater social justice, the Popular Front increased the polarisation of extreme political views. The Communist Party increased its membership from 30,000 to 300,000 between 1933 and 1937. Its credibility was re-established, and it benefited from the failures of Blum's Socialists. The legal dissolution of the fascist leagues by the government resulted either in their re-emergence as legal political parties, such as Jacques Doriot's *Parti Populaire Français* (PPF), or in their crystallisation into sinister secret societies such as Deloncle's 'hooded men'

(*cagoulards*). Just as the Popular Front had declared fascism to be the true threat to France, so the right now retaliated by claiming that anti-bolshevism was the truest form of patriotism, and coining the insidious slogan 'Better Hitler than Blum'.

The optimism and political cohesion of 1936 degenerated into a further flurry of brief ministries, led by Camille Chautemps (June 1937–January 1938), Blum (March–April 1938) and Édouard Daladier (April 1938–March 1940). They were able eventually to stabilise the franc, but unable to do the same for French society, at its moment of greatest peril. Unlike the Weimar Republic, the French Third Republic was not destroyed by domestic dissention and extremism. It was, however, drained of its energy by those factors, and of the will to resist an external enemy that threatened to renew the holocaust of 1914–18.

N French foreign policy aims

The search for security
The central theme uniting the foreign policies of the inter-war French governments is not difficult to identify. It was the search for the security that the peace of 1918 had failed to guarantee, and the attempt to ensure that German recovery would not again subject France to the sufferings of a world war. The apparent continental dominance of France between 1918–33, with Russia preoccupied and Germany defeated, did not deceive many of the nation's leaders. The precondition upon which they based their policies was that renewed foreign conflict would be ruinous for France, even if she emerged victorious, and thus had to be avoided.

The means to achieve these aims were less obvious. The most striking feature of France's foreign position by 1920 was her isolation. With Russia defeated and in the throes of civil war, and with the USA turning her diplomatic back on Europe, the alliance that had saved France from defeat lay in ruins. Even the British showed suspicion of French continental power, and returned to Imperial preoccupations. 'England,' remarked Clemenceau, 'is the lost illusion of my life.' Several possible remedies suggested themselves, but the tragedy of French foreign policy between the wars resulted from a failure consistently to commit the nation to any one course. The first possibility was

to substitute for the vital pre-war alliance with Russia a system of alliances with the eastern European states that had emerged from the collapse of the Habsburg and Romanov empires. Thus France extended material aid and military guarantees (February 1921) to Poland, and concluded similar agreements with the 'Little Entente' of Yugoslavia, Rumania and Czechoslovakia (1922). Considerations of distance, and the comparative weakness of the 'successor states' made it unlikely that these treaties could of themselves form a sound basis for French security.

Enforcement or collective security?
In co-ordination with these anti-German alliances the French government between 1919 and 1924 favoured a policy of 'enforcement'. That is to say, it sought security by ensuring that Germany observed the punitive clauses of the peace treaty to the letter. The culmination of this policy was the occupation of the Ruhr in January 1923 (*see* Chapter 17, section **D**), an action whose superficial success was offset by the resulting increased international isolation of France. It marked the last attempt in the inter-war years to conduct a wholly independent French foreign policy.

Thereafter, French statesmen sought security in one form or another of collective security. The 'grand design' of Aristide Briand from 1925 to 1932 was to construct a series of international agreements which would bind the world's major powers to the maintenance of the status quo. The Locarno Pact, Germany's admittance to the League of Nations, the Dawes and Young Plans, and the apparently naive 'Briand–Kellogg' Pact to outlaw war (*see* Chapter 17, sections **E** and **F**) all belong to the Briand era.

Russia or Italy?
'Briandism' was one of the casualties of the economic crisis of the early 1930s. As her own economy slumped, the USA once again turned her back on Europe, and the collapse of the system of reparations and war debts (*see* Chapter 17, section **G**) renewed French isolation. Worst of all, the advent to power of the rampant nationalism of the Nazis nullified all progress made in reconciliation between France and Germany.

In the last six years of the Third Republic, France sought security primarily through the construction of traditional alliances with other states alarmed at the rise of Germany. In doing so, foreign policy could not escape the chronic divisions of domestic politics.

The reopening of serious diplomatic relations with the Soviet Union by Louis Barthou caused predictable misgivings on the right. After Barthou's death (October 1934), the foundations laid for renewed Franco–Russian co-operation, notably the Mutual Assistance Pact, were neglected by his successor. Pierre Laval's preference for developing existing Franco–Italian understanding was to founder seriously over the question of Italy's assault upon Abyssinia, and over left-wing reaction to Italian involvement in the Spanish Civil War. Meanwhile, French inaction over the German remilitarisation of the Rhineland, and the completion of her Maginot Line fortifications along her eastern and north-eastern borders, seemed to many to betray a purely defensive mentality that promised little to her allies. When Hitler's fortification of the Rhineland further reduced France's capacity for offensive action, she was left largely dependent upon the support and approval of Britain.

The only alternative course was that of friendship with Nazism and Italian fascism. This was preached in the immediate pre-war years by Doriot's PPF and other forces of the extreme right, but was later taken up by some parliamentary conservatives, such as Laval and Flandin. This stultifying combination resulted in French acceptance of the Anschluss, her non-intervention in the Spanish Civil War, and her participation in the Munich agreement.

Foreign policy: conclusions

The precise cause of France's collapse in 1940 has aroused lively controversy. The theses that ascribe responsibility to the domestic tensions within France, to the indecision of Republican politicians after 1933, and to the enormous economic and political factors outside France that placed obstacles in her path, all have some validity. For our present purposes it is sufficient to repeat that French strength in 1919 was illusory, owing most to the weaknesses of potential rivals. As those rivals recovered in the 1920s and 1930s, the Third Republic could find no agreed formula to combat their challenge.

0 Spain: the rival forces

Spain had the weakest democracy of the western European nations disrupted by the economic and ideological tensions of the inter-war decades. Spain's decline from the status of a great imperial power had been a long and painful one, ending only in 1898 with the loss of Cuba, Puerto Rico and the Philippines. The decline of feudal Spain was not offset as in France by the rise of a powerful industrial or mercantile middle class. The country had relatively few mineral resources and, with her chronic political disorders in the 19th century, found it hard to attract foreign capital. Thus the political forces of the old Spain, and those of the new Europe, faced each other across a divide of centuries.

The forces of conservatism

Three sources of intense conservatism should be noted in Spain. The aristocracy remained more of an élite and aloof caste than in any other western state, barricaded behind pedigrees and influence accumulated over hundreds of years. Often the prestige of centuries was supplemented by huge fortunes. The Duke of Medinaceli owned 200,000 acres; the Duke of Penaranda owned 125,000; a total of only 50,000 landowners accounted between them for the ownership of half of Spain.

Secondly, Spanish conservatism drew support from the Church, staffed in the 1930s by 115,000 priests, monks and nuns. Its influence rested upon an almost complete control of education, and very substantial wealth, acquired not only from land, but from a wide variety of investments. Cardinal Segura, Archbishop of Toledo, represented not only the wealth of the Church, with an annual income of 600,000 pesetas, but also its philosophical outlook. He was, wrote R. Oliveira, 'a thirteenth century churchman, who thought that a bath was the invention of heathens if not the devil himself, and who wore a hair shirt like an early monk'.

The spiritual power of the Church was supplemented by the worldly authority of the army. Despite an unenviable record of colonial defeats, the Spanish army maintained a social and political prestige unique in Europe. It was staffed predominantly by the sons of the right, boasting one officer to every six men, and a total of 800 generals.

Largely ill-armed, ill-fed and ill-equipped, it was better suited to keep the peace in Spain than to defeat any external enemy. The exceptions to this depressing rule were the élite units stationed in Spanish Morocco, sharpened by recent successful campaigns against the rebel Moorish leader Abd-el-Krim (1921–26).

Poverty and regionalism

Three sources of opposition confronted this 'old' Spain., of which two were centuries old. The first of these was the deadweight of poverty under which so many Spaniards laboured. H. Rabasseire estimated in 1938 that of a little over 20 million Spaniards, 8 million lived at subsistence level. Of these, 4 to 5 million came into the rural categories of agricultural labourers or tenant farmers, the majority owning no land, or plots of up to 2.5 acres. The circumstances of this peasantry varied, but were especially harsh in Galicia, Léon and Old Castile. Worst of all the provinces was Andalusia which, according to P. Broué, 'probably included some of the most wretched people in Europe, and was also the land of class hatred, of the slave ever ready to revolt against his master'.

A parallel theme of age-old discontent was provided by regionalism, still unextinguished after more than four centuries of nominal national unity. In the Basque region of the north, and in Catalonia, local language and traditions were guarded with special jealousy, and central government was regarded with special distrust. Barcelona was effectively the capital of Spanish political violence in the first quarter of the 20th century. In 1919–23 alone, 700 political assassinations were committed in Catalonia, most of them in Barcelona.

Spanish socialism

The newest, but not the least bitter element in Spanish political divisions was the rise of a divided but intense labour movement. Anarchism enjoyed the greatest impact of the conflicting dogmas that competed for the favour of the Spanish working classes. Influenced by French syndicalism (*see* Chapter 8, section **M**), and by the theories of the Russian, Bakunin, the movement had enjoyed particular success in Barcelona and in Andalusia. From 1911, it found more coherent expression through the CNT (*Confederación Nacional de Trabajo* – National Labour Confederation), whose various wings combined terrorism with revolutionary unionism. Socialism, again largely inspired by the French example, took time to counter the attractions of revolutionary anarchism. The socialist UGT (*Unión General de Trabajadores* – General Workers' Union) boasted some 6,000 members in 1899. By 1918, however, it numbered 200,000, especially in Madrid, Bilbao and the Asturias. They were divided, as were the French socialists, over the question of membership of the Third International. The Spanish movement nevertheless produced, in Largo Caballero, the most prestigious leader of Spanish labour between the wars. Communism came late to Spain, and suffered both from that fact, and from internal divisions that reflected those of the Soviet mother-party. The party gained only one parliamentary seat in the 1933 elections, and was further weakened by the breakaway of the dissident POUM (*Partido Obrero de Unificación Marxista* – Workers' Marxist Unification Party) faction, whose influence became concentrated primarily in Catalonia.

P Spain: rise of the republic

Primo de Rivera

The Second Spanish Republic was born in 1931, less through the great strength of republican political forces than through the persistent weakness of the monarchy. Alfonso XIII, king since his birth in 1886, had worn the mantle of constitutional monarch uneasily, and not always with good faith. He was perhaps lucky that his reign had not ended ten years earlier. Military disaster in July 1921, when a conscript army of 7,000 was massacred by Moorish tribesmen at Annual, in Morocco, had reflected seriously upon the competence of Alfonso and had called the future of the monarchy into question. As usual, however, a major political issue was settled by the attitude of the army. The king was saved from a damaging official enquiry by a coup staged (September 1923) by the military commander of Catalonia, Miguel Primo de Rivera. Profiting from improving economic conditions, Primo de Rivera exercised a 'genial dictatorship' over Spain based, says Raymond Carr, on 'the Nation, Church and King in that order'. His power lasted until January 1929.

In his fall, Primo de Rivera was in part the

victim of general economic depression, but to a greater extent was brought down by purely Spanish factors. He had failed to create a 'new legality', that is, to found his regime upon any firm institutional basis. Above all, he had alienated powerful military elements by his attempts to streamline and modernise the army. To some historians, the period of Primo de Rivera's dictatorship was an inept and almost irrelevant interlude. Raymond Carr, however, has seen it as an episode of the utmost importance in Spain's development, in that it provided 'both a model and a warning to General Franco'. It provided the future dictator with economic, political and institutional ideas, but also convinced him that Spain could only be controlled with a ruthlessness that Primo de Rivera had been unwilling or unable to exercise.

The collapse of the monarchy

Primo de Rivera's resignation brought Spain little comfort. His greatest failing was, as Hugh Thomas has noted, that 'he left behind him no basis for a regime'. The monarchy remained more isolated than ever, unpopular with the left for accepting the 'illegal' dictatorship of the last five and a half years, and with some on the right for dismissing it. The Army and the Church remained lukewarm in their support. Meanwhile, evidence of the revival and growth of republican feeling was provided by widespread student rioting and the so-called Pact of San Sebastian. This was an anti-monarchical agreement concluded by liberal, socialist and Catalan politicians and intellectuals (August 1930). In April 1931, the government decided to hold municipal elections as a means of testing the political atmosphere. In what was effectively a plebiscite, republican candidates received huge votes of confidence in Spain's major cities. The army commanders informed the king that they would not stand against this clear expression of popular opinion, and Alfonso left Madrid for exile on the evening of 14 April.

 ## Spain: the divided republic, 1931–36

The birth of the Republic

In a manner reminiscent of 1848, the Spanish Republic came into being, not through the defeat of conservative forces, but through their unwillingness to defend the old regime. Between 1931 and 1936, therefore, conservative forces lived in uneasy co-existence with the more radical forces supporting the Republic. Political instability was further guaranteed by the divisions among the Republicans. While the left-wing groupings looked upon the constitutional change as merely the prelude to far-reaching social transformation, the centre sought an 'open republic', accommodating all Spaniards regardless of class and previous political record. The political fragmentation of contemporary Spain is well illustrated by the presence of 26 different political parties in the Parliament (*Cortes*) in 1931.

Rural reform and anti-clericalism

From April 1931 until mid-1933, the Spanish Republic was directed by a progressive alliance of Republicans and Socialists under the premierships of Alcalá Zamora (April–December 1931) and Manuel Azaña y Diaz (December 1931–March 1933). Their policies embraced all the prime problems of Spanish politics, but eliminated none of them.

The problem of rural poverty was tackled by an Agrarian Law (1932). This allowed for the distribution to the peasantry of all unworked estates over 56 acres in area. This reform, like others, suffered from the coincidence of social radicalism with international economic depression. With Spanish exports falling by 75 per cent between 1930 and 1934, there were no funds to pay for loans or improvement grants to the peasantry, and the reform changed little. In short, it achieved the worst of both worlds, going far enough to excite conservative fears, but not far enough to prevent the development of frustration and impatience on the left. The projected land reform, concluded E. Malefakis, was the decisive action of the Republic, for it 'seriously threatened the strongest economic class in Spain and awakened the hopes of the impoverished peasantry'.

There was much more in the Republican programme to stimulate conservative fears. Anti-clericalism, for example, was a dominant theme. The Church and the State were separated under Article 26 of the new Spanish constitution. The Jesuit order was expelled and its assets expropriated, divorce was legalised, and the Ministry of Justice was granted powers to suppress any other religious orders that it deemed a threat to the state.

The worst blow was the reaction of the government to the wave of church burnings that swept Madrid and Andalusia in May 1931. Refusing to use force against the insurgents, Azaña remarked provocatively that 'all the convents in Madrid are not worth one Republican life'. Army opinion was offended by the compulsory retirement of 40 per cent of the officer corps, by the appointment of Republican officers, and by the legal reform that made soldiers liable to civil, rather then military law, when they committed civil offences. Nationalists, meanwhile, saw with horror the grants of autonomy to Catalonia (August 1931), which seemed to them to threaten the unity of 'Holy Spain'.

Violence was never far from the surface of contemporary Spanish politics, and could come from either extreme. In August 1932, military unrest was displayed in the unsuccessful 'coup' engineered by General José Sanjurjo, specifically in protest against the grant of Catalonian autonomy. In January 1933, on the other hand, an abortive anarchist rising in Andalusia resulted in a massacre of rebels by Civil Guards in the village of Casas Viejas. This was a combination of threatened revolution and savage repression that alienated right and left alike.

CEDA and the recovery of conservatism

As a reaction to Republican policies and to the threat of revolutionary violence, Spanish conservatism presented a more united front at the elections of November 1933, in the form of the CEDA (*Confederación Espanola de Derechas Autonomas* – Spanish Confederation for Autonomous Rights). Its leader was José-Maria Gil Robles and its inspiration was the Catholic Centre Party in Germany, although its enemies saw a greater resemblance to Mussolini's fascism, and its funds came from the wealth of landowners and of the Church. It marked the beginning of the right-wing solidarity that was to do much to shape the events of the next six years. Although CEDA failed to win an absolute majority, as the largest party in the *Cortes* it was able to force a number of members into the successive cabinets of the premier, Alejandro Lerroux, the leader of the Radical Party.

Between late 1933 and February 1936, therefore, the Republic passed through a phase of conservative government in which the legislative advances of the past three years were slowed and eroded. The salaries of priests, for example, were restored, as was much of the freedom of action of the landowners. This freedom was reflected in a sharp rise in rural evictions, and in an equally sharp drop in rural wages. Predictably, the major outbreaks of anti-Republican violence now originated from the left. Saragossa and Valencia both experienced general strikes lasting for weeks, and numerous incidents and disorders culminated in the attempted national rising of the 'Workers Alliance' in October 1934, a combination of anarchists, socialists and communists. Ill-planned and badly-executed for the most part, it led, however, to two weeks of bitter fighting in the Asturias region. It ended in an estimated 3,000 deaths, many of them summary executions by the victorious army.

R Spain: the descent into violence

The polarisation of Spanish politics

By the time of the new parliamentary elections of February 1936, the concept of the 'open republic' to serve the interests of all Spaniards was effectively dead. It had been killed by the polarisation of politics that was more evident than ever in early 1936. On the right it was clear in the increasing popularity of the *Falange Espanol* ('Spanish Phalanx'). This was a nationalist and élitist group founded (October 1933) by José Antonio Primo de Rivera, son of the former dictator. Influenced by the tactics of Nazism, the Falange vied with the CEDA for the leadership of the right, not by achieving electoral success, but by transferring the ideological battle to the streets. 'A mixture of rhetorical poetry and gang warfare,' Raymond Carr has written, 'its most important contribution was to heighten the atmosphere of violence.' On the left, this polarisation was displayed by the emergence of a 'Popular Front' coalition of Anarchists, Socialists and Communists to fight and win the elections. In fact, these elections witnessed the virtual destruction of the centre parties. They gained only 680,000 votes, against 3.78 million gained by the parties of the right, and 4.21 million polled by the Popular Front.

Although the Popular Front only thinly disguised a 'chaotic incoherence' (Raymond Carr) of left-wing views, its victory, and the consequences of that victory were sufficient to terrify conservatives. They were further alienated by the opening of prisons in Valencia, Oviedo and elsewhere, without governmental authority, to release those imprisoned in 1934. Also there was the dismissal of the moderate Catholic, Alcalá Zamora, as President of the Republic (May 1936). Street violence, strikes and lockouts proliferated. Gil Robles estimated 269 deaths, 1,287 serious injuries, and 381 political attacks upon buildings or premises between February and mid-June 1936.

The 'Generals' rising'

As in 1923 and 1931, all depended upon the attitude of the army. Although military opinion was not united, it now seemed to many officers, and especially to the younger ones, that the whole structure of 'Holy Spain' was threatened by the leftwards lurch of Spanish politics. The resolution of such commanders as General Emilio Mola and General Francisco Franco seems to have been strengthened by the murder (13 July 1936) of Calvo Sotelo, Gil Robles' successor at the head of the CEDA. He was arrested and murdered by an official police detachment in Madrid, apparently in retaliation against the assassination of a senior police officer by Falangists. Five days later, General Franco left his remote posting in the Canary Islands to join the army's crack units in Morocco and the 'generals' rising' began.

Hopes of a neat military 'coup' were frustrated by the prompt reaction of left-wing and Republican organisations throughout Spain. In many places, claimed A. Nin, the army rebellion 'speeded up the revolutionary process by provoking a proletarian revolution more profound than the Russian Revolution itself'. Thus, while Seville and Valladolid fell quickly into military hands, the army rising failed totally in Madrid, Barcelona and Valencia. In late July 1936, therefore, Spain stood divided along class lines, but also along lines of 'geographical loyalty' with Catalonia and the Basque region remaining loyal to the Republic that had given them autonomy.

S Spain: the Civil War

Strengths and weaknesses of the Republic

The relative strengths of the two sides at the out-

break of war appeared evenly balanced. Many of the Republican strengths, however, were illusory. The Republic certainly benefited from the enthusiasm and dedication of tens of thousands of workers. They were armed by their political organisations and, eventually, by a reluctant government. These were weapons, however, of dubious value. Factional rivalries and ideological disagreements, such as those witnessed in Barcelona by George Orwell, severely reduced the efficiency of these militias as a front-line force. Although they often fought bravely in defensive positions, they rarely produced a sustained or co-ordinated offensive. Outbursts of class hatred, and of more positive revolutionary expropriations and collectivisations of estates and factories, completed the alienation of property owners and sent them flocking into Nationalist zones. The task of the Republican leaders was, in Malraux's phrase, 'to organise the Apocalypse'.

The Nationalists

The Nationalists, as supporters of the military rebels chose to call themselves, had the best of the troops and the best of the commanders. The African Army formed the cream of the Spanish forces, and they were soon to enjoy the support of substantial foreign interventionist forces. In particular, the latter factor ensured the Nationalists of air superiority. In contrast to the divided leadership of the Republic, the commander of the African Army, General Franco, soon came to exercise an unparalleled political and military authority. He was aided in this by the deaths in action of such potential rivals as Generals Sanjurjo and Mola, and by the execution by the Republicans of the Falangist leader José Antonio Primo de Rivera. He nevertheless owed much to his own political tact which made him broadly acceptable to Catholic, Monarchist and Falangist factions, and in 1937 he was formally designated head of the Nationalist state. In terms of resources, the Nationalists also controlled the main agricultural regions, quickly causing hardship in the industrial cities. The Republicans' initial economic advantage in controlling those cities faded, however, as resources of raw materials fell into the hands of the Nationalists.

Republican resistance, 1936–37

The first blows of the war were struck in the pursuit of the class struggle. In the Republican zone, an estimated 6,800 priests were murdered as suspected enemy agents. In Nationalist territory the shooting of working-class leaders, and of resisting workers, was a matter of routine. Such events, in Raymond Carr's words, 'put a river of blood between the working class and the gentlemen'. Strategically, the advantage quickly passed to the Nationalists. Advancing north and west, Franco's troops captured Badajoz (August 1936) and linked up with Mola's forces in the north. Meanwhile, the capture of Irun (September 1936) cut off the Basque region from any hope of relief from the French border. At this juncture, Madrid became the focal point of the war. Advancing along the Tagus valley, Nationalist troops were in the suburbs of the capital by the end of September. They were still there in the spring of 1937, denied entry by the heroic defence which made Madrid an international symbol of resistance to fascism. Aided by the arrival of the International Brigades, Republican troops won their first major victories against Franco's troops at the Battle of the Jarama (February 1937) and against Italian forces at Guadalajara (March 1937).

Nationalist triumph, 1937–39

Frustrated, Franco turned his attention north to the Basque region. There he gained greater success. Bilbao (June 1937) and Santander (August 1937) fell, leaving the socialist strongholds of the north with their rich iron ore deposits in Nationalist hands. By the close of 1937 Franco controlled 62 per cent of Spanish territory and half of the nation's population. Further south, a series of Republican offensives succeeded in keeping the Nationalists out of Madrid, but their forces nevertheless struck an important blow with a drive through Aragon to the sea near Valencia (March 1938) which cut Republican territory in two. Although still capable of bold offensives to harass Franco's forces, such as that across the River Ebro (July 1938), the Republican cause was now suffering from crippling handicaps. Military inferiority, material shortages, and desertions in the face of defeat were now capped by political divisions and ideological disputes. Republican resistance in Catalonia crumbled in the face of Nationalist offensives in December and January, and Barcelona fell on 23 January 1939. It was sadly fitting that one of the last acts of the Civil War was an internal feud between Anarchists and Communists that led to the collapse of resistance in Madrid in March 1939, and thus to the end of the conflict.

T Spain: the war and Europe

Intellectual response to the Spanish civil war

Although essentially Spanish in its origins, the Civil War seemed to many observers to be a miniature enactment of the great contemporary tension in Europe, of the great confrontation between the forces of communism and fascism, or between political freedom and totalitarianism. It became, therefore, a major focus of political and intellectual concern throughout Europe. Its impact upon a generation of western intellectuals was fundamental. It seemed, wrote the English poet C. Day Lewis, to be 'a battle between light and darkness'. Most committed writers would have agreed with him that the Republican cause constituted the 'light'. From the Republican side emerged several masterpieces of literature of which the best known are probably Ernest Hemingway's *For Whom the Bell Tolls* and George Orwell's *Homage to Catalonia*. Perhaps the most famous celebration of the war was a painting, Pablo Picasso's great *Guernica*, an abstract protest at the bombing by German planes of a market town in the Basque region.

Political reaction in France and Britain

The politicians of western European democracies were less committed. Although the French Popular Front government appeared willing to extend aid to its Spanish counterpart in July 1936, its attitude quickly changed. In part this was a reaction to the demands of her British ally for caution, but in large part was due to right-wing hostility within France to the idea of aid to the Spanish leftists. 'We are reluctant to believe,' declared the right-wing *L'Echo de Paris*, 'that the government could commit this crime against the nation.' In Britain, too, the distinct preference of some leading political figures for the politics of Franco, and the desire to avoid further confrontation with Italy, contributed towards the eventual policy of 'non-intervention'. In theory, this principle became the official policy of 25 powers who accepted the invitation to join and support (September 1936) the International Committee for the Application of Non-interven-

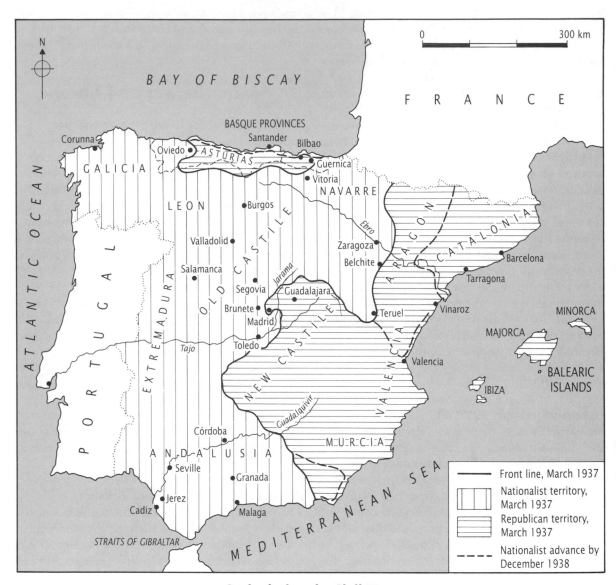

Spain during the Civil War

tion in Spain. Three powers, however, were prominent in flouting that principle.

The reaction of the Soviet Union

The most cautious of these was the Soviet Union. Stalin was torn between his desire to win the trust of the western democracies, and his hostility to Spanish Anarchist and Trotskyite elements and, on the other hand, the need to be seen at the head of world socialism. Thus he committed himself only hesitantly to the Republican cause. Soviet manpower played little part in the war, but her military material was a crucial factor in the Republic's early survival. In March 1937, so American observers estimated, 420 of the Republic's 460 aircraft were Russian. For manpower, however, the Republic had to rely upon the foreign volunteers of the International Brigades. Organised into national units, with Frenchmen and left-wing Italian and German refugees prominent, some 35,000 men fought in Spain from November 1936 onwards. They formed probably the most reliable units of her Republican army, and were prominent in most of the major engagements.

The reactions of Italy and Germany

As with most resources, the most valuable foreign aid was available to the Nationalists. Italian aid had been sought as early as 1934, and began to arrive in substantial quantities as soon as Nationalist troops secured their first successes. Mussolini's motives for intervention were complex. While undoubtedly flattered by the apparent expansion of his fascist creed, his reasons were primarily practical. He wanted to maintain the military prestige of his regime, established in Abyssinia, and to strengthen Italy's Mediterranean status by the establishment of a friendly regime, and perhaps of bases, at the western end of that sea. In all, Italy probably contributed some 70,000 men, about 20 per cent of the total Nationalist forces, some 700 aircraft, and 950 tanks to Franco's cause. It is likely that the total cost to Italy of this intervention was some 14 billion lire and some 11,000 casualties. The contribution of Germany was less ambitious both in terms of motive and of scale. There seems little doubt that Hitler was primarily concerned that Spain should serve as a testing ground for Germany's new and untried armaments. The fact that they would be tested against Soviet material, and that the prolonged war in Spain might stir up pacifism in Britain and France, only added to the attractions of intervention. Nevertheless, it is unlikely that there were ever more than 10,000 Nazi personnel in Spain. The German government compensated, however, by the quality of its aid. The élite Condor Legion, perpetrators of the infamous aerial attack on Guernica, was the most effective airforce unit in the war. Although equipped at first with older aircraft, such as commercial Junker 52s converted to serve as bombers, they later had, in their Heinkel 111 bombers and Messerschmitt 109 fighters, the most advanced planes seen in Spain. It was the Condor Legion that ensured that Spanish civilians were the first in the world to experience the new phenomenon of concentrated aerial bombardment.

The impact of German and Italian aid on the military outcome was fundamental. Its impact on Spain's future political alignment was slight. Although Franco's government concluded economic agreements with her allies, and joined the Anti-Comintern Pact (March 1939), it steadfastly refused to align Spain with fascism and Nazism in the coming conflict. Franco's resistance to Hitler's blandishments at their meeting at Hendaye (October 1940) was so stubborn that the Führer remarked that he 'would rather have three or four teeth yanked out than go through that again'.

U Spain: the price of war

Material damage

The changes wrought in Spain by the Civil War were far-reaching. It was, judged Hugh Thomas, 'the Spanish share in the tragic European breakdown of the 20th century, in which the liberal heritage of the 19th century and the sense of optimism which had lasted since the renaissance, were shattered'. As such, it left scars that time has not yet erased. The most obvious scar was that inflicted by human and material losses. Hugh Thomas has estimated the total human cost of the war at about 500,000 lives. Of these, not more than 40 per cent died in action. The rest were the victims of bombing, executions, reprisals and malnutrition. War damage rendered economic recovery difficult. Destruction of towns and housing was extensive. The 11 million hectares sown with wheat in 1935, for instance, had been reduced to 8 million by 1939. The advent of European war in the wake of civil war meant, furthermore, that Spain had to continue for another decade in isolation and without hope of aid or recovery. To this must be added the bitterness of exile for many Spaniards. No wholly reliable figures exist for the number of Republicans who sought safety across the French border, but by early 1940 there were some 350,000 in France alone. Others had determined to try their luck in South America or even in the USSR. Some had even risked a return to Spain.

The political consequences of the war

Nationalist Spain, meanwhile, faced the twin problems of a domestic political vacuum, and of diplomatic isolation. In the first respect, General Franco had no serious rivals. The war had wiped out not only the whole spectrum of the Spanish left but many of the leading figures of the right. Sanjurjo, Mola, Sotelo, and José Antonio Primo de Rivera had all met violent deaths. Also, in S. Payne's estimate, 60 per cent of all pre-war Falangists had died in the war. Franco was able to exploit this situation cleverly throughout his 36 years of pragmatic dictatorship. Drawing representatives of monarchist, military, ecclesiastical and financial interests into his cabinets, he succeeded in forming governments of the broad right, where the Republic had never succeeded in uniting the broad left. Compromise with his allies went hand-in-hand with unmitigated hostility to those who opposed him. The Italian foreign minister, Count Ciano, spoke of 'a serious and most rigorous purge' in the years after 1939. In his estimate of wartime deaths, Hugh Thomas allowed for 100,000 post-war executions. Diplomatic normality came much more slowly. Although a member of the Anti-Comintern Pact, and recognised after April 1939 by all major powers except the USSR, the allied victory in the Second World War left the Franco regime in renewed ideological isolation. Gradually she was reintegrated into the international community. In 1955 she was admitted to the United Nations, and ten years later benefited from the 'Cold War' between eastern and western blocs by leasing military bases to the USA in return for 1.8 billion dollars in American aid. Only very recently has Spain truly begun to live down the terrible legacy of her civil war, by the proclamation of a constitutional monarchy upon Franco's death (1975), and her membership of the European Union.

Questions

Essay questions

1   Explain why the German democracy of 1919 to 1933 gave way to dictatorship. (UCLES)

2   Why were the opponents of the Weimar Republic so much less effective in the period 1918–1923 than between 1930 and 1934? (AEB)

3   'The collapse of the Weimar Republic was inevitable, but its replacement by Hitler was not.' Discuss. (ULEAC)

4   Who supported the Weimar Republic? (Oxford Entrance)

5   Why did France suffer from political instability in the 1930s? (UCLES)

6   Why did the period of Republican government in Spain (1931–36) end in civil war? (UCLES)

7   To what extent can the Spanish Civil War be described as 'the first chapter in the history of the Second World War'? (WJEC)

8   What was at stake both domestically and internationally in the Spanish Civil War, 1936–39? (Oxford Entrance)

Foreign intervention in the Spanish Civil War

Read the following sources carefully and then answer the questions.

SOURCE A

Negotiations, in which the French took the lead, to get the Non-Intervention Committee started, resulted at last in a first meeting in London on September 9th [1936]. Twenty-six European countries came, including all those with a direct interest in Spanish affairs. The chief contenders, Russia, Germany, Italy and France, chose their Ambassadors to represent them. The thankless task of presiding over this adroit company fell to Great Britain. The first few meetings passed off amiably enough. It was settled that when breaches of the Agreement were alleged, the complaint must be laid by a government which was a party to the Agreement.

From Facing the Dictators, *the memoirs of the British Foreign Secretary Anthony Eden, published in 1962.*

SOURCE B

The Duce is very pleased about Franco's decision to adhere to the Anti-Comintern Pact. The event is of great importance and will influence all future happenings in Europe. Those silly people who tried so hard to criticise our intervention in Spain will one day perhaps understand that on the Ebro, at Barcelona, and at Malaga the foundations for the Roman Mediterranean Empire were laid.

From the diary of Count Ciano, the Italian foreign minister, 22 February 1939.

SOURCE C

1) In the light of past experience, the Führer did not see any end to the hostilities in Spain. If one considered the length of time that Franco's offensives had taken up to now, it was fully possible that the war would continue another three years. On the other hand, a 100 per cent victory for Franco was not desirable either from

the German point of view; rather were we interested in the continuance of the war and in the maintenance of tension in the Mediterranean. Franco in undisputed possession of the Spanish peninsula precluded the possibility of any further intervention on the part of the Italians.

An official transcript of Hitler's view stated in a meeting on policy towards Spain. 1937.

2) We must demand some value in return for our gifts. Shottky indeed very rightly recognised that fact and induced Franco to make deliveries of copper to us to begin with. Now would be the moment to assure ourselves of a basic treaty, which would lay down for a number of years to come what raw materials Spain is to deliver to us and to what extent Spain must buy manufactured goods from us.

Report by Eberhard Messerschmitt, the aircraft manufacturer, following a fact-finding mission to Spain, 1936.

SOURCE D

1) Moscow had a big bureau which did nothing else but devise means of disguising war munitions and the vessels that carried them. They sometimes rebuilt freighters, giving them a false deck, and placed arms between the two decks. Tanks were immersed in the oil of tankers, and so on. But airplanes could scarcely be hidden. I wondered whether big bombers might not fly from the nearest Soviet point to the nearest Loyalist [Republican] airfield. Uritsky said it was physically impossible. Nor could they land in Czechoslovakia. The Czechs would not allow it for fear of antagonising Germany. Uritsky explained that if a Soviet machine made one forced landing anywhere in Europe the whole world would squeal. This made it clear to me that Soviet aid to the Loyalists would remain within the limited legal-illegal bounds of Non-Intervention.

There would be subterfuge and lying and therefore delays and scarcity of supplies. Moscow apparently would not go 'all out on Spain'.

An account by Louis Fischer, a left-wing writer, of conversations held in 1936 with Russian officials in Moscow. Published 1941.

2) Together with Ambassador Rosenberg arrange with Head of Spanish government for the shipment of the gold reserves of Spain to the Soviet Union. This operation must be carried out with the utmost secrecy. If the Spaniards demand from you a receipt for the cargo, refuse, I repeat, refuse to sign anything, and say that a receipt will be issued in Moscow.

Telegram allegedly sent from the Kremlin to the senior NKVD officer in Madrid. 20 October 1936.

a Explain what is meant by the following terms used in the sources:
  i 'the Agreement' (Source A)
  ii 'on the Ebro' (Source B)
  iii 'the whole world would squeal' (Source D).
b Explain briefly why, in 1936–37:
  i Hitler might express an interest in prolonging Italian intervention in the Spanish Civil War (Source C).
  ii The government of Czechoslovakia might be wary of 'antagonising Germany' (Source D).
c Consider Sources A, B and D. Do these sources suggest that the respective governments of Great Britain, Italy and the Soviet Union approached the problem of the Spanish Civil War with a high degree of realism?
d Consider Sources B, C and D. To what extent do these sources support the widespread contemporary feeling that the Spanish Civil War served as a battleground for the major European ideologies of the era?

15
Fascism in Italy

Mussolini delivers a speech, inaugurating work on the draining of the Pontine Marshes.

What characteristic features of Mussolini's style of government are evident in this photograph?

The Historical Debate

Attempts to explain the phenomenon of Italian fascism have been many and varied and were especially numerous in the two decades that followed its collapse. At the centre of much of this work has been the controversy among Italian historians over the links that bound the phenomenon of fascism to the earlier history of Italy. The writings of left-wing historians have been profoundly influenced by the conclusions reached by the leading theorist of Italian communism in the inter-war years, Antonio Gramsci (*Selections from the Prison Notebooks of Antonio Gramsci*, ed. Hoare and Nowell-Smith, 1971). Imprisoned by Mussolini's regime, Gramsci concluded in his writings that fascism was the direct product of the Risorgimento. In that earlier movement genuine, class-based development within Italy had been outflanked and outmanoeuvred by the clever strategies of conservative politicians, giving rise to an Italian state still riddled with unresolved class conflicts. 'The price of this compromise was a permanent breach between the Italian state and Italian civil society, characterised by chronic instability and endemic social disorder' (Lucy Riall). It was in response to this instability that the conservative classes of inter-war Italy allowed themselves to be seduced by the appeal of fascism. The role of capitalism in the development of Italian fascism has, of course, also been a theme eagerly taken up by many Marxist interpreters. P. Alatri (*Biographical Profile of Benito Mussolini*, 1956) may stand as a representative example of the school of thought that sees Mussolini as being, at every turn in his political career, the tool of the interests of monopoly capitalism.

Liberal historians, of course, have been largely unwilling to acknowledge such links between fascism and the creation of the Italian state in the 19th century. The greatest of all Italian liberal historians, Benedetto Croce, insisted upon the essential success of the Risorgimento and assigned blame for the rise of fascism only to later generations of Italian politicians. Other moderate historians have also linked fascism to a short-term crisis in Italian politics, arising from the First World War and economic disruption. As early as the mid-1920s, the movement was placed convincingly in the context of Italy's recent past by L. Salvatorelli (*National Fascism*, 1925), and by Gaetano Salvemini (*The Fascist Dictatorship in Italy*, 1927). Salvatorelli stressed the peculiar combination of economic depression with post-war nationalist disillusionment, while Salvemini emphasised a longer-term conjunction of developing capitalism with wartime militarism.

It is thus less fashionable than it once was to analyse fascism predominantly in terms of the personality of Benito Mussolini himself. In the 1920s and 1930s, of course, this was usually done in the context of 'hero worship' with strong official backing. Such writers as A. Beltramelli (*The New Man: Benito Mussolini*, 1923) and G. Prezzolini (*Benito Mussolini*, 1924) insisted that the doctrine of fascism and its salvation of Italy from economic disaster and Bolshevism

owed everything to the genius of one man. In a more moderate and rational version of the theme, Giorgio Pini and Diulio Susmel (*Mussolini: The Man and His Work*, 1953–55) continued to view fascism as containing and achieving much of value, at least until the mid-1930s, when the disastrous entanglement with Hitler destroyed the true purpose and nature of the regime.

A negative variation of this 'Duce-orientated' theme has been the post-war tendency to view fascism not as the product of Mussolini's genius, but of his fatal weaknesses. G. Dorso (*Mussolini to the Conquest of Power*, 1949) interpreted the rise of fascism as the result of Mussolini's 'vulgar opportunism' in exploiting contemporary political trends. S. W. Halperin (*Mussolini and Italian Fascism*, 1964) could still write that 'fascism was fundamentally nothing but Mussolinianism. Fascism's identity with Mussolini gave the movement tremendous rhetorical dash but also accounted for its extraordinary intellectual poverty'. Modern writers in English have also been drawn to the man more frequently than to his movement. Denis Mack Smith's definitive biography (*Mussolini*, 1981) concentrates upon the extraordinary personality of the Duce and reaches damning conclusions: 'Though the fascist regime may be credited with some positive achievements especially in its early years, its crude belief in political violence and authoritarian repression had negative effects that lasted long after 1945, and its praise of war as something inherently beautiful and beneficial was a cruel absurdity that did untold harm and ultimately turned any positive achievements to dust and ashes'.

The nature of fascism

Probably no historical term has been so abused and misused as the word 'fascism'. In modern political usage the term has too often become one of crude abuse aimed at any political views to the right of one's own and, as M. Kitchen has pointed out, 'to denounce as "fascist" regimes in Latin America ... the practices of the Metropolitan Police, or restrictions on the rights and freedoms of homosexuals ... does nothing to uncover the true nature of the problems under attack'. In the strictest sense, fascism in the 1920s and 1930s could be taken to refer only to the movement led by Mussolini in Italy, which called itself by that name. So many other movements, however, imitated elements of Italian fascism, that it is usual to refer to the fashion for authoritarian right-wing regimes in inter-war Europe as a fashion for fascism.

During its life, and since its decline, a number of general theories of fascism have been devised. To many Marxist theorists, especially those of the contemporary Third International, fascism was interpreted as the last desperate and violent attempts of capitalism to prevent its own collapse. It is a theory that gains some sustenance from the widespread sympathy of 'big business' for fascist and Nazi policies in Italy and Germany, but which suffers from the fact that it is hard to see Italy, Spain or Portugal as societies in which capitalism in the 1920s had reached its highest point of development.

Many western liberals, such as Hannah Arendt and C. J. Friedrich, retaliated in the atmosphere of the east–west 'Cold War' by equating fascism, not with western capitalism, but with Soviet communism. They saw both as manifestations of the wider concept of 'totalitarianism'. Parallels were drawn stressing the common imposition of ideology and a single party system, and the common use of terror as a political tool. This line of approach succeeds as long as one concentrates upon means, but is weaker when one considers ends. The preconceived end product of the Marxist revolution, the classless society, is clearly stated by communist theorists. The final aim of fascism, where it is possible to find one at all, is certainly not the same.

At the root of this problem of definition lies the essential difference between the histories of Marxism and fascism. The first began life as a theory, subsequently modified and adapted when put into practice. Fascism, on the other hand, existed as an emotional form of political action before theories were devised, as by Giovanni Gentile in Italy or Alfred Rosenberg in Germany, to justify or to define it. Essentially, for all its claims to the contrary, fascism was a negative phenomenon. It was not a brave new world, but a reaction against certain elements in the contemporary world.

The roots of fascism in the 1920s
The great political facts of the period were those created by the First World War. The collapse of well-established regimes in central Europe left in their place parliamentary regimes often unable to solve the vast economic and social problems they inherited. They were thus unable to command widespread loyalty or respect. The economic collapse that threatened to follow in the 1920s and early 1930s only heightened the sense of insecurity and instability. In specific cases, as in Germany, Hungary and Italy, the peace terms of 1919 left a burning sense of national injustice. On the other hand, the success of the Bolshevik revolution in Russia offered an alternative vision of the future that horrified the bourgeoisie and those members of the working classes who aspired to bourgeois standards. Sometimes, as Hugh Trevor-Roper has pointed out, response to these factors took the form of a dynamic, if incoherent philosophy, genuinely determined to sweep away existing religious, social and governmental systems, as was the young Mussolini. Sometimes it expressed itself in more traditional conservative forms, such as Franco personified in Spain.

Most 'fascist' regimes in the 1920s and 1930s were coalitions of the two responses. Hence their frequent internal tensions and their divergent forms. On a more practical level, the war and subsequent recession left a further element that was to be a prominent feature of fascist movements. The large numbers of ex-servicemen, brutalised by war and apparently robbed of security in peacetime, formed the basis of the characteristic paramilitary organisations that gave fascism its original physical impact. Such was the case of the SA in Germany and the *Squadristi* in Italy.

Fascism certainly had an ancestry in past political and social philosophy, but it was a confused and incoherent one. The embryos of the authoritarian fascist state and of the charismatic fascist leader can be seen in the work of two men: Hegel (*see* Chapter 1, section **E**), with his views on the dominant role of the state; and Nietzsche, with his belief in the potential of man once freed from the 'slave mentality' of Christianity. Socialism, too, played its role in the genesis of fascism. Mussolini in Italy, Mosley in Britain, Doriot in France, Quisling in Norway, all began their political careers as socialists. On the left of most fascist movements stood men, like the Strasser brothers in Germany, who still cherished ideas of sweeping away the old social and political order, and substituting a new one. This was to be socialist in its social aims, but otherwise still clinging to the principles of nationalism.

Indeed, because nationalism was such a strong element in fascism, it was inevitable that each movement broadly termed 'fascist' should be firmly rooted in the specific historical problems of its own country, and should be dedicated to specifically national aims. In this sense, in Mussolini's words, fascism was truly 'not for export'. For all the shared features of the authoritarian regimes of the 1920s and 1930s, it would be wrong to seek in them uniformity of aims. Nevertheless, we can perhaps accept the broad definition proposed by R. A. H. Robinson of fascism as 'a nationalist, anti-Marxist, mass-mobilising political movement, normally headed by a charismatic leader, aiming at the complete conquest of power and seeking the fullest control possible over all aspects of life in a polity by means of a single-party system'.

A Italy: the bankruptcy of liberalism

The political weaknesses of Italian democracy

Superficially, it might seem surprising that fascism was able to establish itself so firmly in Italy, a state apparently founded throughout its 60 years' existence up to 1920 upon the liberal principles of Cavour and upon the moderate concepts of constitutional monarchy. Behind the achievements of Cavour, however, lurked the illiberal ghost of Mazzini and, as has been indicated in Chapter 4, the liberalism of Cavour was laced with elements of arbitrary government. Since 1870, furthermore, a number of factors had operated to undermine the liberal foundations of the Italian state.

One was the debased and often corrupt form of parliamentary government practised in Italy. It was dominated by 'Transformism', the habit first developed by Cavour of welding together large and sometimes unlikely coalitions in support of ministries. Thus it lacked true party spirit and ruled out any real clash of alternative party principles. It tended merely to facilitate the personal control of those politicians most skilled in the art, and the three longest serving premiers of the period, Agostino Depretis (1881–87), Francesco Crispi (1887–90, 1893–96) and Giovanni Giolitti (1892, 1903–04, 1906 and 1911), were all masters of the practice. All too often, what was justified as a means to political stability became, in Denis Mack Smith's words, 'a common refuge where they laid aside their internal quarrels and joined in parcelling out power and jobbery'.

Although this form of administration was not without its legislative successes, such as the various laws for agricultural improvement (1897–1906) and Giolitti's new electoral law (1912), Italy remained a country of enormous social and economic problems. The southern provinces, especially, remained backward and poverty-stricken. The sociologist L. Franchetti described in 1902 how 'peasant risings, which usually lead to bloodshed, are characteristic and normal events in the public life of the south', which was 'without any middle class, even without workers who are above the poverty level and possess a rudimentary education'. Eighty per cent of Sicilians were illiterate in 1900, and 90 per cent of Sicilian army recruits had to be rejected as medically unfit. The general condition of the Italian working classes expressed itself in the 'haemorrhage' of emigration whereby, in 1914, nearly 6 million Italians out of 41 million lived and worked abroad.

The enemies of Italian democracy

Two major groups regarded the liberal state with almost unrelieved hostility. One was the growing force of socialism, stimulated by the industrial growth of the late 1880s and the early 1890s, and developing its political organisation. By the eve of the First World War, it was capturing 25 per cent of electoral votes. As an alternative to liberalism before the war it was weakened by its constant divisions, and by the preference of many of its leaders for reform rather than revolution. Its many off-shoots, such as the anarchists, the syndicalists, who engineered a highly effective general strike in 1904, and the embryonic communist party, represented altogether a substantial force in opposition to the whole basis of parliamentarianism.

The second hostile force was the Catholic Church. Until the turn of the century the Church maintained the official detachment of Pius IX (*see* Chapter 4, section **N**). It instructed good Catholics to boycott elections, and scarcely any leading figure in national politics was a practising Catholic. When Pius X officially relaxed this boycott in 1904, it was not out of any increased regard for the state, but from fear of the increasing influence of socialism. The Church, therefore, became the potential ally of the more conservative elements in the state. As such, it was equally likely to be an ally, active or passive, of the anti-Marxist forces that arose in the wake of the First World War.

Lastly, in the years immediately before the war, parliamentary government came under attack from a resurgent nationalist party. Although its electoral success was modest, this group enjoyed disproportionate intellectual influence, notably from the support of the writer Gabriele D'Annunzio. The residual nationalism surviving from the Risorgimento received great stimulus from the war of 1911–12 in which Italy secured Libya from Turkey, while the mismanagement and huge cost of the war went further to discredit the existing regime. The entry of Italy into the European war in 1915 naturally enhanced the influence of this movement to an extent unprecedented since the capture of Rome in 1870.

B The rise of Italian fascism

The birth of the fascist movement

The immediate post-war period held considerable promise for an ambitious and flexible politician. The frustrations of the peace treaty, the economic difficulties that produced two million Italian unemployed by November 1919, and the subsequent disillusionment of many ex-servicemen, reduced

the prestige of the liberal regime to a new low ebb. The political format by which Mussolini hoped to exploit this discontent became evident with the formation in Milan (March 1919) of the first 'combat group' (*Fascio di combattimento*). The name of the group, and of the movement, was derived from the *fascio*, the insignia of the lictors of ancient Rome. A bundle of rods with an axe at its centre, the *fascio* was a symbol of unity and strength.

Initially, the programme proposed by these 'fascists' showed the continuing influence of left-wing politics, and especially of French syndicalism (*see* Chapter 8, section **M**). They proposed a republic, the decentralisation of government, the abolition of conscription, the closure of all banks and of the stock exchange, profit sharing and management participation by the workers, and the seizure of Church lands. For Mussolini, however, as Denis Mack Smith has stated, 'fascism was not a system of immutable beliefs but a path to political power'. When the party only polled 4,795 votes in the Milan elections of November 1919, fascist policy began a steady movement to the right.

The nature of fascist support

From 1920 the stress of fascist policy fell instead upon the twin themes of nationalism and anti-Bolshevism. Fervent support for D'Annunzio in his spectacular, illegal seizure of the city of Fiume for Italy (September 1919) seemed almost to annex him to the fascist cause. Meanwhile, the anti-communist violence of the fascist action squads (*Squadristi*) and the new party line in favour of free enterprise went far to reassure the middle classes. The change of direction was a substantial success. Big business was eager to subsidise this valuable anti-communist force, and substantial contributions from such sources as the Fiat motor company, the Pirelli tyre company and the Italian Banking Association put the fascists on a firmer financial footing than most of their rivals.

By late 1921 the party claimed 320,000 members, of whom 18,000 were landowners, 14,000 were small tradesmen, and 4,000 were industrialists. However, many of the party's members were not these, but peasants (36,000) or members of the urban working classes (23,000) seeking a refuge from what they saw as the twin evils of ruthless capitalism and doctrinaire socialism.

Benito Mussolini

Personality and aims

Although the rise of fascism in Italy had deeper and more complex causes than Benito Mussolini, it was his personality that had a profound influence upon the form taken by this alternative to liberalism.

Mussolini was born (29 July 1883) the son of a blacksmith, near Forli in the Romagna. The seeds of his hostility towards bourgeois society, its principles and its standards, which he maintained throughout his political career, may be found in his hard childhood. In the enthusiastic, republican socialism of his father may be found the impetus that propelled him into the ranks of the socialist party in his early days. In his turbulent, violent personality as a young man may be seen the beginnings of the vigorous, often incoherent gestures that later characterised so much of fascist policy. The young Mussolini was expelled four times from his various schools for indiscipline and violence.

His most recent biographer, Denis Mack Smith, has concluded that the innate streak of violence in his character was of as great importance in his development as any of the political philosophers by whom he later claimed to have been influenced.

Failing to find either satisfaction or success in his brief career as a teacher, Mussolini was soon set upon the road of political agitation, organisation and journalism. His success as editor of a provincial socialist journal (1909–12) led to national recognition and to the highly successful editorship of Italy's primary socialist organ *Avanti!* (*Forward!*) in November 1912. In his views during this period can be discerned some of the future bases of fascism. Identified with the left wing of Italian socialism, Mussolini was a violent critic of parliamentary government, and of those socialists who sought parliamentary seats. His solutions to the social and economic problems of contemporary Italy were revolutionary solutions, and he was vitriolic in his attacks upon socialists such as Turati and Bissolati who sought change by moderate reform.

Mussolini's conversion from internationalism and left-wing socialism shortly followed the outbreak of war in 1914. By condemning the Italian policy of neutrality in a sensational editorial in *Avanti!* (18 October 1914), he not only flew in the face of accepted socialist policy, but effectively turned his back on the party for ever. His change of heart has been interpreted in a variety of fashions. His former socialist colleagues, in their sense of betrayal, brought charges of foreign bribery. Other critics have seen it as a cynical acknowledgement that, with his recent election defeat in Forli (October 1913) and the collapse of the revolutionary 'Red Week' riots (June 1914), the political future of socialism seemed bleak. Christopher Hibbert has been more generous in his view that Mussolini was attracted to intervention in the war by the anticipation that it would bring nearer the revolutionary upheaval for which he hoped. There is also much to be said for the interpretation of S. W. Halperin, who has ascribed Mussolini's warlike attitude to 'his temperamental incapacity to abide a neutral stance, to remain a mere spectator, in the midst of world-shaking events'.

Although fascist historians later invented a number of heroic exploits for Mussolini, his military service seems to have been relatively uneventful, apart from an injury received during a training exercise. When he returned to civilian life and journalism, the editorials of his new journal *Il Popolo d'Italia* (*The Italian People*) were distinguished by views easily recognisable as those of embryonic fascism. Prominent among them were the demand that post-war Italy should be governed by those who had fought for her, and the resentment that Italy should be cheated of such fruits of victory as Fiume.

The electoral pact of 1921

The spectacular growth of this fascist faction made it a natural candidate for a place in one of the government's 'Transformist' coalitions: Giolitti had already aided the growth of fascism by turning a blind eye to the excesses of the *Squadristi* when, in May 1921, he accepted Mussolini's offer of an electoral pact. As part of a government alliance, the fascists won 35 parliamentary seats in the elections of that year. This was a small start in a house of 535 seats, but a substantial advance that gave Mussolini and his fellow deputies, as Denis Mack Smith has pointed out, 'a new authority, and respectability and a valuable freedom from arrest'.

C Mussolini's rise to power

It was neither probable, nor desirable to many in the fascist movement, that they should come to power by these parliamentary means. Mussolini himself found his style of oratory ill-suited to parliamentary debate, while other fascist deputies showed their contempt for the institution by brandishing pistols in the chamber and assaulting socialist deputies.

In the event, the crisis in Italian politics continued to operate to the advantage of the fascists. A general strike called by the socialists in August 1922 gave the *Squadristi* a golden opportunity to pose as the country's sole protection against the imminent 'red' threat. The strike, badly organised and ill-led, collapsed within 24 hours. This created the impression that the nation had been saved while the liberal regime stood helplessly by. Simultaneously with the formulation of a plan for the seizure of strategic points in Milan and other major cities, and for a subsequent march on Rome, Mussolini sought to reassure influential sectors of Italian opinion of fascism's regard for the monarchy and for economic liberalism.

The *coup d'état* began on 27 October 1922. In many cities, the active or passive support of local government guaranteed success, but it seemed unlikely that the 26,000 fascists converging on Rome could succeed against the regular troops in their path. Success was, however, guaranteed by the surprising refusal of King Victor Emmanuel III to sign his prime minister's decree of martial law. Historians seeking to explain this fateful timidity have variously stressed the degree of pro-fascist feeling in court circles, and the effect of veiled fascist threats to replace the king with the Duke of Aosta. 'Temperamentally,' wrote Denis Mack Smith, the king 'was drawn to anyone who would take firm decisions and control domestic unrest'. The result was that the ground was cut from beneath the feet of the liberal ministers. Putting aside any doubts, Mussolini exploited his position of strength and had, by 29 October, received a royal summons to form a ministry as the youngest prime minister in Italian history.

The official historians of fascism naturally portrayed the events of October 1922 as a glorious national revolution. More recently it has become fashionable to belittle the fascist insurrection and to stress the surrender of the regime through panic, weakness or self-interest. The truth lies between the two extremes. The insurrection was, indeed, a bold stroke, a substantial risk by its leaders, and carefully and intelligently prepared. On the other hand, it was resistable. Fascism owed its triumph ultimately, not to fascists alone, but to the mass of conservatives, businessmen, army officers, small traders and peasants, who saw Mussolini as the alternative to anarchy.

D The growth of fascist dictatorship

The dismantling of parliamentarianism

It was never likely that the fascist leadership would be content merely to capture the machinery of the liberal state. After an initially conciliatory attitude to other non-socialist parties, therefore, the first years in power were dedicated to the steady destruction of parliamentarianism in Italy. The success of the party's black-shirted *Squadristi* in the early years of the movement was such that Mussolini now transformed them (December 1922) into an official paramilitary body called the Volunteer Militia for National Security. Their wholesale use of violence and intimidation was to be a prominent feature of Italian elections in the 1920s.

The new prime minister also had more subtle means at his disposal. A new electoral law drafted by G. Acerbo (July 1923) aimed to transform fascism's minority status by proposing that any party gaining more votes than any of its rivals, providing that it gained at least 25 per cent of the total, would be entitled to two-thirds of the seats in the assembly. This was in the interests of political stability. It should be noted that this law, like others in the early days of Mussolini's power, became law with the help of liberal votes. This mutilated form of parliamentarianism limped on for five years, until a further electoral law (September 1928) decreed that the whole composition of parliament should be determined by the Fascist Grand Council headed by Mussolini. This body would formulate a list of 400 nominees which the electorate would then be invited to accept or reject *en masse*. Given the means of intimidation in the government's hands, it is perhaps surprising that as many as

136,000 voters rejected the list in 1929. By 1934, however, the number of rejections had fallen to 15,000.

Matteotti's murder and the 'Aventine Secession'

The Acerbo electoral law and the violence of the 1924 elections also precipitated the decisive clash with the party's major rivals, the socialists. A socialist deputy, Giacomo Matteotti, showed great courage in his open defiance and criticism of fascist methods. The result was his kidnap and subsequent murder by fascist thugs. Whether or not he had directly encouraged or ordered the crime, Mussolini clearly bore the moral responsibility for it, and his political position became extremely vulnerable. Two factors aided his survival. Once again, the political tactics of the socialists were naive. Their reaction to the death of Matteotti was to leave parliament in protest. This action became known as the 'Aventine Secession', in commemoration of an incident in ancient Roman history. Their eloquent gesture merely left the fascists in fuller control. Secondly, King Victor Emmanuel, the only man with the constitutional power to dismiss Mussolini, once again shirked a hard decision and accepted the argument of force.

The establishment of authoritarian rule

Initially shaken by the Matteotti crisis, Mussolini now seemed to exploit the new-found strength of his position. F. W. Deakin has stressed the important role in this played by nominal subordinates. Of special importance was the work of the new party secretary, Roberto Farinacci, in overhauling and centralising the party machinery for the tasks of national government. The first months of 1925 saw a miniature 'reign of terror' characterised by house searches, closures of hostile newspapers, harassment of political opponents and constant attacks upon freedom of association and of speech. In November, a plot against Mussolini's life by a former socialist deputy, Zaniboni, provided the pretext for the official suppression of the socialist party.

A series of decrees to strengthen the powers of provincial fascist officers, a formal decree (October 1926) banning all other political parties and the formation (September 1926) of a secret police force, the OVRA, completed the apparatus of political dictatorship.

E The fascist state: the corporative theory

The aims of corporativism

The years 1923–25 formed a period of ambiguous policy statements designed to attract the widest possible support, and of negative assaults upon existing institutions. Only very slowly did the outline of a fascist 'new order' emerge. In theory, this 'new order' owed much to the ideas of syndicalism, but in Italian hands the theories of Sorel had changed significantly. From being a means towards the revolutionary overthrow of capitalism, the 'corporative' system in Italy posed as a solution to the problems of class warfare. It also served as a bridge between the factions of workers and employers in the interests of the fatherland.

The machinery of corporativism

The suppression of existing socialist and Catholic trades unions paved the way for the so-called Rocco Law of April 1926. This law, while outlawing both workers' strikes and employers' lockouts, gave legal recognition to the fascist syndicates. Although these syndicates consisted exclusively either of workers or employers, the law provided for corporations, or 'central liaison organs', to mediate between the two. The actual implementation of this new order was extremely slow. Only in March 1930 was a National Council of Corporations created as an advisory body on the development of the system, and not until 1934 were the corporations actually set up. By 1936 there were 22 of them representing all the major branches of industrial, agricultural, artistic and professional life in Italy. Mussolini claimed to see in these corporations the logical successors to the parliament whose very *raison d'être* had ceased to exist, he claimed, with the death of the multi-party system. Indeed, in 1938–39, the parliamentary system was abolished in name as well as in practice, and replaced by a Chamber of Fasces and Corporations.

The reality of corporativism

In theory, therefore, the government of Italy moved towards a decentralised state in which the varying interests of workers and employers were directly represented through their corporations. In reality, in the words of the contemporary historian G. Salvemini, corporativism was 'an elaborate piece of imposing humbug'. For all their activity in an advisory capacity, the corporations had no role in the formulation of economic policy, which remained firmly in the government's hands. In each corporation, furthermore, the representatives of employers and workers were joined by officials of the Ministry of Corporations, whose task was to ensure that the government's view prevailed. The theory of decentralisation barely masked the reality of rigid fascist control.

F　The fascist state: the reality

The distribution of power

If corporativism did not dominate the Italian state under fascist rule, then what did? As we have seen, much fascist energy in the early years of power was poured into the task of disarming other existing sources of influence such as the other political parties and parliament (*see* section **D**), the trades unions (*see* section **E**) or the Church (*see* section **G**). The powers of the monarchy, already limited, were further restricted by laws that gave Mussolini the power to make laws by decree (January 1926), and deprived Victor Emmanuel of the right to select the prime minister (December 1928). On a local level, elected mayors were replaced by nominated fascist officials known as *podestà*. Even the local powers of the fascist *Ras*, the local party leaders taking their nickname from the semi-independent chieftains of Abyssinia, found themselves subjugated to central authority. They were unable to resist largely because their intense rivalry with each other made them so easy to isolate.

The Fascist Grand Council and its members

Apart from the corporations, the major new constitutional feature of the 1920s was the Fascist Grand Council. This was a body of 56 hierarchs (*gerarchi*), later reduced to 30, whose function as an organ of state came to include determining the succession both to the throne and to the premiership. Even so, the powers defined for it by the laws of 1928–29 make it clear that the Grand Council, too, played only a secondary role. Its membership, times of meetings, even the agenda that it should discuss, all remained the firm prerogative of the Duce. In

short, the end product of the fascist revolution was the personal dictatorship of Benito Mussolini. Two factors help to explain his success in this respect in the 1920s and 1930s. One is the comparative mediocrity of other leading fascists. 'Most of them,' wrote Denis Mack Smith, 'were unintelligent, grasping, jealous and incompetent, and jockeyed for place by telling tales against their rivals.' Of the men closest to the Duce some, like Roberto Farinacci and Italo Balbo, were glorified street fighters, lacking Mussolini's political flair. Some, like Dino Grandi, were too obsequious to consider firm opposition. Others, like the future foreign minister Galaezzo Ciano, who married Mussolini's daughter in 1930, had tied their own fate too closely to that of their leader to risk toppling him. Italian fascism produced no Goering, no Himmler, and certainly no Röhm.

Mussolini's image and leadership

The second factor in Mussolini's favour was his own enormous talent for self-advertisement. He exploited his journalistic talents to the full, not only convincing very many Italians that 'Mussolini is always right', but creating an image, very far from the truth, of a man who possessed all the talents. The controlled press portrayed him as an excellent violinist, fine horseman, daring pilot, bold war hero, and as an intellectual who had mastered all the major philosophies of the day and had found time to memorise whole cantos of Dante. This mastery of publicity, which made him a genius at the art of seizing power, goes far to explain the disappointing record of the fascist government. Denis Mack Smith has summarised Mussolini's failings as an administrator admirably. 'Mussolini's own mental processes never ceased to be governed by slogans and eight-column headlines. He preferred to argue and speechify rather than to penetrate behind words to reality and so never properly dissected a problem. Fascism, which affected to despise speeches and talk, was itself essentially rhetoric and blather.'

G　State and Church

The bases of co-operation

One influential element in Italian life could not be subdued or suppressed by threats and violence.

Relations between fascism and the Catholic Church remained complex and ambiguous throughout the 1920s. While Mussolini and other fascist leaders never lost their fierce anti-clericalism, and both groups remained especially divided over the question of the education and indoctrination of youth, in other respects they shared common ground. Ever the realist, Mussolini never seriously imagined that he could govern Italy successfully in the teeth of Catholic opposition. The Papacy, for all its reservations, still saw fascism as the only alternative to the godless doctrines of socialism.

Despite an interlude of tension in 1927, when the state dissolved the Catholic boy scout movement, Church and state extended olive branches to each other. Gentile's education act (February 1923) restored the compulsory religious education that the liberal regime had abolished in elementary schools. The following year, the Pope did fascism a singular service by withdrawing his support from the Catholic Popular Party, a substantial electoral rival. Always too progressive for the tastes of Pius XI, the party could not survive the blow, and Mussolini was left free of major parliamentary rivals.

The Lateran Accords

These signs of mutual respect reached fruition with the signature of a batch of agreements known as the Lateran Accords (February 1929). For the Church, the Accords settled most of the outstanding conflicts between the Papacy and the Italian state. By creating the tiny state within Rome, known as the Vatican City, the state restored a face-saving vestige of the Papacy's temporal authority. Furthermore, it confirmed catholicism as 'the only state religion', extended compulsory religious education to secondary schools and outlawed divorce. Lastly, the Papacy received a substantial financial compensation, amounting to some 1,750 million lire, for its losses since the Italian seizure of Rome in 1870. Mussolini's gains from the Accords were less tangible, but were perhaps greater. By linking his administration in the popular mind with the immense moral influence of the Church, he entered upon a period of unprecedented national popularity. The Lateran Accords thus represented the greatest political success of his career and the most lasting impact of fascist government on modern Italy.

The limits of Church–state co-operation

It should not be imagined that the agreements of 1929 represent a surrender by either party. Mussolini immediately reminded parliament that the Italian state 'is Catholic, to be sure, but it is above all fascist . . . exclusively, essentially fascist'. In 1931 a further crisis illustrated the lines beyond which neither side would step. In that year, Mussolini declared the disbanding of the youth and student groups affiliated to Catholic Action, an educational and moral organisation highly prized by Pius XI. In the face of a fierce Papal counter-attack Mussolini replaced the dissolution order with lesser limitations on the groups' activities. The incident illustrated the limitations upon fascist absolutism in Italy, the value of even tacit Catholic support to the government and, thereby, the shrewdness of the understanding reached in 1929.

H Education and culture

Fascism and the media

In common with the contemporary Soviet government, fascist Italy demanded in theory that all aspects of the cultural life of the society should support and sustain the regime. For the first time in western Europe, a government attempted to turn the considerable communications machinery of a modern state to a co-ordinated political purpose. The press was steadily subjected to the party line by the suppression of political papers such as *Avanti!* and consistent pressure upon other editors and owners. By 1926 there was no opposition press in Italy, so that E. R. Tannenbaum has referred to the fascist decades as 'the rule of the journalists'.

Fascism and education

The control of education was, of course, considered essential by the fascist regime. In the classroom, the 'fascistisation' of youth involved the strict control of textbooks and of curriculum, and the removal of teachers critical of fascist principles. The primary purpose of the school came to be the inculcation into the young of the fascist virtues, such as manliness, patriotism and obedience. 'A child who asks "Why?",' declared a textbook approved for eight-year-olds, 'is like a bayonet made of milk.' "You must obey because you must," said Mussolini, when explaining the reasons for obedience.' Glorification of the Duce was, of course, another pervasive element. Outside the school, Italy set a pattern for other authoritarian regimes by the law (April 1926) which introduced a system of compulsory youth organisation to coax the male child into the required fascist path. From four to eight he would belong to the 'Sons of the She-Wolf' (*Figli della Lupa*), from eight to fourteen to the *Balilla*, and to the age of eighteen to the 'Vanguard' (*Avanguardisti*). From 1937, the best graduates of this system might join the 'Young Fascists' (*Giovani Fascisti*) until the age of 21. Whatever the political success of the system, the fascist years marked no great advance in conventional educational areas. Illiteracy, which stood at 48.5 per cent in 1901, had been reduced by the liberals to 30 per cent by 1921, but still stood above 20 per cent in 1931.

Fascism and sport

Sport, too, was highly prized by the regime, both as a breeder of fascist virtues and as a source of nationalist propaganda. On a popular level, the *Dopolavoro* organisation was formed in May 1925. It hoped to provide for 'the healthy and profitable occupation of the workers' leisure hours', by means such as cheap holidays, libraries, lectures and theatrical entertainments. On a more élite level, several major sports were reorganised and centralised, and their international successes exploited by the state. In soccer, the 1934 World Cup competition was held in, and won by, Italy. She retained the trophy in 1938, to the great satisfaction of the regime. As boxing was naturally regarded by Mussolini as 'an essentially fascist method of self-expression', the triumph of Primo Carnera (1933) in the World Heavyweight Championship was hailed as a further proof of fascist virility.

The limits of cultural control

Like its ambiguous relationship with the Church, fascism's failure to dominate Italian cultural life illustrates the limits of its absolutism. Although the movement had a considerable appeal in intellectual circles in its early days, this was partly dissipated by its later authoritarianism. The conductor, Arturo Toscanini, a fascist candidate in 1919, left Italy for America in the 1920s. He was followed by the historian Gaetano Salvemini in 1925 and the physicist Enrico Fermi in 1938. Italy's greatest intellectual figure, the philosopher and historian Benedetto Croce, was an opponent of the regime from 1925, when he organised an anti-fascist manifesto. Yet he not only remained in the country throughout Mussolini's years in power, but continued to produce liberal historical works, and to publish his liberal review *La Critica*. Although usually cited as an example of fascist weakness, this might possibly be ascribed to fascist tolerance of an influential rival, putting Croce in the same bracket as the Pope. Certainly, he would not have survived either in Nazi Germany or in Stalin's Russia. A greater failure was the inability to found any true 'fascist culture'. Although Nobel Prizes for literature went to Grazia Deledda (1926) and to Luigi Pirandello (1936), neither was truly a fascist. Despite the much publicised foundation of the Royal Academy of Italy (October 1929), the literature and art encouraged by the regime remained, in E. R. Tannenbaum's words, 'conformist, old-fashioned and lifeless'. Only in the less directly political fields of engineering and music did names of international repute, such as Pier Luigi Nervi and Ottorino Respighi, emerge during the two decades of fascist Italy.

I The fascist economy: economic policy

The policy of De Stefani

Italian fascism inherited a depressing range of economic problems, including a sizeable budget deficit and a total of 500,000 unemployed. Its most consistent success in tackling these was achieved in 1922–25 when, largely for reasons of political expediency, the Ministry of Finance was in the hands of the liberal economist, Alberto De Stefani. His measures included the abolition of price-fixing and of rent controls, and the reduction of government expenditure wherever possible. His achievements included a budget that was in surplus for the first time since 1918, and a reduction in the total of unemployed to only 122,000.

The return to protectionism

Mussolini's motives for departing from this policy, and for replacing De Stefani with the financier and industrialist Giuseppe Volpi, have been the subject of debate. To Marxist commentators, of whom the contemporary French journalist D. Guerin was an extreme example, the reversion to protectionism was proof that Mussolini was doing the bidding of Italian capitalism. Heavy import duties were imposed, for example, upon grain, sugar and milk. Denis Mack Smith, however, is adamant that 'Mussolini was no mere instrument of business and agrarian interests'. He does concede that 'his ignorance of economics and human nature left him an easy target for sharks who wanted protective duties or who extracted money from the state for quite impossible schemes of industrialisation'. An explanation wholly consistent with other areas of fascist policy is that Mussolini was influenced by considerations of political prestige. Certainly, the revaluation of the lire (August 1926) at 90 to the pound, gave it an artificial impression of strength. The immediate result of this swing to protection was that the Italian economy ran into difficulties long before the Wall Street Crash. The low exchange rate of the lire deterred tourist traffic and damaged trade in luxury commodities.

The battles for land and grain

By 1930 the government, tempted by the prospects of domestic prestige and foreign military adventures, had adopted the principle of autarky, that is of economic self-sufficiency. The policy bred some impressive successes, such as the five-fold increase in electricity production between 1917 and 1942, and the spectacular rise in motor production by 1941, when an estimated 34,000 cars were completed. In typically ostentatious fascist fashion, however, the policy was constructed around three great national 'struggles'. The 'battle for grain', officially inaugurated in 1925, was superficially successful. Production figures that had been steady at 40 million 'quintals' since 1870 rose to 60 million in 1930 and to 80 million by 1939. It has been pointed out by agricultural authorities that the official fixation with grain damaged other forms of agricultural output, and kept the relative cost of Italian grain production high. The 'battle for land' was also marked by notable successes. Most famous of the land reclamation schemes was the draining of the Pontine Marshes near Rome to provide hundreds of thousands of acres of new farmland. Much of it, unfortunately, was lost again in 1943–45 due

to the ravages and neglect of war. It is also well worth noting, as Elizabeth Wiskemann does, that fascist attentions to southern Italy resulted in a more effective control of Mafia activities than has been achieved before or since. Also in the same vein of public works, which combined public utility with political propaganda, was the construction of motorways (*autostrada*) between Italy's main urban centres, and the electrification of some 5,000 km of Italy's railway system.

Population trends

Least necessary, and least successful, of the fascist 'struggles' was the 'battle for births'. Imagining that an increased population would provide proof of Italian virility and would support her claims for colonies, Mussolini demanded a rapid rise in the birthrate. Parents of large families were rewarded, while bachelors, with the exceptions of priests and maimed war veterans, were penalised by high taxes (1926). Abortion and contraception, of course, were outlawed. In this aim, so foolish in relation to Italy's limited resources, the Duce suffered bitter disappointment. Although the Italian population rose from 37.5 million (1921) to 44.4 million (1941), two quite different factors were primarily responsible. These were the fall in the death rate, and the restrictions placed upon immigration by the USA.

J The fascist economy: social impact

The absence of socio-economic change

The 'balance sheet' of the policy of autarky was not altogether negative. It produced some durable monuments, and served Italy well when the League of Nations imposed sanctions upon her in the course of the Abyssinian War. In general, its narrow political motives made the period from 1925–40 one of the most stagnant in Italy's economic history, in terms of industrial growth. In those years the annual growth in productivity was only 0.8 per cent, compared with 3.8 per cent in 1901–25 and 3.5 per cent in 1940–52. Cut off from the mainstream of world economics, Italy suffered recession earlier than other European powers, yet drew little benefit from the steady world recovery of the mid-1930s.

The fascist 'revolution' in Italy failed to transform the lives of the ordinary Italians as many of its early supporters had hoped. The 'battle for land', although a potent political symbol, fell far short of any substantial change in the pattern of land ownership in Italy. In 1930, the peasant smallholder still constituted 87.3 per cent of the farming populations, yet held only 13.2 per cent of the farmland. The richest 0.5 per cent of the landed population, on the other hand, still farmed 41.9 per cent of the available land. No significant change occurred in these proportions in the next decade. Smallholders and small businessmen alike found survival increasingly difficult, with an annual average of 7,000 small farms passing to the exchequer as a result of their owners' failure to pay land tax.

Fascism and living standards

Naturally, the fascist period was for most Italians one of stagnant or declining living standards. The task of penetrating fascist statistics is a complex one, and researchers have differed in their conclusions. They have not disputed improvement or decline, but merely about the rate of decline. Professor Chabod has claimed that the Italian farm labourer lost half, and in some cases more, of the real value of his wages, while C. Vannutelli has claimed a drop in the average 'per capita' income of the Italians from 3,079 lire (1929) to 1,829 (1934). The figures have to be set against a falling cost of living and a subsequent rise of the per capita income to return to the 1929 level by 1937.

Workers' rights

One should also note the range of social benefits that the workers' syndicates secured, most of them late in the fascist period. Sick pay was first introduced in 1928, followed ten years later by a 'package' comprising end-of-year bonuses, paid holidays and severance pay.

Although it is possible that the lot of the worker in fascist Italy may have been less severe than it has been painted, the abolition of the right to strike, the failure of the government's 'Charter of Labour' (1927) to guarantee a minimum wage, and an unemployment figure that rose from 110,000 (1926) to over a million (1933), and then levelled off at around 700,000, all show that the years 1923–40 marked little tangible improvement in the worker's life.

K The international influence of fascism

The conquering creed of the inter-war years?

Considering the steady collapse of liberal democratic modes of government throughout Europe in the 1920s and 1930s, it would be tempting to see Mussolini as he sometimes pictured himself, as the founder of the conquering political creed of the era. By the end of the 1930s, indeed, authoritarian government had been established in Germany, Spain, Portugal, Hungary, Austria, Rumania, Yugoslavia and Poland. Even in France democracy was under severe strain. One should not exaggerate, however, the international influence of the Italian fascist form of government which Mussolini himself had declared earlier in his career was 'not for export'.

Many apparent similarities between fascism and these other movements result, not from conscious imitation by the latter, but from common features in the movements' origins. Hungary, like Italy, received a strong nationalist impulse from the supposed injustices of the peace treaties, and the short-lived socialist regime of Bela Kun (1919) which left an even stronger anti-communist feeling than the one which had helped Mussolini to power. The threatening proximity of the Soviet Union also stimulated anti-Marxist passions in Hungary, Poland, Finland and Rumania alike.

Italian influence on the European right

When Italian fascism did directly influence her 'sister' movements, it was in the one area where Mussolini showed true mastery, in the tactics of the seizure and consolidation of power. There can be little doubt of the direct influence upon Hitler of the fascist use of salutes, uniforms and rallies as means of fascinating the public, and of the use of organised violence to terrorise one's enemies. In Germany, however, these tactics remained means to other ends, whereas in Italy they too often appeared as ends in themselves. Much later, Hitler remained fond of referring to Mussolini as 'his only friend', and of claiming that it was the Italian's example that had given him the initial courage to pursue his own political ambitions. In Hitler's consolidation of power many elements, such as the suppression of the press and of the trades unions, had close parallels in Italy. Throughout Europe, especially where fascistic movements still struggled to achieve power, the superficial paraphernalia of Italian fascism was imitated, as for example in Mosley's British Union of Fascists, among the French *Cagoulards*, and in the Rumanian Iron Guards.

The limits of Italian influence

Direct imitations of Italian ideology or methods of government are, however, harder to detect. Corporativism appeared in the right-wing programmes of Salazar in Portugal and of Dollfuss in Austria, while the Italian 'Charter of Labour' (1927) found echoes in Spanish 'Falangist' policy and in Portugal. Neither had any parallel in the Nazi movement. The French *cagoulards* and the Austrian *Heimwehr* were rare in having direct contact with the Italian government. In many cases it is easier to pick out direct contrasts with Italian fascism. The Catholicism that Mussolini tolerated because he could not defeat it was a central factor in the authoritarianism of Dollfuss in Austria and of the Spanish Falange. The Greek Orthodox Church played an equally strong role in the thought of Codreanu, creator of the Rumanian Iron Guard movement. Where Italian fascism had made a virtual prisoner of the monarchy, the Spanish dictator Primo de Rivera was largely motivated by an unswerving loyalty to the crown. Totalitarianism, to which Mussolini aspired, but which only Hitler perfected, was not seriously sought by Primo de Rivera, by Dollfuss, or by Pilsudski in Poland. Their opponents continued to operate in public, albeit often under difficult conditions. In short, it is easy to over-estimate the international influence of Italian fascism, as it is to exaggerate the united nature of right-wing politics as a whole in inter-war Europe. As Elizabeth Wiskemann has remarked, 'Italian fascism was not the conquering creed of the twentieth century', but merely in some superficial respects 'led a political fashion for two decades'.

The influence of Nazism upon Italian fascism

By the late 1930s, there was increasing evidence that fascism itself was coming strongly under the influence of more dynamic forces. Several of the means by which Mussolini sought to revivify his regime appeared, although he strongly denied it, to be reflections of German practices. The Ministry of Popular Culture (*Minculpop*) set up in June 1937 played much the same role as Goebbels' Propaganda Ministry. Above all, the range of anti-Semitic legislation which successively forbade foreign Jews to enter Italy (September 1938), and banned Italian Jews from public, academic and party posts (November 1938), seemed incongruous in a country with so little previous history of anti-Semitism. It could only be seen as an imitation by Mussolini of his more forceful partner. Such a trivial matter as the introduction of the 'goosestep' into the Italian army, under the new title of the 'Roman step' (*Passo Romano*), convinced many of the extent to which, as Elizabeth Wiskemann put it, 'fascism in Italy lost its character and became a poor imitation of German National Socialism'.

L The aims of fascist foreign policy, 1922–34

The bases of foreign policy

Although the details of fascist Italy's international dealings are to be found elsewhere (*see* Chapter 17), it is apt to consider here the broader principles that shaped those dealings. Foreign policy played a leading role in the government of fascist Italy. Not only did the aggressive poses consistently struck by Mussolini and his followers make it essential to pursue a 'dynamic' policy, but there were many in Italy in the 1930s who believed that the government used foreign affairs as a convenient distraction from the stagnation of domestic policies. A leader who declared, as Mussolini did, that 'it is a crime not to be strong', was committed to seek national prestige wherever possible. No parallel in Italian foreign policy, however, can be found to the programme of *Mein Kampf*. Many commentators have concluded that fascist policy was merely incoherent, based upon an opportunistic seeking of advantage wherever it could be found. Those who have seen more consistent purpose in it have usually agreed with the contemporary English statesman, Lord Halifax, who saw in Mussolini's aims 'the classic Italian role of balancing between Germany and the western powers'.

Relations with Britain and France in the 1920s

Certainly, Mussolini carefully pointed out to parliament upon coming to office (November

1922) that, although Italy had 'no intention of abandoning her wartime allies', she did not accept the peace treaties as permanent or perfect. She would not hesitate to seek revision 'if their absurdity becomes evident'.

Neither France nor Britain was a 'natural' ally for fascist Italy. Both were liberal democracies, often highly critical of Mussolini's domestic policies and methods. Also, both had considerable interests in the Mediterranean which, Mussolini told the Italians in the style of the Roman Empire, was *Mare Nostrum* ('Our Sea'). Between Italy and France, the old territorial claims to Corsica, Nice and Savoy, lost in the days of Italy's weakness, still rankled. The years of the Ruhr occupation, of economic crises and the consolidation of the Soviet Union were no time, however, to desert such apparently powerful allies.

Sources of German–Italian tension, 1922–34

Italian relations with Germany remained even more ambiguous. The rise of Nazism excited two conflicting emotions in Mussolini. On the one hand, he was enormously pleased at the triumph of 'his' doctrines in so powerful a state. For many years, furthermore, he badly underestimated the German leader. 'In politics,' he told an associate in the early 1930s, 'it is undeniable that I am more intelligent than Hitler.' On the other hand, the prospect of resurgent German nationalism creating a 'Greater Germany' on Italy's borders horrified him. Austria, indeed, provided one of the keys to Italy's alignment in the 1930s. By 1922, Italy's traditional enemy had been reduced to the status of a weak 'buffer' state between Italy and Germany. Her territory in the South Tyrol had been ceded to Italy and the fascist government had pursued a brutal policy of 'Italianisation'. She forbade the use of German, and changed place names and personal names in what now had to be referred to as the 'Alto Adige'.

The prospect that Austria might become a province of a dynamic German state, committed to rule over all German territories, was the greatest problem facing Italian diplomats in 1925–35. The protection of Italy's frontier on the Brenner Pass was Mussolini's main motive in his co-operation with France and Britain in the Locarno Pacts (*see* Chapter 17, section **F**) and in the subsequent Four Power Pact and Stresa agreement. By way of uni-

lateral action, Mussolini sought to prop up Austria by subsidising, from 1930, the anti-Nazi *Heimwehr* militia. She also concluded the Rome Protocols (March 1934), an agreement to promote trade between Italy, Hungary and Austria.

Italian ambitions in the Balkans and in Africa

Meanwhile, Italy was unwilling to accept the international repose envisaged by the peace treaties and the League of Nations, and so sought to improve her influence and status in traditional areas of involvement. The first of these was on the east cost of the Adriatic. In 1923 Mussolini defied the League of Nations by an invasion of the Greek island of Corfu to exact compensation for the murder of Italians engaged on League business. The eventual withdrawal from Corfu was followed by more permanent gains. Agreement with Yugoslavia (January 1924) allowed Italy to acquire Fiume, designated a 'free city' by the peace treaties. In November 1926, a pact with Albania tied that state to close economic dependence upon Italy. By the time of the conclusion of Mussolini's treaty with Hungary (April 1927), supplying arms and aid to the chief revisionist state in eastern Europe, Mussolini had seemed to become, in the words of Elizabeth Wiskemann, 'the chief anti-democratic conspirator of Europe'. Also, he had established a strong position as patron of the minor states of eastern Europe.

The second area of ambition was Africa. Mussolini's main justification was that imperialism provided relief for Italy's problems of overpopulation. Denis Mack Smith has dismissed this as bogus, preferring to see African expansion as a means of rivalling the Mediterranean influence of Britain and France. Thus, much of the 1920s saw a brutal colonial war in Libya, and a systematic build-up of arms and resources in Somalia. The latter policy betrayed the plans that Mussolini was nursing even then for his major colonial project, the acquisition of Abyssinia (*see* Chapter 17, section **J**).

The failure of fascist foreign policy

Superficially, the confused and hesitant nature of western diplomacy in the 1930s seemed to offer great hopes for this policy of opportunistic aggrandisement. That it ultimately brought disaster was due to three main factors. From 1932, Mussolini was in personal control of foreign policy, free from the restraints of traditional diplomats, and frequently the prisoner of his own rhetoric. He had dismissed Dino Grandi as foreign minister, first taking over the duties himself, and then transferring them to his compliant son-in-law, Count Ciano. Secondly, he badly underestimated Hitler, and by his own destabilisation of European politics, helped to further the projects of the man who was ultimately to destroy fascist Italy. Lastly, for all his warlike slogans, Mussolini totally failed to provide Italy with the means to fight and to win a modern war although he was head of the armed forces by 1932.

In 1939, when the Versailles peace finally collapsed, writes Denis Mack Smith, 'the prosaic truth turned out to be that only ten divisions were ready to fight and these were understrength, with antiquated and inadequate equipment'. The air force, which Mussolini had boasted would 'darken the sky', was described by a contemporary aviation expert as 'irremediably out of date'.

Questions

Essay questions

1 Who, if anyone, in Mussolini's Italy benefited from fascism? (ULEAC)

2 How effective a dictatorship did Mussolini impose on Italy in the years 1922–43? (NEAB)

3 How far did the Italian fascist government have any significant domestic achievements by 1940? (UCLES)

4 Account for the popularity of Mussolini in Italy after 1922. (WJEC)

5 Why did democracy fail in Italy after 1918? (Oxford Entrance)

6 To what extent was the fall of Mussolini in 1943 a consequence of the long-term failures of Italian fascism? (AEB)

Mussolini's fascist empire

Study the following source carefully, and then answer the questions based upon it.

Blackshirts of the Revolution, Italian men and women of the fatherland and in the world, listen! All knots were cut by our gleaming swords, and the African victory remains in the history of the fatherland entire and unsullied. Italy has her empire at last; a fascist empire because it bears the indestructible tokens of the will and of the power of the Roman lictors, because this is the goal towards which, during fourteen years, were spurred on the exuberant and disciplined energies of the young and dashing generations of Italy. An empire of peace, because Italy desires peace, for herself and all men, and she decides upon war only when it is forced upon her by imperious, irrepressible necessities of life. An empire of civilisation and humanity for all the populations of Abyssinia. That is the tradition of Rome, who, after victory, associated the peoples with her own destiny.

The Italian people has created the empire with its blood. It will fertilise it with its labour and will defend it against anybody whomsoever with its arms. In this supreme certainty raise up your weapons and your hearts, to salute after fifteen centuries the reappearance of the empire upon the fateful hills of Rome.

Mussolini's speech on victory in Abyssinia, 9 May 1936.

a i Explain the meaning of the underlined words. [2]
  ii What did Mussolini mean by a victory 'entire and unsullied'? [3]
b i What does the source reveal of the characteristics of the 'fascist empire'? [3]
  ii Explain the contradictions and inconsistencies in Mussolini's argument in favour of the Italian conquest of Abyssinia. [4]
c In what ways does this source contribute to an understanding of Mussolini's imperial ambitions? [8]

(WJEC)

16

The Third Reich

A photomontage composed by the American artist, John Heartfield. It makes use of Hitler's boast that 'millions stand behind me'.

What ambiguity is there in Hitler's claim that 'millions stand behind me'?

How does the artist view the question of where Hitler gained his support?

How accurate do you consider Heartfield's interpretation to be?

The Historical Debate

The volume of literature on the Third Reich, both of general interpretations and of more specialised studies, is enormous, and its fascination shows little sign of diminishing. Through the complexity a number of consistent themes of interpretation may be distinguished. The debate upon the nature of the regime's foreign policy has already been outlined in this chapter (*see* section L) and elsewhere (*see* Chapter 17, section Q). The nature of National Socialism, however, has provoked lively controversy. Four main explanations have been proposed as to the ease with which the German people succumbed to the doctrines of the movement.

Firstly, arising in part from wartime hostility towards Germany, came the view that Nazism was a logical development of the authoritarianism and nationalism evident throughout the previous century or more of German history. As an extension of the unhealthy respect for power evident as early as 1848, Nazism was a specifically German phenomenon. This argument was put forward in England by Rohan Butler (*The Roots of National Socialism*, 1941) and in France by E. Vermeil (*Germany: An Explanatory Essay*, 1945), and is prominent in William Shirer's best-selling *Rise and Fall of the Third Reich* (1960). Similarly, in one of the most popular summaries of modern German history (*The Course of German History*, 1945) A. J. P. Taylor wrote that 'during the preceding eighty years the Germans sacrificed to the Reich all their liberties; they demanded as reward the enslavement of others'.

Naturally, such an interpretation of Germany's past did not prove immediately popular with her own writers. In direct contradiction to Taylor, Gerhard Ritter wrote that 'there is no doubt that the majority of educated Germans were very distrustful of the Hitler propaganda. Very many felt at the time of Hitler's victory that his political system was foreign to them.' Ritter (*The Historical Foundations of the Rise of National Socialism*, 1955) and E. Nolte (*The Three Faces of Fascism*, 1966) were thus among those who favoured the view of Nazism, not as the product of German history, but as the product of the unprecedented social and economic pressures upon Europe in the 1920s and 1930s. Its roots were also those of Italian fascism, and of similar movements in France, Spain and elsewhere. Another prominent German authority, Karl Bracher (*The German Dictatorship*, 1969), actually combines both schools of thought by insisting that 'past research has made clear that an examination of the roots of National Socialism must be conducted simultaneously on two levels; the German and the over-all European'. Relatively close to the 'European' view of Nazism is the Marxist interpretation of the movement proposed in the 1930s and still persisting in some left-wing circles today. In the Marxist view, Nazism should be seen as the last resort of embattled and besieged capitalism in the aftermath of the Russian Revolution and of the Great Depression. As representatives of this school, one might quote the work of F. L. Neumann (*Behemoth:*

The Structure and Practice of National Socialism, 1944) and of R. A. Brady (*The Spirit and Structure of German Fascism*, 1937), both of whom viewed Nazism as a mass middle-class movement confronting and defeating a mass working-class enemy.

A fourth and common approach to the history of the Third Reich concentrates predominantly upon the personality of its founder and leader, Adolf Hitler, and sees him as the evil genius primarily responsible for the disasters of the 1930s and 1940s. Hitler has been the subject of an unprecedented volume of psychological and psychohistorical works, investigating the intricacies of his family relationships, or his sexual make up, to explain the mentality and motivation of the man. Of these, R. G. Waite (*Adolf Hitler: The Psychopathic God*, 1977) and W. Langer (*The Mind of Adolf Hitler*, 1972) may serve as examples. Although such an approach devalues many important factors in the rise of the Third Reich, it is difficult to explain the events of that rise in isolation from Hitler's dynamic personality. Alan Bullock (*Hitler: A Study in Tyranny*, 1952 and *Hitler and Stalin: Parallel Lives*. 1991) is undoubtedly justified, therefore, in his conclusion that 'the evidence leaves no doubt that no other man played a role in the Nazi revolution or in the history of the Third Reich remotely comparable with that of Adolf Hitler'.

A Adolf Hitler as party leader

Hitler as orator and publicist

Hitler's primary qualification for a political career was his extraordinary talent as an orator. In part, this was based upon careful study of all the elements of public speaking, and brilliant mastery of the tactics of dogmatic assertion, sarcasm and emotional appeal. As W. Carr has written, 'a Hitler speech was superb theatre . . . Hitler was his own script writer, choreographer and actor-manager all rolled into one'. His success was not wholly explained, however, by contrived effects, but was largely due to the intense sincerity of his nationalistic outrage, and by his ability to communicate thereby with the outrage and frustration of millions of Germans. Otto Strasser described the effect of a speech as follows. 'He enters a hall. He sniffs the air. For a moment he gropes, feels his way, senses the atmosphere. Suddenly he bursts forth. His words go like an arrow to their target; he touches every private wound on the raw, liberating the mass unconscious, expressing its innermost aspirations, telling it what it most wants to hear.'

Such skills were more than adequate for one who saw himself at first only as a 'Drummer' preparing the way for a greater leader, a John the Baptist, smoothing the way for Germany's true saviour. The stage at which he came to believe in himself as that saviour is unclear; perhaps as he reformulated his political views after the failure of the Munich putsch of 1923 (*see* Chapter 14, section D). The years after 1923, however, saw the emergence of Hitler as unchallenged party leader.

Hitler as 'weak dictator'

He achieved and fulfilled this role in an unorthodox fashion, for his were not the usual talents of political organiser and administrator. Lazy, and often bored by practical detail, he has been called by W. Carr a 'chronic procrastinator', while K. S. Pinson has gone so far as to declare that 'mediocrity was Hitler's most distinguishing characteristic'. Administrative mediocrity, however, was wholly outweighed by a remarkable political instinct, an unconquerable will-power and self-confidence, total ruthlessness, and a talent for winning the dogged devotion of individuals. It is indeed quite probable that he even cultivated his disinterest in

detail and practicalities to maintain party unity, and to present the image that he maintained so well throughout his career as the demi-god, the man of destiny, far above the petty wrangling that disfigured and corrupted mundane politics. Above all, as Hjalmar Schacht described him, Hitler was 'a mass psychologist of really diabolical genius'. These were the talents that transformed Adolf Hitler from the 'nobody of Vienna' into the most dynamic and fateful figure in German history.

B The doctrine of National Socialism

The ancestry of Nazism

The origins of the Nazi Party and its first disastrous bid for power in 1923 have been noted elsewhere (*see* Chapter 14, section D). What concerns us here are the structure and aims of the party as it renewed itself in the decade 1923–33.

The intellectual antecedents of Nazism must be sought in a bewildering variety of locations. Essentially a distillation of resentments and fears, it was philosophically an incoherent rag-bag of elements borrowed from most of the major political tendencies of the last century. From Germany alone it borrowed the conservative *realpolitik* of Bismarck, the nationalism of Fichte and the godless humanism of Nietzsche. Its racial theories leaned heavily upon those of Houston Stewart Chamberlain (*Foundations of the 19th Century*, 1899) and of the Comte de Gobineau (*Essay on the Inequality of the Human Races*, 1855), who had argued from the lunatic fringes of Darwinism that the key to human development lay in the inevitable triumph of the Aryan races over the 'lesser varieties of mankind'.

From further afield, and more recently, came the practical examples provided by Italian fascism with its attractive trappings, and its bold seizure of national power. Also there was the ruthless example of Stalin in his consolidation of power in the Soviet Union. Although he was distanced from Stalin's political aims, Hitler himself could only feel the greatest respect for Stalin's coldly logical methods. 'Stalin and I,' he was to declare, 'are the only ones who see the future.'

The philosophy of *Mein Kampf*

Some semblance of cohesion and consistency was

given to this variety of influences by the initial programme of the National Socialist Party (February 1920) which predated Hitler's dominance over the party and, more importantly, by Hitler's own political testament *My Struggle* (*Mein Kampf*). This was written during his imprisonment after the failure of the 1923 coup, and published in 1925. A rambling and highly personal work, *Mein Kampf* provided no precise manifesto for future government, but made clear the essential precepts upon which the Nazis and their leader intended to proceed.

Central to Hitler's argument was the conviction that the only true basis of the state was, not that of class interest (an invention of Marxism and Judaism) or of community of economic interest, but that of race. It was thus the primary duty of the German state to unite within its borders all those of common racial origin, and to eliminate alien elements that might weaken or corrupt the ethnic community (*Volksgemeinschaft*). In the case of Germany, this meant the elimination of the influence of world Jewry. In Hitler's view their international conspiracy bore the responsibility for all Germany's recent ills. Subsequently, the major duty of the state would be the provision of adequate resources and 'living space' (*Lebensraum*) for the population that dwelt by right within its boundaries. As the preservation of its people was the very reason for the state's existence, it was not only permissible, but positively desirable for the state to acquire this *Lebensraum* by struggle against neighbouring races. Nor did Hitler attempt to dodge the implications of this doctrine in the specific case of Germany. 'History proves, he declared in *Mein Kampf*, 'that the German people owes its existence solely to its determination to fight in the east and to obtain land by military conquest. Land in Europe is only to be gained at the expense of Russia.'

Political authority: the *Führerprinzip*

To provide the dynamism and the unity of purpose necessary for the achievement of such a visionary programme, Nazism defined the 'leader principle' (*Führerprinzip*). Thereby, each level of Nazi organisation was committed to unquestioning obedience to its chief, with ultimate allegiance owed to the man at the apex of the pyramid of command, the Führer. This was to form an essential feature of Nazism. This gave the appearance of consistency

to a divided movement and ensured Hitler's personal authority. The principle also appealed to millions of Germans for whom representative democracy seemed a short road to economic ruin and to national humiliation. This principle allowed the Nazis to pose not merely as the latest candidates for party political power, but also as the appointed guardians of the destiny of the whole German nation. 'The Führer,' wrote the Nazi theorist Ernst Huber in 1933, 'is the bearer of the people's will; he is independent of all groups, associations, and interests . . . In his will the will of the people is realised.'

The socialist element in Nazism

For all this, the views of prominent party members as to Nazi priorities were by no means unanimous when they came to power. To such men as the brothers Otto and Gregor Strasser, and to many of the ex-soldiers who filled the ranks of the SA, the socialist element, the desire to overturn the great capitalist enterprises that had made such a contribution to the economic hardships of the past decade, was central to National Socialism. 'We are enemies,' Gregor Strasser wrote, 'deadly enemies of the present-day capitalist economy with its exploitation of the economically weak, with its unjust wage system, with its immoral evaluation of the individual according to property'. To Hitler such doctrine was divisive, and alienated forces without which German national greatness could scarcely be restored. For him, it remained essential to concentrate upon such vague and emotive concepts as 'Fatherland', '*Volk*', 'loyalty' and 'sacrifice'.

While one can appreciate the reasons for the judgement of D. Schönbaum that Nazism was 'a conglomerate of disparities and contradictions', the movement, like fascism in Italy, retained an element of negative cohesion in its prime targets of hate. The Versailles Treaty, the Weimar Republic, parliamentary liberalism in general, Marxism, and Judaism, all condemned and execrated, were the objects that united the Nazi movement in 1933.

C The Nazis' supporters

The major sources of Nazi support

To whom, therefore, did Nazism appeal and for what reasons? An analysis by M. K. Kater of 4,800 party members in 1923 shows 60 per cent of them to originate from the lower middle, or skilled working classes. These were men who had established some small stake in the world and feared that social and economic chaos would drag them back to the bottom of the ladder. Shopkeepers and small tradesmen (14 per cent), clerks and minor officials (17 per cent), skilled craftsmen (20 per cent) and specialist workers (9 per cent), were prominent on party lists. Two major modifications to this pattern of support had occurred in the years between 1930–33. The first was the emergence of the Nazis as the prime representatives of nationalist politics. This arose from the so-called Harzberg agreement (October 1930) with the Nationalist Party, based upon a common anti-republican campaign in opposition especially to the Young Plan. The co-operation of such Nationalist figures as the industrialist Alfred Hugenberg, Hjalmar Schacht (head of the Reichsbank) and Franz Seldte (head of the *Stahlhelm* veterans' organisation) extended Nazi influence into spheres where it could scarcely have hoped to have penetrated before. Secondly, came the party's remarkably successful campaign to win peasant support, and to infiltrate existing agrarian organisations. H. Gies has shown that the Nazi share of the rural vote rose from 22.6 per cent (1930) to 52.4 per cent (1933), while their share of the urban vote never rose higher than 39.6 per cent (1933).

The upsurge in Nazi support, 1929–33

It is not difficult to understand, therefore, why both party membership and electoral support stagnated during the relative stability of 1924–29, to be regenerated by renewed economic crisis in the wake of the Wall Street Crash. In 1928, the party had 40,000 members, received about 1.03 million votes, and won 12 Reichstag seats. Between 1931–32, those figures rose to 800,000, 16.5 million, and 230 respectively. The motives of these new adherents were undoubtedly similar to those that moved Albert Speer after his first exposure to Hitler's oratory in 1931. 'Here it seemed to me was hope. Here were new ideals, a new understanding, new tasks. The perils of communism could be checked, Hitler persuaded us, and instead of hopeless unemployment, Germany could move towards economic recovery. It must have been during these months that my mother saw an SA parade in the streets of Heidelberg. The sight of discipline in a time of chaos, the impression of energy in an atmosphere of universal hopelessness, seems to have won her over too.'

D   The consolidation of power: legislation

The Reichstag fire and the Enabling Act

Despite their popular pose as a revolutionary party, the Nazis had come to power by wholly constitutional means (*see* Chapter 14, section **G**). It would not be excessive, however, to claim that the years after 1933 witnessed an adaptation of the German state to Nazi needs that was truly revolutionary. Like Mussolini in 1923, Hitler was never likely to be satisfied with power limited by a constitution and by the presence in the state of parties and interests potentially hostile to his own. At first, his tactics for strengthening his position centred upon the Reichstag election to be held in March, for which he prepared with a massive propaganda campaign that stressed the continuity between Nazism and other forms of German conservatism, and by practical measures such as Goering's rapid extension of Nazi control over the police and civil service in Prussia. The result still left the Nazis with the direct support of only 43.9 per cent of the population, but by then a whole new range of possibilities had opened up for Hitler.

The fire that destroyed the Reichstag building (27 February 1933) provided such a convenient crisis for the Nazis that it was supposed for many years that their agents had started it. It now seems, as F. Tobias has demonstrated, that van der Lubbe, the unbalanced Dutch communist who was accused of the crime, really did commit it. The government may merely have exploited the happy coincidence. This powerful illustration of the 'communist threat', upon which Nazi propaganda had long insisted, went far to ensure public acquiescence in the arrest of communist deputies and in the passage of two measures central to the collapse of German democracy. The arrests themselves strengthened Hitler's position in the Reichstag. The Decree for the Protection of People and State (28 February) suspended the essential freedoms of the individual, giving the state unprecedented rights of search, arrest and censorship. The Enabling Law (23

Adolf Hitler

Personality and aims

The tenure of national power of the man who assumed the office of Chancellor in January 1933 lasted only 12 years. His tenure of real international power was shorter by half. The fact that his is undoubtedly the best-known face, and his the best documented political career of the century, bears witness to the extraordinary impact of the man. Yet Hitler's origins were unremarkable in the extreme. Born in the small Austrian town of Braunau am Inn (20 April 1889), he was the son of a customs official already well into middle age. His mother was a young peasant girl to whom Hitler remained so attached that he was later to link her death with Germany's defeat in the First World War, as the two great tragedies of his life. Academically and socially, the young Hitler was a failure. His inability to gain admission to the Academy of Fine Arts in Vienna (1907) formed the

prelude to 'five years of misery and woe' in the Austrian capital, living by odd jobs and occasional artistic work.

Hitler's 'Greater German' nationalism was already formed then, and he later claimed that it was in Vienna that he first formulated the intense and obsessive hatred of Jews and Judaism that was thereafter a central feature of his political beliefs. Convinced of the decadence of the Austro-Hungarian Empire, and of the invincibility of the racially more pure German Reich, Hitler evaded Austrian conscription in 1914 to serve in a Bavarian regiment. After a creditable military

career at the western front, the sudden collapse of the German war effort in November 1918 provided Hitler with perhaps the most traumatic blow of his early life. For him, there could be no other explanation than that the Reich, and all patriotic Germans, had been vilely betrayed by the socialists, Marxists and Jews prominent in the November 'revolution' and in the subsequent Weimar Republic. In subsequent years, Hitler propagated the myth of the 'stab in the back', not because of its propaganda value, but because he was personally convinced of its truth. His natural place thereafter was in the ranks of the extreme nationalist opposition to the Republic. In September 1917 he joined the tiny German Workers' Party which shortly afterwards changed its name to the National Socialist German Workers' Party (NSDAP). By July 1921 Hitler was its chairman.

March), which only the SPD opposed, transferred full legislative and executive power to the Chancellor, Hitler, for a period of four years. Undoubtedly, German democracy was done to death by Hitler, but he was greatly abetted in the crime by so-called democrats who lacked the determination to keep liberty alive.

Gleichschaltung

Long before the expiry of that four-year period, Hitler had destroyed or neutralised all those groups and institutions in a position to impose limits upon his power. This policy was referred to by the euphemism 'co-ordination' (*Gleichschaltung*). In some cases, the weapon used was the naked exercise of state or party power. Thus, the KPD and the SPD were formally outlawed and their property seized, while all other political parties except the Nazis were declared illegal by the Law against the New Formation of Parties. By accepting this law such well-established organisations as the Catholic

Centre Party effectively dissolved themselves and accepted Nazi dictatorship. In January 1934, after preliminary tampering with their constitutions, Hitler abolished the provincial assemblies of the *Länder*. In their places he put Nazi governors (*Reichstatthalter*), and made Germany a centralised, unitary state for the first time. Other institutions weakened their positions by attempts to compromise with the new government. The socialist trades unions had already guaranteed their non-intervention in political questions. They had also accepted the supervision of a Nazi *Reichskommissar* when (2 May 1933) stormtroopers occupied their offices throughout Germany, dissolved them, and began the enrolment of all labour into a German Labour Front. Other institutions lost their independence by a process of subtle infiltration. The Prussian civil service was brought under firmer control by the dismissal of nearly 30 per cent of its officers on racial grounds or on grounds of 'incompetence'. The legal and academic professions became subject to Nazi 'fronts' or 'academies' outside which there was little hope of practice or of professional advancement.

E The consolidation of power

Winning over German industrialists

Three major elements in German society were too powerful to be directly coerced, and perhaps bear more guilt for the accommodations that they reached with Hitler. The support of German industry for Hitler had got seriously underway in 1928–29, when his disciplining of the Strasser 'wing' of the party, and his subsequent alliance with the conservative Nationalist Party had convinced its leaders that the Nazis were not, as the contemporary joke had it, 'like a beefsteak, brown on the outside but red in the middle'. At this early stage substantial financial contributions to the party were made by a variety of banking and mining interests, headed by the great steel magnate Fritz Thyssen. Hitler's consistent policies of anti-socialist legislation and subsequent rearmament earned much wider support in these areas in the years immediately after his seizure of power.

Agreement with the churches

The Catholic Church, too, was quick to seek an arrangement with the new regime, which now found it convenient to play down its essentially anti-Christian nature. The Concordat (July 1933) that it concluded with the Nazi state in an attempt to preserve educational and similar privileges undertook to dissuade Catholic priests from political activity, and did much to hasten the collapse of the Centre Party. Unlike the Lateran Accords (*see* Chapter 15, section **H**) concluded with Mussolini, the Concordat represented an almost complete surrender to the new political leadership. Certain elements in the Lutheran Church, by agreeing to the formation of a Reich Church (*Reichskirche*), surrendered in similarly abject fashion. In this case, however, a breakaway Confessional Church managed with difficulty to survive as a symbol of Christian opposition to Nazism.

Control of the army

Like the major industrialists, the German army (*Reichswehr*) shared a community of interest with

the Nazi Führer. Its commanders had little objection to his declared nationalist aims, while the realisation of those aims seemed unlikely without heavy industry to produce weapons and without soldiers to use them. Although elements of suspicion remained, the army accepted in general the promises as to its future role made to it in February and March 1933. While this gave Hitler the support of the army, he had to wait longer for any substantial element of direct control. The death of President Hindenburg (February 1934) not only made possible the combination of the offices of President and Chancellor in the new office of 'Führer and Chancellor', but gave Hitler the chance to revise his relationship with the army. By imposing a new oath of allegiance upon all ranks (August 1934), he ensured their commitment, not to their superior officers, nor to the Fatherland, but directly to 'the Führer of the German Reich and People, Adolf Hitler'. The later dismissal of the war minister, General von Blomberg (January 1938), over the scandal of his marriage to a former prostitute, and of the Army Commander-in-Chief, General von Fritsch (February 1938), over trumped-up charges of homosexuality, merely consolidated and reinforced Hitler's control over the army at a time of increasing foreign commitment.

F The Night of the Long Knives

The threat from the SA

For all these successes in 'co-ordinating' influential elements in the state into the Nazi system, Hitler could not feel wholly secure by the beginning of 1934. Ironically the greatest surviving threat to him and to his policies came from within the Nazis' own ranks. The paramilitary SA (*Sturmabteilung*) had been formed in the early days of the movement to provide physical protection for Nazi meetings and to disrupt those of their opponents. Its attraction for disorientated former soldiers, as well as for simple hooligans, was enormous, and by late 1933 its numbers had swollen to some 2.5 million men. To its leader, Ernst Röhm, it represented the central weapon of the Nazi Revolution, the German equivalent of Trotsky's Red Army. It would guarantee the radical transformation of German society and, by taking over the functions of the *Reichswehr*, would guarantee the Nazification of the state. To Hitler, in the words of Alan Bullock, the SA was an 'embarrassing legacy of the years of struggle'. It had fulfilled its street-fighting purpose and served now only to scare industrialists and conservative army officers by its radical posturing. Besides, with the SA under his command, Röhm stood as the only man in the Nazi Party realistically able to challenge the power of Hitler.

The elimination of the SA threat

There is much dispute over the process by which Hitler reached the decision to eliminate the threat of the SA. Joachim Fest and Martin Broszat have pictured him upon a deliberate collision course with Röhm since the beginning of 1934, while Alan Bullock is inclined to believe that Hitler would have been willing to delay, had it not been for mounting pressure from the *Reichswehr*. The ill-health of Hindenburg, moreover, made it imperative for Hitler to enjoy full *Reichswehr* support when the opportunity arose for him to take over the dead President's functions. In any case, the decision had been taken by late June when Hitler unleashed the purge known since as the 'Night of the Long Knives' (30 June 1934). This was in response to bogus SA 'revolts' in Berlin and Munich staged by Himmler, Goering and their agents.

The estimates of those murdered by SS (*Schutzstaffel* – Protection Unit) squads with material support from the *Reichswehr* range from a low of 77 to a high of 401. The bulk of these were SA men, including Röhm himself and most of his hierarchy, shot in prison without trial. The opportunity to settle diverse scores with old rivals was, however, too good to miss. The dead also included General von Kahr, who had deserted Hitler in the 1923 *putsch*, Gregor Strasser, who had long opposed him within the party, and a number of other non-Nazi political figures.

The 'Night of the Long Knives' was Hitler's most spectacular and probably his most successful piece of *realpolitik*. For all the initial shock that it caused, it had eliminated the threat from the left of the party and assuaged important conservative interests outside the party. Less than three weeks after the event, 38,000,000 Germans gave their tacit support by accepting in a plebiscite vote Hitler's assumption of the office of 'Führer and Chancellor'.

G The Nazi state

The confusion of administrations within the state

In theory, the far-reaching process of *Gleichschaltung* transformed Germany into a state dominated by its single political party. 'The party,' declared Hitler in mid-1933, 'has now become the state', and that principle was legally enshrined in the Law to Ensure the Unity of Party and State (December 1933). In reality as Gordon Craig has put it, 'the smoothly functioning Nazi state was never much more than a myth', for government consisted largely of a jostling for influence between the old ministerial hierarchies and a variety of party bodies that sought to supervise or to control them. In several cases, ministers who were Nazis only in the sense of collaboration such as von Krosigk at the ministry of finance and Schacht at the ministry of economics, were highly successful in preserving the traditions of their departments.

On the other hand, the minister of the interior, Wilhelm Frick, a Nazi himself, ultimately failed to prevent the infiltration of his department by the Party Chancellery under Martin Bormann. The Foreign Office found itself in competition with the Nazi Bureau for Foreign Affairs, headed by Alfred Rosenberg, and with the specialist agencies headed by Joachim von Ribbentrop, before he himself became foreign minister in 1938. The pattern of 'dualism, struggles over competence, and duplication of function' was repeated at local government level between local administrators and Nazi provincial chiefs (*Gauleiter*). In all cases, a high price was paid in terms of administrative efficiency.

Some have claimed that this confusion arose from Hitler's great failings, his boredom with administrative detail, and his preference for wider questions, especially in foreign affairs. David Irving has even gone so far as to describe him as 'probably the weakest leader Germany has known this century'. More likely Hitler saw the departmental in-fighting as a deliberate means of maintaining his personal power, being the great arbiter in any such dispute. He was satisfied with a system that enabled him to block and nullify any initiative or individual unacceptable to him.

The roles of propaganda and terror

The Nazi state had two great cohesive agents, both

directly responsible to the Führer. One of these was the Ministry of Propaganda under the guidance of Joseph Goebbels. This reached new heights of sophistication through more complex and powerful media than had been available a generation earlier. The second body was the SS (*Schutzstaffel* – Protection Unit), with its secret police offshoot, the 'Gestapo' (*Geheime Staatspolizei* – Secret State Police). Founded in 1925, but transformed four years later with the appointment of Heinrich Himmler as its commander, the SS differed from the SA in several important respects. Whereas the SA was a mass organisation, relying upon force of numbers for its effect, the SS was an élite force, under Hitler's direct control. As such, its role extended rapidly once the Nazis were in power. From 1932 it dominated the party's intelligence work, from 1934 it had effective control of the nation's police system, and under the emergency laws of 1933, the SS controlled the concentration camps which sprang up to receive political opponents of the regime.

If there ever was such a thing as a Nazi state, it was primarily an organism for ensuring the maintenance of power, and the SS was at its centre. Surveying the general incoherence of Nazi administration, Gordon Craig has concluded that 'the force that prevented the regime from dissolving into chaos was terror, and its instrument was the SS'. The activities of the SS therefore expanded further as war increased the need for cohesion in Nazi policy after 1939 . Its members dominated the administration of the occupied territories, and its military wing, the '*Waffen SS*', sought to exert more and more influence over military affairs, resurrecting the threat that the army appeared to have conquered in the 'Night of the Long Knives'.

Thus, as was the case in fascist Italy, the varied and conflicting postures of Nazism amounted in practice in domestic policy to a mechanism for the maintenance of one man's power. The Reichstag after 1934 performed merely formal functions, and the cabinet rarely met. The Nazi theorist Ernst Huber admitted as much in his definition of the Nazi constitution in 1939. 'We must speak, not of state power, but of Führer power, if we want to describe political power in the national Reich correctly . . . The Führer power is not hemmed in by conditions and controls, and jealously guarded individual rights, but is free and independent, exclusive and without restriction.' It cannot be doubted that this power was hugely effective in the negative sense of destroying opposition. What it succeeded in creating now remains to be seen.

H The Nazi economy

The drive for full employment

Whatever the effects of terror and propaganda, the Nazi regime depended for its survival upon the solution of the monstrous economic problems that had caused so many voters to turn to the party in 1929–32. Yet at no time, as Karl Bracher has written, 'did National Socialism develop a consistent economic or social theory'. In place of such a theory, Nazism had a set of fixed and sometimes contradictory commitments. Within the context of those commitments, its economic achievements were considerable.

Firstly, to maintain popular sympathy and industrial support, an expansion of industrial activity and a dramatic reduction of unemployment were necessary. Without departing from the essential principles followed by Papen and Schleicher, the government poured money into public works, the most spectacular example of which was the construction of 7,000 km of motorway (*autobahn*). Aided by the recruitment of many unemployed into the Reich Labour Service, the unemployment figures fell from nearly 6 million to 2.5 million within 18 months of the Nazis' advent to power. With the subsequent expansion of heavy industry to meet the needs of re-armament, and the reintroduction of military conscription (1935), the Nazis could claim almost complete success in this field by 1939, when unemployment figures stood at less than 200,000.

Nazism and the 'little man'

The second range of commitments was met with less consistency and with less obvious success. A complex programme of legislation was introduced to preserve the German peasantry from the twin curses of rising industrial prices and falling prices for their agricultural produce. All peasant debts, totalling 12 billion Reichsmarks, were suspended between March–October 1933, and many imported foodstuffs were subjected to higher tariffs. The Hereditary Farm Law (October 1933) gave the smaller farmer security of tenure by forbidding the sale, confiscation, division or mortgaging of any farm of between 7.5 and 10 hectares, owned by farmers of Aryan stock. While this ensured the permanence of the peasant food producer, the very foundation of the German race in the view of many Nazi theorists, the law militated against the development of larger farming units and new farming methods, and thus ultimately against the self-sufficiency that was a major economic aim of the Nazi state. By 1936 the price of many basic foodstuffs had increased by up to 50 per cent since the Nazi advent to power.

The urban equivalent of the peasant, the small trader or business man, gained still less from the regime that he had helped to bring to power. A number of tentative laws, such as the Law for the Protection of the Retail Trade (May 1933) which was designed to protect the trader against the influence of the larger concerns, were far outweighed by the continued advance of 'big business'. This can be shown by the1500 new cartel arrangements between mid-1933 and the end of 1936. Richard Grunberger has estimated that, whereas only 40 per cent of German production was in the hands of monopolists in 1933, the proportion had grown to 70 per cent by 1937.

Nazism and 'big business'

Ultimately the regime would support the larger enterprises, given that its long-term priority was re-armament and self-sufficiency in all strategic products. This was perhaps the only economic goal towards which Nazi Germany moved with any consistency in the 1930s. The first phase of the policy was supervised by Hjalmar Schacht as President of the Reichsbank (from May 1933) and minister of economics (from June 1934). His major achievement was to limit the drain of Germany's foreign exchange by paying foreign debts in Reichsmarks. Also there was a series of trade agreements notably with Balkan and South American states, whereby Germany paid for her purchases in Reichsmarks, which thus encouraged her trade partners to purchase German goods in return. 'His creation of credit,' wrote William Shirer, 'in a country that had little liquid capital and almost no financial reserves, was a work of genius.' Schacht's great weakness from the Nazi point of view was his financial orthodoxy. His reluctance to spend more

than Germany was earning threatened to put the brake on the process of re-armament. It thus became necessary, by the announcement of the Four-Year Plan (August 1936), which was entrusted to the direction of Hermann Goering, to devise machinery for this task which was directly under the control of the Führer. The primary aim of the Four-Year Plan was to achieve self-sufficiency in strategic industrial and agricultural products, either by increasing production, or by developing synthetic substitutes. The plan had its important 'showpiece' successes, such as the Hermann Goering Steelworks erected at Watenstedt-Salzgitter. It established a complicated system of controls over prices, and the distribution of raw materials, but in some important respects, in fuel, rubber and light metals, Germany remained well short of self-sufficiency in 1939.

Conclusions

By most orthodox economic criteria, the economy of Nazi Germany was chaotic. Her reserves of foreign currency remained low, and her balance of payments remained dramatically in deficit. Karl Bracher and others have painted a picture of the ruination of the economy by Nazi exploitation. On the other hand, B. H. Klein has denied that preparation for war totally dominated German economic activity, stressing that production of consumer goods rose steadily right up to the eve of war in 1939. Certainly, by a mixture of Schacht's clever financing and 'windfalls' such as the confiscation of Jewish property and the seizure of Austrian assets after the Anschluss, the economy produced impressive results (*see* Table 16.1).

Table 16.1 The German economy under the Nazis

	Unemployed (m.)	Coal (m. tons)	Iron ore (m. tons)	Pig iron (m. tons)	Steel (m. tons)	Arms budget (billion RM)
1932	6.042 (Jan) 5.392 (July)	118.6	2.6	6.1	8.2	1.9
1935	2,974 (Jan) 1.754 (July)	143.0	6.0	12.8	16.2	6.0
1938	1.052 (Jan) 0.218 (July)	186.4	12.4	18.1	21.9	17.2

Marxist historians have usually been eager to portray the Nazi regime as a 'front' for the more effective pursuit of the aims of Germany's capitalists. By this theory, the suppression of trades unions and the expansion of heavy industrial output were among the 'tasks allotted by finance – capital to its fascism' (D. Eichholtz). T. W. Mason, on the other hand, speaks for a substantial school of thought in arguing the 'primacy of politics'. He has shown convincingly that, although there was a genuine degree of co-operation between industry and Nazism up to 1936, thereafter all major decisions were taken with the regime's political objectives in view. Often these decisions involved consequences of which the business community heartily disapproved, as in the case of attacks upon Jewish financial and industrial institutions. The decline of Hjalmar Schacht's influence, culminating in his resignation from the Reichsbank (January 1939), typifies the dominance of Nazism in its grim alliance with capitalism. Karl Bracher has supported these views in his conclusion that 'the basic principle of National Socialist economic policy was to use the traditional capitalist structure with its competent economic bureaucracy to move towards its prime objective: acceleration of re-armament'.

I Nazi society: workers and women

The living standards of the German worker

Promise of radical social change probably ranked only a little lower than the prospect of economic recovery and national resurgence as a vote winner for the Nazis in 1929–32. In the event, hopes of a 'social revolution' were frustrated. The dominant classes continued in most cases to exercise their social and economic functions and the Nazi advocates of radical change were eliminated. What change there was served not as a revolutionary end in itself, but as a means towards the broader Nazi aims of the consolidation of power and the preparation of the nation for war.

The emptiness of Nazi promises of a 'social revolution' should not lead one to suppose that German workers gained nothing from their industrial co-operation with Nazi strategy. Although many contemporary commentators, such as R. A. Brady and F. Neumann, stressed the class nature of the Third Reich, seeing it primarily as a middle-class mechanism for the exploitation of the working class, more recent authorities, such as D. Schoenbaum, have indicated instead the solid ben-

efits that accrued to many German workers during this period. Although they lost important rights such as that of union representation, maybe they were awarded prosperity as a consolation prize for the loss of political freedom, as were French workers under Napoleon III. Their greatest gain was, of course, employment. Arguments about the wage levels of the Third Reich are, as Gordon Craig has stressed, academic in view of the fact that six million workers were not receiving a salary of any sort in 1932. In any case there is evidence that, although average wages remained around the 1932 levels, those of skilled workers and workers in strategic industries such as metallurgy, engineering and building benefited markedly from Nazi industrial expansion with wage increases of up to 30 per cent. Production and sales figures for consumer goods in the immediate pre-war years suggest a distinct rise in the standard of living.

Nor should the activities of the 'Strength through Joy' (*Kraft durch Freude*) programme, for all their propaganda content, be dismissed solely as 'window dressing'. In 1938 alone, 180,000 Germans enjoyed holiday cruises under its auspices, while 10 million took holidays of one kind or another. Its activities also extended to evening classes, and a large variety of cultural and sporting activities. Material rewards, however, were often offset by declining conditions of employment. Above all, the German worker frequently put in far longer hours than any of his counterparts in western Europe or the USA. The industrial demands of the regime made 10 per cent increases in hours commonplace, with rises of 25 per cent in some specialised areas of employment. The national average working week lasted 49 hours in 1939, rising to 52 by 1943, with an increase of 150 per cent in the number of industrial accidents in 1933-39, and a 200 per cent increase in occupational diseases. Whether motivated by material gain or by patriotism, it can scarcely be doubted that, as R. Grunberger has put it, 'the working class that Karl Marx had seen as being in the van of the proletarian revolution . . . significantly extended the lifespan of the Third Reich by exertions that came very close to giving it victory'.

The subsidiary role of women in Nazi society

A significant feature of Nazi society in the 1930s was its reactionary view of the place of women.

The duties of women were defined by the party's propaganda in the glib slogan 'Children, Church, Kitchen' (*Kinder, Kirche, Küche*), and every effort was made to eliminate them from leading roles in political and economic life. To an extent this was an ideological aim, based upon the mystical Nazi regard for the breeding and rearing of a pure race. As Richard Grunberger has observed, 'women basked in Nazi esteem between marriage and menopause'. It also had a practical element, in that the removal of women from the competition for jobs would make the full employment of the male population easier. Thus by 1936 only 37 of Germany's 7,000 university teachers were women, while married women were banned by law from the legal and medical professions, from the civil service, and from higher office in the Nazi party. Interest-free loans were made available to newly-weds who undertook that the wife would not seek employment outside the home. The birth rate did indeed rise, from 1,200,000 births in 1934, to 1,410,000 in 1939. While the Nazis claimed this as a success for their methods, T. W. Mason has more recently suggested that it may simply have arisen from the improving economic circumstances in contemporary Germany. In the Nazi attitude to women, as in other areas of Nazi policy, the necessities of politics came eventually to triumph over ideology, and the industrial expansion of the Four-Year Plan once more made female employment unavoidable. Although professional posts remained closed to them, by 1939 women once more constituted 33 per cent of the total German workforce.

J Nazi culture

The rejection of Weimar culture

With the advent of the Nazis to power, one of the most exciting, experimental periods in Germany's cultural history gave way to one of the most stagnant. The 1920s had witnessed a period of unparalleled innovation and experiment in German art. In the aftermath of the collapse of the 'old' Germany, many of the cultural values of that 'old' society were challenged and re-interpreted. The dramatic work and production of Berthold Brecht, the music of Kurt Weill, and the architecture of the Bauhaus movement are only random examples of the inventiveness of 'Weimar' culture. It was immediately evident that artistic freedom played little part in Nazi philosophy and that cultural activity, like all other social and economic functions, was to be 'co-ordinated' to the needs of the regime. This view was aptly summarised by Goebbels in a speech of December 1934, with the judgement that art 'remains free within its own laws of development but it is bound to the moral, social and national principles of the state'. Official taste in the Third Reich had three main distinguishing features. The first was the rejection of internationalism, the response to cultural stimuli from abroad that had characterised the art of the Weimar period. Secondly, in its place, it demanded a stress upon and a glorification of those values that Nazism preached in other areas of policy. Thirdly, it was frequently dominated by a conservatism, often a philistinism, that was apolitical but spoke eloquently of the intellectual mediocrity of many of Germany's new leaders.

The control of culture by the Nazi state

As in all other areas of activity, the Nazis quickly devised a complex machinery to implement this 'co-ordination'. The Reich Chamber of Culture (*Reichskulturkammer* – September 1933), under the presidency of Goebbels, was the central body outside which no 'maker of culture' could legally practise his or her craft. Political undesirables and non-Aryans were automatically excluded. Cruder tactics were necessary to deal with the works of art already executed. 'Exhibitions of Shameful Art' (*Schandausstellungen*) were held, notably in Karlsruhe (1933) and in Munich (1937), with the works of expressionists, cubists and other modern movements prominent. The destruction of rejected books and paintings by fire was widespread. In one conflagration alone, in Berlin in 1939, over 1,000 paintings and 3,700 drawings by leading modern artists were destroyed.

The characteristics of Nazi art

The result of this cultural persecution was to rip the heart out of German art, literature and music. The list of those who abandoned their country to work abroad includes such novelists and playwrights as Thomas and Heinrich Mann, Stefan Zweig and Berthold Brecht, the painter Kokoschka, and the masters of the new art of cinema, Sternberg and Fritz Lang. The majority of those who replaced them were nonentities. In the words of Gordon Craig, most of the products of this cultural 'revolution' were 'of a quality so inferior as to be embarrassing. What passed for Nazi art, when it was not a mere disguise for propaganda, was a reflection of the aesthetic ideals of a culturally retarded lower middle class, full of moral attitudinising and mock heroics and sentimentality and emphasis upon the German soul and the sacredness of the soil'. In literature one might refer to the books of Werner Beumelburg, a specialist in glorifying the spiritual experience of war, or of Hans Blunck, with his emphasis upon Nordic legend. In sculpture, the gigantic evocations of teutonic manhood which were the specialities of Professor Thorak and Arno Breker found particular favour with the Führer himself. Musical taste, of course, was dominated by the German 'giants' of the classical past, by Beethoven and Mozart, and of course by the German epics of Wagner.

Propaganda and the cinema

In one discipline alone did the products of the Third Reich transcend mediocrity. Although the film industry constituted in Goebbels' view 'one of the most modern and scientific methods of influencing the masses', he used it sparingly and intelligently. The most famous films of the era, such as *Hitler Youth Quex* (1933), *The Jew Süss* (1940), and *Ohm Krüger* (1941), an exposé of British atrocities during the Boer War, all had clear political points to make. Yet these were subtly conveyed, and the films were not without artistic merit. The most famous of contemporary German directors, Leni Riefenstahl, showed in her major works, *The Triumph of the Will* (1935), portraying the 1934 Nazi party rally at Nuremberg, and *Olympia* (1937), on the Berlin Olympic Games, that an obvious propaganda message could be conveyed with flair and originality.

Nazism and education

The theme of mediocrity is evident once more in German education under Nazism. The creation of a centralised Reich Education Ministry (May 1934) involved no substantial change in the structure of the educational system, but led to a radical revision of syllabuses. Great stress was now laid upon history, biology and German as the media by which the philosophy of Nazism could best be put across, while the stress upon physical fitness and development raised the gym teacher to a higher level of prestige than he had ever previously enjoyed.

University teaching, too, was subject to haphazard adjustments, such as the dismissal of 'unreliable' teachers, and the banning of such 'Jewish' theses as Einstein's Theory of Relativity. Forty-five per cent of all university posts changed hands between 1933 and 1938. As Nazi agencies competed with established bodies in other spheres, so too in education, youth organisations sought to ensure the indoctrination of the young, to the great detriment of academic standards. From December 1936 it was compulsory for boys to serve in the *Jungvolk* organisation, paralleled by the *Jungmädel* organisation for girls, between the ages of 10 and 14. Thereafter, the boys graduated to the 'Hitler Youth' (*Hitlerjugend*) and the girls to the 'German Girls' League' (*Bund Deutsche Mädchen*) until the age of 18.

K Nazism and the Jews

The motives behind Nazi anti-Semitism

Almost alone among the domestic ideological stances struck by Nazism before its advent to power, anti-Semitism was not sacrificed to the practicalities of power politics. Some writers have tried to see in Nazi anti-Semitism a tool for the achievement of other aims, as in A. J. P. Taylor's phrase 'a showy substitute for social change'. Yet the consistency of Nazi policy, even when it appeared ill-advised in terms of foreign relations or of the economy, can leave us in little doubt that hatred of Jews was central to Hitler's beliefs. 'The Jews,' wrote Lucy Dawidowicz, 'inhabited Hitler's mind. He believed that they were the source of all evil, misfortune and tragedy.' Such views, although of unprecedented viciousness, appealed to a long tradition of German anti-Semitism deriving from economic envy of Jewish commercial success. To this was added intellectual opposition to such 'modern' notions as parliamentarianism and liberalism, through which some Jews had reached political and social emancipation in recent decades.

The early stages of anti-Semitic policy, 1933–34

This is not to say, however, that Nazi anti-Semites had any clear idea in 1933 as to how they would tackle the Jewish 'menace'. Their reasoning dictated that Jews should be excluded from positions of social and political influence, and thus a series of laws (April 1933) banned them from the civil service, the universities and from journalism. Popular emotion, often orchestrated by the SA, led to incoherent outbreaks of violence against Jewish businesses, to the horror of more orthodox nationalists, fearful of foreign reaction and of the breakdown of law and order. For economic reasons, however, Jewish activity in stockbroking and banking remained unimpaired until 1937.

Towards a 'Jew-free' state, 1935–39

From 1935, with increasing domestic security and greater foreign success, the confidence of the Nazis grew. The Nuremberg Laws (September 1935) and the National Law of Citizenship (November 1935), outlawed all marital and sexual contact between Jews and Aryans, and Jews were stripped of their nationality by the stipulation that only Aryan blood entitled one to membership of the German nation. In August 1936, Hitler dictated the principle that the whole Jewish community would be held responsible for the misdeeds of any of its members. The most spectacular application of this principle came on the night of 9–10 November 1938 (*Krystallnacht*) when, in a major pogrom following the murder of a German diplomat by a Jewish student in Paris, 7,000 Jewish businesses were attacked, about 100 Jews were murdered, and thousands more beaten and intimidated. On *Krystallnacht*, as Richard Grunberger has it, 'Germany had passed the point of no return on the path of regression to barbarism'.

Subsequently Nazi policy escalated to include the removal of Jews from the economy and, if possible, from the country itself. The 'Decree on Eliminating Jews from German Economic Life' (November 1938) made it illegal for them to work in sales, services, crafts or management. In January 1939 a Reich Central Office for Jewish Emigration was established to arrange for the expulsion of those with adequate funds and with somewhere to go.

The start of the war in 1939, however, left the majority of Germany's 500,000 Jews stranded without livelihood or political rights in a country that had disowned them. Hitler's apparent conviction that foreign opposition to Germany was part of an international Jewish plot, left them in an even more perilous position. 'If the international Jewish financiers in and outside Europe,' he had told the Reichstag in January 1939, 'should succeed in plunging the nations into a world war, then the result will be . . . the annihilation of the Jewish race in Europe.' True to his propaganda for once, the war years were to witness the formulation at last of a 'final solution' to the 'Jewish problem' (*see* Chapter 18, section **J**).

L Nazi foreign policy: aims and motives

Change or continuity in German foreign policy?

The details of German foreign policy between the wars dominate the narrative of Chapter 17. Here we aim only to consider the broad principles that motivated that policy in the Nazi era.

For Hitler and for many in his party it is probable that foreign affairs represented the true purpose of the Third Reich. The domestic transformation of the first years of Nazi power was primarily carried out to fit Germany for the performance of her international tasks. 'Before conquering the external enemy,' Hitler had written in *Mein Kampf*, 'the enemy at home would have to be eliminated.' It has nevertheless become a matter of some controversy whether the foreign policy of Nazi Germany really did represent a radical change of direction, or whether, in essentials, Hitler merely continued well established traditions of German power politics. The latter view has been put forward by a number of distinguished German historians, such as Friedrich Meinecke and Andreas Hillgrüber, and has received the most enthusiastic support in this country from A. J. P. Taylor. 'In one sphere alone,' writes Taylor of Hitler, 'he changed nothing. His foreign policy was that of his predecessors, of the professional diplomats at the foreign ministry, and indeed of virtually all Germans.' For this school of thought, the terms imposed upon Russia in the Treaty of Brest-Litovsk in 1917 (*see* Chapter 12, section **I**) provide strong evidence of Germany's eastern ambitions long before the advent of Hitler. On the other hand, many contemporaries, as well as more recent writers such as H. A. Jacobsen, saw in Hitler, in his racial doctrines, and in his professions in *Mein*

Kampf, a new and more dangerous force. 'This is not a man of the past,' declared the French ambassador in 1933, 'and his objective is not to restore purely and simply, the state of things in 1914.'

The destruction of the Versailles settlement

The aims laid down in *Mein Kampf* and elsewhere, whether or not they should be regarded as a premeditated and serious programme for Nazi foreign policy (*see* Chapter 17), in fact constitute a combination of familiar projects and new twists. Firstly, as any diplomat of the Weimar Republic would have agreed, Hitler stated the necessity to overturn the Versailles settlement, to destroy the inequalities of Germany's position on armament and reparations, and to regain those portions of her population separated from the Reich by the peace terms. Secondly, he was determined to unite with the Reich those Germans who had previously not been part of it, his fellow Austrians for example, or the Sudetenlanders. This was a deliberate departure from Bismarck's 'Little Germany' in favour of the *Grossdeutschland* that Bismarck had feared and rejected. Thirdly, this *Grossdeutschland* would require 'living space' to provide agricultural and industrial resources for its population, a dangerous and explosive combination of Wilhelmine expansion and newer racial determinism. Alan Bullock has argued further that such an outwardly coherent programme can be further reduced to one simple factor. 'Hitler had only one programme,' he wrote, 'power without limit, and the rest was window dressing.'

The natural enemies of Nazi Germany

The implications for Germany's future foreign relations of a programme such as *Mein Kampf* contained were clear. For Hitler, Russia was the natural enemy, with its combination of inferior Slavic culture, detested Bolshevism, and he thought, Jewish-dominated government. France, too, although a declining power, would be a certain opponent for the future. She was the staunchest supporter of the hated Versailles system, was patron and protector of several of the detested eastern European states, and would have to be dealt with to avoid once more running the risk of war on two fronts. Britain, an essentially maritime and colonial power, and Italy, fascist and with primarily Mediterranean interests, were not natural enemies

of Germany. At an early stage in his career, Hitler envisaged fundamental departures both from Nazi ideology and from traditional German policies, to ensure the acquiescence of Britain and Italy in his general plans. In the case of Britain he showed himself willing to renounce the lost German colonies, subject of so much propaganda after 1919, and in the case of Italy, refrained from claiming the Germans of the South Tyrol as subjects of *Grossdeutschland*.

M Nazi foreign policy: methods

For all the dispute over the originality of Germany's international aims during the Nazi period, there is general unanimity as to the masterly flexibility with which those aims were pursued. The diplomatic methods of the Nazi era fall broadly into two sections. The first three years from 1933 formed a period of caution, dictated by domestic weakness and by widespread foreign distrust. Germany successfully avoided commitments to such international bodies as the League of Nations and the Disarmament Conference, which might have compromised her future freedom of action, and made headway with the disruption of the French system of eastern European alliances, while consistently re-assuring foreign opinion as to her peaceful intentions. Through that period, too, ran the theme of re-armament. The re-introduction of conscription (1935), the agreement with Great Britain over the reconstruction of the German Navy (1935), and the steady re-building of an airforce (*Luftwaffe*) that already boasted 2,000 aircraft by late 1934, all illustrate this theme.

Although the phenomenon has been variously explained as a reaction to greater domestic security or as a response to evident weaknesses in the diplomacy of Hitler's adversaries, the years 1936-37 undoubtedly witnessed a switch to the offensive. If the introduction of the Four-Year Plan (*see* section **H**) prepared the way, the so-called 'Hossbach Conference' (November 1937) is often seen as, in the words of C. Thorne, the 'significant moment in the development of Nazi expansionism'. There, in a meeting with the heads of the armed forces and of the Foreign Ministry, the subject of which is known to us through the minutes recorded by one Colonel Hossbach, Hitler defined the immediate principles of his policy. Repeating the principle of *Lebensraum*, he noted that Germany's present military superiority over her rivals could not be expected to last beyond 1943–45. Thereafter, the obsolescence of German material, and the re-equipment of other armed forces would narrow the gap. Therefore, the minutes report, 'it was his unalterable resolve to solve Germany's problem of space at the latest by 1943–45'. Although the timetable retained some flexibility, the subsequent expansion of armament production, and the removal of such 'doubters' as von Blomberg, Schacht and Neurath from office, clearly indicate that the threats made to the future peace of Europe were not idle.

Questions

Essay questions

1 How, and with what success in the years 1933–39, did Hitler seek to bring about a Nazi revolution within Germany? (JMB/NEAB)

2 Explain the appeal of Fascism in the inter-war years in either Germany or Italy. (UCLES)

3 In what respects can the domestic policy of Hitler be described as radical? (Oxford Entrance)

4 'He gave the German people a new sense of national pride, and he gave them success'. How far does this explain Hitler's dominance within Germany between 1933 and 1941? (NEAB)

5a Identify the principal groups that supported Hitler in Germany in 1933. [4]

 b Explain the popularity of the Nazis in Germany in 1933. [5]

 c To what extent did Hitler's appointment as Chancellor in 1933 signal the failure of parliamentary democracy in Germany? [7]

 d Did Hitler need to extend and consolidate his power within Germany, 1933–34? [9]

6 To what extent, if any, was German society more united in the 1930s than in the 1920s? (AEB)

The Night of the Long Knives

DOCUMENT A

The Brown Shirts advanced from victory to victory with prodigious speed. Their chief weapon was the Terror. Now it is worse than ever, it is more universal, more systematic.

There follows a parade of persecution; of trade union officials; Socialists who accepted the regime; Catholic priests; Protestants; Evangelical clergy; Jews, of course, particularly in the provinces; and pacifists.

Manchester Guardian report, 13 April 1933.

DOCUMENT B

A tremendous victory has been won. But not absolute victory!

The new State did not have to disown the bearers of the will to revolution as the November men had to do. In the new Germany the disciplined brown storm battalions stand side by side with the armed forces.

Not as part of them.

The Reichswehr has its own undisputed task: it is committed to defend the borders of the Reich.

The police have to keep down the law-breakers.

Beside these stand the SA and the SS as the third power factor of the new state with special tasks [for they] are the foundation pillars of the coming National Socialist State. They will not tolerate the German revolution going to sleep or being betrayed at the halfway stage by non-combatants.

If the bourgeois simpletons think that the 'national' revolution has already lasted too long, whether they like it or not, we will continue our struggle with them; if they are unwilling, without them; and if necessary, against them!

Ernst Röhm, Leader of the SA, in a newspaper article, June 1933.

DOCUMENT C

I will suppress every attempt to disturb the existing order as ruthlessly as I will deal with the so-called second revolution, which would lead only to chaos.

Revolution is not a permanent state, [it] must be guided into the secure bed of evolution. A businessman must not therefore be dismissed if he is a good businessman even if he is not yet a good National Socialist; especially not if the National Socialist put in his place knows nothing about business. We must not keep looking round to see what next to revolutionise. The Party has now become the State. All power comes under the authority of the Reich.

Adolf Hitler's speech to the Reich Governors, 6 July 1933.

DOCUMENT D

A militia as Röhm suggested would not be the least bit suitable for national defence. [Hitler] was resolved to raise a people's army, built up on the Reichswehr, rigorously trained and equipped with the most modern weapons. He also rejected a Fascist Militia on the Italian pattern; the SA must confine itself to internal tasks.

Field Marshal von Weich's account of Hitler's speech to the leaders of the SA and most of the senior Reichswehr generals, 28 February 1934.

DOCUMENT E

There appears to be endless talk of a second wave which will complete the revolution; there is much talk about future socialisation. Have we experienced the anti-Marxist revolution in order to carry out the programme of Marxism? For any attempt to solve the social question by collectivising property is Marxism.

No nation that could survive the judgement of history can afford a permanent uprising from below. At some stage the movement must come to an end; at some point there must emerge a firm social structure held together by a legal system secure against pressure and by a State power that is unchallenged.

The State cannot tolerate any dualism and the success of the German revolution and the future of our nation will depend on the discovery of a satisfactory solution for the dualism between Party and State.

Franz von Papen's speech at Marburg University. 17 June 1934.

DOCUMENT F

Without once informing me and at a moment when I had no thought of any such action, Chief of Staff Röhm entered into relations with General Schleicher [who] maintained that:

1. The present regime is not to be tolerated.

2. The Army and all national associations must be united in a single band.

3. The only man to be considered for such a position is Chief of Staff Röhm.

4 Herr von Papen must be removed and he himself would be ready to take the position of Vice-Chancellor.

For fourteen years I have stated consistently that the fighting organisations of the Party are political institutions and have nothing to do with the Army. The supreme head of the Army is none other than the Field Marshal and President of the Reich. The promise I gave him that I would preserve the Army as a non-political instrument of the Reich I hold as binding.

In these circumstances I could make but one decision. If a disaster was to be prevented at all, action must be taken with lightning speed. Only a ruthless and bloody intervention might still perhaps stifle the spread of the revolt.

If anyone reproaches me and asks why I did not resort to the regular courts of justice for the conviction of the offenders, then all I can say to him is this: in this hour I was responsible for the fate of the German people, and thereby I became the Supreme Judge of the German people.

Adolf Hitler's speech to the Reichstag, 13 July 1934.

a   Explain briefly the following references:
i   the November men' (Document B) [1]
ii 'the Reichswehr' (Document B) [1]
iii 'General Schleicher' (Document F) [1]
iv 'The supreme head of the Army is none other than the Field-Marshal and President of the Reich' (Document F) [2]
b   Using only the evidence of these documents, examine the main aims and methods of the SA between 30 January 1933 and 30 June 1934. [6]
c   Röhm was determined not to 'tolerate the German revolution going to sleep or being betrayed' (Document B). With reference to Documents C, D, E and F, how was this determination viewed by Hitler and members of the German establishment? [7]
d   Using these documents, and any other evidence known to you, examine the view that conflict between Hitler and Röhm was inevitable. [7]

(UCLES)

17

The twenty years' truce, 1919–39

Two interpretations of the co-operation between Gustav Stresemann and Aristide Briand in the 1920s. The German version (left) is entitled 'Germany, with her feet bound, dances with the enemy'. The French cartoon (right) is entitled 'The peace in shreds'.

What reservations does each cartoon express about the attempts at Franco–German reconciliation undertaken in the 1920s?

Given that these are contemporary cartoons, what impression do they convey to the historian of the prospects of this policy of reconciliation?

The Historical Debate

The first decade after the conclusion of the Second World War saw a considerable volume of writing on the war's origins. Not much of it, however, could really be described as detached and analytical history. Its arguments tended to reinforce the arguments of wartime and the general conclusions drawn from it were consistent and predictable. In general, it took one of two forms. One form was that of accounts by participants in the war, often members of the defeated sides seeking to set themselves right in the eyes of posterity. The posthumously published work of Count Ciano (*Diary*, 1947) or of von Ribbentrop (*Memoirs*, 1954), both written in prison cells under sentence of death, may stand as representatives of a substantial literature of this kind. Secondly, came official documentary collections, most frequently edited and published by the victors, which naturally, as in the case of the work of E. L. Woodward and Rohan Butler (*Documents on British Foreign Policy*, 1946 onwards), tended to present a relatively favourable view of the policy of the state concerned. Hence E. M. Robertson's characterisation of many of the earlier historians of the origins of the war as 'Intelligence NCOs in plain clothes'. The conclusions reached during this decade varied little. The war was precipitated by a German government dedicated to the principle of overturning the Versailles settlement and fulfilling the racial claims of its leader. T. D. Williams, commenting in 1958 on the work of Sir Lewis Namier *(In the Nazi Era*, 1952) stated that 'he has proved that Hitler wanted war. Nobody would, on the whole, now contest this fact'.

In 1961, however, in *The Origins of the Second World War*, A. J. P. Taylor did, indeed, contest the fact. Briefly summarised, his view was as follows. Refusing to see in *Mein Kampf* anything more than the daydreaming of a frustrated revolutionary, Taylor stressed the continuity between Hitler's foreign policy aims and those of earlier German politicians. Refusing to attach any great importance to the alleged statement of war aims to his generals reported in Colonel Hossbach's memorandum (November 1937), he dismissed the notion of a masterplan for conquest. He viewed Hitler's achievement in 1938–39 primarily as a skillful exploitation of openings offered to him by the errors and hesitations of British, French and Italian leaders. War, in Taylor's view, did not result from Hitler's long-term determination to begin one, but from his short-term miscalculation of allied reaction to the Polish crisis. Although many writers have agreed that Taylor's work has shed important light on details of some of the individual crises that preceded the Second World War, his overall thesis provoked widespread controversy. It has been argued that his presentation has dangerous political implications, in that it could cast doubt on the legitimacy of the verdicts passed on Nazi war criminals at Nuremberg, and could provide encouragement for neo-fascist groups in Germany and elsewhere. It has also been

criticised on grounds of historical method.

Hugh Trevor Roper, in an article in the magazine *Encounter* (1961), refused to accept Taylor's dismissal of *Mein Kampf* and the Hossbach Memorandum, and argued that Hitler considered himself not merely a practical politician, but a thinker, a practical philosopher, the demiurge of a new age of history', and did therefore conceive of a long-term future programme. E. H. Carr (*The Twenty Years Crisis*, 1958) and Elizabeth Wiskemann (*Europe of the Dictators*, 1966) saw *Mein Kampf* as a much more systematic and preconceived plan for national and racial expansion. Others, such as T. W. Mason (article in *Past and Present*, 1964) and A. S. Milward (*The German War Economy*, 1965) stressed that Taylor's preoccupation with diplomacy blinded him to the steady economic and social progress towards a war footing made since 1933. It is interesting to note that much recent German scholarship has tended to suggest that the direction of German policy depended upon more than the will of the Führer. H. A. Jacobsen (*National Socialist Foreign Policy*, 1969) has shown the extent of nationalist demands even among Germans who were not strictly Nazis, and H. Krausnick (*Anatomy of the SS State*, 1968) has demonstrated the depth of popular anti-semitism in contemporary Germany.

Important as the controversy over the Taylor thesis is in terms of detail, it is still possible to find a synthesis of agreement on the broad causes of the Second World War. The responsibility of expansionist elements in German policy has not seriously been questioned, and the less the outbreak is attributed directly to the 'evil genius' of Hitler himself, the more the historian is bound to concentrate on the continuous theme of expansion in recent German history and thought. This theme occupies much of the attention of the American journalist William Shirer in his massive *Rise and Fall of the Third Reich* (1962). Returning finally to Hitler's aims and motives in the late 1930s, sound conclusions, compromising between those of Taylor and those of his opponents, have been drawn by Alan Bullock *(Hitler, A Study in Tyranny*, 1962 and *Hitler and Stalin: Parallel Lives*. 1991) and E. M. Robertson *(The Origins of the Second World War*, ed., 1971). On the question of a Nazi masterplan for aggression and aggrandisement, Bullock concludes that 'Hitler's foreign policy ... combined consistency of aim with complete opportunism in methods and tactics'. The weakness of his opponents, that is, dictated the timing, but not the initial conception of Hitler's policy. On the specific problem of the outbreak of hostilities in 1939, Robertson has tried to resolve the question 'Did Hitler want war?' by the plausible conclusion that he did indeed desire an armed clash with Poland. Where the element of miscalculation and accident occurred was that he had not expected the forceable destruction of Poland to involve him in a general European war with Britain and France.

A The Treaty of Versailles: motives and terms

1919: the fading of allied optimism

November 1918 brought an armistice rather than a definitive peace. Some of its terms, however, such as the withdrawal of German forces beyond the Rhine, and the internment of her fleet, made it a foregone conclusion that Germany would be unable to recommence hostilities. In effect, therefore, the leaders of the four main allied powers, France, Britain, the USA and Italy, were concerned during their six months of deliberation (13 January–28 June 1919) with the preparation of the terms for peace that would be dictated to the representatives of Germany when at last they were allowed to appear in France. Rarely has the preparation of peace been attended by such high hopes and rarely has the feeling been so quickly apparent that the outcome of negotiations had fallen far short of initial expectations. 'We arrived,' wrote the British historian and diplomat Harold Nicolson, 'determined that a peace of justice and wisdom should be negotiated: we left it conscious that the treaties imposed upon our enemies were neither wise nor just.' Others saw the price that Europe would pay for the shortcomings of the peace. 'This is not peace,' Foch is reported to have exclaimed when he heard the terms, 'it is a truce for twenty years.'

The political pressures that formed the peace

The first problem for the leaders of the allied powers was that they were not always free agents.

Lloyd George was in the process of fighting a general election in which popular anger gave rise to such emotive slogans a 'Hang the Kaiser' and 'Squeeze the German orange until the pips squeak'. Clemenceau had to contend with an even more volatile combination of anger and anxiety that the losses of the war should never be repeated. Nor were the delegates united in their purposes. French policy was dominated by an overwhelming desire for future security, for the achievement of which almost no imposition upon the German aggressor would be too great. Britain's view was moderated by a number of considerations. The scuttling of the German fleet at Scapa Flow (31 June 1919) guaranteed her own national security, and her traditional concern with the balance of power on the continent made her wary of weakening Germany excessively, especially as it became ever clearer that the Soviet regime in Russia was there to stay.

Both sets of vested interests, however, were likely to be overridden by the American President, Woodrow Wilson. He hoped to replace the outdated and corrupt criteria of European diplomacy with a lasting and just peace, based upon the satisfaction of justifiable national claims, and outlawing selfish motives. He hoped, in his famous phrase, for 'a peace without victory'. Wilson was the central figure of the peace conference, partly because the USA alone had the manpower and financial resources to continue the struggle if necessary, and partly because of the enormous popularity that he enjoyed as 'the prophet of peace'. He could not, however, expect to impose his views upon the hard-bitten statesmen of Europe.

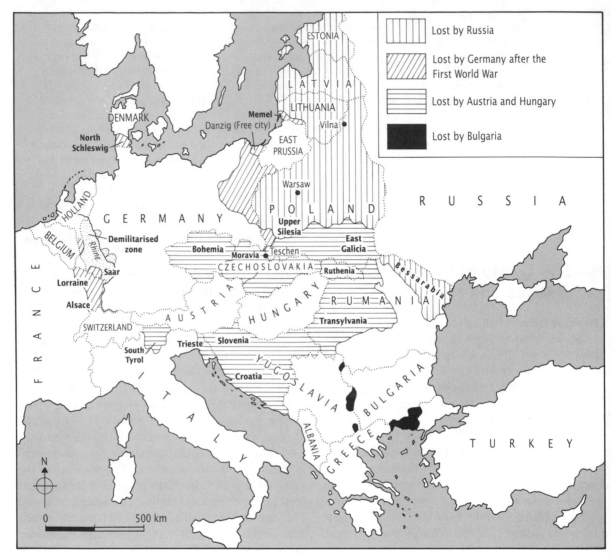

Territorial changes, 1919–24

Punishing Germany

The 440 clauses that constituted the peace treaty between the allies and Germany may be summarised under four general headings. Firstly, although the Treaty of Versailles made allowance for eventual general disarmament, the disarmament of Germany was to be immediate. As her armed forces in future were to cater merely for the defence of her own territory, she was restricted to an army of 96,000 men and 4,000 officers, all serving for a period of 12 years, to prevent the build-up of experienced reserves. These armed forces were forbidden the use of all purely offensive weapons, tanks, heavy artillery, powered aircraft, submarines and capital warships. Secondly, the boundaries of the Reich were adjusted to satisfy the demands of the nationalities that shared her borders. In the west, Alsace-Lorraine returned to France, and the small regions of Eupen and Malmedy became Belgian territory. Ideally France would have wished to make greater inroads for her future security, either to advance her own border to the Rhine, or to create in the Rhineland an independent and neutral state. Both plans met the ideological and pragmatic opposition of Britain and America, and France had to be satisfied with a three-point settlement: a temporary allied occupation of the Rhineland, the permanent banning of all German forces from the Rhineland, and a proposed guarantee of British and American aid in maintaining that settlement. To the north and east, Germany suffered further losses. North Schleswig once more became Danish territory, and territory in Posen and West Prussia was transferred to Poland, notably the infamous 'Polish corridor' giving the new state access to the sea. At the end of the 'corridor', the distinctly German city of Danzig became a 'Free City' with Poland granted the use of its port facilities, her only access to the sea.

The 'war guilt' clause and reparation payment

Central to Germany's resentment of this imposed peace was Clause 231 which forced Germany to acknowledge that the guilt and responsibility for the outbreak of the war was hers. Without this 'war guilt clause' there would have been little moral justification for the fourth imposition upon Germany. The question of reparation payments to the victor by the vanquished had a long tradition in European warfare, but never before had any war been fought on such a scale. Now the allies proposed to charge Germany for the material damage done to them during the hostilities, a very considerable figure in the case of France, and for their future expenses on such items as pensions for their widows and war wounded. This last item alone constituted nearly half the total bill of £6,600 million which was handed to the Germans when the huge task of estimation was eventually completed (May 1921).

The other treaties: redrawing the map

Lastly, although the peace settlement with Germany naturally dominated the attention of European statesmen, it must not be forgotten that it was accompanied by a collection of other treaties with Germany's erstwhile allies, with Austria at St Germain en Laye, with Hungary at Trianon, with Turkey at Sèvres, and with Bulgaria at Neuilly. The disappearance of that dominant feature of central Europe for five centuries, the Habsburg Empire, was central to these treaties. In its place stood the rump German state of Austria, specially forbidden by the treaties to associate with their fellow Germans to the north, and a number of new states, Yugoslavia, Czechoslovakia and Poland, representing the fulfiled national aspirations of nearly

a century. In the cases of Yugoslavia and Czechoslovakia the delegates around Paris had been able to do little but accept the actions of national leaders such as Masaryk, Benes and Trumbic who had seized their opportunities with the collapse of the Austro-Hungarian war effort. Hungary, after a century of increasing national fulfilment, now found herself stripped of Croatia, Slovenia, Slovakia and Ruthenia by these new states. Her resentment of her losses was also to be a significant factor in the politics of central and eastern Europe over the next two decades.

B Implications of Versailles

Patently, the peace settlement of 1919 was unsuccessful. A. J. P. Taylor's blunt judgement that 'the second world war was, in large part, a repeat performance of the first' conveys clearly the extent to which the problems of 1919 were left unresolved. In part, its failure may be ascribed to the enormous complexity of the problems facing the delegates. In 1815 at Vienna the empire of Napoleon had collapsed, but in 1919 at Versailles, it was the empires of Germany, Turkey, Austria-Hungary and Russia that were in ruins. Several other distinct weaknesses in the final drafts of the treaties must also be identified.

The grounds for German resentment

The prime problem that was to haunt Europe for the next two and a half decades was German resentment of the terms imposed upon them. Although on the verge of military defeat in November 1918, German lines were still on foreign soil, and their representatives had approached the allies confident that a settlement would be offered based upon the Fourteen Points. Instead Germans found themselves presented with a dictated peace which stripped the Reich of 25,000 square miles of territory and 7,000,000 inhabitants, about 13 per cent and 10 per cent of her respective totals. She found, furthermore, that in many cases Germany was treated according to principles quite different from those that governed the settlements with other states. Nationality was the proclaimed principle behind most territorial settlements, yet union between Germany and the German-speakers of Austria was specifically forbidden. Germany was disarmed and stripped of her colonies, while the victors retained their weapons and in some cases actually added to their colonial empires. Yet, although Germany was treated as a defeated power, she retained the means to become a great force in the world once more. She was not partitioned, as she was eventually to be in 1945, and she retained nearly 90 per cent of her economic resources. She was deprived of her weapons, but retained the potential to produce modern replacements at a later date. As early as 1925, Germany's production of steel, for instance, was twice that of Great Britain. Her relative position in the European balance of power had hardly suffered, furthermore, from the development that left a collection of relatively weak 'successor states' on her eastern borders.

Enforcement: the end of the wartime alliance

Given this German resentment, the treaty would need to be enforced. Yet, already in 1918, the alliance that had fought the war was in the process of disintegration. By 1920 it was in ruins. Firstly, the great power of Russia, a key factor in the considerations of 1914, was quite excluded from the deliberations of 1919. The Soviet revolution of 1917 removed Russia temporarily from the diplomatic scene, but its eventual success, and its brief imitations in Hungary (March 1919) and Bavaria (April 1919), had profoundly shocked the governing classes of Europe. Their attitudes towards Germany often became, as a result of the revolution, highly ambiguous. With Germany defeated, might not communist Russia now be seen as the major threat to Europe's stability and security? And if a relatively strong, conservative Germany was not preserved as a bulwark in central Europe, what would prevent the westward flow of the communist tide? By mid-1919 it was clear that the United States would not fulfil this role, for she had turned her back on Europe as abruptly as she had intervened in the first place. The considerable prestige of President Wilson at Versailles had hidden the true weakness of his domestic position. Involvement in Europe had never been universally popular, and the prospect of a permanent peace-keeping role there was quite unacceptable to the Senate, which accordingly refused to ratify the treaties that Wilson had negotiated (November 1919). A year later, Wilson's party was out of power, and America was once again firmly on the path of isolationism. In short, the implementation of the peace treaty had to be undertaken from 1919 without the participation of either of the powers who were to decide Europe's fate in 1939–45.

Keynes and the controversy over reparations

There has not been any serious historical dispute on these points. The same cannot be said, however, for the third area of objection that was quickly raised to the peace terms. In an influential work, *The Economic Consequences of the Peace* (1920), the English economist J. M. Keynes denounced what he saw as the folly of the treaty's reparations clauses. By putting such intolerable pressure on the German economy, he concluded, the allies threatened the ability of the whole European economy of which it was part. 'This treaty,' he argued, 'ignores the economic solidarity of Europe, and by aiming at the economic life of Germany, it threatens the health and prosperity of the allies themselves.' Although influential in Britain and in the United States, Keynes' arguments incited great opposition in France, the country most in need of reparations. There they were most effectively answered by E. Mantoux (*The Economic Consequences of Mr. Keynes*, 1944). The crux of his argument was that the productivity of German industry during the 1930s, especially armaments manufacture, showed that the levels of reparations set in 1921 were, after all, within Germany's capacity.

Historical judgements on the Versailles settlement

Mantoux's work is part of a substantial literature since the 1939–45 war which has modified the earlier condemnation of the Versailles treaty. Where Winston Churchill saw 'a turbulent collision of embarrassed demagogues', Keynes saw profound economic ignorance, and Nicolson saw a sad failure to stick to original high ideals, more recent writers have often cited extenuating circumstances. The Frenchman, Maurice Baumont, has stressed that the shortcomings that survived the peace conference should not blind us to the fact that 'as a whole the treaties righted age-old wrongs', especially with regard to the subject nationalities of central Europe. Anthony Adamthwaite has claimed that the main fault in 1919 lay, not with the terms of the treaties, but with the hopes that preceded them, so high that they were bound to be disappointed. 'No peace settlement,' he writes, 'could have fulfiled the millennial hopes of a new heaven and a new earth. It was the destruction of these Utopian hopes that provoked the denunciations of the settlement.' Perhaps the most relevant judgement, however, comes from another Frenchman, Jacques Néré, who finds the fault of the treaty not in its terms but in the failure of its enforcement.

C The League of Nations

The conception of the League

Central to Woodrow Wilson's ideas on the establishment and maintenance of European and world peace was the concept of an international organisation able to transcend the selfish motives and the misunderstandings which, in Wilson's view, were the root causes of international conflict. In general, the idea of a 'League of Nations' was greeted with enthusiasm by the nations represented at the peace conference. Two distinct schools of thought developed, however, as to the form it should take. France took the realistic view that such a body could only be influential if equipped with sufficient armed force to enforce its decisions. This was opposed by Great Britain, uneasy at the idea of an international armed force possibly under French command, and by other states who baulked at the idea of portions of their own forces coming under international control. Above all, President Wilson refused to allow his 'brain child' to become simply another weapon of traditional power politics, or one with which the victors could torment the defeated. Thus, the body whose Covenant, or constitution, was written specifically into each of the peace treaties, and which met for the first time in Geneva in December 1920, was primarily a forum, or agency, to which nations in dispute could bring their problems for advice and settlement.

Aims, machinery and membership

The Covenant of the League of Nations defined four main aims for the organisation. It sought to prevent future wars by peaceful settlement of international disputes, to promote disarmament, to supervise territories referred to it by the peace treaties, such as the former German colonies and the Saarland, and lastly to promote general international co-operation by its various organisations

for social and economic work. Its powers and the obligations of its members in these tasks were also clearly defined. Members in dispute with one another were obliged to refer their differences to one of three processes provided by the League, to the Permanent Court of International Justice, to arbitration or to enquiry by the Council of the League, its executive committee. Failure to do so, or failure to take reasonable account of the resulting decisions rendered offending members liable to sanctions. The allies had been so impressed by the effect of economic embargoes employed against Germany in the war, that economic sanctions were chosen as the League's main weapon. The possibility of military sanctions was admitted, but their extent was left undefined, and they could only ever be applied if a member state agreed to put its own forces at the disposal of the League.

In its 20-year life, the League never once sought to apply military sanctions. Among the 42 states originally subscribing to these terms, there were some notable absentees. The United States, because of the Senate's refusal to ratify the peace terms, was never a member of the organisation inspired by her President. Soviet Russia did not become a member until 1934, the year after Japan left the League. Germany was a member only between 1926 and 1933, her initial absence confirming the impression that, for all Wilson's claims to the contrary, the League in essence stood for the preservation of the 'status quo' established in 1919. None of the several powers dissatisfied with either the terms or the principles of the peace settlement could happily accept or further the aims of the League of Nations.

Successes and failures of the League

Yet the League was not a total failure. When states accepted its mediatory functions it could and did reach notable settlements, as over the Åland Islands claimed by Sweden and Finland (1921), and its border disputes between Greece and Bulgaria (1924) and between Hungary and Yugoslavia (1934). When European statesmen such as MacDonald, Stresemann and Briand worked with it in the late 1920s, it seemed at the centre of European diplomacy, and its international bodies such as the Health Organisation and the Advisory Committee on Traffic in Women and Children, still function today, as the World Health Organisation and

UNICEF. It failed in its primary task, to prevent further war, due to the fact that the League represented a new concept of international relations in a world where most major powers were content to stick to the old selfish methods of force and *Realpolitik*.

In the major confrontations of the inter-war period the League failed, not because it could not find common ground between disputing parties, but because it was totally ignored by one or more of those parties. The League was bypassed in the case of Polish seizure of the town of Vilna (1920), Japanese aggression in Manchuria (1931), Italian attacks on Abyssinia (1935) and all of Hitler's expansionist moves. It had no means in its Covenant to prevent that. Two contemporary verdicts illustrate well the League's weakness in the face of selfish acts of aggression. In all the cases just mentioned the judgement of Lord David Cecil held good that 'the League of Nations has not been tried and found wanting; it has been found inconvenient and not tried'. Prominent among those who found the 'peacemongering' of the League inconvenient was Mussolini. He fully appreciated that, especially in the 1930s, the machinery of the League appealed only to those nations too weak to look after their own interests. 'The League is all right,' he declared, 'when sparrows quarrel. It fails when eagles fall out.'

D   The occupation of the Ruhr

France and the 'policy of enforcement'

In the years immediately after the conclusion of peace, the maintenance of the treaty's terms was primarily a problem for France. For her, the questions of reparation payments, of post-war reconstruction and of German economic potential were not questions of morality or theory, but of national survival. By 1920, however the bases of French security proposed at Versailles lay in ruins. America had withdrawn from European involvement, Britain showed little interest in continuing the co-operation of wartime, and domestic developments in Germany (*see* Chapter 14, section **D**) offered little prospect of her willing acceptance of the settlement. Most serious for France's recovery and prosperity, Germany showed increasing reluctance to maintain her reparation payments. By the

Wiesbaden Accords (October 1921), France agreed to facilitate German payments by accepting a proportion in raw materials and industrial produce, rather than in cash, but in the next year, these payments in kind had also slipped steadily into arrears.

Faced with the choice of using conciliation or confrontation to exact her due from Germany, public and political opinion in France inclined more and more toward the latter solution, the more so with the appointment of Raymond Poincaré as prime minister (January 1922). Poincaré was a hard headed and determined politician, a native of Lorraine who remembered Germany's past offences towards his home region, and was determined that she should not escape her due punishment.

The occupation

The crisis in French–German relations erupted in November 1922 when Germany requested a suspension of her payments for up to four years in the light of domestic economic difficulties. It was her third such request in three years and strongly suggested that the whole question of adherence to the Versailles settlement was at stake. It was thus this vital issue, rather than the trivial pretext of non-delivery of a batch of telegraph poles, that prompted France, with support from Italy and Belgium, to send troops across the Rhine into the industrial heartland of the Ruhr (January 1923). Protesting, with justification, that the invasion of her sovereign territory was against the terms of the peace treaty, the German government of Chancellor Cuno appealed with great success for a policy of passive resistance in the Ruhr. In February 1923, coal production there fell to 2.5 million tons, where 90 million had been mined in 1922. Three iron-smelting furnaces operated in March, where 70 had worked the previous year. Occasional terrorist attacks on troops and military action against German demonstrators raised the overall tension.

To overcome the effects of strikes and passive resistance, Poincaré appealed, with equal success, for unemployed Frenchmen and Belgians to operate mines, furnaces and railways in the Ruhr. Faced with the success of this ploy, with the total collapse of the German currency (*see* Chapter 14, section **D**), and with the ominous spread of separatist movements in Germany, the government conceded defeat. Although it never became official

French governmental policy, commanders in the Ruhr certainly showed some sympathy to political movements that proposed the establishment of an independent Rhineland state. With a united Germany at risk, Gustav Stresemann replaced Cuno as Chancellor in August and decreed the end of passive resistance within a month.

The Ruhr: success or failure?

What, then, had Poincaré achieved in the Ruhr? Economically, he seemed to have triumphed, with France guaranteed 21 per cent of the region's production up to December 1923 and 27 per cent thereafter. Against this, however, Poincaré had reinforced the mistrust and apprehension among his former allies at the French threat to the balance of power, and had made difficult, if not impossible, any future co-operation between France and Germany. 'France,' wrote the Italian minister Count Sforza, 'has committed the supreme error of polarising against her the hostility of all the patriotic elements in the Reich.' The economic gains, important as they were, were largely nullified by France's subsequent political isolation. In his own country Poincaré came under attack, from the left wing for high-handed action in the interests of French capitalists, and from the right, for once more withdrawing when the chance existed finally to break the unity and economic backbone of Germany. In terms of its political consequences it must be considered highly doubtful whether the Ruhr gamble was worth the cost.

E Conciliation: the economy

The Dawes Plan

At least France learned her lesson from the Ruhr adventure. The hostility of British and American reaction, the dramatic decline in the franc (from 70 to the pound in 1922 to 240 to the pound in 1926), and the defeat of the National Bloc in the 1924 elections, all brought home the point that she could not safely rely upon unilateral action. The agreement between France, Britain and the United States (November 1923) to replace the reparations question upon an international footing, represented not only French misgivings, but British and American fears as to where unilateral action might lead in the future.

The result of this decision was the formation of the commission, chaired by the American economist C. C. Dawes, which produced in April 1924 the so-called 'Dawes Plan' for the future regulation of redemption payments. By the Dawes Plan, which was to operate for five years, reparation payments would be guaranteed by two mortgages, one on Germany's railways, and the other on certain German industries, supplemented by deductions from certain German taxes. An American 'General Reparations Agent', Parker Gilbert, was to be installed in Germany to supervise payments. The amounts to be paid by Germany were substantially reduced, but this was outweighed in the French view by the facts that much of her post-war reconstruction was nearing completion, and that the plan once more involved her wartime allies in the collection of reparations. Thus, France accepted the Dawes Plan.

The five years of the Plan's operation have been described as the 'Golden Age' of reparations, with the allies receiving payments, in cash and in kind, with far greater regularity than ever before. It was, however, a temporary expedient, and was still accompanied by German complaints both at the level of payments and that no definite date had been fixed for their end. From the allied point of view, the plan also failed to provide any link between German payments and their own repayment of war debts to the United States.

The Young Plan

The Young Plan (June 1929), proposed to succeed the Dawes Plan, set out to tackle all these questions. Although it further reduced the total to be paid by Germany, it linked French and British debts to the level of German payments, and set 1988 as the final year of reparation payments. It also continued American commitment and involvement in this vital area of European politics. This, in both the Dawes Plan and the Young Plan, was the fatal weakness of these reparation solutions. The operation of both was very largely dependent upon the large sums of foreign capital, two-thirds of it American, that were being invested in Germany in the late 1920s to stimulate and sustain her industries. J. M. Keynes had already written in 1926 that the duration of these arrangements was 'in the hands of the American capitalist'. Within three years, the great crisis of American capitalism was finally to wreck these hopeful prospects of economic reconciliation.

F Conciliation: the diplomatic rehabilitation of Germany

The Locarno Pact

For the German government, the primary objective of their agreement to the reparations plans was to clear their territory of foreign troops and to guard against their return. The first aim was only partially achieved for, although French and Belgian troops had withdrawn from the Ruhr by August 1925, allied troops remained in other Rhineland cities, such as Cologne, under the direct terms of the peace treaty. To complete the process, and to guard against the dangers of separatism in the Rhineland which he took very seriously, Stresemann approached the allies with the boldest proposal of his political career and one that was by no means universally popular in Germany. At a meeting in Locarno, in Switzerland (February 1925), he proposed a voluntary German guarantee of her western borders. For France and Belgium, this meant that Germany freely gave up her claims to Alsace and Lorraine and to Eupen and Malmedy. For Germany, it meant that France would no longer be able to use the weapon of invasion, or harbour hopes of an independent Rhineland state, factors which also made the proposals highly acceptable to Britain.

There were, however, shortcomings in the 'package' from the French viewpoint. Would Germany similarly acknowledge her eastern frontiers? Would she acknowledge the peace treaties as a whole? Italy, also party to the proposals, was equally keen that Stresemann should acknowledge Germany's southern border with Austria. The German government would not go so far, and the Locarno Pact agreed by Germany, France, Britain, Italy and Belgium (October 1925), apart from guaranteeing the current western borders of Germany, merely recognised France's treaty commitments to Poland and Czechoslovakia. France would find these commitments very hard to carry out without violating Germany's western frontiers.

The 'Briand–Kellogg' Pact

It must be understood, however, that the French government accepted the Locarno terms, not because it misunderstood their implications, but because its foreign policy had deliberately rejected attempts to control Germany in favour of attempts to draw her into international undertakings guaranteed by other powers. Locarno has to be seen as part of that programme. Germany's entry into the League of Nations (September 1926) was another essential element in the same programme. So, too, was the 'Briand–Kellogg' Pact (August 1928) whereby the French foreign minister and the American secretary of state agreed to 'the renunciation of war as an instrument of national policy'. Sixty-two of the 64 states invited to subscribe to this agreement did so, Brazil and Argentina being the exceptions, and although it has been widely attacked for its apparent naiveté, the pact was interpreted at the time as an important commitment to peace by the world's leading powers.

1929: optimism and disintegration

By the summer of 1929, when a conference at The Hague reached agreement on the evacuation of the Rhineland, five years earlier than envisaged at Versailles, the policy of reconciliation seemed largely vindicated and its future prospects engendered confidence. Locarno and German membership of the League of Nations seemed to create political stability in Europe; the Dawes Plan and its successor seemed to prove that reparations could be paid on a regular basis; the consultative spirit of the League of Nations seemed to be accepted by all major powers. The disintegration of this reassuring 'scenario' was brutally abrupt. In July, the retirement of Poincaré removed the major source of stability in French politics. On 3 October, Stresemann died of a heart attack, aged 51, and exactly three weeks later, on 'Black Thursday', share values on the Wall Street Stock Market went into a disastrous decline. The 'Great Depression' had begun.

G Economic crisis and the end of reparations

The political impact of economic depression

Details of the impact of the Great Depression upon the individual European states belong elsewhere (*see* Chapter 14). The large-scale withdrawal of American capital from European investment, and the general fall in prices of industrial and agricultural goods also had overall implications in terms of international relations. Any spirit of international co-operation that may have been emerging gave way to a desperate sense of 'every man for himself'. Nation after nation, for example, abandoned the gold standard, and most hurriedly enclosed themselves behind tariff barriers in an attempt to minimise the effects of the crisis upon themselves. By 1931, only France, Italy and Poland of the major European states continued to base their currencies upon gold. We have already seen (*see* Chapter 14, section **G**) the direct role played by the economic crisis in the rise of the Nazi party to power in Germany between 1930 and 1933, but quite apart from aiding the spread of fascism and self-interested nationalism, the Depression also prepared the ground for international appeasement of those forces. As Britain, America and other states slowly recovered, they sought safety in economic entrenchment and carefully balanced budgets. There seemed no room, at a time of careful housekeeping, for heavy arms expenditure, and the expense of another war was unthinkable. Besides, as the domestic affairs of France and Spain showed clearly, the apparent failure of existing regimes to cope with the ills of capitalism caused many to entertain thoughts of Bolshevism or of fascism as an alternative. France, Spain, Belgium and even Britain were not immune from the forces that had engendered fascism in Germany.

The Hoover Moratorium

A direct casualty of the economic catastrophe was the Young Plan for reparation payments. In October 1930, German representatives had approached President Hoover of the United States, as the peace treaty entitled them to do, to request a suspension (or 'moratorium') of reparation payments in the light of increasing economic difficulties. The resultant Hoover Moratorium covered all inter-state debts from mid-1931 to mid-1932. By December 1931, however, it was clear that Europe was not experiencing the 'relatively short depression' for which a moratorium was designed. In that month the powers involved with the Young Plan met in Basle to consider the reparations question and concluded that 'an adjustment of all intergovernmental debts is the only lasting measure which is capable of restoring economic stability and true peace'. The Lausanne Conference (June 1932) agreed that reparation should be ended by a lump-sum payment of 3,000 million marks, relieving Germany of 90 per cent of her outstanding debt. To the anger of the United States, however, her European debtors insisted that their war debt repayments should also end. Even the last payment proposed by the French premier was vetoed by the Assembly. Thus, the financial clauses of the Treaty of Versailles ceased to exist, and if France had gained 'tit for tat' on an economic level, her diplomatic account was left badly in debt by renewed isolation from the United States. The final lump sum payment by Germany, incidentally, was never made.

H The failure of disarmament

The principle of international disarmament was the second major casualty of the early 1930s. It will be recalled that, in theory, the disarmament of Germany was merely a preliminary to a general disarmament. Not until 1926, however, did a 'Preparatory Commission' meet in Geneva, and not until February 1932 did the conference finally gather there to begin serious deliberation. On the surface, the prospects seemed relatively bright, for the renunciation of expensive armaments made good sense at a time of dramatic recession. France, consistently one of the most positive members of the conference, explored three different routes to the goal. The original plan proposed by André Tardieu was that each nation should submit its major offensive weapons, planes, capital ships, heavy artillery, to the control of the League of Nations, to provide a force to oppose aggression. It was, in short, a revival of the 1919 idea of a 'League with Teeth', and fell foul of the same objections about the infringement of national sovereignty. In the face of division among the wartime allies, Germany played her 'trump' card, demanded equal treatment with the allies on the question of armaments, and withdrew from the conference. An agreement without Germany was so pointless that France effectively conceded the radical idea of German equality in her new 'Constructive Plan' (November 1932). This combined the idea of a League of Nations force with the maintenance of national defensive militias, of which Germany was entitled to as large a one as any other state. The principle of German equality was also specifically acknowledged within 'a system which would comprise security for all nations'. Germany returned to the conference but, with Italy, showed little interest in the Constructive Plan. After the failure of a British plan to establish a common limit of 200,000 men on the forces of France, Germany, Italy and Poland, the third French plan came close to success (June 1933). She suggested an eight-year period, during the latter half of which the continental armies would conform to the figures suggested by the British. With Britain, France, Italy and the USA in agreement, and Germany in danger of becoming trapped, Hitler, now in power, withdrew finally from the conference (October 1933). Within five days he turned his back finally on international co-operation by quitting the League of Nations.

I The failure of 'great power' security

The role of Mussolini

The collapse of two essential bases of the collective security envisaged at Versailles caused the major powers of Western Europe to turn to the alternative form of security already explored with some success at Locarno, the security of traditional pacts and alliances. The initiative this time came primarily from Mussolini who, in separate conversations with British and French ministers (March 1933), proposed the idea of a joint undertaking by Italy, France, Germany and Britain to take no unilateral action that might disturb the peace of Europe. The motives of the four powers in following up the suggestion were various. Britain, in the words of then foreign secretary, Sir John Simon, saw Italy as 'the key to European peace', and was willing to work with her to maintain a traditional balance of power. France shared these motives to an extent, although opinion there was by no means united as to the value of such a pact. Germany, at this delicate stage so soon after Hitler's coming to power, was happy to take any step that reassured European opinion while she solved her domestic problems. Only in the case of Italy has there been real disagreement among historians. Those who have generally regarded Mussolini as altogether cynical have seen

his proposals as a means of separating France from her allies in eastern Europe, where Italy of course had ambitions, and perhaps from Britain. Others, following Elizabeth Wiskemann, have regarded Mussolini as genuinely perturbed by the resurgence of Germany. They saw his proposals in 1933 as a genuine attempt to appease Hitler, by recognising Germany's great power status, while restricting her freedom of action by international guarantees.

The Four Power Pact

The Four Power Pact concluded in July 1933 committed the contracting states to co-operation for a period of ten years to preserve the peace of Europe. But, as a further step away from the Versailles settlement, it acknowledged the principle of 'reasonable revision' of the peace treaties. In fact, the pact was a 'dead letter' almost as soon as it was agreed. In October Hitler already felt confident enough to leave the Disarmament Conference and the League of Nations. Within 18 months (March 1935) he had re-introduced conscription in Germany, which promised little for his desire to co-operate with his neighbours. In the light of these events, the Four Power Pact was never ratified by the other powers. Its effects, therefore, were wholly negative, providing a nasty shock for the eastern European states who now found themselves excluded from an apparent great power 'club'. Russia's reaction was to enter negotiations with France for a mutual assistance pact, possibly with a view to splitting this new capitalist bloc. Poland, apparently let down by France, reacted differently and concluded a non-aggression pact with Germany in January 1934.

The Stresa Front

Italy, France and Britain did not yet despair of combined action to preserve their security. Contacts between Mussolini and the pro-Italian foreign Minister of France, Pierre Laval, fuelled by an attempted Nazi 'coup' in Austria (July 1934) resulted in a set of Rome Agreements (January 1935) in which the parties seemed to have reached an understanding on European security and Italian colonial ambitions. With Britain drawn in once more, the Stresa Conference (April 1935) produced a three-sided agreement to oppose 'by all practical means, any unilateral repudiation of treaties, which may endanger the peace of Europe'. In theory, this 'Stresa Front', formed by the leaders of the three powers, was an imposing structure. In reality, it had a number of weaknesses. In effect, far from girding up their loins to fight Hitler, all the members hoped rather that the very existence of the 'Stresa Front' might deter the German dictator from dangerous adventures. Secondly, Mussolini, although his concern at the rise of Germany was undoubtedly genuine, quite specifically desired this agreement to gain such European security as would enable him to pursue Italy's 'imperial destiny'. The reaction of his Stresa partners to his colonial policy was shortly to put this final attempt at a great power equilibrium to the test.

J The conquest of Abyssinia

Italy's colonial motives

In October 1935 Italian forces began the pursuit of Mussolini's colonial plans by an open assault upon the East African state of Abyssinia (also called Ethiopia). The long-term motives for this attack reached back to the 19th century when Italy had marked out this region as her sphere of influence in the general 'scramble for Africa', and had suffered the humiliation of defeat at the hands of Abyssinian tribesmen at Adowa (1896). Not only did national pride demand some compensation for Adowa, but the aggressive nature of Italian fascism demanded, in Mussolini's words, 'war for war's sake, since fascism needs the glory of victory'. Besides, since Britain and France showed no signs of liquidating their empires, was not Italy entitled to equal colonial status? Although evidence suggests that Mussolini had determined his course by 1932, the precise timing of his attack was dictated by several factors: by the rate of military preparation, and especially by Mussolini's conviction that his agreement with France and Britain at Stresa had ensured that Hitler would take no revisionist initiatives while his back was turned.

The defeat of Abyssinia

The new phase of Italian policy opened with a border incident at Wal-Wal (November 1934) and proceeded with a steady and obvious build-up of arms in Italian Somalia and Eritrea. On 2 October 1935, Italian troops invaded Abyssinia on the pretext that they were 'restoring order in a vast country left in the most atrocious slavery and the most primitive conditions of existence'. When local geography and the courage of the local tribesmen caused temporary embarrassment, Mussolini poured huge resources into the fray. Four hundred thousand men fought in Abyssinia, and the full weight of modern weaponry, aerial bombardment and the use of poison gas, was brought to bear. The flight of the Abyssinian Emperor, Haile Selassie, and the capture of his capital, Addis Ababa, confirmed Italy's victory in May 1936.

The diplomatic implications of the invasion

The implications of the conquest of Abyssinia were not, however, confined to East Africa. Unfortunately for Italy, Abyssinia, despite her vague boundaries and semi-feudal government, had been admitted to the League of Nations in 1923 and demanded that the League apply the prescribed economic sanctions against the aggressor. Britain and France thus found themselves committed, with differing degrees of enthusiasm, to a boycott of all Italian goods and to a ban on exports of arms, rubber, and metal ore to Italy. The attempts of their foreign ministers, Hoare and Laval, to buy-off either Mussolini or Haile Selassie ended in embarrassing failure, and their apparent 'double game' of applying sanctions and negotiating at the same time behind the back of the League of Nations effectively dragged down both the League and the Stresa Front. Furthermore, the sanctions were largely ineffective. The vital commodity of oil was not among the prohibited items and, in any case, non-members such as Germany, Japan and the United States were not committed to sanctions. Although his most recent biographer, Denis Mack Smith, draws the conclusion that Mussolini's whole policy over Stresa and Abyssinia was one of calculated duplicity, it seems likely that he was genuinely shocked by the imposition of economic sanctions. His assumption that Laval had granted him a 'free hand' by the Rome Agreements seemed confirmed by British and French silence at Stresa on the Abyssinian question, despite the contemporary build-up of Italian forces in Africa. Surely this had indicated their acquiescence? To Mussolini, a League of Nations that allowed the Japanese to escape unpunished for the aggression in China, and then turned on Italy, was a 'front of conservation, of selfishness, and of hypocrisy'. Whatever their limitations, the 1935 agreements between France, Italy and Britain perished, not necessarily because of Mussolini's deviousness, but because of the extraordinary confusion of British and French foreign policy.

K The remilitarisation of the Rhineland

The remilitarisation and the allied response

The Abyssinian crisis preoccupied European statesmen for eight months (October 1935–May 1936), during which time Hitler struck his first blow at the territorial clauses of the Treaty of Versailles. On 7 March 1936, he ordered a force of 22,000 men into the Rhineland in direct defiance of those treaty terms which declared it a demilitarised zone. As pretext, he claimed that the French pact with the Soviet Union had breached the Locarno understanding. A more realistic explanation of his timing would, of course, take into account Italy's colonial involvement and the resultant weakening of the Stresa Front. Europe was taken by surprise, not by the fact of remilitarisation, but by the method. Diplomats had expected Hitler to negotiate; instead he took swift, decisive action, and offered negotiations afterwards, a method soon to become familiar. The operation succeeded through a combination of Hitler's boldness and French miscalculation. France's military leaders estimated that up to 295,000 German troops were available to Hitler and that their intervention would lead to a major conflict. Her political leaders thus concluded that they could intervene only with British aid. It is now known that the German forces were under direct orders to withdraw if they met resistance. No British aid was forthcoming, however. In Britain and France alike much public opinion felt that confrontation with Germany and Italy at the same time was folly, that French friendship with the Soviet Union was unwise and that, in any case, as a London taxi driver remarked to the British foreign secretary, 'Jerry can do what he likes in his own back garden'. In short, Hitler's move did not cause widespread popular outrage because, in the words of the French historian Maurice Baumont, 'a blow had been aimed, not at French territory, but only at the Treaty of Versailles, in which no one believed any longer'.

The results of the remilitarisation

The implications of the remilitarisation were substantial and complex. In combination with the Abyssinian affair, it seemed to show that the western powers were as unwilling as the League of Nations was unable to act against unilateral revision of the treaties. The effect on France's strategic position was disastrous. Hitler's action provided further disillusionment for such nations as Poland and Czechoslovakia, and the rapid fortification of Germany's frontiers now made it extremely difficult for France to fulfil her eastern pacts by attacks against Germany in the west. French reluctance to act alone also provided proof that she had become the junior partner in her relationship with Britain. Lastly, Hitler's bold gamble, like that of Mussolini in Abyssinia, was invaluable in strengthening his prestige and authority at home, especially in military circles. If Abyssinia destroyed the League of Nations, the remilitarisation of the Rhineland destroyed Locarno, and the way was thus open to the disaster of 1939.

L The Rome–Berlin Axis

Mussolini and Italian isolation

The key feature of European diplomatic relationships, and a major factor in the collapse of the balance of power in Europe after 1935, was the movement of Italy out of the orbit of London and Paris and into that of Berlin. Superficially appealing as the attraction of one fascist dictatorship for another may have been, the coming together of Italy and Germany had little to do with ideology. In the words of Maurice Baumont, Mussolini 'wanted to be on the side of power, the only decisive attraction for him'. In this context of power politics, he had drawn four lessons from the events of 1935–37. Firstly, it had become clear that the statesmen of Britain and France, and still less those of the League of Nations from which Italy withdrew in November 1937, had neither the will nor the means to check the resurgence of Germany. Secondly, it was evident that Italy could not pursue her interests in Abyssinia and in Spain and, at the same time, guard her security in central Europe. Thirdly, involvement in Spain (*see* Chapter 14, section **T**) had badly weakened Italy's international position. It had shown up weaknesses in her army, absorbed half of her foreign currency reserves, and established a gulf between Mussolini and the democrats without guaranteeing any gain or support from General Franco. Lastly, and perhaps most important, just as he became disgusted at the weakness of the western powers, so Mussolini was at once seduced and horrified by the power of Germany. After a relatively unsuccessful visit to Rome in 1934, Hitler had spared no effort to demonstrate German military strength when Mussolini came to Berlin (September 1937).

The development of the German–Italian alliance
This alliance had its origins in the 'October Protocols' signed by Count Ciano in Berlin in 1936. They contained little more than vague anti-Bolshevik phrases, but gave the relationship the name by which it is known to history, by declaring that the Berlin–Rome line was now 'an axis around which can revolve all those European states with a will to collaboration and peace'. In November 1937, shortly after Mussolini's fateful visit to Germany, this 'Axis' took on wider implications when Italy subscribed to the Anti-Comintern Pact, originally concluded between Germany and Japan (November 1936) to present a united front against Bolshevism.

The Pact of Steel
The Anschluss of March 1938, and Italy's meek acceptance of it, did not so much mark a further step towards alliance, as indicate the extent to which Italian policy was already subject to that of Germany. Within two months, Hitler began to pressurise the Italian government to accept a full military alliance. Mussolini's initial reluctance to commit himself was worn down by May 1939, when he allowed Ciano to conclude the alliance, known as the Pact of Steel, which committed both sides to help each other in the event of one of them becoming 'involved in warlike complications'. The terms made no pretence to be merely defensive. The Pact of Steel constituted a triumph for Hitler in his re-orientation of European diplomacy, and completed Mussolini's loss of control over his own policy. 'In point of fact,' as Elizabeth Wiskemann has written, by underwriting all future German schemes, 'Mussolini gave Hitler *carte blanche* to attack Poland and to plunge into the Second World War.'

M The Anschluss

Motives and obstacles, 1920–35
The question of union (*Anschluss*) between Austria and the German Reich was nearly a century old when Hitler came to power. It had its roots in the 19th-century contest for German leadership, seemingly settled by the triumph of Bismarck's Prussia and his careful exclusion of Austria from the German state. The loss of Austria's non-German territories in 1919, and the rise of an ardent pan-Germanist in the person of Hitler, raised the question anew. At the beginning of the 1930s the long-established factors of language and the memory of centuries during which Vienna had been the chief of the German cities, and the more modern consideration that many Austrians would undoubtedly be economically better off as part of a greater state were factors in favour of the Anschluss.

Against Anschluss were the remains of the old spirit of Austrian independence, still resenting the ascendancy of Berlin over Vienna, and the implacable hostility of the Versailles allies, especially of France and Italy. The project for a Customs union between Germany and Austria (March 1931) had foundered upon the rock of French suspicion. 'They must take us for asses,' wrote the French politician, Édouard Herriot, 'if they think that we are able to forget that the political union of Germany was reached by way of a customs union.' The mismanaged 'coup' by Austrian Nazis, with the knowledge of Hitler (July 1934) which ended in the murder of the Austrian Chancellor, Engelbert Dollfuss, foundered upon the prompt action of Mussolini who mobilised the Italian army on the Austrian frontier.

Europe accepts the principle of Anschluss
By the end of 1937 the situation had changed. French inactivity over the advance of German troops to her very frontiers did not suggest that she would act energetically over Austria. Indeed, British and French diplomats, beset with domestic problems, had even indicated to their German counterparts that they had 'no objection to a marked extension of German influence in Austria obtained through evolutionary means'. Most significant was the changed attitude of Italy. Deeply

committed to intervention in the Spanish Civil War, Mussolini was highly impressed by the shows of military power staged for him in Germany and had already begun his drift into Hitler's wake. Count Ciano, his son-in-law and Foreign Minister, expressed the hopelessness of Italy's position over Austrian independence: 'What in fact could we do? Start a war with Germany? At the first shot we fired every Austrian, without exception, would fall in behind the Germans against us.'

The timing of the Anschluss crisis

Despite this, and despite the fact that the very first page of *Mein Kampf* makes clear Hitler's attachment to the principle of German–Austrian unity, A. J. P. Taylor has forwarded a convincing argument to suggest that Hitler did not deliberately set out to absorb Austria in 1938. Although he had hoped to be able to deal first with the question of the Sudetenland, his hand was forced by two factors. Firstly, by continuing agitation by Austrian Nazis led by Arthur Seyss-Inquart, and secondly by the rash decision of the new Austrian Chancellor, Kurt von Schuschnigg, to confront Hitler and force him to disown the agitators.

If Schuschnigg and Seyss-Inquart precipitated the crisis, Hitler nevertheless acted brilliantly to exploit it, partly in the interests of Anschluss, but partly to distract attention from contemporary domestic disagreements. In a violent interview at Berchtesgaten (12 February 1938) Hitler accused Schuschnigg of racial treason, and demanded that Seyss-Inquart be admitted to the Austrian government. Although Schuschnigg accepted this demand he attempted to defend his position by holding a referendum on the question of union with Germany. Unable to risk an anti-German vote, Hitler's hand was now forced. Successively, the German government demanded the postponement of the referendum, the replacement of Schuschnigg by Seyss-Inquart, and finally threatened military intervention. On 11 March, the Austrian Nazi leader, having formed a 'provisional government' of very doubtful legality, requested the dispatch of German troops 'to restore order and save Austria from chaos'. Even so, it is doubtful whether Hitler envisaged more than a 'puppet' government under Seyss-Inquart. On 13 March, however, encouraged by the enthusiastic reception from Austrian crowds at Linz, and by Mussolini's meek acceptance of the principle of Anschluss, Hitler proclaimed the formal union of his native Austria with the German Reich.

Reactions and implications

The Anschluss marked a clear escalation in Nazi policy as it involved the actual obliteration of an independent state set up by the peace treaties. Still, Hitler's action did not excite united European condemnation. The approval registered in the referendums Hitler now held, 99.08 per cent in Germany and 99.75 per cent in Austria, probably had a sound basis in pan-German feeling. Nevertheless, they were obviously in part the result of pressure and fear. 'In Austria,' claimed Goering at Nuremberg in 1945, 'we were not met with rifle shots and bombs; only one thing was thrown at us, flowers.' The British government merely made a formal protest. There was no French government. Chautemps had resigned four days earlier and Blum had yet to take office. Once again, rapid and risky action had reaped a rich reward. Hitler's confidence in such action was now to put the peace of Europe in increasing danger.

N The Sudeten question

Czechoslovakia and the Sudetenland

If Hitler were serious in his desires either to unite all Germans in a single Reich, or to expand the territories of that Reich eastwards, the state of Czechoslovakia constituted a substantial obstacle in his path. She possessed a mountainous and easily defensible frontier with Germany, an army of 34 divisions well supplied by the giant Skoda arms factories at Pilsen, and enjoyed membership of a diplomatic system comprising France, Britain, Poland and the Soviet Union.

She also, however, had her weaknesses. She was, for instance, a state of minority groups. Apart from the uneasy union of Czechs and Slovaks at the heart of the state, Hungarians, Poles and Ukrainians had been placed under the authority of Prague to give the new creation territorial and economic viability. Thirty-five per cent of the population, in fact, was neither Czech nor Slovak. The greatest of these minorities were the Germans of the Sudetenland, an irregular ribbon of territory around the northern, western and southern periphery of

Bohemia and Moravia. Spread through these regions were 3.25 million Germans, resentful that they no longer enjoyed the privileges that had been theirs under Habsburg rule, and regarded with suspicion by the Czech government.

Furthermore, the events of the mid-1930s isolated Czechoslovakia and increased her vulnerability. She had no border with friendly states such as France and the Soviet Union, could expect no help from Italy, as Austria had received none and, after the Anschluss, had a southern border with the enlarged Reich devoid of any natural defences.

The escalation of Sudeten demands

As with Austria, Hitler did not so much cause a crisis over Czechoslovakia, as exploit one that was already developing. A key factor was the Sudeten Party, formed in 1935 by Konrad Henlein, whose political demands had escalated by the time of Henlein's 'Karlsbad Programme' (April 1938) from a claim for equal treatment with the Czechs to a demand for full independence from Czechoslovakia. Still relatively confident of French and British backing, the Czech President, Edvard Benes, was happy to confront and defy the Sudeten Germans. Hitler, more confident than ever after his Austrian successes, had no objection to confrontation, and was greatly aided by a new turn in British and French policy.

Munich and the bankruptcy of appeasement

Britain and France were committed by the second half of 1938 to a policy of persuading Benes to grant Sudeten demands. They were convinced by the events in Austria and by rumours of German troop movements (May 1938) that, if Hitler was determined to support Henlein, the choice lay between Czech concessions and a general war. Henlein's policy, however, and that of Hitler, was to 'demand so much that we never can be satisfied'. When the Czech President conceded the principal demands of the Sudeten Germans, their leaders precipitated unsuccessful risings in Karlsbad, Eger and other centres (13 September) to sustain the tension. The danger that Hitler would intervene as he had in Austria broke the British and French nerve and their respective premiers, Chamberlain and Daladier, plunged into direct negotiations with Hitler. At Berchtesgaten (15 September) and at Bad Godesberg (22 September), Chamberlain heard Hitler's demands escalate through direct German annexation of the Sudetenland, to immediate military occupation. Dramatically, six days later, Hitler agreed to a conference between himself, Chamberlain and Daladier, to be held in Munich with Mussolini as mediator. It has been variously suggested that he had become aware of the lack of enthusiasm in Germany for a military solution, that he was disturbed by Mussolini's reluctance to give military support, or simply that he now knew that his shaken opponents were willing now to allow him the bulk of his demands. Certainly the Munich Conference (29–30 September 1938) granted Hitler far more than he had been demanding a few weeks earlier. It was agreed between the powers that, although Germany would receive all Czech territory where Germans were in a majority, the transfer would be by stages, and under international supervision. In none of these negotiations was the Czech government consulted or allowed to participate. It was simply presented with the alternatives of acceptance or single combat with Germany.

The implications of Munich

Both morally and practically, the implications of the Munich agreement were enormous. The allies, especially the French with their direct treaty obligations, had betrayed Czechoslovakia. Although Britain, France, Italy and Germany all formally guaranteed her remaining territory, the state was in fact doomed by the loss of her defensible frontier, the loss of 70 per cent of her iron and steel resources, the loss of the Skoda works, and also by the encouragement that Sudeten success gave to other separatists. Hungary and Poland both revived claims to Czech territory, and the cause of Slovak separatism took on a new lease of life. In March 1939, having failed to cause the collapse of Czechoslovakia by the Sudeten crisis, Hitler was to precipitate a new crisis over the Slovak demands, and to force the Czechs to accept a German 'protectorate' over Bohemia and Moravia, while Hungary, Poland and the Slovaks achieved their desires. Czechoslovakia, therefore, like Poland in the past, died of partition. The tremendous popular relief at the avoidance of war was short-lived, and certainly did not survive Hitler's seizure of Prague in March. Despite the weakness displayed at Munich, and the loss of Czechoslovakia's

34 divisions to their cause, the subsequent military co-ordination between Britain and France, and their renewal of guarantees to Poland, Greece and Rumania (March–April 1939) strongly suggested that the next crisis would be confronted with greater resolution.

O   Ribbentrop–Molotov Pact

The Soviet Union and the western allies

An undoubted casualty of the Munich surrender was the relationship between the western democracies and the Soviet Union. The relationship had suffered from mutual suspicion for a decade; suspicion on the Soviet side that the British and French secretly preferred German resurgence to the existence of a stable Soviet regime; suspicion in London and Paris either that Stalin still favoured the international spread of communism, or that his vicious domestic purges (*see* Chapter 13, section **K**) had destroyed Russia's viability as an ally. The Munich agreement, made without any reference to the Soviet Union, showed at best that the diplomacy of the western powers was incapable of checking German ambitions, and at worst represented a tacit agreement to Germany's quest for 'living space' in eastern Europe. Either way, the Soviet Union could no longer trust for her security to Paris and London. 'We nearly put our foot on a rotten plank,' declared a prominent Soviet diplomat. 'Now we are going elsewhere.'

The shaping of the German-Soviet pact

The first Soviet overtures for a more positive relationship with Nazi Germany came in May 1938, when the new ambassador to Berlin, A. Meretalov, received instructions to press for better commercial relations. At a time when he was increasingly preoccupied with the problem of Czechoslovakia, Hitler reacted favourably to anything that might separate the Soviet Union from his immediate enemies. In July, the governments reached an oral agreement on the ending of their mutually hostile press campaigns. With the allied abandonment of Czechoslovakia, the Soviet government began to knock harder on Germany's door. The replacement of Maxim Litvinov as commissar for foreign affairs by Vacheslav Molotov (May 1939) was invested with great significance by foreign observers. Molotov, as a member of the Politburo, had the necessary power to engineer major policy changes, whereas Litvinov had been a persistent advocate of collective security, and was furthermore a Jew. Nevertheless, it was widely agreed that Stalin at this stage was still merely keeping open his option of choosing between Germany and the western democracies. It was in mid-August, when British–French–Soviet military negotiations in Moscow collapsed over the reluctance of Poland to allow Soviet troops to cross her territory in the event of an attack on Germany, that Stalin and his advisors drew the conclusion that they had only one remaining option for their national security.

Hitler responded far more rapidly and favourably than the allies had, for his short-term purposes were also served by a change of policy. With his sights now set on Poland, and with Britain and France renewing their pledges to the Poles, it was an urgent priority to ensure that his ambitions would not encounter Soviet opposition. This, and Stalin's desire for greater security for the Soviet frontiers, resulted in the startling agreement reached after only one day's negotiation in Moscow between Molotov and the German foreign minister, Joachim von Ribbentrop (23 August 1939).

The terms of the German–Soviet pact

To the outside world, the Ribbentrop–Molotov Pact took the form of a non-aggression treaty lasting ten years. Secretly, however, it divided the territories between the German and Soviet borders into 'spheres of influence'. Germany's comprised Poland, west of the rivers Narew, Vistula and San, and part of Lithuania. The Soviet zone comprised the rest of Poland and Lithuania, and the states of Estonia, Latvia and Finland. Germany, furthermore, expressed her disinterest in the Balkans and recognised Russia's interest in the Rumanian territory of Bessarabia. Hitler, in short, received tacit Soviet approval to fulfil his designs on Danzig and the Polish 'corridor'. In return, Stalin not only triumphantly reversed the losses suffered by Russia during the Revolution and Civil War 20 years earlier, but seemed to have won a breathing space in terms both of time and of territory. With the Soviet occupation of their sphere of influence between June–August 1940, the amount of territory between a future invader and the vital centres of Leningrad and Moscow was increased by 300 km.

The German-Soviet pact: conclusions

To western commentators, as to Maurice Baumont, this was seen as 'one of the most cynical treaties in world history', a complete reversal of the ideologies of both states. As A. J. P. Taylor has commented, however, 'it is difficult to see what other course Soviet Russia could have followed' in the light of western indifference. It was difficult, too, to see why their part in the destruction of Poland was worse than that of the allies in the destruction of Czechoslovakia. Doubtless both Hitler and Stalin believed that the pact ensured that the Polish question could now be solved without general war. In the event, by giving Hitler the confidence to attack Poland, without diverting Britain and France from their renewed guarantees, Stalin's signature made war in Europe inevitable.

P Poland and the onset of war

The issue of Danzig

The collapse of Czechoslovakia left, in the German view, one major limiting element of the Versailles Treaty standing in eastern Europe. Antipathy between Germans and Poles had a far longer history than the life of the post-war Polish state, but the treaty had created a new focus of hostility in the forms of the 'Free City' of Danzig, and the 'corridor' of territory transferred in 1919 from Germany to Poland to connect Danzig with the Polish heartland. Although the treaty gave the Poles complete control of Danzig's docks, its customs duties, its railway system and foreign relations, Danzig was undeniably a German city, inhabited by 400,000 Germans and without a name in Polish until 'Gdansk' was invented for it in 1919. Similarly, the 'corridor' contained the homes of one million Germans. It was not a settlement that the majority of Germans were willing to tolerate freely.

The dual threat to Poland

Successive Polish governments remained fully aware of this hostility. She was trapped between an unforgiving Germany to the west and a resentful Russia to the east, from which she had newly won her independence (*see* Chapter 12, section **L**). Poland's apprehension was heightened by the Russo–German agreement at Rapallo and the failure of the Locarno Pact to guarantee Germany's eastern borders. Thus Poland sought security through her own armed forces and through her treaties with France.

By the mid-1930s, however, her international position had been greatly complicated by the rise of Hitler, the bankruptcy of French policy towards eastern Europe, and the entry of the Soviet Union into the diplomatic arena. In general, under the direction of General Beck between 1932 and 1939, the Polish foreign ministry proceeded upon the assumption that the Soviet Union posed the greater threat to Poland. 'With the Germans,' he reputedly declared, 'we risk losing our liberty. With the Russians we lose our souls.' From this line of thought sprang the Polish–German non-aggression pact of 1934 and the persistent refusal to allow passage to Soviet troops across Polish territory in the event of war. Furthermore, overestimation of his nation's strength led Beck into the cynical policy whereby Poland participated in the partition of Czechoslovakia, gaining the region of Teschen (March 1939) and staking an unsuccessful claim to Slovakia.

Throughout this period Danzig, its local government in the hands of the local Nazi party since May 1933, remained a canker in Polish–German relations. From the completion of his destruction of Czechoslovakia, the signs accumulated that Hitler intended next to turn his attentions towards Poland As with Austria and Czechoslovakia, his initial policy was that of a war of nerves. In April 1939, Hitler not only repudiated Germany's non-aggression pact with Poland, but renewed German claims to Danzig. In May, the 'Pact of Steel' agreement committed Italy to follow Hitler's path, and by August he was assured that the Soviet Union would not stand in his way. Meanwhile, the German press conducted a persistent campaign of accusations concerning alleged persecution of Poland's German minority. Surely, under these circumstances, Britain and France would not risk themselves on Poland's behalf?

The crisis of August/September 1939

The last week of August 1939 was occupied by Anglo–French efforts to persuade Poland to sacrifice Danzig. This time, however, the situation differed in important respects from that at Munich the previous year. Poland, aware that surrender had not saved Czechoslovakia, refused now to compromise her national sovereignty. The two democratic governments, although eager to avoid war, refused to repeat their Munich performances. Perhaps they were encouraged by increasing evidence of Mussolini's un-fascist reluctance to commit himself to war. Perhaps, as A. J. P. Taylor has stressed, the political conservatives of Britain and France, rather than being terrified by the Russo–German agreement, became more hostile to Hitler now that he no longer posed as a bulwark against communism. Maybe Chamberlain and Daladier merely recognised the futility of their Munich policy. General war, in the event, resulted from the conviction of both sides that the other was bluffing. 'The men I met at Munich,' Hitler declared to his generals, 'are not the kind to start another world war.' Thus, on 1 September, German troops invaded Poland on the false pretext of Polish border violations. Only two days later did Britain and France issue separate ultimatums for German withdrawal, perhaps encouraging Hitler by their delay. Nevertheless, upon the expiry of the ultimatums, both powers declared war on Germany, ending almost exactly to Foch's prediction, the 'Twenty Years' Truce'.

Questions

Essay questions

1   Discuss the view that the peace settlement following the First World War was a 'fatal blend of idealism and revenge'. (UCLES)

2   'France had a bark but no bite'. How apt is this comment on the attitude displayed by France towards Germany in the inter-war years? (NEAB)

3   Would you agree with the view that Hitler's conduct of foreign policy was 'purely opportunist'? Explain your answer fully. (WJEC)

4   Did the policy of appeasement pursued by Britain and France in the 1930s reflect more their realism or their cowardice? (ULEAC)

5   Why was there such limited resistance in continental Europe to German recovery and expansion in the period 1925–1941? (AEB)

6   How far did the extent and rapidity of German territorial expansion in the period 1938–1941 result from the shortcomings of the Versailles settlement? (AEB)

Documentary Question

Study the following source carefully, and then answer the questions based upon it.

In my opinion there are three great tasks that confront German foreign policy in the more immediate future.

In the first place, the solution of the Reparations question in a sense tolerable for Germany, and the assurance of peace, which is an essential prerequisite for the recovery of our strength.

Secondly, the protection of Germans abroad, those ten to twelve millions of our kindred who now live under a foreign yoke in foreign lands.

The third great task is the readjustment of our Eastern frontiers: the recovery of Danzig, the Polish corridor, and a correction of the frontier in Upper Silesia.

In the background stands the union with German Austria, although I am quite clear that this not merely brings no advantages to Germany but seriously complicates the problems of the German Reich.

If we want to secure these aims, we must concentrate on these tasks. Hence the Security Pact, which guarantees us peace, and makes England and Italy, if Mussolini consents to cooperate, guarantors of our Western frontiers. The pact also rules out the possibility of any military conflict with France for the recovery of Alsace-Lorraine. This is a renunciation on the part of Germany, but, so far, it possesses only a theoretical character, as there is no possibility of a war with France.

The question of a choice between East and West does not arise as the result of our joining the League. Such a choice can only be made when backed by military force. That, alas, we do not possess.

Gustav Stresemann to the former German Crown Prince (7 September 1925).

a i   Explain the meaning of the underlined phrases. [2]

  ii   What did Stresemann mean by 'the union with German Austria'? [3]

b i   What evidence is there in the source of Germany's discontent with her role in international affairs in the 1920s? [3]

  ii   What does the source reveal about Stresemann's attitude towards international agreements and organisations? [4]

c   How far does the source contribute to an understanding of Weimar foreign policy? (You are advised to use in your answer relevant background knowledge as well as information derived from the source.)

(WJEC)

18

The Second World War

A Soviet cartoon published in 1944. The original caption read: 'The general from the Eastern Front seeks orders, and the Führer deliberates.'

Even if it were not dated, what elements in the cartoon indicate that it was published in the latter stages of the war?

Why would the Soviet government have been unlikely to publish this form of anti-German propaganda in 1941 or 1942?

Unlike the conflict of 1914–18, the war that began in 1939 was to become a true world war. The First World War was, in fact, global mainly in the sense that the imperialist interests of some of the combatants caused European powers to clash in distant regions. The Second World War was to include campaigns in the Pacific and in East Asia in which European power was indirectly concerned, if at all. These conflicts, however, must remain beyond our present scope, and the aim of this chapter will only be to describe and explain those elements of the Second World War that had the most direct impact upon the political, social and economic structure of the continent of Europe itself.

A The state of the powers

The relative strengths of the major European powers in 1939 may be judged from Table 18.1. Such figures tell part of the story accurately enough, but they do not tell the whole story. As the lessons of the 1914–18 war should have taught, the importance of the 'big battalions' was now outweighed by technical and tactical superiority. In these respects German leadership was indisputable. Under the influence of such commanders as Guderian and Rommel she had adopted the principles of mechanised warfare, of rapid thrusts against a slow-moving enemy to cut his lines of supply and of retreat, far more effectively than her opponents. Germany enjoyed a distinct advantage in the areas vital to this 'lightning war' (*Blitzkrieg*), in the design and deployment of her tanks and the use of aerial support. She had turned her enforced disarmament of 1919 to her own ends, building modern weapons while her opponents laboured under the weight of obsolete equipment. The most modern of the Luftwaffe's planes were faster and more manoeuvrable than anything possessed by the French or the Poles and, although her 3,200 tanks did not represent a numerical superiority, models such as the PkwIII and the PkwIV were superior to their counterparts.

Despite the entreaties in the earlier 1930s of a young tank officer, Colonel Charles de Gaulle, French military commanders continued to think of the tank as a form of mechanised horse, supporting the all-important infantry advances. Neither they nor their allies appreciated the value of the weapon used in massed formations. Their plans and their armies proceeded at the pace of the foot soldier in a military world dominated by the internal combustion engine. Most ominous of all for the allies' immediate prospects in the autumn of 1939 were the weaknesses of the Polish armed forces, largely unchanged since their successes against the Russians 20 years before.

Table 18.1 The military balance of power in Europe, 1939

	Army divisions	Air strength	Capital ships	Submarines
Germany	125	4,210	5	65
Italy	73	1,531	4	104
USSR	125	3,361	3	18
France	86	1,234	7	78
Great Britain	4	1,750	15	57
Poland	40	500	–	–

From A. Adamthwaite, *The Coming of the Second World War*.

B *Blitzkrieg* and phoney war

The defeat of Poland
'Although Hitler blundered,' wrote A. J. P. Taylor, 'in supposing that the two western powers would not go to war at all, his expectation that they would not go to war seriously turned out to be correct.' Poland received no material support from her allies and the tactics of all three powers contrasted starkly with those of the invaders. Poland became the first victim of the *Blitzkrieg* perfected by the German forces as, pitching armoured columns and overwhelming aerial superiority against an army that continued to trust in the mobility of large cavalry forces, the *Wehrmacht* made rapid progress eastwards, encircling the defending forces in a great pincer movement. On 17 September the fate of Poland was sealed when Soviet forces began their occupation of her eastern regions. Within ten days the German and Soviet forces had reached the line agreed in the Ribbentrop–Molotov Pact, and the Polish state ceased to exist.

The mentality of the 'phoney war'
In the west, meanwhile, a very different kind of war was being waged. The leading contemporary military historian, Sir Basil Liddell Hart, has argued strongly that the allies, with 85 French divisions alone, could have taken effective action against a German frontier guarded by only 43 divisions,

without tanks, aircraft or substantial supplies. Yet nothing positive was done. This was largely due to the outmoded thinking of the French commanders, still wedded to the defensive strategy of the previous war, but also in part to the hesitation of political leaders who had still not wholly overcome the appeasement mentality of the last decade. Thus, when allied bombers did fly over German industrial towns, it was to drop propaganda leaflets rather than bombs. This curious state of suspended hostility was christened the 'Phoney War'. To the Germans it became the 'sitting-down war' (*Sitzkrieg*) in ironic contrast to the more effective tactics of the eastern front.

Allied strategies during the 'phoney war'

Illogically, the attention of allied strategists during this 'Phoney War' turned towards Scandinavia. There, in the mines of Sweden and Norway, lay the source of 51 per cent of Germany's supplies of iron ore. That, in itself, provided a sound justification for allied attempts to entice Norway and Sweden into the war on their side. However, with the opening of the Soviet Union's 'Winter War' with Finland (November 1939–March 1940), it is hard to resist the conclusion that the allied governments continued to be as much concerned with the Soviet threat as with that posed by Germany. Similarly, French actions in the Middle East against Hitler's Caspian oil supplies were as much anti-Soviet in conception as anti-German. Once more, allied action proved hesitant and half-hearted. While they debated the mining of neutral Norwegian waters to prevent the passage of ore to Germany, Hitler ordered the extension of operations to Scandinavia to safeguard his supplies. The invasion of Denmark (April 1940), necessary for the purposes of communication, was an immediate success, but the simultaneous assault on Norway encountered stiffer resistance aided by allied forces. However, by the end of June all allied forces had been forced to withdraw, leaving Norway in German hands.

C   The Fall of France

German strategy

The 'Phoney War' ended abruptly on 10 May 1940 with the launching of the German offensive into France and the Low Countries. Despite the months that had been available for preparation, the defending forces were taken largely unaware, not only by the speed and power of the German attack, but also by its strategy. Expecting an offensive like that of 1914, based upon a drive through central Belgium, allied strategy centred upon an advance into Belgium to check the enemy's right wing short of the French frontier while the rest of his forces dashed themselves against the defences of the Maginot Line. Indeed, until January 1940, Belgium had played a leading role in *Wehrmacht* plans. Only then, upon the suggestion of General von Manstein, had a daring new strategy been introduced. Manstein, aware that the allies regarded the hilly and wooded region of the Ardennes, beyond the flank of the Maginot Line, as virtually impassable, and that it was thus only lightly defended, proposed a massive armoured attack across the river Meuse and into this weakest sector of the allied line.

The German offensive

In the event, the German offensive contained both elements. For the first ten days Holland and Belgium bore the brunt of aerial bombardment and assault by infantry, artillery and airborne troops. In particular, the bombing of Rotterdam, where nearly 1,000 civilians died within a few minutes, was unparalleled in European experience and created a profound psychological impression. The Dutch government capitulated on 15 May. The breaching of Belgium's defences drew British and French forces onto her territory to check the German advance and when, on 12 May, the massive armoured force under General von Kleist broke through the Ardennes and breached the French line near Sedan, these advanced allied forces were threatened with encirclement. This breakthrough, although it did not end the battle for France, effectively decided its eventual outcome. Faced with the alternatives of evacuation or annihilation, the British forces, with some 10,000 French troops, retreated to the Channel at Dunkirk. Here, by a combination of heroism, good fortune and puzzling German tactics, they were transported back to Britain by a fleet of 860 assorted vessels hastily assembled for the task (26 May–4 June). The operation owed much, perhaps everything to Hitler's curious decision to hold back tanks and aircraft that could have destroyed the allied forces and their rescuers on the beaches. Variously explained as a temporary loss of nerve, or as evidence of a continuing hope that Britain would still conclude a separate peace, Hitler's decision allowed an escape which, in the popular mind, did something to obscure the magnitude of the allied defeat.

Collapse and armistice

The new French line, along the rivers Aisne and Somme, was attacked on 5 June and broke two days later. Thereafter, disaster piled upon disaster. The government abandoned Paris for the safety of the south (9 June). Any remaining hope of national survival vanished the following day when, with the main fighting done and the spoils there for the taking, Mussolini judged the moment ripe for Italy, too, to declare war on France. From their retreat near Bordeaux the French government, now led by the hero of the First World War, Marshal Philippe Pétain, rejected the option of flight to Africa and requested Germany's terms for an armistice. Considering the extent of the military defeat the terms dictated at Rethondes (21 June), in the same railway carriage used for the German surrender in 1918, were moderate. In 46 days of fighting, France had lost 84,000 men dead, 120,000 injured and 1,500,000 taken prisoner. Yet, with the exception of strategic areas in the north and along the Atlantic coast, French officials were to be allowed to retain responsibility for civil administration while the French government retained complete sovereignty over the southern 40 per cent of the country free from German military occupation. No territory was earmarked for annexation by Germany, although Italy claimed the return of Nice and Savoy, and France kept control of her fleet and of her Empire. The fact remained, as the future would show, that with total military domination, Hitler could take what he did not now claim whenever he felt the need.

The significance of the French defeat

The astonishing collapse of France had many causes, among which the confused foreign policy of the last two decades, the deep domestic divisions of recent years, and the extraordinary incompetence of commanders who neglected airpower, mechanised forces and modern communications, are prominent. Although the transformation of this European conflict into a true world war was eventually to reverse the outcome of 1940, the significance of the German victory in purely European terms must not be underestimated. A nation that had held the first place in the affairs of the continent for three centuries had been rendered impotent within five weeks, and the rise of German power, checked at great cost in 1918, seemed after all to have reached its logical conclusion. Peter Calvocoressi has summarised the impact of these events in his judgement that 'the fall of France opened an abyss of uncertainty for the whole continent and shook the imagination as perhaps nothing had shaken it since the victory of the Turks at Mohacs in 1526'.

D   The Battle of Britain

British resistance and the German response

The collapse of France seemed likely to end the war in western Europe. Britain's chances of continuing the war seemed hopeless. Her land forces, although extricated from Dunkirk, had lost most of their equipment, and the defence of 3,000 km of coastline posed enormous problems. Yet, stiffened by the extraordinary leadership and resolution of the new prime minister, Winston Churchill, Britain did not sue for peace. Instead, Churchill announced his determination that 'we shall fight on the beaches, we shall fight on the landing grounds, we shall fight in the hills; we shall never surrender'.

Hitler's response to this decision seems to have been conditioned by three factors. Firstly, although it is unlikely that Britain could have resisted an invasion, no definite plans had been prepared for one, so sure was the German High Command that the fall of France would end the western campaign. Secondly, Hitler professed a persistent reluctance to treat a 'Germanic' civilisation in the same way that he had treated the Poles. Lastly, if Britain still needed to be prodded towards peace, the commander of the *Luftwaffe*, Hermann Goering, was determined that his forces should be allowed to demonstrate their effectiveness.

The defeat of the *Luftwaffe*

Unlike the Battle of France, therefore, the Battle of Britain took the form of a concentrated aerial attack, firstly upon Britain's airfields, to gain total air supremacy, and then upon London and other centres to break the resistance of the civilian population. Neither effort was successful. The numerical superiority of the *Luftwaffe*, about 1,200 bombers and 1,000 fighters based in France to some 900 British fighters, was offset by several factors. The relatively light German bombers such as the Heinkel 111 and the Dornier 217 were vulnerable without substantial fighter support, and the range of such fighters as the Messchersmitt 109E was only sufficient to give them a few minutes of combat over British targets.

On the British side, the Spitfire and Hurricane fighters were formidable weapons, fast, manoeuvrable, heavily armed, and with the advantage of fighting over their own territory. The rapid development of radar and its establishment along the southern and eastern costs provided valuable early warning of the bombers' approach. Thus, in the main phase of the engagement (early August–late September 1940), the *Luftwaffe* lost over 1,100 aircraft, against a British loss of 650. Hitler, half-hearted in his campaign from the outset, and impatient to turn against his 'real' enemy in the east, suspended the plan for invasion on 17 September, and reduced *Luftwaffe* operations over Britain at the end of the month. Although the struggle was decided as much by German errors and miscalculations as by British strengths, the Battle of Britain represented a first checking of Germany's triumphant military progress, and the beginning of that overstretching of her military resources that was to be her downfall.

E The conflict spreads

The Mediterranean and the Balkans

In mid-1940, the conflict that we now call the Second World War was a strictly limited one, tightly confined to areas of western and northern Europe. The failure of Germany in that summer to eliminate British opposition began a process of proliferation which transformed this into a truly global war. Firstly, after the failure of aerial warfare, the Atlantic Ocean became the major theatre of Anglo–German conflict as the German navy sought, with submarines, surface raiders and mines, to cut British supply lines. Secondly, the entry of Italy into the war inevitably spread the conflict to those areas that Mussolini considered to

be his sphere of influence: the Balkans, the Mediterranean, and North Africa. That German troops became involved in these regions was the result of two factors. The failure of Italian forces to sustain their offensive against Greece (October 1940) and the British decision to send aid to the Greeks seriously threatened interests that Germany had carefully built up in that region. By a mixture of bullying and diplomacy, Hitler had ensured that Hungary, Rumania and Yugoslavia would remain sympathetic to German ambitions in eastern Europe, valuable sources of strategic supplies and potential assembly areas for anti-Soviet forces.

The hope that General Franco might repay his debt from the Spanish Civil War by supporting Axis interests in the Mediterranean collapsed in a series of discussions in October and November in which the Spanish leader made it very clear that his priority was domestic consolidation and reconstruction. Thus, with Italian forces checked in Greece and later in North Africa, and with the pro-German government of Yugoslavia overthrown by a *coup d'état* (March 1941), Hitler found himself forced into large-scale intervention. Although militarily successful, with Greece cleared of hostile troops by late April and the island of Crete captured in May, the commitment of 28 divisions to the Balkans and of several mechanised divisions to North Africa forced a postponement of the planned Russian offensive and the establishment of a costly and lasting 'side show' for the Germans.

The entry of the United States

Of far greater significance, however, was the gradual involvement of the United States in the conflict. American isolationism, re-established by the Senate's refusal to ratify the Versailles Treaty, and confirmed by three Neutrality Acts (1935–36–37), was only slowly eroded by the influence of Churchill's close personal relationship with President Franklin D. Roosevelt, and by a growing public awareness that events in the world were beginning to pose a direct threat to American interests. The fall of France, for instance, presented the prospect of an Atlantic ocean dominated by hostile fleets at the same time as Japanese influence spread in the Pacific Ocean. The Battle of the Atlantic, with its extensive German submarine action, not only confirmed this prospect, but posed a definite danger to American shipping. Thus there was sufficient support in the United States for the 'Destroyer Deal' (September 1940), which placed 50 older ships in British hands, and for the more important 'Lend-Lease' agreement (March 1941), whereby British purchase of war materials from American companies was financed by the American government regardless of Britain's current dollar reserves. By late 1941, therefore, the United States, largely due to the influence of Roosevelt himself, had taken up an ambiguous position. She was clearly sympathetic to Germany's opponents, but not openly committed to war.

This position was changed dramatically on 7 December 1941 by the Japanese air attack upon the American Pacific fleet at Pearl Harbor. The American declaration of war upon Japan was followed almost immediately (11 December) by Hitler's declaration of war upon the United States. Many have since followed Alan Bullock in regarding this declaration as 'the greatest single mistake of his career'. Peter Calvocoressi and others have, on the other hand, noted Hitler's previous efforts to avoid provoking the United States into intervention in Europe, and have interpreted his declaration of war as a simple acceptance of American hostility to Germany.

F   The invasion of the USSR

German motives and strategy

Although increasingly committed to secondary theatres of war, Hitler would not postpone the major element in his policy, the assault upon Soviet Russia, beyond June 1941. Although this assault was dictated by long-term hostility to Bolshevism and by theories of *Lebensraum*, there were also logical short-term factors that dictated its timing. An attack now upon the Soviet Union would leave Britain with no prospect of future support in Europe, and would leave Japan without any distraction in her impending confrontation with the United States. Besides, Hitler was convinced that his successes in eastern Europe would, sooner or later, cause Stalin to take action to redress the balance, and it made no sense to delay until the Soviet Army had had time to fortify the territories occupied in 1939. Thus on 22 June 121 divisions of the *Wehrmacht*, with massive aerial support, were launched across the frontier. Dismissing his generals' insistence upon a direct assault upon Moscow,

Hitler made the Soviet capital only one of three objectives for his army. An attack upon Leningrad would secure his Baltic flank with Finnish aid, while a thrust into the Ukraine would secure valuable industrial and agricultural resources.

The initial success of the German offensive

Although German forces were no greater than those that faced them, indeed the Red Army had more men, more tanks, and more aircraft, the invaders enjoyed several substantial advantages. They enjoyed a great element of surprise, for Soviet propaganda had allowed no word to escape of worsening German–Soviet relations. They attacked an army which, although it had learned much from the difficult war with Finland a year earlier, had not yet had time fully to implement the necessary improvements in command and materials. The Red Army, uncertain which enemy constituted the greater threat, still divided its forces between its frontier with the Germans and that in the east with Japan.

Thus, the initial success of the German offensive was staggering. Soviet resistance was as brave as always, but it lacked the co-ordination to contain the enemy advance for any considerable period. In the north, Leningrad found itself surrounded and besieged by September. In the south, a Soviet force of 600,000 was surrounded and the key Ukrainian city of Kiev fell in the same month. By mid-October the *Wehrmacht* had pushed over 650 km into central Russia and was within 80 km of the Soviet capital. Soviet losses had been huge; perhaps three million men and 18,000 tanks in three months. Ominously, however, the rate of German casualties, some 750,000 of them, was also far higher than in any previous campaign.

G   Moscow, Leningrad, Stalingrad

Soviet recovery and resistance

Great as these successes were, none of the objectives of the invasion had been completely secured by the beginning of the autumn, and signs were evident that the tide was turning. The first factor in the Soviet recovery, as in the Napoleonic invasion of 1812, was the weather. Heavy rain in October blocked the German advance with seas of mud, and heavy frosts in November exposed them to all the horrors of a winter campaign in Russia. Frostbite claimed 100,000 victims. Aircraft, tanks, lorries and guns could not operate for want of antifreeze, and men were reduced to stuffing their uniforms with paper to keep out temperatures as low as 40° below freezing.

Secondly, the German forces encountered astonishing resistance from military and civilians alike. Although reinforced by fear of retribution from their own side from the NKVD, this resistance was primarily a manifestation of intense patriotism, of reaction to ill-advised German behaviour in the territories they occupied, and of an acute awareness of the nature of the German threat. In his first wartime address to the nation, Stalin declared that the enemy 'is out to seize our lands watered by the sweat of our brows, to seize our grain and oil, secured by the labour of our hands . . . , to restore the rule of the landlords'.

The siege of Leningrad

In the north, too, German plans were narrowly frustrated. Of the seven Soviet cities awarded the title 'Hero City' after the war, none deserved it more than Leningrad. The siege, a product of Hitler's determination to destroy the cradle of Bolshevism, lasted from September 1941 to January 1944. Desperately short of food and precariously supplied by routes built over the ice of Lake Ladoga and by rail routes open to constant German attack, the inhabitants suffered constant bombardment and the permanent threat of starvation. It is possible that the total casualty figures for the siege may have been as high as 1.5 million, most of them civilians. That Leningrad never fell was due to the heroism of the inhabitants, to the shrewd defensive organisation of the greatest Soviet soldier of the war, G. K. Zhukov, who was backed by the local party machinery, and to the eventual need of the *Wehrmacht* to divert substantial resources of men and material to the south-west of the USSR.

The Battle of Stalingrad

This region was the key theatre of the European war in 1942. Given the industrial potential of the world's largest state (*see* section **H**) and the failure of the 1941 campaign to crush her resistance, time was against Hitler. It was essential that Germany should complete her conquest of the oil-rich regions between the Black Sea and the Caspian as quickly as possible. In a fateful strategic decision, Hitler resolved to divide his southern forces between a drive against the Caucasian oilfields to the south and an assault upon the important communications centre of Stalingrad, on the Volga River, to the east. The personal links between Stalin and the city that bore his name gave the ensuing battle special significance in the eyes of both sides. From September 1942 until January 1943, the streets, houses and factories of the city were the scene of constant and bitter fighting. This continued until the German Sixth Army, surrounded since November but specifically forbidden to retreat by Hitler, finally submitted. The battle cost the Germans 70,000 casualties, over 100,000 prisoners and vast quantities of guns and vehicles. The Soviet victory forced the retreat of those German forces further south that now faced the danger of being cut off. Worst of all, the invincible reputation of the *Wehrmacht* and the impetus of two years of *Blitzkrieg* campaigns in the east also died.

H The new balance of power

The Soviet war effort

In this transformed war, in which Germany and her allies no longer faced an Anglo–French alliance, but a coalition that included the world's two largest states, the balance of industrial and economic forces would now only admit one eventual outcome.

The Soviet Union brought enormous industrial resources and a centralised political authority uniquely capable of mobilising and directing them. In the Kremlin, a frantic revision of pre-war principles was now undertaken in the interests of national unity, that included the rehabilitation of the Orthodox church, and the re-introduction of the privileges of higher military ranks to ensure their undivided loyalty in the struggle. Industrially, the Soviet Union had lost much in the early months of the war, including some 60 per cent of her coal and iron production and as much as 25 per cent of her workforce. The process of industrial re-organisation had begun before the war, however, when the Third Five-Year Plan had dictated the establishment of many new industrial concentrations in the region of the Ural Mountains and in

Siberia. Happily these plants were beyond the reach of German attacks. Now they were supplemented at remarkable speed by the transfer of factories from the vulnerable western regions. One thousand three hundred and sixty factories moved eastwards in 1942 and 2,250 new units of production arose there between 1942 and 1944.

The astonishing nature of this achievement is conveyed by this description by Peter Calvocoressi. 'At the new sites wooden structures were thrown up to house machinery, but there was often neither time nor materials to build houses for the workers ... , they slept on the floor by their machines. Mortality was high, output poor. The wonder is that they were not worse.' Eventually, results were outstanding in regions old and new. The Moscow coalfield, reduced to an output of 590 tons per day in January 1942, was back to its pre-war norm of 35,000 tons per day by the following October. The trans-Ural regions, at their peak, were producing at 2.5 times the rate of the whole of Soviet industry in 1940. Russian military production overhauled that of Germany in 1943 to reach a peak of 30,000 tanks and 40,000 aircraft in that year.

The contribution of the United States

The merest glance at the industrial capacity of the United States suffices to show the vital role that nation played in the outcome of the Second World War. American increases in armament production in the war years were prodigious, from 6,000 aircraft in 1940 to 96,000 in 1945, from under a thousand tanks in 1940 to 21,000 in 1943. Much of this went, of course, to fight the war in the Pacific, but the American contribution to the European theatre of war remained invaluable. On D-Day the British army operated 3,300 Sherman tanks and 86,000 American motor vehicles. Some 20 per cent of the RAF's strength in 1943–45 was also made up of American planes. The USSR benefited largely from 'Lend-Lease' agreements (October 1941 and June 1942) similar to that negotiated with Britain, and which provided 2,000 tanks and 1,300 planes by mid-1942 at the height of the Soviet crisis.

British war production

Nor was the contribution of Great Britain herself negligible. Like the Soviet Union she had won time to mobilise her resources and she did so effectively. From four divisions ready for combat in 1939, she could count on 60 by mid-1941, 20 of them from the Empire and Dominions. Domestic resources were also fully exploited. In 1940–42 British aircraft production was actually higher than that of Germany, and by the time Germany regained the lead in 1944, American and Soviet production had already put the issue of industrial supremacy beyond doubt.

The German war effort from 1942

Against these overwhelming forces, the German economy performed miracles, but laboured under a variety of insuperable obstacles. It had never been geared for a long war, only for the production of materials for *Blitzkrieg*, and Germany needed to undergo a miniature 'industrial revolution' to meet its new crisis. Central figures in this process were Fritz Todt, minister of armaments and munitions until his death in February 1942, and his successor, Albert Speer. As a relatively civilised and realistic figure surrounded by Nazi extremists, Speer has since received lenient treatment both from the Nuremberg judges and from historians, but his role in equipping Germany to fight the war in 1942–45 was of great importance. Aircraft production reached a peak of 25,285 in 1944, as against 3,744 in 1940, and the rebuilding of factories to protect them from air raids was so effective that 5,000 new aircraft were still produced in the first four months of 1945 even as the allies were in the process of over-running Germany. Speer could not, however, overcome Germany's severe political and geographical disadvantages. She was subjected to bombing from two sides while American and Siberian factories lay beyond her reach. There was in Germany no central authority to co-ordinate production. While Hitler specialised in oratory, Speer had frequently to struggle against the influence of Goering, the chiefs of various state agencies, and the local jealousies of the *Gauleiters*, over questions of policy and resources. Resources, such as the coal and iron of the Ruhr and of Silesia, shrank as allied forces advanced.

I Hitler's new order

The government of occupied Europe

For four years, Nazi Germany dominated the mainland of Europe more completely than it had ever been dominated before. In the west, in France, Norway and Denmark, 'puppet' governments were installed, checked at every turn by German military commanders and representatives of the security forces, to ensure that German interests were served. Puppet governments also operated in the Balkans, Greece, Yugoslavia and Rumania. In eastern Europe, where the Slavs could not be afforded even this limited freedom, direct German government was the rule. Poland was placed under the arbitrary authority of a German Governor-General (Hans Frank), and Bohemia and Moravia under that of a Protector (first Neurath, then Heydrich, then Frick). The territories of Ostland and the Ukraine, created from captured Soviet territory, came under the authority of the Reichsminister for the East, the fanatical Nazi theorist Alfred Rosenberg.

The 'new order' that these regimes advertised and imposed had a dual nature. In Nazi propaganda, especially in western Europe, it took the form of a gigantic union of European states to combat the alien menace of Judaism and its political offshoot, Bolshevism. It was a highly successful interpretation which found a living expression in the many international units assembled in occupied countries, such as the French 'Legion of Volunteers Against Bolshevism' and the Belgian 'Flemish Legion', to join the *Wehrmacht* on the eastern front. In reality, of course, the 'new order' took the form of a colossal plundering of European resources for the exclusive benefit of Germany. This could be explained as a necessity imposed by the continuing war, but in large part it belonged to the plans of Nazi theorists. Hitler's aims in the Soviet union were not merely to defeat its communist leadership, but to 'Germanise the country by the settlement of Germans and treat the natives as redskins'. Germany would provide the industrial heartland of this new Europe, and would in turn be fed by the less developed, largely agricultural territories that surrounded her.

The economic exploitation of occupied Europe

The occupation administrations had the two main tasks of the economic exploitation of the conquered territories for the war effort, and the breaking of local political and intellectual structures. The first function was dominated by two central figures, Hermann Goering, as Commis-

sioner of the Five-Year Plan, and Fritz Sauckel, the official responsible for the supply of labour to German industries. It took a number of forms, including the exploitation of local resources, such as the coal deposits of Silesia, the adaptation of local plant to German requirements, the transfer of some of that plant to German factories, and the recruitment of foreign labour for service in Germany. In the west, this last task was often tackled by relatively subtle enticements, such as the promise of higher wages or the placing of obstacles in the way of local employment, but in eastern Europe sheer physical force was the norm. Seven million foreign workers had been transferred to German factories by 1944, not more than 200,000 of them as volunteers, and foreign resources in the same year supplied some 20–25 per cent of the rations consumed by German civilians.

Although the system was effective in terms of quantity it had its drawbacks. Forced labour was bound to be unreliable, especially in more skilled jobs, and the system provided tremendous problems for a transport network also committed to supplying troops on several fronts. As Norman Rich has pointed out, the two tasks of the occupation administrations frequently clashed with each other, when the military advantages of a friendly local population were sacrificed to the economic and ideological demands for suppression and exploitation.

The use of terror in occupied Europe

Terror, of course, was a standard feature of the 'new order'. Sometimes it was deliberately applied as a matter of policy, as by the special SS squads (*Einsatzgruppen*) whose specific task in some eastern areas was to purge undesirable groups. The 33,000 Jews murdered at Babi Yar in the Ukraine (September 1941) were some of the victims of these groups. Sometimes, atrocities were a means of reprisal following local opposition or resistance. Proclaiming that 'wars are not won by the methods of the Salvation Army', Hitler fully approved of General Keitel's infamous 'Night and Mist' (*Nacht und Nebel*) order (December 1941) which prescribed death as the automatic punishment for any act of sabotage or resistance, and advised summary execution. Most occupied territories suffered some example of the German tactic of destroying whole communities, often at random, as reprisals for

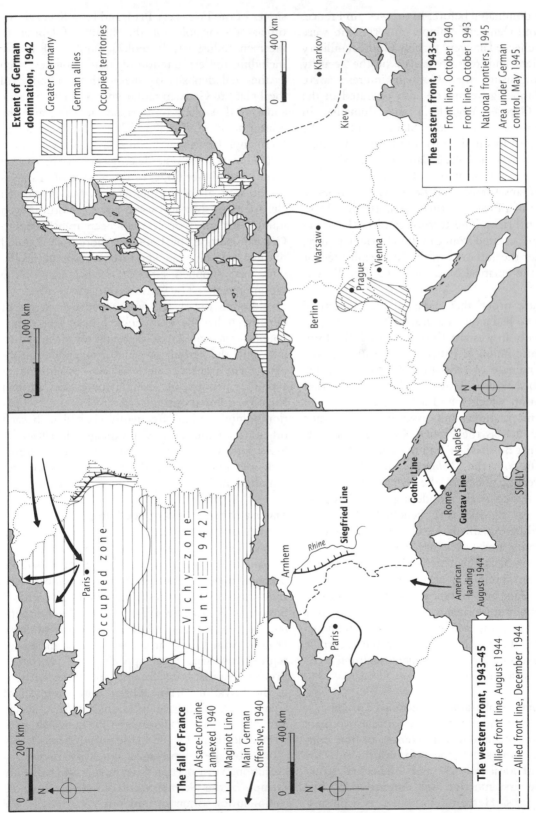

Extent of German domination, 1942

- Greater Germany
- German allies
- Occupied territories

1,000 km

The eastern front, 1943–45

- Front line, October 1940
- Front line, October 1943
- National frontiers, 1945
- Area under German control, May 1945

400 km

N

Kharkov

Kiev

Berlin

Warsaw

Prague

Vienna

The fall of France

- Alsace-Lorraine annexed 1940
- Maginot Line
- Main German offensive, 1940

200 km

N

Occupied zone

Vichy zone (until 1942)

Paris

The western front, 1943–45

- Allied front line, August 1944
- Allied front line, December 1944

400 km

N

Arnhem

Rhine

Siegfried Line

Gothic Line

Naples

Rome

Gustav Line

American landing August 1944

Paris

SICILY

The Second World War in Europe, 1939–45

attacks upon German personnel. The deaths of nearly 200 innocent civilians at Lidice in Czechoslovakia (May 1942) and of 642 at Oradour sur Glane in France (July 1944) are the most notorious examples. To the list could be added Palmiry, near Warsaw, Televaag, in Norway, Boves, in Italy, and Putten, in the Netherlands.

J   The fate of the Jews

The prelude to the 'final solution'

The unprecedented domination that Nazi Germany enjoyed over the continent also provided her with the opportunity to give prolonged attention to the obsessive anti-Semitism of the Nazi movement. Hitler's anti-Semitism, like his foreign policy, was a mixture of unswerving principle and uncertain means. For all his hostility towards them, Hitler still had little clear idea in 1939 what he intended to do with the Jews. The most likely official plan was that which called for the shipment of European Jews to the island of Madagascar in the Indian Ocean, which would be demanded from France for that purpose after that nation's defeat.

The first two years of warfare, however, caused the rethinking of this plan. Firstly, although France was defeated, the continuing hostility of Britain made regular sea access to Madagascar difficult. Secondly, the fall of Poland amplified the Jewish 'problem' dramatically. Whereas the Reich in 1939 had a Jewish population of about 357,000, the large number of Polish Jews multiplied by ten the number of Jews in the Greater Reich in 1940. Between the invasion of Poland and that of the Soviet Union, concentration camps, not exclusively for Jews, but also for Poles, communists, gypsies, and others, were established in Poland at Auschwitz, Chelmno, Treblinka, Sobibor and Belsen. Even so, it was not until 1941, when continued Soviet resistance ruled out the interim plan of dumping the Jews in Siberia, that it was officially resolved that the 'final solution' to the 'Jewish question' was to consist of wholesale and systematic extermination.

The 'final solution' in the context of the war

The insane intensity of this anti-Semitism is illustrated, not only by the scale of the slaughter, but by the fact that, while locked in an increasingly unsuccessful war, the German government still saw fit to devote substantial resources of manpower, communications and technology to this horrible task. In the midst of the eastern campaigns in 1942, trainloads of Jews from France, Belgium and the Netherlands were being shipped the length of Europe to the eastern camps. In 1943 and 1944, the SS was still expanding its programme to deal with Greek and Hungarian Jews. Only in October 1944, with the Red Army threatening to overrun the camps, did Himmler give the order for them to cease their dreadful routine.

The scale of the 'final solution'

Between 1941 and 1944 technological refinements such as the special Cyclon-B gas and specially designed ovens for incineration, that routine proceeded with awful efficiency. Chelmno, with 1,000 victims a day in late 1941, was outrun by Treblinka, which managed up to 6,000 a day at its peak, while Auschwitz was responsible for the murder of some three million people in the course of three years. The German government declared in November 1943, although it was not entirely correct, that there were no Jews left in the Greater Reich. By the end of the war, 50 per cent of Belgian Jews, 66 per cent of Rumanian Jews and 75 per cent of the Dutch community were dead. The best records for the protection of Jews were those of Denmark and of France, although in the latter case the government only preserved the lives of French Jews by assisting the capture and deportation of those who were not French citizens.

Lucy Dawidowicz, in her standard history of this genocide, has settled upon a figure of 5.93 million as the final toll of Jewish victims, estimating that it embraces 67 per cent of occupied Europe's pre-war Jewish population. Nor should it be forgotten that some three million non-Jews, mainly Slavs, and political opponents of Nazism, also died in extermination camps. These camps were responsible for the destruction in the most horrible circumstances, of some 7.5 million human lives. Such, ultimately, is the monument to the 'new order' of Nazism.

K   Collaboration

The case of France

Resistance to this Nazi 'new order', especially in

the first two years of the war, remained the prerogative of a brave but very small minority. The apparent finality of the German victories up to the end of 1941 dictated that the main problem of the conquered was how to live with the conquerors. In general, as Norman Rich has concluded, 'the response of the European peoples to Nazi dominion reflects an instinct of people everywhere to cling to life and to seek physical and economic security for themselves and their families'.

This was especially evident in France where Pierre Laval, foreign minister from October 1940 and premier from April 1942, showed particular enthusiasm for co-operation with Germany. Although this made him the special butt of allied propaganda and led to his execution in 1945, Laval's fault was really short-sightedness, an inability to appreciate the international extent of the conflict, rather than any true sympathy with Nazi aims. Laval's motives were, indeed, simple. They were to save France from the fate of Poland, from dismemberment and disintegration, and to do this it was necessary to co-operate with the new masters of Europe. Others had more positive motives, springing from an actual sympathy with the aims of Nazism, sometimes anti-Semitic, sometimes anti-British, often anti-communist. Thirdly, of course, many collaborated simply because the Germans were the winners, with the money, the resources, business contracts and influence that men still sought in war as in peace.

Collaboration in 'nordic' Europe

Although France provided a rare example of an established government, staffed by credible pre-war politicians, collaborating enthusiastically with the Germans, western Europe provided many other examples of puppet administrations and national fascist bodies willing to co-operate for opportunist or ideological reasons. The Netherlands had a Nazi party, under A. A. Mussert, which claimed a membership of 50,000 during the war, and Belgium had its Flemish nationalists under Staf de Clercq, who saw collaboration with the Germans as a means of breaking the power of the French-speaking Walloons.

In Norway, the government of Vidkun Quisling, whose name gave a new word to the English language to describe such collaborators, enthusiastically supported the ideology of Nazism, but generally failed to convince the Norwegian people of its value. In all of these cases, the relationship with Germany ended in frustration as it became clear that Hitler sought, not ideological support, but unconditional domination.

Collaboration in eastern Europe

If open collaboration was rarer in eastern Europe, it was because Nazi theory generally forbade co-operation with the 'sub-human' Slavs. Some such co-operation, however, still existed. Even in the USSR racial minorities such as Tartars and Chechens sought German aid against Soviet oppression, and a Russian Liberation Army under General A. A. Vlasov numbered 50,000 men by the end of the war. Similarly, the anti-communist attitudes of Dmitri Mihailovic and his *chetnik* force, and of Ante Pavelic in Yugoslavia offered possibilities for the German and Italian occupiers, which were generally thrown away because of the brutal and callous attitudes of Nazism towards the Slavs.

What did collaboration achieve?

The benefits of collaboration varied. In France, the policy of Laval bore little fruit. It did not greatly hasten the return of prisoners of war, did not prevent a 50 per cent rise in the mortality rate due largely to cases of malnutrition and did not save France from total occupation when German interests demanded it (November 1942). On the other hand, it served the Germans well. Thirty-seven per cent of all German materials and finances from foreign sources came from France, tanks and army trucks rolled off the production lines of Renault and Berliet, and 45,000 Frenchmen joined the paramilitary Milice force that combated the resistance and attempted to maintain domestic stability in the last years of the occupation.

Elsewhere, the results were sometimes better. Norman Rich has cited the cases of Slovakia, which was spared a German occupation by the co-operation of Tiso's government, while Admiral Horthy ensured that Hungary escaped quite lightly from the war. Denmark succeeded in preserving its monarchy, part of its army, and even most of its Jews. In short, it was sometimes possible after the war to justify collaboration in terms of short-term local successes. In the wider context of Nazi inhumanity, the policy was always much harder to justify.

L Resistance

The motives for resistance

The motives that led a select and highly honourable minority into resistance to the Nazi 'New Order' were many and complex. Perhaps a simple national pride was at the basis of the other motives. 'They resisted,' wrote A. Werth of the French movements after 1941, 'because it was a matter of ordinary self respect to do so. They were unwilling to accept that while London was "taking it", or that while the Red Army was fighting the Battle of Stalingrad, France was doing nothing.' Secondly, the brutality of German policy in the occupied territories convinced many of the need for resistance. This was especially true in the eastern territories, where the callous recruitment of forced labour, and the determination of 'treat the natives like redskins' made resistance the surer means towards survival.

In France, too, it was the recruitment of labour that drove many young men into the countryside, where their groups took their names from the shrub-like bushes (*maquis*) that gave them shelter. Thirdly, the entry into the war of the Soviet Union played a dual role. Not only did it make resistance a more attractive prospect by offering some alternative to a German victory, but it set the communist parties of the occupied countries, previously nonplussed by the Russo–German Pact of 1939, in opposition to the invaders. In September 1941, General Keitel, as chief of staff, ordered that all acts of resistance or sabotage should be ascribed to communists and that batches of alleged communists should be executed as reprisals. Communists, or those likely to be suspected of party membership thus had little to lose by active resistance.

Forms of resistance

Resistance, similarly, took many forms. The most simple, and the safest, was the refusal of social contact with the occupier. Norway provided a fine example of passive resistance when her bishops and High Court judges resigned *en masse*.

The dissemination of war news and propaganda was another important, but highly dangerous function. In Belgium alone some 300 illegal journals were published, and over 1,000 such papers appeared in France between 1940–44. Belgium was also the centre of a complex network of groups specialising in the sheltering of allied airmen shot down over Europe, and in smuggling them back to home bases. Some 10,000 individuals were involved, and the number of aircrew thus returned to active service numbered about 3,500. Similar networks in Poland and in Czechoslovakia did valuable work by providing intelligence on German troop movements to allied forces.

Next came acts of violence against specific Germans. Such activities, however, entailed costs out of all proportion to their strategic value. The assassination of Reinhard Heydrich, 'Protector' of Bohemia and Moravia, for example, was paid for with 1,500 Czech lives and the destruction of the villages of Lidice and Lezaky.

Guerrilla warfare, 1942–45

It was with the weakening of the German war effort, and in co-operation with advancing allied forces, that resistance groups achieved their greatest impact. By mid-1942 there were an estimated 150,000 partisan fighters operating behind German lines in the Soviet Union, disrupting communications and tying down large numbers of regular troops. In the west, resistance actions delayed and weakened important German units moving to combat the Normandy landings. Finally, with the German disintegration, these forces formed the basis of resurgent national armies. Sixty thousand Czech partisans fought with the Soviet Army, the French FFI (*Forces Françaises de l'Interieur*) played a role in the liberation of several French cities and in the final thrust into Germany, and partisan forces played a major part in the liberation of Belgrade, and of many of the cities of northern Italy.

What did the resistance movements achieve?

In an area that has proved of great interest to recent historians, disagreement has arisen as to how much was actually achieved by the various resistance movements. A. S. Milward has put forward the view that in no case did a resistance movement seriously defeat German intentions. The crushing of the Warsaw Rising (August 1944) and the heavy losses of the French resistance at Vercors (June 1944) showed the relative impotence of resistance forces when not backed by allied troops. The price exacted by the Germans in reprisals leads Milward to his conclusion that resistance 'seems to have been seldom effective, sometimes stultifying, frequently dangerous, and almost always too costly'.

M. R. D. Foot, although not seriously challenging this view of the strategic contribution of the resistance movements, detects a wider value in their activities. 'The greatest good that resistance did,' he concludes, 'lay in the hearts of the people who took part in it.' The greatest contribution of resistance, in other words, lay not so much in what it achieved during the war, as in the contribution that it made after the war to the re-establishment of national self-confidence and self-respect in such a country as France, where the traumatic shock of defeat and occupation had been devastating, and where its scars still exist.

M The collapse of the Axis: Italy

The opening of a 'southern front'
The clearance of German and Italian troops from North Africa by combined British and American forces by May 1943 left the southern flank of fascist Europe exposed. The daunting task of renewing the offensive against 'Fortress Europe' began (10 July 1943) with an allied assault upon Sicily, at the southern tip of Italy, which was not strongly resisted by the Axis forces. Within six weeks the island was in allied hands. The decision to proceed from Sicily to the Italian mainland was an unpopular one with Stalin, who preferred an attack upon German forces in France, to relieve pressure upon the Soviet Union, but it was based upon sound strategic sense. Italy was clearly the weakest point of the Axis, and by her elimination from the war the Mediterranean could be secured, and bases could be won for a future assault upon Germany.

The collapse of the fascist government
The capture of Sicily precipitated the final crisis for the fascist government of Italy, and transformed the position of Italy in the war. Having joined Hitler's war effort when success seemed certain, Mussolini now faced an invasion of Italian territory, deprived of the services of 200,000 troops killed or captured in North Africa, and of a further million committed to distant theatres of war. Resistance to the allies would now be possible only at the cost of turning the country over to the

Germans, clearly a terrible price to pay, and a negation of all that fascist nationalism had stood for. Mussolini's failure to extricate himself from the disastrous German alliance caused the collapse of his political position which was wrecked by strikes and demonstrations, by the withdrawal of the support of the Fascist Grand Council (24 July 1943), and by his dismissal as prime minister by the king (25 July). Briefly, fascist government survived the fall of Mussolini under the leadership of Marshal Badoglio. His government had two primary aims, to maintain the credibility of fascism, and to lead Italy into the allied camp without substantial German reprisals. On both counts it failed. While anti-fascist partisan forces reduced parts of Italy to a state of virtual civil war, and Italian forces disintegrated in the confusion, the German High Command took the decision to defend as much of the country as possible from the allied forces now (9 September 1943) landed on the mainland.

German resistance and the impact upon Italy
Defending first the Gustav Line, midway between Naples and Rome, then the Gothic Line 190 km farther north, the *Wehrmacht* ensured that the allies would have to fight for every foot of Italian soil. Mussolini, sensationally rescued from his imprisonment, and installed as head of the 'Italian Social Republic' in the north, found himself reduced to the 'puppet' status of many would-be allies of Germany. It was perhaps the logical outcome of his 'savage friendship' with Hitler. Rome, expected to fall by the end of 1943, was not occupied by the allies until 4 June 1944, and German troops continued to resist in Milan and other northern cities long after allied troops had crossed the Rhine.

If the price paid by the allies for the 18 months of warfare in Italy was high, for Italy herself that period constituted the final disaster of fascism. A further 100,000 Italians died in military action and bombing raids not only added high civilian casualties, but caused great damage to the cultural heritage of the nation. The destruction of the great Benedictine monastery of Monte Cassino was only the worst example of many. Inflation and the cost-of-living index soared, the latter from a base of 100 in 1938 to 5,313 in October 1947. On top of this came political collapse. Badoglio's government collapsed in June 1944 and King Victor Emanuel III abdicated in May 1946. Forty-three days later a referendum in favour of a republic ended 85 years of Italian monarchy. Mussolini did not live to see all this. Captured by partisans as he tried to flee into Switzerland, he was shot without trial, and his body hanged from a meathook in a Milan square (28–29 April 1945).

N The collapse of the Axis: the western front

'Operation Overlord'

By the beginning of 1944 the British and American commanders were able to concentrate men and materials for their greatest undertaking, the re-invasion of France. The technical difficulties facing 'Operation Overlord' were enormous, including the laying of oil pipelines across the Channel, and the designing of artificial 'Mulberry' harbours to provide anchorages for subsequent supply ships. German hopes of resisting the invasion depended entirely on checking it on the landing beaches. That the High Command failed to do so owed much to the element of surprise, for they had judged an invasion more likely in the region of Calais, rather than in Normandy, and much to the enormous air superiority of the allies.

Beginning on 6 June 1944, D-Day, the allies landed 326,000 men in six days along a 80-km beachhead. Within a month, a million men had landed, suffering only 9,000 fatal casualties. Stiff German resistance around Caen and Falaise could not be sustained after a further American landing in the south (15 August) and the collapse of German control in France was subsequently rapid. Paris was occupied, appropriately by Free French forces, on 24 August, Brussels and Antwerp were liberated in the first week of September, and by the onset of autumn, German forces were manning the defences of the Siegfried Line on their own frontiers.

From Normandy to the Rhine

German resistance, however, was not quite exhausted. Sir Basil Liddell Hart has stressed the decision of the allies to demand unconditional surrender. He claims that this was a factor that made it easier for Hitler, even after such defeats, to rally stiff defence. In the last days of 1944 the *Wehrmacht* enjoyed its last successes on the western front,

defeating an allied attempt to outflank the Siegfried Line at Arnhem (17–24 September), and temporarily regaining ground in the Ardennes by the counter attack known as the 'Battle of the Bulge' (16 December 1944–13 January 1945). The first months of 1945, however, were a period of steady disintegration. The *Wehrmacht* had to make good its losses by the conscription of raw teenagers, fuel supplies were on the brink of exhaustion, and the *Luftwaffe* had finally lost the struggle for air supremacy. Brilliant new weapons, such as the Messerschmitt 262 jet fighter and the V1 and V2 rockets, came too late to save the Reich.

The last stages of the German collapse

The surviving German units proved quite insufficient to prevent an allied crossing of the Rhine (7–23 March 1945), and thereafter the main cities of Germany fell regularly to the advancing allied forces until (25 April 1945) advanced units of the American forces made contact with the Soviet army at Torgau in Saxony. Hitler's vision of a defeated Germany destroying itself in a Wagnerian 'Twilight of the Gods' came to nothing. Civilian morale was severely strained by the 'Thousand Bomber' raids on Dresden (13–14 February). Also the planned yard-by-yard resistance of the German 'Home Guard' (*Volkssturm*) failed to materialise, and local and central officials at last showed open defiance of Hitler's will by disobeying orders to destroy strategic buildings and important industrial plant.

O The collapse of the Axis: the eastern front

The liberation of Soviet territory

A major contribution to the rapid allied successes in the west was, of course, made by the heavy German commitment to the Russian front. There, the campaigns of 1943 continued to be fought deep into Soviet territory, but with the Soviet army steadily developing both numerical and technical superiority. A German counter-attack at Kharkov (February 1943) achieved considerable success, but could not be sustained, and an attempt to force back Soviet forces at Kursk (July 1943) was thwarted in the biggest tank battle of the war. In the south, the Soviet army's own counter-attacks after the Battle of Kursk drove the German forces back to the river Dnieper and cut off those units occupying the Crimea.

In 1944 it was the turn of the northern units of the *Wehrmacht* to feel the weight of the Soviet offensive. In 1943 they had held a defensive line from Orel to Leningrad relatively comfortably, an illustration perhaps of the error of Hitler's offensive strategy in the south. Now, a series of massive Soviet campaigns finally broke the encirclement of Leningrad (January 1944), re-occupied Minsk in White Russia (July), and drove into Poland and the Baltic territories (August), capturing 30 German divisions in the process. In the second half of the year southern offensives cleared Soviet soil of German troops and caused the surrender of Germany's Rumanian (August) and Bulgarian (September) allies.

The Soviet thrust into Germany

In the east, too, the beginning of 1945 saw allied troops poised for the final thrust into the Greater German Reich. Although more heavily manned and equipped than in the west, Germany was similarly in no shape to resist. Hitler himself was now ravaged by nervous disease, in a state where, as Alan Bullock describes him, 'his orders became wilder and more contradictory, his demands more impossible, his decisions more arbitrary. His answer to every proposal was: No withdrawal'. He himself had shattered his own High Command. Such able generals as Manstein and Rundstedt had been dismissed for their failures to carry out impossible tasks, and Kluge and Rommel had both committed suicide when their roles in an officers' plot to murder Hitler and set the war upon a sounder footing (July 1944) were discovered. The final assault, by four armies on a front from the Baltic to the Carpathian mountains, thus made rapid progress. In March, Soviet forces crossed the Oder river, driving beyond Berlin to ensure that it was their forces, and not those of their allies, that occupied the German capital. Although he has been much criticised for it since, the commander of the western forces, General Eisenhower, adhered strictly to the spheres of influence agreed by the political leaders (*see* section **P**) and there was no race for Berlin.

The week from 30 April to 7 May 1945 witnessed the last rites of the Third Reich.

Fulminating against the incompetence of his generals, and repeating his doctrines of anti-Semitism and of the German need for *Lebensraum*, Hitler killed himself on 30 April and had his body burned to ensure that it could not be treated as that of Mussolini had been. On 7 May, after several unsuccessful attempts to negotiate separate peace treaties and so to divide the allies, the German government, now in the hands of Admiral Doenitz, surrendered unconditionally to the combined allied forces, thus ending the war in Europe.

P Teheran to Yalta

The genesis of post-war Europe

Although Germany and her allies entered the war with complex but quite well-defined aims, her opponents, especially Britain and the Soviet Union, fought originally for no other reason than that war was forced upon them by German aggression. At first, their war aims were simple and largely negative; to survive, and to destroy Nazism as a means to survival.

Only in 1942 did it become practical and practicable to consider in detail the settlement that the allies should pursue in the event of their victory. In the diplomatic discussions that followed, three main European issues were at stake; the treatment of Germany after her defeat, the fate of eastern Europe, and the means of ensuring future stability. General principles 'for common action to preserve peace and resist aggression in the post-war period' had been laid down in an Anglo-Russian treaty of May 1942, and by British agreements with America. Only in November 1943 did the allied leaders, Churchill, Roosevelt and Stalin, meet at Teheran in Iran, to begin to define details. Although the Teheran meeting was preoccupied with military strategy against Germany, it contained the seeds of the post-war settlement and gave early indications of Soviet ambitions. Roosevelt suggested that post-war Germany be divided into five sectors, with her industrial heartlands of the Ruhr, the Saar, Hamburg and the Kiel Canal, placed under international control. Stalin, determined that the Soviet Union would no longer be threatened by the instability of her immediate European neighbours, produced a 'shopping list' that stipulated future Soviet influence in East

Prussia, and in most of those territories gained as a result of the 1939 pact with Germany.

The establishment of post-war spheres of influence

The next meeting of the allied leaders was over a year later, at Yalta in the Crimea (4 February 1945). By then, German resistance was on the verge of collapse, and much of eastern Europe was, in any case, in the hands of the Soviet Army. Roosevelt and Churchill have since incurred much criticism for their apparent acquiescence in the establishment of a substantial Soviet sphere of influence, but the considerations behind the creation of such a sphere were primarily practical. Only by force could eastern Europe be wrested from Soviet control, and even then it seems unlikely that forceful tactics could have succeeded. Thus, Stalin emerged from Yalta with confirmation of his dominance in Rumania, Bulgaria, Hungary and Poland. The lesser degree of Soviet influence in Yugoslavia, and its absence in Greece, also resulted from practical considerations, for their Mediterranean position made them as much subject to Anglo–American sea power as to Soviet land power. In return for this agreement, to which the Soviet Union adhered quite closely, Stalin agreed wholesale to American proposals for a four zone occupation of Germany, with a zone allocated to the French, and for the establishment of a United Nations Organisation. The last great tripartite meeting, at Potsdam (July 1945), was mainly concerned with the detailed implementation of the Yalta agreements.

The genesis of the United Nations

The broad concept of a 'World Organisation' to replace the League of Nations had arisen at Teheran, and at a separate meeting of foreign ministers in Moscow (November 1943). Its specific format was thrashed out at an interallied conference at Dumbarton Oaks, Washington, in August–October 1944 where, among other decisions, it was agreed that the major powers sitting permanently on the central Council of the organisation could employ a veto over any measure that displeased them. Between April and June 1945 delegates of 50 nations met in San Francisco to draft what has become the United Nations Charter. The decision that the seat of the United Nations Organisation should be in New York was perhaps symbolic of the fact that Europe was no longer the focal point of world politics.

Q Consequences

The cost of the war

The Second World War's impact upon the next generation of Europeans was twofold: unparalleled physical and economic destruction, and revolutionary political change. Table 18.2, including non-European powers for purposes of comparison, shows the enormous cost of the war.

Table 18.2 Costs of the Second World War

	Probable military casualties	Probable civilian casualties	Probable cost (£ m.)
USSR	13,600,000	7,700,000	23,253
Germany	3,480,000	3,890,000	53,084
Japan	1,700,000	360,000	10,317
Great Britain	452,000	60,000	12,446
Italy	330,000	85,000	5,267
USA	295,000	-	62,560
France	250,000	360,000	27,818
Poland	120,000	5,300,000	not known

From T. G. Charman, *Modern European History Notes*, Telles Langdon Publications.

Comparisons with the war of 1914–18 may be fruitful. The human losses of the USSR alone in 1941–45 were equal to the total casualty toll of the earlier conflict, and German losses were double those of the first war. The nature of the warfare in the Second World War meant that British and French losses were lighter than in the first war, but the devastation of those areas that saw the bulk of the fighting exceeded all precedents. Again, the Soviet Union and Germany suffered most. In the USSR between half and three quarters of all living quarters in the theatre of war were destroyed. In addition to her casualties, Europe faced the problem between 1939 and 1947 of some 16 million refugees rendered homeless by the fighting.

Although the war made no such impact upon the map of Europe as the Napoleonic Wars and the First World War had done, its effect upon the political balance of the continent was revolutionary. Fascism and Nazism, proclaimed by Mussolini and Hitler as the dominant doctrines of the next millenium, vanished and have made no significant reappearance.

Even more remarkable was that Germany, the central features of the last century of European history, also vanished. She was replaced by two states, the Federal Republic of Germany and the German Democratic Republic, both closely tied to one of the two power blocs that now dominated world politics. The dominance that Germany had long aspired to and had briefly enjoyed now clearly passed to the Soviet Union. Although not dominating the eastern European states in the same fashion as Germany had done, her military and economic superiority over the socialist republics that arose with direct Soviet assistance in Czechoslovakia, Poland, Hungary, Bulgaria and Rumania, survived intact for over 40 years with only two serious challenges. Although Yugoslavia avoided such direct influence from Moscow, her socialist philosophy affiliated her, too, to this formidable eastern bloc.

Indeed, the Soviet Union could claim to have emerged from the war, not only as the main European power, but perhaps as the only European power of world stature. The intercontinental empires of Britain, France, Italy, Belgium and the Netherlands were racked with difficulties before 1939, but the defeats of these powers, or the vast economic strain of their eventual victories, has meant that the post-war history of these empires has been one of steady liquidation. As a result, the whole nature of political confrontation in the world had changed. It no longer centred around the economic and political ambitions of a few European states, but rather around the different conceptions of human freedom and democracy represented by the two great world powers, one created by refugees from Europe, the other as much Asian as European in its culture and history.

A history of Europe between 1848–1945 touches upon many issues that affected the lives of people all over the globe, but European global dominance was one of the major casualties of the last great European war. At the heart of this new confrontation lay another great product of this war. The nuclear arms race dates from the dropping by the United States of the first atomic bomb on the Japanese city of Hiroshima (6 August 1945), the culmination of the increasing sophistication of weaponry during the war. In so many respects we may truly paraphrase Guérard's judgement on 1848, and conclude that a new era of European and world history began in 1945.

Questions

Essay questions

1 'The weaknesses of Germany's opponents were more responsible for Hitler's military successes than were his Blitzkrieg tactics, 1939–41.' Discuss. (WJEC)

2 To what extent was the outcome of the Second World War in Europe determined by the use of air power? (AEB)

3 To what extent did the fighting between Germany and Russia determine the outcome of the Second World War? (JMB/NEAB)

4 Was the entry of the USA into the Second World War the decisive turning point in the conflict? (Oxford Entrance)

5 Why did Hitler agree to a non-aggression pact with Stalin in 1939 and then attack the USSR in 1941? (UCLES)

Wartime collaboration in France

Read the sources carefully and answer the questions that follow.

SOURCE A

It is with honour, and to maintain ten centuries of French unity within the context of the new European order, that I enter today upon the path of collaboration. This collaboration must be sincere. It must involve patient and confident effort. The present armistice is not a peace settlement. France is bound by many obligations with regard to her conqueror. At least she retains her sovereignty. That sovereignty obliges her to defend her soil, to extinguish divergences of opinion, to reduce dissent in her colonies. This is my policy. The ministers are responsible to me alone. It is I whom history shall judge.

Marshal Pétain's broadcast to the French people, 30 October 1940.

SOURCE B

My desire is to re-establish normal and trusting relations with Germany and with Italy.

A new Europe will inevitably arise from this war. One often speaks of 'Europe'. It is a word that the French are not yet accustomed to. One loves one's country because one loves one's village. For myself, Frenchman as I am, I wish that in the future we may be able to love a Europe in which France will have a place worthy of her.

I wish for a German victory because, without her, Bolshevism will establish itself everywhere. When I say that this policy is the only one that can ensure the status of France and guarantee her development in the peace to come, you must believe me and follow me. This war, as I have already said, is not like other wars. It is a revolution from which a new world will spring. You have nothing to fear and everything to hope for from the regime that is now established in our country. A younger Republic, stronger and more humane, will be born; socialism will be established everywhere in Europe, and the form that it will take in France will be determined by our national character.

Speech by Pierre Laval, outlining his policy upon his return to office, 22 June 1942.

SOURCE C

Registered and listed, French Jews were driven out bit by bit from all the jobs, the shops, the offices, and the administrative structures. Jews were forbidden to take part in certain economic activities (virtually all of them in effect), by the German ordinance of 26 April 1941. They were forbidden to use the telephone, to frequent places of entertainment or other public establishments: restaurants, swimming baths, cafés, libraries, squares, race courses, etc.

The list published by Oberg, head of the SS and of the police is astonishing in its variety. From the telephone booth to the castle, from the stadium to the camping site, everything is covered. Thus one would see the old university professor roaming outside the libraries where he was no longer allowed to study, and men risking arrest by buying a postage stamp in a café.

Henri Amouroux, La Vie des Françaises sous l'Occupation, published 1961.

SOURCE D

	Wheat	Potatoes	Meat	Milk	Dried vegetables
(in kilograms for solids, and in litres for milk)					
1938	241	415	40.9	241	6.9
1939	168	343	37.5	243	5.6
1940	132	253	24.9	188	5.9
1941	151	180	19.9	174	4.4
1942	133	180	18.6	160	3.9
1943	156	173	15.5	162	3.5
1944	159	196	16.0	139	3.6
1945	121	155	21.0	154	3.4

Table showing the consumption of foodstuffs, per head of the population, in France. 1938–45. From Mouvement économique en France de 1938 à 1948 (Published 1950).

SOURCE E

2. Avoid speaking of Alsace-Lorraine. Do not use that expression and do not get involved in any discussion on the issue.

3. You are reminded that you should avoid speaking of 'Anglo-Saxons'. Use the term 'Anglo-Americans'.

8. Say nothing about the costs of occupation.

11. Avoid giving prominence to anything that involves the restrictions and the sacrifices demanded of the population.

17. In obituaries, do not mention that the deceased died in captivity.

25. Do not speak of the divergences of opinion and the differences that may exist between Monsieur Laval and other political groups (Doriot etc).

38. Do not give any global figures for the number of workers leaving to work in Germany. Equally, do not give any figures concerning the categories of prisoners of war who are liberated.

41. Do not publish anything concerning acts of sabotage or other acts of violence.

Notice issued to French journalists by the German Propagandastaffel [Propaganda authority]. 18 February 1943.

---

a Explain the following passages that occur in these sources:
  i 'to reduce dissent in her colonies' (Source A).
  ii 'Avoid speaking of Alsace-Lorraine' (Source E).
  iii 'workers leaving to work in Germany' (Source E).
b Compare the forms of collaboration envisaged by Pétain (Source A) and by Laval (Source B). How similar are the motives of the two men?
c In the light of Sources C, D and E, how realistic are the following statements made in Sources A and B?
  i 'At least she [France] retains her sovereignty' (Source A).
  ii 'My desire is to re-establish normal and trusting relations with Germany' (Source B).
  iii 'A younger Republic, stronger and more humane, will be born' (Source B).
d 'On balance, French interests were well served by the policy of collaboration'. How far do these sources, and any other evidence known to you, lead you to question this statement?

Glossary

This glossary does not include terms that are defined in detail in the text.

Anarchism (Greek *Anarchia* - Non-rule). Political doctrine advocating abolition of organised authority, and regarding all forms of government as oppressive.

Anti-clericalism Social-political view based upon hostility to the organised church, and especially to the power and privileges of the clergy.

Anti-Semitism Hostility to Jews.

Autarky (or **Autarchy**) Economic policy aiming at national self-sufficiency in terms of raw materials and other essential economic resources.

Authoritarianism Political system favouring or enforcing obedience to the authority of the state, to the detriment of personal liberty.

Autocracy Absolute government in which the power of the ruler or rulers is not limited by the constitutional rights of the governed.

Blitzkrieg (German – *lightning war*). War decided by rapid and devastating strategic blows.

Bolshevik Member of that branch of the Russian communist movement favouring the form of strictly organised, élite political party advocated by V. I. Lenin.

Bonapartist Supporter of Napoleon Bonaparte or, subsequently, of Napoleon III. Broadly in favour of stable, prosperous government, preserving the moderate gains of the French Revolution, but resisting the dangers of more radical social reconstruction.

Bourgeoisie That stratum of society beneath the aristocracy whose wealth and prosperity derives from industrial and mercantile enterprise, or from investment.

Capitalism Economic system under which social/political influence lies largely in the hands of the social class controlling the means of industrial production and distribution.

Cartel Organisation of industrial manufacturers with a view to the control of production, marketing, prices etc. to their mutual benefit.

Comintern International Organisation of National Communist Parties: founded in Moscow in 1919 to exert Russian Soviet influence over international socialism.

Concordat Agreement or treaty between the Papacy and a secular government.

Corporativism System of government propounded by Benito Mussolini in which trade and professional organisations, or corporations, are the basis of society and political activity.

Coup d'état Sudden change of government brought about by force.

Duma The semi-constitutional assembly in Russia between 1906–17.

Entente (French – *understanding*). A friendly agreement between two states, which falls short of a formal alliance.

Franchise The right to vote. Those who possess this right are said to be enfranchised.

Free trade Economic policy which does not protect home industries against foreign competition by imposing high tariffs upon foreign goods, but allows free import and export of all goods.

Führer (German – *Leader*).

Gold Standard Currency system whereby the value of a state's currency is guaranteed by quantities of gold held by the state.

Grossdeutsch (German – *great German*). A variant of German nationalism which believed that the German state should include all members of the German race.

Imperialism The practice whereby a state acquires economic and/or political power over other territories, usually with a view to commercial/ industrial expansion.

Informal empire Form of imperialism in which the imperial power does not directly rule the colonised territory, but leaves it nominally independent while pursuing economic penetration and exploitation of the territory.

Junker Member of the hereditary Prussian aristocratic class, which dominated the army and government from a basis of landed wealth.

Kadets Russian political group of liberal tendencies, supported by progressive landowners, middle classes and intellectuals.

Kleindeutsch (German - *little German*). Variant of German nationalism which accepted the concept of a German state which contained only a section of the total German-speaking population of Europe. In practice this came to mean a German state dominated by Prussia rather than by Austria.

Kulak (Russian – *fist*). A prosperous peasant, regarded by communists, and sometimes by fellow peasants as flourishing at the expense of his poorer neighbours.

Lebensraum (German – *living space*). That foreign territory which, in the view of extreme German nationalists, had to be seized for the proper future maintenance of the German race.

Legitimist Monarchist supporting the claims of a dynasty which he regards as having a divine right to rule, e. g. a supporter of the Bourbon dynasty in France.

Levant Collective term for the territories in the eastern part of the Mediterranean.

Luftwaffe German air force.

Menshevik Member of that branch of the Russian communist movement which favoured a more popular, loose-knit form of party organisation and discipline, with more democratic leadership.

Octobrists Russian political group favouring limited political reform within the framework of Nicholas II's October Manifesto.

Orleanist French monarchist supporting the claim to the throne of Louis Philippe and his descendants. In more general terms, a supporter of moderate conservatism in France, based upon a constitutional monarchy.

Ottoman The ruling dynasty of the Turkish Empire. Hence Turkey was frequently referred to as the Ottoman Empire.

Pan-germanism The political belief that all German-speaking peoples should be brought together into one political unit.

Pan-slavism The belief that all Slav peoples should be brought together in one political unit under the protection of Russia.

Papal infallibility The belief that, due to his position as God's representative on earth, the Pope's judgement and pronouncement in all matters of Church government and doctrine is necessarily and unquestionably correct.

Particularism Political view stressing and favouring the independence of smaller political units within larger ones, e.g. the independence of the smaller German states within the German Confederation.

Politburo The committee of ministers responsible for policy making within the Soviet Union.

Populism Russian social and political movement based upon an appeal to the peasantry, which it saw as the only viable basis for a socialist society within Russia.

Positivism Philosophy preaching that all true knowledge is scientific, and thus rejecting all views and beliefs based upon moral or religious abstractions.

Protectionism Economic policy whereby a state's industries and commerce are protected from foreign competition by high tariffs placed upon imported foreign products.

Putsch (German - *coup d'état*).

Realpolitik (German – *realistic policy*). Political policies that are not guided by moral or abstract considerations, but by practical application of the available means.

Reichsfeind (German – *enemy of the Empire*). Term applied to a party or group identified as a threat to the interests of the German state. The supposed threat from such groups might be used by the state power as a common threat to rally other groups in support of the state.

Reichstag Imperial German parliament.

Reichswehr Imperial German army.

Reparations Payments made by a defeated state to compensate the victorious state(s) for damage or expenses caused by war.

Serfdom A form of servitude in which the landowner physically owns the peasants who live and work on his estates, and can regulate their labour, their lives and their persons at will.

Slavophilism Russian social and political doctrine preaching the superiority of Slav (and especially of Russian) institutions over those of western Europe.

Soviet (Russian – *council*). Term applied to the communist form of government in Russia based upon the representation of workers' interests through a hierarchy of local and regional councils.

Syndicalism Militant trade union movement aiming at the transfer and control of the means of production, not to the state, but to the workers themselves through the medium of their unions.

Totalitarianism A form of government centred upon a dictatorial, single-party system, extending its influence over all areas of public and private life within the state and society.

Ultramontanism Politico-religious attitude which accepts the authority of the Pope in matters affecting the Church and society within one's own state.

Wehrmacht Official designation of the German armed forces at the time of the Third Reich.

Weltpolitik (German – *world policy*). Policy pursued by the government of Kaiser Wilhelm II, insisting that German influence should be felt in all world issues, and should not be limited to continental affairs. This also involved the establishment of German colonies beyond Europe.

Zemstvo Elective rural council established in Russia as part of the reforms of Tsar Alexander II.

Zollverein (German - *customs union*). The customs union established between various German states under the presidency of Prussia in 1834.

Further reading

General

France
R. Magraw, *France 1815–1914. The Bourgeois Century*, Fontana, 1983.
G. Wright, *France in Modern Times*, Norton, 1981.

Italy
H. Hearder, *Italy in the Age of the Risorgimento 1790–1870*, Longman, 1984.

Germany
W. Carr (ed.), *A History of Germany 1815–1945*, Edward Arnold, 1969.
G. A. Craig, *Germany 1866–1945*, Oxford, 1978.

Russia
H. Seton-Watson, *The Russian Empire 1801–1917*, Oxford, 1967.
J. N. Westwood, *Endurance and Endeavour: Russian History 1812–1980*, Oxford (2nd edn), 1981.

Austria-Hungary
C. A. Macartney, *The Habsburg Empire: 1790–1918*, Weidenfeld and Nicolson, 1971.
A. J. P. Taylor, *The Habsburg Monarchy, 1809–1918*, Penguin, 1964.

By Chapter

Chapter 1
L. R. Berlanstein, *The Industrial Revolution and Work in Nineteenth Century Europe*, Routledge, 1992.
D. Caute, *The Left in Europe*, Weidenfeld and Nicolson, 1966.
J. Droz, *Europe Between Revolutions*, Fontana, 1967.
E. J. Hobsbawm, *The Age of Revolution: Europe 1789 to 1848*, Weidenfeld and Nicolson, 1962.
D. S. Landes, *The Unbound Prometheus*, Cambridge, 1970.
G. Lichtheim, *A Short History of Socialism*, Weidenfeld and Nicolson, 1970.
A. Sked (ed.), *Europe's Balance of Power 1815–48*, Macmillan, 1979.

Chapter 2
E. Eyck (ed.), *The Revolutions of 1848–49*, Oliver and Boyd, 1972.
P. Jones, *The 1848 Revolutions*, Longman, 1981.

Chapter 3
J. P. T. Bury, *Napoleon III and the Second Empire*, English University Press, 1964.
J. F. McMillan, *Napoleon III*, Longman, 1991.

A. Plessis, *The Rise and Fall of the Second Empire. 1852–1871*, Cambridge, 1985.
W. H. C. Smith, *Second Empire and Commune: France 1848–1871*, Longman, 1985.

Chapter 4
D. Beales, *The Risorgimento and the Unification of Italy*, Allen and Unwin, 1972.
H. Hearder, *Italy in the Age of the Risorgimento 1790–1870*, Longman, 1984.
D. Mack Smith, *Cavour*, Methuen, 1985.
D. Mack Smith, *Mazzini*, Yale, 1994.
S. Woolf, *A History of Italy 1700–1860: the Social Constraints of Political Change*, Routledge, 1986.

Chapter 5
E. Eyck, *Bismarck and the German Empire*, Allen and Unwin, 1968.
Lothar Gall, *Bismarck, the White Revolutionary*, (2 vols), Allen and Unwin, 1986.
A. J. P. Taylor, *Bismarck: the Man and the Statesman*, New English Library, 1968.
D. G. Williamson, *Bismarck and Germany 1862–1890*, Longman, 1986.

Chapter 6
W. Bruce Lincoln, *Nicholas I*, Allen Lane, 1978.
M. E .Falkus, *The Industrialisation of Russia 1700–1914*, Macmillan, 1972.
Maureen Perrie, *Alexander II, Emancipation and Reform in Russia 1855–1881*, Historical Association, 1989.
David Saunders, *Russia in the Age of Reaction and Reform 1801–1881*, Longman, 1992.

Chapter 7
As for Chapter 5, plus:
Gordon Martel (ed.), *Modern Germany Reconsidered 1870–1945*, Routledge, 1992.
Hans-Ulrich Wehler, *The German Empire 1871–1918*, Berg, 1985.

Chapter 8
R. Anderson, *France 1870–1914*, Routledge, 1977.
R. Gildea, *The Third Republic from 1870 to 1914*, Longman, 1988.
J.-M. Mayeur and M. Rebérioux, *The Third Republic from its Origins to 1914*, Cambridge, 1984.
D. Thomson, *Democracy in France since 1870*, Oxford, 1969.
T. Zeldin, *France 1848–1945*, Oxford, 1973.

Chapter 9
M. E. Falkus, *The Industrialisation of Russia 1700–1914*, Macmillan, 1972.
L. Kochan, *The Making of Modern Russia*, Penguin, 1977.
H. Rogger, *Russia in the Age of Modernisation and Revolution. 1881–1917*, Longman, 1983.

J. N. Westwood, *Endurance and Endeavour: Russian History 1812–1980*, Oxford, 1981.

Chapter 10

G. A. Craig, *Germany 1866–1945*, Oxford, 1978.

R. J. Evans (ed.), *Society and Politics in Wilhelmine Germany*, Croom Helm, 1978.

F. Fischer, *From Kaiserreich to Third Reich: Elements of Continuity in German History 1871–1945*, Unwin Hyman, 1986.

R. A. Kann, *History of the Habsburg Empire 1526–1918*, University of California, 1974.

J. W. Mason, *The Dissolution of the Austro-Hungarian Empire 1867–1918*, Longman, 1985.

H.-U. Wehler, *The German Empire 1871–1918*, Berg, 1985.

Chapter 11

M. Ferro, The Great War 1914–18, Routledge, 1973.

H. W. Koch (ed.), Origins of the First World War, Macmillan, 1972.

G. Martel, The Origins of the First World War, Longman, 1987.

A. J. P. Taylor, *The Struggle for Mastery in Europe 1848–1918*, Oxford, 1971.

A. J. P. Taylor, *The First World War: An Illustrated History*, Penguin, 1966.

Chapter 12

J. Bradley, *Civil War in Russia 1917–1920*, Batsford, 1975.

E. H. Carr, *A History of Soviet Russia 1917–1929*, Penguin, 1966.

M. McCauley, *The Soviet Union Since 1917*, Longman, 1981.

J. D. White, *The Russian Revolution 1917–1921*, Edward Arnold, 1994.

A. Wood, *The Russian Revolution*, Longman, 1979.

Chapter 13

A. Bullock, *Hitler and Stalin: Parallel Lives*, Harper-Collins, 1991.

R. Conquest, *The Great Terror: A Reassessment*, Pimlico, 1992.

I. Deutscher, *Stalin: A Political Biography*, Penguin, 1966.

M. McCauley, *Stalin and Stalinism*, Longman, 1983.

A. Nove, *An Economic History of the USSR*, Penguin, 1969.

A. Ulam, *Stalin*, Allen Lane, 1973.

Chapter 14

R. Carr, *Spain 1808–1939*, Oxford, 1966.

J. Hiden, *The Weimar Republic*, Longman, 1974.

G. Martel (ed.) *Modern Germany Reconsidered, 1870–1945*, Routledge, 1992.

W. L. Shirer, *The Collapse of the Third Republic*, Simon and Schuster, 1969.

H. Thomas, *The Spanish Civil War*, Penguin, 1968.

Chapter 15

M. Clark, *Modern Italy, 1871–1982*, Longman, 1984.

D. Mack Smith, *Mussolini's Roman Empire*, Penguin, 1977.

D. Mack Smith, *Mussolini*, Weidenfeld and Nicolson, 1981.

E. R. Tannenbaum, *Fascism in Italy: Society and Culture, 1922–1945*, Allen Lane, 1973.

E. Wiskemann, *Fascism in Italy: Its Development and Influence*, Macmillan, 1969.

S. J. Woolf, *European Fascism*, Weidenfeld and Nicolson, 1970.

Chapter 16

K. D. Bracher, *The German Dictatorship*, Penguin, 1978.

M. Broszat, *The Hitler State*, Longman, 1981.

A. Bullock, *Hitler: A Study in Tyranny*, Penguin, 1962.

A. Bullock, *Hitler and Stalin: Parallel Lives*, Harper-Collins, 1991.

L. Dawidowicz, *The War Against the Jews, 1933–45*, Penguin, 1977.

J. C. Fest, *Hitler*, Penguin, 1977.

R. Grunberger, *A Social History of the Third Reich*, Penguin, 1974.

G. Martel (ed.), *Modern Germany Reconsidered, 1870–1945*, Routledge, 1992.

D. G. Williamson, *The Third Reich*, Longman, 1982.

Chapter 17

A. Adamthwaite, *The Making of the Second World War*, Allen and Unwin, 1977.

A. Bullock, *Hitler: a Study in Tyranny*, Penguin, 1962.

M. Gilbert and R. Gott, *The Appeasers*, Weidenfeld and Nicolson, 1963.

K. Hildebrand, *The Foreign Policy of the Third Reich*, Batsford, 1973.

C. J. Lowe and F. Marzari, *Italian Foreign Policy, 1870–1940*, Routledge, 1975.

J. Néré, *The Foreign Policy of France from 1914 to 1945*, Routledge, 1975.

R. J. Overy, *The Origins of the Second World War*, Longman, 1987.

A. J. P. Taylor, *The Origins of the Second World War*, Hamish Hamilton, 1961.

Chapter 18

P. Calvocoressi and G. Wint, *Total War*, Penguin, 1974.

M. R. D. Foot, *Resistance*, Methuen, 1976.

A. S. Milward, War, *Economy and Society 1939–1945*, Allen Lane, 1977.

N. Rich, *Hitler's War Aims*, André Deutsch, 1973.

Index